Deviance

THE REYNOLDS SERIES IN SOCIOLOGY

Deviance

A Symbolic Interactionist Approach

NANCY J. HERMAN
Central Michigan University

GENERAL HALL
A Division of
ROWMAN & LITTLEFIELD PUBLISHERS, INC.
Lanham • Boulder • New York • Oxford

GENERAL HALL
A Division of Rowman & Littlefield Publishers, Inc.
4720 Boston Way
Lanham, MD 20706
www.rowmanlittlefield.com

12 Hid's Copse Road
Cumnor Hill, Oxford OX2 9JJ, England

Library of Congress Catalog Card Number: 95-78984

ISBN: 1-882289-38-2 (pbk.)
       1-882289-39-0 (cloth)

Printed in the United States of America

DEC 1 3 2010

⊖™ The paper used in this publication meets the minimum requirements of American
National Standard for Information Sciences—Permanence of Paper for Printed Library
Materials, ANSI/NISO Z39.48–1992.

In loving memory of
My Father, Michael J. Herman

Contents

PART VII
ORGANIZING DEVIANTS —
SUBCULTURES AND DEVIANT ACTIVITIES

ACKNOWLEDGEMENTS

Books are not the product of solitary endeavors. Rather, they are collective enterprises. This edited collection is the result of efforts and contributions on the part of many individuals. In particular, I wish to thank Ravi Mehra, President of General Hall Inc. for his interest in this book. Additionally, I wish to thank Larry T. Reynolds for his intellectual support and editorial expertise. Moreover, I am indebted to those who wrote original contributions for this book. I also wish to thank Julie Blaha for her outstanding typing services and proofreading skills. Further, I wish to thank my colleague Rod Kirk for coming to my rescue to deal with various computer disasters. Finally, I wish to thank Bridget Saunders and Ken Laundra for their painstaking efforts at proofreading this manuscript.

The editor and publisher also wish to thank the following who have kindly given permission for use of copyright materials.

"Criminology: An Integrationist Perspective," Diane Fishbein, original contribution.

"Psychological Theories of Deviance," Allen Liska. Pp. 10–12 in *Perspectives on Deviance*, 2nd edition. Englewood Cliffs, New Jersey: Prentice-Hall, 1980.

"The Normal and the Pathological," Emile Durkheim. Pp. 65–72. Reprinted with the permission of The Free Press, a division of Simon & Schuster from The Rules of Sociological Method by Emile Durkheim, translated by Sarah A. Solovay and John H. Mueller. Edited by George E.G. Catlin Copyright 1938 by George E.G. Catlin; copyright renewed 1966 by Sarah A. Solovay, John H. Mueller, and George E.G Catlin, 1938.

"Illegitimate Means and Delinquent Subcultures," Richard Cloward and Lloyd Ohlin. Pp. 145–52, in *Delinquent and Opportunity*. New York: The Free Press: a Division of MacMillan, 1960.

"Evaluation of Structural Functionalism," Alex Thio. Pp. 32–34, in Alex Thio, *Deviant Behavior*. New York: Harper and Row. Reprinted with permission of Harper Collins, Inc., 1988.

"The Theory of Differential Association," Edwin Sutherland, Donald R. Cressey and David F. Luckenbill. Pp. 86–90, in *Principles of Criminology*, eleventh edition. Dix Hills, New York: General Hall Publishers. Reprinted with permission.

"Evaluation of Differential Association Theory," Alex Thio. Pp. 40–42, in Alex Thio *Deviant Behavior*. New York; Harper and Row. Reprinted with permission of Harper Collins, Inc., 1988.

"A Control Theory of Delinquency," Travis Hirschi. Pp. 16–26, in *Causes of Delinquency*, Los Angeles: University of California Press, 1969.

"Evaluation of Social Control," Alex Thio. Pp.48–50, in Alex Thio, *Deviant Behavior*. New York: Harper and Row. Reprinted with permission of Harper Collins, Inc., 1988.

"Group Conflict Theory as an Explanation of Crime," George B. Vold. Pp. 270–276, in *Theoretical Criminology*. London: Oxford University Press, 1958.

"A Radical Perspective on Crime," Jeffrey Reiman. Pp. 123–129, in *The Rich Get Richer and the Poor Get Prison*, New York: MacMillan, 1979. Reprinted with permission.

"Evaluation of Conflict Theory," Alex Thio. Pp. 76–78, in Alex Thio *Deviant Behavior*. New York: Harper and Row. Reprinted with permission of Harper Collins, Inc., 1988.

"Secondary Deviance and Role Conceptions," Edwin Lemert. Pp. 75–78, in *Social Pathology*, New York: McGraw-Hill, 1951.

"Outsiders," Howard S. Becker. Pp. 8–10, 12–14, and 31–33, in *Outsiders*. New York: The Free Press, 1963. Reprinted with permission.

"Evaluation of Labeling Theory," Alex Thio. Pp. 58–61, in Alex Thio, *Deviant Behavior*. New York: Harper and Row 1988. Reprinted with permission of Harper Collins, Inc.

"Accessing the Stigmatized: Gatekeeper Problems, Obstacles and Impediments to Social Research," Nancy J. Herman. original contribution.

"Personal Safety in Dangerous Places," Terry Williams, Eloise Dunlap, Bruce D. Johnson and Ansley Hamid. *Journal of Contemporary Ethnography* Vol. 21 #3: 343–74, 1992. Reprinted with permission of Sage Publications.

"Moral Entrepreneurs: The Creation and Enforcement of Deviant Categories," Howard S. Becker. Pp. 148–161 in *Outsiders*. New York: The Free Press, 1961. Reprinted with permission.

"The Social Construction of Deviance: Experts on Battered Women," Donileen Loseke and Spencer Cahill, *Social Problems* 31(3): 290–310, 1984. Reprinted with permission of the University of California Press.

"The 'Discovery' of Child Abuse," Stephen J. Pfohl, *Social Problems* 24(3): 315–21, 1977. Reprinted with the permission of the University of California Press.

"The Legislation of Morality: Creating Drug Laws," Troy Duster. Reprinted with the permission of The Free Press, a division of Simon & Schuster from *The Legislation of Morality* by Troy Duster. Copyright 1970 by The Free Press.

"Medicine as an Institution of Social Control," Peter Conrad and Joseph R. Schneider, Pp. 251–60 in *Deviance and Medicalization*. Philadelphia, Pa: Temple University Press, 1983. Reprinted with permission.

"The Making of Blind Men," Robert Scott, Pp. 76–87 in *The Making of Blind Men: A Study of Adult Socialization*. New York: Russell Sage Foundation, 1969. Reprinted with permission.

"Record-keeping Practices in the Policing of Deviants," Albert J. Meehan, *Urban Life* 18 #1: 70–102, 1986. Reprinted with permission of Sage Publications.

"Constructing Probationer Careers," Douglas Thomson, original contribution.

"The In-patient Phase in the Moral Career of the Psychiatric Patient: The Context Within Which Self is Mortified," Nancy J. Herman, original contribution.

"Being Sane in Insane Places," D.L. Rosenhan, *Science* vol. 179 (January): 250–58, 1973. Reprinted with permission of the American Association for the Advancement of Science.

"The 'Mixed Nutters' and Looney Tuners:" The Emergence, Development, Nature, and Functions of Two Informal, Deviant Subcultures of Chronic Expsychiatric Patients," Nancy J. Herman, *Deviant Behavior* 8: 232–58, 1987. Reprinted with permission of Taylor & Francis Inc.

"Constructing Women and Their World: The Subculture of Female Impersonation," Richard Tewksbury, original contribution.

"Into the Darkness: An Ethnographic Study of Witchcraft and Death," Wendy Lozano and Tanice Foltz, *Qualitative Sociology* 13 #3: 211–34, 1990. Reprinted with permission of Human Sciences Press.

"The Urban Speed Gang: An Examination of the Subculture of Young Motorcyclists" Stephen L. Muzzatti, original contribution.

"The Culture of Gangs in the Culture of the School," Daniel J. Monti, *Qualitative Sociology* 16 #4: 383–404, 1993. Reprinted with permission.

"Parade Strippers: A Note on Being Naked in Public," Craig J. Forsyth, *Deviant Behavior* 13: 391–403, 1992. Reprinted with permission of Taylor and Francis Inc.

"Policing Morality: Impersonal Sex in Public Places," Frederick J. Desroches, original contribution.

"Knives and Gaffs: Definitions in the Deviant World of Cockfighting," Steve Worden and Donna Darden. *Deviant Behavior* 13: 271–289, 1992. Reprinted with permission of Taylor and Francis Inc.

"Paranoia and the Dynamics of Exclusion," Edwin Lemert, *Sociometry* 25(1): 2–5, 7–15, 18–20, 1962. Reprinted with permission.

"Creating Crazies/Making Mentals: The Pre-patient Phase in the Career of the Psychiatric Patient," Nancy J. Herman, original contribution.

"A Model of Homosexual Identity Formation," Richard Troiden, Pp. 35–60 in *Gay and Lesbian Identity: A Sociological Analysis*. Dix Hills, New York: General Hall, 1988.

"Becoming an Addict/Alcoholic," Jack Haas, original contribution.

"Drifting into Dealing: Becoming a Cocaine Seller," Sheigla Murphy, Dan Waldorf and Craig Reinarman, *Qualitative Sociology* 13(4): 321–43, 1990. Reprinted with permission of Human Sciences Press.

"Becoming a Hit Man: Neutralization in a Very Deviant Career," Ken Levi, *Urban Life* 10#1:47–63, 1981. Reprinted with permission of Sage Publications.

"Stigma and Social Identity," Erving Goffman, Pp. 2–9 in *Stigma*. New Jersey: Prentice-Hall, 1963.

"Deviance Disavowal: the Management of Strained Interaction by the Visibly Handicapped," Fred Davis, *Social Problems* 9(2): 120–32, 1961. Reprinted with permission of the Society for the Study of Social Problems.

"Return to Sender: Reintegrative Stigma-Management Strategies of Ex-Psychiatric Patients," Nancy J. Herman, *Journal of Contemporary Ethnography* 22 #3, 1993. Reprinted with permission of Sage Publications.

"Double Stigma and Boundary Maintenance," Mark R. Kowalewski, *Journal of Contemporary Ethnography* 17 #2: 211–228, 1988. Reprinted with permission of Sage Publications.

"Ostomates: Negotiating an Involuntary Identity," Mark Nagler, 1990. Reprinted with permission of the author.

"The 'Post' Phase of Deviant Careers: Reintegrating Drug Traffickers," Patricia Adler, *Deviant Behavior* 13: 103–126, 1992. Reprinted with permission of Taylor and Francis Inc.

"Becoming Normal: Certification as a Stage in Exiting from Crime," Thomas Meisenhelder, *Deviant Behavior* 3:137–53, 1982.

"Recovery Through Self-Help," Jack Haas, original contribution.

"Gaining and Losing Weight: Identity Transformations," Cliff English, *Deviant Behavior* 14: 227–41, 1993. Reprinted with permission of Taylor and Francis Inc.

Part I

Introduction

What is deviant behavior?

Why should we even bother to ask the question. Don't we all agree that deviance has to do with "nuts, sluts and preverts"(Liazos, 1972). Not necessarily. Every year for the past seven years, at the start of each class in deviant behavior, I conduct a small exercise wherein I ask undergraduate students to write down on a piece of paper a list of persons or behaviors that they regard as deviant.[1] The results have indicated that there is tremendous variability as to what is considered deviant and what is not. In fact, among the three hundred and twenty two students sampled, they mentioned over 347 different persons and types of acts as deviant. These deviants included, for example: Charles Manson, homosexuals, Madonna, those who chew tobacco, deer hunters, those engaging in oral sex, Canadians, George Bush, drug dealers, income tax evaders, politicians, those engaging in bestiality, professors, drug users, rapists, Jeffrey Dahmer, Christians, streakers, those who view pornographic materials, vegetarians, murderers and Republicans. Certainly this list is by no means exhaustive or all-inclusive. You are perhaps surprised by, and no doubt, probably disagree with some of the aforementioned choices. Most likely, many of the behaviors that you conceive of as deviant behavior are not even mentioned on this partial list.

Administration of this exercise indicates that there exists very *little* consensus among students as to the conception of deviant behavior. I would argue that this disagreement parallels the level of disagreement among the public.

If at this juncture you can appreciate the diversity of phenomena defined by individuals as deviant, you can also appreciate the difficulties others have when attempting to answer the question, "What is deviant behavior?"

I would argue that there is a similar lack of consensus among natural and social scientists as well.

Biological Theories of Deviance

Biological explanations of deviance and criminality are cyclical in popularity. Essentially, they assume that certain biological structures or processes cause individuals to commit norm violations. In the nineteenth century, the Italian criminologist, Cesare Lombroso argued that criminals were "evolutionary throwbacks", a biological state that manifested itself in terms of certain characteristics such: as an over-hanging brow, high cheekbones, and heavy jaws. Such characteristics were also found in "savages" and apes. Enrico Ferri, Lombroso's student, argued that such biological states are inherited. Lombroso's theory of skull shapes has long been

1

disproved but in the 1940's, William Sheldon, a psychologist made similar such claims for body types. Basically, Sheldon argued that certain kinds of germ plasm caused certain physiological states which are subsequently manifested into certain psychological and physical characteristics. For example, agile, energetic, muscular types (mesomorphs) are more likely to become criminals than are thin, delicate types (ectomorphs) or soft, round types (endomorphs). This theory has also been disproved.

During the 1960's and 1970's, researchers discovered a chromosomal abnormality that they thought caused norm violations. Normal males possess an XY chromosome pattern, while normal females have an XX pattern. It was discovered that some prisoners had an extra male chromosome (in a XYY configuration). Studies argued that XYY males were aggressive, tall, and had histories of criminal behavior. However, further investigation revealed, to the contrary, that these persons were much less aggressive than other prisoners, but were also less intelligent (Shah and Roth, 1974; Witkin et al., 1976).

A more current area of biological research has focussed on identical twins who share identical genes. Arguing for a "nature" as opposed to a "nurture" stance, Bartollas and Dinitz (1989) in their research on samples from the United States and Europe suggest that criminality of adopted twins more likely follows the behavior of the biological parents as opposed to the adopted parents.

In the first selection "*Criminology: An Integrationist Perspective*," Diana Fishbein presents current research from numerous behavioral sciences such as genetics, physiological psychology, psychopharmacology and endocrinology illustrating the significance of biological factors in the development of deviant behavior. The author maintains that integrating biological perspectives with sociological perspectives yields a fuller understanding regarding the processes underlying deviant or antisocial behavior.

Psychological and Personality Theories

Psychological explanations of deviant behavior essentially focus on the individual, on child-rearing factors and past social experiences that cause the person to develop certain personality traits—traits leading to the violation of societal norms.

Sigmund Freud and his psychoanalytic colleagues argue that the human infant is largely self-centered, greedy, oversexed, with no regard for others. These *"id"* centered primitive, aggressive sexual instincts which are inborn, gradually become contained by the *"ego"* (memory, perception, reason) and the *"superego"* components of self. (norms and values). According to psychological theories, our urge to commit deviant behavior arises from the id, but the ego and superego serve to hold it in check—to inhibit it or channel it into culturally appropriate behaviors. In short, we are all born deviants; some of us learn to control our tendencies, while others do not.

A great deal of research has also been conducted by psychologists in an effort to link various types of deviance to abnormal features of the personality. Researchers have employed various personality tests in an effort to distinguish between criminals and non-criminals, or normal individuals and deviants. Some psychologists argue that in certain cases, incomplete or faulty socialization may create a "psychopathic personality."—an individual causing violence with no regard for self or others.

Hans Toch (1969) has focused his efforts on aggressive behavior. He discovered that men who engaged in repeated incidences of violence and assault possessed very low self-esteem. Toch asserts that this psychological trait made males resentful of all criticisms, however minor or slight. Their violent outbursts were rooted in their fear of loss of face, coupled with their self-perception that others held them in low esteem.

Expanding on Toch's work, Leonard Berkowitz (1978) asserted that these males had such fragile self-esteems that they flew into violent rages even when no one else was present. In certain cases, audience members would precipitate even more violent responses on the part of the individual.

The selection by Allen Liska entitled, *"Psychological Theories of Deviance,"* presents a description of the logic underlying psychogical theories and a brief summary of the major theoretical approaches in psychology that attempt to account for abnormal, maladaptive or deviant behavior.

Sociological Theories

Although sociologists have proposed a number of different definitions and theories of deviant behavior, they can be classified into two groups: (1) the *Objectivist or Traditional Approach* —also referred to as the positivist, determinist, normative perspective—in which deviance is conceptualized as a norm violation and (2) the *Subjectivist or Contemporary Approach* —also referred to as the anti-positivist, definitionist, relativist approach—in which deviance is conceived as a social definition. Let us discuss each perspective in detail.

(1) The Objectivist or Traditional Perspective

Proponents of the Objectivist perspective define deviance as a norm violation. Examine the following statements on deviance:
Robert K. Merton:

> Deviant behavior refers to conduct that departs significantly from the norms set for people in their social statuses (1966:805).

and Albert Cohen:

> ...behavior which violates institutionalized expectations—that is, expectations that are shared and recognized as legitimate within a social system (1955:62).

According to these theorists, there exists in society an overall consensus as to what is considered deviant and what is not. Thus, social researchers, and anyone else for that matter can identify an act of deviance by comparing this behavior to society's listing of *"do's"* and *"don't's"* or norms. Norms represent an objective standard by which deviance can be scientifically defined. Shared rules function to channel behavior into culturally-appropriate behavioral patterns. Behavior deviating from these normative patterns, is deviant behavior, so that deviants, in this view, are people who violate the normative consensus of society.

Moreover, deviant behavior typically leads to negative societal responses such as ostracism, legal sanctions, etc. Punishment functions to reaffirm common cultural values, goals and norms.

Further, sociologists advocating this perspective center on a deterministic view of deviance—that is, it is caused by something. It is the task of the sociologist then, to attempt to figure out what causal factors gave rise to acts of deviance, whether it be social environment, family background, social class, religion, gender, etc.

The Subjectivist or Contemporary Approach

The traditional perspective dominated sociology until the late 1950's when another group of sociologists developed a different conception of deviant behavior—not as a norm violation, but as a social definition. These theorists shifted concerns from what *caused* individuals to commit deviant acts to the process by which actors come to be *defined* and *treated* as deviant. Thus, focus shifted to others reactions which were now treated as subjectively problematic.

Subjectivist theorists contend that deviance is an act that has been labeled by others (a social audience) as deviant. According to this approach, societal reactions then, are the means for identifying deviant behavior. These theorists argue that there is no overall societal consensus as to what is considered deviant or non-deviant. Because we live in a complex, industrialized society, and come from different ethnic, religious and social class backgrounds, it is unrealistic to believe that we *all* share the same set of norms, values and beliefs. People will often have competing and conflicting beliefs rather than shared goals and interests. Instead of being the product of consensus, organized behavior may be the result of self-interested negotiations between two parties or of coercion on the part of more powerful individuals.

Such a perspective then, emphasizes that existing social arrangements are always in the process of change, thus highlighting the dynamic aspects of social life. The static concept of "norm" utilized by traditional theorists overlooks the emergent nature of social life.

Adopting a relativist stance then, defining an act as deviant depends on such factors as: who does the defining, when the circumstances occurred, the social groups involved, the tolerance level of the community, etc. Howard S. Becker writes:

> From this point of view, deviance is not a quality of the act a person commits, but rather, a consequence of the application by others of rules and sanctions to an "offender." The deviant is one to whom the label has successfully been applied; deviant behavior is behavior that people so label (1962:9).

and John Kitsuse (1962:253) states:

> Forms of behavior *per se* do not differentiate deviants from non-deviants;
> it is the responses of the conventional and conforming members of
> society who identify and interpret behavior as deviant which sociologi-
> cally transform persons into deviants.

Social deviants then, are individuals who have been successfully labelled by an audience. The successful assignation of a deviant label necessarily involves a complex process wherein others' reaction to a particular act, may involve unofficial and official third parties, official processing, and eventually leads to the individual internalizing the new deviant identity and corresponding status proffered him or her.

This edited book adopts the subjectivist or contemporary perspective, that is, it conceives of deviance as a social definition, an orientation giving primacy to the values and expectations of those who judge various behaviors or beliefs to be deviant. Depending on who is watching us and their morals and standards, we are all potentially deviant. The format of this book then, follows the contemporary approach we have just outlined. We begin this section with selections dealing with biological and psychological approaches to the study of deviant behavior. In Parts II and III, we introduce the reader to various traditional and contemporary sociological theories that attempt to answer the question, "What is deviant?" Criticisms of each theory are discussed.

In Part IV, we deal with the manner by which sociologists go about studying the phenomenon of deviance. Particular attention is paid to participant observation/ ethnographic research, a methodological orientation yielding a rich and detailed understanding of the phenomenon under investigation.

Part V centers on the deviant-making enterprise. Specifically, in this section we address the social processes by which deviant categories are created and the consequences of their application.

In Part VI of the reader we examine the formal regulation of deviance. In particular, we shall examine various formal deviance processing institutions, their "theory of the office," and the dynamics involved in the processing of those individuals adjudged or labelled deviant.

Part VII deals with deviant subcultures, deviant acts and deviant gangs. Some deviants, as a consequence of institutional processing, possess a stigma—an attribute limiting their future participation in society. Persons, such as ex-cons and ex-mental patients often enter into, or perhaps even form a subculture—a group providing its members with substantial economic, physical and psychological benefits. Other individuals, such as strippers, punk rockers and motorcycle gang members enter into deviant subcultures not as a result of institutional processing, but as a matter of choice. We shall examine these two variant career patterns.

In Parts VIII-X, we turn attention to the complex social processes through which deviant identities are developed, maintained and transformed. Specifically, the readings in these sections focus on the effects of labelling from the subjective standpoints of the individuals so tagged. How do individuals respond when first labelled "deviant?" Do they automatically accept this new identity and corresponding status? Do they reject it? If so, are they successful in doing so? If not, why not? We shall focus on the role of institution processing in stripping individuals of their former, non-deviant self-conceptions and identities, and the processes by which individuals gradually come to accept the image and identity pro-offered them. We shall focus on how deviants attempt to "manage" their new identities, what Goffman (1963) refers to as a "spoiled identity"—that is, what techniques and stratagems do deviants employ in order to mitigate the stigma potential of their "failing."

Once individuals leave the prison, mental institution, etc., many desire to transform their deviant identities. Many deviants desire to abandon their deviant identities and statuses and resume normal identities, roles and statuses that they once held. The readings in this section will address the problem of identity transformation and the individual and collective stratagems ex-deviants employ to aid their cause.

References

Bartollas, C., and S. Dinitz 1989. *Introduction to Criminology—Order and Disorder*. New York: Harper.

Becker, Howard S., 1962 *Outsiders: Studies in the Sociology of Deviance*. New York: Free Press.

Berkowitz, Leonard, 1978. "Is Criminal Violence Normative Behavior?" *Journal of Research in Crime and Delinquency* 15:148-161.

Cohen, Albert, 1955. *Delinquent Boys*. Glencoe, Illinois: The Free Press.

Goffman, Erving 1963. *Stigma*. Englewood Cliffs, New Jersey: Prentice-Hall.

Kitsuse, John, 1962. "Societal Reaction to Deviant Behavior." *Social Problems* 9:247-256.

Liazos, Alexander, 1972. "The Poverty of the Sociology of Deviance: Nuts, Sluts and Preverts." *Social Problems* 20:103-120.

Robert K. Merton, 1966. "Social Problems and Sociological Theory." Pp. 775-827 In Robert K. Merton and Robert Nisbet, eds., *Contemporary Social Problems*. New York: Harcourt Brace and World.

Shah, Saleem A., and Loren H. Roth. "Biological and Psychophysiological Factors in Criminology." In Daniel Glaser, ed., *Handbook of Criminology*. Chicago: Rand McNally.

Simmons, Jerry L., 1969. *Deviants*. New York: Glendessary.

Toch, Hans 1969. *Violent Man: An Inquiry into the Psychology*. Chicago: Aldine.

Witkin, Herman, et al., "Criminality in XYY and XXY Men." *Science* 193:547-555.

NOTES

1. A similar study was conducted by Simmons (1969).

Chapter 1

CRIMINOLOGY: AN INTEGRATIONIST PERSPECTIVE

Diana H. Fishbein

Consistent observations that a small percentage of offenders are responsible for a preponderance of serious violent crime (Hamparin et al., 1978; Moffitt et al., 1989; Wolfgang, 1972) suggest that this particular population is unusually vulnerable to repetitive antisocial behavior. Numerous studies report that chronically violent criminals have an early history of crime and aggression (Loeber and Dishion, 1983; Moffitt et al., 1989); in fact, the best predictor of present and future behavior is past behavior. Findings that conduct disorders and delinquent acts precede drug abuse and related criminal behaviors (see Fishbein, 1991) provide further fuel for the suggestion that a subgroup of offenders are at high risk for many forms of antisociality. The possibility that biological conditions may play a role in the development of antisocial and criminal behavior is accentuated by these reports and has spurred a search for biological markers in "vulnerable" subgroups (Fishbein, 1990; Mednick et al., 1987).

Recently, biological aspects of criminal behavior have been investigated by behavioral scientists employing a multidisciplinary approach that promises to substantially enhance the rigor of findings. Scientists in such fields as genetics, biochemistry, endocrinology, neuroscience, immunology, and psychophysiology have been intensively studying aspects of human behavior that are relevant to the criminologist and the criminal justice practitioner. Due to the technical and field-specific language of this research, findings generated from these works are often neglected in criminological literature reviews. The relative lack of interdisciplinary communication has resulted in a lack of awareness of data pertinent to the study of criminal behavior.

The primary purpose of this chapter is to present a more balanced view of antisocial behavior which integrates findings from various behavioral sciences relevant to the study of crime. The central question addressed is "Given similar environmental and socio-cultural experiences, why does only a subgroup engage in antisocial and sometimes violent behavior?" Sociological research has well established the link between particular adverse environmental and social conditions, but has been unable to explain individual differences in vulnerability to these conditions. Using this "integrationist" approach, reliable biological aspects of criminal behavior may be incorporated into sociological paradigms to provide a comprehensive understanding of antisociality. This chapter provides only a condensed introduction to the vast amount of work accomplished in the behavioral sciences.

Theoretical and Methodological Parameters

A theoretical framework within which the interaction between biological and sociological influences can be understood will be presented first in order to (1) establish the relevancy of biology to the study of crime, (2) develop the groundwork for including biological data in criminological theories, and (3) determine the boundaries of practical applications of biological findings. The sections to follow discuss pertinent issues that arise within that frame of reference that both clarify and exemplify the integrationist perspective, including nature versus nurture, free will versus determinism and learning theory.

Theoretical Framework

The development of a framework for including biological perspectives in criminology requires that we first identify behaviors of interest. This exercise is essential given that not all "illegal" behaviors are dysfunctional or antisocial and not all "legitimate" behaviors are moral, acceptable, or adaptive. The term "criminality" includes behaviors that do not necessarily offend all members of society, such as certain "victimless" acts, and it excludes behaviors that may be antisocial or illegal but that are not detected by the criminal justice system. Antisocial behaviors, on the other hand, are costly to citizens and society overall. Such behaviors do not necessarily violate legal norms or come to official attention, however. Antisocial individuals have a high probability of being labeled as delinquent or criminal, but being so labeled is not a sufficient criterion to be identified as antisocial. For example, schizophrenics' behavior is poorly regulated, detrimental to their own well-being, and considered "deviant", but they rarely engage in crime. Individuals identified as psychopathic, conversely, are at risk for crime by virtue of their behavior. Yet, there are psychopathic individuals who find legal, albeit not always ethical, avenues for channeling their behavioral tendencies (e.g., some of those involved in competitive sports, high-risk activities, corporate life, and politics). The focus of this chapter is on antisocial behaviors, including both criminal and undetected behaviors, that are detrimental to the individuals affected and/or their milieu; in other words, behaviors that increase risk for criminal stigmatization, e.g., violence.

The theoretical framework presented herein is consistent with the diathesis-stress model (see Tarter and Edwards, 1987) constructed to explain many forms of antisocial behavior. According to this model, individuals vary considerably with respect to their biological strengths and weaknesses. Biological weaknesses, referred to as a "vulnerability", are influential in an individual's risk for antisocial behavior. Rather than acting alone, however, these biological features operate by setting the stage for how adaptively an individual will respond to personal stressors. In other words, a stressful environment is more likely to contribute to some form of psychopathology when it is received by a biological system that is somehow compromised. Learning disability, brain damage or functional irregularity, drug exposure, genetic predisposition to temperamental disturbances, and other biological disadvantages lay the groundwork for a pathological response to stress. Prior learning experiences contribute further by either increasing or decreasing the risk.

Although the probability of a pathological response is a function of the number of these risk factors present, the probability is even greater in the presence of an adverse environment with severe stressors (e.g., poverty, unemployment, crime and drug infestation, poor parenting, lack of education, abuse/neglect, and social immobility). For example, hyperactive children may function well given appropriate intervention. In the presence of family instability, alcoholism, absence of educational programs, and a delinquent peer group, however, the child may be more prone to antisocial behavior, possibly resulting in criminal acts. Thus, environmental factors play a facilitating role in determining an antisocial outcome in vulnerable persons. Environmental factors may be even more potent determinants of antisociality than strictly biological vulnerabilities when the environment is unusually harsh or conducive to such behavior, as we may readily observe in our inner cities. Once again, however, not all inner city residents engage in antisocial behavior; that outcome remains somewhat dependent on individual vulnerability. The reverse may be also apply — even in the presence of a protective environment, a biological disadvantage may be so severe as to overwhelm the positive environmental influence. An example of that particular outcome may be seen in fetal alcohol syndrome, when the biological odds frequently outweigh prosocial influences.

Nature or Nurture?

In beginning to apply the above framework to research in criminology, the age-old question of whether human behavior is a product of nature or nurture must be updated. Those on the nature side of the debate claimed that behavior is a result of inherited predispositions, and genetic influences were considered responsible for most of the variance in complex human behaviors. The argument that nurture is the impetus for behavior contended that environmental inputs are primarily responsible for the final behavioral product, and manipulations of external conditions were thought to effectively modify behavior.

A growing consensus has emerged that the "truth" lies somewhere in between— a "nature plus nurture" perspective (see Plomin, 1990). Numerous studies on alcoholism, temperament, violence, depression, and mental illness have established a solid role for genetic and biological influences. Although the separate, relative contributions of biology and social learning to behavior have yet to be estimated, their impact on antisocial behavior is particularly relevant to the criminologist.

Evidence for an interaction between nature and nurture comes from both animal and human studies, which demonstrate the importance of the link between biological and acquired traits. One example of this interaction involves chemical messengers in the brain called neurotransmitters, which fluctuate in response to an environmental situation, thus altering behavior. Serotonin in particular is high in dominant monkeys and humans in leadership positions (Raleigh et al., 1984). Levels of serotonin tend to decline when a dominant individual becomes subordinate and when exposed to stressful situations. Conversely, drugs that lower serotonin cause a dominant male to behave like a submissive one (Fairbanks and McGuire, 1979; McGuire et al., 1982; Raleigh et al., 1980; 1984). When serotonin is low, due to external influences or biological abnormality, behavior is altered and the likelihood of antisocial behavior increases (Fishbein et al., 1989a).

Another example of this interaction is illustrated by recent reports that gender differences in cognitive ability, a fundamentally neural process, are decreasing (see Geary, 1989). In an effort to explain changing trends in a seemingly immutable biological process, researchers are discovering that cultural and experiential conditions directly influence cognitive abilities. For example, activity patterns (e.g., frequency of rough and tumble play) may alter cognitive ability (e.g., spatial skills) by modifying processes of brain development.

Although intellectual capacity is largely considered to be stable and intractible, an individual's intellect partially depends upon fluctuating environmental conditions. Even in the presence of low birth weight, intellectual abilities can be manipulated with subsequent nurturing, including proper nutrition, tactile stimulation, and other forms of intensive personal attention. Temperamental traits, such as extraversion, depression, dominance, and neuroticism, have also been shown to have heritable components in humans (Biederman et al., 1986; DeFries and Plomin, 1978; Ghodsian-Carpey and Baker, 1987; Rowe, 1987; Rushton et al., 1986). The behavioral outcome is contingent upon various stressors in the environment, prior life experiences and present opportunities. A withdrawn and shy child, for instance, can alter his/her introverted temperament with self-awareness and training, given the availability of necessary personal and external resources.

The dynamic interaction between natural and acquired traits in a given environment must always be considered inseparable in the evaluation of complex phenomena such as human behavior. These illustrations remind us that as evidence for a substantial genetic influence grows we must be cautious not to replace environmental explanations with biologically deterministic views. Instead, a more accommodating, balanced approach will carry more empirical weight.

Free Will or Determinism?

Invariably, the question arises as to whether humans are able to make free will decisions if behavior is influenced by biological processes. Although some behavioral scientists are deterministic in their views, attributing behavior to everything from socioeconomic conditions to neurochemical events, most individuals prefer to credit their own free will for their behavior. There is, however, a compromise reflecting a more accurate position on the forces behind human behavior, that is widely accepted—the theory of "conditional free will" (Fishbein, 1990).

Conditional free will theory is based on the laws of probability in which numerous factors interplay in a dynamic fashion, increasing the likelihood of a particular behavior. It is rarely the case that a behavior can be associated with only one cause — an ever-changing interaction of causes is responsible for the final result. Indeed, social human behavior is contingent on a countless number of possible decisions from among which the individual may choose. Not all of those decisions are feasible, however, nor are the resources available that are required to act on them. Choosing a course of action, therefore, is limited by preset boundaries, which narrow the range of possibilities substantially. Decision-limiting factors include current circumstances and opportunities, learning experiences, physiological abilities, and genetic predispositions. Each one of these conditions collaborates physically and environmentally to produce a final action. The behavioral result is thus restricted to options available within these limitations, yet behavior still cannot be precisely predicted. Nevertheless, stable individuals generally behave with some degree of expectability; certain patterns of behavior are more probable than others in a given situation in a given individual.

The principle of conditional free will postulates that when conditions are suitable for rational thought, we are accountable for our actions. Given "rational" thought processes, calculation of risks versus the benefits, and the ability to judge the realities that exist, the result is likely to be an adaptive response, that is, the behavior will be beneficial for the individual and the surrounding environment. On the other hand, if one or more conditions to which the individual is exposed are disturbed or irregular, the individual is more likely to choose a disturbed or irregular course of action. Thus, the risk of such a response increases as a function of the number of deleterious conditions.

Integrated Learning Theory and the Developmental Course Model

The process of social learning operates as the functional bridge between biology and the environment in that the learning process is the embodiment of concepts fundamental to both criminology and behavioral biology. Integrated learning theory incorporates underlying assumptions about human behavior in general and applies the previously described model to improve the explanation of how antisocial behaviors develop specifically. In essence, integrated learning theory accommodates well-established findings in the social, psychological *and* biological sciences. This section discusses the importance of the learning process, firmly entrenched in the findings of all three disciplines.

Individuals are not inherently criminal, nor do they suddenly become homicidal maniacs (except under unusual circumstances). Antisocial behavior has many precursors[1]. Manifestations of a problem are frequently observed in childhood when innate tendencies toward antisocial behavior or other risk factors are compounded by suboptimal environmental and social conditions (Denno, 1988; Lewis et al., 1979, 1985; Mednick et al., 1984). These early seeds for antisocial behavior are commonly ignored, inappropriately treated, or not recognized as complications that warrant intervention. Over time, behavioral difficulties become compounded and, to some extent, reinforced once the child has established mechanisms to protect him/herself and cope with his/her liabilities. In such cases, the severity of the condition and resultant behaviors are well advanced by adolescence and adulthood. By the time the criminal justice system becomes involved, the problem is already significantly compounded and difficult to treat, costing society both money and victims. Thus, antisocial behavior is a function of a cumulative, developmental process. According to this "developmental course" model of human behavior, criminal behavior is virtually always secondary to an underlying problem(s). Evidence for a developmental phenomenon in antisocial behavior highlights the dire need for early detection and intervention (Kazdin, 1987). Both biological and social behavior are learned. Thus, biological traits and proclivities are not stationary characteristics; they are reinforced or, in some cases, altered through social learning processes. For example, temperamental traits may be reinforced by external rewards or expectations or may, on the other hand, be overcome by modeling. Thus, the actualization and longevity of this trait depend on environmental experiences or stressors.

When an individual is exposed to either a biological or social stimulus, permanent changes occur in the structure and function of the brain. This process is referred to as "memory," experiences coded and stored for retrieval. Bodily functions involved in memory are multifaceted. In particular, attention and arousal prepare the individual to receive stimuli and react to them selectively. Motivational processes operate so that the individual attends to and later retrieves information. And motor systems permit a response to a memory or experience. When stimuli are received and remembered, all future behaviors are modified, and perception is altered. Thus, humans interrelate current experiences with information previously learned, and the future response to an equivalent stimulus may be different. The integrity of each of the above activities determines whether the learning experience will result in accurately encoded memories to produce an appropriate behavioral response.

The learning process of comparing new information with memories to produce a response results in "behavioral conditioning." There is an innate foundation for learning in our biological structure that sets contingencies for behavioral conditioning in an individual, consistent with the premise of conditional free will. Consequently, behavioral sequences are neither programmed nor innate; they are acquired. The two forms of behavioral conditioning, classical and instrumental, both directly involve biological mechanisms. Classical conditioning refers to the response to a neutral stimulus that becomes associated with the acquisition of a reward or the avoidance of harm, for example, when a cocaine user sees talcum powder or a bill, craving for cocaine ensues.

When an individual is instrumental in causing a stimulus to occur, operant or instrumental conditioning is at work. The stimulus being elicited either satiates a drive or permits one to avoid a noxious result. For example, if we learn that stealing results in a reward, the behavior will continue. On the other hand, if we are consistently punished for such behavior, we are unlikely to repeat the action. Thus, both forms of conditioning revolve around the same contingencies (biological drives to avoid pain and seek pleasure, known as hedonism) which reinforce our behavior. In general, the criminal justice system is founded on the principle of behavioral conditioning in its application of deterrent measures to curb crime. Deterrence relies on the association made between specific, in this case illegal, behaviors and the application of a punitive sanction which generally involves curtailing freedom and exposure to unpleasant living conditions. The painful stimulus must be temporally associated with the behavior, consistently applied, and intense enough to prevent further such behaviors. The individual must not learn that the intrinsic reward properties of the behavior are greater or more consistent than the punishment. Also, opportunities for preferred modes of behavior must be available. Due to the prevalence of low clearance rates, trial delays, inconsistently applied dispositions, legal loopholes, the learning of improper reward and punishment contingencies and a lack of available legitimate opportunities, the criminal justice system has been unable to meet the criteria set above for deterrence. The experience of a painful consequence being associated with a behavior is encoded into memory and when we calculate the consequences of repeating that behavior we are deterred by the possible negative response. The impetus for such behavioral change resides in our nervous systems. We feel anxiety when the threat of a negative repercussion exists due to the learned association between the behavior and its likely consequence. Subjective feelings of anxiety are a result of autonomic nervous system responses, a portion of the nervous system that regulates emotional state and functions not under our conscious control, e.g., increased heart rate, blood pressure, and hormone release. Thus, the brain initiates a release of hormones that stimulates feelings of stress whenever we contemplate a behavior that we have been conditioned to avoid. Individuals with a properly functioning nervous system become conditioned to avoid stressful situations given the learned contingencies discussed above. Most of us, for example, would experience psychological and physical discomfort at the thought of picking a pocket or burglarizing a convenience store. Thus, we make a rational choice based on a calculation of costs and benefits and deterrence is most likely achieved.

The learning and conditioning of behavior occur differentially among individuals given their neurological status. For example, psychopaths are relatively unemotional, impulsive, immature, thrill-seeking and "unconditionable" (Cleckley, 1964; Moffitt, 1983; Quay, 1965; Zuckerman, 1983), and have been characterized as having low levels of perceptible anxiety and physiological responses during stressful events (Hare and Schalling, 1978; House and Milligan, 1976; Syndulko et al., 1975; Venables, 1987; Yeudall et al., 1985). Theoretically, psychopaths do not sufficiently experience the discomfort of anxiety associated with a proscribed behavior because they have an underaroused autonomic nervous system, and thus, they are not easily conditioned or deterred (Hare and Schalling, 1978). They make a rational choice based on the calculation that the benefits of the act (e.g., monetary gain) outweigh the costs (e.g., anxiety of detection). Accordingly, we would expect that psychopaths encountered by the criminal justice system would be resistant to most deterrence programs.

Rewards and punishments influence behavior directly through brain mechanisms. Centers responsible for pain and pleasure are located within the brain's limbic system. Not surprisingly, memories are encoded, stored, and retrieved in this same system. Direct electrical stimulation of certain areas within the limbic system is inherently reinforcing, even in the absence of a biological or social drive (Olds and Milner, 1954). An animal quickly learns to seek this stimulation due to its drive-inducing and intensely pleasurable effect. In humans, these areas are naturally stimulated when a behavior results in increases in specific neurotransmitters and peptides responsible for either pleasure (i.e., dopamine) or the reduction of pain (i.e., serotonin or beta-endorphins)[2]. This pain and pleasure mechanism is illustrated by the use of cocaine, which directly stimulates the release of dopamine in structures of the limbic system responsible for pleasure (Wise, 1984). The user quickly learns that cocaine is biologically rewarding and he/she will be more likely to crave and reuse the drug. This is an example of both classical and instrumental conditioning.

Imbalances of the limbic system may alter proper stimulation of pain and pleasure centers. Some psychopaths experience intense pleasure from thrill-seeking or risk-taking activities and have a high pain threshold (Blackburn, 1978). Behaviors that involve an element of danger are not only exciting to these individuals, but may be addictive in the conventional sense, producing feelings of euphoria and then discomfort when not engaging in such activities (Quay, 1965). The possibility that psychopaths have a disturbance in pain and pleasure centers is consistent with studies showing that they have low levels of anxiety and are relatively "unconditionable". There is ample support for the proneness of these individuals to become involved in criminal activities (see Wilson and Herrnstein, 1985), again due to biological traits that are reinforced through social learning.

In sum, social rewards remain secondary to biological rewards; our desire for money is social, but it is secondary to being a means for obtaining food and shelter. Thus, social behavior satisfies biological needs and drives by providing adaptive mechanisms for reproduction, mating, rearing, defense, and numerous other biological functions. Even though these strategies are fundamentally biological, how we behave to satisfy them relies heavily on learning.

The following discussion concentrates on biological aspects of this multifaceted relationship. A variety of disciplines have examined antisocial behaviors, and at least one example from each topical area will be discussed. Note that the majority of so-called multidisciplinary studies have examined only a few variables in isolation, without accounting for interactive effects between biological and socio-environmental conditions. A truly collaborative research project promises to yield more informative results regarding bio-socio-environmental influences on antisocial behavior. (See Fishbein, 1990 and Mednick et al., 1987 for detailed critiques of biological approaches.)

Selected Studies of the Biology of
. Antisocial Behavior Genetic Contributions

As a rule, what is inherited is not a behavior; rather, it is the way in which an individual responds to the environment—it provides an orientation, predisposition, or tendency to behave in a certain fashion. Also, genetic influences on human behavior are polygenic—no single gene effect can be identified for most behaviors.

Intellectual deficits (Bouchard and McGue, 1981; Cattell, 1982), temperamental traits and personality types that increase the risk for antisocial behavior have been shown to have heritable components in humans, e.g., extraversion, depression, alcoholism, dominance, neuroticism, mania, impulsivity, hyperactivity, conduct disorder, sensation seeking, and hyperemotionality (Biederman et al., 1986; Cadoret et al., 1985; DeFries and Plomin, 1978; Ghodsian-Carpey and Baker, 1987; Plomin et al., 1989; Rowe, 1987; Rushton et al., 1986). Individuals with such personality dispositions have an increased familial incidence of similar behavioral problems and show differences, along with their family members, in certain biochemical, neuropsychological, and physiological parameters (Biederman et al., 1986; Cadoret et al., 1975; DeFries and Plomin, 1978; Hare and Schalling, 1978; Plomin et al., 1989; Rushton et al., 1986; Tarter et al., 1985; Zuckerman, 1983).

Numerous studies have attempted to estimate genetic contributions to the development of criminality, delinquency, aggression, and antisocial behavior, using one of four methods: family, twin, adoption and molecular genetics studies. Because it is difficult to isolate genetic factors from developmental events, cultural influences, early experiences, and housing conditions, genetic studies of criminal behavior have been criticized (Mednick et al., 1987; Plomin et al., 1989; Rowe and Osgood, 1984; Walters and White, 1989; Wilson and Herrnstein, 1985). This research suffers from a high level of abstraction because "criminal behavior" is a legalistic label, not descriptive of actual behavior. Instead, research should focus on actual acts that can be consistently and accurately measured. Accordingly, genetic effects may be more directly associated with particular traits and behaviors that act as risk factors for criminal behavior. Violence, depression, alcoholism, and antisocial or psychopathic behavior more aptly reflect an actual behavioral pattern to which specific criteria for their identification can be applied (Plomin et al., 1989). Genetic research designs and selected studies are briefly described below.

Family Studies

Family studies seek to identify genetic influences on behavioral traits by evaluating similarities among family members. Cross-generational linkages have been reported for personality and behavioral attributes related to criminal behavior, including temper outbursts (Mattes and Fink, 1987), sociopathy (Cloninger et al., 1975; 1978; Guze et al., 1967), delinquency (Robins et al., 1975; Rowe, 1986), hyperactivity and attention deficit disorder (Cantwell, 1979), conduct disorder, aggression, violence and psychopathy (Bach-y-Rita et al., 1971; Stewart et al., 1980; Stewart and DeBlois, 1983; Stewart and Leone, 1978; Twito and Stewart, 1982).

Despite conclusions from these studies that genetic effects are largely responsible for criminal behavior, this method does not directly assess genetic contributions. Environmental influences on measures of behavior may be common to parents and offspring, and thus, large environmental correlations among relatives cannot be accounted for. Diet, environmental toxins, neighborhood conditions, and television-viewing habits are only a few examples of environmental factors that similarly influence family members. We may conclude only that the incidence of criminal and related behaviors appears to have a familial basis.

Twin Studies

The classic twin design involves the testing of identical (monozygotic or MZ) and fraternal (dizygotic or DZ) twins. MZ twins share genetic material from the biologic parents and are, thus, considered genetically identical. DZ twins are approximately 50% genetically alike, as are regular siblings. The extent to which MZ twins share a characteristic as compared to DZ twins provides evidence for a genetic influence on the variable. To the extent that there is still some degree of DZ resemblance after genetic influences have been accounted for, there is evidence for the influence of common family environment on the trait. For example, if a sample of MZ twins is 60% similar for IQ and a matched sample of DZ twins is 25% similar for IQ, we can conclude that IQ is largely a function of heredity.

Overall, twin studies provide strong evidence for a genetics-environment interaction, showing that MZ twins were more alike in their antisocial activity than DZ twins (see reviews by Christiansen 1977 and Raine 1993). Significant genetic effects have been found for both self-report and official rates of delinquent or criminal behavior (Rowe, 1983; Rowe and Osgood, 1984) and personality or temperamental traits related to criminal behavior, for example, aggression (Coccaro et al., 1993; Ghodsian-Carpey and Baker, 1987; Rowe, 1986; Rushton et al., 1986; Tellegen et al., 1988), although discrepant studies exist (Owen and Sines, 1970; Plomin et al., 1981). Plomin et al. (1988) examined numerous twin studies of criminal/delinquent behavior and aggression and noted that the results were highly inconsistent, possibly because no uniform measure of self-reported aggression and its constructs has been applied. Twin studies commonly suffer from a number of unique methodological weaknesses (see Plomin et al., 1980). In particular, the twin method can only examine the level of genetic contribution, thus, there is contamination from an unknown amount of environmental contribution.

Adoption Studies

This method examines individuals who were raised from infancy by nonrelated adoptive parents rather than biological relatives. To the extent that subjects resemble biological relatives and not nonbiologic relatives, heredity is thought to play a contributory role. The adoption study method provides richer information about the relative contribution of heredity to behavioral traits and for genetics-environment interactions. Nevertheless, the method also has some weaknesses (see Mednick, et al., 1984; Plomin et al., 1989; Walters and White, 1989).

Fourteen adoption studies indicate noteworthy genetic effects on criminal or delinquent behavior and related psychopathology, i.e., psychopathy (See Raine, 1993). For the most part, these studies suggest that biological relatives of criminal or antisocial probands have a greater history of criminal convictions or antisocial behavior than the biological relatives of noncriminal control adoptees. In general, family environment, including such indices as social class, rearing styles, and parental attitudes, played a smaller role than did purported genetic effects. Surprisingly, 3 of these studies indicate that property offending is more heritable than violent crime (Bohman et al., 1982; Mednick et al., 1984; Sigvardsson et al., 1982). This is likely due to the failure of researchers to examine repetitively violent offenders; infrequently violent offenders do not show a chronic pattern of aggressiveness and their crimes may be more situational.

Genetic influences on criminality may differ for those who are also alcoholic (Bohman et al., 1982). Specifically, when the biological parents are both criminal and alcoholic, crimes of adoptees tend to be more violent. Cadoret et al. (in press) further demonstrated a strong effect of a biologic parent with both alcohol problems and antisocial personality on the eventual substance abuse and antisocial behavior in the adopted-away offspring. Antisocial personality in individuals with biologic antisocial parents is first manifested in childhood and adolescence as a conduct disorder, followed by the early onset of substance use. The factor most predictive of drug abuse was aggressivity and was correlated with biological parent antisocial personality.

Adoption studies highlight the importance of gene-environment interaction models (Rowe and Osgood, 1984). Having a criminal adoptive parent most profoundly affects those with a genetic propensity for criminality (Mednick et al. (1984). In other words, those who inherited certain antisocial personality and temperamental traits are more likely to manifest criminal behaviors in the presence of deleterious environmental conditions, e.g., criminal parents.

Molecular Genetic Studies

While family, twin and adoption studies have predominated efforts to assess genetic contributions to antisocial behavior, they do not directly identify the actual biological features being inherited. Molecular genetic techniques are increasing our understanding of causal links between genetics, brain function, temperament, and the behavioral outcome. Investigators have isolated DNA from blood to identify specific genetic features that may be involved (Comings et al., 1994; Noble et al., 1993). Genetic defects in two neurotransmitters, dopamine and serotonin, have been identified in certain drug abusers and appear to play a role in forms of excessive and compulsive behaviors, including aggressivity, conduct disorder, obsessive-compulsive disorder, and post-traumatic stress disorder, all of which are associated with violence. The sensitivity of brain regions to both abusable drugs and aggressive behavior is a function of these neurotransmitters. Thus, the use of drugs and/or aggressivity may provide relief from or stimulation to systems that are chronically imbalanced. Theoretically, vulnerable individuals may attain a "neurological high" from both drug use and antisocial or violent behavior (Gove and Wilmoth, 1990).

Biological Contributions

Genetic foundations for behavior are manifested in the resulting, visible expression of a genetic trait. Although we can rarely trace a behavioral disorder to a specific gene, we can measure the manifestation of a genetic blueprint in nervous system features. Other biological traits associated with behavioral problems are not directly genetic in origin; they may be due to genetic mutations, biochemical exposures, or a deleterious social environment. All of these conditions, from the genetic to the environmental, exert their influence on the nervous system and, thus, can be examined. The following correlates of behavioral disorders illustrate selected ways in which genetic and environmental factors impact on the nervous system to alter behavior.

Biochemical Correlates

A number of biochemical differences have been found between controls and individuals with psychopathy, antisocial personality, violent behavior, conduct disorder, and other behaviors associated with criminal behavior. These groups have been discriminated on the basis of levels of certain hormones, neurotransmitters, peptides, toxins, and metabolic processes (Brown et al., 1979; Comings et al., 1994; Davis et al., 1983; Eichelman and Thoa, 1973; Fishbein et al., 1989a; Mednick et al., 1987; Rogeness et al., 1987; Roy et al., 1986; Valzelli, 1981; Virkkunen and Narvanen, 1987).

Current investigations of biochemical mechanisms of aggressiveness focus on the study of neurotransmitter systems. Animal and human studies, for example, indicate that serotonin globally inhibits behavioral responses to emotional stimuli and modulates aggression (Muhlbauer, 1985; Soubrie, 1986; van Praag et al., 1987). Several indicators of lower levels of serotonin activity in individuals characterized as violent or impulsive, in comparison with those who are not, have been reported (Brown et al., 1979; Coccaro, 1989; Coccaro and Astill, 1990; Fishbein et al., 1989a; Linnoila et al., 1983; Virkkunen et al., 1987, 1989). These studies indicate that serotonin functioning is altered in some types of human aggressiveness and violent suicidal behavior. Specifically, a decrease in serotonin activity is disinhibiting in both brain mechanisms and behavior and results in increased aggressiveness or impulsivity.

Biological factors contributing to individual differences in temperament, arousal, or vulnerability to stress may be important in the etiology of female criminal behavior (Widom, 1978). Socioenvironmental influences may differentially interact with biological sex differences to produce variations in male and female criminality (see, for example, Ellis and Ames, 1987). For example, in males, high levels of the male sex hormone testosterone may increase aggressive behavior (Kreuz and Rose, 1971; Olweus et al., 1988; Rada et al., 1983; Schiavi et al., 1984), although discrepant studies exist (Coe and Levine, 1983). Sex hormones may also contribute to antisocial behavior in some women. Premenstrual and postpartum periods have been associated with elevated levels of aggressivity and irritability in some women. These phases of the cycle are marked by a hormonal upset which may trigger both physical and psychological impairments in a subgroup of women, e.g.,sharp changes in mood, depression, irritability, aggression, difficulty in concentration, and substance abuse (Haskett, 1987; Trunnell and Turner, 1988). A significant number of females imprisoned for aggressive criminal acts were found to have committed their crimes during the premenstrual phase, and female offenders were found to be more irritable and aggressive during this period (see Ginsburg and Carter, 1987 for review). Despite methodological shortcomings (see Harry and Balcer, 1987), there remains a general impression that a small percentage of women appear to be vulnerable to cyclical hormonal changes which cause them to be more prone to anxiety and hostility (Carroll and Steiner, 1987; Clare, 1985; Ginsburg and Carter, 1987).

Exposure to toxic trace elements is yet another factor that has been shown to interfere with brain function and behavior. Exposure to lead, for example, has a deleterious effect on brain function by damaging organ systems, impairing intellectual development, and subsequently interfering with the regulation of behavior. Sources of lead include our diet and environment, and contamination among children may be grossly underestimated (Bryce-Smith and Waldron, 1974; Moore and Fleischman, 1975). Resulting impairments may be manifested as learning disabilities and cognitive deficits (hyperactivity and attention deficit disorder), particularly in measures of school achievement, verbal and performance IQ, and mental dullness (see Benignus et al., 1981; Lester and Fishbein, 1987; Needleman et al., 1979; Pihl and Parkes, 1977), all risk factors for delinquency. Research has also demonstrated that lead intoxication is significantly associated with violence (Pihl et al., 1982). Accumulating evidence strongly suggests that lead exposure substantially increases the risk for antisocial behavior (see Rimland and Larson, 1983, for review).

Psychophysiological Correlates

Psychophysiological variables are quantifiable indices of nervous system function, e.g., heart rate, blood pressure, attention and arousal levels, skin conductance, and brain waves. These measurable conditions directly reflect emotional responses. Studies have repeatedly found psychophysiological evidence for mental abnormality and central nervous system disturbances as putative markers for antisocial behavior. For example, psychopaths have been found to differ from nonpsychopathic controls in several physiological parameters. These indices include (a) electroencephalogram (EEG) differences, (b) cognitive and neuropsychological impairment, and (c) electrodermal, cardiovascular, and other nervous system measures (see Raine, 1993 for review).

In particular, psychopathic individuals have been found to show relatively more slow wave activity in their EEG compared with controls, which may be related to differences in cognitive abilities (Fishbein et al., 1989b; Hare, 1970; Howard, 1984; Pincus and Tucker, 1974; Syndulko, 1978). Relatively high levels of EEG slowing found in psychopathic subjects may reflect a maturational lag in brain function (Kiloh et al., 1972; Pontius and Ruttiger, 1976). Thus, EEG slowing among individuals who also demonstrate immature behavior and an inability to learn from experience reflects a developmental delay. EEG slowing among some psychopaths is consistent with findings of hypoaroused autonomic function (see above) and other differences in psychophysiologic parameters. Their need for external stimulation may be higher and more difficult to satisfy than in other populations due to a lower level of internal stimulation.

Psychopharmacological Inducements

Psychopharmacology is the study of the psychological and behavioral aspects of drug effects on brain activity. Certain psychoactive drugs are reported to increase aggressive responses (see Fishbein and Pease, in press), for example, amphetamines, cocaine, alcohol, and phencyclidine (PCP). The actual expression of aggressive behavior depends on the dose, route of administration, genetic factors, and type of aggression.

Several biological mechanisms have been proposed as explanations for alcohol-induced aggression: (1) pathological intoxication, sometimes involving psychomotor epilepsy or temporal lobe disturbance (Bach-y-Rita et al., 1970; Maletsky, 1976; Marinacci, 1963); (2) hypoglycemic reactions (low blood sugar; Cohen, 1980; Coid, 1979; Wallgren and Barry, 1970); and (3) alterations in neurotransmitter activity (Weingartner et al., 1983). Because most drinkers do not become aggressive, indications are that alcohol either changes the psychological state or the psychological state has an effect on the behavioral outcome of alcohol consumption. In the second scenario, alcohol would stimulate an existing psychiatric condition or psychological predisposition to aggress or misbehave (Pihl and Ross, 1987). Because serotonin appears to modulate drinking behavior, individuals with low serotonin may be more likely to drink to excess and equally more likely to exhibit aggressive behavior. Hence, alcohol does not appear to "cause" aggression, but rather permits its expression under specific circumstances and biological conditions.

Chronic use of PCP (phencyclidine) has been repeatedly associated with extreme violence to self and others (Aronow et al., 1980; Fauman and Fauman, 1980; Linder et al., 1981; Schuckit and Morrissey, 1978; Seigal, 1978; Smith and Wesson, 1980). Violent reactions appear to be an extension of PCP toxic psychosis, which affects some users (Fauman and Fauman, 1980). Because only a subpopulation of users manifest violent behavior, additional research is needed to determine the nature of the vulnerability that causes certain individuals to be particularly susceptible to that behavioral effect. PCP-related aggression may be due to influences on hormonal and neurotransmitter activity (Domino, 1978, 1980; Marrs-Simon et al., 1988). Also, neuropsychological impairments have been observed that minimally reflect a temporary organic brain syndrome (Cohen, 1977; Smith and Wesson, 1980). Studies of PCP users indicate that factors in the user's background, personality, and drug history are also important determinants of the drug-related experience (Fauman and Fauman, 1980; McCardle and Fishbein, 1989). The behavioral consequences of PCP use are determined by a number of individual factors, including the pharmacological, psychological, and situational.

Implications of Biological Findings for CJ Practices

In order to determine the relevance and significance of biological perspectives for criminology, researchers must estimate the incidence of biological disorders among antisocial populations, identify etiologic mechanisms, assess the dynamic interaction among biological and socioenvironmental factors, and determine whether improvements in behavior follow large-scale therapeutic manipulations.

We are beginning to identify markers of antisocial behavior using biological tests (e.g., EEG slowing, body lead burden, neurotransmitter imbalance). Some of these correlations may prove to be spurious, but at present, several of these factors appear to influence an individual's risk status in combination with environmental conditions. Demands in the criminal justice system for evaluation of causal relationships are made in decisions regarding the granting of bail, release on personal recognizance, competency, guilty pleas, sentencing options, probation and parole, and proclivity to recidivate. Conclusions and prognoses regarding the role of biological factors, however, are not definitive at this time, regardless of the informational source.

To further establish the relevance of biology to criminology, we must demonstrate the ability to reliably predict antisocial behavior using a combination of biological and social variables. The central question thus becomes, Can we explain more of the variance in the incidence of antisocial behavior with an integrated approach than with a unidisciplinary perspective? Many clinicians and researchers have concluded that predicting antisocial behavior with social or legal variables is inherently unreliable (Cocozza and Steadman, 1974; Gottfredson, 1986; Monahan, 1981; Wenk et al., 1972). Prediction studies incorporating biological measures into sociological data bases will facilitate the isolation of significant predictors of antisocial behavior and enhance explanatory power (Brizer and Crowner, 1989; Denno, 1988; Virkunnen et al., 1989).

Denno (1988) conducted a comprehensive study of the effects of numerous environmental and biological variables on criminal behavior, juvenile delinquency, and disciplinary problems. Denno concluded that "biological and environmental variables exert strong and independent influences on juvenile crime" and that "crime appears to be directly related to familial instability and, most important, a lack of behavioral control associated with neurological and central nervous system disorders" (p. 659). She cautions, however, that behavior should be predicted in terms of a series of probabilities of expected behavior, not in terms of cause and effect. An approach that neither neglects nor places undue emphasis on socioenvironmental or biological features of behavior provides considerable promise as the direction of future research into practical problems in criminology.

At the very least, the inclusion of biological measures holds promise of explaining individual variation within a social context. Why is it, for example, that not all children exposed to child abuse become violent as adults? Research suggests that whether child abuse contributes to violent behavior partially depends on the presence of a biological vulnerability, e.g., brain damage (Lewis et al., 1979). Perhaps abused children without concomitant or resultant brain damage would be less aggressive and more in control of their impulses. Research yet to be conducted may also show that individuals with biological "disadvantages" respond with more violent or criminal behavior in a criminogenic environment than those equipped with biological "insulators," for example, high intelligence or adequate serotonergic activity.

We are closer to enacting prevention programs aimed at populations who are at risk for exposure to biological and socioenvironmental hazards that are known to increase the incidence of behavioral problems. Factors that may prove to be important contributors to relevant behavioral disorders could subsequently be manipulated on a wide scale to prevent the onset of behavioral disorders in the general population. Early detection programs could be implemented by school systems, and parents could be educated to recognize signs of an impairment. Screening clinics, regulating environmental toxins, school programs, prenatal care facilities, and public educational programs are only a few of the preventative measures possible. The number of "risk" factors could, in essence, be reduced or minimized.

An excellent example of this strategy was suggested by Moffitt et al. (1989) in their review of minor physical anomalies (MPAs), that is, observable minor malformations that result from a disturbance in fetal development. MPAs are reflective of other hidden anomalies, such as central nervous system impairment, that may result from some perinatal trauma (e.g., illness, poor diet, drug use, stress). A relatively large number of MPAs have been observed among hyperactive and violent populations. There is no acceptable mode of individual remediation in such cases, particularly because of the remote association of MPAs with behavior. These consistent observations, however, emphasize the need for a global effort to provide proper prenatal care. Such programs may reduce the incidence of developmental deficits related to behavioral disorders.

Criminal justice policies must be based on well-founded theories and findings that survive scientific scrutiny. The application of scientific findings to criminal justice programs that are well recognized and accepted by the discipline have more value than trial and error approaches in preventing or minimizing antisocial behavior. Although biological techniques in the assessment of human behavior are still under the miscroscope and definitive answers have yet to surface, the foregoing description of biological foundations for behavior provides evidence of their applicability and value. By undertaking a collaborative strategy, we can develop more effective prevention and therapeutic programs and develop a legal system that reflects public consensus, meets human needs, and maintains an ethical and organized social structure.

REFERENCES

Aronow, R., Miceli, J.N. and Done, A.K. 1980. "A therapeutic approach to the acutely overdosed patient." *Journal of Psychedelic Drugs*, 12, 259–268.

Bach-y-Rita, G., Lion, J.R. and Ervin, F. R. 1970. "Pathological intoxication. Clinical and electroencephalographic studies." *American Journal of Psychiatry* 127: 698–703.

Bach-y-Rita, G., Lion, J.R., Climent, C.E. and Ervin, F.R. 1971. "Episodic dyscontrol: A study of 130 violent patients." *American Journal of Psychiatry* 127: 1473–1478.

Benignus, V.A., Otto, D.A., Muller, K.E. and Seiple, K.J. 1981. "Effects of age and body lead burden on CNS function in young children. II: EEG spectra." *Electroencephalography and Clinical Neurophysiology* 52: 240–248.

Biederman, J., Munir, K., Knee, D., Habelow, W., Armentano, M., Autor, S., Hoge, S.K. and Waternaux, C. 1986. "A family study of patients with attention deficit disorder and normal controls." *Journal of Psychiatric Research* 204: 263–274.

Blackburn, R. 1978. "Psychopathy, arousal and the need for stimulation." Pp. 74–93. In R.D. Hare and D. Schalling (Eds.), *Psychopathic Behavior: Approaches to Research*. Chichester, England: Wiley.

Bouchard, T.J., Jr. and McGue, M. 1981. "Familial studies of intelligence: A review." *Science* 212: 1055–1059.

Bohman, M., Cloninger, C.R., Sigvardson, S. and von Knorring, A.L. 1982. "Predisposition to petty criminality in Swedish adoptees: I. Genetic and environmental heterogeneity." *Archives of General Psychiatry* 41: 872–878.

Brizer, D.A. and Crowner, M. 1989. *Current Approaches to the Prediction of Violence*. Washington, D.C.: American Psychiatric Press.

Brown, G.L., Goodwin, F.K., Ballenger, J.C., Goyer, P.F. and Major, L.F. 1979. "Aggression in humans correlates with cerebrospinal fluid amine metabolites." *Psychiatry Research* 1(2): 131–139.

Bryce-Smith, D. and Waldron, H.A. 1974. "Lead, behavior, and criminality." *The Ecologist* 4: 367–377.

Cadoret, R., Cunningham, L., Loftus, R. and Edwards, J. 1975. "Studies of adoptees from psychiatrically disturbed biologic parents. II. Temperament, hyperactive, antisocial and developmental variables." *Journal of Pediatrics* 87: 301–306.

Cadoret, R.J., O'Gorman, T.W., Troughton, E. and Heywood, E. 1985. "Alcoholism and antisocial personality: Interrelationships, Genetic and environmental factors." *Archives of General Psychiatry* 42: 161–167.

Cadoret, R.J., Yates, W.R., Troughton, E., Woodworth, G., and Stewart M.A. (in press). "Adoption study demonstrating two genetic pathways to drug abuse."

Cantwell, D.P. 1979. "Minimal brian dysfunction in adults: Evidence from studies of psychiatric illness in the families of hyperactive children." Pp. 37–44 in L. Bellak (Ed.), *Psychiatric Aspects of Minimal Brain Dysfunction in Adults*. New York: Grune and Stratton.

Carroll, B.J. and Steiner, M. 1987. "The psychobiology of premenstrual dysphoria: The role of prolactin." *Psychoneuroendocrinology* 3: 171–180.

Cattell, R.B. 1982. *The Inheritance of Personality and Ability: Research Methods and Findings*. New York: Academic Press.

Christiansen, K.O. 1977. "A review of studies of criminality among twins." In S.A. Mednick and K.O. Christiansen (Eds.), *Biosocial Bases of Criminal Behavior*. New York: Garnder Press.

Clare, A.W. 1985. "Hormones, behavior and the menstrual cycle." *Journal of Psychosomatic Research* 29 (3): 225–233.

Cleckley, H. 1964. *The Mask of Sanity*, 4th ed. St. Louis: Mosby.

Cloninger, C.R., Reich, T., and Guze, S.B. 1975. "The multifactorial model of disease transmission: II. Sex differences in the familial transmission of sociopathy (Antisocial personality)." *British Journal of Psychiatry* 127: 11–22.

Cloninger, C.R., Christiansen, K.O., Reich, T., and Gottesman, I.I. 1978. "Implications of sex differences in the prevalence of antisocial personality, alcoholism, and criminality for familial transmission." *Archives of General Psychiatry* 35: 941–951.

Coccaro, E.F. 1989. "Central serotonin and impulsive aggression." *British Journal of Psychiatry* 115 (Suppl. 8): 52–62.

Coccaro, E.F. and Astill, J.L. 1990. "Central serotonergic function inparasuicide." *Progress in Neuropsychopharmacology and Biological Psychiatry* 14: 663–674.

Coccaro, E.F., Bergeman, C.S. and McClearn, G.E. 1993. "Heritability of Irritable impulsiveness: A study of twins reared together and apart." *Psychiatry Research* 48: 229–242.

Cocozza, J.J. and Steadman, H.J. 1974. "Some refinements in the measurement and prediction of dangerous behavior." *American Journal of Psychiatry* 131: 1012–1014.

Coe, C.L. and Levine, S. 1983. "Biology of aggression." *Bulletin of the American Academy of Psychiatry Law* 11: 131–148.

Cohen, S. 1977. "Angel dust." *Journal of the American Medical Association* 238: 515–516.

Cohen, S. 1980 "Alcoholic hypoglycemia." *Drug Abuse and Alcoholism Newsletter* 9 (2): 1–4.

Coid, J. 1979. "Mania a potu: A criminal review of pathological intoxication." *Psychological Medicine* 9: 709–719.

Comings, D.E., Muhleman, D., Ahn, C., Gysin, R., and Glanagan, S. 1994. "The dopamine D2 receptor gene: A genetic risk factor in substance abuse." *Drug and Alcohol Dependence*, 34: 175–180.

Davis, B.A., Yu, P.H., Boulton, A.A., Wormith, J.S. and Addington, D. 1983. "Correlative relationship between biochemical activity and aggressive behavior." *Progress in Neuro-Psychopharmacology and Biological Psychiatry* 7: 529–535.

DeFries, J.C. and Plomin, R. 1978. "Behavioral genetics." *Annual Reviews in Psychology* 29: 473–515.

Denno, D.W. 1988. "Human biology and criminal responsibility: Free Will or Free Ride?" *University of Pennsylvania Law Review* 137 (2): 615–671.

Domino, E.F. 1978. "Neurobiology of Phencyclidne - An Update." Pp. 5–14. In R.C. Peterson and R.C. Stillman (Eds.) *PCP Phencyclidine Abuse: An Appraisal*, National Institute on Drug Abuse Research Monograph Series 21.

Domino, E.F. 1980. "History and pharmacology of PCP and PCP-related analogs." *Journal of Psychedelic Drugs*, 12, 223–227.

Eichelman, B.S. and Thoa, N.B. 1972. "The aggression monoamines." *Biological Psychiatry* 6 (2): 143–163.

Ellis, L. and Ames, M.A. 1987. "Neurohormonal functioning and sexual orientation: A theory of homosexuality-heterosexuality." *Psychological Bulletin* 101: 233–258.

Fairbanks, L.A. and McGuire, M.T. 1979. "Inhibition of control role behaviors in captive vervet monkeys." *Behavioral Processes* 4: 145–153.

Fauman, M.A. and Fauman, B.J. 1980. "Chronic phencyclidine (PCP) abuse: A psychiatric perspective." *Journal of Psychedelic Drugs*, 12, 307–314.

Fishbein, D.H. 1990. "Biological Perspectives in Criminology." *Criminology* 28: 27–72.

Fishbein, D.H. 1991. "Medicalizing the Drug War." *BehavioralSciences and the Law* 9: 323–344.

Fishbein, D.H., Lozovsky, D. and Jaffe, J.H. 1989a. "Impulsivity, aggression and neuroendocrine responses to serotonergic stimulation in substance abusers." *Biological Psychiatry* 25: 1049–1066.

Fishbein, D.H., Herning, R., Pickworth, W., Haertzen, C., Hickey, J. and Jaffe, J. 1989b. "Spontaneous EEG and Brainstem Evoked Response Potentials in Drug Abusers with Histories of Aggressive Behavior." *Biological Psychiatry* 26:595–611.

Fishbein, D.H. and Pease, S. (in press). *The Dynamics of DrugAbuse*. Allyn and Bacon, Inc.

Geary, D.C. 1989. "A model for representing gender differences in the patten of cognitive abilities." *American Psychologist* 44: 1155–1156.

Ghodsian-Carpey, J. and Baker, L.A. 1987. "Genetic and environmental influences on aggression in 4 to 7 year old twins." *Aggressive Behavior* 13: 173–186.

Ginsburg, B.E. and Carter, B.F. 1987. *Premenstrual Syndrome:Ethical and Legal Implications in a Biomedical Perspective*. New York: Plenum Press.

Gottsfredson, S. 1986. "Statistical and actual considerations." In F. Dutile and C. Foust (Eds.), *The Prediction of Criminal Violence*. Springfield: Charles C. Thomas.

Gove, W.R. and Wilmoth, C. 1990. "Risk, crime and physiological highs: A consideration of neurological processes which may act as positive reinforcers." Pp. 262–93. In L. Ellis and H. Hoffman (Eds.), *Evolution, The Brain and Criminal Behavior: A Reader in Biosocial Criminology*. New York: Praeger.

Guze, S.B., Wolfgram, E.D., McKinney, J.K., and Cantwell, D.P. 1967."Psychiatric illness in the families of convicted criminals: A study of 519 first-degree relatives." *Diseases of the Nervous System* 28: 651–659.

Hamparin, D.M., Schuster, R., Dinitz, S., and Conrad, J.P. 1978. *The Violent Few: A Study of Dangerous Juvenile Offenders*. Lexington, Mass., Lexington/D.C. Heath.

Hare, R.D. 1978. "Electroderman and cardiocascular correlates of psychopathy." Pp. 107–143 in R.D. Hare and D. Schalling (Eds.), *Psychopathic Behavior*. New York: Wiley.

Harry, B. and Balcer, C. 1987. "Menstruation and Crime: A critical review of the literature from the clinical criminology perspective." *Behavioral Sciences and the Law* 5 (3): 307–322.

Haskett, R.F. 1987. "Premenstrual Dysphoric disorder: Evaluation, pathophysiology and treatment." *Progress in Neuro-Psychopharmacology and Biological Psychiatry* 11: 129–135.

House, T.H. and Milligan, W.L. 1976. "Autonomic responses to modeled distress in prison psychopaths." *Journal of Personality and Social Psychology* 34: 556–560.

Howard, R.C. 1984. "The clinical EEG and personality in mentally abnormal offenders." *Psychological Medicine* 14: 569–580.

Kadzin, A.E. 1987. "Treatment of antisocial behavior in children: Current status and future directions." *Psychological Bulletin* 102: 187–203.

Kiloh, L.G., McComas, A.J. and Osselton, J.W. 1972. *Clinical Electroencephalography*, 3rd ed. Butterworths, London.

Kreuz, L.E. and Rose, R.M. 1971. "Assessment of aggressive behavior and plasma testosterone in a young criminal population." *Psychosomatic Medicine* 34: 321–332.

Lester, M.L. and Fishbein, D.H. 1987. "Nutrition and Neuropsychological Development in Children." Pp. 291–335. In R. Tarter and K. Edwards (Eds.), *Medical Neuropsychology: The Impact of Disease on Behavior*. New York: Plenum Press.

Lewis, D.O., Shanok, S.S. and Balla, D.A. 1979. "Perinatal difficulties, head and face trauma and child abuse in the medical histories of serious youthful offenders." *American Journal of Psychiatry*, 136: 419–423.

Lewis, D.O., Shanok, S.S. and Pincus, J.N. 1981. "The neuropsychiatric status of violent male delinquents." Pp. 67–88 in D.O. Lewis (Ed.), *Vulnerabilities to Delinquency*. New York: Spectrum.

Linder, R.L., Lerner, S.E., and Burns, R.S. 1981. "The experience and effects of PCP abuse." In *The Devil's Dust: Recognition, Management, and Prevention of Phencyclidine Abuse*. Belmont, California: Wadsworth Publishing Company.

Linnoila, M., Virkkunen, M., Scheinin, M., Nuutila, A., Rimon, R. and Goodwin, F.K. 1983. "Low cerebrospinal fluid 5–hydroxyindoleacetic acid concentration differentiates impulsive from nonimpulsive violent behavior." *Life Sciences* 33: 2609–2614.

Loeber, R. and Dishion, T. 1983. "Early predictors of male delinquency: A review." *Psychological Bulletin* 94: 68–99.

Maletsky, B.M. 1976. "The diagnosis of pathological intoxication." *Journal of Studies of Alcohol* 37: 1215–1228.

Marinacci, A.A. 1963. "Special types of temporal lobe seizures following ingestion of alcohol. *Bulletin of the Los Angeles Neurological Society* 28: 241–250.

Marrs-Simon, P.A., Weiler, M., Santangelo, M.A., Perry, M.T. and Leikin, J.B. 1988. "Analysis of sexual disparity of violent behavior in PCP intoxication." *Veterinary and Human Toxicology* 30 (1): 53–55.

Mattes, J.A. and Fink, M. 1987. "A family study of patients with temper outbursts." *Journal of Psychiatric Research* 21: 249–255.

McCardle, L. and Fishbein, D.H. 1989. "The self-reported effects of PCP on human aggression."*Addictive Behaviors* 4 (4):465–72.

McGuire, M.T., Raleigh, M.J. and Brammer, G.L. 1982. "Sociopharmacology." *Annual Review of Pharmacology and Toxicology* 22: 643–661.

Mednick, S.A., Moffitt, T.E. and Stack, S.A. 1987. *The Causes of Crime: New Biological Approaches.* New York: Cambridge University Press.

Mednick, S.A., Gabrielli, W.F. and Hutchings, B. 1984. "Genetic influences in criminal convictions: Evidence from an adoption cohort." *Science* 224: 891–894.

Moffitt, T.E. 1983. "The learning theory model of punishment: Implications for delinquency deterrence." *Criminal Justice and Behavior* 10: 131–158.

Moffitt, T.E., Mednick, S.A. and Gabrielli, W.F. 1989. "Predicting careers of criminal violence: Descriptive data and predispositional factors." In D.A. Brizer and M. Crowner (Eds.), *Current Approaches to the Prediction of Violence.* Washington, D.C.: American Psychiatric Press.

Monahan, J. 1981. *The Clinical Prediction of Violent Behavior.* Rockville, MD: U.S. Department of Health and Human Services.

Moore, L.S. and Fleischman, A.I. 1975. "Subclinical lead toxicity."*Orthomolecular Psychiatry* 4: 61–70.

Muhlbauer, H.D. 1985. "Human aggression and the role of central serotonin." *Pharmacopsychiatry* 18: 218–221.

Needleman, H.L., Gunnoe, C., Leviton, A., Reed, P., Peresie, H., Maher, C. and Barrett, P. 1979. "Deficits in psychologic and classroom performance of children with elevated dentine lead levels." *New England Journal of Medicine* 300: 689–695.

Noble, E.P., Blum, K., Khalsa, M.E., Ritchie, T., Montgomery, A., Wood, R.C., Fitch, R.J., Ozkartagoz, T., Sheridan, P.J., Anglin, M.D., Paredes, A., Treiman, L.J., and Sparkes, R.S. 1993. "Allelic association of the D2 dopamine receptor gene with cocaine dependence." *Drug and Alcohol Dependence* 33: 271–285.

Olds, J. and Milner, P. 1954. "Positive reinforcement produced by electrical stimulation of septal area and other regions of rat brain." *Journal of Comparative and Physiological Psychology* 47: 419–427.

Olweus, D., Mattsson, A., Schalling, D., Low, H. 1988. "Circulating testosterone levels and aggression in adolescent males: A causal analysis." *Psychosomatic Medicine* 50: 261–272.

Owen, D. and Sines, J.O. 1970. "Heritability of personality in children." *Behavior Genetics* 1: 235–248.

Patterson, G.R., Debaryshe, B.D., and Ramsey, E. 1989. "A developmental perspective on antisocial behavior." *American Psychologist* 44: 329–335.

Pihl, R.O. and Parkes, M. 1977. "Hair element content in learning disabled children." *Science* 198: 204.

Plomin, R., DeFries, J.C. and McClearn, G.E. 1980. *Behavioral Genetics: A Primer.* San Francisco: W.H. Freeman.

Plomin, R., Pedersen, N.L., McClearn, G.E., Nesselroade, J.R., and Bergeman, C.S. 1988. "EAS temperaments during the last half of the life span: Twins reared apart and twins reared together." *Psychology and Aging* 3: 43–50.

Plomin, R., Nitz, K. and Rowe, D.C. 1990. "Behavioral Genetics and Aggressive Behavior in Childhood." Pp. 119–133 in M. Lewis and S.M. Miller (Eds.), *Handbook of Developmental Psychopathology.* New York: Plenum Press.

Pontius, A.A. and Ruttinger, K.F. 1976. "Frontal lobe system maturational lag in juvenile delinquents shown in narrative test." *Adolescence* XI (44): 509–518.

Quay, H.C. 1965. "Psychopathic personality as pathological stimulation seeking." *American Journal of Psychiatry* 122: 180–183.

Rada, R.T., Laws, D.R., Kellner, R., Stivastava, L. and Peake, G. 1983. "Plasma androgens in violent and nonviolent sex offenders." *Bulletin of the American Academy of Psychiatry Law* 11: 149–158.

Raine, A. 1993. *The Psychopathology of Crime: Criminal Behavior as a Clinical Disorder.* New York: Academic Press.

Raleigh, M.J., Brammer, G.L. and Yuwiler, A. 1980. "Serotonergic influences on the social behavior of vervet monkeys (Cercopithecus aethiops sabaeus)." *Experimental Neurology* 68: 322–334.

Raleigh, M.J., McGuire, M.T., Brammer, G.L. and Yuwiler, A. 1984. "Social and environmental influences on blood serotonin concentrations in monkeys." *Archives of General Psychiatry* 41: 405–410.

Rimland, B. and Larson, G.E. 1983. "Hair mineral analysis and behavior: An analysis of 51 studies." *Journal of Learning Disabilities* 16: 279–285.

Robins, L.N., West, P.A. and Herjanic, B.L. 1975. "Arrests and delinquency in two generations: A study of black urban families and their children." *Journal of Child Psychology and Psychiatry* 16: 125–140.

Rogeness, G.A., Javors, M.A., Maas, J.W., Macedo, C.A. and Fischer, C. 1987. "Plasma dopamine-B-hydroxylase, NVA, MHPG, and conduct disorder in emotionally disturbed boys." *Biological Psychiatry* 22: 1155–1158.

Rowe, D.C. 1983. "Biometrical genetic models of self-reported delinquent behavior: A twin study." *Behavior Genetics* 13: 473–489.

Rowe, D.C. 1986. "Genetic and environmental components of antisocial behavior: A study of 265 twin pairs." *Criminology* 24 (3): 513–532.

Rowe, D.C. and Osgood, D.W. 1984. "Heredity and sociological theories of delinquency: A reconsideration." *American Sociological Review* 49: 526–540.

Rowe, D.C., Clapp, M. and Wallis, J. 1987. "Physical attractiveness and the personality resemblance of identical twins." *Behavior Genetics* 17: 191–201.

Roy, A., Virkkunen, M., Guthrie, S., Poland, R., and Linnoila, M. 1986. "Monoamines, glucose metabolism, suicidal and aggressive behaviors." *Psychopharmacology Bulletin* 22 (3): 661–665.

Rushton, J.P., Fulker, D.W., Neale, M.C., Nias, D.K.B., and Eysenck, H.J. 1986. "Altruism and Aggression: The heritability of individual differences." *Journal of Personality and Social Psychology* 50 (6): 1192–1198.

Schiavi, R.C., Theilgaard, A., Owen, D.R., and White, D. 1984. "Sex chromosome anomalies, hormones, and aggressivity." *Archives of General Psychiatry* 41: 93–99.

Schuckit, M.A. and Morrissey, M.A. 1978. "Propoxyphene and phencyclidine (PCP) use in adolescents." *Journal of Clinical Psychiatry* 39: 7–13.

Seigel, R.K. 1978. "Phencyclidine, criminal behavior, and the defense of diminished capacity." Pp. 272–288 in R.C. Peterson and R.C. Stillman (Eds.), *Phencyclidine (PCP) Abuse: An Appraisal,* NIDA Research Monograph 21. Rockville, MD: National Institute on Drug Abuse.

Sigvardsson, S., Cloninger, C.R., Bohman, M. and von Knorring, A.L. 1982. "Predisposition to petty criminality in Swedish adoptees. III. Sex Differences and validation of the male typology." *Archives of General Psychiatry* 39: 1248–1253.

Smith, D.E. and Wesson, D.R. 1980. "PCP Abuse: Diagnostic and pharmacological treatment approaches." *Journal of Psychedelic Drugs* 12: 293–299.

Soubrie, P. 1986. "Reconciling the role of central serotonin neurons in human and animal behavior." *The Behavioral and Brain Sciences* 9: 319–364.

Stewart, M.A. and de Blois, C.S. 1983. "Father-son resemblances in aggressive and antisocial behavior." *British Journal of Psychiatry* 142: 78–84.

Stewart, M.A., de Blois, C.S. and Cummings, C. 1980. "Psychiatric disorder in the parents of hyperactive boys and those with conduct disorder." *Journal of Child Psychology and Psychiatry* 21: 283–292.

Syndulko, K. 1978. "Electrocortical investigations of sociopathy." Pp. 115–143. In R.D. Hare and D. Schalling (Eds.). *Psychopathic Behavior: Approaches to Research.* Chichester, England: Wiley.

Syndulko, K., Parker, D.A., Jens, R., Maltzman, I. and Ziskind, E. 1975. "Psychophysiology of sociopathy: Electrocortical measures." *Biological Psychology* 3: 185–200.

Tarter, R.E., Alterman, A.I., and Edwards, K.L. 1985. "Vulnerability to alcoholism in men: A behavior-genetic perspective." *Journal of Studies on Alcoholism* 46 (4): 329–356.

Tellegen, A., Lykken, D.T., Bouchard, T.J., Wilcox, K., Segal, N. and Rich S. 1989. "Personality similarity in twins reared apart and together." *Journal of Personality and Social Psychology* 54 (6): 1031–1039.

Trunnell, E.P. and Turner, C.W. 1988. "A comparison of the psychological and hormonal factors in women with and without premenstrual syndrome." *Journal of Abnormal Psychology* 97: 429–436.

Twito, T.J. and Stewart, M.A. 1982. "A half-sibling study of aggressive conduct disorder." *Neuropsychobiology* 8: 144–150.

Valzelli, L. 1981. *Psychobiology of Aggression and Violence.* New York, NY: Raven Press.

Van Praag, H.M., Kahn, R.S., Asnis, G.M., Wetzler, S., Brown, S.L., Bleich, A. and Korn, M.L. 1987. "Denosologization of biological psychiatry or the specificity of 5-HT disturbance in psychiatric disorders." *Journal of Affective Disorders,* 13: 1–8.

Venables, P.H. 1987. "Autonomic nervous system factors in criminal behavior." Pp. 110–130. In S.A. Mednick, T. Moffitt and S. Stack (Eds.), *The Causes of Crime: New Biological Approaches.* New York: Cambridge University Press.

Virkkunen, M. and Narvanen, S. 1987. "Plasma insulin, tryptophan and serotonin levels during the glucose tolerance test among habitually violent and impulsive offenders." *Neuropsychobiology* 17:19–23.

Virkkunen, M., Nuutila, A., Goodwin, F.K. and Linnoila, M. 1987. "Cerebrospinal fluid monoamine metabolite levels in male arsonists." *Archives of General Psychiatry* 44: 241–247.

Virkkunen, M., DeJong, J., Bartkko, J., Goodwin, F.K., and Linnoila, M. 1989. "Relationship of psychobiological variables to recidivism in violent offenders and impulsive fire setters." *Archives of General Psychiatry* 46: 600–603.

Wallgren, H. and Barry, H. 1970. *Action of Alcohol, Vols. 1 and 2.* New York: Elseview.

Walters, G.D. and White, T.W. 1989. "Heredity and crime: Bad genes or bad research?" *Criminology* 27: 455–486.

Weingartner, H., Rudorfer, M.V., Buchsbaum, M.S. and Linnoila, M. 1983. "Effects of serotonin on memory impairments produced by ethanol." *Science* 221: 472–474.

Wenk, E.A., Robison, J.O. and Smith, G.W. 1972. "Can violence be predicted?" *Crime and Delinquency,* Oct.:294–321.

Widom, C.S. 1978. "Toward an understanding of female criminality." *Progress in Experimental Personality Research* 8: 245–308.

Wilson, J.Q. and Herrnstein, R.J. 1985 *Crime and Human Nature.* New York: Simon and Schuster.

Wise, R. 1984. "Neural mechanisms of the reinforcing action of cocaine." NIDA Research Monograph 50. Washington, D.C., pp. 15–33.

Wolfgang, M.E., Figlio, R.M. and Sellin, T. 1972. *Delinquency in a Birth Cohort.* University of Chicago, Chicago.

Yeudall, L.T., Fedora, O. and Fromm, D. 1985. *A Neuropsychosocial Theory of Persistent Criminality: Implications for Assessment and Treatment.* Alberta Hospital, Edmonton, Research Bulletin #97.

Zuckerman, M. 1983. "A biological theory of sensation seeking." Pp. 62–76 in M. Zuckerman (Ed.), *Biological Basis of Sensation Seeking, Impulsivity and Anxiety.* Hillsdale, NJ: Lawrence Erlbaum Associates, Inc.

NOTES

[1] Antisocial children have a high incidence of adjustment problems, for example, low academic achievement, temper tantrums, conduct disorders, and negative attitudes (see Patterson et al., 1989).

[2] See Gove and Wilmoth, 1990, for a discussion of neurological processes that reinforce behavior. The authors suggest that risky and dangerous criminal behaviors stimulate neurological systems that act as positive reinforcers for continuing those forms of dangerous or criminal behaviors. A learning theory of behavior based on biological reward systems is presented. See Gove and Wilmoth, 1990 for a discussion of neurological processes that reinforce behavior. The authors suggest that risky and dangerous criminal behaviors stimulate neurological systems that act as positive reinforcers for continuing those forms of dangerous or criminal behaviors. A learning theory of behavior based on biological reward systems is presented.

Chapter 2

PSYCHOLOGICAL THEORIES OF DEVIANCE

Allen Liska

Psychological theories ignore the study of deviance as a social definition and focus on norm violations. They explain norm violations in terms of processes and structures of the individual psyche, which in turn are generally explained in terms of past social experiences.

As a subtype of psychological theories, personality theories have been very significant. They analyze people in terms of general psychic characteristics (tendencies, needs, motives, and drives) assumed to affect behavior over a variety of social situations. A considerable amount of effort has gone into constructing personality scales, such as the Minnesota Multiphasic Personality Inventory, examining how people develop specific personality characteristics like aggressiveness and sociability and studying how such characteristics influence behavior in a variety of social situations. The immediate social situation is viewed as having relatively little influence on behavior other than to provide a medium for the expression of general personalty characteristics.

In respect to norm violations, personality theories can be classified into two general types. One type explains norm violations as an outcome of normal characteristics which also causes conformist behavior. For example, homicide is sometimes explained as a manifestation of an aggressive personality, and homosexuality is sometimes explained as a manifestation of psychological dependency. These theories, however, do not clearly explain why only a small percentage aggressive personalities commit homicide and why only a small percentage of dependent personalities become homosexuals. To circumvent this problem, some theorists have argued that certain personalities violate certain norms in certain social situations while in other situations they conform.

The McCords' (1960) theory of alcoholism is one such example. They argue that all people have dependency needs, generally satisfied during childhood in parent-child relationships. In some cases these childhood needs are not satisfied and must be satisfied in adolescence and adulthood. This is particularly a problem in the United States, where adolescent and adult males are expected to be independent. The personality need for dependence clashes with the social demands for independence, creating a psychological conflict. Alcoholism relieves the associated guilt and anxiety and relaxes social inhibitions, thereby permitting the expression of dependency needs.

Another example is intelligence. Since the turn of the century, researchers have attempted to link deviance and crime with low intelligence. More recently Gordon

28

(1967) argues that low intelligence leads to crime because it inhibits the socialization process; that is, people of low intelligence simply fail to learn the rules of society. On the other hand, Hirschi and Hindelang (1977) argue that low intelligence leads to delinquency because it leads to frustration in school, which turns juveniles away from school and toward delinquent peers for social acceptance.

Another type of personality theory explains norm violations as expressions abnormal personalities, termed psychopathic and sociopathic personalities. The meaning of these concepts is vague (Hakeem, 1958; Mechanic, 1969), generally referring to a variety of "undesirable" psychological characteristics, such as acting on impulse, misrepresenting reality and lacking the capacity to feel shame and remorse. Cason (1943) recorded fifty-five such characteristics in the literature, and Cleckley (1950) recorded sixteen. The link between these characteristics and norm and law violations is equally vague. Frequently, norm violations are used to infer the existence of psychopathology and sociopathology, which are then used to explain norm and law violations are used to infer the existence of psychopathology and sociopathology as "wastebasket" or "residual" concepts, referring to no clear psychological entities and used to describe a variety of otherwise unclassifiable psychological states and socially problematic behaviors.

Various researchers have attempted to more precisely identify and categorize abnormal personalities. By comparing hospitalized psychiatric patients with normal residents, researchers have developed ten different scales (Minnesota Multiphasic Personality Inventory) of psychiatric disorders, such as hysteria, paranoia, and schizophrenia. However, Hathaway and Monachesi (1957; 1963) report that these scales do not, either individually or collectively, predict delinquency very well.

Generally, efforts to explain norm violation in terms of personality characteristics, normal or abnormal, have not been very successful, although relationships between norm violations and personality characteristics are frequently reported. Schuessler and Cressey (1950), examining 113 studies using thirty different personality tests, report that 42 percent of the studies found some personality differences between criminals and noncriminals. Updating this study, Waldo and Dinitz (1967) examined ninety-four studies using twenty-nine tests between 1950 and 1965, and report that 81 percent of the studies found some differences between these two groups. Finally, updating both studies, Tennenbaum (1977) examined forty-four studies and fifty-two different tests and reported that 82 percent of the studies found some differences between criminals and non criminals. These reports, however, are not very convincing, for in many of the studies the differences are quite minor, and in most it is not clear whether the personality characteristics caused the violations or the violations caused the characteristics. For example, being publicly identified and convicted as a regular drug user may cause a good deal of anxiety and psychological disorder, thereby producing a relationship between anxiety and drug use.

Generally, personality theories have been criticized for emphasizing rare and abnormal personalities in explaining norm violations, for ignoring or at least deemphasizing the present social situation in explaining norm violations, and for ignoring the study of evidence as a social definition.

REFERENCES

Cason, Hulsey 1943. "The psychopath and the psychopathic." *Journal of Criminal Psychopathology* 4" 522–27.

Cleckley, Henry M. 1950. *The mask of sanity.* St. Louis, Mo,: C.V. Mosby.

Gordon, Robert A. 1967. "Social level, social disability and gang interaction." *American Journal of Sociology* 73:42–62.

Hakeem, Michael 1958. "A critique of the psychiatric approach to crime and corrections." *Law and Contemporary Problems* 22: 681–82.

Hardt,Robert H., and Sandra Peterson-Hardt 1977. "Self-reporting of delinquency." *Journal of Research of Crime and Delinquency* 14: 247–61.

Hathaway, Stanke R., and Elio D. Monachesi 1963. *Adolescent personality and behavior: MMPI patterns of normal, delinquent, dropout and other outcomes.* Minneapolis: University of Minnesota Press.

_____. 1957. "The personalities of predelinquent boys." *Journal of Criminal Law, Criminology and Police Science* 48:149–63.

Hirschi, Travis and Michael Hingelang 1977. "Intelligence and delinquency: A revisionist review." *American Sociological Review* 42:571–86.

McCord, William and Joan McCord 1960. *Origins of Alcoholism.* Stanford: Stanford University Press.

Mechanic, David 1969. *Mental Health and social policy.* Englewood Cliffs, New Jersey: Prentice-Hall.

Schuessler, Karl and Donald Cressey 1950. "Personality characteristics of criminals." *American Journal of Sociology* 55:476–84.

Tennenbaum, David J. 1977. "Personality and criminality." *Journal of Criminal Justice* 5:1–9.

Waldo, Gordon, and Simon Dinitz 1967. "Personality attributes of the criminal: An analysis of research studies, 1950–1965." *Journal of Research in Crime and Delinquency* 4: 185–202.

Part II

Traditional Theories of Deviance

In this section, we will examine specific traditional social theories of deviance. Traditional theories of deviance can be divided into the following:

(1) Structural-Functionalism; (2) Anomie Theory; (3) Differential Association Theory; and (4) Social Control Theory.

The Structural-Functionalist Perspective

Examination of structural-functionalist theory reveals that it is based on the following underlying assumptions:

(1) all human interaction occurs in systems and has to be understood in those terms.

(2) the system is comprised of parts that are functionally interdependent in nature. Such parts derive their meaning only in terms of the whole, and function to realize the system's (society's) values and goals.

(3) the entire system (society) is based on order, integration and stability, and desires to remain in a state of equilibrium.

(4) there is a universal agreement of the parts within the system. Consensus, according to this model represents a kind of unity *not* willed by the individual parts but is an element of the system as a whole.

(5) deviance is conceived as a persistent, normal feature of society functioning to maintain the existing social order.

For structural-functionalists, there exists a high level of normative consensus, integration and order in society. Taking social order as a fact of life, these normative theorists focus upon the means responsible for the persistence of this stability in society. In their holistic, abstract theoretical perspective, functionalists employ an updated image of society as a system[1] comprised of parts (social structures) that are interrelated and interdependent to form a functional whole. According to these theorists, it is *not* the individual actors who are interdependent, but aspects of their behavior—their motivations, roles and values. In this paradigm, the system possesses a set of culturally-shared, structured symbols that are accepted by most societal members—symbols that provide primary social meanings, a normative orientation that imposes social order by constraining individuals to act within the conventions of the symbolic system. In short then, for structural functionalists, society is made possible because its actors organize their goals and behaviors around shared moral standards.

Assuming that the parts (social structures and patterns of behavior) do not persist unless they perform some social function for the whole, deviant behavior—a persistent form of behavior, is explained by identifying its social functions. Accord-

31

ing to this model, deviance performs vital social functions in terms of contributing to the continuity of the social order. Specifically, deviance serves the two-fold function of defining the boundaries of right and wrong as well as acting as a safety valve to drain off excess energy generated by the pressures of institutional routines.

In terms of the methodological orientation of this theory, structural-functionalists, in their efforts to omit subjective bias from their paradigm, adopt a rigorous "scientific" methodology—an objective positivist methodology based on the canons of deductive logic. In contrast to other theoretical perspectives on deviance based on analytic induction that begin with no overarching hypotheses, gather data on deviant subjects firsthand through observation and subsequently construct generalizations and hypotheses[2], structural-functionalists, employing axiomatic or deductive logic, begin with broad *apriori* theoretical assumptions concerning the relationship among certain phenomena. From these general statements substantive hypotheses are then constructed. Concepts are operationally defined and the hypothesized relationships among variables are statistically tested using secondary source data. Empirical testing of this manner serves to either confirm or refute the validity of the hypotheses.

The Structural-Functionalist— Emile Durkheim:
Deviance as Social Deregulation

The structural-functionalist perspective of deviant behavior can be traced back to the writings of French sociologist, Emile Durkheim. In contrast to Max Weber's *verstehende* methodology—an orientation that examined social phenomena from the subjective points of view of the actors themselves[3], Durkheim, through his positivist approach, attempted to understand social phenomena from an objective, external point of view irrespective of the subjective states of individual actors. For Durkheim (1950), the proper unit of analysis was not the individual, but rather, the social whole. In this model, society is considered a reality *sui generis*—the whole system is greater than the sum of the parts, and cannot be explained in terms of the parts, but only in terms of itself.

Durkheim (1950) felt that the major problem with sociology in his day was that it lacked a scientific foundation for analyzing social phenomena. Thus, he took it upon himself to develop a sociological theory based upon deductive logic and scientific principles. In terms of the latter, modelling his theory after biology, he conceived of society as an organism comprised of functionally-interdependent parts (social structures and institutions). In terms of the former, Durkheim began with a general theory of society from which specific hypotheses were constructed and made subject to statistic analysis for confirmation or refute. In so doing, Durkheim hoped to avoid the subjective bias he felt existed in other perspectives.

Adopting such a methodological orientation required Durkheim to adopt the theoretical position that social facts were "things" in their own right, amenable to objective investigation. For Durkheim then, the rightful subject matter for sociology were social facts—facts not reducible to the level of the individual, but rooted in the collective life of the group, external to the individual and endowed with power and coercion.

The nature of man, according to Durkheim's (1951) theory, was a creature with appetites, drives, sensations and desires that are insatiable. As Durkheim (1951:248) states: "The more one has, the more one wants, since satisfactions received only stimulate instead of filling needs." It follows from this natural insatiability of the human animal that his desires can only be held in check by external control—by societal control or what Durkheim termed, "the collective conscience." The collective conscience is "the totality of beliefs and sentiments common to average citizens of the same society," (Durkheim, 1933:79). Such sentiments and values are generally accepted and shared by all societal members. In this holistic model, Durkheim conceived of the collective conscience as more than merely the sum of its parts. It is not simply the sum of all the individual consciences. Individual conscience, within this paradigm is somewhat variable—it is not merely a duplication of the individual conscience. Durkheim conceived of the individual conscience as only one moment of the collective conscience. Regulating forces then, it remains external to the individual, existing within the normative structures of society.

According to Durkheim (1960), the strength and weakness of the collective conscience is inextricably tied to the historical development of societies—specifically, the division of labor within societies. In his discussion of primitive or agricultural society, he contended that it is based upon homogeneity. Individuals are generally involved in similar activities; the division of labor is minimal. As a result, such individuals form similar goals and values—a strong collective conscience is formed which functions to regulate the society. However, with extensive division of labor in industrial societies, there exist a number of interest groups with numerous competing realities of what is right and wrong—each exerting minimal control over the individual. A weak collective conscience brings about a decrease in social control. Such deregulation leads to deviant behavior.

Durkheim (1960) argued that the social regulatory forces are at their lowest point during the transitional period from primitive, agricultural society to industrial society. During this time period, old normative structures are disbanded, but new regulatory forces are not fully established. This lack of formal rules, coupled with industrial society's emphasis on individual wants and motives, leads to the condition Durkheim (1951) refers to as "anomie." Anomie represents a state of normlessness or social deregulation. It is in this context that deviance arises. Specifically, in positing a theory of suicide, Durkheim found that where low levels of social regulation exist, this leads to a high level of suicide among certain social groups.[4]

Such a perspective on suicide and deviant behavior in general, does *not* imply that such phenomena are pathological entities. Working from the assumption that behaviors do not persist unless they perform some social function, and since deviant behavior is a persistent entity, Durkheim thus conceived of these phenomena as normal entities and studied them in terms of their functions in maintaining the existing social order. In his classic essay, *"The Normal and the Pathological"*, Durkheim contends that crime and deviance are present in all societies. Such behavior serves the following functions for society: (1) it functions as a boundary maintenance mechanism; it defines the boundaries of right conduct; (2) it also functions to reconfirm the solidarity of society—it reemphasizes the norms and values of society, strengthening collective sentiments against infringements of the norm; (3) deviance and criminal behavior functions to initiate social change. According to this theorist (1950:71), "Where crime exists, collective sentiments are sufficiently flexible to take on a new form, and crime sometimes helps to determine the form they will take. How many times, indeed, it is only an anticipation of future morality—a step toward what will be."

Robert Merton: Social Structure and Anomie

Merton accepted a basic premise of Durkheim's theory that society is characterized by external, normative structures comprised of shared attitudes, values and norms. In Merton's paradigm, such norms and values are implanted in an individual's goals and ambitions. In contrast to Durkheim however, who conceived of human beings with "insatiable" and bottomless desires, Merton (1957:31) suggests that "the image of man as an untamed bundle of impulses begin to look more like a caricature than a portrait." While Durkheim contended that anomie resulted from social deregulation, and thus, took as his major focus, the analysis of breakdowns in the social order, Merton, by contrast, introducing a class variable, focuses his theory on the imperfections in the social order—specifically, the inconsistencies between cultural goals and the means for achieving them. The essay by Merton entitled, "*Social Structure and Anomie*" centers around this idea of "structured strain"—the general forces and pressures in the social system that push individuals into deviation.

According to Merton (1957), social life is comprised of two elements: (1) the social situation—sets of relationships among individuals; and (2) the cultural situation—socially approved goals to which people aspire and the institutional means for achieving such goals. Anomie, for Merton, arises not as a result of social deregulation, but from a disjunction between socially-approved goals and the institutional means for achieving them. While both the goals and means are pre-scribed by culture, when society over-emphasizes the goals in proportion to the means (or when the means become inaccessible for certain social classes), Merton contends that a state of anomie or demoralization results which expresses itself in deviant behavior of various forms. In short, where approved means to approved goals are not available, Merton argues that the following deviant adaptations may emerge. *Type I* adaptation consists of conforming behavior. Such an adaptation occurs where the culturally-approved goals and means of achieving them are pursued successfully. *Type II* adaptation, innovation, occurs when the culturally-approved goals are accepted but the institutionalized means are absent. Merton states: "[innovation]...occurs when the individual has assimilated the cultural emphasis upon the goal without equally internalizing the institutional norms governing ways and means for its attainment." This adaptation is common to the lower social and economic classes. *Type III* adaptation, ritualism, occurs when the culturally-approved goals are not accepted but the institutionalized means are accepted. The ritualist, frequently a member of the lower middle class has given up all hope of achieving societal goals, but nevertheless, clings to the institutionalized means of achieving them. *Type IV* adaptation, retreatism, occurs when the socially-approved goals and approved means for achieving such goals are both rejected. The retreatist is a social outcast—he is a vagrant, tramp, alcoholic etc. *Type V* adaptation, rebellion, occurs when both the approved goals and means are rejected, and new goals and means are substituted in their place. Specifically, this adaptation represents an organized struggle for social change, functioning to "introduce a social structure in which the cultural standards of success would be sharply modified and provision would be made for a closer correspondence between merit, effort, and reward" (Merton, 1957:155).

In short, Merton's perspective on deviance expanded upon Durkheim's theory in two directions. First, through his introduction of the concept of anomie as a disjunction between goals and means, Merton was able to posit an association between limited institutional means and deviant behavior. Second, through the introduction of a class variable, Merton was able to posit that the amount of deviance varied as a result of the degree of disjunction between means and goals in different social classes—a disjunction which Merton contended occurred more frequently among the lower class.

Richard Cloward and Lloyd Ohlin: Deviance as Differential Opportunity

Cloward and Ohlin, in their paper, *"Differential Opportunity and Delinquent Subcultures,"* provide an extension and application of Merton's theory which includes the concept of "differential opportunity." In reaction against Merton's implicit statement that individuals who do not have access to legitimate means will automatically have access to illegitimate means, Cloward and Ohlin contend, to the contrary, that becoming a deviant requires more than motivations and pressures. Specifically, it requires the *opportunity* to learn deviant roles and enact them. The potential criminal "must have access to a learning environment and, once having been trained, must be allowed to perform his role" (Cloward and Ohlin, 1960:147).

According to Cloward and Ohlin, individuals are located in two opportunity structures: one being legitimate, and the other illegitimate. Given limited access to societal goals by legitimate means, the nature of the deviant response will vary according to the availability of various illegitimate opportunities. Specifically, these theorists contend that these varying illegitimate opportunities lead to three types of deviant lifestyles: (1) the stable criminal career; (2) a conflict pattern; and (3) a retreatist pattern. The stable criminal career pattern occurs where there is a coordination between persons in both legitimate and illegitimate roles. In order to develop a stable criminal career pattern, this requires that contacts be made in both the deviant subculture as well as in the legitimate culture. The delinquent, moving toward a stable career pattern, interacts with established criminals, the police, lawyers, prosecuting attorneys, etc. Such interactions serve to expand the potential criminal's knowledge and skills, thereby leading to new opportunities for more protected and rewarding acts: "the criminal, like the occupant of a conventional role, must establish relationships with other categories of persons, all of whom contribute in one way or another to the successful performance of criminal activity."

In terms of the second type of deviant lifestyle, Cloward and Ohlin assert that violence disrupts not only legitimate activities but also affects criminal activities; thus, in order for both legitimate and illegitimate opportunities to exist, the occurrence of violence must be constrained. Where both legitimate and illegitimate opportunity structures are missing, where controls on violence are absent, Cloward and Ohlin contend that a pattern of conflict arises: "As long as conventional and criminal opportunity structures remain closed, violence continues unchecked."

In terms of the third type of deviant lifestyle, the retreatist lifestyle, Cloward and Ohlin suggest that this lifestyle emerges as a result of an individual's 'double-failure'—a delinquent who has failed in his/her experiences with both legitimate and illegitimate opportunity structures. As a result, such a person retreats from both realms of society.

In contrast to Merton who conceived of deviants as unconscious participants in the direction of their fate, Cloward and Ohlin contend that such persons are actively aware of the injustices of their class-related social experiences. Gradually, the individuals become aware of such injustices: "...he perceives his failure to gain access to opportunities as an injustice in the system rather than as a deficiency in himself" (1960:118). Such an attitude allows an individual to join forces with other deviants without feeling guilty about his behavior.

Differential Association Theory
Edwin Sutherland and Donald Cressey

Edwin Sutherland, in 1939, published the third edition of his book, *Principles of Criminology*, a work having a major impact on the fields of deviance and criminology. He termed his theory, "differential association."

In their essay, *"The Theory of Differential Association"*, Sutherland and Cressey maintain that "deviance is a group product, the result of an excess of definition unfavorable to violation of the law". Further, such definitions are learned in a normal learning process with other individuals who are in a process of communication. The chief source for learning criminal behavior occurs within small, intimate groups. This learning process includes techniques of committing the crime, the specific direction of motives, drives, rationalizations and attitudes. The efficiency of this learning process is a function of the frequency, duration, priority and intensity of differential association. In sum, for these theorists, deviant behavior is *not* caused by biological or genetic processes, nor is it discovered accidentally. It involves a learning process that one person passes on to others; people who develop deviant careers differentially associate with others who condone deviant/illegal activities. Individuals engage in deviance because of an excess of definitions favorable to the violation of law over definitions unfavorable to the violation of law.

Social Control Theory: Travis Hirschi

Social control theory is a major theory of deviant behavior although it has been utilized primarily in the study of delinquent behavior. In contrast with other traditional theories of deviance which ask the question, "Why do people commit deviant acts?", social control theorists ask, "Why *don't* they do it?"

Social control theorists begin with the assumption that we all find deviance attractive, enticing, lucrative, etc. Why is it, then, that most people do not engage in deviant behavior? Why don't they break the law and become criminals?

As Hirschi elaborates in *"A Control Theory of Delinquency,"* the answer lies in the *bonds* or *ties* we have with conventional society. If these bonds are weak or broken, we will be free to deviate from the norm. In short, it is our lack of ties to conventional society that leads to deviance and delinquency.

Control Theory has four essential elements: (1) *attachment* (2) *commitment* (3) *involvement* and (4) *belief*. Hirschi argues that the more attached we are to normal conventional members of society such as our parents, teachers, employers, clergy, etc., the less likely we will commit deviant behavior; the more committed we are to the conventional social institutions such as school, our family, work, church, etc., the less likely we will commit deviant behavior. Further, the more involved we are in culturally-sanctioned activities, such as the boy scouts and organized little league, the less likely we will commit deviance. Finally, the more deeply we believe in societal norms, the less likely we will commit deviant and delinquent acts.

In sum then, deviance, for social control theorists, is held in check or contained by social bonds to conventional institutions, persons, activities and beliefs. The stronger are such bonds, the less likely will individuals deviate.

References

Cohen, Albert. 1965. "The sociology of the deviant act: Anomie theory and beyond." *American Sociological Review* 30: 5–14.

Cressey, Paul. 1932. *The Taxi–Dance Hall*. Chicago: University of Chicago Press.

Dahrendorf, Ralf. 1958. *Class and Class Conflict in Industrial Society*. Stanford, California: Stanford University Press.

———. 1959. "Out of utopia: Toward a reorientation of sociological analysis." *American Journal of Sociology*. 64: 115–27.

Durkheim, Emile. 1950. *The Rules of the Sociological Method*. Translated and edited by Solovay and Mueller. Edited by G.E.G. Catlin. Illinois: Free Press of Glencoe.

———. 1951. *Suicide*. Translated by J. Spaulding and G. Simpson. Edited by G. Simpson. Illinois: The Free Press.

———. 1960. *The Division of Labour in Society*. Translated by G. Simpson. New York: Macmillan.

Marx, Karl. 1964. *Selected Writings in Sociology and Social Philosophy*, edited by T. Bottomore and M. Rubel. New York: McGraw-Hill.

Merton, Robert. 1957. *Social Theory and Social Structure*. New York: Free Press.

Sutherland, Edwin. 1934. *Criminology*. Philadelphia: Lippincott Company.

Sutherland, Edwin, and Donald R. Cressey. 1966. *Principles in Criminology*. Philadelphia: Lippincott, 7th ed.

Weber, Max. 1964. *Basic Concepts in Sociology*. New York: Citadel.

NOTES

[1] The structural-functionalists borrowed this conception from the biological sciences.

[2] See Weber (1964:29) for a discussion of this methodological orientation.

[3] See Weber (1964:29) for a discussion of this methodological orientation.

[4] Durkheim found that high levels of suicide occurred among those individuals who were unmarried, those who were Protestant, and those not involved in political groups. For Durkheim, suicide varied inversely with the degree of integration in religious society (with Catholics being more integrated than Protestants; it also varies inversely with the degree of integration of domestic society; further, it varies inversely with the degree of integration in political society.

Chapter 3

THE NORMAL AND THE PATHOLOGICAL

Emile Durkheim

Crime is present not only in the majority of societies of one particular species but in all societies of all types. There is no society that is not confronted with the problem of criminality. Its form changes; the acts thus characterized are not the same everywhere; but, everywhere and always, there have been men who have behaved in such a way as to draw upon themselves penal repression. If, in proportion as societies pass from the lower to the higher types, the rate of criminality, i.e., the relation between the yearly number of crimes and the population, tended to decline, it might be believed that crime, while still normal, is tending to lose this character of normality. But we have no reason to believe that such a regression is substantiated. Many facts would seem rather to indicate a movement in the opposite direction. From the beginning of the [nineteenth] century, statistics enable us to follow the course of criminality. It has everywhere increased. In France the increase is nearly 300 percent. There is, then, no phenomenon that presents more indisputably all the symptoms of normality, since it appears closely connected with the conditions of all collective life. To make of crime a form of social morbidity would be to admit that morbidity is not something accidental, but, on the contrary, that in certain cases it grows out of the fundamental constitution of the living organism; it would result in wiping out all distinction between the physiological and the pathological. No doubt it is possible that the crime itself will have abnormal forms, as, for example, when its rate is unusually high. This excess is, indeed, undoubtedly morbid in nature. What is normal, simply, is the existence of criminality, provided that it attains and does not exceed, for each social type, a certain level, which it is perhaps not impossible to fix in conformity with the preceding rules.[1]

Here we are, then, in the presence of a conclusion in appearance quite paradoxical. Let us make no mistake. To classify crime among the phenomena of normal sociology is not to say merely that it is an inevitable, although regrettable phenomenon, due to the incorrigible wickedness of men; it is to affirm that it is a factor in public health, an integral part of all healthy societies. This result is, at first glance, surprising enough to have puzzled even ourselves for a long time. Once this first surprise has been overcome, however, it is not difficult to find reasons explaining this normality and at the same time confirming it.

In the first place crime is normal because a society exempt from it is utterly impossible. Crime, we have shown elsewhere, consists of an act that offends certain very strong collective sentiments. In a society in which criminal acts are no longer committed, the sentiments they offend would have to be found without exception in

38

all individual consciousness, and they must be found to exist with the same degree as sentiments contrary to them. Assuming that this condition could actually be realized, crime would not therefore disappear; it would only change its form, for the very cause which would thus dry up the sources of criminality would immediately open up new ones.

Indeed, for the collective sentiments which are protected by the penal law of a people at a specified moment of its history to take possession of the public conscience or for them to acquire a stronger hold where they have an insufficient grip, they must acquire an intensity greater than that which they had hitherto had. The community as a whole must experience them more vividly, for it can acquire an intensity greater than that which they had hitherto had. The community as a whole must experience them more vividly for it can acquire from no other source the greater force necessary to control these individuals who formerly were the most refractory. For murderers to disappear, the horror of bloodshed must become greater in those social strata from which murderers are recruited; but, first it must become greater throughout the entire society. Moreover, the very absence of crime would directly contribute to produce this horror; because any sentiment seems much more respectable when it is always and uniformly respected.

One easily overlooks the consideration that these strong states of the common consciousness cannot be thus reinforced without reinforcing at the same time the more feeble states, whose violation previously gave birth to mere infraction of convention—since the weaker ones are only the prolongation, the attenuated form, of the stronger. Thus robbery and simple bad taste injure the same single altruistic sentiment, the respect for that which is another's. However, this same sentiment is less grievously offended by bad taste than by robbery; and since, in addition, the average consciousness has not sufficient intensity to react keenly to the bad taste, it is treated with greater tolerance. That is why the person guilty of bad taste is merely blamed, whereas the thief is punished. But, if this sentiment grows stronger, to the point of silencing in all consciousness the inclination which disposes man to steal, he will become more sensitive to the offenses which, until then, touched him but lightly. He will react against them, then, with more energy; they will be the object of greater opprobrium, which will transform certain of them from the simple moral faults that they were and give them the quality of crimes. For example, improper contracts, or contracts improperly executed, which only incur public blame or civil damages, will become offenses in law.

Imagine a society of saints, a perfect cloister of exemplary individuals. Crimes, properly so called, will there be unknown; but faults which appear venial to the layman will create there the same scandal that the ordinary offense does in ordinary consciousness. If, then, this society has the power to judge and punish, it will define these acts as criminal and will treat them as such. For the same reason, the perfect and upright man judges his smallest failings with a severity that the majority reserve for acts more truly in the nature of an offense. Formerly, acts of violence against persons were more frequent than they are today, because respect for individual dignity was less strong. As this has increased, these crimes have become more rare; and also, many acts violating this sentiment have been introduced into the penal law which were not included there in primitive times.[2]

In order to exhaust all the hypotheses logically possible, it will perhaps be asked why this unanimity does not extend to all collective sentiments without exception. Why should not even the most feeble sentiment gather enough energy to prevent all dissent? The moral consciousness of the society would be present in its entirety in all the individuals, with a vitality sufficient to prevent all acts offending it—the purely conventional faults as well as the crimes. But a uniformity so universal and absolute is utterly impossible; for the immediate physical milieu in which each one of us is placed, the hereditary antecedents, and the social influences vary from one individual to the next, and consequently diversify consciousness. It is impossible for all to be alike, if only because each one has his own organism and that these organisms occupy different areas in space. That is why, even among the lower peoples, where individual originality is very little developed, it nevertheless does exist.

Thus, since there cannot be a society in which the individuals do not differ more or less from the collective type, it is also inevitable that, among these divergences, there are some with a criminal character. What confers this character upon them is not the intrinsic quality of a given act but that definition which the collective conscience lends them. If the collective conscience is stronger, if it has enough authority practically to suppress these divergences, it will also be more sensitive, more exacting; and, reacting against the slightest deviations with the energy it otherwise displays only against more considerable infractions, it will attribute to them the same gravity as formerly to crimes. In other words, it will designate them as criminal.

Crime is, then, necessary; it is bound up with fundamental conditions of all social life, and by that very fact it is useful, because these conditions of which it is a part are themselves indispensable to the normal evolution of mortality and law.

Indeed, it is no longer possible today to dispute the fact that law and mortality vary from one social type to the next, nor that they change within the same type if the conditions of life are modified. But, in order that these transformations may be possible, the collective sentiments at the basis of morality must not be hostile to change, and consequently must have but moderate energy. If they were too strong, they would no longer be plastic. Every pattern is an obstacle to new patterns, to the extent that the first pattern is inflexible. The better a new structure is articulated, the more it offers a healthy resistance to all modification; and this is equally true of functional, as of anatomical, organization. If there were no crimes, this condition could not have been fulfilled; for such a hypothesis presupposes that collective sentiments have arrived at a degree of intensity unexampled in history. Nothing is good indefinitely and to an unlimited extent. The authority which the moral conscience enjoys must not be excessive; otherwise no one would dare criticize it, and it would too easily congeal into an immutable form. To make progress, individual originality must be able to express itself. In order that the originality of the idealist whose dreams transcend his century may find expression, it is necessary that the originality of the criminal, who is below the level of his time, shall also be possible. One does not occur without the other.

Nor is this all. Aside from this indirect utility, it happens that crime itself plays a useful role in this evolution. Crime implies not only that the way remains open to necessary changes but that in certain cases it directly prepares these changes. Where crime exists, collective sentiments are sufficiently flexible to take on a new form, and crime sometimes helps to determine the form they will take. How many times, indeed, it is only an anticipation of future morality—a step toward what will be! According to Athenian law, Socrates was a criminal, and his condemnation was no more than just. However, his crime, namely, the independence of his thought, rendered a service not only to humanity but to his country. It served to prepare a new morality and faith which the Athenians needed, since the traditions by which they had lived until then were no longer in harmony with the current conditions of life. Nor is the case of Socrates unique; it is reproduced periodically in history. It would never have been possible to establish the freedom of thought we now enjoy if the regulations prohibiting it had not been violated before being solemnly abrogated. At that time, however, the violation was a crime, since it was an offense against sentiments still very keen in the average conscience. And yet this crime was useful as a prelude to reforms which daily became more necessary. Liberal philosophy had its precursors the heretics of all kinds who were justly punished by secular authorities during the entire course of the Middle Ages and until the eve of modern times.

From this point of view the fundamental facts of criminality present themselves to us in an entirely new light. Contrary to current ideas, the criminal no longer seems a totally unsociable being, a sort of parasitic element, a strange and inassimilable body, introduced into the midst of society.[3] On the contrary, he plays a definite role in social life. Crime, for its part, must no longer be conceived as an evil that cannot be too much suppressed. There is no occasion for self-congratulation when the crime rate drops noticeably below the average level, for we may be certain that this apparent progress is associated with some social disorder. Thus, the number of assault cases never falls so low as in times of want.[4] With the drop in the crime rate, and as a reaction to it, comes a revision, or the need of a revision in the theory of punishment. If, indeed, crime is a disease, its punishment is its remedy and cannot be otherwise conceived; thus, all the discussions it arouses bear on the point of determining what the punishment must be in order to fulfill this role of remedy. If crime is not pathological at all, the object of punishment cannot be to cure it, and its true function must be sought elsewhere.

NOTES

[1]From the fact that crime is a phenomenon of normal sociology, it does not follow that the criminal is an individual normally constituted from the biological and psychological points of view. The two questions are independent of each other. This independence will be better understood when we have shown, later on, the difference between psychological and sociological facts.

[2]Calumny, insults, slander, fraud, etc.

[3]We have ourselves committed the error of speaking thus of the criminal, because of a failure to apply our rule (*Division du travail social:* 395–6).

[4]Although crime is a fact of normal sociology, it does not follow that we must not abhor it. Pain itself has nothing desirable about it; the individual dislikes it as society does crime, and yet it is a function of normal physiology. Not only is it necessarily derived from the very constitution of every living organism, but it plays a useful role in life, for which reason it cannot be replaced. It would, then, be a singular distortion of our thought to present it as an apology for crime. We would not even think of protesting against such an interpretation, did we not know to what strange accusations and misunderstandings one exposes oneself when one undertakes to study moral facts objectively and to speak of them in a different language from that of the layman.

Chapter 4

SOCIAL STRUCTURE AND ANOMIE

Robert K. Merton

There persists a notable tendency in sociological theory to attribute the malfunction-
ing of social structure primarily to those of man's imperious biological drives which
are not adequately restrained by social control. In this view, the social order is solely
a device for "impulse management" and the "social processing" of tensions. These
impulses which break through social control, be it noted, are held to be biologically
derived. Nonconformity is assumed to be rooted in original nature.[1] Conformity is by
implication the result of a utilitarian calculus or unreasoned conditioning. This point
of view, whatever its other deficiencies, clearly begs one question. It provides no
basis for determining the nonbiological conditions which induce deviations from
prescribed patterns of conduct. In this paper, it will be suggested that certain phases
of social structure generate the circumstances in which infringement of social codes
constitutes a "normal" response.[2]

The conceptual scheme to be outlined is designed to provide a coherent,
systematic approach to the study of socio-cultural sources of deviate behavior. Our
primary aim lies in discovering how some social structures *exert a definite pressure*
upon certain persons in the society to engage in nonconformist rather than conformist
conduct. The many ramifications of the scheme cannot all be discussed; the problems
mentioned outnumber those explicitly treated.

Among the elements of social and cultural structure, two are important for our
purposes. These are analytically separable although they merge imperceptibly in
concrete situations. The first consists of culturally defined goals, purposes, and
interests. It comprises a frame of aspirational reference. These goals are more or less
integrated and involve varying degrees of prestige and sentiment. They constitute a
basic, but not the exclusive, component of what Linton aptly has called "designs for
group living." Some of these cultural aspirations are related to the original drives of
man, but they are not determined by them. The second phase of the social structure
defines, regulates, and controls the acceptable modes of achieving these goals. Every
social group invariably couples its scale of desired ends with moral or institutional
regulation of permissible and required procedures for attaining these ends. These
regulatory norms and moral imperatives do not necessarily coincide with technical
or efficiency norms. Many procedures which form the standpoint of *particular
individuals* would be most efficient in securing desired values, e.g., illicit oil-stock
schemes, theft, fraud, are ruled out of the institutional area of permitted conduct. The
choice of expedients is limited by the institutional norms.

To say that these two elements, culture goals and institutional norms, operate
jointly is not to say that the ranges of alternative behaviors and aims bear some

constant relation to one another. The emphasis upon certain goals may vary independently of the degree of emphasis upon institutional means. There may develop a disproportionate, at times, a virtually exclusive, stress upon the value of specific goals, involving relatively slight concern with the institutionally appropriate modes of attaining these goals. The limiting case in this direction is reached when the range of alternative procedures is limited only by technical rather than institutional considerations. Any and all devices which promise attainment of the all important goal would be permitted in this hypothetical polar case.[3] This constitutes one type of cultural malintegration. A second polar type is found in groups where activities originally conceived as instrumental are transmuted into ends in themselves. The original purposes are forgotten, and ritualistic adherence to institutionally prescribed conduct becomes virtually obsessive.[4] Stability is largely ensured while change is flouted. The range of alternative behaviors is severely limited. There develops a tradition-bound, sacred society characterized by neophobia. The occupational psychosis of the bureaucrat may be cited as a case in point. Finally, there are the intermediate types of groups where a balance between culture goals and institutional means is maintained. These are the significantly integrated and relatively stable, though changing, groups.

An effective equilibrium between the two phases of the social structure is maintained as long as satisfactions accrue to individuals who conform to both constraints, viz., satisfactions from the achievement of the goals and satisfactions emerging directly from the institutionally canalized modes of striving to attain these ends. Success, in such equilibrated cases, is twofold. Success is reckoned in terms of the product and in terms of the process, in terms of the outcome and in terms of activities. Continuing satisfactions must derive from sheer *participation* in a competitive order as well as from eclipsing one's competitors if the order itself is to be sustained. The occasional sacrifices involved in institutionalized conduct must be compensated by socialized rewards. The distribution of statuses and roles through competition must be so organized that positive incentives for conformity to roles and adherence to status obligations are provided *for every position* within the distributive order. Aberrant conduct, therefore, may be viewed as a symptom of dissociation between culturally defined aspirations and socially structured means.

Of the types of groups which result from the independent variation of the two phases of the social structure, we shall be primarily concerned with the first, namely, that involving a disproportionate accent on goals. This statement must be recast in a proper perspective. In no group is there an absence of regulatory codes governing conduct, yet groups do vary in the degree to which these folkways, mores, and institutional controls are effectively integrated with the more diffuse goals which are part of the culture matrix. Emotional convictions may cluster about the complex of socially acclaimed ends, meanwhile shifting their support from the culturally defined implementation of these ends. As we shall see, certain aspects of the social structure may generate countermores and antisocial behavior precisely because of differential emphases on goals and regulations. In the extreme case, the latter may be so vitiated by the goal-emphasis that the range of behavior is limited only by considerations of technical expediency. The sole significant question then becomes, which available means is most efficient in netting the socially approved value?[5] The technically most feasible procedure, whether legitimate or not, is preferred to the institutionally prescribed conduct. As this process continues, the integration of the society becomes tenuous and anomie ensues.

Thus, in competitive athletics, when the aim of victory is shorn of its institutional trappings and success in contests becomes construed as "winning the game" rather than "winning through circumscribed modes of activity," a premium is implicitly set upon the use of illegitimate but technically efficient means. The star of the opposing football team is surreptitiously slugged; the wrestler furtively incapacitates his opponent through ingenious but illicit techniques; university alumni covertly subsidize "students" whose talents are largely confined to the athletic field. The emphasis on the goal has so attenuated the satisfactions deriving from sheer participation in the competitive activity that these satisfactions are virtually confined to a successful outcome. Through the same process, tension generated by the desire to win in a poker game is relieved by successfully dealing oneself four aces, or, when the cult of success has become completely dominant, by sagaciously shuffling the cards in a game of solitaire. The faint twinge of uneasiness in the last instance and the surreptitious nature of public derelicts indicate clearly that the institutionally rules of the game are *known* to those who evade them, but that the emotional supports of these rules are largely vitiated by cultural exaggeration of the success-goal.[6] They are microcosmic images of the social macrocosm.

Of course, this process is not restricted to the realm of sport. The process whereby exaltation of the end generates a *literal demoralization*, i.e., a deinstitutionalization, of the means is one which characterizes many[7] groups in which the two phases of the social structure are not highly integrated. The extreme emphasis upon the accumulation of wealth as a symbol of success[8] in our own society militates against the completely effective control of institutionally regulated modes of acquiring a fortune.[9] Fraud, corruption, vice, crime, in short, the entire catalogue of proscribed behavior, becomes increasingly common when the emphasis on the *culturally induced* success-goal becomes divorced from a coordinated institutional emphasis. This observation is of crucial theoretical importance in examining the doctrine that antisocial behavior most frequently derives from biological drives breaking through the restraints imposed by society. The difference is one between a strictly utilitarian interpretation which conceives man's ends as random and an analysis which finds these ends deriving from the basic values of the culture.[10]

Our analysis can scarcely stop at this juncture. We must turn to other aspects of the social structure if we are to deal with the social genesis of the varying rates and types of deviate behavior characteristic of different societies. Thus far, we have sketched three ideal types of social orders constituted by distinctive patterns of relations between culture ends and means. Turning from these types of *culture patterning*, we find five logically possible, alternative modes of adjustment or adaptation *by individuals* within the culture-bearing society or group.[11] These are schematically presented in the following table, where (+) signifies "acceptance," (−) signifies "elimination," and (±) signifies "rejection and substitution of new goals and standards."

Our discussion of the relation between these alternative responses and other phases of the social structure must be prefaced by the observation that persons may

		Culture Goals	*Institutionalized Means*
I.	Conformity	+	+
II.	Innovation	+	−
III.	Ritualism	−	+
IV.	Retreatism	−	−
V.	Rebellion[12]	±	±

shift from one alternative to another as they engage in different social activities. These categories refer to role adjustment in specific situations, not to personality *in toto*. To treat the development of this process in various spheres of conduct would introduce a complexity unmanageable within the confines of this paper. For this reason, we shall be concerned primarily with economic activity in the broad sense, "the production, exchange, distribution, and consumption of goods and services" in our competitive society, wherein wealth has taken on a highly symbolic cast. Our task is to search out some of the factors which exert pressure upon individuals to engage in certain of these logically possible alternative responses. This choice, as we shall see, is far from random.

In every society, Adaptation I (conformity to both culture goals and means) is the most common and widely diffused. Were this not so, the stability and continuity of the society could not be maintained. The mesh of expectancies which constitutes every social order is sustained by the modal behavior of its members falling within the first category. Conventional role behavior oriented toward the basic values of the group is the rule rather than the exception. It is this fact alone which permits us to speak of a human aggregate as comprising a group or society.

Conversely, Adaptation IV (rejection of goals and means) is the least common. Persons who "adjust" (or maladjust) in this fashion are, strictly speaking, *in* the society but not *of* it. Sociologically, these constitute the true "aliens." Not sharing the common frame of orientation, they can be included within the societal population merely in a fictional sense. In this category are *some* of the activities of psychotics, psychoneurotics, chronic autists, pariahs, outcasts, vagrants, vagabonds, tramps, chronic drunkards, and drug addicts.[13] These have relinquished, in certain spheres of activity, the culturally defined goals, involving complete aim-inhibition in the polar case, and their adjustments are not in accord with institutional norms. This is not to say that in some cases the source of their behavioral adjustments is not in part the very social structure which they have in effect repudiated nor that their very existence within a social area does not constitute a problem for the socialized population.

This mode of "adjustment" occurs, as far as structural sources are concerned, when both the culture goals and institutionalized procedures have been assimilated thoroughly by the individual and imbued with affect and high positive value, but where those institutionalized procedures which promise a measure of successful attainment of the goals are not available to the individual. In such instances, there results a two-fold mental conflict insofar as the moral obligation for adopting institutional means conflicts with the pressure to resort to illegitimate means (which may attain the goal) and inasmuch as the individual is shut off from means which are both legitimate *and* effective. The competitive order is maintained, but the frustrated and handicapped individual who cannot cope with this order drops out. Defeatism, quietism, and resignation are manifested in escape mechanisms which ultimately lead the individual to "escape" from the requirements of the society. It is an expedient which arises from continued failure to attain the goal by legitimate measures and from an inability to adopt the illegitimate route because of internalized prohibitions and institutionalized compulsives, *during which process the supreme value of the success-goal has as yet not been renounced.* The conflict is resolved by eliminating *both* precipitating elements, the goals and means. The escape is complete, the conflict is eliminated, and the individual is associated.

Be it noted that where frustration derives from the inaccessibility of effective institutional means for attaining economic or any other type of highly valued "success," that Adaptations II, III, and V (innovation, ritualism, and rebellion) are also possible. The result will be determined by the particular personality, and thus, the *particular* cultural background, involved. Inadequate socialization will result in the innovation response whereby the conflict and frustration are eliminated by relinquishing institutional means and retaining the success-aspiration; an extreme assimilation of institutional demands will lead to ritualism wherein the goal is dropped as beyond one's reach but conformity to the mores persists; and rebellion occurs when emancipation from the reigning standards, due to frustration or to marginalist perspectives, leads to the attempt to introduce a "new social order."

Our major concern is with the illegitimacy adjustment. This involves the use of conventionally proscribed but frequently effective means of attaining at least the simulacrum of culturally defined success—wealth, power, and the like. As we have seen, this adjustment occurs when the individual has assimilated the cultural emphasis on success without equally internalizing the morally prescribed norms governing means for its attainment. The question arises, which phases of our social structure predispose toward this mode of adjustment? We may examine a concrete instance, effectively analyzed by Lohman,[14] which provides a clue to the answer. Lohman has shown that specialized areas of vice in the near north side of Chicago constitute a "normal" response to a situation where the cultural emphasis upon pecuniary success has been absorbed, but where there is little access to conventional and legitimate means for attaining such success. The conventional occupational opportunities of persons in this area are almost completely limited to manual labor. Given our cultural stigmatization of manual labor, and its correlate, the prestige of white collar work, it is clear that the result is a strain toward innovational practices. The limitation of opportunity to unskilled labor and the resultant low income cannot compete *in terms of conventional standards of achievement* with the high income from organized vice.

For our purposes, this situation involves two important features. First, such antisocial behavior is in a sense "called forth" by certain conventional values of the culture *and* by the class structure involving differential access to the approved opportunities for legitimate, prestige-bearing pursuit of the culture goals. The lack of high integration between the means-and-end elements of the cultural pattern and the particular class structure combine to favor a heightened frequency of antisocial conduct in such groups. The second consideration is of equal significance. Recourse to the first of the alternative responses, legitimate effort, is limited by the fact that actual advance toward desired success-symbols through conventional channels is, despite our persisting open-class ideology,[15] relatively rare and difficult for those handicapped by little formal education and few economic resources. The dominant pressure of group standards of success is, therefore, on the gradual attenuation of legitimate, but by and large ineffective strivings and the increasing use of illegitimate, but more or less effective expedients of vice and crime. The cultural demands made on persons in this situation are incompatible. On the one hand, they are asked to orient their conduct toward the prospect of accumulating wealth and on the other, they are largely denied effective opportunities to do so institutionally. The consequences of such structural inconsistency are psychopathological personality, and/or antisocial conduct, and/or revolutionary activities. The equilibrium between culturally designated means and ends becomes highly unstable with the progressive emphasis on attaining the prestige-laden ends by any means whatsoever. Within this context, Capone represents the triumph of amoral intelligence over morally prescribed "failure," when the channels of vertical mobility are closed or narrowed[16] *in a society which places a high premium on economic affluence and social ascent for all its members.*[17]

This last qualification is of primary importance. It suggests that other phases of social structure besides the extreme emphasis on pecuniary success must be considered if we are to understand the social sources of antisocial behavior. A high frequency of deviate behavior is not generated simply by "lack of opportunity" or by this exaggerated pecuniary emphasis. A comparatively rigidified class structure, a feudalistic or caste order, may limit such opportunities far beyond the point which obtains in our society today. It is only when a system of cultural values extols, virtually above all else, certain *common* symbols of success *for the population at large* while its social structure rigorously restricts or completely eliminates access to approved modes of acquiring these symbols *for a considerable part of the same population* that antisocial behavior ensues on a considerable scale. In other words, our egalitarian ideology denies by implication the existence of noncompeting groups and individuals in the pursuit of pecuniary success. The same body of success-symbols is held to be desirable for all. These goals are held to *transcend class lines*, not to be bounded by them, yet the actual social organization is such that there exists class differentials in the accessibility of these *common* success-symbols. Frustration and thwarted aspiration lead to the search for avenues of escape from a culturally induced intolerable situation; or unrelieved ambition may eventuate in illicit attempts to acquire the dominant values.[18] The American stress on pecuniary success and ambitiousness for all thus invites exaggerated anxieties, hostilities, neuroses, and antisocial behavior.

This theoretical analysis may go far toward explaining the varying correlations between crime and poverty.[19] Poverty is not an isolated variable. It is one in a complex of interdependent social and cultural variables. When viewed in such a context, it represents quite different states of affairs. Poverty as such, and consequent limitation of opportunity, are not sufficient to induce a conspicuously high rate of criminal behavior. Even the often mentioned "poverty in the midst of plenty" will not necessarily lead to this result. Only insofar as poverty and associated disadvantages in competition for the culture values approved for *all* members of the society are linked with the assimilation of a cultural emphasis on monetary accumulation as a symbol of success is antisocial conduct a "normal" outcome. Thus, poverty is less highly correlated with crime in southeastern Europe than in the United States. The possibilities of vertical mobility in these European areas would seem to be fewer than in this country, so that neither poverty *per se* nor its association with limited opportunity is sufficient to account for the varying correlations. It is only when the full configuration is considered, poverty, limited opportunity, and a commonly shared system of success-symbols, that we can explain the higher association between poverty and crime in our society than in others where rigidified class structure is coupled with *differential class symbols of achievement*.

In societies such as our own, then, the pressure of prestige-bearing success tends to eliminate the effective social constraint over means employed to this end. "The-end-justifies-the-means" doctrine becomes a guiding tenet for action when the cultural structure unduly exalts the end and the social organization unduly limits possible recourse to approved means. Otherwise put, this notion and associated behavior reflect a lack of cultural coordination. In international relations, the effects of this lack of integration are notoriously apparent. An emphasis upon national power is not readily coordinated with an inept organization of legitimate, i.e., internationally defined and accepted, means for attaining this goal. The result is a tendency toward the abrogation of international law, treaties become scraps of paper, "undeclared warfare" serves as a technical evasion, the bombing of civilian populations is rationalized,[20] just as the same societal situation induces the same sway of illegitimacy among individuals.

The social order we have described necessarily produces this "strain toward dissolution." The pressure of such an order is upon outdoing one's competitors. The choice of means within the ambit of institutional control will persist as long as the sentiments supporting a competitive system, i.e., deriving from the possibility of outranking competitors and hence enjoying the favorable response of others, are distributed throughout the entire system of activities and are not confined merely to the final result. A stable social structure demands a balanced distribution of affect among its various segments. When there occurs a shift of emphasis from the satisfactions deriving from competition itself to almost exclusive concern with successful competition, the resultant stress leads to the breakdown of the regulatory structure.[21] With the resulting attenuation of the institutional imperatives, there occurs an approximation of the situation erroneously held by utilitarians to be typical of society generally wherein calculations of advantage and fear of punishment are the sole regulating agencies. In such situations, as Hobbes observed, force and fraud come to constitute the sole virtues in view of their relative efficiency in attaining goals—which were for him, of course, not culturally derived.

It should be apparent that the foregoing discussion is not pitched on a moralistic plane. Whatever the sentiments of the writer or reader concerning the ethical desirability of coordinating the means-and-goals phases of the social structure, one must agree that lack of such coordination leads to anomie. Insofar as one of the most general functions of social organization is to provide a basis for calculability and regularity of behavior, it is increasingly limited in effectiveness as these elements of the structure become dissociated. At the extreme, predictability virtually disappears and what may be properly termed cultural chaos or anomie intervenes.

This statement, being brief, is also incomplete. It has not included an exhaustive treatment of the various structural elements which predispose toward one rather than another of the alternative responses open to individuals; it has neglected, but not denied the relevance of, the factors determining the specific incidence of these responses; it has not enumerated the various concrete responses which are constituted by combinations of specific values of the analytical variables; it has omitted, or included only by implication, any consideration of the social functions performed by illicit responses; it has not tested the full explanatory power of analytical scheme by examining a large number of group variations in the frequency of deviate and conformist behavior; it has not adequately dealt with rebellious conduct which seeks to refashion the social framework radically; it has not examined the relevance of cultural conflict for an analysis of culture-goal and institutional-means malintegration. It is suggested that these and related problems may be profitably analyzed by this scheme.

NOTES

[1] E.g., Ernest Jones, *Social Aspects of Psychoanalysis*, 28, London, 1924. If the Freudian notion is a variety of the "original sin" dogma, then the interpretation advanced in this paper may be called the doctrine of "socially derived sin."

[2] "Normal" in the sense of a culturally oriented, if not approved, response. This statement does not deny the relevance of biological and personality differences which may be significantly involved in the *incidence* of deviate conduct. Our focus of interest is the social and cultural matrix; hence we abstract from other factors. It is in this sense, I take it, that James S. Plant speaks of the "normal reaction of normal people to abnormal conditions." See his *Personality and Cultural Pattern*, 248, New York, 1937.

[3] Contemporary American culture has been said to tend in this direction. See Andre Siegfried *America Comes of Age*, pp.26–37, New York, 1927. The alleged extreme(?) emphasis on the goals of monetary success and material prosperity leads to dominant concern with technological and social instruments designed to produce the desired result, inasmuch as institutional controls become of secondary importance. In such a situation, innovation flourishes as the *range of means* employed is broadened. In a sense, then, there occurs the paradoxical emergence of "materialists: from an "idealistic" orientation. Cf. Durkheim's analysis of the cultural conditions which predispose toward crime and innovation, both of which are aimed toward efficiency, not moral norms. Durkheim was one of the first to see that "contrairement aux idees courantes le criminel n'apparait plus comme un etre radicalement insociable, comme une sorte d'element parasitaire, de corps etranger et inassimilable, introduit au sien de la societe, c'est un agent regulier de la vie sociale." See *Les Regales de la Methode Sociologique*, 86–89, Paris, 1927.

[4] Such ritualism may be associated with a mythology which rationalizes these actions so that they appear to retain their status as means, but the dominant pressure is in the direction of strict ritualistic conformity, irrespective of such rationalizations. In this sense, ritual has proceeded farthest when such rationalizations are not even called forth.

[5] In this connection, one may see the relevance of Elton Mayo's paraphrase of the title of Tawney's well-known book. "Actually the problem *is not that of the sickness of an acquisitive society; it is that of the acquisitiveness of a sick society.*" *Human Problems of an Industrial Civilization*, 153, New York, 1933. Mayo deals with the process through which wealth comes to be a symbol of social achievement. He sees this as arising from a state of anomie. We are considering the unintegrated mortary-success goal as an element in producing anomie. A complete analysis would involve both phases of this system of interdependent variables.

[6] It is unlikely that interiorized norms are completely eliminated. Whatever residuum persists will induce personality tensions and conflict. The process involves a certain degree of ambivalence. A manifest rejection of the institutional norms is coupled with some latent retention of their emotional correlates. "Guilt feelings," "sense of sin," "pangs of conscience" are obvious manifestations of this unrelieved tension; symbolic adherence to the nominally repudiated values or rationalizations constitute a more subtle variety of tensional release.

[7] "Many," and not all, unintegrated groups, for the reason already mentioned. In groups where the primary emphasis shifts to institutional means, i.e., when the range of alternatives is very limited, the outcome is a type of ritualism rather than anomie.

[8] Money has several peculiarities which render it particularly apt to become a symbol of prestige divorced from institutional controls. As Simmel emphasized, money is highly abstract and impersonal. However acquired, through fraud or institutionally, it can be used to purchase the same goods and services. The anonymity of metropolitan culture, in conjunction with this peculiarity of money, permits wealth, the sources of which may be unknown to the community in which the plutocrat lives, to serve as a symbol of status.

[9] The emphasis upon wealth as a success-symbol is possibly reflected in the use of the term "fortune" to refer to a stock of accumulated wealth. This meaning becomes common in the late sixteenth century (Spenser and Shakespeare). A similar usage of the Latin *fortuna* comes into prominence during the first century B.C. Both these periods were marked by the rise to prestige and power of the "bourgeoisie."

[10] See Kingsley Davis, "Mental Hygiene and the Class Structure." *Psychiatry*, 1928, 1: esp. 62–63; Talcott Parsons, *The Structure of Social Action*, 59–60, New York, 1937.

[11] This is a level of intermediate between the two planes distinguished by Edward Sapir; namely, culture patterns and personal habit systems. See his "Contribution of Psychiatry to an Understanding of Behavior in Society," *American Journal of Sociology*, 1937, 42:862–70.

[12] This fifth alternative is on a plane clearly different from that of the others. It represents a *transitional* response which seeks to *institutionalize* new procedures oriented toward revamped cultural goals shared by the members of the society. It thus involves efforts to *change* the existing structure rather than to perform accommodative actions *within* the structure, and introduces additional problems with which we are not at the moment concerned.

[13] Obviously, this is an elliptical statement. These individuals may maintain some orientation to the values of their particular differentiated groupings within the larger society or, in part, of the conventional society itself. Insofar as they do so, their conduct cannot be classified in the "passive rejection" category (IV). Nels Anderson's description of the behavior and attitudes of the bum, for example, can readily be recast in terms of our analytical scheme. See *The Hobo*, 93–8, *et passim*, Chicago, 1923.

[14] Joseph D. Lohman, "The Participant Observer in Community Studies," *American Sociological Review*, 1937, 2:890–8.

[15] The shifting historical role of this ideology is a profitable subject for exploration. The "office-boy-to-president" stereotype was once in approximate accord with the facts. Such vertical mobility was probably more common then than now, when the class structure is more rigid. (See the following note.) The ideology largely persists, however, possibly because it still performs a useful function for maintaining the *status quo*. For insofar as it is accepted by the "masses," it constitutes a useful sop for those who might rebel against the entire structure, were this consoling hope removed. This ideology now serves to lessen the probability of Adaptation V. In short, the role of this notion has changed from that of an approximately valid empirical theorem to that of an ideology, in Mannheim's sense.

[16] There is a growing body of evidence, though none of it clearly conclusive, to the effect that our class structure is becoming rigidified and that vertical mobility is declining. Taussig and Joslyn found that American business leaders are being *increasingly* recruited from the upper ranks of our society. The Lynds have also found a "diminished chance to get ahead" for the working classes in Middletown. Manifestly, these objective changes are not alone significant; the individual's subjective evaluation of the situation is a major determinant of the response. The extent to which this change in opportunity for social mobility has been recognized by the least advantaged classes is still conjectural, although the Lynds present some suggestive materials. The writer suggests that a case in point is the increasing frequency of cartoons which observe in a tragi-comic vein that "my old man says everybody can't be President. He says if ya can get three days a week on steady on W.P.A. work ya ain't doin' so bad either." See F.W. Taussig and C.S. Joslyn,

American Business Leaders, New York, 1932; R.S. and H.M. Lynd, *Middletown in Transition*, 67, ff., ch. 12, New York, 1937.

[17] The role of Negro in this respect is of considerable theoretical interest. Certain elements of the Negro population have assimilated the dominant caste's values of pecuniary success and social advancement, but they also recognize that social ascent is at present restricted to their own caste almost exclusively. The pressures upon the Negro which would otherwise derive from the structural inconsistencies we have noticed are hence not identical with those upon lower class whites. See Kingsley Davis, op. cit., 63; John Dollard, *Caste and Class in a Southern Town*, 66 ff., New Haven, 1936; Donald Young, *American Minority Peoples*, 581, New York, 1932.

[18] The physical coordinates of these processes have been partly established by the experimental evidence concerning *Anspruchniveaus* and levels of performance. See Kurt Lewin, *Vorsatz, Willie, and Bedurfnis*, Berlin, 1926; N.F. Hope, "Erfolg und Misserfolg," *Psychology Forsschung*, 1930, 14:1–63; Jerome D. Frank, "Individual Differences in Certain Aspects of the Level of Aspiration," *American Journal of Psychology*, 1935, 47:119–28.

[19] Standard criminology texts summarize the data in this field. Our scheme of analysis may serve to resolve some of the theoretical contradictions which P.A. Sorokin indicates. For example, "not everywhere nor always do the poor show a greater proportion of crime...many poorer countries have had less crime than the richer countries...The [economic] improvement in the second half of the nineteenth century, and the beginning of the twentieth, has not been followed by a decrease of crime." See his *Contemporary Sociological Theories*, 560–1, New York, 1928. The crucial point is, however, that poverty has varying social significance in different social structures, as we shall see. Hence, one would not expect a linear correlation between crime and poverty.

[20] See M.W. Royse, *Aerial Bombardment and the International Regulation of War*, New York, 1928.

[21] Since our primary concern is with the socio-cultural aspects of this problem, the psychological correlates have been only implicitly considered. See Karen Horney, *The Neurotic Personality of Our Time*, New York, 1937, for a psychological discussion of this process.

Chapter 5

DIFFERENTIAL OPPORTUNITY AND DELINQUENT SUBCULTURES

Richard A. Cloward
Lloyd E. Ohlin

The Availability of Illegitimate Means

Social norms are two-sided. A prescription implies the existence of a prohibition, and *vice versa*. To advocate honesty is to demarcate and condemn a set of actions which are dishonest. In other words, norms that define legitimate practices also implicitly define illegitimate practices. One purpose of norms, in fact, is to delineate the boundary between legitimate and illegitimate practices. In setting this boundary, in segregating and classifying various types of behavior, they make us aware not only of behavior that is regarded as right and proper but also of behavior that is said to be wrong and improper. Thus the criminal who engages in theft or fraud does not invent a new way of life; the possibility of employing alternative means is acknowledged, tacitly at least, by the norms of the culture.

This tendency for proscribed alternatives to be implicit in every prescription, and *vice versa*, although widely recognized, is nevertheless a reef upon which many a theory of delinquency has floundered. Much of the criminological literature assumes, for example, that one may explain a criminal act simply by accounting for the individual's readiness to employ illegal alternatives of which his culture, through its norms, has already made him generally aware. Such explanations are quite unsatisfactory, however, for they ignore a host of questions regarding the *relative availability* of illegal alternatives to various potential criminals. The aspiration to be a physician is hardly enough to explain the fact of becoming a physician; there is much that transpires between the aspiration and the achievement. This is no less true of the person who wants to be a successful criminal. Having decided that he "can't make it legitimately," he cannot simply choose among an array of illegitimate means, all equally available to him. As we have noted earlier, it is assumed in the theory of anomie that access to conventional means is differentially distributed, that some individuals, because of their social class, enjoy certain advantages that are denied to those elsewhere in the class structure. For example, there are variations in the degree to which members of various classes are fully exposed to and thus acquire the values, knowledge, and skills that facilitate upward mobility. It should not be startling, therefore, to suggest that there are socially structured variations in the availability of illegitimate means as well. In connection with delinquent subcultures, we shall be concerned principally with differentials in access to illegitimate means within the lower class.

Many sociologists have alluded to differentials in access to illegitimate means without explicitly incorporating this variable into a theory of deviant behavior. This is particularly true of scholars in the "Chicago tradition" of criminology. Two closely related theoretical perspectives emerged from this school. The theory of "cultural transmission," advanced by Clifford R. Shaw and Henry D. McKay, focuses on the development in some urban neighborhoods of a criminal tradition that persists from one generation to another despite constant changes in population.[1] In the theory of "differential association," Edwin H. Sutherland described the processes by which criminal values are taken over by the individual.[2] He asserted that criminal behavior is learned, and that it is learned in interaction with others who have already incorporated criminal values. Thus the first theory stresses the value systems of different areas; the second, the systems of social relationships that facilitate or impede the acquisition of these values.

Scholars in the Chicago tradition, who emphasized the processes involved in learning to be criminal, were actually pointing to differentials in the availability of illegal means—although they did not explicitly recognize this variable in their analysis. This can perhaps best be seen by examining Sutherland's classic work, *The Professional Thief*. "An inclination to steal," according to Sutherland, "is not a sufficient explanation of the genesis of the professional thief."[3] The "self-made" thief, lacking knowledge of the ways of securing immunity from prosecution and similar techniques of defense, "would quickly land in prison;...a person can be a professional thief only if he is recognized and received as such by other professional thieves." But recognition is not freely accorded: "Selection and tutelage are the two necessary elements in the process of acquiring recognition as a professional thief...A person cannot acquire recognition as a professional thief until he has had tutelage in professional theft, *and tutelage is given only to a few persons selected from the total population.*" For one thing, "the person must be appreciated by the professional thieves. He must be appraised as having an adequate equipment of wits, front, talking-ability, honesty, reliability, nerve, and determination." Furthermore, the aspirant is judged by high standards of performance, for only "a very small percentage of those who start on this process ever reach the stage of professional thief..." Thus motivation and pressures toward deviance do not fully account for deviant behavior any more than motivation and pressures toward conformity account for conforming behavior. The individual must have access to a learning environment and, once having been trained, must be allowed to perform his role. Roles, whether conforming or deviant in content, are not necessarily freely available; access to them depends upon a variety of factors, such as one's socioeconomic position, age, sex, ethnic affiliation, personality characteristics, and the like. The potential thief, like the potential physician, finds that access to his goal is governed by many criteria other than merit and motivation.

What we are asserting is that access to illegitimate roles is not freely available to all, as is commonly assumed. Only those neighborhoods in which crime flourishes as a stable, indigenous institution are fertile criminal learning environments for the young. Because these environments afford integration of different age-levels of offender, selected young people are exposed to "differential association" through which tutelage is provided and criminal values and skills are acquired. To be prepared for the role may not, however, ensure that the individual will ever discharge it. One important limitation is that more youngsters are recruited into these patterns of differential associations than the adult criminal structure can possibly absorb. Since there is a surplus of contenders for these elite positions, criteria and mechanisms of selection must be evolved. Hence a certain proportion of those who aspire may not be permitted to engage in the behavior for which they have prepared themselves.

Thus we conclude that access to illegitimate roles, no less than access to legitimate roles, is limited by both social and psychological factors. We shall here be concerned primarily with socially structured differentials in illegitimate opportunities. Such differentials, we contend, have much to do with the type of delinquent subculture that develops.

Learning and Performance Structures

Our use of the term "opportunities," legitimate or illegitimate, implies access to both learning and performance structures. That is, the individual must have access to appropriate environments for the acquisition of the values and skills associated with the performance of a particular role, and he must be supported in the performance of the role once he has learned it.

Tannenbaum, several decades ago, vividly expressed the point that criminal role performance, no less than conventional role performance, presupposes a patterned set of relationships through which the requisite values and skills are transmitted by established practitioners to aspiring youth:

> It takes a long time to make a good criminal, many years of specialized training and much preparation. But training is something that is given to people. People learn in a community where the materials and the knowledge are to be had. A craft needs an atmosphere saturated with purpose and promise. The community provides the attitudes, the point of view, the philosophy of life, the example, the motive, the contacts, the friendships, the incentives. No child brings those into the world. He finds them here and available for use and elaboration. The community gives the criminal his materials and habits, just as it gives the doctor, the lawyer, the teacher, and the candlestick-maker theirs.[4]

Sutherland systematized this general point of view, asserting that opportunity consists, at least in part, of learning structures. Thus "criminal behavior is learned" and, furthermore, it is learned "in interaction with other persons in a process of communication." However, he conceded that the differential-association theory does not constitute a full explanation of criminal behavior. In a paper circulated in 1944, he noted that "criminal behavior is partially a function of opportunities to commit [i.e., to perform] specific classes of crime, such as embezzlement, bank burglary, or illicit heterosexual intercourse." Therefore, "while opportunity may be partially a function of association with criminal patterns and of the specialized techniques acquired, it is not determined entirely in that manner, and consequently differential association is not the sufficient cause of criminal behavior.[5]

To Sutherland, then, illegitimate opportunity included conditions favorable to the performance of a criminal role as well as conditions favorable to the learning of such a role (differential associations). These conditions, we suggest, depend upon certain features of the social structure of the community in which delinquency arises.

We believe that each individual occupies a position in both legitimate and illegitimate opportunity structures. This is a new way of defining the situation. The theory of anomie views the individual primarily in terms of the legitimate opportunity structure. It poses questions regarding differentials in access to legitimate routes to success-goals; at the same time it assumes either that illegitimate avenues to success-goals are freely available or that differentials in their availability are of little significance. This tendency may be seen in the following statement by Merton:

> Several researchers have shown that specialized areas of vice and crime constitute a "normal" response to a situation where the cultural emphasis upon pecuniary success has been absorbed, but where there is little access to conventional and legitimate means for becoming successful. The occupational opportunities of people in these areas are largely confined to manual labor and the lesser white-collar jobs. Given the American stigmatization of manual labor *which has been found to hold rather uniformly for all social classes,* and the absence of realistic opportunities for advancement beyond this level, the result is a marked tendency toward deviant behavior. The status of unskilled labor and the consequent low income cannot readily compete *in terms of established standards of worth* with the promises of power and high income from organized vice, rackets and crime...[Such a situation] leads toward the gradual attenuation of legitimate, but by and large ineffectual, strivings and the increasing use of illegitimate, but more or less effective, expedients.[6]

The cultural-transmission and differential-association tradition, on the other hand, assumes that access to illegitimate means is variable, but it does not recognize the significance of comparable differentials in access to legitimate means. Sutherland's "ninth proposition" in the theory of differential association states:

> *Though criminal behavior is an expression of general needs and values, it is not explained by those general needs and values since non-criminal behavior is an expression of the same needs and values.* Thieves generally steal in order to secure money, but likewise honest laborers work in order to secure money. The attempts by many scholars to explain criminal behavior by general drives and values, such as the happiness principle, striving for social status, the money motive, or frustration, have been and must continue to be futile since they explain lawful behavior as completely as they explain criminal behavior.[7]

In this statement, Sutherland appears to assume that people have equal and free access to legitimate means regardless of their social position. At the very least, he does not treat access to legitimate means as variable. It is, of course, perfectly true that "striving for social status," "the money motive," and other socially approved drives do not fully account for either deviant or conforming behavior. But if goal-oriented behavior occurs under conditions in which there are socially structured obstacles to the satisfaction of these drives by legitimate means, the resulting pressures, we contend, might lead to deviance.

The concept of differential opportunity structures permits us to unite the theory of anomie, which recognizes the concept of differentials in access to legitimate means and the "Chicago tradition," in which the concept of differentials in access to illegitimate means is implicit. We can now look at the individual, not simply in relation to one or the other system of means, but in relation to both legitimate and illegitimate systems. This approach permits us to ask, for example, how the relative availability of illegitimate opportunities affects the resolution of adjustment problems leading to deviant behavior. We believe that the way in which these problems are resolved may depend upon the kind of support for one or another type of illegitimate activity that is given at different points in the social structure. If, in a given social location, illegal or criminal means are not readily available, then we should not expect a criminal subculture to develop among adolescents. By the same logic, we should expect the manipulation of violence to become a primary avenue to higher status only in areas where the means of violence are not denied to the young. To give a third example, drug addiction and participation in subcultures organized around the consumption of drugs presuppose that persons can secure access to drugs and knowledge about how to use them. In some parts of the social structure, this would be very difficult; in others, very easy. In short, there are marked differences from one part of the social structure to another in the types of illegitimate adaptation that are available to persons in search of solutions to problems of adjustment arising from the restricted availability of legitimate means.[8] In this sense, then, we can think of individuals as being located in two opportunity structures—one legitimate, the other illegitimate. Given limited access to success-goals by legitimate means, the nature of the delinquent response that may result will vary according to the availability of various illegitimate means.[9]

Varieties of Delinquent Subculture

As we have noted, there appear to be three major types of delinquent subculture typically encountered among adolescent males in lower-class areas of large urban areas. One is based principally upon criminal values; its members are organized primarily for the pursuit of material gain by such illegal means as extortion, fraud, and theft. In the second, violence is the keynote; its members pursue status ("rep") through the manipulation of force or threat of force. These are the "warrior" groups that attract so much attention in the press. Finally, there are subcultures which emphasize the consumption of drugs. The participants in these drug subcultures have become alienated from conventional roles, such as those required in the family or the occupational world. They have withdrawn into a restricted world in which the ultimate value consists in the "kick." We call these subcultural forms "criminal," "conflict," and "retreatist," respectively.[10]

These shorthand terms simply denote the *principal* orientation of each form of adaptation from the perspective of the dominant social order; although one can find many examples of subcultures that fit accurately into one of these three categories, subcultures frequently appear in somewhat mixed form. Thus members of a predominantly conflict subculture may also on occasion engage in systematic theft; members of a criminal subculture may sometimes do combat in the streets with rival gangs. But this should not obscure the fact that these subcultures tend to exhibit essentially different orientations.

The extent to which the delinquent subculture organizes and controls a participant's allegiance varies from one member to another. Some members of the gang are almost totally immersed in the perspectives of the subculture and bring them into play in all their contacts; others segregate this aspect of their lives and maintain other roles in the family, school, and church. The chances are relatively slight, however, that an adolescent can successfully segregate delinquent and conforming roles for a long period of time. Pressures emanate from the subculture leading its members to adopt unfavorable attitudes towards parents, school teachers, policemen, and other adults in the conventional world. When he is apprehended for delinquent acts, the possibility of the delinquent's maintaining distinctly separate role involvements breaks down, and he is confronted with the necessity of choosing between law-abiding and delinquent styles of life. Since family, welfare, religious, educational, law-enforcement, and correctional institutions are arrayed against the appeal of his delinquent associates, the decision is a difficult one, frequently requiring either complete acceptance or complete rejection of one or the other system of obligations.[11]

At any one point in time, however, the extent to which the norms of the delinquent subculture control behavior will vary from one member to another. Accordingly, descriptions of these subcultures must be stated in terms of the fully indoctrinated member rather than the average member. Only in this way can the distinctiveness of delinquent styles of life be made clear. It is with this understanding that we offer the following brief empirical characterizations of the three main types of delinquent subculture.

The Criminal Pattern

The most extensive documentation in the sociological literature of delinquent behavior patterns in lower-class culture describes a tradition which integrates youthful delinquency with adult criminality.[12] In the central value orientation of youths participating in this tradition, delinquent and criminal behavior is accepted as a means of achieving success-goals. The dominant criteria of in-group evaluation stress achievement, the use of skill and knowledge to get results. In this culture, prestige is allocated to those who achieve material gain and power through avenues defined as illegitimate by the larger society. From the very young to the very old, the successful "haul"—which quickly transforms the penniless into a man of means—is an ever-present vision of the possible and desirable. Although one may also achieve material success through the routine practice of theft or fraud, the "big score" remains the symbolic image of quick success.

The means by which a member of a criminal subculture achieves success are clearly defined for the aspirant. At a young age, he learns to admire and respect older criminals and to adopt the "right guy" as his role-model. Delinquent episodes help him to acquire mastery of the techniques and orientation of the criminal world and to learn how to cooperate successfully with others in criminal enterprises. He exhibits hostility and distrust toward representatives of the larger society. He regards members of the conventional world as "suckers," his natural victims, to be exploited when possible. He sees successful people in the conventional world as having a "racket"—e.g., big businessmen have huge expense accounts, politicians get graft, etc. This attitude successfully neutralizes the controlling effect of conventional norms. Toward the in-group the "right guy" maintains relationships of loyalty, honesty, and trustworthiness. He must prove himself reliable and dependable in his contacts with his criminal associates although he has no such obligations toward the out-group of noncriminals.

One of the best ways of assuring success in the criminal world is to cultivate appropriate "connections." As a youngster, this means running with a clique composed of other "right guys" and promoting an apprenticeship or some other favored relationship with older and successful offenders. Close and dependable ties with income-producing outlets for stolen goods, such as the wagon peddler, the junkman, and the fence, are especially useful. Furthermore, these intermediaries encourage and protect the young delinquent in a criminal way of life by giving him a jaundiced perspective on the private morality of many functionaries in conventional society. As he matures, the young delinquent becomes acquainted with a new world made up of predatory bondsmen, shady lawyers, crooked policemen, grafting politicians, dishonest businessmen, and corrupt jailers. Through "connections" with occupants of these half-legitimate, half-illegitimate roles and with "big shots" in the underworld, the aspiring criminal validates and assures his freedom of movement in a world made safer for crime.

The Conflict Pattern[13]

The role-model in the conflict pattern of lower-class culture is the "bopper" who swaggers with his gang, fights with weapons to win a wary respect from other gangs, and compels a fearful deference from the conventional adult world by his unpredictable and destructive assaults on persons and property. To other gang members, however, the key qualities of the bopper are those of the successful warrior. His performance must reveal a willingness to defend his personal integrity and the honor of the gang. He must do this with great courage and displays of fearlessness in the face of personal danger.

The immediate aim in the world of fighting gangs is to acquire a reputation for toughness and destructive violence. A "rep" assures not only respectful behavior from peers and threatened adults but also admiration for the physical strength and masculinity which it symbolizes. It represents a way of securing access to the scarce resources for adolescent pleasure and opportunity in underprivileged areas.

Above all things, the bopper is valued for his "heart." He does not "chicken out," even when confronted by superior force. He never defaults in the face of a personal insult or a challenge to the integrity of his gang. The code of the bopper is that of the warrior who places great stress on courage, the defense of his group, and the maintenance of honor.

Relationships between bopping gang members and the adult world are severely attenuated. The term that the bopper uses most frequently to characterize his relationships with adults is "weak." He is unable to find appropriate role-models that can designate for him a structure of opportunities leading to adult success. He views himself as isolated and the adult world as indifferent. The commitments of adults are to their own interests and not to his. Their explanations of why he should behave differently are "weak," as are their efforts to help him.

Confronted by the apparent indifference and insincerity of the adult world, the ideal bopper seeks to win by coercion and the attention and opportunities he lacks and cannot otherwise attract. In recent years the street-gang worker who deals with the fighting gang on its own "turf" has come to symbolize not only a recognition by conventional adult society of the gang's toughness but also a concession of opportunities formerly denied. Through the alchemy of competition between gangs, this gesture of attention by the adult world to the "worst" gangs is transformed into a mark of prestige. Thus does the manipulation of violence convert indifference into accommodation and attention into status.

The Retreatist Pattern

Retreatism may include a variety of expressive, sensual, or consummatory experiences, alone or in a group. In this analysis, we are interested only in those experiences that involve the use of drugs and that are supported by a subculture. We have adopted these limitations in order to maintain our focus on subcultural formations which are clearly recognized as delinquent, as drug use by adolescents is. The retreatist preoccupation with expressive experiences creates many varieties of "hipster" cult among lower-class adolescents which foster patterns of deviant but not necessarily delinquent conduct.

Subcultural drug users in lower-class areas perceive themselves as culturally and socially detached from the life-style and everyday preoccupations of members of the conventional world. The following characterization of the "cat" culture, observed by Finestone in a lower-class Negro area in Chicago, describes drug use in the more general context of "hipsterism."[14] Thus it should not be assumed that this description in every aspect fits drug cultures found elsewhere. We have drawn heavily on Finestone's observations, however, because they provide the best descriptions available of the social world in which lower-class adolescent drug cultures typically arise.

The dominant feature of the retreatist subculture of the "cat" lies in the continuous pursuit of the "kick." Every cat has a kick—alcohol, marijuana, addicting drugs, unusual sexual experiences, hot jazz, cool jazz, or any combination of these. Whatever its content, the kick is a search for ecstatic experiences. The retreatist strives for an intense awareness of living and a sense of pleasure that is "out of this world." In extreme form, he seeks an almost spiritual and mystical knowledge that is experienced when one comes to know "it" at the height of one's kick. The past and the future recede in the time perspective of the cat, since complete awareness in the present experience is the essence of the kick.

The successful cat has a lucrative "hustle" which contrasts sharply with the routine and discipline required in the ordinary occupational tasks of conventional society. The many varieties of the hustle are characterized by a rejection of violence or force and a preference for manipulating, persuading, outwitting, or "conning" others to obtain resources for experiencing the kick. The cat begs, borrows, steals, or engages in some petty con-game. He caters to the illegitimate cravings of others by peddling drugs or working as a pimp. A highly exploitative attitude toward women permits the cat to view pimping as a prestigeful source of income. Through the labor of "chicks" engaged in prostitution or shoplifting, he can live in idleness and concentrate his entire attention on organizing, scheduling, and experiencing the esthetic pleasure of the kick. The hustle of the cat is secondary to his interest in the kick. In this respect the cat differs from his fellow delinquents in the criminal subculture, for whom income-producing activity is a primary concern.

The ideal cat's appearance, demeanor, and taste can best be characterized as "cool." The cat seeks to exhibit a highly developed and sophisticated taste for clothes. In his demeanor, he struggles to reveal a self-assured and unruffled manner, thereby emphasizing his aloofness and "superiority" to the "squares." He develops a colorful, discriminating vocabulary and ritualized gestures which express his sense of difference from the conventional world and his solidarity with the retreatist subculture.

The word "cool" also best describes the sense of apartness and detachment which the retreatist experiences in his relationships with the conventional world. His reference group is the "society of cats," an "elite" group in which he becomes isolated from conventional society. Within this group, a new order of goals and criteria of achievement are created. The cat does not seek to impose this system of values on the world of the square. Instead, he strives for status and deference within the society of cats by cultivating the kick and the hustle. Thus the retreatist subculture provides avenues to success-goals, to the social admiration and the sense of well-being or oneness with the world which the members feel are otherwise beyond their reach.

NOTES

[1] See esp. C.R. Shaw, *The Jack-Roller* (Chicago: University of Chicago Press, 1930); Shaw, *The Natural History of a Delinquent Career* (Chicago: University of Chicago Press, 1931); Shaw, et al., *Delinquency Areas* (Chicago: University of Chicago Press, 1940); and Shaw and H.D. McKay, *Juvenile Delinquency and Urban Areas* (Chicago: University of Chicago Press, 1942).

[2] E.H. Sutherland, ed., *The Professional Thief* (Chicago: University of Chicago Press, 1937); and Sutherland, *Principles of Criminology*, 4th ed., (Philadelphia: Lippincott, 1947).

[3] All quotations on this page are from *The Professional Thief*, pp. 211–13. Emphasis added.

[4] Frank Tannenbaum, "The Professional Criminal," *The Century*, Vol. 110 (May-Oct. 1925), p.577.

⁵ See A.K. Cohen, Alfred Lindesmith, and Karl Schuessler, eds., *The Sutherland Papers* (Bloomington, Ind.: Indiana University Press, 1956), pp.31–5.

⁶ R.K. Merton, *Social Theory and Social Structure*, Rev. and Enl. Ed. (Glencoe, Ill.: Free Press, 1957), pp.145–6.

⁷ *Principles of Criminology*, op. cit., pp.7–8.

⁸ For an example of restrictions on access to illegitimate roles, note the impact of racial definitions in the following case: "I was greeted by two prisoners who were to be my cell buddies. Ernest was a first offender, charged with being a 'hold-up' man. Bill, the other buddy, was an older offender, going through the machinery of becoming a habitual criminal, in and out of jail...The first thing they asked me was, 'What are you in for?' I said, 'Jack-rolling.' The hardened one (Bill) looked at me with a superior air and said, 'A hoodlum, eh? That's all they're good for. Kid, jack-rolling's not a white man's job.' I could see that he was disgusted with me, and I was too scared to say anything." (Shaw, *The Jack-Roller*, op. cit., p.101).

⁹ For a discussion of the way in which the availability of illegitimate means influences the adaptations of inmates to prison life, see R.A. Cloward, "Social Control in the Prison," *Theoretical Studies of the Social Organization of the Prison*, Bulletin No.15, (New York: Social Science Research Council, March 1960), pp.20–48.

¹⁰ It should be understood that these terms characterize these delinquent modes of adaptation from the reference position of conventional society; they do not necessarily reflect the attitudes of members of the subculture. Thus the term "retreatist" does not necessarily reflect the attitude of the "cat." Far from thinking of himself as being in retreat, he defines himself as among the elect.

¹¹ Tannenbaum summarizes the community's role in this process of alienation by the phrase "dramatization of evil" (Frank Tannenbaum, *Crime and Community* [New York: Columbia University Press, 1938], pp.19–21). For a more detailed account of this process, see Chap.5, *infra*.

¹² See esp. C.R. Shaw, *The Jack-Roller* (Chicago: University of Chicago Press, 1930); Shaw, *The Natural History of a Delinquent Career* (Chicago: University of Chicago Press, 1940); Shaw and H.D. McKay, *Juvenile Delinquency and Urban Areas* (Chicago: University of Chicago Press, 1942); E.H. Sutherland, ed., *The Professional Thief* (Chicago: University of Chicago Press, 1937); Sutherland, *Principles of Criminology*, 4th ed. (Philadelphia: J.P. Lippincott Co., 1947); and Sutherland, *White Collar Crime* (New York: Dryden Press, 1949).

¹³ For descriptions of conflict groups, see Harrison Salisbury, *The Shook-up Generation* (New York: Harper & Bros., 1958); *Reaching the Unreached*, a Publication of the New York City Youth Board, 1952; C.K. Myers, *Light in the Dark Streets* (Greenwich, Conn.: Seabury Press, 1957); Walter Bernstein, "The Cherubs are Rumbling," *The New Yorker*, Sept. 21, 1957; Sam Glane, "Juvenile Gangs in East Side Los Angeles," *Focus*, Vol.29, (Sept. 1959), pp.136–41; Dale Kramer and Madeline Karr, *Teen-Age Gangs* (New York, Henry Holt, 1953); S.V. Jones, "The Cougars—Life with a Brooklyn Gang," *Harper's*, Vol.,209, (Nov. 1954), pp.33–43; P.C. Crawford, D.I. Malamund, and J.R. Dumpson, *Working with Teen-Age Gangs* (New York Welfare Council, 1950); Dan Wakefield, "The Gang That Went Good," *Harper's*, Vol. 216 (June, 1958), pp.36–43.

¹⁴ Harold Finestone, "Cats, Kicks, and Color," *Social Problems*, Vol.5 (July 1957), pp.3–13.

Chapter 6

EVALUATION OF STRUCTURAL-FUNCTIONALIST
AND ANOMIE THEORIES

Alex Thio

First, there is no reliable evidence to support anomie theory's claim that people of lower classes are more likely than those of other classes to engage in deviant behavior.[1] It is true that the official statistics on crime and delinquency, which anomie theorists rely on, do support the theory. But the official statistics are largely unreliable and invalid. They are unreliable because law enforcers are much more likely to catch lower-class criminals and delinquents. They are invalid because they do not reflect the total picture of deviance—they measure instead a very small portion of the totality of deviance, namely, the relatively serious types. If we modify the theory and say that lower-class people are more likely to commit what society considers *serious* types of deviance, then the theory does have adequate empirical support from both the official and unofficial reports on criminality and delinquency.

Second, there is no evidence to support the assumption of anomie theory that lower-class people tend to hold the same level of success aspirations as do upper- and middle-class people. On the contrary, both theoretical analysis and empirical data show that lower-class people hold a significantly lower level of success aspirations. It is true, as anomie theorists claim, that American society does encourage lower-class people to embrace high success goals. But it is not necessarily true, as anomie theorists assume, that lower-class people will in fact embrace high success goals. Merton and other anomie theorists appear to have ignored the fact that the manifest intended function of success ideology (to get all classes of people to entertain high aspirations) is *not* the same as its latent, unintended consequence (people of higher social classes end up holding far higher aspirations than do people of lower classes).

Third, related to the preceding criticism is the doubt cast upon Merton's assumption of value consensus. Many sociologists question Merton's assumption that the same set of cultural goals (i.e., success goals) governs various groups of individuals in the society. They point out that this assumption fails to jibe with the pluralistic and conflicting nature of American society. Recognition of this *value pluralism* may reveal the limitation of anomie theory. Thus many minority groups in our society have their own cultural values, so they may engage in deviant acts without having been influenced by the cultural goal of success. Their deviant acts may include:

> Violations of fish and game laws by Indians; common law marriage, statutory rape, marihuana use, and carrying concealed weapons by Mexican migrants; common law marriage, "totin'" (petty theft) and

assault by rural Negro migrants; gambling and opium use by Chinese; informal sororal polygyny, gambling and statutory rape ("sex sixteen" cases) among Hawaiians; drunkenness among older Japanese in Hawaii; and cockfighting among Filipinos.[2]

Fourth, anomie theory has been criticized for overdrawing the picture of lower-class delinquents as sorry kids who are forced into unpleasant deviant activities by the lack of success opportunity. This, Gwynn Nettler argues, slights the fact "that lower-class ways of life may have a rationale and a definition of 'how things ought to be' that have their own validity." Nettler assumes that the delinquents may have no interest at all in achieving success. He concludes:

This structural explanation [anomie theory] is blind, therefore, to the *fun* that is involved in being delinquent—fun like skipping school, rolling drunks, snatching purses, being chased by the police, staying out till all hours, going where one wants, and doing what one wants without adult supervision.[3]

Fifth, despite all these shortcomings, anomie theory does have some very important redeeming value, aside from its being considered by many sociologists as highly interesting. For one thing, anomie theory has contributed greatly to the sociological idea that the society, not the individual, causes deviant behavior. Before the theory was first presented in 1938, many sociologists tended to seek the causes of crime and delinquency within the individual rather than without. The fact that today many sociologists take for granted the notion of deviance as caused by society is a testament to the contribution of anomie theory.

Also, anomie theory seems to have a valid premise: the discrepancy between aspirations and the opportunity to realize these aspirations produces pressures toward deviation. This premise appears valid as long as we do not do what Merton has done—use it to make the unwarranted generalization that the lower classes are more pressured toward deviation than are other classes. Instead, we may use the premise to suggest that anybody, regardless of his or her class, tends to engage in deviance if he or she experiences a significant gap between aspiration and opportunity. Indeed, research has shown that wherever the aspiration-opportunity gap strikes, it tends to generate deviation. This has occurred, for example, in such diverse areas as an interdisciplinary scientific research team, the professions, an orthodox Jewish community, and a military prison,[4] as well as in the army, a governmental bureaucracy, and a Soviet firm.[5]

NOTES

[1] For a more detailed discussion of this and some of the other following points, see Alex Thio, " A Critical Look at Merton's Anomie Theory." *Pacific Sociological Review 18* (April 1975): 139-158.

[2] Edwin M. Lemert, 1967, *Human Deviance, Social Problems, and Social Control.* Englewood Cliffs, New Jersey: Prentice-Hall:8.

[3] Gwynn Nettler 1978, *Explaining Crime.* New York: MacGraw-Hill:232.

[4] Studies on these are cited in Merton, 1957 *Social Theory and Social Structure.* New York: The Free Press:181.

[5] Findings on deviance in these areas are discussed by Cohen 1966, *Deviance and Control.* Englewood Cliffs, New Jersey: Prentice-Hall:78-82.

Chapter 7

THE THEORY OF DIFFERENTIAL ASSOCIATION

Edwin H. Sutherland
Donald R. Cressey
David Luckenbill

The Problem for Criminological Theory

If criminology is to be scientific, the heterogenous collection of factors known to be associated with crime and criminality must be organized and integrated by means of explanatory theory which has the same characteristics as the scientific theory in other fields of study. That is, the conditions which are said to cause crime should be present when crime is present, and they should be absent when crime is absent. Such a theory or body of theory would stimulate, simplify, and give direction to criminological research, and it would provide a framework for understanding the significance of much of the knowledge acquired about crime and criminality in the past. Furthermore, it would be useful in minimizing crime rates, provided it could be "applied" in much the same way that the engineer "applies" the scientific theories of the physicist.

There are two complementary procedures which may be used to put order into criminological knowledge. The first is logical abstraction. Blacks, males, urban-dwellers, and young adults have comparatively high crime rates. What do these persons have in common that results in these high crime rates? Research has shown that criminal behavior is associated, in greater or lesser degree, with such social and personal conditions as poverty, slum-residence, lack of recreational facilities, inadequate and demoralized families, mental retardation and emotional instability. What do these conditions have in common that apparently produces excessive criminality? Research has also demonstrated that many individuals faced with these conditions do not commit crimes and that individuals in the upper socioeconomic classes frequently violate the law, although they do not live in poverty, do not lack recreational facilities, and are not mentally retarded or emotionally unstable. Obviously, it is not the conditions themselves that cause crime, for they are sometimes present when criminality does not occur, and they also are sometimes absent when criminality does occur. An explanation of crime and criminality can be reached by logically abstracting the conditions and processes which are common to the rich and the poor, the males and the females, the blacks and the whites, the urban dweller and the rural dwellers, the young adults and the older adults, and the emotionally stable and the emotionally unstable who do commit crimes.

In developing such an explanation, criminal behavior must be precisely defined and carefully distinguished from noncriminal behavior. Criminal behavior is human behavior, and it has much in common with noncriminal behavior. An explanation of

64

criminal behavior should be consistent with a general theory of other human behavior, but the conditions and processes said to produce crime and criminality should be specific. Many things that are necessary for behavior are not important criminality. In differentiating for example respiration, is necessary for any behavior, but the respiratory process cannot be used in an explanation of criminal behavior, for it does not differentiate criminal behavior from noncriminal behavior.

The second procedure for putting order into criminological knowledge is differentiation of levels of analysis. The explanation must be limited, largely in terms of chronology, and in this way held at a particular level. When Renaissance physicists stated the law of falling bodies, they were not concerned with the reasons why a body began to fall except as this might affect the initial momentum. Galileo did not study the "traits" of falling objects themselves, as Aristotle might have done. Instead, he noted the relationship of the body to its environment while it was falling freely or rolling down an inclined plane, and it made no difference to his generalization whether a body began to fall because it was dropped from the hand of an experimenter or because it rolled off the ledge of a bridge due to vibration caused by a passing vehicle. It also, was not significant for the law of falling bodies that a round object would roll off the bridge more readily than a square object. Such facts were considered as existing on a different level of explanation and being irrelevant to the problem of explaining the behavior of falling bodies.

Much of the confusion regarding crime and criminal behavior stems from a failure to define and hold constant the level at which they are explained. By analogy, many criminologists concerned with understanding crime would attribute some degree of causal power to the roundness of the object in the above example. In the heterogenous collection of factors associated with crime and criminal behavior, one factor often occurs prior to another in much the way that roundness occurs prior to vibration, and vibration occurs prior to rolling off a bridge. However, consideration of time sequences among the conditions associated with crime and criminology could lead to simplicity of statement can be made without referring to those early factors. By holding the analysis at one level, the early factors are combined with or differentiated from later factors, thus reducing the number of variables which must be considered in a theory.

In a classic tale two boys who were engaged in a minor theft the ran when they were discovered. One boy had longer legs, escaped, and later became a priest; the other had shorter legs, was caught, and committed to a reformatory, and later became a gangster. In this comparison, the boy who became a criminal was differentiated from the one who did not become a criminal by the length of his legs. But "length of legs" need not be considered a criminological theory because it is obvious that this condition does not determine criminality and has no necessary relation to criminality. In the illustration, the differential in the length of the boys' legs apparently was significant to subsequent criminality or noncriminality only to the degree that it determined the subsequent experiences and associations of the two boys. It is in these experiences and associations, then, that the mechanisms and processes which are important to criminality or noncriminality are to be found.

Two Types of Explanations of Criminal Behavior

Scientific explanations of criminal behavior may be stated either in terms of the processes which are operating at the moment of the occurrence of crime or in terms of the processes operating in the earlier history of the criminal. In the first case, the explanation may be called "situational," or "dynamic"; in the second case, "historical" or "developmental." Both types of explanation are desirable. The situational type of explanation has been favored by physical and biological scientists, and it probably could be the more efficient type of explanation of criminal behavior. However, criminological explanation of the situational type have been, for the most part, unsuccessful because they have been formulated largely in connection with attempts to isolate personal and social pathologies among criminals. Still, work from this point of view has results in the conclusion that the immediate determinants of criminal behavior lie in person-situation complex (see Gibbons, 1971).

The objective situation is important to criminality largely to the extent that it provides an opportunity for a criminal act. A thief may steal from a display case when the clerk is not in sight but refrain when the clerk is present; a burglar may attack a bank which is poorly protected but refrain from attacking a bank that is well protected. But in another sense, the situation is not exclusive of the person, for the situation which is important is the situation as defined by the person who is involved. That is, some persons define a situation in which a clerk is out of sight as a "crime committing" situation, while others do not. Furthermore, the events in the person-situation complex at the time a crime occurs cannot be separated from the prior life experiences of the criminal. This means that the situation is defined by the person in terms of the inclinations and abilities which he or she has acquired. Thus, while a person could define a situation in such a manner that criminal behavior would be the inevitable result, past experiences would, for the most part, determine the way in which he or she defined the situation. An explanation of criminal behavior made in terms of these past experiences is a historical or developmental explanation.

The following section states such a developmental theory of criminal behavior on the assumption that a criminal act occurs when a situation appropriate for it, as defined by the person, is present. The theory should be regarded as tentative, and it should be tested by the factual information presented in the later chapters to follow and by all other factual information and theories which are applicable.

The Theory of Differential Association Behavior

The following statements refer to the process by which a particular person comes to engage in criminal behavior:

1. *Criminal behavior is learned.* Negatively, this means that criminal behavior is not inherited, as such. Also, the person who is not already trained in crime does not invent criminal behavior, just as a person who has had no training in mechanics does not make mechanical inventions.

2. *Criminal behavior is learned in interaction with other persons in a process of communication.* This communication is verbal in many respects, but it also includes "the communication of gestures."

3. *The principal part of the learning of criminal behavior occurs within intimate personal groups.* Negatively, this means that the interpersonal agencies of communication, such as movies and newspapers, play a relatively unimportant part in the genesis of criminal behavior.

4. *When criminal behavior is learned, the learning includes (a) techniques of committing the crime, which are sometimes very complicated, sometimes very simple; (b) the specific direction of motives, drives, rationalizations, and attitudes.*

5. *The specific direction of motives and drives is learned from definitions of the legal codes as favorable or unfavorable.* In some societies the individual is surrounded by persons who invariably define the legal codes as rules to be observed, while in others he is surrounded by persons whose definitions are favorable to the violation of the legal codes. In our American society these definitions are almost always mixed, with the consequence that we have culture conflict in relation to the legal codes.

6. *A person becomes delinquent because of an excess of definitions favorable to violation of law over definitions unfavorable to violation of law.* This is the principle of differential association. It refers to both criminal and anticriminal associations and involves *with* counteractions forces. When persons become criminal, they do so because of contact with criminal behavior patterns and also because of isolation from anticriminal patterns. Any person inevitably assimilates the surrounding culture unless other patterns are in conflict; a southerner does not pronounce r because other southerners do not pronounce r. Negatively, this proposition of differential association means that associations which are neutral so far as crime is concerned have little or no effect on the genesis of criminal behavior. Much of the experience of a person is neutral in this sense, for instance, learning to brush one's teeth. This behavior has no negative or positive effect on criminal behavior except that it may be related to associations which are concerned with the legal codes. This neutral behavior is important especially as an occupier of the time of a child so that he or she is not in contact with criminal behavior during the time the child is so engaged in the neutral behavior.

7. *Differential associations may vary in frequency, duration, priority, and intensity.* This means that associations with criminal behavior and also associations with anticriminal behavior vary in those respects. Frequency and duration as modalities of associations are obvious and need no explanation. Priority is assumed to be important in the sense that lawful behavior developed in early childhood may persist throughout life, and also that delinquent behavior developed in early childhood may persist throughout life. This tendency, however, has not been adequately demonstrated, and priority seems to be important principally through its selective influence. Intensity is not precisely defined, but it has to do with such things as the prestige of the source a criminal or anticriminal pattern and with emotional reactions related to the associations. In a precise description of the criminal behavior of a person, these modalitites would be rated in quantitative form and a mathematical ratio would be reached. A formula in this sense has not been developed, and the development of such a formula would be extremely difficult.

8. *The process of learning criminal behavior by association with criminal and anticriminal patterns involves all of the mechanisms that are involved in any other*

learning. Negatively, this means that the learning of criminal behavior is not restricted to the process of imitation. A person who is seduced, for instance, learns criminal behavior by association, but this process would not ordinarily be described as imitation.

9. *While criminal behavior is an expression of general needs and values, it is not explained by those general needs and values, since noncriminal behavior is an expression of the same needs and values.* Thieves generally steal in order to secure money, but likewise honest laborers work in order to secure money. The attempts by many scholars to explain criminal behavior by general drives and values, such as the happiness principle, striving for social status, the money motive, or frustration, have been, and must continue to be, futile, since they explain lawful behavior as completely as they explain criminal behavior. Such drives are similar to respiration, which is necessary for any behavior, but which does not differentiate criminal from noncriminal behavior.

It is not necessary, at this level of explanation, to explain why persons have the associations they have; this certainly involves a complex of many things. In an area where the delinquency rate is high, a boy who is sociable, gregarious, active, and athletic is very likely to come in contact with the other boys in the neighborhood, learn delinquent behavior patterns from them, and become a delinquent. In the same neighborhood an emotionally disturbed boy who is isolated, introverted, and inactive may remain at home, not become acquainted with the other boys in the neighborhood, and not become delinquent. In another situation, the sociable, outgoing, active boy may become a member of a scout troop and not become involved in delinquent behavior. The person's associations are determined in a general context of social organization. A child is ordinarily reared in a family; the place of residence of the family is determined largely by family income; and the delinquency rate is in many respects related to the rental value of the houses. Many other aspects of social organization affect the associations a person has.

The preceding explanation of criminal behavior purports to explain the criminal and noncriminal behavior of individual persons. As indicated earlier, it is possible to state sociological theories of criminal behavior which explain the criminality of a community, nation, or other group. The problem, when thus stated, is to account for variations in crime rates, which involves a comparison of the crime rates of different groups or the crime rates of a particular group at different times. The explanation of a crime rate must be consistent with the explanation of the criminal behavior of the person, since the crime rate is a summary statement of the number of persons in the group who commit crimes and the frequency with which they commit crimes. One of the best explanations of crime rates from this point of view is that a high crime rate is due to social disorganization. The postulate on which this theory is based, is that crime is rooted in the social organization and is an expression of that social organization. A group may be organized for criminal behavior or organized against criminal behavior. Most communities are organized for both criminal and anticriminal behavior, and, in that sense, the crime rate is an expression of the differential group organization. Differential group organization as an explanation of variations in crime rates is consistent with the differential association theory of the processes by which persons become criminals.

Chapter 8

EVALUATION OF DIFFERENTIAL ASSOCIATION THEORY

Alex Thio

First, differential association theory is mainly applicable to criminals and delinquents who commit crime and delinquency in groups. The theory is less applicable to those who often commit crimes alone, such as "rural offenders, landlords, trust violators, check forgers, and white-collar criminals."[1]

Second, it is difficult to determine precisely what differential association or "excess of criminal patterns over anticriminal patterns" is in real life situations. Many researchers have found that people often cannot identify the persons from whom they have learned criminal and anticriminal behavior patterns, much less determine whether one behavior pattern has occurred more often than the other in their lives.[2]

The difficulty in finding an empirical indicator of differential association is, from the scientific point of view, extremely damaging to the theory. This is because the theory may become a useless statement of circular reasoning. Since it is convenient to identify individual criminality as the empirical indicator of "the excess of criminal patterns over anticriminal patterns," then it is tautological to say that "the excess of criminal patterns over anticriminal patterns" *causes* individual criminality.

But Cressey does not accept this criticism. He says: "It should be noted that these damaging criticisms of the theory of differential association as a precise statement of the mechanism by which persons become criminals do not affect the value of the theory as a general principle which organizes and makes good sense of the data on crime rates. A theory accounting for the distribution of crime, delinquency, or any other phenomenon can be valid even if a presumably coordinate theory specifying the process by which deviancy occurs in individual cases is *incorrect*, let alone untestable."[3] In this quote, Cressey apparently believes that, if it cannot successfully explain *individual* criminality, the theory can at least account for *group* criminality. Can it? This leads us to the next point.

Third, it also appears difficult for the theory to account scientifically for group criminality. The theory can explain group criminality, but in a tautological way. As quoted earlier, Sutherland said: "The formal statement of the theory indicates, for example, that a high crime rate in urban areas can be considered the end product of criminalistic traditions in those areas."[4] Note that a criminalistic tradition is supposed to explain a high crime rate or that the former is the cause and the latter is the effect. It is difficult to observe criminalistic tradition. But it is easy to observe a high crime rate. We may use this as the observable indicator of a criminalistic tradition. Yet it would be an exercise in circular reasoning if we say that the criminalistic tradition is the *cause* of a high crime rate.

Fourth, in emphasizing the importance of learning how to become criminal or delinquent, Sutherland's theory may have assumed that some special skills must be learned in order to pull off a criminal or delinquent act. Some sociologists have severely criticized this part of the theory. Sheldon Glueck, for example, attacks it this way:

> What is there to be learned about simple lying, taking things that belong to another, fighting, and sex play? Do children have to be taught such natural [delinquent] acts? If one takes account of the psychiatric and criminological evidence that involves research into the early childhood manifestations of antisocial behavior, one must conclude that it is not delinquent behavior that is learned; that comes naturally. It is rather *non*-delinquent behavior that is learned. Unsocialized, untamed, and uninstructed, the child resorts to lying, slyness, subterfuge, anger, hatred, theft, aggression, attack, and other forms of social behavior in its early attempts of self-expression and ego formation.[5]

You may see that the child's delinquent acts listed in this quote are basically so unsophisticated that one need not learn a skill in order to be able to commit them. You could add to that list some adult crimes which are also unsophisticated, such as murder, forcible rape, aggravated assault, and other such crimes of impulse and passion—which need not be learned, either.

Fifth, Glaser's differential identification theory appears to have been supported by some empirical data. Victor Matthews, for example, found that high school boys who identified with delinquent friends were likely to become delinquent themselves.[6] But there is no conclusive evidence that identification with delinquent friends is the cause of delinquency or occurs before a person becomes delinquent....

Sixth, although it is difficult (as the second point has suggested) to determine the exact, empirical meaning of differential association, numerous sociologists have nonetheless found that their research data appear to suport Sutherland's theory. But this need not be surprising. For those sociologists have found empirical support not exactly be Sutherland's theory, but instead for their own interpretations of the theory. As James Short, who has done much research attempting to test the theory, concludes: "Much support has been found for the principle of differential association *if* the liberties taken in the process of its operationalization [translation into empirical or testable terms] are granted."[7] Most frequently, researchers have translated the principle of differential association into an intellectualized version of the popular "bad companions" theory, which says in effect that a person who runs around with bad companions will more likely become bad than another who does not.[8] One of these researchers, for example, gives this concluding statement about his research: "On the basis of this research, it is clear that adolescents who associate extensively with delinquent friends report more delinquent behavior than those whose contact with delinquent peers is minimal."[9] At any rate, all this shows that Sutherland's differential association theory has inspired a good deal of research, which may make the theory more empirically testable and thus a better scientific theory.

NOTES

[1] Sutherland, Edwin and Paul Cressey, 1978. *Criminology.* Philadelphia: Lippincott: 88.

[2] *Ibid.,*:91–92.

[3] *Ibid.*

[4] *Ibid.,*:94.

[5] Glueck, S. 1956. "Theory and Fact in Criminology." *British Journal of Delinquency* 7:94.

[6] Matthews, V.M. 1968. "Differential Identification: An Empirical Note." *Social Problems* 14:376–83.

[7] Short, J.F. Jr. 1960. "Differential Association as a Hypothesis: Problems of Empirical Testing." *Social Problems* 8:24.

[8] Sutherland would have considered this an error, as his emphasis on criminal *patterns and definitions* made clear.

[9] Voss, H.L. 1964. "Differential Association and Reported Delinquent Behavior: A Replication." *Social Problems* 12:85. See also J.F. Short, "Differential Association with Delinquent Friends and Delinquent Behavior." *Pacific Sociological Review* 1:20–25; D. Glaser. 1960. "Differential Association and Criminological Research." *Social Problems* 8:6–14; A.J. Reiss & L.A. Rhodes. 1964. "An Empirical Test of Differential Association Theory." *Journal of Research in Crime and Delinquency* 1:5–18.

Chapter 9

A CONTROL THEORY OF DELINQUENCY

Travis Hirschi

Control theories assume that delinquent acts result when an individual's bond to society is weak or broken. Since these theories embrace two highly complex concepts, the *bond* of the individual to *society*, it is not surprising that they have at one time or another formed the basis of explanations of most forms of aberrant or unusual behavior. It is also not surprising that control theories have described the elements of the bond to society in many ways, and that they have focused on a variety of units as the point of control...

Elements of the Bond Attachment

In explaining conforming behavior, sociologists justly emphasize sensitivity to the opinion of others.[1] Unfortunately,...they tend to suggest that man *is* sensitive to the opinion of others and thus exclude sensitivity from their explanations of deviant behavior. In explaining deviant behavior, psychologists, in contrast, emphasize insensitivity to the opinion of others.[2] Unfortunately, they too tend to ignore variation, and, in addition, they tend to tie sensitivity inextricably to other variables, to make it part of a syndrome or "type," and thus seriously to reduce its value as an explanatory concept. The psychopath is characterized only in part by "deficient attachment to or affection for others, a failure to respond to the ordinary motivations founded in respect or regard for one's fellow";[3] he is also characterized by such things as "excessive aggressiveness," "lack of superego control," and "an infantile level of response."[4] Unfortunately, too, the behavior that psychopathy is used to explain often becomes part of the *definition* of psychopathy. As a result, in Barbara Wootton's words: "[The psychopath] is...*par excellence*, and without shame or qualification, the model of the circular process by which mental abnormality is inferred from anti-social behavior while anti-social behavior is explained by mental abnormality."[5]

The problems of diagnosis, tautology, and name-calling are avoided if the dimensions of psychopathy are treated as causally and therefore problematically interrelated, rather than as logically and therefore necessarily bound to each other. In fact, it can be argued that all of the characteristics attributed to the psychopath follow from, are effects of, his lack of attachment to others. To say that to lack attachment to others is to be free from moral restraints is to use lack of attachment to explain the guiltlessness of the psychopath, the fact that he apparently has no conscience or superego. In this view, lack of attachment to others is not merely a symptom of psychopathy, it *is* psychopathy; lack of conscience is just another way of saying the same thing; and the violation of norms is (or may be) a consequence.

72

For that matter, given that man is an animal, "impulsivity" and "aggressiveness" can also be seen as natural consequences of freedom from moral restraints. However, since the view of man as endowed with natural propensities and capacities like other animals is peculiarly unpalatable to sociologists, we need not fall back on such a view to explain the amoral man's aggressiveness.[6] The process of becoming alienated from others often involves or is based on active interpersonal conflict. Such conflict could easily supply a reservoir of *socially derived* hostility sufficient to account for the aggressiveness of those whose attachments to others have been weakened.

Durkheim said it many years ago: "We are moral beings to the extent that we are social beings."[7] This may be interpreted to mean that we are moral beings to the extent that we have "internalized the norms" of society. But what does it mean to say that a person has internalized the norms of society? The norms of society are by definition shared by the members of society. To violate a norm is, therefore, to act contrary to the wishes and expectations of other people. If a person does not care about the wishes and expectations of other people—that is, if he is insensitive to the opinion of others— then he is to that extent not bound by the norms. He is free to deviate.

The essence of internalization of norms, conscience, or superego thus lies in the attachment of the individual to others.[8] This view has several advantages over the concept of internalization. For one, explanations of deviant behavior based on attachment do not beg the question, since the extent to which a person is attached to others can be measured independently of his deviant behavior. Furthermore, change or variation in behavior is explainable in a way that it is not when notions of internalization or superego are used. For example, the divorced man is more likely after divorce to commit a number of deviant acts, such as suicide or forgery. If we explain these acts by reference to the superego (or internal control), we are forced to say that the man "lost his conscience" when he got a divorce; and, of course, if he remarries, we have to conclude that he gets his conscience back.

This dimension of the bond to conventional society is encountered in most social control-oriented research and theory. F. Ivan Nye's "internal control" and "indirect control" refer to the same element, although we avoid the problem of explaining changes over time by locating the "conscience" in the bond to others rather than making it part of the personality.[9] Attachment to others is just one aspect of Albert J. Reiss's "personal controls"; we avoid his problems of tautological empirical *observations* by making the relationship between attachment and delinquency problematic rather than definitional.[10,11] Finally, Scott Briar and Irving Piliavin's "commitment" or "stake in conformity" subsumes attachment, as their discussion illustrates, although the terms they use are more closely associated with the next element to be discussed.

Commitment

"Of all passions, that which inclineth men least to break the laws, is fear. Nay, excepting some generous natures, it is the only thing, when there is the appearance of profit or pleasure by breaking the laws, that makes men keep them."[12] Few would deny that men on occasion obey the rules simply from fear of the consequences. This rational component in conformity we label commitment. What does it mean to say that a person is committed to conformity? In Howard S. Becker's formulation it means the following:

> First, the individual is in a position in which his decision with regard to some particular line of action has consequences for other interests and activities not necessarily [directly] related to it. Second, he has placed himself in that position by his own prior actions. A third element is present though so obvious as not to be apparent; the committed person must be aware [of these other interests] and must recognize that his decision in this case will have ramifications beyond it.[13]

The idea, then, is that the person invests time, energy, himself, in a certain line of activity—say, getting an education, building up a business, acquiring a reputation for virtue. When or whenever he considers deviant behavior, he must consider the costs of this deviant behavior, the risk he runs of losing the investment he has made in conventional behavior.

If attachment to others is the sociological counterpart of the superego or conscience, commitment is the counterpart of the ego or common sense. To the person committed to conventional lines of action, risking one to ten years in prison for a ten-dollar holdup is stupidity, because to the committed person the costs and risks obviously exceed ten dollars in value. (To the psychoanalyst, such an act exhibits failure to be governed by the "reality-principle.") In the sociological control theory, it can be and is generally assumed that the decision to commit a criminal act may well be rationally determined—that the actor's decision was not irrational given the risks and costs he faces. Of course, as Becker points out, if the actor is capable of in some sense calculating the costs of a line of action, he is also capable of calculational errors: ignorance and error return, in the control theory, as possible explanations of deviant behavior.

The concept of commitment assumes that the organization of society is such that the interest of most persons would be endangered if they were to engage in criminal acts. Most people, simply by the process of living in an organized society, acquire goods, reputations, prospects that they do not want to risk losing. These accumulations are society's insurance that they will abide by the rules. Many hypotheses about the antecedents of delinquent behavior are based on this premise. For example, Arthur L. Stinchcombe's hypotheses that "high school rebellion...occurs when future status is not clearly related to present performance"[14] suggests that one is committed to conformity not only by what one has but also by what one hoped to obtain. Thus "ambition" and/or "aspiration" play an important role in producing conformity. The person becomes committed to a conventional line of action, and he is therefore committed to conformity.

Most lines of action in a society are of course conventional. The clearest examples are educational and occupational careers. Actions thought to jeopardize one's chances in these areas are presumably avoided. Interestingly enough, even nonconventional commitments may operate to produce conventional conformity. We are told, at least, that boys aspiring to careers in the rackets or professional thievery are judged by their "honesty" and "reliability"—traits traditionally in demand among seekers of office boys.[15]

Involvement

Many persons undoubtedly owe a life of virtue to a lack of opportunity to do otherwise. Time and energy are inherently limited: "Not that I would not, if I could, be both handsome and fat and well dressed, and a great athlete, and make a million a year, be a wit, a bon vivant, and a lady killer, as well as a philosopher, a philanthropist, a statesman, warrior, and African explorer, as well as a 'tone-poet' and saint. But the thing is simply impossible."[16] The things that William James here says he would like to be or do are all, I suppose, within the realm of conventionality, but if he were to include illicit actions he would still have to eliminate some of them as simply impossible.

Involvement or engrossment in conventional activities is thus often part of a control theory. The assumption, widely shared, is that a person may be simply too busy doing conventional things to find time to engage in deviant behavior. The person involved in conventional activities is tied to appointments, deadlines, working hours, plans, and the like, so the opportunity to commit deviant acts rarely arises. To the extent that he is engrossed in conventional activities, he cannot even think about deviant acts, let alone act out his inclinations.[17]

This line of reasoning is responsible for the stress placed on recreational facilities in many programs to reduce delinquency, for much of the concern with the high school dropout, and for the idea that boys should be drafted into the army to keep them out of trouble. So obvious and persuasive is the idea that involvement in conventional activities is a major deterrent to delinquency that it was accepted even by Sutherland: "In the general area of juvenile delinquency it is probable that the most significant difference between juveniles who engage in delinquency and those who do not is that the latter are provided abundant opportunities of a conventional type for satisfying their recreational interests, while the former lack those opportunities or facilities."[18]

The view that "idle hands are the devil's workshop" has received more sophisticated treatment in recent sociological writings on delinquency. David Matza and Gresham M. Sykes, for example, suggest that delinquents have the values of a leisure class, the same values ascribed by Veblen to *the* leisure class: a search for kicks, disdain of work, a desire for the big score, and acceptance of aggressive toughness as proof of masculinity.[19] Matza and Sykes explain delinquency by reference to this system of values, but they note that adolescents at all class levels are "to some extent" members of a leisure class, that they "move in a limbo between earlier parental domination and future integration with the social structure through the bonds of work and marriage."[20] In the end, then, the leisure of the adolescent produces a set of values, which, in turn, leads to delinquency.

Belief

Unlike the cultural deviance theory, the control theory assumes the existence of a common value system within the society or group whose norms are being violated. If the deviant is committed to a value system different from that of conventional society, there is, within the context of the theory, nothing to explain. The question is, "Why does a man violate the rules in which he believes?" It is not, "Why do men differ in their beliefs about what constitutes good and desirable conduct?" The person is assumed to have been socialized (perhaps imperfectly) into the group whose rules he is violating; deviance is not a question of one group imposing its rules on the members of another group. In other words, we not only assume the deviant *has* believed the rules, we assume he believes the rules even as he violates them.

How can a person believe it is wrong to steal at the same time he is stealing? In the strain theory, this is not a difficult problem. (In fact,...the strain theory was devised specifically to deal with this question.) The motivation to deviance adduced by the strain theorist is so strong that we can well understand the deviant act even assuming the deviator believes strongly that it is wrong.[21] However, given the control theory's assumptions about motivation, if both the deviant and the nondeviant believe the deviant act is wrong, how do we account for the fact that one commits it and the other does not?

Control theories have taken two approaches to this problem. In one approach, beliefs are treated as mere words that mean little or nothing if the other forms of control are missing. "Semantic dementia," the dissociation between rational faculties and emotional control which is said to be characteristic of the psychopath, illustrates this way of handling the problem.[22] In short, beliefs, at least insofar as they are expressed in words, drop out of the picture; since they do not differentiate between deviants and nondeviants, they are in the same class as "language" or any other characteristic common to all members of a group. Since they represent no real obstacle to the commission of delinquent acts, nothing need be said about how they are handled by those committing such acts. The control theories that do not mention beliefs (or values), and many do not, may be assumed to take this approach to the problem.

The second approach argues that the deviant rationalizes his behavior so that he can at once violate the rule and maintain his belief in it. Donald R. Cressey had advanced his argument with respect to embezzlement,[23] and Sykes and Matza have advanced it with respect to delinquency.[24] In both Cressey's and Sykes and Matza's treatments, these rationalizations (Cressey calls them "verbalizations," Sykes and Matza term them "techniques of neutralization occur prior to the commission of the deviant act. If the neutralization is successful, the person is free to commit the act(s) in question. Both in Cressey and in Sykes and Matza, the strain that prompts the effort at neutralization also provides the motive force that results in the subsequent deviant act. Their theories are thus, in this sense, strain theories. Neutralization is difficult to handle within the context of a theory that adheres closely to control theory assumptions, because in the control theory there is no special motivational force to account for the neutralization. This difficulty is especially noticeable in Matza's later treatment of this topic, where the motivational component, the "will to delinquency," appears *after* the moral vacuum has been created by the techniques of neutralization.[25] The question thus becomes: Why neutralize?

In attempting to solve a strain-theory problem with control-theory tools, the control theorist is thus led into a trap. He cannot answer the crucial question. The concept of neutralization assumes the existence of moral obstacles to the commission of deviant acts. In order plausibly to account for a deviant act, it is necessary to generate motivation to deviance that is at least equivalent in force to the resistance provided by these moral obstacles. However, if the moral obstacles are removed, neutralization and special motivation are no longer required. We therefore follow the implicit logic of control theory and remove these moral obstacles by hypothesis. Many persons do not have an attitude of respect toward the rules of society; many persons feel no moral obligation to conform regardless of personal advantage. Insofar as the values and beliefs of these persons are consistent with their feelings, and there should be a tendency toward consistency, neutralization is unnecessary; it has already occurred.

Does this merely push the question back a step and at the same time produce conflict with the assumption of a common value system? I think not. In the first place, we do not assume, as does Cressey, that neutralization occurs in order to make a specific criminal act possible.[26] We do not assume, as do Sykes and Matza, that neutralization occurs to make many delinquent acts possible. We do not assume, in other words, that the person constructs a system of rationalizations in order to justify commission of acts he *wants* to commit. We assume, in contrast, that the beliefs that free a man to commit deviant acts are *unmotivated* in the sense that he does not construct or adopt them in order to facilitate the attainment of illicit ends. In the second place, we do not assume, as does Matza, that "delinquents concur in the conventional assessment of delinquency."[27] We assume, in contrast, that there is *variation* in the extent to which people believe they should obey the rules of society, and, furthermore, that the less a person believes he should obey the rules, the more likely he is to violate them.[28]

In chronological order, then, a person's beliefs in the moral validity or norms are, for no teleological reason, weakened. The probability that he will commit delinquent acts is therefore increased. When and if he commits a delinquent act, we may justifiably use the weakness of his beliefs in explaining it, but no special motivation is required to explain either the weakness of his beliefs or, perhaps, his delinquent act.

The keystone of this argument is of course the assumption that there is variation in belief in the moral validity of social rules. This assumption is amenable to direct empirical test and can thus survive at least until its first confrontation with data. For the present, we must return to the idea of a common value system with which this section was begun.

The idea of a common (or perhaps better, a single) value system is consistent with the fact, or presumption, of variation in the strength of moral beliefs. We have not suggested that delinquency is based on beliefs counter to conventional morality; we have not suggested that delinquents do not believe delinquent acts are wrong. They may well believe these acts are wrong, but the meaning and efficacy of such beliefs are contingent on other beliefs and, indeed, on the strength of other ties to the conventional order.[29]

NOTES

[1]Books have been written on the increasing importance of interpersonal sensitivity in modern life. According to this view, controls from within have become less important than controls from without in *producing* conformity. Whether or not this observation is true as a description of historical trends, it is true that interpersonal sensitivity has become more important in *explaining* conformity. Although logically it

should also have become more important in explaining nonconformity, the opposite has been the case, once again showing that Cohen's observation that an explanation of conformity has to be an explanation of deviance cannot be translated as "an explanation of conformity has to be an explanation of deviance." For the view that interpersonal sensitivity currently plays a greater role than formerly in producing conformity, see William J. Goode, "Norm Commitment and Conformity to Role-Status Obligations," *American Journal of Sociology*, LXVI (1960), 246–58. And, of course, also see David Reisman, Nathan Glazer, and Rouel Denney, *The Lonely Crowd* (Garden City, New York: Doubleday, 1950), especially Part I.

[2] The literature on psychopathy is voluminous. See William McCord and Joan McCord, *The Psychopath* (Princeton: D. Van Nostrad, 1964).

[3] John M. Martin and Joseph P. Fitzpatrick, *Delinquent Behavior* (New York: Random House, 1964), p.30.

[4] Ibid. For additional properties of the psychopath, see McCord and McCord, *The Psychopath*, pp.1–22.

[5] Barbara Wootton, *Social Science and Social Pathology* (New York: Macmillan, 1959), p.250.

[6] "The logical untenability [of the position that there are forces in man 'resistant to socialization] was ably demonstrated by Parsons over 30 years ago, and it is widely recognized that the position is empirically unsound because it assumes [!] some universal biological drive system distinctly separate from socialization and social context—a basic and intransigent human nature" (Judith Blake and Kingsley Davis, "Norms, Values, and Sanctions," *Handbook of Modern Sociology*, ed. Robert E.L. Faris [Chicago: Rand McNally, 1964], p.471).

[7] Emile Durkheim, *Moral Education*, trans. Everett K. Wilson and Herman Schnurer (New York: The Free Press, 1961), p.64.

[8] Although attachment alone does not exhaust the meaning of internalization, attachments and beliefs combined would appear to leave only a small residue of "internal control" not susceptible in principle to direct measurement.

[9] F. Ivan Nye, *Family Relationships and Delinquent Behavior* (New York: Wiley, 1958), pp.5–7.

[10] Albert J. Reiss, Jr., "Delinquency as the Failure of Personal and Social Controls," *American Sociological Review*, XVI(1951), 196–207. For example, our observations show...that delinquent recidivists are less often persons with mature ego ideals or nondelinquent social roles" (p.204).

[11] Scott Briar and Irving Piliavin, "Delinquency, Situational Inducements, and Commitment to Conformity," *Social Problems* XIII(1965):41–42. The concept "stake in conformity" was introduced by Jackson Toby in his "Social Disorganization and Stake in Conformity: Complementary Factors in the Predatory Behavior of Hoodlums," *Journal of Criminal Law, Criminology and Police Science*, XLVIII (1957), 12–17. See also his "Hoodlum or Business Man: An American Dilemma," *The Jews*, ed. Marshall Sklare (New York: The Free Press, 1958), pp. 542–550. Throughout the text, I occasionally use "stake in conformity" in speaking in general of the strength of the bond to conventional society. So used, the concept is somewhat broader than is true for either Toby or Briar and Piliavin, where the concept is roughly equivalent to what is here called "commitment."

[12] Thomas Hobbes, *Leviathan*, (Oxford: Basil Blackwell, 1957), p.195.

[13] Howard S. Becker, "Notes on the Concept of Commitment." *American Journal of Sociology*, LXVI (1960), pp.35–6.

[14] Arthur L. Stinchcombe, *Rebellion in a High School* (Chicago: Quadrangle, 1964), p.5.

[15] Richard A. Cloward and Lloyd E. Ohlin, *Delinquency and Opportunity* (New York: The Free Press, 1960), p.147, quoting Edwin H. Sutherland, ed., *The Professional Thief* (Chicago: University of Chicago Press, 1937), pp.211–13.

[16] William James, *Psychology* (Cleveland: World Publishing Co., 1948), p.186.

[17] Few activities appear to be so engrossing that they rule out contemplation of alternative lines of behavior, at least if it estimates the amount of time men spend plotting sexual deviations have any validity.

[18] *The Sutherland Papers*, ed. Albert K. Cohen, et al. (Bloomington: Indiana University Press, 1956), p.37.

[19] David Matza and Gresham M. Sykes, "Juvenile Delinquency and Subterranean Values," *American Sociological Review*, XXVI (1961), 712–19.

[20] Ibid., p.718.

[21] The starving man stealing the loaf of bread is the image evoked by most strain theories. In this image, the starving man's belief in the wrongness of his act is clearly not something that must be explained away. It can be assumed to be present without causing embarrassment to the explanation.

[22] McCord and McCord, *The Psychopath*, pp.12–15.

[23] Donald R. Cressey,

[24] Gresham M. Sykes and David Matza, "Techniques of Neutralization: A Theory of Delinquency," *American Sociological Review*, XXII (1957), pp.664–70.

[25] David Matza, *Delinquency and Drift* (New York: Wiley, 1964), pp.181–91.

[26] In asserting that Cressey's assumption is invalid with respect to delinquency, I do not wish to suggest that it is invalid for the question of embezzlement, where the problem faced by the deviator is fairly specific and he can reasonably be assumed to be an upstanding citizen. (Although even here the fact that the embezzler's nonsharable financial problem often results from some sort of hanky-panky suggests that "verbalizations" may be less necessary than might otherwise be assumed.)

[27] *Delinquency and Drift*, p.43.

[28] This assumption is not, I think, contradicted by the evidence presented by Matza against the existence of a delinquent subculture. In comparing the attitudes and actions of delinquents with the picture painted by delinquent subculture theorists, Matza emphasizes—and perhaps exaggerates—the extent to which delinquents are tied to the conventional order. In implicitly comparing delinquents with a supermoral man, I emphasize—and perhaps exaggerate—the extent to which they are not tied to the conventional order.

[29] The position taken here is therefore somewhere between the "semantic dementia" and the "neutralization" positions. Assuming variation, the delinquent is, at the extremes, freer than the neutralization argument assumes. Although the possibility of wide discrepancy between what the delinquent professes and what he practices still exists, it is presumably much rarer than is suggested by studies of articulate "psychopaths."

Chapter 10

EVALUATION OF SOCIAL CONTROL THEORY

Alex Thio

First, although it has been criticized for having some vague concepts, control theory has generally enjoyed a good deal of empirical support. But we should note that these supporting data are largely about adolescent, unsophisticated delinquent behavior. There is no evidence that the theory can also explain adult or more sophisticated deviant acts. In fact, we may argue that the theory cannot. Let us elaborate on this as our second point.

Second, control theory has used lack of ambition as one explanation of juvenile delinquency. It is true, as Hirschi's data has pointed out, that juvenile delinquents are more likely than nondelinquents to lack ambition. But this does not necessarily mean that the lack of ambition, which reflects the lack of social and intellectual skills, causes delinquency. Instead, it simply means that for an adolescent to become delinquent he or she does not have to be ambitious or to acquire social and intellectual skills. Why not? Because of the simple fact that delinquent acts are so uncomplicated and unsophisticated that children can easily commit them.[1]

Now, there is a big difference between the world of childhood and that of adulthood. Generally, adults' deviant acts are more complicated and sophisticated than those of juveniles. In order to commit the complicated and sophisticated acts, adult deviants cannot afford to be like juvenile delinquents, namely, unambitious or lacking in social and intellectual skills. For example, such adult deviants as former Attorney General John Mitchell, former Presidential Assistants John Ehrlichman and Bob Haldeman, and other Watergate criminals are extremely ambitious and highly skilled.

Also, it is true, as demonstrated by Hirschi's data, that frustrated aspirations do not provoke juvenile delinquency.[2] But this may be false in generalized to more sophisticated, adult deviance. There is research to suggest that frustrated aspirations do provoke adult deviance.[3] This is not to imply that all adults will engage in relatively sophisticated deviant acts if they experience frustrated aspirations. Indeed, it seems that, just as the experience of frustrated aspirations does not provoke delinquency among juveniles, neither does it provoke deviance among *some* adults. This is likely to be true on two conditions: if the word *deviance* refers to such unsophisticated acts as murder, forcible rape, and aggravated assault—namely acts that are quite similar to the unsophisticated ones committed by juvenile delinquents; and if the word *adults* refers to those who are quite like juveniles in being powerless members of society— namely, poor, socioeconomically deprived, or socially and intellectually unskilled adults. In other words, powerless or childlike adults do not have to experience frustrated aspirations in order to commit deviant acts that are as unsophisticated as juveniles' delinquency. Yet frustrated aspirations may easily provoke many relatively powerful adults into sophisticated forms of deviance such as tax evasion, fraudulent advertising, and the like. In sum, although it is useful for explaining juveniles' unsophisticated delinquent acts, control theory is less useful for explaining adults' sophisticated deviant behavior.

Third, control theory presents an inadequate view of social control. This view may accurately reflect the world of childhood but not that of adulthood. Again, there is a big difference between the world that juveniles live in and the world that adults live in—the former being comparatively simple and the latter complicated. In the more simple world of childhood, it is often the case that things are either black or white, people are either good guys or bad guys, and rules are so clear-cut that the distinction between obeying them (conformity) and violating them (deviance) can easily be established. It is somewhat like the wonderful world of Walt Disney movies, which tend to portray a clear contrast or contest between good and evil. In such a simple world, the nature of social control is unmistakably clear: social control works against evil so that good will prevail.

Thus, in attempting to control juveniles' animal—evil or deviant—impulses, parents as society's social control agents socialize their charges to become civilized: to dress properly, to respect property, to be polite, considerate, and well-behaved—in other words, to acquire conforming behavior. In this process of acquiring conforming behavior, juveniles do not simultaneously acquire the tendency to perform deviant acts. This is because conformity and deviance, or good and evil, are clearly distinguishable from and clearly opposed to each other. The acquirement of conformity is categorically the prevention of deviance.

On the other hand, the world of adulthood is far more complicated. In the adult world, the acquirement of conformity is *not* categorically the prevention of deviance. When adults learn some conforming behavior, they simultaneously acquire the tendency to perform deviant acts. There are two reasons for this. One is that the ability and opportunity to perform deviant acts depend on the ability and opportunity to perform conforming acts. If adults learn how to manage a bank, they also acquire the ability and opportunity to embezzle money from the bank; if adults become government officials, they also acquire the ability and opportunity for bribery; if adults become physicians, they also acquire the ability and opportunity to get involved in medical malpractice. So, unlike a juvenile, an adult must learn and have the opportunity to become deviant, and this ability to be deviant and the opportunity for it result from becoming an accomplished conformist.

Another reason for the overlap between conforming and deviant behavior is that social rules pertaining to adults are more ambiguous. It may be easy for us to define a juvenile's behavior (say, stealing or buying an apple) as either absolutely delinquent or absolutely nondelinquent, but it is far more difficult to define an adult's behavior (say, giving a gift to a public official or to a friend) as either a criminal act of bribery or a noncriminal act of friendship. Consequently, when an adult appears to be performing a conforming act, he or she may actually be perpetrating a deviant act.

But, as has been implied before, not all adults have the same problem. There are adults who are almost as powerless as juveniles, such as the poor, uneducated, unsophisticated, and unskilled. Having been thrust by birth and socioeconomic circumstance into a world very much like the juvenile's world, the powerless adults do not have to learn how to commit such unsophisticated deviant acts as murder, forcible rape, and aggravated assault. Also, the rules which the powerful establishment applies to powerless adults are like those applied to juveniles. Those rules are generally so clear-cut that it is easy for a social control agent to establish what constitutes the observance of them (conformity) as opposed to what constitutes the violation of them (deviance). The law against homicide, for example, is far more clear-cult than the law against corporate tax evasion. As a result, it is far much easier—assuming that there is evidence for the act—for the court to determine the guilt or innocence of a powerful adult accused of corporate tax evasion.

Yet, most adults, being unlike powerless juveniles, are constantly faced with ambiguous rules and constantly exposed, through conforming activities, to deviant opportunities. There is, then, a difference between the complex world of adults and the simple world of juveniles. We may conclude that the view of social control as presented by control theory may be relevant to juveniles, but less so to adults.

Gary Marx has also criticized, but in a different way, the simplistic view of social control. He suggests that the control theorists, by emphasizing social control as a preventer of deviance, fail to see it as a cause of deviance. Marx offers many instances in which the very process of social control directly triggers law-breaking acts. Some of the control agents' crime-causing actions are unintentional, as in the familiar case of the police officer taking action against a suspect and thereby causing the latter to commit such criminal acts as resisting arrest or assaulting an officer. Other criminogenic acts on the part of the crime controllers are intentional. These may include law enforcers posing as drug peddlers or buyers, as tourists seeking prostitutes, as streetwalkers soliciting customers, as homosexuals finding partners, as fences buying stolen goods, as hit men taking a contract, as criminals trying to bribe prosecutors, as entrepreneurs running pornographic bookstores, and as Arab sheiks trying to offer congressmen money in return for favors. Each of these acts, though designed to control crime, involves control agents purposely encouraging certain people to commit crime.[4]

NOTES

[1] This is why it makes sense for control theorists to assume that "conformity, *not* deviation, must be learned" (Nye, *Family Relationships*, p.5; emphasis added).

[2] Hirschi, T. *Causes of Delinquency*, pp.162–86.

[3] As cited earlier: Merton, *Social Theory*, p.181; Cohen, *Deviance*, pp.78–82.

[4] Marx, G.T. 1981. "Ironies of Social Control: Authorities as Contributors to Deviance Through Escalation, Nonenforcement, and Covert Facilitation." *Social Problems* 28:221–46.

Part III

CONTEMPORARY THEORIES OF DEVIANCE

All of the traditional perspectives on deviance discussed in the previous section examined the causal factors leading individuals to violate social norms. Two later perspectives, namely conflict theory and labeling theory, depart from this tradition and conceive of deviance in a radically different manner. Instead of focusing on the study of norm violations, these perspectives focus on social definitions.

Conflict Theory

Abandoning the idea of consensus, conflict theorists conceive of society as being characterized by conflict. This perspective focuses on the creation of rules, especially criminal law. It examines the processes whereby certain values and norms become converted into law, why some laws are enforced against certain people, and why certain people become defined as "criminals." In short, conflict theory studies the legal order itself.

Karl Marx and Ralph Dahrendorf

Examination of contemporary conflict theories of criminality and deviance reveal that they are clearly rooted in the works of Marx and Dahrendorf (Liska, 1981). In terms of the former, Marx (1964) contended that conflict between the social classes is a basic process of society itself. Such conflicts are of major importance in understanding the nature of man, society and social change. According to Marx, there exist two classes of individuals: the *proletariat* and the *bourgeoisie*. The latter refers to those who own the means of production; the former refers to those who are employed by, and paid a wage-labor by, the bourgeoisie. These classes differ from each other in terms of their own interests, values, styles of life, and most importantly, political power. Those who control the means of production, the bourgeoisie or "oppressors", have a vested interest in maintaining this arrangement of economic relations; but this class inevitably becomes an obstacle to the progressive development of the productive forces. The "oppressed" or proletariat, become increasingly aware of their exploitative position, and naturally commit themselves to a new system of social relations, one which would favor the maximum growth of the productive forces. Conflict then, arises in the interactions between these two classes, each with diametrically-opposed goals: "The history of all hitherto existing society is the history of class struggles" (Marx, 1964).

83

In Marx's schema, the economic relationships exert a major influence on the educational, familial, political and religious institutions of society. Governments, the law, educational institutions, religions—components of the superstructure are developed by the bourgeoisie in order to protect their own interests.

Examination of Dahrendorf's (1958, 1959) work indicates that, in contrast to Marx's emphasis on the ownership of the means of production, he instead places emphasis on "power" as the major divisive factor. For Marx, (1964) power is obtained from the ownership of the means of production; for Dahrendorf (1958), in industrial society, power is conceived as being divorced from such ownership of the means of production. Rather, it is based on authority:

> If we define classes by relations of authority, it is *ipso facto* evident that 'economic classes,' i.e., classes within economic organizations, are but a special case of the phenomenon of class. Furthermore, even within the sphere of industrial production it is not really economic factors that give rise to class formation, but a certain type of social relations which we have tried to comprehend in the notion of authority (Dahrendorf, 1959:139).

Authority then, for Dahrendorf is the central source of dissensus in society—he focuses on the division between those who have and those who have not the authority to exercise control over behavior. In this scheme, economic structures play a less important role in the development of political, cultural and religious institutions (as Marx asserted). In short, for Dahrendorf (1959:171), authority relationships in one institution do not necessarily exert an influence over other institutions:

> There are a large number of imperatively coordinated associations in any given society. Within every one of them we can distinguish the aggregates of those who dominate and those who are subjected. But since domination in industry does not necessarily involve domination in the State or a church, or other associations, total societies can present a picture of a plurality of competing dominant (and, conversely, subjected) aggregates.

The theories of Marx and Dahrendorf did not deal extensively with deviant and criminal behavior; rather, they centered on social conflict or dissensus within society. Contemporary conflict theorists have developed their theories of crime based upon the general ideas concerning social conflict as expounded by Marx and Dahrendorf. Specifically, modern conflict theorists focus on the following issues:

(a) why the norms of certain groups or classes are transformed into law, thereby creating criminals out of conflicting groups or classes;

(b) why certain laws are enforced but not others, thereby making criminals out of those who violate such laws but not others;

(c) why laws are enforced against certain social groups and classes, thus, creating criminals out of certain rule violators but not others (Liska, 1981:174).

In short then, the conflict perspective examines the social and political processes whereby certain norms are converted into laws, certain laws are enforced, and certain people become criminalized. Rather than examining why some individuals commit deviant or illegal acts, proponents of the conflict model focus on the legal order itself.

George B. Vold—Culture or Group Conflict Theory

Culture or group conflict theory developed in the 1930's within the early Chicagoan school of sociology. In their research on the city of Chicago, researchers observed and documented cultural differences among various ethnic immigrants. Thorsten Sellin (1938) felt that ethnic diversity was a major cause of deviance. He argued that those individuals who adhere to the traditional norms and values of their homeland frequently come into conflict with the normative order of the society to which they immigrated.

The selection by George B. Vold entitled, *"Group Conflict Theory as an Explanation of Crime,"* is representative of this perspective. Vold contends that group conflict can be employed to explain certain types of crime. He characterizes society as being in a state of equilibrium of "balanced forces in opposition." Often when the purposes, norms, and values of one group clashes with another, conflict is the end result. As the two groups conflict with one another, they seek assistance from the State. For Vold, legislation and law enforcement is a reflection of the deep-seated conflicts between individual groups and their general struggle for control of the police state. In this selection, Vold examines the ability of one group to have the power to transform its values into laws, thus having the power to make criminals out of those who express conflicting values.

William Chambliss, Richard Seidman, Richard Quinney, Ian Taylor, Paul Walton and Jock Young—Radical-Conflict Theory

Chambliss and Seidman—Law and Power

Chambliss and Seidman (1971) begin their theory with the fundamental assumption that society is comprised of social groups with widely varying values, sentiments and norms; for these theorists, there is no overall societal and normative consensus; rather, society is based on dissensus.

In their discussion concerning social conflict, Chambliss and Seidman (1971) state that this phenomenon is not, or ever was, present in all societies; rather, these theorists maintain that in the primitive, less complex societies, internal disputes are often resolved through reconciliation and compromise, thereby allowing for a high level of consensus. However, as societies become more developed, more complex and stratified in nature, such a reconciliation becomes more difficult, and the enforcement of norms becomes more apparent. In modern, industrial societies, these legal norms reflect the interests of powerful political-economic groups. Laws defining deviance and criminality then, are the results of efforts of such groups to impose their own values and definitions on the larger society. Specifically, Chambliss and Seidman (1971), in their discussion concerning the emergence of laws assert that laws arise in order to maintain stable and smooth relationships. For these theorists, the expression of the law is not value-neutral in nature; rather, it is reflective of the interests of the power group. In short then, such laws serve to "benefit" one group—namely those in power. Chambliss and Seidman (1971) contend that these "benefits" are temporally variable—that is, they may alter from time to time; certain laws may be dropped, revived, or amended. Specifically, using the example of the law concerning vagrancy, Chambliss and Seidman (1971) state that in England during the twelfth century, the Black Death Plague coupled with the Crusades reduced the agricultural labor supply to fifty percent; moreover, the commercialization and industrialization of the urban areas enticed the serfs to leave the rural areas. Chambliss and Seidman (1971) suggest that vagrancy laws were created in conjunction with the interests of the landed aristocracy to control their labor supply. In short, with the establishment of such laws, it became illegal to accept or give charity, and to travel. Moreover, their research also indicates that the passage of vagrancy laws was in the interest of the Church of England, who, due to the Crusades, were in financial difficulty. The passing of vagrancy laws served to absolve the Church of its traditional obligation to offer aid to the poor. By the sixteenth century, according to Chambliss and Seidman (1971) such laws were revived to protect the interests of the new commercial class in order that trade be conducted in an orderly manner. Specifically, these laws were employed to eradicate "undesirables"—those who were unemployed and considered as being sources of trouble (Liska, 1981).

Turning to the issue of discretion in the law and its relationship to inequality, Chambliss and Seidman (1971) contend that discretion in applying the law arises from the symbols used and the nature of the language employed. The core meaning of the law is indefinite in nature. The rules covering the laws are, according to Chambliss and Seidman (1971) not only vague and ambiguous, but often contradictory in nature. The value and normative system of the groups in power who exert control over the law specifically provide law enforcement agencies with as few norms as possible—thereby providing room for discretionary interpretation and application of the law "as needed".

Discussing the nature of the judicial system, these authors assert that the application of the law in terms of sentencing practices and adjudication is also subject to discretion and inequality. Specifically, such discretion occurs as a result of the nature of the sentencing procedures as well as from a lack of uniform sentencing practices. Inequality, according to Chambliss and Seidman (1971) arises out of a number of sources. That is, it arises as a result of the beliefs and sentiments of the magistrates themselves—those whose training reflects middle-class conservative biases. Moreover, the matters with which the judicial system deals, are of great concern to the powerful classes. The high cost of litigation functions to close off access to the courts to all but wealthy individuals. In short then, in Chambliss and Seidman's conceptualization, inputs into the judicial system are conservative, reflecting the interests of the dominant powerful groups in society. Outputs, in the form of sentencing practices, also reflect the interests of the powerful classes—they serve to maintain the status quo (Chambliss and Seidman, 1971:181).

Richard Quinney—(a) The Social Reality of Crime; and (b) Radical Criminology

Quinney's work can be divided into two sections: that published prior to 1971 and that published after 1971 (Liska, 1981). In terms of the former, Quinney (1970) in his work, *The Social Reality of Crime* conceives of society (similar to Turk, 1969) in terms of competing interests. Specifically, Quinney's (1970) early work attempts to link the formulation and application of criminal labels with the actual occurrence of such behaviors. According to Quinney (1970:21), there exist four sources of criminal behavior: (1) structured opportunities; (2) learning experiences; (3) interpersonal associations and identifications; and (4) self-conceptions. The initial two conditions, indicate that class-based differences in behaviors are ontologically prior to the legal response defining such actions as being criminal. For Quinney (1970:21): "persons in the segments of society whose behavior patterns are not represented in formulating and applying criminal definitions are more likely to act in ways that will be defined as criminal than those in the segments that formulate and apply criminal definitions."

In terms of the latter two conditions, interpersonal associations, identifications and self-conceptions, Quinney (1970) asserts that class-based behavior patterns that are defined as deviant or criminal, exist as a *response* to interactions with the legal authorities: "...those who have been defined as criminal begin to conceive of themselves as criminal; as they adjust to the definitions imposed upon them, they learn to play the role of the criminal" (Quinney, 1970:21–22).

Quinney (1970) contends that these four sources of criminal behavior are brought together by the *conceptions* of such behavior adhered to by the powerful social classes. According to Quinney (1970:23) conceptions of crime held by the powerful become real in their effects—that is, they ultimately determine "the social reality of crime:"

> In general then, the more the power segments are concerned with crime, the greater the probability that criminal definitions will be created and that behavior patterns will develop in opposition to criminal definitions. The formulation and application of criminal definitions and the development of behavior patterns related to criminal definitions are thus joined in full circle by the construction of criminal conceptions...The social reality of crime is constructed by the formulation and application of criminal definitions, the development of behavior patterns related to criminal definitions, and the construction of criminal conceptions.

Upon examination of Quinney's later works, (specifically Quinney, 1974:1977), it is apparent that this theoretical paradigm is more explicitly Marxian in nature. Specifically, Quinney (1974:1977) contends that a basic social conflict exists between those who own the means of production and those who do not. Those exerting control over economic relationships represent the ruling class—a class which also exerts control over other spheres such a familial, educational, cultural and religious institutions. For Quinney (1974) such institutions function to serve the interests of the ruling class.

In his discussion concerning the formulation and application of criminal law, Quinney (1974:1977) states that criminal law is an instrument of the State and ruling class to maintain and perpetuate the existing social and economic order. For Quinney, law is conceived as a "political instrument"; individuals become criminal or deviant because the dominant social class has the power to formulate certain laws and apply them. Similar to Marx, ruling class is defined as those who own and control the means of production.

Moreover, Quinney (1974:1977) argues that the interests of the ruling class determine when such laws are enforced and to whom they are applied. Specifically, this theorist states that such legal norms are enforced against individuals who pose a threat to those who control the means of production; however when individuals belonging to the ruling class violate laws, such violations are not rigorously enforced. This may be true partially because the ruling class infrequently violate laws that are strictly enforced—rather, they focus their efforts on such norm violations as stock manipulation, anti-trust, etc.—laws that are not rigorously enforced. However, even when such persons violate laws that are strictly enforced, these laws are *not* as rigorously enforced against them in comparison to lower class individuals committing the same offense. In short, Quinney accounts for the differential rate of enforcement in terms of the ability of the ruling class to resist enforcement.

Turning to other institutions besides the government, Quinney (1974:1977) argues that such social institutions as religions, education, mass media, etc.) are also organized so as to reflect the interests of the dominant social order. Specifically, Quinney focuses on the development and perpetuation of a moral order that functions to legitimize the legal order of the ruling class; moreover, he focuses on the role of various social institutions in maintaining this order. Through such institutions, individuals who do not own the means of production, gradually accept the ruling class definitions of morality and learn to pattern their actions so to conform with such definitions; as a result, according to Quinney (1977), the interests of the ruling class also become the interests of the subordinates.

Ian Taylor, Paul Walton and Jock Young—The New Criminology

Taylor, Walton and Young (1973) do not provide an *explicit, fully-developed* theoretical perspective on criminology; rather, their theoretical stance is found implicitly in their critiques of structural-functionalism; symbolic interactionists, and the new conflict theories. For Taylor et al., (1973) each of these theoretical perspectives possesses a number of deficiencies. Thus, in their place, Taylor et al., argue for an alternative perspective—a Marxist approach to the study of law and deviant behavior. Specifically, these theorists call for a perspective to be built upon the fundamental tenet that the development of legal norms, their enforcement and adjudication are *not* the result of various interest groups; rather, they are the product of the conditions of labor and production:

> The structure and function of law as a whole in advanced capitalist society can be seen as a reflection of this epic (the ethic of individualism),

rather than as the cumulation of the activities of independent and autonomous interest groups arising in different historical periods.(Taylor et al., 1973:264)

Secondly, these theorists (1973:264–65) state that it is of crucial importance to recognize formal law as being connected with the alliance of capital and the state; the sanctioning of actions as criminal and the ability to enforce the law is inextricably tied to the control of the state. Such a structuring of formal law, according to Taylor et al., (1973) produces two kinds of citizenship and responsibility: the labor forces of industrial society—controlled by penal sanctions and criminal law; and the state and the owners or the means of production—controlled by civil law. In sum then, for Taylor et al., (1973:264) a theory of law must not only focus on the content of the law, but also on its structural form—specifically on how the state and the owners of capital are placed above incrimination and criminal sanctioning:

> It is not only that there is differential application of law: it is also that the state and the owners of capital and labor—irrespective of particular battles between interest groups at particular moments of historical development—are beyond incrimination and, most significantly, beyond the criminal sanction.

Following Taylor, Walton, and Young's thesis, Jeffrey Reiman, in *"A Radical Perspective on Crime"*, provides a detailed discussion of the radical conflict model. Reiman argues that the laws and criminal justice system operate to maintain the status quo, the established economic and social order. Focusing on the individual deviant/criminal or "blaming the victim" is a way to achieve this end result. By so doing, Reiman argues that this shifts our attention away from the problems with the social order and absolves society from any guilt. Moreover, Reiman illustrates how various institutional and societal structures *benefit* from the perpetuation of individual failure.

The Labeling Perspective

Frank Tannenbaum, Edwin Lemert, Howard S. Becker, Thomas Scheff

In reaction against traditional theories of deviance such as those discussed previously which were based on an underlying assumption of normative stability and consensus—entities provide a reference point from which behaviors could be judged as conventional or unconventional, sociologists developed an alternative approach to the study of deviant behavior. Such an approach focuses on the emerging, changing and conflicting nature of social norms. Without a specific reference point from which to judge behavior, deviance became reconceptualized as a social definition. Specifically, for labeling theorists, deviance is regarded as a social definition that has been successfully applied to an individual by others who so label him. Emphasis then, is placed not on the causes of various forms of deviance (as do traditional theories), but on the societal reaction to deviant acts.

The labeling perspective, emerging in the 1960's, developed out of ideas first expounded by Frank Tannenbaum in 1938. Stressing the importance of societal reaction in the development of a criminal identity, Tannenbaum (1938:19) states:

> The first dramatization of the "evil"—the act of defining and reacting which separates the child out of his group for specialized treatment plays a greater role in making the criminal than perhaps any other experience...He has been tagged....The process of making the criminal, therefore, is a process of tagging, defining, identifying, segregating, describing emphasizing and making conscious and self-conscious.

In a more systematic attempt at theoretical explication, Lemert (1951:22–23) provides much of the infrastructure upon which current labeling theory is constructed:

> ...we start with the idea that persons and groups are differentiated in various ways, some of which result in social penalties, reaction and segregation. These penalties and segregative reaction of society or the community are dynamic factors which increase, decrease and condition the form which the initial differentiation or deviation takes...The deviant person is one whose role, status, function and self-definition are importantly shaped by how much deviation he engages in, by the degree of its social visibility, by the particular exposure he has to the societal reaction, and by the nature and strength of the societal reaction.

Examination of the underlying assumptions of the labeling perspective reveals that it is clearly rooted within an interactionist framework. A major tenet of the labeling perspective asserts that one is not able to fully comprehend deviant behavior in terms of the actions themselves, but only if it is realized that deviant behavior, like 'normal' behavior involves social interaction with others. For advocates of this perspective, deviance is conceptualized as a product of social interaction between an individual committing a deviant act and the audience who respond to such behavior. In short, a fundamental assumption of the labeling approach focuses not on action *per se* but on societal reaction.

Conceiving of deviance as a 'reaction process' of society leads to a second, related assumption of the labeling approach which asserts that the demarcation between deviant and non-deviant behavior is disputable and ambiguous. As Scheff (1975:10) suggests, labeling is not an automatic process: whether one is defined as 'deviant' is contingent upon several factors such as:

(1) the visibility of the rule violation;

(2) the power of the rule-violator in relation to the individuals responding to this violation;

(3) the severity of the violation;

(4) the tolerance level of the community;

(5) the availability of the society to channel the reaction to something other than labeling.

For proponents of the labeling approach then, there exists a reciprocal relationship between the actor and his/her audience. "Processes of social interaction must be inspected to ascertain the conditions under which deviance is defined and what consequences flow from that definition" (Rubington and Weinberg, 1973:1–2).

In contrast to the structural-functionalist perspective, conceiving of deviance as "objectively given" and based on deductive logic—a theory that began with *a priori* assumptions about the nature of man and society and collected data (largely from the official records) to confirm causal hypotheses, the labeling perspective, conceiving of such phenomena as "subjectively problematic", is based on inductive logic. Adopting a *versthende* approach, labeling theorists seek to gain an understanding of deviance from the subjective points of view of the actors themselves—understanding which can be achieved by sharing in their 'definitions of the situation' (Thomas, 1931:41) and 'constructions of reality' (Berger and Luckmann, 1966).

In order to achieve such an aim, proponents of the labeling perspective adopt an open-ended, inductive, methodological scheme. Specifically, such persons, beginning without any preconceptions or overarching hypotheses, gather descriptive data firsthand through participant observation techniques—data which can be subsequently analyzed and upon which generalizations can be made. As Becker (1961:18) states: (labeling theorists) "use methods that would allow us to discover phenomena whose existence we were unaware of at the beginning of the research."

Conceiving of deviance as subjectively problematic, labeling theorists focus on the following: (1) those who define an individual as deviant; and (2) the individual who has been negatively labelled and stigmatized by others. In terms of the former, proponents of this perspective focus on: (i) the conditions under which an individual is segregated and labelled as deviant; (ii) how the individual is cast into the deviant role; (iii) the behavior of others toward this redefined person; and (iv) the positive or negative value others place on the facts of deviance (Rubington and Weinberg, 1973:2).

In terms of the latter, labeling theorists center upon the actor him/herself who has been negatively labelled and stigmatized by others as deviant. Specifically, theorists focus on: (i) the reaction of the actor to the label bestowed upon him; (ii) the manner by which he/she adopts the deviant role; and (iii) the extent to which the actors adopt this new conception of self (Rubington and Weinberg, 1973:3).

Edwin Lemert—Deviance as a Social Label

While Lemert himself disclaims being categorized as a labeling theorist, his work, however, provides some of the underlying tenets upon which labeling theory has been constructed. Lemert's (1951;1967) paradigm focuses on the societal reaction to deviance and its effects upon self-images and identities. Specifically, attention is directed at the social processes through which an individual comes to be defined as deviant and its effects on the development of deviant identified and deviant careers.

The terms "primary" and "secondary" deviance are central to Lemert's (1967) thesis. Primary deviance, according to this theorists, refers to norm violations that are caused by a number of factor and are transitory in nature—such behavior which does not affect the person's psychological structure and performance of normal social roles:

> Primary deviance is assumed to arise in a wide variety of social, cultural and psychological contexts and at best has only marginal implications for the psychic structure of the individual; it does not lead to symbolic reorganization at the level of self-regarding attitudes and social roles...Primary deviation...is polygenetic, arising out of a variety of social, cultural, psychological and physiological factors, either in adventitious or recurring combinations (Lemert, 1967:17, 40).

Secondary deviance, by contrast is conceived by Lemert (1967) as deviance which is a response to the conditions caused by the societal reaction to primary deviation—such deviance is prolonged in nature and affects the psychological structure of the individual and his/her performance of social roles:

> Secondary deviation is deviant behavior or social roles based upon it which becomes a means of social defense, attack or adaption to the overt and covert problems created by the societal reaction to primary deviance... Secondary deviation refers to a special class of socially defined responses which people make to problems created by the societal reaction to their deviance...When a person begins to employ his deviant behavior or role based upon it as a means of defense, attack, or adjustment to the overt and covert problems created by the consequent societal reaction to him, his deviation is secondary(Lemert, 1967:17, 40).

For Lemert, primary deviance does not necessarily result in secondary deviance; rather, the latter is a societal reaction to the former. Being reacted to and defined as deviant, Lemert (1967) asserts, is socially stigmatizing for the individual and negatively affects his/her future relationships and opportunities. As Lemert suggests, such labeling alters social relationships, as "normals" are unwilling (for the most part) to associate with deviants; Moreover, it functions to decrease employment opportunities, as employers are not willing to hire such persons. Further, Lemert's thesis states that if individuals are defined as deviant, they will ultimately come to see themselves in this manner and act accordingly.

The above ideas are an integral part of Lemert's (1962) theory concerning the development of paranoia. The selection by Edwin Lemert, *"Secondary Deviance and Role Conceptions"*, illustrates the social interactional processes taking place between actors and audiences in the definitional process. Specifically, in reaction against Cameron's (1943) conception of the paranoid as one who engages in open conflict with a supposed or "pseudo" community he perceives as conspiring against him—conflict leading to temporary or permanent isolation, Lemert (1962) maintains that this view is largely incorrect. While he states that the paranoid's perception of individuals conspiring against him may or may not be initially accurate, by the time the paranoid's behavior has been crystallized into a stable pattern, his perceptions are firmly grounded in reality. According to Lemert (1962), while the paranoid individual responds differently to his social environment, the environment also react differently to him—such persons are, in fact, involved in covert and conspiratorial actions.

Discussing the development of paranoia, Lemert (1962) asserts that it typically begins with an individual experiencing persistent interpersonal difficulties—such persons are perceived by others as having "problems". Others, according to Lemert (1962:8) observe that "there is something odd about him," or "he must be upset," or that "he is just ornery." However, when the tolerance limit is reached, such persons alter their interactions with the individual:

> At some point in the chain of interactions, a new configuration takes place in perceptions others have of the individual, with shifts in figure-group relations... From a normal variant the person becomes "unreliable," "untrustworthy," "dangerous" or someone with whom others "do not wish to be involved"....Once the perceptual reorientation takes place...interaction changes qualitatively....it becomes spurious, distinguished by patronizing, evasions, "humoring," guiding conversations onto selected topics, underreaction, and silence, all calculated wither to prevent intense interaction or to protect individual and group values by restricting access to them.

This shift in figure-group relations, initiates the process through which an individual is moved from inclusion within a group to exclusion with concomitant alterations in the person's self-identity. The ultimate result of this process is the confirmation of the paranoid individual's expectations leading to the development of secondary deviation, or even the development of a paranoid career.

Howard Becker—Deviance as a Social Status

In his classic work, *"Outsiders"*, Becker (1963) focuses upon two issues: (1) the manner by which societal rules are constructed and applied to particular people, thereby labeling them as outsiders; (2) the consequences of such labeling in terms of social statuses and identities.

In terms of the former, Becker (1963) focuses on the processes by which rules are created. Specifically, he centers on the moral entrepreneurial activities of individuals who feel that the existing rules are unsatisfactory—there is some evil out there that needs to be stopped through the creation of a new rule or set of rules. As Becker (1963) states, the moral entrepreneurs conceive of themselves as moral crusaders—such persons typically believe that their "mission is a holy one." "The crusader is not only interested in seeing to it that other people do what he thinks right. He believes that if they do what is right it will be good for them. Or he may feel that his reform will prevent certain kinds of exploitation of one person by another" (Becker, 1963:148).

While Becker (1963:152) emphasizes that not all crusades achieve success, those that do, result in the establishment of a new rule or set of rules, usually with the concomitant enforcement machinery. (We shall discuss in greater detail Becker's concept of moral entrepreneurs in Section V of this reader).

Once rules come into existence, Becker (1963) asserts, they can be applied to certain individuals, thereby creating groups of deviants or outsiders. However, the person who is judged to be deviant may not be in accord with this issue:

...the person who is thus labelled an outsider may have a different view of the matter. He may not accept the rule by which he is being judged and may not regard those who judge his as either competent or legitimately entitled to do so. Hence, a second meaning of the term emerges: the rule-breaker may feel his judges are outsiders (Becker, 1963:2–3).

For Becker (1963:9), deviance is "a consequence of the application by others of rules and sanctions to an 'offender.' The deviant is one to whom the label has been *successfully* applied."

Becker (1963) contends that patterns of deviance are best comprehended in terms of career-like progressions.[1] Career contingencies are central to the movement from one stage to another. Such contingencies include both changes in the motives, desires, and sentiments of the individuals as well as the objective facts of social structure. The major career contingency of the deviant career, according to Becker (1963:31) is the application of the deviant label: "One of the most crucial steps in the process of building a stable pattern of deviant behavior is likely to be the experience of being caught and publicly labelled as deviant." Such an event sets in motion the processes leading to the transformation of self-images and identities: "treating a person as though he were generally rather than specifically deviant produces a self-fulfilling prophecy. It sets in motion several mechanisms which conspire to shape the person in the image people have of him" (Becker, 1963:34).

For Becker (1963, 1964), a deviant label functions in a manner similar to a social status in that it serves to structure the course of social interaction. Upon being defined as deviant, treated within the confines of an institution and subsequently released, the discharged person often experiences stigma with respect to finding employment and also in maintaining relationships with "normals." For some ex-deviants, their public deviant identity becomes what Becker (1964) refers to as a "master status"—a status overriding all others in affecting social interaction.

REFERENCES

Anderson, Nels, 1923. *The Hobo*. Chicago: University of Chicago Press.

Becker, Howard S. 1963. *Outsiders*. New York: Free Press.

———. 1964. *The Other Side: Perspective on Deviance*. New York: The Free Press.

———. 1967. "Whose side are we on?" *Social Problems*, 14, 3: 239–47.

Berger, Peter and Thomas Luckmann. 1966. *The Social Construction of Reality*. London: Penguin/Allen Lane.

Box, Steven, 1971. *Deviance, Reality and Society*. London: Holt, Rinehart and Winston Ltd.

Cameron, N., 1943. "The Paranoid Pseudocommunity." *American Journal of Sociology*, 46: 33–38.

Chambliss, William J., 1964. "A sociological analysis of the law of vagrancy," *Social Problems* 12: 67–77.

————. 1969. *Crime and the Legal Process.* New York: McGraw-Hill.

Chambliss, William J., and Robert B. Seidman,1971. *Law, Order and Power.* Reading, Mass.: Addison-Wesley.

Dahrendorf, Ralph, 1958. *Class and Class Conflict in Industrial Society.* Stanford, Calif.: Stanford University Press.

————. 1959. "Out of utopia: Toward a reorientation of sociological analysis." *American Journal of Sociology* 64: 115–27.

Denisoff, R. Serge, and Donald McQuarie, 1975. "Crime Control in capitalist society: A reply to Quinney." *Issues in Criminology,* 10: 109–19.

Fine, Bob, 1977. "Labeling theory: an investigation into the sociological critique of deviance." *Economy and Society.* 6 #2: 166–190.

Gibbs, Jack P., 1966. "Conceptions of deviant behavior: The old and the new." *Pacific Sociological Review,* 9: 9–14.

Gove, Walter, 1970. "Societal Reaction as an Explanation of Mental Illness: An Evaluation." *American Sociological Review,* 35: 873–884.

Hughes, Everett C., 1958. *Men and Their Work.* New York: Free Press.

Kitsuse, John, 1962. "Societal Reactions to Deviant Behavior: Problems of Theory and Method," *Social Problems,* 9: 247–56.

Lemert, Edwin, 1951. *Social Pathology.* New York: McGraw-Hill.

————. 1962. "Paranoia and the Dynamics of Exclusion." *Sociometry,* vol. 25 no. 1: 2–22.

————. 1964. "Social Structure, social control and deviation." In M. Clinard, ed., *Anomie and Deviant Behavior.* New York: Free Press.

————. 1967. *Human Deviance, Social Problems and Social Control.* New Jersey: Prentice-Hall.

Liska, Allen E., 1981. *Perspectives on Deviance.* New Jersey: Prentice-Hall.

Marx, Karl, 1964. *Selected Writings in Sociology and Social Philosophy,* ed. by T. Bottomore and M. Rubel. New York: McGraw-Hill.

Miller, Walter B.,1958. "Lower Class Culture as a Generating Milieu of Gang Delinquency." *Journal of Social Issues,* v. 14, no. 3.

Petrunik, Michael, 1977. "The rise and fall of labeling theory: the construction and destruction of a sociological strawman." *Canadian Journal of Sociology,* 5(3): 213–233.

Quinney, Richard, 1970. *The Social Reality of Crime.* Boston: Little Brown.

————. 1974. *Critique of Legal Order.* Boston: Little Brown.

————. 1977. *Class, State and Crime.* New York: David McKay.

Rubington, Earl, and Martin S. Weinberg, 1973. *Deviance: The Interactionist Perspective.* (2nd edition). New York: MacMillan.

Schur, Edwin, 1971. *Labeling Deviant Behavior: Its Sociological Implications.* New York: Harper and Rowe.

————. 1973. *Radical Non-Intervention.* New Jersey: Prentice-Hall.

Sellin, Thorsten, 1938. *Culture Conflict and Crime.* New York: Social Science Research Bulletin no. 41.

Szasz, Thomas, 1960. "The Myth of Mental Illness." *American Psychologist,* 15: 113–118.

Tannenbaum, F., 1938. *Crime and the Community.* Boston: Ginn.

Taylor, Ian, Paul Walton and Jock Young, 1973. *The new criminology: for a social theory of deviance.* London: Routledge & Kegan Paul.

Thomas, W.I., 1931. *The Unadjusted Girl.* Boston: Little Brown.

Turk, Austin, 1969. *Criminality and the Legal Order.* Chicago: Rand McNally.

Weber, Max, 1964. *Basic Concepts in Sociology.* New York: Citadel.

Whyte, William Foote, 1943. *Street Corner Society.* Chicago: University of Chicago Press.

Wirth, Louis, 1938. "Urbanism as a way of life." *American Journal of Sociology* 40: 46–63.

NOTES

[1]This term is borrowed from Hughes (1958).

Chapter 11

GROUP CONFLICT THEORY AS EXPLANATION OF CRIME

George B. Vold

Basic Considerations in Conflict Theory

The social-psychological orientation for conflict theory rests on social interaction theories of personality formation and the "social process" conception of collective behavior.[1] Implicit to this view is the assumption that man always is a group-involved being whose life is both a part of, and a product of, his group associations. Implicit also is the view of society as a congerie of groups held together in a shifting but dynamic equilibrium of opposing group interests and efforts.[2]

This continuity of group interaction, the endless series of moves and counter-moves, of checks and cross checks, is the essential element in the concept of social process. It is this continuous on-going of interchanging influence, in an immediate and dynamically maintained equilibrium, that gives special significance to the designation "collective behavior," as opposed to the idea of simultaneously behaving individuals.[3] It is this fluid flow of collective action that provides opportunity for a continuous possibility of shifting positions, of gaining or losing status, with the consequent need to maintain an alert defense of one's position, and also always with the ever-present and appealing chance of improving on one's status relationship. The end result is a more or less continuous struggle to maintain, or to defend, the place of one's own group in the interaction of groups, always with due attention to the possibility of improving its relative status position. Conflict is viewed, therefore, as one of the principal and essential social processes upon which the continuing on-going of society depends.[4]

As social interaction processes grind their way through varying kinds of uneasy adjustment to a more or less stable equilibrium of balanced forces in opposition, the resulting condition of relative stability is what is usually called social order or social organization. But it is the adjustment, one to another, of the many groups of varying strengths and of different interests that is the essence of society as a functioning reality.

The normal principle of social organization is that groups are formed out of situations in which members have common interests and common needs that can be best furthered through collective action.[5] In other words, groups arise out of important needs of group members, and groups must serve the needs of the members or they soon wither away and disappear. New groups are therefore continuously being formed as new interests arise, and existing groups weaken and disappear when they no longer have a purpose to serve.[6]

96

Groups come into conflict with one another as the interests and purposes they serve tend to overlap, encroach on one another, and become competitive. In other words, conflicts between groups occur principally when the groups become competitive by attempting to operate in the same general field of interaction. There is never any serious conflict between groups whose operations can be channeled so that they perform satisfactorily without moving in on one another's territory of common interests and common purposes.[7]

The danger that any existing group must protect itself against, when in contact with any other group in the same area of interests and needs, is the ever-present one of being taken over, of being replaced. A group must always be in a position to defend itself in order to maintain its place and position in the world of constantly changing adjustments. The principal goal, therefore, of one group in contact with another is to keep from being replaced. Where there is no problem of competition and replacement, there is little likelihood of serious intergroup conflict, be it between nations, races, religions, economic systems, labor unions, or any other type of group organization.

Groups become effective action units through the direction and coordination of the activities of their members. For the members, the experience of participation in group activity and the sharing of troubles and satisfactions operate to make the individual a group-conscious person. It is out of this experience background that group identification and group loyalty become psychological realities. The loyalty of the group member to his group is one of the most profoundly significant facts of social psychology, though there is no assured explanation of *why* the loyalty and identification develop. Both loyalty and identification tend to be emotionally toned attachments not closely related to any rational understanding the individual may have of the place or significance of a particular group in the general scheme of things.[8]

It has long been realized that conflict between groups tends to develop and intensify the loyalty of the group members to their respective groups.[9] This is clearly one of the important elements in developing *esprit de corps* and "group-mindedness" attitudes on the part of individual members. The individual is most loyal to the group for which he has had to fight the hardest, and to which he has had to give the greatest measure of self for the common end of group achievement.[10]

Nothing promotes harmony and self-sacrifice within the group quite as effectively as a serious struggle with another group for survival. Hence, patriotic feeling runs high in war time, and the more desperate the situation (short of collapse and the chaos of defeat and despair) in battle, the higher runs the feeling that nothing is too great a sacrifice for the national good. A group crisis, in which the member must stand up and be counted, is an age-old device for separating the men from the boys. It needs to be remembered that groups have always paid tribute to "service beyond the call of duty." Thus it is that some of our finest ideals of character and manhood are the offshoots of group conflict where the individual has had opportunity to serve the common purpose and not merely to serve his own selfish ends.[11]

The logical outcome of group conflict should be either on the one hand, conquest and victory for one side with the utter defeat and destruction or subjugation for the other side; or, on the other hand, something less conclusive and decisive, a stalemate of compromise and withdrawal to terminate the conflict with no final settlement of the issues involved. It should be noted that, generally speaking, there is never any compromise with a position of weakness — the weak, as a rule, are quickly overwhelmed, subjugated to and integrated with the victors in some subordinate and inferior capacity. The group that will survive and avoid having to go down in defeat is the one strong enough to force some compromise settlement of the issues in conflict. This general pattern has been a commonplace occurrence in the conflicts between national groups and also between political factions within the nation.[12]

Crime and the Conflict Process

The foregoing brief sketch of some of the elements involved in the conflicts of groups should be sufficient to alert the thoughtful reader to further applications of these general group relationships to more specific situations. For example, politics, as it flourishes in a democracy, is primarily a matter of finding practical compromises between antagonistic groups in the community at large.[13] The prohibitionist wishes to outlaw the manufacture and sale of alcoholic beverages; the distillers and brewers wish unrestricted opportunity to make and sell a product for which there is a genuine economic demand (i.e. "demand" in the sense of not only having a desire for the product but also having the ability to pay for it). The complicated collection of regulations that American communities know so well, including special taxes, special licensing fees and regulations, special inspections, and special rules for closing hours, etc., are all part of the compromise settlement in the clash of these incompatible interests in the political organization of society.

As political groups line up against one another, they seek the assistance of the organized state to help them defend their "rights" and protect their interests. Thus the familiar cry, "there ought to be a law" (to suppress the undesirable) is understandable as the natural recourse of one side or the other in a conflict situation. Yet for exactly the same reason such action has a necessary logical opposition which resists the proposed legislation. Whichever group interest can marshal the greatest number of votes will determine whether or not there is to be a new law to hamper and curb the interests of some opposition group.[14]

Suppose, for purposes of illustration, that a new law has been enacted by a normal, legal, legislative majority. Those who opposed it and fought it before adoption are understandably not in sympathy with its provisions, and do not take kindly to efforts at law enforcement. In other words, the whole political process of law making, law breaking, and law enforcement becomes a direct reflection of deep-seated and fundamental conflicts between interest groups and their more general struggles for the control of the police power of the state. Those who produce legislative majorities win control over the police power and dominate the policies that decide who is likely to be involved in violation of the law.[15]

The struggle between those who support the law and those who violate it existed in the community before there was legislative action; it was the basis for the battle in the legislature; it is then continued through the judicial proceedings of prosecution and trial; and it culminates eventually in the prison treatment of the violators by those who wish to have the law enforced. The principle of compromise from positions of strength operates at every stage of this conflict process. Hence, there is bargaining in the legislature to get the law passed; there is bargaining between prosecution and defense in connection with the trial; between prison officials and inmates; and between parole agent and parolee. This is the background for Sutherland's famous "sociological definition" of crime as a social situation, as a set of relationships rather than as an act of behavior under specific legal definition.[16]

NOTES

[1]Cf. Robert E. Park and Ernest W. Burgess, *Introduction to Science of Sociology*, University of Chicago Press, Chicago, 1924. "Competition," pp. 504–510; "Conflict," pp. 574–9; "Collective Behavior," pp. 865–74.

[2]Cf. Arthur F. Bentley, *The Process of Government*, University of Chicago Press, Chicago, 1908, "Social Pressures," pp. 258–96.

[3]R.E. Park and E.W. Burgess, op. cit. p. 865, also Muzafer Sherif, op. cit. ch. 5, "Properties of Group Situations," pp. 98–121.

[4]For a discussion of the relation between the principal social processes and the resulting social order, see R.E. Park and E.W. Burgess, op. cit., pp. 506–10.

[5]Cf. Albion W. Small, *General Sociology*, University of Chicago Press, Chicago, 1905, pp. 495–500.

[6]Cf. Charles H. Cooley, *Social Organization*, Scribner, New York, 1924. "Primary Aspects of Organization," pp. 3–57.

[7]Charles H. Cooley, op. cit., "Hostile Feelings Between Classes," pp. 301–9.

[8]Muzafer Sherif, *An Outline of Social Psychology*, Harper, New York, 1948, ch.13, "Adolescent Attitudes and Identification," pp. 314–38.

[9]Walter Bagehot, *Physics and Politics*, 1869, reprinted by Knopf, New York, 1948, "The Use of Conflict," pp. 44–84.

[10]Muzafer Sherif, op. cit., ch. 7, "The Formation of Group Standards or Norms," pp. 156–82.

[11]Ibid., ch. 12, "Ego-Involvement in Personal and Group Relationships," pp. 282–313; also ch. 16, "Men in Critical Situations," pp. 401–24.

[12]Cf. Park and Burgess, op. cit., p. 575; also Hadley Cantril *The Psychology of Social Movements*, Wiley, New York, 1941, chs. 8 and 9, "The Nazi Party," pp. 210–70.

[13]Walter Bagehot, op. cit., chs. 3 and 4, "Nation-Making," pp. 85–160.

[14]E.H. Sutherland and Donald R. Cressy, *Principles of Criminology*, 5th ed., Lippincott, New York, 1955, ch.1, "Criminology and the Criminal Law," pp. 2–22.

[15]E.H. Sutherland, "Crime and the Conflict Process," *Journal of Juvenile Research*, 13:38–48, 1929.

[16]Sutherland and Cressy, op. cit., p.15

Chapter 12

A RADICAL PERSPECTIVE ON CRIME

Jeffrey H. Reiman

The Implicit Ideology of Criminal Justice

Every criminal justice system conveys a subtle, yet powerful message in support of established institutions. It does this for two interconnected reasons.

First, because it concentrates on *individual* wrongdoers. This means that *it diverts our attention away from our institutions, away from consideration of whether our institutions themselves are wrong or unjust or indeed "criminal."*

Second, because the criminal law is put forth as the *minimum neutral ground rules* for any social living. We are taught that no society can exist without rules against theft and violence, and thus the criminal law is put forth as politically neutral, as the minimum requirements of *any* society, as the minimum obligations that any individual owes his fellows to make social life of any decent sort possible. Thus, it not only diverts our attention away from the possible injustice of our social institutions, but *the criminal law bestows upon those institutions the mantle of its own neutrality.* Since the criminal law protects the established institutions (e.g., the prevailing economic arrangements are protected by laws against theft, etc.), attacks on those established institutions become equivalent to violations of the minimum requirements for any social life at all. In effect, *the criminal law enshrines the established institutions as equivalent to the minimum requirements for any decent social existence — and it brands the individual who attacks those institutions as one who has declared war on all organized society and who must therefore be met with the weapons of war.*

This is the powerful magic of criminal justice. By virtue of its focus on *individual* criminals, it diverts us from the evils of the *social* order. By virtue of its presumed neutrality, it transforms the established social (and economic) order from being merely *one* form of society open to critical comparison with others into *the* conditions of *any* social order and thus immune from criticism. Let us look more closely at this process.

What is the effect of focusing on individual guilt? Not only does this divert our attention from the possible evils in our institutions, but it puts forth half the problem of justice as if it were the *whole* problem. To focus on individual guilt is to ask whether or not the individual citizen has fulfilled his obligations to his fellow citizens. *It is to look away from the issue of whether his fellow citizens have fulfilled their obligations to him.*

To look only at individual responsibility is to look away from social responsibility. To look only at individual criminality is to close one's eyes to social injustice and to close one's ears to the question of whether our social institutions have exploited or violated the individual. *Justice is a two-way street—but criminal justice is a one-way street.*

Individuals owe obligations to their fellow citizens because their fellow citizens owe obligations to them. Criminal justice focuses on the first and looks away from the second. *Thus, by focusing on individual responsibility for crime, the criminal justice system literally acquits the existing social order of any charge of injustice!*

This is an extremely important bit of ideological alchemy. It stems from the fact [that] the same act can be criminal or not, unjust or just, depending on the conditions in which it takes place. Killing someone is ordinarily a crime. But if it is in self-defense or to stop a deadly crime, it is not. Taking property by force is usually a crime. But if the taking is just retrieving what has been stolen, then no crime has been committed. Acts of violence are ordinarily crimes. But if the violence is provoked by the threat of violence or by oppressive conditions, then, like the Boston Tea Party, what might ordinarily be called criminal is celebrated as just. This means that when we call an act a crime *we are also making an implicit judgement about the conditions in response to which it takes place. When we call an act a crime, we are saying an implicit judgement about the conditions in response to which it takes place.* When we call an act a crime, we are saying that the conditions in which it occurs are not themselves criminal or deadly or oppressive or so unjust as to make an extreme response reasonable or justified, that is, to make such a response non-criminal.

This means that when the system holds an individual responsible for a crime, *it is implicitly conveying the message that the social conditions in which the crime occurred are not responsible for the crime,* that they are not so unjust as to make a violent response to them excusable. The criminal justice system conveys as much by what it does not do as by what it does. By holding the individual responsible, *it literally acquits the society of criminality or injustice.*

Judges are prone to hold that an individual's responsibility for a violent crime is diminished if it was provoked by something that might lead a "reasonable man" to respond violently and that criminal responsibility is eliminated if the act was in response to conditions so intolerable that any "reasonable man" would have been likely to respond in the same way. In this vein, the law acquits those who kill or injure in self-defense and treats lightly those who commit a crime when confronted with extreme provocation. The law treats leniently the man who kills his wife's lover and the woman who kills her brutal husband, even when neither has acted directly in self-defense. By this logic, when we hold an individual completely responsible for a crime, we are saying that the conditions in which it occurred are such that a "reasonable man" should find them tolerable. In other words, by focusing on individual responsibility for crimes, *the criminal justice system broadcasts the message that the social order itself is reasonable and not intolerably unjust.*

Thus the criminal justice system serves to focus moral condemnation on individuals and to deflect it away from the social order that may have either violated the individual's rights or dignity or literally pushed him or her to the brink of crime. This not only serves to carry the message that our social institutions are not in need of fundamental questioning, but it further suggests that the justice of our institutions is obvious, not to be doubted. Indeed, since it is deviations from these institutions that are crimes, the established institutions become the implicit standard of justice from which criminal deviations are measured.

This leads to the second way in which a criminal justice system always conveys an implicit ideology. It arises from the presumption that the criminal law is nothing but the politically neutral minimum requirements of any decent social life. What is the consequence of this?

Obviously, as already suggested, this presumption transforms the prevailing social order into justice incarnate and all violations of the prevailing order into injustice incarnate. This process is so obvious that it may be easily missed.

Consider, for example, the law against theft. It does indeed seem to be one of the minimum requirements of social living. As long as there is scarcity, any society—capitalist or socialist—will need rules preventing individuals from taking what does not belong to them. But the law against theft is more: it is a law against stealing what individuals *presently* own. *Such a law has the effect of making present property relations a part of the criminal law.*

Since stealing is a violation of the law, this means that present property relations become the implicit standard of justice against which criminal deviations are measured. Since criminal law is thought of as the minimum requirements of any social life, this means that present property relations become equivalent to the minimum requirements of *any* social life. And the criminal who would alter the present property relations becomes nothing less than someone who is declaring war on all organized society. The question of whether this "war" is provoked by the injustice or brutality of the society is swept aside. Indeed, this suggests yet another way in which the criminal justice system conveys an ideological message in support of the established society.

Not only does the criminal justice system acquit the social order of any charge of injustice, it specifically cloaks the society's own crime-producing tendencies. I have already observed that by blaming the individual for a crime, the society is acquitted of the charge of injustice. I would like to go further now and argue that by blaming the individual for a crime, the society is acquitted of the charge of complicity in that crime! This is a point worth developing, since many observers have maintained that modern competitive societies such as our own have structural features that tend to generate crime. Thus, holding the individual responsible for his or her crime serves the function of taking the rest of society off the hook for their role in sustaining and benefiting from social arrangements that produce crime. Let us take a brief detour to look more closely at this process.

Cloward and Ohlin argue in their book *Delinquency and Opportunity*[1] that much crime is the result of the discrepancy between social goals and the legitimate opportunities available for achieving them. Simply put, in our society everyone is encouraged to be a success, but the avenues to success are open only to some. The conventional wisdom of our free enterprise democracy is that anyone can be a success if he or she has the talent and the ambition. Thus, if one is not a success, it is because of their own shortcomings: laziness or lack of ability or both. On the other hand, opportunities to achieve success are not equally open to all. Access to the best schools and the best jobs is effectively closed to all but a few of the poor and begins to open wider only as one goes up the economic ladder. The result is that many are called but few are chosen. And many who have taken the bait and accepted the belief in the importance of success and the belief that achieving success is a result of individual ability must cope with the feelings of frustration and failure that result when they find the avenues to success closed. Cloward and Ohlin argue that one method of coping with these stresses is to develop alternative avenues to success. Crime is such an alternative. Crime is a means by which people who believe in the American dream pursue it when they find the traditional routes barred. Indeed, it is plain to see that the goals pursued by most criminals are as American as apple pie. I suspect that one of the reasons that American moviegoers enjoy gangster films—movies in which gangsters such as Al Capone, Bonnie and Clyde, or Butch Cassidy and the Sundance Kid are the heroes, as distinct from police and detective films whose heroes are defenders of the law—is that even where they deplore the hero's methods, they identify with his or her notion of success, since it is theirs as well, and respect the courage and cunning displayed in achieving that success.

It is important to note that the discrepancy between success goals and legitimate opportunities in America is not an aberration. It is a structural feature of modern competitive industrialized society, a feature from which many benefits flow. Cloward and Ohlin write that

> ...a crucial problem in the industrial world...is to locate and train the most talented persons in every generation, irrespective of the vicissitudes of birth, to occupy technical work roles...Since we cannot know in advance who can best fulfill the requirements of the various occupational roles, the matter is presumably settled through the process of competition. But how can men throughout the social order be motivated to participate in this competition?... One of the ways in which the industrial society attempts to solve this problem is by defining success-goals as potentially accessible to all, regardless of race, creed, or socioeconomic position.[2]

But since these universal goals are urged to encourage a competition to weed out the best, there are necessarily fewer openings than seekers. And since those who achieve success are in a particularly good position to exploit their success to make access for their own children easier, the competition is rigged to work in favor of the middle and upper classes. As a result, "many lower-class persons...are the victims of a contradiction between the goals toward which they have been led to orient themselves and socially structured means of striving for these goals."[3]

> [The poor] experience desperation born of the certainty that their position in the economic structure is relatively fixed and immutable—a desperation made all the more poignant by their exposure to a cultural ideology in which failure to orient oneself upward is regarded as a moral defect and failure to become mobile as proof of it.[4]

The outcome is predictable. "Under these conditions, there is an acute pressure to depart from institutional norms and to adopt illegitimate alternatives."[5]

In brief, this means that the very way in which our society is structured to draw out the talents and energies that go into producing our high standard of living has a costly side effect: it produces crime. But by holding individuals responsible for crime, those who enjoy that high standard of living can have their cake and eat it. They can reap the benefits of the competition for success and escape the responsibility of paying for the costs of that competition. By holding the poor crook legally and morally guilty, the rest of society not only passes the costs of competition on to the poor, but they effectively deny that they (the affluent) are the beneficiaries of an economic system that exacts such a high toll in frustration and suffering.

Willem Bonger, the Dutch Marxist criminologist, maintained that competitive capitalism produces egotistic motives and undermines compassion for the misfortunes of others and thus makes human beings literally *more capable of crime*—more capable of preying on their fellows without moral inhibition or remorse—than earlier cultures that emphasized cooperation rather than competition.[6] Here again, the criminal justice system relieves those who benefit from the American economic system of the costs of that system. By holding criminals morally and individually responsible for their crimes, we can forget that the motives that lead to crime—the drive for success at any cost, linked with the beliefs that success means out-doing others and that violence is an acceptable way of achieving one's goals—are the same motives that powered the drive across the American continent and that continue to fuel the engine of America's prosperity.

David Gordon, a contemporary political economist, maintains "that nearly all crimes in capitalist societies represent perfectly *rational* responses to the structure of institutions upon which capitalist societies are based."[7] That is, like Bonger, Gordon believes that capitalism tends to provoke crime in all economic strata. This is so because most crime is motivated by a desire for property or money and is an understandable way of coping with the pressures of inequality, competition, and insecurity, all of which are essential ingredients of capitalism. Capitalism depends, Gordon writes,

> ...on basically competitive forms of social and economic interaction and upon substantial inequalities in the allocation of social resources. Without inequalities, it would be much more difficult to induce workers to work in alienating environments. Without competition and a competitive ideology, workers might not be inclined to struggle to improve their relative income and status in society by working harder. Finally, although rights of property are protected, capitalist societies do not guarantee economic security to most of their individual members. Individuals must fend for themselves, finding the best available opportunities to provide for themselves and their families...Driven by the fear of economic insecurity and by a competitive desire to gain some of the goods unequally distributed throughout the society, many individuals will eventually become "criminals."[8]

To the extent that a society makes crime a reasonable alternative for a large number of its members from all classes, that society is itself is not very reasonably or humanely organized and bears some degree of responsibility for the crime it encourages. Since the criminal law is put forth as the minimum requirements that can be expected of any "reasonable man," its enforcement amounts to a denial of the real nature of the social order to which Gordon and the others point. Here again, by blaming the individual criminal, the criminal justice system serves implicitly but dramatically to acquit the society of its criminality.

The Bonus of Bias

We turn now to consideration of the additional ideological bonus that is derived from the criminal justice system's bias against the poor. This bonus is a product of the association of crime and poverty in the popular mind. This association, the merging of the "criminal classes" and the "lower classes" into the "dangerous classes," was not invented in America. The word "villain" is derived from the Latin *villanus*, which means a farm servant. And the term "villein" was used in feudal England to refer to a serf who farmed the land of a great lord and who was literally owned by that lord.[9] In this respect, our present criminal justice system is heir to a long and hallowed tradition.

The value of this association was already seen when we explored the "average citizen's" concept of the Typical Criminal and the Typical Crime. It is quite obvious that throughout the great mass of middle America, far more fear and hostility are directed toward the predatory acts of the poor than the rich. Compare the fate of politicians in recent history who call for tax reform, income redistribution, prosecution of corporate crime, and any sort of regulation of business that would make it better serve American social goals with that of politicians who erect their platform on a call for "law and order," more police, less limits on police power, and stiffer prison sentences for criminals—and consider this in light of what we have already seen about the real dangers posed by corporate crime and business-as-usual.

In view of all that has been said already, it seems clear that Americans have been systematically deceived as to what are the greatest dangers to their lives, limbs, and possessions. The very persistence with which the system functions to apprehend and punish poor crooks and ignore or slap on the wrist equally or more dangerous individuals is testimony to the sticking power of this deception. That Americans continue to tolerate the gentle treatment meted out to white-collar criminals, corporate price fixers, industrial polluters, and political-influence peddlers, while voting in droves to lock up more poor people faster and longer, indicates the degree to which they harbor illusions as to who most threatens them. It is perhaps also part of the explanation for the continued dismal failure of class-based politics in America. American workers rarely seem able to forget their differences and unite to defend their shared interests against the rich whose wealth they produce. Ethnic divisions serve this divisive function well, but undoubtedly the vivid portrayal of the poor— and, of course, the blacks—as hovering birds of prey waiting for the opportunity to snatch away the worker's meager gains serves also to deflect opposition away from the upper class. A politician who promises to keep their communities free of blacks and their prisons full of them can get their votes even if the major portion of his or her policies amount to continuation of favored treatment of the rich at their expense. Surely this is a minor miracle of mind control.

The most important "bonus" derived form the identification of crime and poverty is that it paints the picture that the threat to decent middle Americans comes from those below them on the economic ladder, not those above. For this to happen the system must not only identify crime and poverty, but *it must also fail to reduce crime so that it remains a real threat.* By doing this, it deflects the fear and discontent of middle Americans, and their possible opposition, away from the wealthy. The two politicians who most clearly gave voice to the discontent of middle Americans in the post-World War II period were George Wallace and Spiro Agnew. Is it any accident that their politics were extremely conservative and their anger reserved for the poor (the welfare chiselers) and the criminal (the targets of law and order)?

There are other bonuses as well. For instance, if the criminal justice system functions to send out a message that bestows legitimacy on present property relations, the dramatic impact is mightily enhanced if the violator of the present arrangements is propertyless. In other words, the crimes of the well-to-do "redistribute" property among the haves. In that sense, they do not pose a symbolic challenge to the larger system in which some have much and many have little or nothing. If the criminal threat can be portrayed as coming from the poor, then the punishment of the poor criminal becomes a morality play in which the sanctity of legitimacy of the system in which some have plenty and others have little or nothing is dramatically affirmed. It matters little who the poor criminals really rip off. What counts is that middle Americans come to fear that those poor criminals are out to steal what they own.

There is yet another and, I believe, still more important bonus for the powerful in America, produced by the identification of crime and poverty. It might be thought that the identification of crime and poverty would produce sympathy for the criminals. My suspicion is that it produces or least reinforces the reverse: *hostility toward the poor.*

Indeed, there is little evidence that Americans are very sympathetic to criminals or poor people. I have already pointed to the fact that very few Americans believe poverty to be a cause of crime. Other surveys find that most Americans believe that police should be tougher than they are now in dealing with crime (83 percent of those questioned in a 1972 survey); that courts do not deal harshly enough with criminals (75 percent of those questioned in a 1969 survey); that a majority of Americans would like to see the death penalty for convicted murderers (57 percent of those questioned in November 1972); and that most would be more likely to vote for a candidate who advocated tougher sentences for law-breakers (83 percent of those questioned in a 1972 survey).[10] Indeed, the experience of Watergate seems to suggest that sympathy for criminals begins to flower only when we approach the higher reaches of the ladder of wealth and power. For some poor ghetto youth who robs a liquor store, five years in the slammer is our idea of tempering justice with mercy. When a handful of public officials try to walk off with the U.S. Constitution, a few months in a minimum security prison will suffice. If the public official is high enough, resignation from office and public disgrace tempered with a $60,0000-a-year pension is punishment is enough.

My view is that since the criminal justice system—in fact and fiction—deals with *individual legal* and *moral guilt*, the association of crime with poverty does not mitigate the image of individual moral responsibility for crime, the image that crime is the result of an individual's poor character. My suspicion is that it does the reverse: it generates the association of poverty and individual moral failing and thus *the belief that poverty itself is a sign of poor or weak character*. The clearest evidence that Americans hold this belief is to be found in the fact that attempts to aid the poor are regarded as acts of charity rather than as acts of justice. Our welfare system has all the demeaning attributes of an institution designed to give handouts to the undeserving and none of the dignity of an institution designed to make good on our responsibilities to our fellow human beings, If we acknowledged the degree to which our economic and social institutions themselves breed poverty, we would have to recognize our own responsibilities toward the poor. If we can convince ourselves that the poor are poor because of their own shortcomings, particularly moral shortcomings like incontinence or indolence, then we need acknowledge no such responsibility to the poor. Indeed, we can go further and pat ourselves on the back for our generosity and handing out the little that we do, and of course, we can make our recipients go through all the indignities that mark them as the undeserving objects of our benevolence. By and large, this has been the way in which Americans have dealt with the poor.[11] It is a way that enables us to avoid asking the question of why the richest nation in the world continues to produce massive poverty. It is my view that this conception of the poor is subtly conveyed by the way our criminal justice system functions.

Obviously, no ideological message could be more supportive of the present social and economic order than this. It suggests that poverty is a sign of individual failing, not a symptom of social or economic injustice. It tells us loud and clear that massive poverty in the midst of abundance is not a sign pointing toward the need for fundamental changes in our social and economic institutions. It suggests that the poor are poor because they deserve to be poor, or at least because they lack the strength of character to overcome poverty. When the poor are seen to be poor in character, then economic poverty coincides with moral poverty and the economic order coincides with the moral order—as if a divine hand guided its workings, capitalism leads everyone getting what they morally deserve!

If this association takes root, then when the poor individual is found guilty of a crime, the criminal justice system acquits the society of its responsibility not only for the crime *but for poverty as well.*

With this, the ideological message of criminal justice is complete. The poor rather than the rich are seen as the enemies of the mass of decent middle Americans. Our social and economic institutions are held to be responsible for neither crime nor poverty and thus are in need of no fundamental questioning or reform. The poor are poor because they are poor of character. The economic order and the moral order are one. And to the extent that this message sinks in, the wealthy can rest easily—even if they cannot sleep the sleep of the just.

Thus, we can understand why the criminal justice system creates the image of crime as the work of the poor and fails to stem it so that the threat of crime remains real and credible. The result is ideological alchemy of the highest order. The poor are seen as the real threat to decent society. The ultimate sanctions of criminal justice dramatically sanctify the present social and economic order, and *the poverty of criminals makes poverty itself an individual moral crime!*

Such are the ideological fruits of a losing war against crime whose distorted image is reflected in the criminal justice carnival mirror and widely broadcast to reach the minds and imaginations of America.

NOTES

[1]Richard A. Cloward and Lloyd E. Ohlin, *Delinquency and Opportunity: A theory of Delinquent Gangs* (New York: The Free Press, 1960), esp. pp. 77–107.

[2]Ibid., p. 81.

[3]Ibid., p. 105.

[4]Ibid., p. 107.

[5]Ibid., p. 105.

[6]Willem Bonger, *Criminality and Economic Conditions*, abridged and with an introduction by Austin T. Turk (Bloomington, Indiana: Indiana University Press, 1969), pp. 7–12, 40–47. Willem Adrian Bonger was born in Holland in 1876 and died by his own hand in 1940 rather than submit to the Nazis. His *Criminalite et Conditions Econonomiques* first appeared in 1905. It was translated into English and published in the United States in 1916. Ibid., pp. 3–4.

[7]David M. Gordon, "Capitalism, Class, and Crime," *Crime and Delinquency* (April 1972), p.174.

[8]Ibid., p.174.

[9]William and Mary Morris, *Dictionary of Word and Phrase Origins*, II (New York: Harper & Row, 1967), p.282.

[10]*Sourcebook*, pp.203, 204, 223, 207; see also p.177.

[11]Historical documentation of this can be found in David J. Rothman, *The Discovery of the Asylum: Social Order and Disorder in the New Republic* (Boston: Little, Brown, 1971)' and in Frances Fox Piven and Richard A. Cloward, *Regulating the Poor: The Functions of Public Welfare* (New York: Pantheon, 1971), which carries the analysis up to the present.

Chapter 13

EVALUATION OF CONFLICT THEORY

Alex Thio

A number of sociologists have criticized conflict theory. First of all, traditional sociologists have argued that, contrary to what its proponents seem to imply, conflict theory cannot apply to *all* kinds of deviant behavior. As Ronald Akers observes, "the conflict approach seems more appropriate to the analysis of the behavior of groups and individuals involved in *ideological and political confrontations*. It is less appropriate to the analysis of the behavior of those involved in many types of common-law crimes, usual deviations, and vices."[1] In this quote, Akers means that conflict theory is correct if it is taken to suggest that political crimes emerge from group conflict, but that the theory is not correct if it is taken to mean that such nonpolitical, ordinary crimes as murder, theft, burglary, rape, and arson result from group conflict. At first glance, this criticism appears perfectly valid. It certainly was many years ago, but today it seems less valid. The reason is that today an increasing number of "common criminals" tend to see their crimes as essentially political in nature. Akers may also appear correct in observing that conflict theory is not applicable to trivial deviations and vices—because they are, in his view, not serious enough for the powerful to get politically excited and to pass laws against them. But even here the reality is not necessarily what it appears to be. As John Hepburn perceptively observes, such usual deviations as illicit sex, gambling, drinking, loitering, and truancy do threaten powerful people's vested interests by challenging the underlying values of capitalism. Examples of these capitalist values are sobriety, individual responsibility, deferred gratification, industriousness, and the belief that the true pleasures in life can only be found in honest, productive labor. Laws against those "trivial" deviant acts, then, serve to preserve these capitalist values, the capitalist system, and hence the dominant position of the powerful.[2]

Second, conflict theory seems to hold the unconvincing assumption that in the utopian, socialist society, such nasty human acts as killing, robbing, raping, and otherwise hurting one another will disappear after the power to criminalize them is abolished. We may argue that the abolition of the power to criminalize does not necessarily lead to the abolition of humans' capacity to hurt one another. It may be more realistic to assume that if full social equality were achieved, the serious forms of human nastiness would greatly decrease rather than completely disappear. With the abolition of poverty in a fully egalitarian society there would not be any poor people to produce, as they do now, a comparatively large number of serious crimes, and thus this volume would greatly shrink. This is because the formerly poor people and the new, full egalitarian society would have as small a tendency to commit those serious crimes as the rich in the present, inegalitarian society.

Third, from the standpoint of understanding the making and enforcing of norms, rules, or laws, conflict theory does offer us a solid contribution. As Akers, a traditional sociologist, admits, "This perspective leads us to ask and suggests why certain values and norms become dominant and others do not. For this reason the conflict approach is *potent as an explanation of the formation and enforcement of the norms themselves*."[3] There is also some research evidence to support this aspect of the theory.[4] But other traditional sociologists have criticized conflict theorists for overlooking "the large number of laws that are supported by societal consensus [popular opinion]."[5] These critics, however, fail to appreciate the complex, subtle ways in which even the law that appears to serve all people may actually serve the ruling elite's interests more than the masses'.[6] The critics also fail to appreciate the positive link between popular opinion and the elite's values, as expressed by the Marxist dictum that the ruling ideas of a society are the ideas of the ruling class.

Finally, the Marxist theory about the causation of deviance is highly plausible. Its suggestion that unemployment causes crime among the surplus population is particularly reasonable: it is in fact consistent with popular belief. Unfortunately, numerous studies that have been conducted in the last 140 years have not consistently demonstrated the link between unemployment and crime. Some studies have revealed such a link while others have not. Even recent attempts to test the theory have yielded conflicting findings.[7] All this does not necessarily mean that the Marxist theory is invalid. The problem is basically methodological: "the methods used have not always been carefully devised, and the measures of both crime and business conditions have varied widely, with the result that no positive, definite, and valid generalizations can be made."[8]

NOTES

[1] Akers, R.L. 1977. *Deviant Behavior: A Social Learning Approach*, 2nd ed. Belmont, CA: Wadsworth. (p.28).

[2] Hepburn, J.R. 1977. "Social Control and the Legal Order: Legitimated Repression in a Capitalist State." *Contemporary Crises* 1:84.

[3] Akers, *Deviant Behavior*, p.29.

[4] .See, for example, K.R. Williams and S. Drake. 1980. "Social Structure, Crime, and Criminalization: An Empirical Examination of the Conflict Perspective." *The Sociological Quarterly* 21:563–75.

[5] Gibbons, D.C. 1979. *The Criminological Enterprise: Theories and Perspectives*. Englewood Cliffs, NJ: Prentice-Hall. (p.188)

[6] For an analysis of how this may be the case, see John R. Hepburn, 1977, "Social Control and the Legal Order." *Contemporary Crises* 1:77–90.

[7] See, for example, D. Wallace and D. Humphries, "Urban Crime and Capitalist Accumulation: 1950–1971," Pp. 140–56 IN David Greenberg, ed., *Crime and Capitalism*. Palo Alto, California: Mayfield: 140–56; Kirk R. Williams and Susan Drake, "Social Structure, Crime and Criminalization." *Sociological Quarterly* 21: 563–75.

[8] Sutherland, E.H. & D.R. Cressey. 1978. *Criminology*, 10th ed. Philadelphia: Lippincott :235.

Chapter 14

SECONDARY DEVIANCE AND ROLE CONCEPTIONS

Edwin M. Lemert

Primary and Secondary Deviation

There has been an embarrassingly large number of theories, often without any relationship to a general theory, advanced to account for various specific pathologies in human behavior. For certain types of pathology, such as alcoholism, crime, or stuttering, there are almost as many theories as there are writers on these subjects. This has been occasioned in no small way by the preoccupation with the origins of pathological behavior and by the fallacy of confusing *original* causes with *effective* causes. All such theories have elements of truth, and the divergent viewpoints they contain can be reconciled with the general theory here if it is granted that original causes or antecedents of deviant behaviors are many and diversified. This holds especially for the psychological processes leading to similar pathological behavior, but it also holds for the situational concomitants of the initial aberrant conduct. A person may come to use excessive alcohol not only for a wide variety of subjective reasons but also because of diversified situational influences, such as the death of a loved one, business failure, or participating in some sort of organized group activity calling for heavy drinking of liquor. Whatever the original reasons for violating the norms of the community, they are important only for certain research purposes, such as assessing the extent of the "social problem" at a given time or determining the requirements for a rational program of social control. From a narrower sociological viewpoint the deviations are not significant until they are organized subjectively and transformed into active roles and become the social criteria for assigning status. The deviant individuals must react symbolically to their own behavior aberrations and fix them in their socio-psychological patterns. The deviations remain primary deviations or symptomatic and situational as long as they are rationalized or otherwise dealt with as functions of a socially acceptable role. Under such conditions normal and pathological behaviors remain strange and somewhat tensional bedfellows in the same person. Undeniably a vast amount of such segmental and partially integrated pathological behavior exists in our society and has impressed many writers in the field of social pathology.

Just how far and how long a person may go on dissociating his sociopathic tendencies so that they are merely troublesome adjuncts of normally conceived roles is not known. Perhaps it depends upon the number of alternative definitions of the same overt behavior that he can develop; perhaps certain physiological factors (limits) are also involved. However, if the deviant acts are repetitive and have a high visibility, and if there is a severe societal reaction, which, through a process of

111

identification is incorporated as part of the "me" of the individual, the probability is greatly increased that the integration of existing roles will be disrupted and that reorganization based upon a new role or roles will occur. (The "me" in this context is simply the subjective aspect of the societal reaction.) Reorganization may be the adoption of another normal role in which the tendencies previously defined as "pathological" are given a more acceptable social expression. The other general possibility is the assumption of a deviant role, if such exists; or, more rarely, the person may organize an aberrant sect or group in which he creates a special role of his own. *When a person begins to employ his deviant behavior or a role based upon it as a means of defense, attack, or adjustment to the covert problems created by the consequent societal reaction to him, his deviation is secondary.* Objective evidences of this change will be found in the symbolic appurtenances of the new role, in clothes, speech, posture, and mannerisms, which in some cases heighten social visibility, and which in some cases serve as symbolic cues to professionalism.

Role Conceptions of the Individual Must Be Reinforced by Reactions of Others

It is seldom that one deviant act will provide a sufficiently strong societal reaction to bring about secondary deviation, unless in the process of introjection the individual imputes or projects meanings into the social situation which are not present. In this case anticipatory fears are involved. For example, in a culture where a child is taught sharp distinctions between "good" women and "bad" women, a single act of questionable morality might conceivably have a profound meaning for the girl so indulging. However, in the absence of reactions by the person's family, neighbors, or the larger community, reinforcing tentative "bad-girl" self-definition, it is questionable whether a transition to secondary deviation would take place. It is also doubtful whether a temporary exposure to a severe punitive reaction by the community will lead a person to identify himself with a pathological role, unless, as we have said, the experience is highly traumatic. Most frequently there is a progressive reciprocal relationship between the deviation of the individual and the societal reaction, with a compounding of the societal reaction out of the minute accretions in the deviant behavior, until a point is reached where ingrouping and outgrouping between society and the deviant is manifest.[1] At this point a stigmatizing of the deviant occurs in the form of name calling, labeling, or stereotyping.

The sequence of interaction leading to secondary deviation is roughly as follows: (1)primary deviation; (2)social penalties; (3)further primary deviation; (4)stronger penalties and rejections; (5)further deviation, perhaps with hostilities and resentment beginning to focus upon those doing the penalizing; (6)crisis reached in the tolerance quotient, expressed in formal action by the community stigmatizing of the deviant; (7)strengthening of the deviant conduct as a reaction to the stigmatizing and penalties; (8)ultimate acceptance of deviant social status and efforts at adjustment on the basis of the associated role.

As an illustration of this sequence the behavior of an errant schoolboy can be cited. For one reason or another, let us say excessive energy, the schoolboy engages in a classroom prank. He is penalized for it by the teacher. Later, due to clumsiness, he creates another disturbance and again he is reprimanded. Then, as sometimes happens, the boy is blamed for something he did not do. When the teacher uses the tag "bad boy" or "mischief maker" or other invidious terms, hostility and resentment are excited in the boy, and he may feel that he is blocked in playing the role expected of him. Thereafter, there may be a strong temptation to assume his role in the class as defined by the teacher, particularly when he discovers that there are rewards as well as penalties deriving from such a role. There is, of course, no implication here that such boys go on to become delinquents or criminals, for the mischief-maker role may later become integrated with or retrospectively rationalized as part of a role more acceptable to school authorities.[2] If such a boy continues this unacceptable role and becomes delinquent, the process must be accounted for in the light of the general theory of this [work]. There must be a spreading corroboration of a sociopathic self-conception and societal reinforcement at each step in the process.

The most significant personality changes are manifest when societal definitions and their subjective counterpart become generalized. When this happens, the range of major role choices becomes narrowed to one general class.[3] This was very obvious in the case of a young girl who was the daughter of a paroled convict and who was attending a small Middle Western college. She continually argued with herself and with the author, in whom she had confided, that in reality she belonged on the "other side of the railroad tracks" and that her life could be enormously simplified by acquiescing in this verdict and living accordingly. While in her case there was a tendency to dramatize her conflicts, nevertheless there was enough societal reinforcement of her self-conception by the treatment she received in her relationship with her father and on dates with college boys to lend it a painful reality. Once these boys took her home to the shoddy dwelling in a slum area where she lived with her father, who was often in a drunken condition, they abruptly stopped seeing her again or else became sexually presumptive.

NOTES

[1]Mead, G. "The Psychology of Punitive Justice." *American Journal of Sociology* 23:577-602.

[2]Evidence for fixed or inevitable sequences from predelinquency to crime is absent. Sutherland, E.H. *Principles of Criminology*, 1939, 4th ed., p.202.

[3]Sutherland seems to say something of this sort in connection with the development of criminal behavior. Ibid. p.86.

Chapter 15

OUTSIDERS

Howard S. Becker

(One theoretical approach)...defines deviance as the infraction of some agreed-upon rule. It then goes on to ask who breaks rules, and to search for the factors in their personalities and life situations that might account for the infractions. This assumes that those who have broken a rule constitute a homogeneous category, because they have committed the same deviant act.

Such an assumption seems to me to ignore the central fact about deviance: it is created by society. I do not mean this in the way it is ordinarily understood, in which the causes of deviance are located in the social situation of the deviant or in "social factors" which prompt his action. I mean, rather, that *social groups create deviance by making the rules whose infraction constitutes deviance,* and by applying those rules to particular people and labeling them as outsiders. From this point of view, deviance is *not* a quality of the act the person commits, but rather a consequence of the application by others of rules and sanctions to an "offender." The deviant is one to whom the label has successfully been applied; deviant behavior is behavior that people so label.[1]

Since deviance is, among other things, a consequence of the responses of others to a person's act, students of deviance cannot assume that they are dealing with a homogeneous category when they study people who have been labeled deviant. That is, they cannot assume that those people have actually committed a deviant act or broken some rule, because the process of labelling may not be infallible; some people may be labeled deviant who in fact have not broken a rule. Furthermore, they cannot assume that the category of those labeled deviant will contain all those who actually have broken a rule, for many offenders may escape apprehension and thus fail to be included in the population of "deviants" they study. Insofar as the category lacks homogeneity and fails to include all the cases that belong in it, one cannot reasonably expect to find common factors of personality or life situation that will account for the supposed deviance. What, then, do people who have been labeled deviant have in common? At the least, they share the label and the experience of being labeled as outsiders. I will begin my analysis with this basic similarity and view deviance as the product of a transaction that takes place between some social group and one who is viewed by that group as a rule-breaker. I will be less concerned with the personal and social characteristics of deviants than with the process by which they come to be thought of as outsiders and their reactions to that judgment....

The point is that the response of other people has to be regarded as problematic. Just because one has committed an infraction of a rule does not mean that others will respond as though this had happened. (Conversely, just because one has not violated a rule does not mean that he may not be treated, in some circumstances, as though he had).

The degree to which other people will respond to a given act as deviant varies greatly. Several kinds of variation seem worth noting. First of all, there is variation over time. A person believed to have committed a given "deviant" act may at one time be responded to much more leniently than he would be at some other time. The occurrence of "drives" against various kinds of deviance illustrates this clearly. At various times, enforcement officials may decide to make an all-out attack on some particular kind of deviance, such as gambling, drug addiction, or homosexuality. It is obviously much more dangerous to engage in one of these activities when a drive is on than at any other time. (In a very interesting study of crime news in Colorado newspapers, Davis found that the amount of crime reported in Colorado newspapers showed very little association with actual changes in the amount of crime taking place in Colorado. And, further, that people's estimate of how much increase there had been in crime in Colorado was associated with the increase in the amount of crime news but not with any increase in the amount of crime).[2]

The degree to which an act will be treated as deviant depends also on who commits the act and who feels he has been harmed by it. Rules tend to be applied more to some persons than others. Studies of juvenile delinquency make the point clearly. Boys from middle-class areas do not get as far in the legal process when they are apprehended as do boys from slum areas. The middle-class boy is less likely, when picked up by the police, to be taken to the station; less likely when taken to the station to be booked; and it is extremely unlikely that he will be convicted and sentenced.[3] This variation occurs even though the original infraction of the rule is the same in the two cases. Similarly, the law is differentially applied to Negroes and whites. It is well known that a Negro believed to have attacked a white woman is much more likely to be punished than a white man who commits the same offense; it is only slightly less well known that a Negro who murders another Negro is much less likely to be punished than a white man who commits murder.[4] This, of course, is one of the main points of Sutherland's analysis of white-collar crime: crimes committed by corporations are almost always prosecuted as civil cases, but the same crime committed by an individual is ordinarily treated as a criminal offense.[5]

Some rules are enforced only when they result in certain consequences. The unmarried mother furnishes a clear example. Vincent[6] points out that illicit sexual relations seldom result in severe punishment or social censure for the offenders. If, however, a girl becomes pregnant as a result of such activities the reaction of others is likely to be severe. (The illicit pregnancy is also an interesting example of the differential enforcement of rules on different categories of people. Vincent notes that unmarried fathers escape the severe censure visited on the mother).

Why repeat these commonplace observations? Because, taken together, they support the proposition that deviance is not a simple quality, present in some kinds of behavior and absent in others. Rather, it is the product of a process which involves responses of other people to the behavior. The same behavior may be an infraction of the rules at one time and not at another; may be an infraction when committed by one person, but not when committed by another; some rules are broken with impunity, others are not. In short, whether a given act is deviant or not depends in part on the nature of the act (that is, whether or not it violates some rule) and in part on what other people do about it.

Some people may object that this is merely a terminological quibble, that one can, after all, define terms any way he wants to and that if some people want to speak of rule-breaking behavior as deviant without reference to the reactions of others they are free to do so. This, of course, is true. Yet it might be worthwhile to refer to such behavior as *rule-breaking behavior* and reserve the term *deviant* for those labeled as deviant by some segment of society. I do not insist that this usage be followed. But it should be clear that insofar as a scientist uses "deviant" to refer to any rule-breaking behavior and takes as his subject of study only those who have been *labeled* deviant, he will be hampered by the disparities between the two categories.

If we take as the object of our attention behavior which comes to be labeled as deviant, we must recognize that we cannot know whether a given act will be categorized as deviant until the response of others has occurred. Deviance is not a quality that lies in behavior itself, but in the interaction between the person who commits an act and those who respond to it....

In any case, being branded as deviant has important consequences for one's further social participation and self-image. The most important consequence is a drastic change in the individual's public identity. Committing the improper act and being publicly caught at it place him in a new status. He has been revealed as a different kind of person from the kind he was supposed to be. He is labeled a "fairy," "dope fiend," "nut" or "lunatic," and treated accordingly.

In analyzing the consequences of assuming a deviant identity let us make use of Hughes' distinction between master and auxiliary status traits.[7] Hughes notes that most statuses have one key trait which serves to distinguish those who belong from those who do not. Thus the doctor, whatever else he may be, is a person who has a certificate stating that he has fulfilled certain requirements and is licensed to practice medicine; this is the master trait. As Hughes points out, in our society a doctor is also informally expected to have a number of auxiliary traits: most people expect him to be upper middle class, white, male, and Protestant. When he is not, there is a sense that he has in some way failed to fill the bill. Similarly, though skin color is the master status trait determining who is Negro and who is white, Negroes are informally expected to have certain status traits and not to have others; people are surprised and find it anomalous if a Negro turns out to be a doctor or a college professor. People often have the master status trait but lack some of the auxiliary, informally expected characteristics; for example, one may be a doctor but be a female or Negro.

Hughes deals with this phenomenon in regard to statuses that are well thought of, desired and desirable (noting that one may have the formal qualifications for entry into a status but be denied full entry because of lack of the proper auxiliary traits), but the same process occurs in the case of deviant statuses. Possession of one deviant trait may have a generalized symbolic value, so that people automatically assume that its bearer possesses other undesirable traits allegedly associated with it.

To be labeled a criminal one need only commit a single criminal offense, and this is all the term formally refers to. Yet the word carries a number of connotations specifying auxiliary traits characteristic of anyone bearing the label. A man who has been convicted of housebreaking and thereby labeled criminal is presumed to be a person likely to break into other houses; the police, in rounding up known offenders for investigation after a crime has been committed, operate on this premise. Further, he is considered likely to commit other kinds of crimes as well, because he has shown himself to be a person without "respect for the law." Thus, apprehension for one deviant act exposes a person to the likelihood that he will be regarded as deviant or undesirable in other respects.

There is one other element in Hughes' analysis we can borrow with profit: the distinction between master and subordinate statuses.[8] Some statuses, in our society as in others, override all other statuses and have a certain priority. Race is one of these. Membership in the Negro race, as socially defined, will override most other status considerations in most other situations; the fact that one is a physician or middle-class or female will not protect one from being treated as a Negro first and any of these other things second. The status of deviant (depending on the kind of deviance) is this kind of master status. One receives the status as a result of breaking a rule, and the identification proves to be more important than most others. One will be identified as a deviant first, before other identifications are made....

NOTES

[1] The most important earlier statements of this view can be found in Frank Tannenbaum, *Crime and the Community* (New York: Columbia University Press, 1938), and E.M. Lemert, *Social Pathology* (New York: McGraw-Hill Book Co., 1951). A recent article stating a position very similar to mine is John Kitsuse, "Societal Reaction to Deviance: Problems of Theory and Method," *Social Problems*, 9(Winter, 1962), 247–256.

[2] F. James Davis, "Crime News in Colorado Newspapers," *American Journal of Sociology*, LVII (January, 1952), 325–330.

[3] See Albert K. Cohen and James F. Short, Jr., "Juvenile Delinquency," P. 87 IN Robert K. Merton and Robert A. Nisbet, eds., *Contemporary Social Problems*. New York: Harcourt, Brace and World, 1961.

[4] See Harold Garfinkel, "Research Notes on Inter- and Intra-Racial Homicides," *Social Forces* 27 (May, 1949):369–81.

[5] Edwin Sutherland "White Collar Criminality," *American Sociological Review* V (February, 1940):1–12.

[6] Clark Vincent, *Unmarried Mothers* (New York: The Free Press of Glencoe, 1961):3–5.

[7] Everett C. Hughes "Dilemmas and Contradictions of Status." *American Journal of Sociology* L (March, 1945): 353–359.

[8] *Ibid.*

Chapter 16

EVALUATION OF LABELING THEORY

Alex Thio

Labeling theory has enjoyed tremendous popularity among sociologists. But it has also drawn considerable criticism.

First of all, many sociologists criticize labeling theory for not being able to answer the etiological question about (primary) deviance—the question being: What causes deviance? Jack Gibbs, for example, points out that labeling theory cannot provide adequate answers to these three etiological questions: "(1) Why does the incidence of a particular act vary from one population to the next? (2) Why do some persons commit the act while others do not? (3) Why is the act in question considered deviant and/or criminal in some societies but not in others?"[1]

This criticism misses the mark because the theory was never intended to be etiological, to deal with causation. The plain fact is that the theory is basically nonetiological, not concerned with causal questions. This has much to do with labeling theorists' antideterministic or voluntaristic stance.

But some of the more recent advocates of labeling theory seem to have changed the originally noncausal content of the theory into a causal one. This shift is especially apparent in their empirical studies on secondary deviance. As we have noted, the original proponents, Lemert in particular, strongly emphasized the voluntaristic element in the process of a person's becoming a secondary deviant—through *active* interaction with the labelers. But many of Lemert's followers have tended to present the secondary deviant as a *passive* object whose behavior is totally determined by the labelers. So this has prompted David Bordua to observe that labeling theory "assumes an essentially empty organism, or at least one with little or no autonomous capacity to determine conduct. The process of developing deviance seems all societal response and no deviant stimulus."[2]

More recently, Frances Piven has also questioned the assumption that the deviant is basically passive. She argues that the deviant is actually quite active: "The impact of societal reactions on deviant action is complex because it interactive. Rule violators are not simply the passive objects of societal reactions; they are active, responding subjects."[3] All this means that some people, when labeled deviant, do not passively accept the stigmatizing label but instead actively, indignantly, or angrily reject it.[4] The increasing number of this kind of deviant in the 1970s and 1980s has indeed surprised Kitsuse, one of the major proponents of labeling theory. As he says:

> Given our sociological conceptions of the effects of societal reactions on deviants, who would have thought that prostitutes would lobby the halls of legislative bodies to denounce "your tired old ethics"; or that mental

patients would organize to demand discharge from institutions that provide only custody but not treatment; or that paraplegics would be able to leave the mark of their political clout on so many street corners across the nation; or that marijuana would openly be used at "puff in" demonstrations on the steps of government buildings; or that American Nazis would claim the right to parade down the predominantly Jewish community of Skokie, Illinois; or that the police chief of San Francisco would sponsor a program of recruiting gay men and women for positions on the force?

Kitsuse goes on to call these people "tertiary deviants" because of their assertiveness as opposed to secondary deviants' supposed passivity: "Whereas the tertiary deviant might say, 'Here I am, warts and all; these warts have nothing to do with my right to life, liberty, and the pursuit of happiness,' the secondary deviant's message is more nearly, 'Here I am with these warts, but I've done all I can to keep them respectably under control and out of public view.'"[5]

Labeling theory has also been criticized for grossly oversimplifying and distorting the real world, as well as for exaggerating the significance of labeling in the making of a deviant career.[6] Nanette Davis has made a related point: "Labeling theory, characteristically oriented within a symbolic interaction framework, has suffered from a 'methodological inhibition' often associated with this social psychological approach. Conceptual impoverishment is facilitated by an absorption with general imagery, with unsystematic, elusive, and suggestive empirical presentations, rather than definitive tests of the interaction framework."[7]

These criticisms are indeed well taken. But they simply point out that labeling theory is largely humanistic in character. The things that have been mentioned— oversimplification, distortion, exaggeration, elusiveness, suggestiveness, vagueness, lack of definitive tests, and the like—are normally the by-product of a humanistic work.[8] They do not necessarily diminish the value of labeling theory as a humanistic product. According to Robert Bierstedt's humanistic viewpoint, a work, argument, or theory should be judged for its *cogency* rather than its truth.[9] If we accept this humanistic criterion, we may have to regard labeling theory as a very good theory. For it seems highly cogent, as its acceptance by numerous sociologists can testify. The cogency of labeling theory seems to lie primarily in the fact that its core idea— that the use of a label, definition, or symbol in social interaction has significant influence on human behavior—is something that all of us can feel and witness in our daily lives.

Although labeling theory is very convincing, we should put it in proper perspective by noting its limitations. The first point of labeling theory is that it is the more powerful people who typically impose the deviant label on the less powerful. This is obviously true, but it tends to lead us, as it has led labeling theorists, to study the powerful as labelers only—and ignore them as deviants. Failure to deal with the powerful as deviants may reinforce and perpetuate the conventional false belief that deviance abounds among the lower classes but not among the middle and upper classes.

The second point of labeling theory is that being labeled deviant produces negative consequences for the person so labeled. More specifically, the deviant label tends to lead the person into further deviant involvement. This point appears very sensible but has not been consistently supported by research findings. Some studies show that labeling encourages further deviance, while many others fail to demonstrate this. David Farrington and his fellow researchers, for example, found that juvenile delinquents who are publicly labeled (convicted in court for an offense) tend to commit more delinquent acts than their nonlabeled peers.[10] But Charles Tittle found in his survey of sixteen longitudinal studies that recidivism rates among released prisoners range from 24 to 68 percent with the average being 44 percent—not high enough, in Tittle's view, to support the labeling argument.[11]

We should therefore not attribute too much importance to labeling. It is not all-powerful nor the only process in determining the outcome of a deviant experience. If labeling theory suggests that the stigma of being an ex-con leads to encourage the individual to commit more crimes, this should not be taken to mean that all or even most of the released prisoners will do so. But it is fair to say that labeling does have *some* impact. Even if "only" an average of 44 percent of the prisoners in the studies reviewed by Tittle committed new crimes after their release from prison, this figure certainly demonstrates the impact of labeling. We should not, however, expect labeling alone to make magical transformations in deep-seated personalities, long-standing habits, and the like. Such an expectation is bound to lead to disappointment, as it has for a critic who writes:

> There *are* personality differences that are reliably associated with behavioral differences and that are remarkably persistent. These persistent ways of feeling and acting are not readily changeable with changes in the labels attached to them. Regardless of what we have been called, *most of us continue to be what we have been a long time becoming*...The point is made in the autobiography of the playwright S.N. Behrman, who, after years of failure and impoverished struggle, wrote a play that was a hit. Behrman comments: "With the production of a successful play...you acquire overnight a new identity—a public label. But this label is pasted on you. It doesn't obliterate what you are and have always been—doesn't erase the stigmata of temperament."[12]

While labeling theory can still be used for explaining some of the problem of recidivism, it seems largely applicable to powerless, not powerful, deviants. The experience of being labeled deviant may have a deviance-encouraging effect on the powerless, but the same experience may have the opposite effect on the powerful. As suggested by research evidence, legal punishments such as imprisonment may provoke powerless deviants such as drug addicts and public drunks to more deviance, while similar punishment discourages powerful deviants like corporate and other white-collar criminals from further deviance.[13]

The third point of labeling theory is that labeling others as deviant creates positive consequences for the individuals, groups, or communities that apply the label. The major positive consequence is the preservation and consolidation of social order and social stability. This appears to be true, but true only because of two significant factors: (1) The labelers represent the more powerful forces of society, while the labeled are such powerless deviants as robbers, murderers, rapists, and other so-called common criminals. (2) By recruiting and punishing these powerless deviants, the more powerful, conventional members and law-enforcing agents of the society champion law and order, so that they themselves are unlikely to commit robbery, murder, rape, and other crimes commonly perpetrated by powerless people. Thus the third point of labeling theory is apparently correct insofar as labeling some powerless people as criminals may ensure social order by deterring other powerless people— as well as the more powerful ones and their law-enforcing agents—from committing those dangerous crimes. But labeling theorists fail to mention that, behind the facade of social order, the more powerful persons, including lawmakers and law enforcers, may be tempted to commit the more sophisticated, more devious, and more undetectable types of crime. This is primarily because so much public attention and law enforcement are focused on powerless deviants that powerful deviants are left alone and thus encouraged to "do their thing."

A number of sociologists have also taken issue with labeling theorist Erikson's contention that crime may strengthen social stability and solidarity. John Conklin, for example, argues that crime weakens rather than strengthens social solidarity.[14] He illustrates this point by citing, among others, the case of a small town called Boise. The Boise residents were shocked by news about homosexual relations between adults and teenagers in their midst. "The overall effect of the scandal on the community," writes Conklin, "was divisive. Single men were stigmatized and suspect, the police were blamed for their ineffectiveness in dealing with the problem, and some teenagers were labeled as corrupted if not actually deviant."[15] In other words, the labeling of homosexuality as a crime divides rather than unites the community—by creating distrust and suspicion. This criticism seems valid, but Erikson may also be correct if his concept of social stability is taken to mean a low rate of deviance among the community's conventional members, resulting, as Erikson has suggested, from their attempts to separate themselves as "good guys" from the "bad guys" they have condemned. In fact, we can see this in the Boise case, too: "By reacting very negatively, people were able to show others that they were not at all like the deviants. One Boise resident said that 'the night with the boys' disappeared, and that 'you never saw so many men going out to the bars at night with their wives and girlfriends.'"[16]

Recently Frances Piven criticized labeling theorists for assuming that the labeling process discourages deviance by showing the powerless the distinction between good and evil:

> What evidence is there that people do not already know, just for having lived in their society, where the line between good and evil is drawn? If I take [this] assumption at face value, I would have to conclude that the hooded mob with cross, rope, and torch is part of some societal mechanism to instruct southern black men that white women are inaccessible to them, thus marking a crucial caste boundary. It seems to me much more reasonable to trust that people know the terms of their domination and understand where the lines are drawn. They understand because the shape of domination is imprinted upon their consciousness by every daily transaction between those with power and those without it. It is the

experience of domination that teaches the rules upon which domination depends. To suppose that southern black men need repetitive examples of lynchings in order to be properly instructed that white women are excluded from their sexual universe is to imagine them as imbeciles.[17]

But we may argue in defense of labeling theory that the southern whites did intend the repetitive use of lynchings to be an "instruction" against raping white women. The extreme cruelty of such an instruction also implies that the dominant whites regarded the oppressed blacks as imbeciles or worse. All this is part of "the experience of domination that teaches the rules upon which domination depends."

However, labeling theorists—and their critics—fail to see the other function of the good-verus-evil "lesson." As suggested by our criticism above, the labeling of powerless people as deviants "instructs" law enforcers to focus their attention on powerless deviants but not on powerful ones. The upshot is that powerful people are encouraged to commit and to continue committing the kinds of crime that law enforcers ignore. Thus the southern whites who lynched blacks could repeatedly do so because they were not labeled criminal—only the black victims were.

NOTES

[1] Gibbs, J.B. 1966. "Conceptions of Deviant Behavior: The Old and the New." *Pacific Sociological Review* 9:12.

[2] Bordua, D.J. 1967. "Recent Trends: Deviant Behavior and Social Control." *Annals of American Academy of Political and Social Science* 369:153.

[3] Piven, F.F. 1981. "Deviant Behavior and the Remaking of the World." *Social Problems* 28:503.

[4] Rogers, J.W. & M.D. Buffalo. 1974. "Fighting Back: Nine Modes of Adaptation to a Deviant Label." *Social Problems* 22:101–18; T.E. Levitin. 1975. "Deviants as Active Participants in the Labeling Process: The Visibly Handicapped." *Social Problems* 22:548–57.

[5] Kitsuse, J.I. 1980. "Coming out all over: Deviants and the Politics of Social Problems." *Social Problems* 28:2, 10.

[6] Gibbons, D.C. & J.F. Jones. *The Study of Deviance: Perspectives and Problems.* Englewood Cliffs, NJ: Prentice-Hall.

[7] Davis, N.J. 1972. "Labeling Theory in Deviance Research: A Critique and Reconsideration." *The Sociological Quarterly* 13:459.

[8] This kind of criticism may also aptly describe the basically humanistic works of Marx, Freud, Weber, and Durkheim. See R. Bierstedt. 1960. "Sociology and Humane Learning." *American Sociological Review* 25:3–9.

[9] Ibid., p.7.

[10] Farrington, D.P. 1977. "The Effects of Public Labelling." *British Journal of Criminology* 17:112–25; and D.P. Farrington, S.G. Osbourn, & D.J. West. 1978. "The Persistence of Labeling Effects." *British Journal of Criminology* 18:277–84.

[11] Tittle, C.R. 1980. "Labelling and Crime: An Empirical Evaluation." In W. Gove, ed., *The Labeling of Deviance: Evaluating a Perspective.* Beverly Hills: Sage.

[12] Nettler, G. 1978. *Explaining Crime*, 2nd ed. New York: McGraw-Hill, p.258.

[13] Chambliss, W.J. 1969. *Crime and the Legal Process.* New York: McGraw-Hill, p.302.

[14] Conklin, J.E. 1975. *The Impact of Crime.* New York: Macmillan, pp.50–72.

[15] Ibid., p.63.

[16] Ibid.

[17] Piven, "Deviant Behavior," p.499.

Part IV

STUDYING DEVIANCE

How do sociologists go about studying deviance and criminality? What do they study? How do they measure acts of deviance and criminality? In this section, we shall attempt to answer these questions.

Researchers studying deviance and criminality can gather data in the following manners: through the employment of:

(1) official statistics

(2) non-official agency data

(3) unofficial measures, such as victimization surveys, self-report questionnaires and field research or participant observation.

I. Official Statistics—Counting Crime Officially

As Nettler (1978), Barlow (1984) and others argue, official statistics are one of the most popular measurements of crime and deviance. Nettler asserts that the measurement of deviance and criminality is a "socially-organized activity with socially-correlated purposes." It involves two components: (a) those committing criminal and deviant acts; and (2) those producing information about such acts. People create criminal and deviant behaviors while others produce information about it.

The official counting of crime and deviance is done by a number of organizations and institutions in our society. These include the police, mental hospitals, the FBI, our legal system—the courts, probation officers, prisons, etc.

These official criminal records serve one important function: they indicate the extent to which, and the method whereby, official agencies of social control define and regulate the deviance they define.

As scholars point out, there exist a number of problems with the production of official agency data. One major problem centers on miscalculation of numbers in the processing of criminals and deviants. So, for example, overworked probation officers will make mistakes in their statistical record-keeping practices. Moreover, agencies or organizations will sometimes "fudge" or distort statistics regarding their processing of deviants or criminals. Specifically, some mental health agencies will alter recidivism rates—making them appear far lower than in actuality—for the sole purpose of ensuring that their funding will be renewed for the next fiscal year.

Apart from deliberate attempts at distortion of the data or accidental counting mistakes made, official statistics as a major measure of deviance and crime, are also subject to other problems. A great amount of behavior escapes the scrutiny of others and remains known only to the actor. We are all secret deviants, some of us are closet criminals, yet, because no one has seen us committing the act, we do not become a part of the official statistics. This leads to an underreporting of certain crimes in the criminal records.Moreover, in many cases, even if acts are viewed by an audience, they are nevertheless reported. Consider the case of rape. According to the official records, nearly 70 out of every 100,000 American women are raped annually; the experts contend that the true rate of victimization is far greater than this, perhaps two to ten times greater (Griffin, 1971). The same is true of spousal abuse and acts of incest. Hence, there is an underreporting of these acts in the official criminal records.

Further, even though some behaviors are reported to the officials, such persons may not label the behavior as deviant or criminal. Why? Sometimes, this is due to the fact that according to strict legal definitions, such acts cannot be labelled. Apart from this fact however, official agents have a great deal of discretion in their exercise of the application of deviant/criminal labels. The police, for example, in dealing with juvenile delinquents, use a great deal of discretion. Some persons, by virtue of their gender, age, demeanor, family background, race, etc., will not be defined as delinquents, but rather, labelled a "precocious kid" and told to go home. Research by Cicourel (1969) and others, unmasks the myth of objectivity in statistics by illustrating the stereotypical notions employed by the police in labelling and apprehending youths. In a similar vein, Piliavin and Briar's (1964) research on this topic underscores the importance of demeanor in determining whether one will be labelled juvenile or not.

In short, individuals engage in criminal and deviant acts and other people spend their time producing information about these acts—such information is subject to bias and distortion.

II Non-Official Agency Data

A second way that researchers study deviance and criminality is by employing "non-official" agency data. Hospitals keep mortality records on its patients—records used to estimate the prevalence of mental illness, alcoholism, drug abuse, domestic violence etc. Security firms and private policing agencies also provide researchers with a source of data. Barnes security officers, for example, keep shoplifting and robbery records on individuals that they have apprehended.

While this data may help to expand our knowledge, it is nevertheless riddled with biases and problems. Depending on the coroner's social definition of the official cause of death, perhaps a suicide victim (at the request of his Catholic family) is listed in the records as some other cause of death. This also leads to an underreporting of certain activities in the official records.

Security officers, just as police officers, also often handle cases in an informal matter, thus, "Johnny Green", son of the CEO of a major bank, is not charged with shoplifting, but is sent home to his parents.

III Unofficial Measures

(a) Victimization Surveys

In order to recover information lost through non-reporting, some researchers rely on victimization surveys. This method of data collection emerged in the United States in the 1960's where researchers conducted their studies on a house-to-house basis. Since 1973, under the auspices of the federal government, national victimization data have been gathered by the *National Crime Survey*. These studies provide valuable information about the deviance process from the perspectives of the victims—their experiences. Despite this merit, this measure of crime and deviance possesses certain shortcomings. First, such surveys have centered on a very limited subject matter, dealing primarily with criminal acts committed against property or individuals. These studies did not focus on victimless crimes such as drug abuse, mental illness, etc. A second problem centers on the accuracy of the statements reported by the victim. These responses may be subject to bias and distortion. Individuals forget all the details of the crime due to memory problems. They may also purposely lie or omit certain details. Further, they may suffer from "forward telescoping"—a condition where the subject remembers incidents as more recent than they actually are.

(b) Self-Report Questionnaires

In addition to the measures discussed above, researchers may attempt to recover lost data by asking members of the public to tell about their own involvement in deviance and criminal activities. The notion behind these studies is to attempt to establish more reasonable estimates of such behaviors. This self-report instrument lists a variety of deviant, illegal and delinquent behaviors. Individuals are asked to check if they have engaged in any of these during a specified time period. These questionnaires are often administered to Sociology 100 classes or incarcerated delinquents. As with the victimization surveys, these self-report questionnaires are also subject to biasing. Individuals may forget how many times they committed a carjacking—was it 22 or 57? Respondents also lie with respect to their responses. In some cases, as Walker (1971) notes, respondents will exaggerate about their participation in illegal or deviant activities—they will admit to acts that they have never committed or admitted to acts more serious than the ones in which they were involved.

(c) Field Research/Participant Observation

In an effort to overcome the problems and biases associated with the aforementioned measures of crime and deviance, researchers have employed the method of field research or participant observation. Researchers contend that such an approach yields more valid, reliable, and richer data.

The Chicagoan sociologist, Robert Park is quoted as having stated to his students:

> You have been told to go grubbing in the library, thereby accumulating a mass of notes and a liberal coating of grime. You have been told to choose problems wherever you can find musty stacks of routine records based on trivial schedules prepared by tired bureaucrats...This is called, *"getting your hands dirty in real research"*.....But one more thing is needed: first hand observation. Go and sit in the lounges of the luxury

hotels and on the doorsteps of the flophouses; sit on the Gold Coast settees and on the slum shakedowns. In short, go get the seats of your pants dirty in real research (McKinney, 1966:71).

Park and others argued that, in order to understand human behavior, one must abandon the official statistics, the non-agency data, the victimization surveys and alike. Rather, the researcher must immerse herself in the world of her subjects, must examine individuals "in their own terms", must grasp the symbolic meanings that the people themselves define as important and real. This method, known variously as "field research," "ethnographic research," "Chicago school research," and "participant observation," "signifies the relation which the human enters in some fashion in the experience and action of those he observes" (Blumer, 1966:vi).

As Rosalie Wax (1971) points out, the history of fieldwork can be traced back to Greek and Roman times, when travellers, intrigued with cultural differences, documented their observations, albeit in an ethnocentric fashion. In the early twentieth century, professionals (mainly doctors, lawyers and government officials), gathered firsthand information on segments of their own society.

Ethnographic research has had a long history of use among cultural anthropologists. Franz Boas, often referred to as the founder of modern cultural anthropology, did fieldwork with the Inuit of Baffin Island, and subsequently with the North American Indians. Boas argued for the importance of developing detailed accounts of the natives' experiences and interpreting their practices within the cultural contexts in which they were situated. Unfortunately, most of Boas' experiences in the field were rather short; he relied heavily on interpreters and native informers. By contrast, Malinowski (1922) lived with a tribe in the Trobriand Islands for an "extended period of time, during which he participated in their activities and ceremonial customs, learned their language, ate their foods, and traced genealogies and kinship systems. The task of the ethnographer is to describe a culture from the native's point of view. As Malinowski (1922:25) put it, the goal of ethnography is "to grasp the native's point of view, his relation to life, to realize his vision of his world."

In the 1920's, at the University of Chicago, a group; of sociologists began doing firsthand fieldwork, participant observation studies of various social groups, not located in some far-off land but in their own society. In his now classic study, *Street Corner Society*, William Foote Whyte (1943) spent over three years studying Cornerville, a lower-class Italian neighborhood in Boston's North end.

Similarly, Herbert Gans (1962) moved into Levittown, another Italian neighborhood in Boston, where he not only made detailed observations but actively participated in the lives of his subjects.

The community studies discussed above constitute only one small arena in which participant observation has been utilized. In the field of deviance, this method has been used widely. Such studies include: Adler's (1987) work on drug dealers; Denzin's (1987) research on alcoholics; Goffman's (1959) classic study on the mental institution, Lofland's investigation of the "Doomsday Cult", Sutherland's (1966) research on the professional thief, and Weinberg's (1960) examination of the nudist subculture.

In all of these cases, the researchers "penetrated beneath the veil" (Boas, 1923), immersed themselves in the natural settings of their subjects, joked with them, empathized with them, shared their joys and sorrows.

In my own research with ex-psychiatric clients (Herman, 1986, 1987, 1989), for over a four-year period, I interacted with them on street-corners, played cards with them at drop-in centers, shot billiards with them, attended their medical appointments, ate countless donuts and thousands of cups of coffee with them at a local coffee shop, interacted with many at homeless shelters, boarding homes, etc. I became friends not only with the ex-patients, but also with many of their family members.

The Major Features of Participant Observation

The primary component of participant observation research is the ethnographic account. Detailed accounts of what goes on in the everyday lives of subjects are derived from fieldnotes taken by the researcher. Fieldnotes are the "meat" of any study; the study is only as good as the quality of the notes taken. Fieldnotes should be written immediately following every trip into the field, every setting in which the researcher interacts with the subjects. There are many different prescriptions on how to "take notes." Some ethnographers, for example, (Bodgan and Taylor, 1975; Shaffir et al. 1987) argue that researchers should wait until they have left the setting and then commence recording their observations and conversations. Others (Festinger et al., 1956) secretly record a number of observations while in the field, and later translate their notes into full-fledged fieldnotes. In my own research on the psychiatric ward, (Herman, 1981b) I did both. For the most part, I waited until I left the setting, went home and then wrote up my complete fieldnotes of what has transpired that day. Sometimes, however, while in the setting, a respondent said something particularly complex or thought-provoking, or made a statement that I though was central to my study. In these instances, I excused myself, went to the rest room, and wrote down the entire conversation on pieces of toilet paper which I shoved into my pockets. (On some nights, I am sure the patients thought I had chronic diarrhea, as I excused myself a number of times.) Some researchers keep fieldnotes by taking a tape recorder into the setting. There are both pros and cons to using a tape recorder. Certainly, its use eliminates the researcher's need to try to remember every conversation verbatim, or in sequence. However, sometimes one's subjects feel inhibited by this mechanical device and will "hold back" on information, especially if you are dealing with highly sensitive information. In my own research on the psychiatric ward, at some point in my research I had become overwhelmed with the wealth of information being told to me during my sessions on the ward. So, on my next excursion into the field, I decided to take a tape recorder. I asked my subjects' permission to use it—to do otherwise, would have been unethical. When permission was granted, I chit chatted with them and, when I felt they were at ease, I turned the machine on. From that moment on, the patients "froze." They were very much inhibited by the tape recorder. Although it was placed inconspicuously, my subjects stared at it, bent over to talk directly into the machine. Their answers were short and robot-like in tone. Clearly, our interactions were constrained by the tape recorder. Hence, I didn't use it again. I relied on my memory, and taking notes on toilet paper. As soon as I left the setting, on my ride back to my house, I turned on the tape recorder in my car and began recounting, in temporal sequence-every conversation, verbatim, the facial grimaces, smirks, all sights, sounds, smells-everything that had occurred on the ward.

Gold (158) had identified four major roles a researcher may take in order to collect data: (1) the complete participant; (2) the participant as observer; (3) the observer as participant; and (4) the complete observer. Let us briefly examine each.

Complete participant—In this role, the researcher enters a setting without disclosing any aspects of the project or the researcher's true identity. The researcher is a covert observer whose scientific or professional aims are unknown to the subjects. The subjects are led to believe that the researcher is "one of them." Wallis (1977), for example secretly studied a religious group, the Scientologists. Lofland and Lejeune (1960) conducted secret observations on several Alcoholics Anonymous groups; Dalton (1959) conducted secret research on several large corporations; Humphreys (1970) covertly observed men engaging in sex in public rest rooms.

Researchers justifying the covert research role, (Douglas, 1976) make the argument that entry might otherwise be denied if their true identities as sociologists were presented to the group prior to the study. Taking an ethical relativist stance, these sociologists feel that they have the "right" to study all groups whether they desire to be studied or not. Another justification made is that subjects alter their behavior if they know they are being studied; thus, covert data collection yields more valid data. The majority of social researchers vehemently oppose covert research on both ethical and pragmatic grounds (Davis, 1961; Erikson, 1965; Gold, 1958; Johnson, 1976; Shils, 1959). In response, these sociologists, taking an ethical absolutist stance, argue that social scientists have no right to invade the privacy of individuals; and deliberate disguising of the intentions of research can potentially cause harm to the subjects. Further, opponents of covert research, or taking on a complete participant role, argue that difficulties undoubtedly arise with researchers recording their observations. Obviously, note pads cannot be visible, nor could tape recorders be used. Resorting to using hidden tape recorders also raises certain ethical issues. A further problem centers on the research being constrained within certain social roles. That is, as a complete participant, the researcher is forced to act in a certain way—to play a part, to say certain things, to have a great deal of knowledge about the group, its structure, its ideology, etc. The researcher is unable to ask the types of questions a non-member might ask for fear of being discovered and perhaps forced to leave the group. As Gold (1958) concludes, "While the complete observer role offers possibilities of learning about aspects of behavior that might otherwise escape a field observer, it places him in pretended role which call for delicate balances of role and self."

Participant-as-Observer—A second role that a researcher may assume is that of participant-as-observer. In contrast to the complete observer, the participant observer role is one in which the researcher has received consent from the subjects to participate and observe them in their natural environments. All of the subjects are aware of the scientific study and the role of the researcher. The researcher negotiates a bargain—a set of mutual obligations and promises agreed upon at the outset of the research. In some cases, the researcher negotiates the bargain with the subjects themselves, in other cases, negotiation occurs with the gatekeepers (see Herman

1981a; Haas and Shaffir, 1980). The type of bargain that is struck is crucial to the research endeavor. Time, setting, or sample constraints imposed by the subjects or gatekeepers at the outset may seriously hamper the study or the quality of data collected. The aim of the researcher is to negotiate for free rein within the setting, to stay for an extended period of time, to interact with whoever wishes to speak with her.

Once access has been granted, the researcher begins to participate in the natural setting(s) of the subjects. During the first days (perhaps even weeks) in the field, the researcher may feel uncomfortable, anxious, or afraid. As Geer (1964) points out, such feelings are completely normal. Researchers inevitably make mistakes at work, especially during the first days in the field—they may say or do something that proves embarrassing. Bogdan and Taylor (1975) and others suggest that it is best to remain fairly passive during this time. They advise that one do more observing than participating. As the researcher begins to acquaint herself with the setting and participants, she will become more comfortable interacting.

During the early stages of fieldwork, subjects are sometimes wary or even hostile. The aim of the researcher is to develop rapport and establish their trust. Such a relationship is not built over night. It may take several weeks or months to acquire a relationship wherein subjects will be open and honest. In my own research on hospitalized mental patients (Herman, 1981b) trust was established in about one month. The patients asked me countless questions—many of which were quite embarrassing and highly personal in nature. They were as interested in my life as I was in theirs. Failure to open up and share with them would have hampered our relationship. Moreover, as subjects will sometimes do in the early stages of fieldwork, I was given a series of "tests" to see "whose side" I was on—tests to evaluate my trustworthiness. At the outset, I had ensured my subjects confidentiality and anonymity with respect to anything they told me. However, during the first days, I was "fed" tidbits of information—information such as ways to escape from the institution and ways to secure sex, drugs, and other commodities. My subjects wanted to see if I would report such information to the staff. When I did not, I passed their test and they certified me trustworthy. A bond developed between they and me. Once rapport has been established, the researcher is accepted as a member of the group, the task now centers on "learning the ropes" (Shaffir et al., 1987; Geer et al., 1968; Lofland, 1971)—obtaining intimate familiarity with the group, acquiring their perspectives, learning the meanings and symbols that the group defines as important and real. While there are no magical formulas for learning the ropes, the researcher must participate actively in the social world of her subjects.

At some point, affected by time, financial, and other constraints, the researcher makes the decision to leave the field and begin analyzing the data and writing up the findings. At this stage, known as "the disengagement process," the investigator is often faced with several difficulties (Maines et al., 1987; Letkemann, 1987; Altheide, 1987). Although I had told my subjects on a number of occasions of my impending leave, when I no longer returned to the psychiatric ward my subjects felt abandoned and cheated. Over the two years, I had become a large part of their lives and I was missed. I, too, felt a void in my life when I no longer visited them on a regular basis. In retrospect, it would have been better had I gradually phased myself out of their lives rather than leaving cold-turkey.

Observer-as-Participant—In this role, the researcher typically interacts with the subjects only one or, perhaps, two times. In contrast to the previously described role in which the researcher may interact in the setting for several months or even several years, the observer as participant has brief contact with the subject. The researcher may orally administer a formal questionnaire (Miall, 1984); there is no attempt to establish rapport or develop a relationship between the two parties. (We shall discuss their method more fully in the next section, on interviewing.)

Complete Observer—A fourth role is that of complete observer, wherein the investigator is completely removed from interacting with the subjects. The reader studies individuals in a laboratory environment. All variables are strictly controlled by the investigator who will observe and record behavior behind a one-way mirror (Brehm and Weintrab, 1977; Couch, 1988; Couch et al., 1986a, 1986b). We shall turn to a detailed discussion of this researcher role in our section on the social experiment.

The selections in this reader are based on participant observation/fieldwork studies of various deviants. Participant observation is the major method utilized by labelling theorists because it allows the researchers to examine the manner by which social definitions are constructed, the manner by which persons are affected by others' reactions, the social processes by which they are labelled deviant, the negotiative and communicative processes occurring between individuals and their audiences, and the effect of labelling upon the self-images, and identities of the individuals.

In the following two selections by Herman entitled, *"Accessing the Stigmatized: Gatekeeper Problems, Obstacles and Impediments to Social Research."* and Williams et al., entitled, *"Personal Behavior in Dangerous Places,"* we are provided with a detailed understanding of some of the concerns and problems associated with conducted fieldwork on deviant populations. In the Herman piece, the author discusses some of the problems she faced when attempting to gain access to studying the institutionalized mentally ill. Specifically, Herman documents the dilemmas and roadblocks she encountered when attempting to negotiate a "bargain" with "gatekeepers" of a large, state, psychiatric institution. The author points out that the bargaining stage of research is more accurately conceptualized as a continuous struggle between the researcher and the gatekeeper, each attempting to gain control over "definitions of the situation" and "constructions of reality."

In the Williams et al., paper, the authors address another important issue, that of personal safety. Drawing from numerous years of participant observation research in studying crack dealers in New York City, the authors discuss the various strategies by which fieldwork can be conducted safely, even in dangerous settings with dangerous people.

REFERENCES

Adler, Patricia. 1985. *Wheeling and Dealing*. New York: Columbia University Press.
Altheide, David L. 1974. "Leaving the Newsroom." Pp. 301–310 In William Shaffir, Robert A.Stebbins, and A. Turowetz, editors, *Fieldwork Experience: Qualitative Approached to Social Research.* New York: St. Martin's Press.
Anderson, N. 1923. *The Hobo*. Chicago: University of Chicago Press.

Barlow, Hugh, 1984., *Introduction to Criminology*. Boston: Little Brown.

Bogdan, Robert and Steven Taylor. 1975. *Introduction to Qualitative Research Methods*. New York: John Wiley.

Cicourel, Aaron, 1969. *The Social Organization of Juvenile Justice*. New York: John Wiley.

Douglas, Jack D. 1976. *Investigative Social Research*. Beverly Hills, CA: Sage.

———. 1985. *Creative Interviewing*. Beverly Hill, CA: Sage.

Festinger, Leon, Henry W. Riecken, And Stanley Schacter. 1956. *When Prophecy Fails*. New York: Harper and Row.

Fine, Gary Allen. 1987. "Cracking Diamonds: Observer Role in Little League Baseball Settings and the Acquisition Social Competence." Pp. 117–132, In Wm. Shaffir, et al., editors, *Fieldwork Experience: Qualitative Approaches to Social Research*. New York: St. Martin's Press.

Gans, H. 1962. *The Urban Villagers*. New York: Free Press.

Geer, B. 1969. "First Days in the Field." In G.M. McCall and J. L. Simmons, eds., *Issues in Participant Observation*. New York: Random House.

Goffman, E. 1961. *Asylums: Essays on the Social Situation of Mental Patients and Other Inmates*. Garden City, NY: Random House.

Griffin, Susan, 1971. "Rape: The All-American Crime." *Ramparts* 10:34–35.

Gold, R.L. 1958. "Roles in Sociological Field Observations." *Social Forces* 36:217–223.

Haas, J., ViVona C., Miller, S.J., Woods, C. and Becker, H.S. 1968. "Learning the Ropes: Situational Learning in Four Occupational Training Programs." Pp. 209–233, In I. Deutscher and E.P. Thompson, eds., *Among the People: Encounters with the Poor*. New York: Basic Books, Inc.

Haas, Jack and William Shaffir. 1977. "The Professionalism of Medical Students: Developing Competence and a Cloak of Competence." *Symbolic Interaction* 1:71–88.

———. 1980. "Fieldworkers' Mistakes at Work: Problems in Maintaining Research and Researcher Bargains." Pp. 244–255, In William Shaffir et al., eds., *Fieldwork Experience: Qualitative Approaches to Social Research*. New York: St. Martin's Press.

Herman, N.J. 1981. *The Making of a Mental Patient: An Ethnographic Study of the Processes and Consequences of Institutionalization Upon Self-Images and Identities*. Unpublished Master's thesis, McMaster University, Hamilton, Ontario, Canada.

Humphreys, Laud. 1970. *Tearoom Trade: Impersonal Sex in Public Places*. Chicago: Aldine.

Johnson, John M. 1975. *Doing Fieldwork Research*. New York: Macmillan.

Letkemann, Peter. 1978. "Crime as Work: Leaving the Field." Pp. 292–301, In William Shaffir et al., eds., *Fieldwork Experience: Qualitative Approaches to Social Research*. New York: St. Martin's.

Liebow, E. 1967. *Tally's Corner*. Boston: Little, Brown.

Lofland, John. *Doomsday Cult: A Study of Conversion, Proselytization, and Maintenance of Faith*. Englewood Cliffs, N.J.: Prentice-Hall.

Maines, David R., William Shaffir, and Allan Turowetz. 1973. "Leaving the Field in Ethnographic Research: Reflections on the Entrance-Exit Hypothesis." Pp. 261–281 in William Shaffir et al., eds., *Fieldwork Experience: Qualitative Approached to Social Research*. New York: St. Martin's.

Malinowski, Bronsilaw. 1922. *Argonauts of the Western Pacific*. London: Routledge and Kegan Paul.

Miall, Charlene. 1984. *Women and Involuntary Childlessness: Perceptions of Stigma Associated with Infertility and Adoption*. Unpublished Ph.D. Dissertation, York University, Department of Sociology.

Nettler, Gwynn, 1978. *Explaining Crime*. New York: McGraw-Hill.

Piliavin, Irving and Scott Briar, 1964. "Police Encounters with Juveniles." *American Journal of Sociology* 70:206–14.

Shaffir, W. 1974. *Life in a Religious Community: The Lubavitcher Chassidism in Montreal*. Toronto: Holt, Rinehart, and Winston.

Thomas, William I. and Florian Znaniecki. 1918–1920. *The Polish Peasant in Europe and America* (Volumes I–V). Boston: Richard Badger.

Wax, Rosalie. 1971. *Doing Field Work*. Chicago: University of Chicago Press.

Weinberg, Martin S. 1966. "Becoming a Nudist." *Psychiatry: Journal for the Study of Interpersonal Processes* 29:15–24.

Whyte, W.F. 1955. *Street Corner Society*. Chicago: University of Chicago Press.

Chapter 17

ACCESSING THE STIGMATIZED: GATEKEEPER PROBLEMS, OBSTACLES, AND IMPEDIMENTS TO SOCIAL RESEARCH

Nancy J. Herman

Introduction

An essential precondition for conducting field research whether with "*deviant*" or "*non-deviant*" groups, involves "getting in"—gaining access to the social setting and the individuals one desires to study.

Examination of previous studies detailing how entre was obtained, indicates that there appears to be differential access to research settings and research populations. While some researchers have managed to gain access expediently and with relative ease,[1] others have been confronted with numerous difficulties that occurred over extended periods of time.[2]

Successful access into the research setting is dependent upon a number of variables,[3] one of which centers on the type of "bargain" that is made—"the written or unwritten agreement between the gatekeeper(s)[4] and/or the subjects, and the researcher that defines the obligations they have to one another" (Bogdan and Taylor, 1975:35). Typically, the researcher seeks to make a bargain that will secure him/her a free hand in the setting; however, in actual fact, such an aim is often difficult to achieve. Examination of previous studies reveal that while some researchers, in the context of the research bargain are given total freedom, others are frequently restricted within the setting, and are sometimes even forced to discontinue the study.[5]

When field researchers typically conceive of the "bargaining stage" of research, it is often thought of as a rather *static* phase. The underlying tenet is that the researcher is able to enter a setting, make a bargain, develop rapport with his/her respondents, and no further negotiation is necessary. My fieldwork experience (similar to that of others)[6] reveals that the bargaining stage is more accurately conceptualized as a *continuous process*, a process in which negotiation and renegotiation continues throughout the entire research endeavor.

This article reviews my experiences in attempting to gain access to conduct participant observation and informal interviewing with a "stigmatized" population, namely, a group of psychiatric patients, institutionalized in a state mental hospital. In particular, it focuses on the problems encountered in attempting to make and maintain research bargains with gatekeepers of a "*powerful*" institution, namely the professional staff of a large psychiatric hospital.[7]

This research project was impeded by a number of factors including: (1) the state's objection to the project, (2) their initial denial of access, (3) their attempts to

132

assist in defining the nature and method of the project, (4) their continual attempts to assert authority and control over the data and the research process in general, (5) their efforts to deny access to respondents, (6) their insistence on access to confidential fieldnotes, and (7) their efforts to control publication rights.

Making and Maintaining Research Bargains

Examination of the series of negotiations and renegotiations between the gatekeepers of the psychiatric institution and myself revealed that both parties were struggling for superiority. Each party sought to gain control of the situation.[8]

As Becker (1964:272) notes, an irreconcilable dichotomy exists between the interests of the researcher and the individuals representing the institution under investigation. Every institution, when under examination seeks to control the outsiders' study of their behavior. The institution wants to ensure that the results of the study are consonant with its official ideology, hence allowing the organization to remain in a positive light. Often if a researcher attempts to study the so-called "overdogs" or higher-level subjects of an organization he/she meets no problems when attempting to make a bargain; however, if he/she so desires to study the "underdogs" or lower-level subjects (as I sought to do), he/she is often confronted with numerous problems.

I encountered several problems when attempting to make a bargain with a large, state psychiatric hospital. My interest in studying the social worlds of mental patients from their points of view was responded to by the gatekeepers in an extremely negative and wary manner.

In order to receive permission to conduct this research, an initial series of meetings occurred between an administrative official in charge of the educational services of the institution and myself. During the first meeting, I introduced myself and outlined my research interests in a general manner.[9] I continued to explain that the study would be strictly confidential in terms of both the identity of the hospital and the patients involved. Moreover, I indicated that the research would be unobtrusive in nature. At no time would the fieldwork interfere with the formal treatment activities of the patients. I also stressed that the study would be non-evaluative in nature. My aim as a sociologist was not to evaluate the treatment programs or the general conditions of the hospital; rather, the aim of the proposed study would seek to understand the social worlds of mental patients as they subjectively experience it.

Subsequent to this initial meeting, a research proposal was requested and submitted to the gatekeeper providing a detailed description of the aims, the theoretical and methodological orientation and anticipated significance of the study. The administrative official objected to the proposed project on several grounds:[10]

(1) the study was too "broad" and "vague." The project was "unscientific"—it lacked rigorous design. The proposed project did not possess specific hypotheses that could be empirically tested;

(2) the proposed study was invalid. The gatekeeper felt that the study possessed no validity because it was not examining the *biological* and *genetic* factors affecting mental illness;

(3) the unobtrusiveness of the research was questioned. The gatekeeper felt that the patients' rights would be violated by such an investigation—the study would undoubtedly be "disruptive for the patients";

(4) the safety of the researcher was also a major issue—it was conceived that I might be seriously injured if allowed to conduct research on a psychiatric ward;

(5) the gatekeeper suggested that the ward staff might object to my presence on the ward;

(6) finally, the gatekeeper felt that the research lacked significance for the hospital—the hospital would not benefit in any way from a *sociological study*" (Interview #1).

Although I had expected that my proposal would be critically examined, I did not anticipate the number of obstacles that were placed in front of me. I had no idea that an institution which heralded itself as an *"Accredited Teaching Hospital"* would be so unsympathetic to alternative types of research focusing on mental patients and on mental health care facilities in general. From the outset of our negotiations, very little attempt on the part of the gatekeeper was made to understand the sociological significance of the proposed project. The inductive nature of the research was viewed by the gatekeeper *not* as a scientifically valid methodological orientation within which one gathers descriptive data on human behavior; rather, it was interpreted as a lack of knowledge about the nature of mental illness on the part of the researcher. In order to clarify my perspective, I repeatedly emphasized the theoretical and methodological orientation of the research and stressed why it was of utmost importance to begin the study with no preconceived hypotheses in mind. But to professionals schooled in the natural sciences and who approach the study of phenomena from a positivist stance, my proposal seemed "too vague" and "meaningless."

A second major objection to the research proposal centered on the validity of the study. Specifically, it was felt (by two ward psychiatrists and an administrative official) that my study was invalid because "mental illness or the process of mental illness (was) not being considered." The administrative gatekeeper emphasized that the proposed study lacked validity because it did not focus upon the biological or genetic bases of mental illness. Adopting the medical model of mental illness,[11] the gatekeepers flatly rejected the sociological model of mental illness[12]—the model upon which the proposed study was based. In response to this objection, I argued that while the medical model may have some credibility in terms of explaining the nature of mental illness, it is of *equal* importance to examine the nature of mental illness from a sociological perspective.

Regarding the issue of patient rights, it was repeatedly stressed by the gatekeeper that my participant observation would undoubtedly "upset" the patients. Conceiving of sociologists in a negative manner, the gatekeeper told me at one of our initial meetings:

> All they (sociologists) do is come in and disturb everyone...From my experiences with anthropologists and sociologists, all they do is get everyone upset. Even clergymen coming in, when they try to talk religion to the patients, they just upset them because they (the patients) end up

having religious delusions....If you were qualified and experienced with the patients, I might let you in, but I'm afraid that you would only upset them. (Interview #1)

I assured the gatekeeper that my presence would not upset the patients. I would only converse with the patients if they so desired. We would talk about subjects that the patients themselves defined as being important and real. No attempt would be made to pry into areas they did not wish to discuss.

Another major problem to the proposed study concerned my own safety. Throughout our negotiations it was repeatedly expressed that this study would be potentially "dangerous" to me. Every attempt was made to point out to me that "there are three hundred *psychotic patients* in this hospital." It seemed apparent that the gatekeeper was employing a scare tactic in the hope that I would become apprehensive about conducting the study. However, I assured the gatekeeper that I was not afraid to conduct fieldwork in this setting. Moreover, I expressed that if the hospital was worried about the legal obligations of my safety, I would agree to sign a statement releasing the institution of any liabilities.

Regarding the problem of the anticipated objection of the ward staff, I offered to speak with both the ward supervisor and ward psychiatrist fully detailing the aims of the project.

One final objection recurred throughout the negotiation process relating to the anticipated significance of the proposed study. Specifically, the official gatekeepers repeatedly asked: "What will the hospital get out of this study?" "There doesn't seem to be anything in it for us."[13] Rosalie Wax (1952:34) addresses this problem:

> "Why should anybody in this group bother to talk to me? Why should this man take time out from his work, gambling, or pleasant loafing to answer my questions?" I suggest that as the field worker discovers the correct answers he will improve not only his technique in obtaining information but also his ability to evaluate it. I suggest, moreover, that the correct answers to these questions will tend to show that whether an informant likes, hates, or just doesn't give a hoot about the field worker, he will talk because he and the field worker are *making an exchange, are consciously or unconsciously giving each other something they both desire or need.*

In terms of my study, I argued that its anticipated significance was threefold: it had significance for sociologists, social psychologists, psychiatrists, and all who were interested in obtaining a fuller understanding of social problems of which mental patients are a part. Secondly, I emphasized that the proposed study had practical significance in that certain processes which may come to light as a result of this fieldwork may be taken to a higher level of abstraction and utilized to understand other social groups. Finally, I contended that through this study both the researcher and the hospital would gain an understanding of the processes and consequences of institutionalization upon the self-images and identities of mental patients.

The initial series of negotiations, prior to the commencement of field research, lasted approximately one month, with the researcher formulating and reformulating research proposals in an attempt to clarify and "sell" the proposed project. During this time, a meeting was held among the ward supervisor, ward psychiatrist, and myself during which the theoretical and methodological orientation of the study was discussed. Similar to my earlier meetings with the administrative gatekeeper, these gatekeepers treated the project in much the same negative manner. At this time, two things were suggested to me: (1) that I "go home and rethink the project and come back some other time"; or (2) that I "should go and study some other group outside this institution such as an ex-mental patient group in the community".[14] Despite these patronizing and evasion tactics, I did not discourage. After presenting the administrative gatekeeper with an extensive, revised research proposal, providing solutions to *each* objection raised, a bargain was finally made. Still, in one final attempt for the institution to gain control over the situation, the gatekeeper "suggested" the he be given access to my fieldnotes in order to "give direction" to my research:

> ...I think that you will need some *guidance*. You know, Nancy, you could easily get lost in this institution. I don't mean physically, but you could be out there (he points into space) trying to collect data but in the process you get lost in the shuffle. I think that I should be your *advisor*. You should report to me once a month with your fieldnotes so that I can *direct* your research. If you are going down a wrong path, I can set you straight.

In response to the gatekeeper's request for access to my fieldnotes, I emphasized that as an ethical researcher I had an obligation to protect the patients under investigation. Under no circumstances would the gatekeeper be allowed to examine the fieldnotes— they were strictly confidential and would remain the sole property of the researcher. I expressed the point of view that sharing the fieldnotes would be a violation of the researcher's code of ethics, specifically protecting patient confidences and anonymity. Through the "give and take" process[15] that researchers and gatekeepers engage in when bargaining, it was finally agreed that fieldnotes would remain the property of the researcher, but I would meet with the gatekeeper on a regular basis to discuss my research in a "general" manner.

After this arduous series of negotiations during which both parties continually struggled for superiority, a bargain was achieved. I was finally granted permission to conduct fieldwork on the ward. Although I thought that the negotiations had been completed at this point, (approximately one month later), I was notified by the administrative gatekeeper that a meeting was scheduled to "discuss the *proposed* project"—this time the meeting would involve the ward supervisor, ward psychiatrist, administrative official, my advisor from the university and myself. Further, I was also informed that I was suspended from conducting fieldwork until after this meeting. During this meeting, we again discussed the theoretical underpinnings of the study and its methodological orientation. Addressing my advisor, one of the gatekeepers expressed his central concerns and reservations about the study:

> In our previous discussion with Nancy, I expressed concern with her study on the grounds that it was *abstract* and possessed certain contradic-

tions. I find it difficult to deal with this notion of "understanding"...
(Interview #10).

The gatekeeper felt that one could not gain an understanding of what it is like to be a mental patient from the inductive type of study proposed. He contended that the research would "just be detailing what a researcher thinks it is like to be a patient." Moreover, the gatekeeper stated that this study could not possibly be non-evaluative in nature—the researcher would not be objective. In response to these areas of concern, my advisor argued that our aim as social scientists is to understand. We were not interested in evaluating the conditions of the setting or the treatment approaches. He explained that we were not journalists interested in publishing our findings in popular magazines or newspapers. We, instead are *scientists*, attempting to *understand* social phenomena. He further pointed out that we were interested in examining social processes—my study would be an attempt to examine the processes of institutionalization and its effects on patient self-images and identities. This study would attempt to look at *reality* in terms of what the patients, individually and/or collectively, define as important and real.

Despite my advisor's efforts to win over the gatekeepers, they still viewed the study in a negative manner. My advisor asked the gatekeepers if they had ever read any sociological studies which adopt a "symbolic interactionist perspective."[16] As we anticipated, they had not. As a result, I handed the gatekeepers a book of readings that adopted this theoretical stance, along with a brief introduction to symbolic interactionism.[17] In a rather reserved tone, one of the gatekeepers replied:

Well, I will have to examine these ideas further. Maybe through further reading, I will come to grips with this...(Interview #10)

A second gatekeeper concern centered on the learning objectives discussed in the proposal—the same proposal which was agreed to by the administrative gatekeeper one month prior to this meeting. Once again, the gatekeepers wanted to know how the "hospital would benefit" from the study. I described the theoretical and practical significance of the project pointing out that both the hospital and myself would undoubtedly learn about the processes and consequences of institutionalization upon the patient's self-concept. Because of the institution's interest in "getting something out of the research," I offered to give a seminar to the ward staff on completion of the study, outlining my findings in a general manner. This offer was responded to by the gatekeepers in a favorable way.

A third concern was expressed concerning my role on the ward. One of the gatekeepers stated that the ward staff were concerned about my identity and the objectives of the study:[18]

The staff are concerned about your role, what it is that you're doing here. You have to realize that you're different, Nancy. You are not the conventional student coming onto the ward. We usually have nursing students, medical students who have specific objectives to meet...We have a very regimented structure here.... Your proposal is *very different* (Interview #10)

In response to this area of concern, I stated that, in violation of our original agreement in which both the administrative gatekeeper and the ward supervisor agreed to inform the staff about my presence and the aims of the study, nevertheless, they were confused about my role; hence, I was being treated very coldly by the staff. Essentially, the staff had the misconception that I was conducting an "evaluative" study of them, despite my efforts to explain what I was actually doing.[19] And this placed me in a precarious position—I was afraid that my interacting with the staff (in informing them of my identity and study) would seriously harm my rapport with the patients (who would label me as a "traitor" for interacting with the staff). Upon expressing this concern, the gatekeepers agreed to clear up the situation immediately—one of the gatekeepers would personally ensure that *every* staff member was informed of my presence. (Unfortunately, this promise never carried through for throughout the entire fieldwork experience, I was continually faced with individuals to which I had to explain my role and objectives).[20]

One final concern was expressed by one gatekeeper, specifically related to the problem of "transference." The gatekeeper stated that he had some reservations about the manner in which data would be collected. It was felt that, conducting a study from a "subjective" point of view, participating with the patients and coming to an empathetic understanding, would undoubtedly result in myself "going native"[21] or associating myself with the patients. I attempted to assure the gatekeeper that this would not happen; I explained that while the participant observer actively participates in the lives of his informants, at the same time he has the capacity to remain detached and objective.[22]

After long deliberation, I was *once again* granted access into the hospital. Walking out the door, I remarked to my advisor that I never thought that the bargaining stage was a *continuous* process that occurred throughout the research endeavor—a process in which agreements shifted and altered. One of the gatekeepers, overhearing this statement replied in a half-joking manner:

This is only the beginning, Nancy. I told you this wasn't going to be easy (he chuckles). You ain't seen nothin' yet! (Interview #10).

Ignoring this warning, I assured myself that I was finally allowed access into the research setting—this time, the bargain had been made for good. I was sure that no further negotiations would be necessary between the gatekeepers and myself, but I was wrong!

Trouble loomed once more approximately two months after this second bargain was made. I was informed by the administrative gatekeeper's assistant that she had received an alarming phone call from an "*anonymous source*" regarding my research:

Nancy, I had this call yesterday from an *hysterical* woman who was saying some disturbing things...This woman said that your reports (fieldnotes) were being given out to the thirty people in your class and that they were also available to anyone else who wanted them. She told us that these reports were *derogatory* to the hospital—they stated that there were all kinds of suicides and escapes going on that no one knows about...This woman expressed that she didn't want to phone us but her conscience was bothering her and she said that *we have to stop you* (Interview #14, November 27, 1979:1).

I was shocked when I learned of this news. In response to these allegations, I emphasized to the gatekeeper that my fieldnotes were *not* being distributed to "anyone who wanted them." The only individuals allowed to see the fieldnotes were my professor, myself, and my fellow classmates taking a qualitative methods course with me and who had taken an oath of confidentiality. I pointed out that at present I had no reason to believe that anyone violated this oath. I stressed that:

> We can't deal with heresay evidence here. My fieldnotes are not an attempt to damage the hospital in any way....I am not interested in conducting an expose of the hospital. I think that this phone call represents an effort to damage myself, rather than to damage the hospital (Interview #10).

The gatekeeper agreed with this point but emphasized that because the anonymous phone caller specifically identified my name and the research class I was in, this phone call could not be disregarded. The gatekeeper's assistant wondered if the phone caller might be one of the patients that I was interviewing who "became upset with my questioning." But because the caller gave my name in full, knew details about the qualitative methods course in which I was enrolled, and asked for the administrative official with whom I was bargaining, the gatekeeper's assistant felt (as I did) that this person was probably someone from my class who was attempting to sabotage the research. Nevertheless, the institution could not ignore this phone call—to them, this call indicated that the institution's positive identity was being threatened.

In response to this phone call and thereafter, the institution made a serious, forceful attempt to gain control of the situation—to gain control over constructions of reality. Specifically, it was suggested that I discontinue my fieldwork until a meeting could be set up between the administrative gatekeeper and myself during which time a decision would be reached regarding *if* the project should be allowed to continue. I argued that it would be impossible for me to stop conducting fieldwork at this time because it would seriously destroy the rapport I had worked so hard to establish with my subjects. Reluctantly, the gatekeeper's assistant allowed me to continue the study in the interim.

In the following week, I met with the administrative official one more time. During our earlier negotiations, an attempt was made on the part of the gatekeeper to establish a somewhat collegial relationship with me; however, from this meeting onward, a gradual breakdown in collegiality and cooperation occurred. The gatekeeper responded to my research in an extremely negative manner. In an attempt to convince the gatekeeper that the allegations made against my research were simply not true, I stated:

> You know, I am just as upset about this telephone incident as you are, Mr.
> _____. My professor and I have questioned the credibility of this phone
> call on several grounds. First of all, this call was said to have been made
> by a "doctor's wife." If so, why didn't this woman identify herself? It
> seems to me that anyone who is willing to give such information would
> not be afraid to give her name, unless these accusations are false...this
> woman claimed that my reports were being circulated throughout the
> university—this is simply not true. Only the people in my class were
> allowed to see these notes and my professor swore them to confidential-
> ity. In terms of the content of the notes, nowhere was there anything
> written that was meant to be degrading to the hospital (Interview #16)

I explained to him that careful examination of this unfortunate incident indicated that
someone in my class deliberately set out to undermine my fieldwork. I was aware that
some of my fellow classmates were jealous of my research and earnest efforts, and
had even made threats that they were going to sabotage the study, but I never thought
that they would follow through on their threats. I emphasized to the gatekeeper that:

> ...this call was merely aimed at getting *me* into trouble. What I'm trying
> to say is that you cannot see this incident as an effort to damage the
> hospital, but rather, it represents a blatant effort to *damage myself* and *my
> professor*; we are clearly the victims here! (Interview #16).

However, the gatekeeper was not convinced by this explanation and offered an
alternative interpretation of the incident:

> This is all very interesting, I mean, this idea that people in your class made
> this phone call, but I have a different perception of this incident. I think
> that your advisor and you are missing the point. You are attempting to
> rationalize the irrational. I think that this is one of the downfalls of
> sociology. My perception of all of this is that if a person is doing this to
> you in class, he/she must be *mentally ill*. Perhaps the way in which you
> are discussing the topic of mental illness in your notes is upsetting to the
> person. I try to listen to what the irrational is saying to me. I see this
> incident as an irrational person's way of crying out for help. They do this
> by phoning the hospital. Obviously, there is something in your fieldnotes
> that is wrong; you are probably missing talking about what mental illness
> is...I'm not interested about who in your class did this. What is important
> is this "message" and I'm going to have to follow it. When I get messages
> like this, they are usually telling me something important (Interview
> #16).

To ensure strictest confidentiality, I informed the gatekeeper that no one in my
class would receive further fieldnotes. I would only discuss my research with my
advisor. The gatekeeper, in another effort to gain control over the research requested
that he be given access to my fieldnotes. I flatly denied his request on the basis of an

ethical obligation to protect my informants. Realizing that I possessed this strong conviction to protect my subjects, the gatekeeper reluctantly changed the subject. He handed me a counter-proposal written by two psychiatrists who critiqued my original research proposal—the *same* proposal to which one of the two psychiatrists had agreed two months earlier. This counter-proposal presented a critique of my entire theoretical and methodological framework. Specifically, the psychiatrists expressed two central concerns:[23]

(1) they felt that the study would undoubtedly be evaluative in nature. It was expressed that "participant observation studies are affected by the biases of the investigator more than other kinds of studies and the "facts" emerging from such a study could be merely affirmation of the biases" ; (2) they felt that the study was invalid because it was not looking at the subject of mental illness. As a result of these concerns, it was requested that I only conduct fieldwork during recreational and self-care activities. I was no longer granted permission to conduct participant observation during formal therapy sessions—a violation of one of the conditions of our original bargain. Having no choice in the matter but to abide by the gatekeeper's request, I agreed to this alteration of our original agreement.

Examination of this entire bargaining experience from a symbolic interactionist perspective reveals that the representatives of the institution attempted to "discourage" me from conducting this research from the outset; however, through persistence, I was reluctantly granted access. Throughout our negotiations and renegotiations, the institution's representatives struggled to gain control of the situation—especially in this latter attempt to gain control of the researcher's fieldnotes. While I managed to successfully resist, the institution did not concede. Although the institution was not able to control reality in terms of exerting control over the *nature* of the data being collected, its representatives still managed to control me "spatially"—that is, they attempted to control the *areas* and *activities* which I was allowed to observe.

From a labelling perspective, this bargaining experience can be conceptualized as an on-going struggle of the researcher against being negatively labelled by the gatekeepers of the psychiatric institution. Specifically, the gatekeepers equated the inductive nature of the research with a lack of knowledge on the part of the researcher, thereby attempting to bestow upon me the label, "incompetent researcher." Moreover, possessing the misconception that all sociologists conduct "expose-types" of research, and that the researcher was going to conduct such a study that would present the hospital in a negative light, these gatekeepers sought to attach to me the label, "troublemaker." Through my persistent efforts, I attempted to prove my competence as a qualitative researcher by justifying the methodological orientation of the study. I emphasized and re-emphasized the non-evaluative nature of the study. I was not interested in "exposing" the conditions or treatment facilities of the institution. While my efforts partially convinced the gatekeepers of the clarity and rigor of the research design, nevertheless they still conceived of me as a "troublemaker." As a result, they attempted to control *when* and *where* I was allowed to conduct my fieldwork.

During subsequent weeks, I conducted fieldwork as many times as possible. I sensed that the hospital was attempting to do something in order to terminate the study. I was correct, for I received by mail a new research proposal (written by the hospital) detailing an entirely new set of conditions to which I was advised to agree.

No attempt was made to explain why such a new proposal was developed. A note was merely attached to this proposal stating that both my advisor and myself should sign this agreement and return it immediately. While it would be too lengthy to discuss this new proposal in its entirety, suffice it to say that the new additions were simply unacceptable—I was being further restricted in the hospital setting which would make it extremely difficult, if not impossible, to achieve the aims of my research. The document stated that I was to call the ward to arrange a weekly schedule with the ward supervisor when it would be "convenient for the ward to have me."

Moreover, this new proposal stated that, "all records (fieldnotes) will be viewed as the *property* of Springville Psychiatric Hospital and will be treated with respect and discretion"—a condition that I could not agree to under any circumstances.

Further, in another effort to hamper the research process, they drafted a statement downgrading the capabilities of the research and the quality of the study:

> The image of the hospital will be *maintained* and any discussion that fails
> to emphasize the *strengths* of the hospital or tends toward *sensationalism*
> will be avoided.

A final condition of the proposal stressed that the paper resulting from this fieldwork would *not* be published. Under the conditions of our original bargain, at some later date should I decide to do so, I would allow the hospital pre-publication criticism rights, but not control over such rights.

In response to this new proposal, I formulated a letter criticizing *every* element that was unacceptable. I stressed the fact that the institution reneged on our original bargain and attempted a formal *fait a accompli* which represented a serious breech of professional ethics. I emphasized that such a unilateral power play was offensive to both my advisor and myself. I pointed out that I tried to cooperate with the hospital submitting numerous research proposals and that I was subsequently granted access and "cooperation" from the institution. The letter was concluded by stating that this set of violations of our original agreement and the attachment of a new set of conditions reflected unprofessional and unethical conduct unbecoming of representatives of an academically-affiliated institution.

Upon receipt of my letter, the administrative gatekeeper suggested that another meeting take place—this time among the gatekeeper, my advisor, myself, and the medical director of the institution. I was emphatically told that:

> This is not meant to sound like a threat....but we have to get this letter of
> agreement signed (their new proposal) or we'll be forced to terminate
> your placement! (Interview #32)

The institution was asserting its authority one final time—its representatives were no longer interested in negotiating. The issued an ultimatum: either I would agree to the set of conditions outlined in the new proposal or be forced to leave the setting. I received this ultimatum after seven months in the field, after which time I managed to collect a wealth of information regarding the institutionalization of mental patients. Thus, it would not seriously affect the research if the fieldwork was terminated at this point. After discussing the situation with my advisor, it was mutually agreed that the best strategy would be for me to leave the field. I phoned the administrative gatekeeper and informed him that my fieldwork was now complete; therefore, it would not be necessary to have another meeting. In response, the gatekeeper argued:

> Well, I think there is a reason for this meeting...There are so many things that need to be cleared up at this meeting...We have to clear things up regarding publication. Nancy, you may think that you're finished but we have yet to get a letter of agreement saying that you won't publish. Right now, *we have no control over you* and I don't like that....(Interview #33).

This was a final attempt on the part of the institution to gain control over the situation. I stressed that according to our original bargain, it was stated that my immediate aim was not to publish; however, if I should decide to do so, I would allow the hospital pre-publication criticism rights. I emphasized that I had cooperated with the hospital at all times. I had fulfilled every obligation of our original bargain. My fieldwork was now completed; therefore, I saw no reason for further negotiations. I thanked the gatekeeper and said goodbye.

In summary, the preceding discussion focused upon my negotiations and renegotiations with "powerful people" in a "powerful institution."[24] From an interactionist perspective, it represents the continuous struggle between the researcher and the gatekeepers, each party attempting to gain control over "constructions of reality" and "definitions of the situation." From a labelling perspective, it represents an on-going struggle of the "incompetent researcher," a "troublemaker," who, through her research, would undoubtedly destroy the positive image of the hospital.

This bargaining experience lends support to the view that the research bargain is more accurately conceptualized as a continual *process* that occurs throughout the entire research endeavor. While this long series of negotiations and renegotiations was sometimes discouraging and anxiety-provoking for the researcher, in retrospect, this experience was highly instructive about the problematics of negotiations with "powerful people" in "powerful institutions."

REFERENCES

Argyris, C. 1952. "Diagnosing Defenses Against the Outsider." *Journal of Social Issues*, 8:24–34.

Barber, B. 1973. "Research on Human Subjects: Problems of Access to a Powerful Profession." *Social Problems*, 21:103–12.

Becker, H.S. 1964. "Problems in the Publication of Field Studies." Pp. 267–84 IN *Reflections on Community Studies*, edited by A.J. Vidich, J. Bensman, and M.R. Stein. New York: Wiley.

_____. 1970. *Sociological Work: Methods and Substance*. Chicago: Aldine.

Becker, H.S., B. Geer, E.C. Hughes, and A.L. Strauss *Boys in White:* Student Culture in Medical School. Chicago: University of Chicago Press.

Blankenship. R.L. 1977. *Colleagues in Organizations: The Social Construction of Professional Work.* New York: Wiley.

Blau, Peter M. 1963. *The Dynamics of Bureaucracy*. Chicago: University of Chicago Press.

Blumer, H. 1969. *Symbolic Interactionism: Perspective and Method*. New Jersey: Prentice-Hall.

Bogdan, R. 1972. "Learning to Sell Door-to-Door." *The American Behavioral Scientist*, (September/ October): 55–64.

Bogdan, R. and S. Taylor. 1975. *Introduction to Qualitative Research Methods*. New York: Wiley.

Bruyn, S.T. 1966. *The Human Perspective in Sociology: The Methodology of Participant Observation.* New Jersey: Prentice-Hall.

Diamond, S. 1964. "Nigerian Discovery: The Politics of Field Work." Pp.119–54 IN A. Vidach, J. Bensman, and M.R. Stein, editors, *Reflections on Community Studies.* New York: Wiley.

Erikson, K.T. 1957. "Patient Role and Social Uncertainty—A Dilemma of the Mentally Ill." *Psychiatry,* 20(August): 263–74.

_____. 1964. "Notes on the Sociology of Deviance." IN Howard S. Becker (ed.), *The Other Side: Perspectives on Deviance.* New York: The Free Press.

Freidson, E. 1975. *Doctoring Together: A Study of Professional Social Control.* New York: Elsevier.

Geer, B. 1970. "Studying a College." IN Robert Habenstein (ed.), *Pathways to Data.* Chicago: Aldine.

Goffman, E. 1961. *Asylums.* Chicago: Aldine.

Gullahorn, J. and G. Strauss. 1954. "The Field Worker in Union Research."*Human Organization,* 13:28–32.

Haas, J. and W. Shaffir. 1980. "Fieldworkers' Mistakes at Work: Problems in Maintaining Research and Researcher Bargains." Pp. 244–55 IN W. Shaffir, R. Stebbins and A. Turowetz, editors, *Fieldwork Experience: Qualitative Approaches to Social Research.* New York: St. Martin's Press.

Habenstein, R. (ed.) 1970. *Pathways to Data: Field Methods for Studying On-going Social Organizations.* Chicago: Aldine.

Johnson, J.M. 1975. *Doing Field Research.* New York: Free Press.

Keyser, R. 1977. "Becoming a Teacher: Reenacting Yesterday Today for Use Tomorrow." M.A. Thesis. Sociology department, McMaster University.

Larson, M.S. 1977. *The Rise of Professionalism: A Sociological Analysis.* Berkeley: University of California Press.

Lewis, A. 1967. *The State of Psychiatry.* New York: Science House.

Manis, J. and B. Meltzer (eds). 1967. *Symbolic Interaction.* Boston: Allyn and Bacon.

Miller, S.M. 1952. "The Participant Observer and 'Over-Rapport.'" *American Sociological Review* 17:97–9.

Rose, A. 1962. A Systematic Summary of Symbolic Interaction Theory." In A Rose, (ed.),*Human Behavior and Social Processes,* Boston: Houghton Mifflin.

Scheff, T. 1966. *Being Mentally Ill.* Chicago: Aldine.

_____. 1967. *Mental Illness and Social Processes.* New York: Harper and Row.

_____. 1975. *Labeling Madness.* New Jersey: Prentice-Hall.

Schwab, J. and M. Schwab. 1978. *Sociocultural Roots of Mental Illness: An Epidemiologic Survey.* New York: Plenum.

Schwartz, M.S. and C.G. Schwartz. 1955. "Problems in Participant Observation." *American Journal of Sociology* 60:343–54.

Siegler, M. and H. Osmond. 1974. *Models of Madness, Models of Medicine.* New York: MacMillan Publishing Company.

Spradley, J.P. and D.W. McCurdy. 1975. *Anthropology: The Cultural Perspective.* New York: Wiley and Sons.

Wax, R. 1952. "Reciprocity as a Field Technique." *Human Organization* 11:34–7.

Whybrow, P.C. 1972. "The Use and Abuse of the 'Medical Model' as a Conceptual Frame in Psychiatry." *Psychiatry in Medicine* 3:333–42.

Whyte, W.F. 1955. *Street Corner Society.* Chicago: University of Chicago Press.

Zimmerman, D.H. 1966. "Paper Work and People Work." Ph.D. dissertation, Department of Sociology, University of California, Los Angeles.

NOTES

[1]See Becker, et. al., (1961); Begde, (1972):55–64; Geer,(1970); Keyser, (1977).

[2]See for example, Haas and Shaffir, (1980):244–55; Habenstein, (1970); Whyte, (1955); Zimmerman, (1966).

[3] These variables include: the nature of the research project (whether it is overt or covert), the organization of the research setting, the personality of the fieldworker, and whether the subjects feel that the potential project will be "beneficial" to them. For a detailed discussion of these and other variables affecting access, see Johnson, (1975):50–81.; and Shaffir et. al., eds., (1980): 23–29.

[4] Becker (1970).

[5] See for example, Argyris, (1952):24–34; Blau (1963); Diamond, (1964); Gullahorn and Strauss (1954):28–32; Haas and Shaffir, (1980): 244–55; Habenstein (1970).

[6] See Geer, (1970): 81–96; and Haas and Shaffir, op. cit.

[7] From September, 1979 to August, 1980, fieldwork was conducted on institutionalized psychiatric patients at a state mental hospital in Southern Ontario, Canada, herein designated as "Springville Psychiatric Hospital." In order to gather data on the social worlds of institutionalized patients, participant observation was conducted on an "admission ward" in this facility. The ward had a fluctuating patient population of between forty to eighty patients, both male and female, ranging in age from seventeen to mid-seventies. The length of stay on this ward varied from a few weeks to several months, after which they were either discharged or transferred to another ward for further treatment. In terms of the admission status of the patients, the ward contained a mixture of "first admissions" and "readmissions", the majority of which were admitted involuntarily

[8] See Blankenship (1977); Friedson (1975); Haas and Shaffir, op. cit., and Larson (1975).

[9] Bogdan and Taylor (1975): 34 suggest that it is the best strategy to outline the study in *general* terms. "Observers need not explain their substantive or theoretical interests or their specific techniques in great detail. In fact, it is probably unwise for researchers to volunteer elaborate details concerning the precision with which notes will be taken."

[10] See Zimmerman, op. cit. for a discussion of similar problems faced when attempting to gain access.

[11] For a discussion of the medical model of mental illness, see: Siegler and Osmond (1974); Schwab and Schwab (1978); Lewis, (1967):179–94; Whybrow (1972).

[12] For a discussion of the sociological model of mental illness, see: Erikson (1957), (1964), (1966); Goffman (1961), Scheff, (1966), (1967), (1975).

[13] Gatekeepers often ask how *they* (the institution) will benefit from the research project. This question was frequently asked of me during my negotiations and renegotiations with the gatekeepers. Researchers (both anthropologists and sociologists) are often criticized for going into the field, collecting data on aspects of human behavior, leaving the field and then writing their data—without giving the people under investigation anything in return. Due to this fact, coupled with the persistence of the gatekeepers, I felt an obligation to give the institution something in return; thus, I offered to give the institutional officials a copy of the resulting study as well as an oral presentation of my findings to the ward staff, in order that both parties would benefit from the research experience.

[14] This action is an illustration of an institution's attempt to "pass the buck." Because the research project was incompatible with the interests of the institution, its representatives actively attempted to "channel" my interests elsewhere.

[15] For a discussion of this "give and take" of the exchange process, see: Johnson (1975).

[16] For a discussion of the interactionist perspective, see: Blumer (1969); Rose (1962); Manis and Meltzer (1967).

[17] Johnson, op cit., contends that it is a good strategy to take along publications of the researcher, along with articles that outline the (where's the rest of this endnote, Nancy-pooh?)

[18] See Haas and Shaffir (1980):244–55 for a similar discussion.

[19] For a similar discussion regarding misconceived researcher aims and identities, see: Johnson (1975):71–2.

[20] Every time I went to do fieldwork on the ward, I was forced to explain my identity to each of the staff. The ward staff operated on a rotation basis whereby each month they were transferred to another ward—thus, each time I arrived, I was confronted with an entirely different set of "ward gatekeepers" who were unaware of my identity and the aims of the study. As a result, I was forced to spend time explaining to them who I was and what I was doing on the ward—actions which threatened to destroy the thrust of the patients that I had worked so hard to establish. Specifically, my interaction with the staff was interpreted by the patients as being traitorous and it was only through perseverance that I was able to regain my informants' trust.

[21] For a discussion on the subject of "going native" or "over-rapport," see: Spradley and McCurdy (1975):60; Miller (1952:97–9).

[22] See Bruyn (1966); and Schwartz and Schwartz (1955):343–54.

[23] Each of these concerns was fully dealt with previously and resolved. Yet at subsequent meetings, the gatekeepers raised these same problems.

[24] For a discussion regarding similar problems of gaining access, see: Barber (1973):103–12; Habenstein (1970); Haas and Shaffir (1978).

Chapter 18

PERSONAL SAFETY IN DANGEROUS PLACES

Terry Williams
Eloise Dunlap
Bruce D. Johnson
Ansley Hamid

A serious problem confronting many social scientists is assuring the physical safety of ethnographers and other staff conducting research among potentially violent persons who are active in dangerous settings. Of equal concern is attempting to assure the personal safety of potential research subjects. Even when extensive ethnographic experience shows that physical violence against ethnographers has rarely occurred, researchers may have considerable difficulty convincing others (including colleagues and family members) that they can safely conduct fieldwork.

Some ethnographic research may be a dangerous enterprise. Howell's (1990) discussion of safety offered an extensive discussion of common law crimes (robbery, theft, rape) in the field. Field-workers have encountered illness, injury, or death in the course of fieldwork due to natural and criminal causes. It is often unclear whether the fieldworkers were harmed by research subjects and other members of the social networks or whether they were merely victimized like any other citizen (Howell, 1990).

The question of personal safety is rarely addressed as a methodological issue in its own right (Howell, 1990; Sluka, 1990), particularly in regard to the social milieu in which ethnographers carry out their work. There is relatively little discussion about how to minimize risks and dangers that ethnographers may face in the field, with suggestions to help ensure their personal safety. Some hints about safety may be gleaned from the extensive methodological literature in ethnography (Agar, 1980; Fetterman, 1989) that deals with such topics as gaining access and recruiting subjects (Johnson, 1990), striking a research bargain (Carey, 1972), entering the field, making observations (Broadhead and Fox, 1990), selecting roles to pursue in the field (Adler and Adler, 1987), building and maintaining rapport (Dunlap et al., 1990; Rose, 1990), conducting interviews (McCracken, 1988), and writing field notes (Fetterman, 1989). In practice, paying attention to the personal safety of ethnographers goes hand in hand with learning and applying skills in these areas.

The lack of good guidelines and methodological strategies for conducting safe ethnographic fieldwork in potentially violent social settings is especially noteworthy. In one of the few articles addressing safety issues, Sluka (1990) provided a systematic discussion of the risks and dangers facing ethnographers in a politically charged, potentially violent setting by studying supporters of the Irish Republican Army in Belfast. His suggestions are strikingly relevant for ethnographers in the substance abuse field and for those who study street- and upper-level crack dealers. Sluka (1990:115) called for "foresight, planning, skillful maneuver, and a conscious effort at impression management" to minimize personal risk and danger in potentially violent settings. He further suggested that field-workers become well-acquainted in the community, cultivate well-respected persons who vouch for them, avoid contacts with police, be truthful about the purpose of the research, and be flexible concerning research objectives. He proposed that successful fieldwork in dangerous settings "can be done by recognizing how people are likely to define you, avoiding acting in ways that might reinforce these suspicions, and being as honest and straightforward as possible about who you really are and what you are really doing" (Sluka, 1990:121).

Sluka's advice about personal safety is among the best available at the present time. In this article we will conceptually extend and apply his and others' (e.g. Adler and Adler, 1987; Denzin, 1970; Douglas, 1972) ideas to ethnographic research in inner-city settings. We focus on issues of personal safety while conducting fieldwork in potentially dangerous settings. Closely related ethnographic issues—rapport, recruiting subjects, ethnographer roles, reciprocity, personal experiences with contacts, and so on—are briefly included in the discussion. While recognizing that ours is but one approach to doing ethnographic research we contribute to the literature on ethnographic methods by underscoring themes and practices for personal safety that may be of interest to all ethnographers and staff conducting research in dangerous settings—or even in "safe" settings.

Method

This article emerges from the authors' many years of experience in conducting both quantitative (Johnson, 1973; Elmoghazy and Dunlap, 1990; Johnson, et al., 1985, 1988) and qualitative (Carpenter et al., 1988; Dunlap, 1988; Dunlap et al., 1990; Hamid, 1979, 1990, 1992; Johnson, Hamid, and Sanabria, 1991; Williams, 1978, 1989, 1991; Williams and Kornblum, 1985) research among abusers and sellers of marijuana, heroin, cocaine, and crack. All of the authors have done much of their work among low-income and minority populations (Dunlap, et al., 1990; Hamid, 1990; Johnson, et al., 1985; Johnson, Williams, et al., 1990; Williams, 1989, 1991; Williams and Kornblum, 1985). These professional ethnographers (Dunlap, Hamid, Sanabria, and Williams) have extensive experience in qualitative field research on drug-related issues and other topics in New York City, Latin America, and the Caribbean. Four staff members (Arnold, Beddoe, Randolf, and Miller) are ex-drug users and/or ex-dealers who developed wide networks among upper-level dealers. Collectively, the staff have many years of experience working in or researching various aspects of drug use and dealing. The authors are professional researchers and ethnographers whose primary careers are built around research funded by grants. We recognize that many academic ethnographers do not have resources for hiring staff, paying subjects, and other support available via grants.[1] Yet the strategies and approaches reported here are vital for and applicable to our academic colleagues in that they have been assembled from years of professional ethnographic experience in dangerous locations.

Building on this experience, we systematically trained staff members on issues of personal safety during an ongoing study called "Natural History of Crack Distribution."[2] This was a qualitative study about the structure and functioning of crack distribution, including the careers of dealers in New York City (Johnson, Williams, et al., 1990; Johnson, et al., 1991). During the fieldwork phase of this study, November 1989–March 1991, the ethnographic staff spent an average of 15–20 hours per week in several of New York City's most dangerous locales interacting with numerous street people. Staff members conducted intensive fieldwork in four New York City neighborhoods (Harlem, Washington Heights, Brownsville, and Williamsburg). They wrote field notes that contain observations and references to over 300 different crack distributors. They also conducted open-ended life history interviews (5–15 hours long) with 80 distributors. Fifteen of these were upper-level dealers buying and selling kilograms of cocaine; the remainder were independent sellers. To obtain this information, they conducted three or more sessions with most dealers. All interviews were recorded and transcribed. Our data and analyses rely on the strategies and experiences of ourselves and our ethnographic staff for maintaining their own personal safety as well as on specific experiences reported by other ethnographers in the drug abuse field.

Laypeople and ethnographers anticipate and are fearful about several potential sources of physical danger associated with the use and sale of crack (Brownstein and Goldstein, 1990a, 1990b; Goldstein, 1985; Goldstein, et al., 1990, 1991a, 1991b; *New York Newsday*, 1990; *New York Times*, 1990a, 1990b; *Washington Post*, 1990): Crack abusers may be paranoid and behave irrationally; dealers routinely use violence and may threaten subjects who talk to ethnographers; use of guns lead to "random" shootings; researchers may be robbed or have articles stolen. The mass media typically feature the most violent and extreme activities of crack distributors (Reinarman and Levine, 1989), so laypersons are led to believe that severe violence occurs all the time in this business. Despite these fears, ethnographic research in dangerous settings has been safely conducted for years. Our staff and many other researchers (Adler, 1985; Biernacki, 1988; Feldman, 1974; Goldstein, et al., 1990; Hanson, et al., 1985; Spunt, 1988; Morales, 1989; Smith and Kornblum, 1991) have met, talked with, and interviewed many potentially violent persons over long periods and have *never* been physically assaulted.[3]

Styles of Safety

Researchers can create "safety zones" in which to conduct research in dangerous settings so as to protect themselves and the persons with whom they are interacting from physical harm or violence during the research endeavor. The following sections are organized according to conceptual themes regarding styles of safety that emphasize demeanor, protector roles, safety zones, neutrality, and common sense during fieldwork.

Style and Demeanor

Style and demeanor are central to safety. First impressions are very important. Wearing clothes appropriate to the setting prevents drawing undue attention and exhibits a sense of belonging in the setting. Researchers' attire can be viewed as an extension and manifestation of their personalities as well as a willingness to fit into the social setting. As ethnographers enter and attempt to establish a presence in the field, they explain the purpose of research, exhibit personal interest in others, and avoid drug use or sales (Adler and Adler, 1987; Agar, 1980; Horowitz, 1986; Johnson, 1990). Failure to establish this presence, and especially being perceived as a victim, by those in the drug business for instance, may greatly increase personal dangers of theft/robbery and difficulty in establishing rapport with potential subjects. Although various roles have been employed by ethnographers in a variety of settings (Becker, 1960; Adler and Adler, 1987), those conducting field research among drug abusers generally employ a variation of friendly stranger (Agar, 1980) or friendly outsider. This role is partially mandated by a professional code of ethics forbidding illegal behavior[4] and institutional requirements to obtain informed consent from research subjects.

Purpose and Access

Once accepted as an ordinary person in the area, initial conversations are the first step in seeking persons with whom to develop rapport. Williams has been conducting research among cocaine users since 1974. During a 17–year career, he has visited hundreds of after-hours clubs, base houses, crack houses (Williams, 1978, 1989, 1991), number holes,[5] and other settings where illegal and legal activities occur. Williams explained several strategies for gaining entry into such locales:[6]

> Initially I prefer to be taken into a crack house or dealing location by someone who is known there. They vouch that I'm OK and no cop. When initially approaching a crack house without someone to introduce me, I'll claim to be sent by someone they may know, like Robby, KeeKay, or someone else with a common street name. When I get inside, I may explain that I am writing a book on crack houses (or another topic). I usually have a copy of a book I've written to show people. This approach goes a long way toward convincing skeptical persons that I'm an author and serious about my intentions.

After gaining initial entry and some rapport with one or more persons in the setting, Dunlap found it necessary to arrange a meeting with one or more drug dealers to explain herself, to seek their permission and informed consent to conduct long life-history interviews, and to strike the research bargain (see Carey, 1972). The dealers can also examine the project's Certificate of Confidentiality.[7] Dunlap explained:

> I begin by telling them about myself, my life, and why I'm interested in them. I spend much time explaining how their identity will be concealed and how our interviews will be protected and never be available to police or law enforcement agencies. I explain the risks and benefits of the research to them in terms of their participation and obtain their informed

consent. Even after these lengthy explanations, most subjects tend to remain tense and somewhat terse in their answers. Only during and after the first session of the in-depth interview do they begin to relax and talk openly about themselves. Such conversations would not even begin, however, without the assurances of confidentiality and the promise of benefits.

The end result is that ethnographers have built substantial rapport with one or more persons, carefully explained the purpose of the research, provided assurances of protection and safety, and obtained informed consent from persons who will become potential research subjects. Of course, the ethnographer must continue to meet with and show a genuine personal interest and friendliness to such persons. Such further conversations and interactions help build strong rapport with subjects.

The "Victim" Role

As ethnographers, we need a "mind set" that assumes safety and does not lead to fearful behavior. Street people act on their intuitions and are experts in reading behavior. Dunlap expressed the critical importance of not being perceived as a victim ("vic"):

> The ethnographer's state of mind on entering the field must not include fear about studying violent people; at least such fears must not be at the front of one's mind. Overconcern about violence may cause ethnographers to appear afraid or react inappropriately to common street situations and dangers that do not involve themselves. Fearful behavior is easily inferred by violent persons from the way one walks and the way one interacts with others. Fearful behavior may place an ethnographer in the "vic" category to be targeted by others as a true victim of crimes like robbery and assault.

Not exhibiting fearful behavior does not mean abandoning choices about a sensible course of action. Rather, the mindset we have found appropriate is cautious, friendly, understanding, and open. This mindset emphasizes a degree of determination and self-confidence that does not leave room for ethnographers to be labeled as "vics." Likewise, *not* using or selling drugs is also important for avoiding the "vic" role. If potential subjects observe ethnographers buying or selling illicit drugs, they may be suspected of being undercover agents, or expect them to be potential customers, or people who will share or provide drugs. Further decisions about whether to enter specific locales or meet certain persons must be made deliberately and based on the other themes discussed below.

Locator and Protector Roles

Two roles are especially important in conducting research among upper-level and in many instances among lower-level drug sellers. The roles of *locator* and *protector* are vital to the safety of persons working in the illicit drug industry. Locating the individuals who can perform these roles can be critical to ethongoraphers' safety with and access to upper-level dealers. The ethnographic literature (Agar, 1980; Johnson, 1990; Liebow, 1967; Whyte, 1955, 1984) provides advice about finding one or more key informants who can provide access to others in the setting and who give much information about the phenomena being studied. Classical ethnographers have assumed that such representatives can be found or that they will come forth voluntarily so that ethnographers need only cultivate and build rapport with them.

Crack sellers and upper-level dealers, however, have very good reasons to insulate their identities, locales, and illegal activities from everyone (excepting their trusted co-workers). They are concerned with avoiding detection and arrest and with preventing robbery or injury by other street persons. They systematically evade conversations that may build close relationships (Adler, 1985). Yet to conduct their business safely, they must rely on others who perform a variety of roles such as steerers, touts, guards, lookouts, connections, runners, and muscle men (Johnson, Williams et al., 1990; Johnson et al., 1991).[8] Approaching a crack dealer directly (without an intermediary) threatens the dealer, as it proves his identity is known or suspected. Ethnographers will always be suspected initially of being a "cop" or an "informer," thus elevating the probability of personal risk and possible harm from the dealer or his associates.

Ethnographers can seek access to drug dealers through someone performing a *locator role* and rely on others to play a *protector role* as access is gained. Experience has indicated that access to crack dealers was most successful when ethnographers worked with a highly trusted former associate of the dealer who performed both the locator and the protector roles. The same person, however, need not perform both roles.

Critical in studies with drug dealers is someone who will perform the locator role of introducing the ethnographers into a setting where dealers are present. Recovered substance abusers who have had management roles in drug-selling organizations or have been incarcerated for several years for drug distribution crimes are particularly valuable in such roles. These ex-dealers typically have a large network of current sellers and dealers, know how to negotiate with active dealers, and can be trained to assist with fieldwork. They can locate and introduce ethnographers to several dealers (the locator role), provide protection in dangerous settings (the protector role), become systematic observers and interviewers (field-worker or interviewer role), and explain many of the informally understood norms to a professional ethnographer (the "expert" role).[9]

Proper Introductions

At the early stages of fieldwork among crack sellers, ethnographers generally do not attempt to enter a setting alone. Someone familiar with the locale is recruited or hired to assist in arranging "proper introductions" of the ethnographers to dealers as well as to provide protection. As a paraprofessional staff member, Arnold contacted several dealers and helped arrange interviews with our ethnographers. He stated that

152   DEVIANCE

"the contact person has a major affect for the ethnographer upon people in the setting." From his network of acquaintances, he had initial contacts and helped persuade dealers to talk with the ethnographer.

Another paraprofessional, Beddoe, explained why and how proper introductions occur among street dealers:

> They [good contact persons] tend to have contact across time in the given area. Most street dealers are middle men. They will continue to work together and routinely rely on each other. Introductions by one dealer who vouches to other dealers that someone is "right" and "not a cop" is a vital part of street life and everyday dealing hustles. If an ethnographer gets a positive reference from a dealer, another dealer will still be a little suspicious. They study how you handle yourself in the field and then decide whether to talk more.

Having the appropriate person provide an introduction to a dealer is vital. Group members respond according to the reputation of the individual who provides the introduction. If that person is not trusted, the ethnographer will not be trusted. Dunlap's field notes recorded why she was unable to gain access to several dealers in one Harlem block:

> My early contact on this block was Chief, a female who worked for several dealers, mainly as a "fill-in-seller" at the street level. Chief had committed some act which had deemed her untrustworthy to most of her suppliers. She was only trusted to sell small portions of drugs at a time, never large amounts. When she attempted to introduce me to one of her bosses, it was disastrous. The dealer refused to even meet me. Seeing this, other street sellers whom I had informally met at the same time ceased interacting with me. From this and other experiences, I learned that lower-level crack users/dealers can seldom provide good introduction to their bosses or suppliers.

When a respected and trusted former dealer provided the introduction to other dealers only a few blocks away, several meetings and interviews were the outcome. Arnold reported:

> I contacted several dealers who had trusted me because we had done prison time for drug sales. After explaining the study to them, they were willing to attend a meeting. I set up the meetings and got them there, so that she [Dunlap] could explain it in more detail and build some relationship with them. This resulted in several interviews.

Dunlap reflected on her experience with recruitment of several upper-level dealers:

Contact with middle- and upper-level dealers comes only through the dealer's trusted and limited circle who continuously work to assure his personal safety. Although the dealer may be known by several persons in his or her area, a "proper introduction" of the ethnographer to the dealer can only be provided by someone the dealer trusts.[10] Only through that person will an initial audience be granted, so to speak. The trusted contact is someone who has worked with the dealer for many years (either working directly with the dealer or selling drugs at the same time). Prison is also an important place where dealers have met persons whom they can trust as "safe." One dealer commented, "Serving time tells what a man is made of." The norms among prisoners and ex-prisoners eliminated the chance that the individual is an informant or an undercover cop.

The Protector

Ethnographers usually assume that they do not need protection from persons in a social setting. In the context of the drug business, this usual assumption is false; everyone must arrange protection to assure their personal safety. Once ethnographers are properly introduced into a setting, finding someone to perform the protector role is usually not difficult. Everyone in a drug dealer's network is expected to "watch backs" (i.e., help each other avoid possible dangers). Even freelance sellers competing for customers on the same block quickly reach agreement to "divide up" the territory and to "watch backs" for each other in case of physical danger (Johnson, et al., 1991). Williams reported:

> In every field setting, some person always appears to perform a protector role and "watches the back" of the ethnographer; he discourages violence among others in the setting "because the Man [ethnographer] is here." If I leave the street for a month, it feels like a year. I need to maintain regular visits. Because I rely on them for protection, my best protectors in the street are enemies of the police: drug dealers, con men, robbers.

After gaining experience in similar settings, ethnographers can enter another site and expect to rapidly encounter someone who will perform the protector role. Usually, the protector will be among the first to speak to the ethnographer. In the event that a protector does not emerge or cannot be found (see "safety zone" next), or if a feeling of safety is lacking (see "sixth sense" below), researchers are encouraged to leave that setting.

Field Roles

Ethnographers have an anomalous position that potential contacts may find unfamiliar or unclear. While conducting field research, they occupy roles that are "betwixt and between" (Jackson, 1990) their own professional roles and the roles enacted by potential subjects in the field setting. The dual role of observer and participant (Adler and Adler, 1987) played by the friendly outsider (Agar, 1980) is unfamiliar to most subjects. Rather, subjects tend to project familiar roles unto ethnographers.

In fact, field roles are fluid and changing during a typical day and during the course of the field research (Denzin, 1970; Spradley, 1980). In conversation and interaction with individual subjects and groups, ethnographers can listen closely for the roles that others assign to them. This is helpful in designing one or more field roles that are compatible with the research, yet understood by subjects and protectors. During this study, several subjects referred to Dunlap as "auntie," "mom," "sister," or other fictive kin; Williams was perceived as "book author" and a "sharp dude;" Hamid and Curtis (1990) were "voyeurs" when conducting research in a "freakhouse" (where crack use and sexual activity occur). These subject-assigned roles were effective because they permitted access to the setting, were used by the protector to briefly explain the ethnographer's presence, and permitted informal conversation, questioning, and direct observations to occur—without suspicion that the ethnographer was a cop or a police informer.

As a single female living in a crack dealing neighborhood, Dunlap did not want research subjects to know where she lived, but she had to return home during early morning hours when only drug dealers and street people were awake. Dunlap described how she created and maintained a "right citizen" role with five regular crack dealers who helped assure her safety when she returned home very late:

> I first observed who had the most respect from others and who appeared to have control over various situations—this was usually crack dealers. Then I walked by and said, "How you doing?" and engaged in "nonsensical" conversations about such things as the music on the street, street language, the drunk leaning against a fire hydrant. We avoided conversations about what they were doing or about what I did. I also avoided talking to the drug users. By being friendly with the drug dealers, hey quickly accepted me as someone who would do them no harm. In return, they protected me in little ways. For example, one night after speaking briefly to my local dealer, a crack user began to approach me for some money; the dealer told her to "move on" and not bother me. If some threatening situation were to arise, I feel certain they would act to protect me or intervene if necessary.

Dunlap also practiced this role in other research settings when interacting with persons who were not to be approached as research subjects.

During the past 6 years, many ethnographers and paraprofessionals have assumed the role of health worker doing outreach on AIDS prevention projects (e.g., Broadhead and Fox, 1990). The "AIDS outreach worker" is an effective street role for ethnographers; it has become well known and respected among street people in several communities. The AIDS outreach worker role clearly "sides" with subjects and potential subjects and provides a basis for interaction with a variety of persons. Such persons express concern about subjects' health, facilitate referrals to other health service agencies, and help ethnographers to avoid being seen in a law enforcement role.

Safety Zones

When conducting research in settings that may be dangerous, or among persons who may be suspicious or hostile toward researchers, a first order of business is to create and maintain a physical and social environment in which ethnographers and potential subjects accept each other's presence.

In settings where many persons are present, effort should be made to include several persons as protectors in a safety zone. This is conceptualized as a physical area extending a few feet around the researcher, in which researchers and other persons within this area feel comfortable. The safety zone has three major components. First, researchers must have a feeling of "psychological safety"; that is, they must not feel endangered, they must experience some degree of acceptance by others, and they must be willing to stay in the location (see "sixth sense"). Second, other persons in this zone should accept the ethnographers' presence, trusting that they are "right" and "not a cop." Third, the physical environment must not be hazardous (e.g., the floors should not be likely to collapse; the ceiling should not be likely to fall).[11]

When entering a locale, ethnographers can quickly scan the physical environment for obvious signs of danger. They should test steps and flooring, especially in abandoned buildings, and be cognizant of all exits. By introducing ethnographers to others at the site, the protector can facilitate social acceptance. Ethnographers must then establish their own right to be present in the locale during subsequent conversation with others. Such interaction typically brings about an implicit (and sometimes explicit) agreement, thus creating a shared sense of psychological acceptance or a "safety zone."

During the initial visit to a setting, ethnographers can state plans to return in the future and attempt to judge how others in the locale feel about this. If a good relationship has been developed with a key person at the site (apartment resident, owner/manager of a crack house, street dealer), ethnographers can return to the location without the initial contact and rely on people in the setting to provide protection and help maintain the safety zone. Beddoe suggested:

> Look at how they talk with each other, and how they deal with each other, and try to copy their style. This will help you get to other people in the social circle. Any conversation is generally better than none.

When entering a new setting, Dunlap generally located potential exits and figured out who was in charge:

> This is accomplished in a subtle and gradual way in order not to cause suspicion or make anyone feel they are being watched. I call this getting the feeling of the place, people, and conditions. Try to fit in by taking a

comfortable stance, giving the impression of familiarity with various situations or scenarios.

Williams usually created the safety zone by paying careful attention to the setting and peoples' activities:

> Use your own style and smooth approach. Usually don't be aggressive. Try to figure who is available for a conversation and talk to them when [they're] ready; otherwise wait. They communicate with each other via certain physical gestures which can be learned, especially when "thirsty" for smoke [crack]. Let them know that you really want to talk to other people and meet others. You don't want to create enemies out in the field. You have to be constantly improvisational in the setting. Don't overstay your welcome. Three to 4 hours in one place is too long, so move on. You have to be aware of who you are [a researcher] and where you are at. This is not a recreational place; it is a place where you are conducting research but others are buying and selling illegal cocaine. One should follow the rules of the street—which is surviving.

As rapport with persons in such settings is increased, a safety zone is created among those present. Norms usually include strong expectations of reciprocity. Dunlap described how she responded to these expectations:

> Be counted on to "do the right thing" for them personally, even though [you're] not taking part in what is happening (you do not sell or smoke crack). I was always prepared to participate in ethically more appropriate exchanges. I would accept a cigarette but more frequently provided them to those present. I would provide food or coffee that was shared by all or help a person read something. On the other hand, I avoided sharing drugs and declined to chip in to buy drugs.

This safety zone is a short-term agreement among persons in a concrete locale about the right of other persons to be present. Such temporary agreements do not imply that the potential subjects present have provided ethnographers with informed consent, acceptance, rapport, or a willingness to be interviewed. The safety zone only provides a locale and time during which ethnographers can begin to obtain further cooperation from some of those present.

Humor and Neutrality

Even when ethnographers function within a safety zone, a variety of tense interactions and situations may arise in specific locales. The effective use of humor and neutrality in these settings by ethnographers may also have important benefits for persons in these settings.

Ethnographers' neutrality in tense social situations is well described (Fetterman, 1989; Agar, 1980; Adler and Adler, 1987), but it is sometimes a source of tension between their subjects and themselves (Broadhead and Fox, 1990). Humor can defuse such tense situations and build solidarity among group members (Seckman and

Couch, 1989). Less well documented is the way in which humor and neutrality may help in dangerous situations (Carpenter et al., 1988).

Crack houses and drug-dealing locales are characterized by high levels of mistrust, paranoia, and potential violence. At the same time, these locales are at least partially organized to reduce violence and informally control persons (*New York Times*, 1991) who act aggressively. Hamid described the dangers:

> In crack houses, users constantly argue and accuse others of using too much or hiding or stealing crack or money. Street sellers face frequent arguments about money, the quality of crack or other drugs, threats of robbery, and other topics. Usually these arguments are resolved by the disputants reaching some kind of agreement, but other persons (guards, boss, owner) may occasionally intervene if the argument begins to escalate to physical violence.

After establishing a safety zone and acquiring protectors, ethnographers in a crack house or crack sale location may introduce an element of stability and safety. Ethnographers are not under the influence of drugs or alcohol and can think swiftly and clearly. They do not want to buy crack or sell drugs or to be used for such purposes. They are neutral in the various disputes between persons and attempt to maintain communication with all. They have requested and generally been granted protection and safety while in the location. Moreover, ethnographers are sophisticated in interpersonal relationships and can deal with tense situations. Hamid described how he sometimes intervenes:

> When two crackheads are arguing about who got the most crack or stole it [the truth is, they've both used it up], and the dispute is heading toward a physical fight, I begin telling an outrageously funny story that has nothing to do with the conflict. The disputants are distracted from their conflict, they laugh and separate; usually the dispute is forgotten. Humor is a major way that tense arguments between crackheads or distributors may be resolved without blows and without any loss of face by either party.

Dunlap explained how she has deliberate conversations with crack users while they are "straight" to reduce the potential for subsequent violence:

> Many crack users try to convince themselves and others that they drug does not affect them. They claim their behavior remains the same after they smoke crack as it is before they smoke crack. I always bring this discussion up when the individual is sober, before he or she has ingested any drug. When their behavior begins to change after smoking, I can usually bring them back to normal behavior by remarking that they are acting differently by smoking crack. Persons will try to prove that the drug does not affect them in various ways, and that they can handle the drug. While restating these claims, they generally abandon the various

kinds of behavior associated with crack intoxication. Also, I never take sides in any disagreement. Let the situation work itself out. If I feel the situation is becoming too dangerous, I leave.

By remaining neutral but interested parties, ethnographers gain respect from people in these settings. In many potentially violent situations, ethnographers may be the only "neutral" person who is not high and may become a mediator between individuals and groups. Such neutrality involves not engaging in personal (especially sexual) relationships with subjects during the study as well as avoiding alignment with only one group. Ethnographers' personal "safety zone" is frequently extended to protect subjects and potential subjects from the possible dangers that their own behavior and willingness to use violence may bring about. Thus the presence of ethnographers probably reduces the risk of violence among crack users and sellers in crack houses and dealing locations rather than increasing the potential for violence.

"Sixth Sense" and Common Sense

Not all conflicts and issues in dangerous settings can be resolved by neutrality and humor. Ethnographers need to be prepared to respond effectively in a variety of potentially dangerous circumstances (paranoia, sexual approaches, robbery, theft, shootings, police raids, and arrests) that actually occur infrequently but are a major fear among nonethnographers. Reliance on prudence, common sense, and a "sixth sense" can help reduce physical violence to a minimum. Different kinds of potentially dangerous situations can be handled by evasion and movement away from the danger, controlled confrontation, or rapid departure from the setting. The ability to handle a variety of situations requires both a "sixth sense" for danger and skill in moving away from and evading physical harm. Dunlap provided an illustration:

> Acting from the "sixth sense" is relatively easy. We use it all the time in everyday life when we walk into new situations. There is an uneasiness, an inability to verbalize what is wrong. You may be able to explain everything that is taking place, do not see anything out of the ordinary, but still feel uncomfortable. This is a warning that something may go wrong. When such discomfort occurs, leave as soon as possible. For example, I had planned to hang around Ross and his family on a particular weekend. Each time I made preparations to leave, this uneasy feeling arose—I did not want to go and could not explain it, so I did not see him until the following week. Upon arrival, Ross reported that one of his partners had been shot and killed. If I had gone that weekend, I might have been next to Ross, who was sitting beside his drug-selling partner when the latter was shot by the father of a crack customer.

When and if ethnographers get a feeling of discomfort without reason, they will be safer by leaving the setting and returning another time—even though they may fail to gather some data and violence may not actually occur. But if their "sixth sense" has extracted them from the locale, they will not be harmed during those rare occasions when serious violence does occur.

Crack-Related Paranoia

Cocaine and crack induce a short-term paranoia in which users are very suspicious of others around them. They may believe others are enemies out to arrest or harm them. If challenged, pushed, or threatened, they may become unreasonably aggressive or violent. Yet crack users opt for avoidance and nonconfrontation to handle such short-term paranoia exhibited by other crack users. Williams has dealt with crack induced paranoia in many settings:

> When people are smoking crack, they go through different stages, one of which is paranoia. The crackhead may comment, "I don't like to be around people who don't get high" or "Why are you watching me?" This person may even be your sponsor or protector but is no longer the rational person you came with. The easy solution is to move away and not watch. Above all else, don't confront or challenge them. Usually you can find another person who is in a talkative stage where they want to talk. After a while, the first person's paranoia will subside and the person is open to conversation again—with no or little recollection of his comments or implicit threats while high.

Sexual Approaches

While using crack, a person may express a desire for physical closeness or sexual intimacy and approach others (including the ethnographer) for satisfaction. Williams explained how he responded to various levels of physical closeness:

> There are touchers; persons who seek affection while they ingest drugs and smoke crack. They seek such affection and closeness when they get high, just before the effect wears off. Usually, I just move away or shift to conversation with someone else. What do you do when sexually approached? Be forceful and let them know that you aren't available for sex play; they usually will not pursue it further.

Several female ethnographers have had their fieldwork severely constrained or have had to terminate it completely (Horowitz, 1986; Adler and Adler, 1987; Howell, 1990; Warren, 1989) due to the sexual expectations and demands of subjects or other males in the research setting. The threat of sexual assault or rape is a real concern for most female ethnographers and staff members. As a woman, Dunlap followed several strategies to reduce vulnerability to sexual approaches:

Smoking crack causes many individuals to be stimulated sexually. Yet when first developing rapport, potential subjects frequently assign a fictive-kin-role.[12] I may seem like a sister, cousin, mother, or aunt to them. Assuming such roles leads individuals to become "close friends" and share many behaviors they would not otherwise exhibit. When projecting such roles to me, they place me "off limits" for sexual approaches and affairs. Enough crack-using women are available for sexual affairs; neither male nor female subjects need me for sex and usually agree to protect me from advances by others. The crack-sex link focuses on the sexual act, not personal relationships. Even women who routinely exchange sex for crack or money will refuse sexual foreplay and intimacy for short periods during their crack consumption cycles; both men and women leave them alone at those times.

The value of the protector role was evident one evening while Dunlap was observing several prostitutes with whom she had established good rapport:

I was standing on the sidewalk talking with Lisa (a prostitute who used crack), when a John (customer) drove up and started talking dirty to us. Lisa talked back to him while I listened. When Lisa said she wants $20 for a blowjob, the man replied, "I don't want you. How much is she [referring to me]?" Lisa exploded: "She ain't one of us. You leave her alone and keep your fuckin' hands off her ." She started kicking and pounding the car. The man looked surprised and drove off quickly.

Abandoned Buildings and Other Dangerous Locales

Most ethnographic research is conducted where the physical environment is structurally safe. Assuming such safety can be dangerous when researchers are studying crack dealers. Crack dealers may set booby traps to slow police or potential robbers. The sale and use of crack often occurs in abandoned buildings, rundown tenements, and hidden locations (e.g., under bridges or tunnels). Such locations are best approached only with a protector who knows it well. Even then, visits should occur only when the ethnographer feels comfortable. Dunlap recalled her trepidations:

A street contact said, "Let's go to a place where a friend lives. I'm doing this as a favor to you." She took me into an abandoned building where her friend gave us a back room. I could have been robbed. But nothing happened. The interview went well but the place was unheated and filthy. On other occasions, I have rented apartments or hotel rooms for interviews because I didn't want to go into particularly bad abandoned buildings where subjects lived. If I enter an abandoned building (most have serious structural defects like broken steps or holes in the floor), I do so only with people who know their way around defects that could cause serious harm.

The presence of a protector who can vouch for the safety of the premises and serves as a guide around several obstacles is critical in deciding whether to go into abandoned buildings or outdoor locales that researchers perceive as dangerous. Typically, ethnographers and subjects prefer more neutral settings like a coffee shop, restaurant, storefront, or apartment of a friend (which usually have comfortable chairs, heat, and some privacy).

Crimes and Threats Involving Money

Robbery, burglary, and theft from field staff are uncommon but do occur (Spunt, 1988). In fact, many crack distributors are frequent and proficient robbers, burglars, and thieves (Johnson, Elmoghazy, and Dunlap, 1990). Furthermore, crack users are constantly broke and in need of money. Thus we have developed strategies to minimize criminal victimization and monetary losses. Ethnographers and field staff can expect to be constantly approached for money, "loans," and "advances" (Johnson et al., 1985, 205–6). When these are not provided, implicit threats may be made. Dunlap defused threats by trying to provide balanced reciprocation:

> While declining to provide cash to the "kitty" towards the next purchase of drugs, providing cigarettes, candy, food, drinks, and refreshments will usually satisfy one's social obligation to contribute to shared group activities in a crack house or among drug sellers.

Usually, persons in protector roles will prevent threats from becoming robbery attempts. Johnson described one simple precaution that may reduce the magnitude of monetary losses if a robbery or theft occurs:

> While in the field, wear clothing with a lot of pockets. Distribute the money into different pockets and keep $10 in a shoe for emergencies. While in the field, only take money from one pocket—conveying the impression that all my money is in that pocket. If someone observes and actually attempts a hold-up [which has not happened yet], give the contents from only that one pocket. When the money in that pocket gets low, go to a private place (e.g., a bathroom) and transfer money into the spending pocket.

In prior or concurrent research projects (Johnson, 1990; Johnson et al., 1985; Goldstein et al., 1990), some staff members have been robbed, and in one case, a physical assault without serious injury (Spunt, 1988) occurred. When crimes occurred, staff members usually report them to police to indicate that such violations will have consequences. Several thefts of tape recorders and minor personal possessions were not reported, due mainly to lack of police interest.

Fights

A physical fight or show of weapons may break out without warning so that ethnographers have little chance to use humor and neutrality to prevent it. Almost always, such weapons and fights have nothing to do with the ethnographers' presence. Rather, they are linked to disputes with other crack abusers in the locale. Williams followed several strategies for dealing with such occurrences:

Sometimes knives or guns appear, more frequently as a display of possessions (like gold chains or sneakers) than as a means of threatening persons. If they seek approval for their new possession, I may comment about how nice it is, but add, "Guns aren't my favorite thing. Could you put it away?" I've been in hundreds of crack houses and dealing locations where weapons were widely evident, but I've never been present when guns were used in a threatening manner. If such an event were to occur, I'd leave as soon as possible, and not get involved as an intermediary.

Stickup Men and Drive-by Shootings

Perhaps the most dangerous situation is a "rip off." This occurs when robbers surprise the occupants at a crack-dealing locale with the clear intention of taking all cash and drugs present. Likewise, when two or more drug dealer groups are competing for a good selling location, they may try to "warn" others by street shootouts. These are not situations for mediation or humor, only for getting out of the way or following orders. Beddoe noted:

Stickup men have usually cased the location and are quite certain who is present before coming in. They want money and drugs. Keep quiet and provide what they want.

Williams noted that ethnographers who have good rapport with dealers may be relatively safe:

How do you know a territorial dispute is going on? Generally, someone will let you know so you can stay out of the way 'til some order has been reestablished. You have more warning of trouble than ordinary citizens in the contested area. Your contacts can provide information later— without your being present.

Violence and shooting in the drug culture/business is unpredictable and without warning because surprise is frequently a major element in its use. But most violence by crack dealers is intentionally directed at specific persons and occurs in a concealed setting (so no witnesses are present). Drive-by shooting/machine-gunning of people on street corners and "stray bullets" that kill children remain the exception in drug-related violence, even though they are a major feature of sensationalizing mass media coverage (*Daily News*, 1990; *New York Newsday*, 1990; *New York Times*, 1990a, 1990b).

Contacts with the Police

Since 1983, police task forces directed against dealers have frequently engaged in surprise raids against dealers and crack houses. Despite concerns about police action and fear of arrest, ethnographers who avoid using and selling drugs themselves are rarely involved with the police. The police are authorized to use force only when a person resists physically, so ethnographers contacted by the police are rarely arrested (Bourgois, 1990). Particularly in street settings, ethnographers must be careful in dealings with police. Informal conversations with police should be avoided so that subjects and potential subjects do not have a basis for believing that the ethnographer is talking to or "informing" the police. When the police behave unprofessionally toward subjects, ethnographers who are observed to "stand up" to police gain respect in the eyes of potential subjects. Williams reported one such incident:

> One night I was on the streets with a white ethnographer in a copping area. One police officer came up and asked, "Say, white boy, why don't you buy drugs in your own neighborhood?" and pushed him against the squad car to search him. After producing identification showing that he lived within a couple of blocks, he got off with no further hassle. People in the community saw this as harassment by police and concluded that the ethnographer was not a police officer.

Despite many hours and days spent with crack dealers in crack sales locations where police were observed several times a day, our research staff have never been present when "busts" occurred. During a parallel study of sex-for-crack in Miami in 1989, however, Inciardi (personal communication) walked through the back door of a crack house as a police raid came through the front door. He and others present were taken to detention where he was held for 5 hours; he was released at booking without formal arrest following the procedures outlined below. He did not, however, return to that crack house or others in its general vicinity.

On a parallel research project evaluating the impact of Tactical Narcotics Teams (TNT), ethnographers at Vera Institute (in cooperation with the New York City police) have been instructed about appropriate procedures to follow in the event of being caught in a police sweep or raid. The ethnographers are not to resist arrest or attempt to talk to police officers at the arrest location. Rather, they are to follow instructions, let police gain control, and allow themselves to be handcuffed and taken to the station house. At the point of booking, ethnographers should present identification as a researcher working for a nonprofit organization and ask the booking sergeant to call the principal investigator or let the researcher make such a call. If possible, staff members try to arrange the researchers' release at booking, without formal arrest charges. Otherwise, senior staff or a lawyer will be present at arraignment and will attempt to persuade the judge to drop charges or provide bail money. Subsequent efforts will be made to have charges dismissed or the conviction overturned. To date, researchers at Vera Institute or Narcotic and Drug Research, Inc. have not been arrested while conducting research during the 1980s. Narcotic and Drug Research, Inc. now retains a lawyer to act quickly to represent staff, both ethnographers and paraprofessionals, arrested during fieldwork or AIDS outreach activities....

164   DEVIANCE

REFERENCES

Adler, P.A. 1985. *Wheeling and Dealing*. New York: Columbia University Press.

Alder, P.A. and P. Adler. 1987. *Membership Roles in Field Research*. Newbury Park, CA: Sage.

Agar, M.H. 1980. *The Professional Stranger*. New York: Academic Press.

Becker, H. 1960. "Participant Observation: The Analysis of Qualitative Field Data." Pp. 267–89 In R.N. Adams and J.J. Price eds., *Field Relations and Techniques*. Homewood, IL: Dorsey.

Biernacki, P. 1988. *Pathways from Heroin Addiction*. Philadelphia: Temple University Press.

Bourgois, P. 1990. "In Search of Horatio Alger: Culture and Ideology in the Crack Economy." *Contemporary Drug Problems*, 16: 619–50.

Broadhead, R.S. and K.J. Fox. 1990. "Takin' It to the Streets: AIDS Outreach as Ethnography." *Journal of Contemporary Ethnography*, 19:322–48.

Brownstein, H.H. and J.P. Goldstein. 1990a. "A Typology of Drug Related Homicides." Pp. 171–92 In Ralph Weisheit, ed., *Drugs, Crime, and the Criminal Justice System*. Cincinnati, OH: Anderson.

_____. 1990b. "Research and the Development of Public Policy: The Case of Drugs Violent Crime." *Journal of Applied Sociology*, 7:77–92.

Carey, J.T. 1972. "Problems of Access and Risk in Observing Drug Scenes." Pp. 71–92 In Jack D. Douglas, ed., *Research on Deviance*. New York: Random House.

Carpenter, C., B. Glassner, B.D. Johnson, and J. Loughlin. 1988. *Kids, Drugs, and Crime*. Lexington, MA: Lexington Books.

Daily News. 1990. "Slaughter of the Innocents." October 19: 1.

Denzin, Norman K. 1970. *The Research Act*. Chicago: Aldine.

Douglas, J.D., ed. 1972. *Research on Deviance*. New York: Random House.

Dunlap, E. 1988. "Male-Female Relations and the Black Family." Ph.D. dissertation, University of California, Berkeley.

Dunlap, E., E.D. Johnson, H. Sanabria, et al. 1990. "Studying Crack Users and Their Criminal Careers: The Scientific and Artistic Aspects of Locating Hard-to-Reach Subjects and Interviewing Them About Sensitive Topics." *Contemporary Drug Problems*, 17:121–44.

Feldman, H. 1974. *Street Status and the Drug Researcher: Issues in Participant Observation*. Washington, DC: Drug Abuse Council.

Feldman, H.W., M.H. Agar, and G.M. Beschner. 1979. *Angel Dust: An Ethnographic Study of PCP Users*. Lexington, MA: Lexington Books.

Fetterman, D.M. 1989. *Ethnography: Step by Step*. Newbury Park, CA: Sage.

Goldstein, P.J. 1985. "The Drugs/Violence Nexus: A Triparite Conceptual Model." *Journal of Drug Issues* 15:493–506.

Goldstein, P.J., B. Spunt, T. Miller, and P.A. Bellucci. 1990 "Ethnographic Field Stations." Pp. 80–95 In Elizabeth Lambert, ed., *The Collection and Interpretation of Data from Hidden Populations*. Research Monograph 98. Rockville, MD: National Institute on Drug Abuse.

Goldstein, P.J., P.A. Bellucci, B. Spunt, and T. Miller. 1991a. "Volume of Cocaine Use and Violence: A Comparison Between Men and Women." *Journal of Drug Issues* 21:345–68.

_____. 1991b. "Frequency of Cocaine Use and Violence: A Comparison Between Men and Women." Rockville, MD: National Institute on Drug Abuse.

Hamid, A. 1990. "The Political Economy of Crack-Related Violence." *Contemporary Drug Problems* 17:31–78.

_____. 1990. "The Political Economy of Crack-Related Violence." *Contemporary Drug Problems* 17:31–78.

_____. 1992. *The Political Economy of Drugs*. New York: Plenum.

Hamid, A. and R. Curtis. 1990. "Beaming up: Contexts for Smoking Cocaine and Sex-for-Drugs in the Inner-City and What They Mean." Manuscript, John Jay College, New York.

Hanson, B., G. Beschner, J. Walters, and E. Bovelle, eds. 1985. *Life with Heroin: Voices from the Inner City*. Lexington, MA: Lexington Books.

Howell, N., ed. 1990. *Surviving Fieldwork: A Report of the Advisory Panel on Health and Safety in Fieldwork*. Washington, DC: American Anthropological Association.

Horowitz, R. 1986. "Remaining an Outsider: Membership as a Threat to Research Rapport." *Urban Life* 14:409–30.

Jackson, J.E. 1990. "Deja entendu: The Liminal Qualities of Anthropological Field Notes." *Journal of Contemporary Ethnography* 19:8–43.

Johnson, B.D. 1973. *Marihuana Users and Drug Subcultures*. New York: Wiley.

Johnson, B.D., B. Frank, J. Schmeidler, R. Morel, M. Maranda, and C. Gillman. 1988. "Illicit Substance Use Among Adults in New York State's Transient Population." *Statewide Household Survey of Substance Abuse, 1986*. New York: Division of Substance Abuse Services.

Johnson, B.D., P.J. Goldstein, E. Preble, J. Schmeidler, D.S. Lipton, B. Spunt, and T. Miller.1985. *Taking Care of Business: The Economics of Crime by Heroin Abusers*. Lexington, MA: Lexington Books.

Johnson, B.D., A. Hamid, and Sanabria. 1991. "Emerging Models of Crack Distribution." Pp. 56–78 In Tom Mieczkowski, ed., *Drugs and Crime: A Reader*. Boston: Allyn and Bacon.

Johnson, B.D., T. Williams, K. Dei, and H. Sanabria. 1990. "Drug Abuse in the Inner City: Impact on Hard Drug Users and the Community." Pp. 9–67 in *Drugs and Crime*, edited by Michael Tonry and James Q. Wilson. Chicago: University of Chicago Press.

Johnson, J.C. 1990. *Selecting Ethnographic Informants*. Newbury Park, CA: Sage.

Liebow, E. 1967. *Tally's Corner: A Study of Negro Streetcorner Men*. Boston: Little, Brown.

McCracken, G. 1988. *The Long Interview*. Newbury Park, CA: Sage.

Morales, E. 1989. *Cocaine: White Gold Rush in Peru*. Tuscon: University of Arizona Press.

New York Newsday. 1990. "Stray Bullets Kill 7 in New York in 1990." December 28: 4.

New York Times. 1989. "Drug Wars Don't Pause to Spare the Innocent." December 28:4.

_____. 1990a. "Woman Is Killed in Bronx Drive-by Shooting. October 7:40.

_____. 1990b. "Record Year for Killings Jolts Officials in New York." December 31:25.

_____. 1991. "In a Crack House: Dinner and Drugs on the Stove." April 6:1. 24.

Preble, E.J. and J.J. Casey. 1969. "Taking Care of Business: The Heroin User's Life on the Street." *International Journal of Addictions* 4(1):1–24.

Reinarman, C. and H.G. Levine. 1989. "Crack in Context: Politics and Media in the Making of a Drug Scare." *Contemporary Drug Problems* 16:535–78.

Rose, D. 1990. *Living the Ethnographic Life*. Newbury Park, CA: Sage.

Seckman, M.A. and Couch, C.J. 1989. "Jocularity, Sarcasm, and Relationships." *Journal of Contemporary Ethnography* 18:237–34.

Sluka, J.A. 1990. "Participant Observation in Violent Social Contexts." *Human Organization* 49(2):114–26.

Smith, C. and W. Kornblum, eds. 1991. *In the Field: Readings on the Field Research Experience*. Westport, CT: Praeger.

Spradley, J.P. 1980. *Participant Observation*. New York: Holt, Rinehart, and Winston.

Spunt, B. 1988. "Backstage at an Ethnographic Field Station." Paper presented at the Annual Meeting of the American Society of Criminology, Chicago.

Washington Post. 1990. "Violence in the '90s: Drugs Deadly Residue." October 14:A1, A12.

Warren, C. 1989. *Gender Issues in Field Research*. Newbury Park, CA: Sage.

Whyte, W.F. 1955. *Street Corner Society*. 2nd ed. Chicago: University of Chicago Press.

_____. 1984. *Learning from the Field: A Guide from Experience*. Beverly Hills, CA: Sage.

Williams, T. 1978. "The Cocaine Culture in After Hours Clubs." Ph.D. dissertation, City University of New York.

_____. 1989. *The Cocaine Kids*. New York: Addison-Wesley.

_____. 1991. *The Crack House*. New York: Addison-Wesley.

Williams, T. and W. Kornblum. 1985. *Growing up Poor*. Lexington, MA: Lexington Books.

NOTES

[1]Many researchers have conducted studies without funding. Other ethnographers conducting research on drug-related topics without substantial funding have made important contributions (Adler, 1985; Bourgois, 1990). Ethnographers (Feldman, Agar, and Beschner, 1979; Biernacki, 1988; Preble and Casey,

1969) in the drug field have attained significant government or foundation support over the past 3 decades. Ehtnographic methods have had a very substantial impact on AIDS intervention efforts (Broadhead and Fox, 1990). Professional ethnographers have obtained and administered millions of dollars in federal and state grants to provide AIDS outreach efforts in field settings to drug abusers.

[2] The issue of paying subjects is not addressed here because it is not directly related to safety. Some academic researchers are concerned that money payments to subjects may corrupt the field for other researchers. Our stand is that paying subjects for their time and information demonstrates clear reciprocity and appreciation for that person's life experiences and expertise about the topic being studied. Moreover, we feel strongly that it is unethical to expect poor persons in particular (the most vulnerable and accessible) to spend time with us and provide information about their lives without compensation. Ethnographers almost always provide some form of reciprocal benefits. Money is only one form; services and referrals are others. It is a matter of preference about how to reciprocate for cooperation provided by subjects.

[2] Future papers will report substantive findings from this project.

[3] In addition, ethnographers may be verbally threatened with physical assault and perhaps shoved or pushed; such threats constitute respect for the ethnographer by the person doing so and are usually a direct request to leave. We honor these immediately. The principles suggested in this article have also been adapted from standard tactics for personal safety widely employed by crack abusers/dealers and other street people to protect themselves while engaging in illegal activities. Howell (1990) documented several common law crimes, homicides, and other hazards that have occurred to anthropologists in the field, but she was not always able to distinguish between crimes that occurred during fieldwork and those that occurred to anthropologists when functioning in their citizen roles.

[4] Ethical standards of anthropology and sociology generally prohibit researchers from engaging in illegal behavior, including the use and sale of illegal drugs. Moreover, the use, possession, or sale of drugs exposes ethnographers to arrest and potential legal consequences. Most persons without criminal records who do not possess drugs and have not been observed selling them are released even if their arrest occurred in a crack house.

[5] After-hours clubs are private clubs where patrons can buy (illegally) alcohol and use cocaine (mainly via nasal inhalation—Williams, 1978). Base houses are apartments where someone freebased cocaine powder into cocaine for smoking. Crack houses are places where crack can be used with others in barter-exchange situations. Number holes are locales where the numbers racket (illegal betting) does business.

[6] In all of the following quotes, ethnographers' statements have been edited for the sake of clarity and flow. Subjects' names are pseudonyms.

[7] This is a formal letter issued by the federal government that provides legal protection to all subjects of a research study. It states that the data collected cannot be admitted or used against subjects in a federal court, state court, or administrative hearing. The certificate, which has been supported by court precedent, must be applied for and is granted by several agencies in the Department of Health and Human Services. Similar protection is automatically extended to subjects in all grants funded by the Department of Justice. When conducting research with early crack sellers, Williams (1989) showed his federal certificate to a key subject, who commented, "We didn't know you were with the Feds." The term "federal" had a very different and unfavorable referent for dealers.

[8] A variety of roles have different names in other localities; New York terms are used here. Streeters refer buyers to sellers, touts locate customers for sellers, cop men transport money and drugs between buyers and sellers who never meet, guards and muscle men provide protection and security, lookouts warn of the approach of police or enemies, and runners transport drugs from one locale to another.

[9] Difficulties in training, monitoring, supervising, and firing such paraprofessional workers have also been noted (Johnson et al., 1985; Spunt, 1988, Goldstein et al., 1989; Broadhead and Fox, 1990).

[10] Of course, some dealers do not trust anyone and choose not to talk bout their lives and activities. Such persons do not become research subjects.

[11] Ethnographers need not like the physical setting. The setting may be unattractive and even filthy by ordinary standards. Most sites are not organized for the comfort of crack users or researchers.

[12] In many low-income communities, persons who are unrelated by blood frequently assume fictive kin relationships. Adolescents and young adults who grew up in foster care or with emotionally distant parents are very likely to seek affection and support from any adult (including ethnographers) and expect them to behave as fictive kin (e.g., "aunt," "uncle," or "cousin" role).

Part V

THE DEVIANCE-MAKING ENTERPRISE

In examining deviant behavior, a major question needs to be asked, "How, and under what circumstances do behaviors come to be defined as deviant?"

In order to answer this question, we must examine how deviance is defined, how these social definitions are maintained, and how rule-violators are treated and subsequently processed. Such an approach then, involves, from an historical perspective, an intensive examination of the political and legal processes that affect the creation and alteration of deviant categories.

A major focal point must be those in society who have the power and resources to create social definitions and their abilities to have them enforced.

Moral Entrepreneurs, Moral Crusades, Rule-Makers and Rule-Breakers

In his paper, *"Moral Entrepreneurs: The Creation and Enforcement of Deviant Categories"*, Howard S. Becker provides a detailed discussion of the evolution of deviant categories (norms). A key component of his thesis is the role of "moral entrepreneurs"—people involved in the rule-creation process. Becker divides moral entrepreneurs into two types: (1) rule creators; and (2) rule enforcers. The former, according to Becker refers to individuals who view someone or a certain activity as "morally evil" in their own eyes, and feel that this evil can only be stamped out by legislating against it. These individuals go on a "moral crusade", lobbying societal members and politicians to agree with their view. If their lobbying activities are successful, a new deviant category is created along with a set of rules for enforcing it.

Rule-creating activities can be conducted by a solitary individual, such as Tipper Gore, campaigning to label heavy metal music; however, it is much more common that individuals band together in order to have deviant categories created. MADD—Mothers Against Drunk Drivers, Pro-Life and Pro-Choice, and MAG—Mothers Against Gangs, represent collective moral entrepreneurial activities. As a collectivity, such groups can pressure others to change/create laws. They are also more likely, by virtue of their group efforts, to bring about a moral conversion of others in society.

Once a deviant category has been created and the concomitant norms of enforcement, it is the task of the second type of moral entrepreneur—the rule enforcers to ensure that the rules are being applied against an "offender."

The articles in this section deal with various moral entrepreneurial activities, the creation of, and consequences of various deviant social categories.

Donileen Loseke and Spencer Cahill, in *"The Social Construction of Deviance: Experts on Battered Women"*, contend that abused spouses have been the central object of deviant definitions. In the 1970's, the women's movement brought to the forefront the problem of family violence. Overnight, there emerged a group of "experts" who claim to be exerts on spousal abuse. The major concern of the experts was with women who remained in abusive relationships—a focus defining the problem in terms of the women's inability to leave. In short, as Loseke and Cahill point out, the experts did not seek to explain abusive behavior in terms of the behavior of the husbands, but instead, as a failure on their parts to leave their assailants. It was along these lines that experts created a new deviant category, "the abused wife." In their analysis, experts cited a number of reasons why women failed to leave their husbands: economic dependency, lack of support from friends and family, etc. Apart from these external constraints, experts also cited such internal constraints, as: poor self-concept, emotional dependency, traditional conceptions of women etc.—all of which made it difficult for women to leave. In their paper, Loseke and Cahill demonstrate that the so-called experts' accounts are largely based on questionable evidence. A more plausible explanation is provided for why women stay in abusive relationships.

Stephen J. Pfohl in his article, *"The 'Discovery' of Child Abuse,"* provides an excellent historical overview of how societal definitions can be altered in a rather short period of time. Until the 1960, there were no deviant labels related to child abuse. The societal attitude was primarily one of tolerance for the abuser. The author details the moral entrepreneurial activities lead by radiologists and other interested persons, and the various organizational and social factors leading to the labelling of "child abuse" and its subsequent criminalization.

Troy Duster provides another historical analysis, in *The Legislation of Morality: Creating Drug Laws."* Focusing on the Harrison Narcotics Act of 1914, the author illustrates the interrelationship between entrepreneurial morality and legislation. He documents that although the public has been concerned with such drugs as marijuana and LSD, it was opium that "most dominated and colored the American conception of narcotics." Morphine, a derivative of opium was used widely during and after the Civil War, and for many years there existed no state or federal laws restricting its sale and distribution. Duster contends that approximately 3 percent of the population was addicted to morphine—such an addiction upset members of the medical profession. It was during this time that heroin was also being manufactured—a derivative of morphine. Initially heroin was thought to be non-addictive but in 1989, the medical journals pronounced otherwise. The medical profession, acting as moral entrepreneurs lobbied to have legislation passed that would regulate the manufacture and distribution of narcotics. In 1914, Congress passed the Harrison Narcotics Act.

The final selection by Schneider and Conrad entitled, *"Medicine as an Institution of Social Control"*, details the role of the medical profession in the definition or categorization and treatment of various types of behaviors. *Medicalization of deviance* refers to defining behavior as a medical problem or an illness and mandating doctors to provide treatment for it. Alcoholism, drug addiction, and hyperkinesis are examples of the medicalization of deviance. The authors discuss the positive and negative social consequences of the medicalization of deviance and how medicine has become an agency of social control with its increasing medical knowledge and expanding technology. Given such conditions, Schneider and Conrad conclude that, in the future, it is highly probable that more deviant behavior will be medicalized and medicine's social control will be further increased.

Chapter 19

MORAL ENTREPRENEURS:
THE CREATION AND ENFORCEMENT OF DEVIANT CATEGORIES

Howard S. Becker

Rules are the products of someone's initiative and we can think of the people who exhibit such enterprise as *moral entrepreneurs*. Two related species—rule creators and rule enforcers—will occupy our attention.

Rule Creators

The prototype of the rule creator, but not the only variety as we shall see, is the crusading reformer. He is interested in the content of rules. The existing rules do not satisfy him because there is some evil which profoundly disturbs him. He feels that nothing can be right in the world until rules are made to correct it. He operates with an absolute ethic; what he sees is truly and totally evil with no qualification. Any means is justified to do away with it. The crusader is fervent and righteous, often self-righteous.

It is appropriate to think of reformers as crusaders because they typically believe that their mission is a holy one. The prohibitionist serves as an excellent example, as does the person who wants to suppress vice and sexual delinquency or the person who wants to do away with gambling.

These examples suggest that the moral crusader is a meddling busybody, interested in forcing his own morals on others. But this is a one-sided view. Many moral crusades have strong humanitarian overtones. The crusader is not only interested in seeing to it that other people do what he thinks right. He believes that if they do what is right it will be good for them. Or he may feel that his reform will prevent certain kinds of exploitation of one person by another. Prohibitionists felt that they were not simply forcing their morals on others, but attempting to provide the conditions for a better way of life for people prevented by drink from realizing a truly good life. Abolitionists were not simply trying to prevent slave owners from doing the wrong thing; they were trying to help slaves to achieve a better life. Because of the importance of the humanitarian motive, moral crusaders (despite their relatively single-minded devotion to their particular cause) often lend their support to other humanitarian crusades. Joseph Gusfield has pointed out that:

> The American temperance movement during the 19th century was a part
> of a general effort toward the improvement of the worth of the human
> being through improved morality as well as economic conditions. The
> mixture of the religious, the equalitarian, and the humanitarian was an

outstanding facet of the moral reformism of many movements. Temperance supporters formed a large segment of movements such as sabbatarianism, abolition, women's rights, agrarianism, and humanitarian attempts to improve the lot of the poor....

In its auxiliary interests the WCTU revealed a great concern for the improvement of the welfare of the lower classes. It was active in campaigns to secure penal reform, to shorten working hours and raise wages for workers, and to abolish child labor and in a number of other humanitarian and equalitarian activities. In the 1880's the WCTU worked to bring about legislation for the protection of working girls against the exploitation by men.[1]

As Gusfield says,[2] "Moral reformism of this type suggests the approach of a dominant class toward those less favorably situated in the economic and social structure." Moral crusaders typically want to help those beneath them to achieve a better status. That those beneath them do not always like the means proposed for their salvation is another matter. But this fact—that moral crusades are typically dominated by those in the upper levels of the social structure—means that they add to the power they derive from the legitimacy of their moral position, the power they derive from their superior position in society.

Naturally, many moral crusades draw support from people whose motives are less pure than those of the crusader. Thus, some industrialists supported Prohibition because they felt it would provide them with a more manageable labor force.[3] Similarly, it is sometimes rumored that Nevada gambling interests support the opposition to attempts to legalize gambling in California because it would cut so heavily into their business, which depends in substantial measure on the population of Southern California.[4]

The moral crusader, however, is more concerned with ends than with means. When it comes to drawing up specific rules (typically in the form of legislation to be proposed to a state legislature or the Federal Congress), he frequently relies on the advice of experts. Lawyers, expert in the drawing of acceptable legislation, often play this role. Government bureaus in whose jurisdiction the problem falls may also have the necessary expertise, as did the Federal Bureau of Narcotics in the case of the marihuana problem.

As psychiatric ideology, however, becomes increasingly acceptable, a new expert has appeared—the psychiatrist. Sutherland, in his discussion of the natural history of sexual psychopath laws, pointed to the psychiatrist's influence.[5] He suggests the following as the conditions under which the sexual psychopath law, which provides that a person "who is diagnosed as a sexual psychopath may be confined for an indefinite period in a state hospital for the insane,"[6] will be passed.

First, these laws are customarily enacted after a state of fear has been aroused in a community by a few serious sex crimes committed in quick succession. This is illustrated in Indiana, where a law was passed following three or four sexual attacks in Indianapolis, with murder in two. Heads of families bought guns and watch dogs, and the supply of locks and chains in the hardware stores of the city was completely exhausted....

A second element in the process of developing sexual psychopath laws is the agitated activity of the community in connection with the fear. The attention of the community is focused on sex crimes, and people in the most varied situations envisage dangers and see the need of and possibility for their control....

The third phase in the development of these sexual psychopath laws has been the appointment of a committee. The committee gathers the many conflicting recommendations of persons and groups of persons, attempts to determine "facts," studies procedures in other states, and makes recommendations, which generally include bills for the legislature. Although the general fear usually subsides within a few days, a committee has the formal duty of following through until positive action is taken. Terror which does not result in a committee is much less likely to result in a law.[7]

In the case of sexual psychopath laws, there usually is no government agency charged with dealing in a specialized way with sexual deviations. Therefore, when the need for expert advice in drawing up legislation arises, people frequently turn to the professional group most closely associated with such problems:

In some states, at the committee stage of the development of a sexual psychopath law, psychiatrists have played an important part. The psychiatrists, more than any others, have been the interest group back of the laws. A committee of psychiatrists and neurologists in Chicago wrote the bill which became the sexual psychopath law of Illinois; the bill was sponsored by the Chicago Bar Association and by the state's attorney of Cook County and was enacted with little opposition in the next session of the State Legislature. In Minnesota all the members of the governor's committee except one were psychiatrists. In Wisconsin the Milwaukee Neuropsychiatric Society shared in pressing the Milwaukee Crime Commission for the enactment of a law. In Indiana the attorney-general's committee received from the American Psychiatric Association copies of all of the sexual psychopath laws which had been enacted in other states.[8]

The influence of psychiatrists in other realms of the criminal law has increased in recent years.

In any case, what is important about this example is not that psychiatrists are becoming increasingly influential, but that the moral crusader, at some point in the development of his crusade, often requires the services of a professional who can draw up the appropriate rules in an appropriate form. The crusader himself is often not concerned with such details. Enough for him that the main point has been won; he leaves its implementation to others.

By leaving the drafting of the specific rule in the hands of others, the crusader opens the door for many unforeseen influences. For those who draft legislation for crusaders have their own interests, which may affect the legislation they prepare. It is likely that the sexual psychopath laws drawn by psychiatrists contain many features never intended by the citizens who spearheaded the drives to "do something about sex crimes," features which do however reflect the professional interests of organized psychiatry.

The Fate of Moral Crusades

A crusade may achieve striking success, as did the Prohibition movement with the passage of the Eighteenth Amendment. It may fail completely, as has the drive to do away with the use of tobacco or the anti-vivisection movement. It may achieve great success, only to find its gains whittled away by shifts in public morality and increasing restrictions imposed on it by judicial interpretations; such has been the case with the crusade against obscene literature.

One major consequence of a successful crusade, of course, is the establishment of a new rule or set of rules, usually with the appropriate enforcement machinery being provided at the same time. I want to consider this consequence at some length later. There is another consequence, however, of the success of a crusade which deserves mention.

When a man has been successful in the enterprise of getting a new rule established—when he has found, so to speak, the Grail—he is out of a job. The crusade which has occupied so much of his time, energy, and passion is over. Such a man is likely, when he first began his crusade, to have been an amateur, a man who engaged in a crusade because of his interest in the issue, in the content of the rule he wanted established. Kenneth Burke once noted that a man's occupation may become his preoccupation. The equation is also good the other way around. A man's preoccupation may become his occupation. What started as an amateur interest in a moral issue may become an almost full-time job; indeed, for many reformers it becomes just this. The success of the crusade, therefore, leaves the crusader without a vocation. Such a man, at loose ends, may generalize his interest and discover something new to view with alarm, a new evil about which something ought to be done. He becomes a professional discoverer of wrongs to be righted, of situations requiring new rules.

When the crusade has produced a large organization devoted to its cause, officials of the organization are even more likely than the individual crusader to look for new causes to espouse. This process occurred dramatically in the field of health problems when the National Foundation for Infantile Paralysis put itself out of business by discovering a vaccine that eliminated epidemic poliomyelitis. Taking the less constraining name of The National Foundation, officials quickly discovered other health problems to which the organization could devote its energies and resources.

The unsuccessful crusade, either the one that finds its mission no longer attracts adherents or the one that achieves its goal only to lose it again, may follow one of two courses. On the one hand, it may simply give up its original mission and concentrate on preserving what remains of the organization that has been built up. Such, according to one study, was the fate of the Townsend Movement.[9] Or the failing movement may adhere rigidly to an increasingly less popular mission, as did the Prohibition Movement. Gusfield has described present-day members of the WCTU as "moralizers in retreat."[10] As prevailing opinion in the United States becomes increasingly anti-temperance, these women have not softened their attitude toward drinking. On the contrary, they have become bitter at the formerly "respectable" people who no longer will support a temperance movement. The social class level from which WCTU members are drawn has moved down from the upper-middle class to the lower-middle class. The WCTU now turns to attack the middle class it once drew its support from, seeing this group as the locus of acceptance of moderate drinking. The following quotations from Gusfield's interviews with WCTU leaders give some of the flavor of the "moralizer-in-retreat":

> When this union was first organized, we had many of the most influential ladies of the city. But now they have got the idea that we ladies who are against taking a cocktail are a little queer. We have an undertaker's wife and a minister's wife, but the lawyer's and the doctor's wife shun us. They don't want to be thought queer.
>
> We fear moderation more than anything. Drinking has become so much a part of everything—even in our church life and our colleges.
>
> It creeps into the official church boards. They keep it in their iceboxes....The minister here thinks that the church has gone far, that they are doing too much to help the temperance cause. He's afraid that he'll stub some influential toes.[11]

Only some crusaders, then, are successful in their mission and create, by creating a new rule, a new group of outsiders. Of the successful, some find that they have a taste for crusades and seek new problems to attack. Other crusaders fail in their attempt and either support the organization they have created by dropping their distinctive mission and focusing on the problem of organizational maintenance itself or become outsiders themselves, continuing to espouse and preach a doctrine which sounds increasingly queer as time goes on.

Rule Enforcers

The most obvious consequence of a successful crusade is the creation of a new set of rules. With the creation of a new set of rules we often find that a new set of enforcement agencies and officials is established. Sometimes, of course, existing agencies take over the administration of the new rule, but more frequently a new set of rule enforcers is created. The passage of the Harrison Act presaged the creation of the Federal Narcotics Bureau, just as the passage of the Eighteenth Amendment led to the creation of police agencies charged with enforcing the Prohibition Laws.

With the establishment of organizations of rule enforcers, the crusade becomes institutionalized. What started out as a drive to convince the world of the moral necessity of a new rule finally becomes an organization devoted to the enforcement of the rule. Just as radical political movements turn into organized political parties and lusty evangelical sects become staid religious denominations, the final outcome of the moral crusade is a police force. To understand, therefore, how the rules creating a new class of outsiders are applied to particular people we must understand the motives and interests of police, the rule enforcers.

Although some policemen undoubtedly have a kind of crusading interest in stamping out evil, it is probably much more typical for the policeman to have a certain detached and objective view of his job. He is not so much concerned with the content of any particular rule as he is with the fact that it is his job to enforce the rule. When the rules are changed, he punishes what was once acceptable behavior just as he ceases to punish behavior that has been made legitimate by a change in the rules. The enforcer, then, may not be interested in the content of the rule as such, but only in the fact that the existence of the rule provides him with a job, a profession, and a *raison d'etre*.

Since the enforcement of certain rules provides justification for his way of life, the enforcer has two interests which condition his enforcement activity: first, he must justify the existence of his position and, second, he must win the respect of those he deals with.

These interests are not peculiar to rule enforcers. Members of all occupations feel the need to justify their work and win the respect of others. Musicians, as we have seen, would like to do this but have difficulty finding ways of successfully impressing their worth on customers. Janitors fail to win their tenants' respect, but develop an ideology which stresses the quasi-professional responsibility they have to keep confidential the intimate knowledge of tenants they acquire in the course of their work.[12] Physicians, lawyers, and other professionals, more successful in winning the respect of clients, develop elaborate mechanisms for maintaining a properly respectful relationship.

In justifying the existence of his position, the rule enforcer faces a double problem. On the one hand, he must demonstrate to others that the problem still exists: the rules he is supposed to enforce have some point, because infractions occur. On the other hand, he must show that his attempts at enforcement are effective and worthwhile, that the evil he is supposed to deal with is in fact being dealt with adequately. Therefore, enforcement organizations, particularly when they are seeking funds, typically oscillate between two kinds of claims. First, they say that by reason of their efforts the problem they deal with is approaching solution. But, in the same breath, they say the problem is perhaps worse than ever (though through no fault of their own) and requires renewed and increased effort to keep it under control. Enforcement officials can be more vehement than anyone else in their insistence that the problem they are supposed to deal with is still with us, in fact it is more with us than ever before. In making these claims, enforcement officials provide good reason for continuing the existence of the position they occupy.

We may also note that enforcement officials and agencies are inclined to take a pessimistic view of human nature. If they do not actually believe in original sin, they at least like to dwell on the difficulties in getting people to abide by rules, on the characteristics of human nature that lead people toward evil. They are skeptical of attempts to reform rule-breakers.

The skeptical and pessimistic outlook of the rule enforcer, of course, is reinforced by his daily experience. He sees, as he goes about his work, the evidence that the problem is still with us. He sees the people who continually repeat offenses, thus definitely branding themselves in his eyes as outsiders. Yet it is not too great a stretch of the imagination to suppose that one of the underlying reasons for the enforcer's pessimism about human nature and the possibilities of reform is that fact that if human nature were perfectible and people could be permanently reformed, his job would come to an end.

In the same way, a rule enforcer is likely to believe that it is necessary for the people he deals with to respect him. If they do not, it will be very difficult to do his job; his feeling of security in his work will be lost. Therefore, a good deal of enforcement activity is devoted not to the actual enforcement of rules, but to coercing respect from the people the enforcer deals with. This means that one may be labeled as deviant not because he has actually broken a rule, but because he has shown disrespect to the enforcer of the rule.

Westley's study of policemen in a small industrial city furnishes a good example of this phenomenon. In his interview, he asked policemen, "When do you think a policeman is justified in roughing a man up?" He found that "at least 37% of the men believed that it was legitimate to use violence to coerce respect."[13] He gives some illuminating quotations from his interviews:

> Well, there are cases. For example, when you stop a fellow for a routine questioning, say a wise guy, and he starts talking back to you and telling you you are no good and that sort of thing. You know you can take a man in on a disorderly conduct charge, but you can practically never make it stick. So what you do in a case like that is to egg the guy on until he makes a remark where you can justifiably slap him, and then, if he fights back, you can call it resisting arrest.
>
> Well, a prisoner deserves to be hit when he goes to the point where he tries to put you below him.
>
> You've gotta get rough when a man's language becomes very bad, when he is trying to make a fool of you in front of everybody else. I think most policemen try to treat people in a nice way, but usually you have to talk pretty rough. That's the only way to set a man down, to make him show a little respect.[14]

What Westley describes is the use of an illegal means of coercing respect from others. Clearly, when a rule enforcer has the option of enforcing a rule or not, the difference in what he does may be caused by the attitude of the offender toward him. If the offender is properly respectful, the enforcer may smooth the situation over. If the offender is disrespectful, then sanctions may be visited on him. Westley has shown that this differential tends to operate in the case of traffic offenses, where the policeman's discretion is perhaps at a maximum.[15] But it probably operates in other areas as well.

Ordinarily, the rule enforcer has a great deal of discretion in many areas, if only because his resources are not sufficient to cope with the volume of rule-breaking he is supposed to deal with. This means that he cannot tackle everything at once and to this extent must temporize with evil. He cannot do the whole job and knows it. He takes his time, on the assumption that the problems he deals with will be around for a long while. He establishes priorities, dealing with things in their turn, handling the most pressing problems immediately and leaving others for later. His attitude toward his work, in short, is professional. He lacks the naive moral fervor characteristic of the rule creator.

If the enforcer is not going to tackle every case he knows of at once, he must have a basis for deciding when to enforce the rule, which persons committing which acts to label as deviant. One criterion for selecting people is the "fix." Some people have sufficient political influence or know-how to be able to ward off attempts at enforcement, if not at the time of apprehension then at a later stage in the process. Very often, this function is professionalized; someone performs the job on a full-time basis, available to anyone who wants to hire him. A professional thief described fixers this way:

> There is in every large city a regular fixer for professional thieves. He has no agents and does not solicit and seldom takes any case except that of a professional thief, just as they seldom go to anyone except him. This centralized and monopolistic system of fixing for professional thieves is found in practically all of the large cities and many of the small ones.[16]

Since it is mainly professional thieves who know about the fixer and his operations, the consequence of this criterion for selecting people to apply the rules to is that amateurs tend to be caught, convicted, and labeled deviant much more frequently than professionals. As the professional thief notes:

> You can tell by the way the case is handled in court when the fix is in. When the copper is not very certain he has the right man, or the testimony of the copper and the complainant does not agree, or the prosecutor goes easy on the defendant, or the judge is arrogant in his decisions, you can always be sure that someone has got the work in. This does not happen in many cases of theft, for there is one case of a professional to twenty-five or thirty amateurs who know nothing about the fix. These amateurs get the hard end of the deal every time. The coppers bawl out about the thieves, no one holds up his testimony, the judge delivers an oration, and all of them get credit for stopping a crime wave. When the professional hears the case immediately preceding his own, he will think, "He should have got ninety years. It's the damn amateurs who cause all the heat in the stores." Or else he thinks, "Isn't it a damn shame for that copper to send that kid away for a pair of hose, and in a few minutes he will agree to a small fine for me stealing a fur coat?" But if the coppers did not send the amateurs away to strengthen their records of convictions, they could not sandwich in the professionals whom they turn loose.[17]

Enforcers of rules, since they have no stake in the content of particular rules themselves, often develop their own private evaluation of the importance of various kinds of rules and infractions of them. This set of priorities may differ considerably from those held by the general public. For instance, drug users typically (and a few policemen have personally confirmed it to me) that police do not consider the use of marihuana to be as important a problem or as dangerous a practice as the use of opiate drugs. Police base this conclusion on the fact that, in their experience, opiate users commit other crimes (such as theft or prostitution) in order to get drugs, while marihuana users do not.

Enforcers, then, responding to the pressures of their own work situation, enforce rules and create outsiders in a selective way. Whether a person who commits a deviant act is in fact labeled a deviant depends on many things extraneous to his actual behavior: whether the enforcement official feels that at this time he must make some show of doing his job in order to justify his position, whether the misbehaver shows proper deference to the enforcer, whether the "fix" has been put in, and where the kind of act he has committed stands on the enforcer's list of priorities.

The professional enforcer's lack of fervor and routine approach to dealing with evil may get him into trouble with the rule creator. The rule creator, as we have said, is concerned with the content of the rules that interest him. He sees them as the means by which evil can be stamped out. He does not understand the enforcer's long-range approach to the same problems and cannot see why all the evil that is apparent cannot be stamped out at once.

When the person interested in the content of a rule realizes or has called to his attention the fact that enforcers are dealing selectively with the evil that concerns him, his righteous wrath may be aroused. The professional is denounced for viewing the evil too lightly, for failing to do his duty. The moral entrepreneur, at whose instance the rule was made, arises again to say that the outcome of the last crusade has not been satisfactory or that the gains once made have been whittled away and lost.

Deviance and Enterprise: A Summary

Deviance—in the sense I have been using it, of publicly labeled wrongdoing—is always the result of enterprise. Before any act can be viewed as deviant, and before any class of people can be labeled and treated as outsiders for committing the act, someone must have made the rule which defines the act as deviant. Rules are not made automatically. Even though a practice may be harmful in an objective sense to the group in which it occurs, the harm needs to be discovered and pointed out. People must be made to feel that something ought to be done about it. Someone must call the public's attention to these matters, supply the push necessary to get things done, and direct such energies as are aroused in the proper direction to get a rule created. Deviance is the product of enterprise in the largest sense; without the enterprise required to get rules made, the deviance which consists of breaking the rule could not exist.

Deviance is the product of enterprise in the smaller and more particular sense as well. Once a rule has come into existence, it must be applied to particular people before the abstract class of outsiders created by the rule can be peopled. Offenders must be discovered, identified, apprehended and convicted (or noted as "different" and stigmatized for their nonconformity, as in the case of legal deviant groups such as dance musicians). This job ordinarily falls to the lot of professional enforcers who, by enforcing already existing rules, create the particular deviants society views as outsiders.

It is an interesting fact that most scientific research and speculation on deviance concerns itself with the people who break rules rather than with those who make and enforce them. If we are to achieve a full understanding of deviant behavior, we must get these two possible foci of inquiry into balance. We must see deviance, and the outsiders who personify the abstract conception, as a consequence of a process of interaction between people, some of whom in the service of their own interests make and enforce rules which catch others who, in the service of their own interests, have committed acts which are labeled deviant.

NOTES

[1] Joseph R. Gusfield, "Social Structure and Moral Reform: A Study of the Women's Christian Temperance Union," *American Journal of Sociology*, LXI (November, 1955), p.223.

[2] Ibid.

[3] See Raymond G. McCarthy, editor, *Drinking and Intoxication* (New Haven and New York: Yale Center of Alcohol Studies and The Free Press of Glencoe, 1959), pp.395–6.

[4] This is suggested in Oscar Lewis, *Sagebrush Casinos: The Story of Legal Gambling in Nevada* (New York: Doubleday and Co., 1953), pp.233–4.

[5] Edwin H. Sutherland, "The Diffusion of Sexual Psychopath Laws," *American Journal of Sociology* LVI (September, 1950), pp.142–8.

[6] Ibid., p.142.

[7] Ibid., pp.143–5.

[8] Ibid., pp.145–6.

[9] Sheldon Messinger, "Organization Transformation: A Case Study of a Declining Social Movement," *American Sociological Review*, XX (February, 1955), pp.3–10.

[10] Gusfield, *op. cit.*, pp.227–8.

[11] Ibid., pp.227, 229–30.

[12] See Ray Gold, "Janitors Versus Tenants: A Status-Income Dilemma," *American Journal of Sociology*, LVII (March, 1952), pp.486–93.

[13] William A. Westley, "Violence and the Police," *American Journal of Sociology*, LIX (July, 1953), p.39.

[14] Ibid.

[15] See William A. Westley, "The Police: A Sociological Study of Law, Custom, and Morality" (unpublished Ph.D. dissertation, University of Chicago, Department of Sociology, 1951).

[16] Edwin H. Sutherland (editor), *The Professional Thief* (Chicago: University of Chicago Press, 1937), pp.87–8.

[17] Ibid., pp.91–2.

Chapter 20

THE SOCIAL CONSTRUCTION OF DEVIANCE:
EXPERTS ON BATTERED WOMEN

Donileen R. Loseke
Spencer E. Cahill

Like previous examinations of wife assault, this article is primarily concerned with the question of why battered women remain in relationships with abusive mates. However, we focus not on the behavior of battered women *per se* but on the experts who ask this question. The question "Why do they stay?" implicitly defines the parameters of the social problem of battered women. By asking this question, the experts imply that assaulted wives are of two basic types: those who leave their mates and those who do not. Not only are possible distinctions among assaulted wives who remain with their mates implicitly ignored, but so, too, are the unknown number of assaulted wives who quickly terminate such relationships. By focusing attention on those who stay, the experts imply that assaulted wives who remain with their mates are more needy and deserving of public and expert concern than those who do not. In fact, some of the experts have explicitly defined battered women as women who *remain* in relationships containing violence (Ferraro and Johnson, 1983; Pizzey, 1979; Scott, 1974; Walker, 1979).

Moreover, the experts' common and overriding concern with the question of why assaulted wives stay reveals their shared definition of the normatively expected response to the experience of battering. To ask why assaulted wives remain with their mates is to imply that doing so requires explanation. In general, as Scott and Lyman (1968) have noted, normatively expected behavior does not require explanation. It is normatively unanticipated, untoward acts which require what Scott and Lyman term an "account." By asking why battered women stay, therefore, the experts implicitly define leaving one's mate as the normatively expected response to the experience of wife assault. Staying, on the other hand, is implicitly defined as deviant, an act "which is perceived (i.e., recognized) as violating expectations" (Hawkins and Tiedman, 1975:59).

In other words, once the experts identify a woman as battered, normative expectations regarding material stability are reversed. After all, separated and divorced persons are commonly called upon to explain why their relationships "didn't work out" (Weiss, 1975). It is typically marital stability "staying," which is normatively expected and marital instability, "leaving," which requires an account. However, as far as the experts on battered women are concerned, once wife assault occurs, it is marital stability which requires explanation.

In view of the experts' typifications of relationships within which wife assault occurs, this reversal of normative expectations seems only logical. Although research indicates that the severity and frequency of wife assault varies considerably across couples (Straus et al., 1980), the experts stress that, *on the average*, wife assault is more dangerous for victims than is assault by a stranger (U.S. Department of Justice, 1980). Moreover, most experts maintain that once wife assault has occurred within a relationship, it will become more frequent and severe over time (Dobash and Dobash, 1979), and few believe that this pattern of escalating violence can be broken without terminating the relationship.[1] It is hardly surprising, therefore, that the experts on battered women define "leaving" as the expected, reasonable, and desirable response to the experience of wife assault.[2] Staying, in contrast, is described as "maladaptive choice behavior" (Waites, 1977–78), "self-destruction through inactivity" (Rounsaville, 1978), or, most concisely, "deviant" (Ferraro and Johnson, 1983). For the experts, battered women who remain with their mates pose an intellectual puzzle: Why are they so unreasonable? Why do they stay?

To ask such a question is to request an account. Experts who provide answers to this question are, therefore, offering accounts on behalf of battered women who remain with their mates. According to Scott and Lyman (1968), two general types of accounts are possible: justifications and excuses. A justification is an account which acknowledges the actor's responsibility for the behavior in question but challenges the imputation of deviance ("I did it, but I didn't do anything wrong"). An excuse, on the other hand, acknowledges the deviance of the behavior in question but relieves the actor of responsibility for it ("I did something wrong, but it wasn't my fault").

Clearly, these different types of accounts elicit different kinds of responses. If the behavior in question is socially justifiable, then the actor was behaving reasonably, as normatively expected. The actor's ability or competence to manage everyday affairs without interference is not called into question (Garfinkel, 1967:57). In contrast, excusing behavior implies that the actor cannot manage everyday affairs without interference. Although the behavior is due to circumstances beyond the actor's control, it is admittedly deviant. By implication, assistance from others may be required if the actor is to avoid behaving similarly in the future. In order to fully understand the experts' responses to battered women who remain with their mates, it is necessary, therefore, to determine which type of account they typically offer on behalf of such women.

The Experts' Accounts

Experts on battered women are a diverse group. This diversity is reflected in the emphasis each expert places on various accounts, in the number of accounts offered, and in how series of accounts are combined to produce complex theoretical explanations. Despite such diversity, however, there is a sociologically important similarity among the experts' accounts. None of the experts argues that "staying" is justifiable. "Staying" is either explicitly or implicitly defined as unreasonable, normatively unexpected, and therefore, deviant. By implication, the accounts offered by the experts are excuses for women's deviant behavior, and they offer two basic types.[3] Battered women are said to remain with their mates because of external constraints on their behavior or because of internal constraints. In either case, the accounts offered by the experts acknowledge the deviance of staying but relieve battered women of responsibility for doing so.

External Constraints

Almost all contemporary experts on battered women maintain that staying is excusable due to external constraints on women's behavior (Dobash and Dobash, 1979; Freeman, 1979; Langsley and Levy, 1977; Martin, 1979; Pagelow, 1981a, 1981b; Pizzey, 1979; Ridington, 1977–78; Roy, 1977; Shainess, 1977).

> Why does she not leave? The answer is simple. If she has children but no money and no place to go, she has no choice. (Fleming, 1979:83).

Clearly, such accounts are based on the assumption that battered women who stay are economically dependent upon their mates. If a woman has no money and no place to go, she cannot be held responsible for the unreasonable act of staying. She has no choice.

Although this excuse is the most prevalent in the literature on battered women, further elaboration is necessary. In its simplest form, such an account can be easily challenged: What about friends, family, the welfare system, and other social service agencies? In response to such challenges, experts must offer accounts which will excuse women for not taking advantage of such assistance. Experts meet these challenges with at least two further accounts of external constraints. First, experts claim that most battered women are interpersonally isolated. Even if they are not, family and friends are said to typically blame women for their problems instead of providing assistance (Carlson, 1977; Dobash and Dobash, 1979; Fleming, 1979; Hilberman and Munson, 1977–78; Truninger, 1971). Second, experts claim that social service agencies typically provide little, if any, assistance. In fact, experts maintain that the organization of agencies (bureaucratic procedures and agency mandates to preserve family stability) and the behavior of agency personnel (sexism) discourage battered women who attempt to leave (Bass and Rice, 1979; Davidson, 1978; Dobash and Dobash, 1979; Higgins, 1978; Martin 1976, 1978; McShane, 1979; Pizzey, 1979; Prescott and Letko, 1977; Truninger, 1971). In other words, the experts maintain that battered women can expect little assistance in overcoming their economic dependency.

Although the external constraint type of excuse acknowledges that staying is unreasonable, it relieves battered women of the responsibility for doing so. Battered women who remain with their mates are portrayed as "more acted upon than acting" (Sykes and Matza, 1957:667). The implication, of course, is that women would leave (i.e., they would be reasonable) if external constraints could be overcome. The experts provide a warrant, therefore, for intervention in battered women's everyday affairs. In order to act reasonably and leave, battered women must overcome the external constraint of economic dependency, which they cannot do without the assistance of specialized experts.

Despite the prevalence of external constraint accounts in the literature on battered women, most experts consider such excuses as insufficient. Instead of, or in addition to, such accounts, the experts maintain that battered women face a second type of constraint on their behavior.

Internal Constraints

Some experts have proposed that biographically accumulated experiences may lead women to define violence as "normal" and "natural" (Ball, 1977; Gelles, 1976; Langley and Levy, 1977; Lion, 1977). Likewise, according to some experts, women define violence as a problem only if it becomes severe and/or frequent "enough"[4] (Carlson, 1977; Gelles, 1976; Moore, 1979; Rousanville and Weissman, 1977–78). If violence is not subjectively defined as a "problem," then women have no reason to consider leaving.

For the most part, experts have focused their attention on documenting internal constraints which are said to prevent women from leaving their mate *even when* violence is subjectively defined as a problem. Experts suggest two major sources of such internal constraints: femininity and the experience of victimization.

To many experts, the primary source of internal constraints is the femininity of battered women. Attributes commonly regarded as "feminine" are automatically attributed to battered women, especially when these characteristics can conceivably account for why such women might remain with their mates. For example, women who stay are said to be emotionally dependent upon their mates (Dobash and Dobash, 1979; Fleming, 1979; Freeman, 1979; Langley and Levy, 1977; Moore, 1979; Pizzey, 1979; Roy, 1977); to have a poor self-image or low self-esteem (Carlson, 1977; Freeman, 1979; Langley and Levy, 1977; Lieberknecht, 1978; Martin, 1976; Morgan, 1982; Ridington, 1977–78; Star et al., 1979; Truninger, 1971); and to have traditional ideas about women's "proper place."[5] In isolation or in combination, these so-called feminine characteristics are said to internally constrain women's behavior. According to the experts, women find it subjectively difficult to leave their mates even when violence is defined as a problem.

Internal constraints are also said to follow from the process of victimization itself. According to the experts, battered women not only display typically feminine characteristics, but they also develop unique characteristics due to the victimization process. For example, some experts have argued that once a woman is assaulted she will fear physical reprisal if she leaves (Lieberknecht, 1978; Martin, 1979; Melville, 1978). Other physical, emotional, and psychological after-effects of assault are also said to discourage battered women from leaving their mates (Moore, 1979; Roy, 1977). Indeed, battered women are sometimes said to develop complex psychological problems from their victimization. These include the "stress-response syndrome" (Hilberman, 1980), "enforced restriction of choice" (Waites, 1977–78), "learned helplessness" (Walker, 1979), or responses similar to those of the "rape trauma syndrome" (Hilberman and Munson, 1977–78). A symptom common to all such diagnostic categories is that sufferers find it subjectively difficult to leave their mates.

As with external constraint excuses, these internal constraint accounts also acknowledge the deviance of remaining in a relationship containing violence while, at the same time, relieving battered women of responsibility for doing so. They function in this way, as excuses, because the various internal constraints attributed to battered women are identified as beyond their personal control. Clearly, battered women are not responsible for their gender socialization or for the physical violence they have suffered. In other words, both external and integral constraint accounts portray battered women who stay with their mates as more acted upon than acting. What women require, "for their own good," is assistance in overcoming the various barriers which prevent them from acting reasonably. Thus, both types of accounts offered by the experts on behalf of battered women who stay provide grounds for expert intervention in these women's everyday affairs.

As Scott and Lyman (1968) have pointed out, the criteria in terms of which accounts are evaluated vary in relation to the situation in which they are offered, the characteristics of the audience, and the identity of the account provider. In the present context, the identity of the account provider is of particular interest. Experts who speak on behalf of others are expected to do so on the basis of uncommon knowledge. If, therefore, the evidence which the experts offer in support of their accounts for why battered women stay fails to confirm the expectation of uncommon knowledge, then their claim to be speaking and acting on such women's behalf is open to question.

The Evidence for Experts' Accounts

How do experts obtain their knowledge about the experiences and behavior of battered women? In order to explore the experts' claim to uncommon knowledge, we address three questions: From whom is evidence obtained (the issue of generalizability)? By what means is evidence obtained (the issue of validity)? How consistently does the evidence support the accounts offered (the issue of reliability)?

Generalizability

Experts on battered women claim to have knowledge of the experiences and behavior of women who remain in relationships containing violence. Yet, while there is general agreement that many battered women suffer in silence, with few exceptions the experts have studied only those assaulted wives who have come to the attention of social service agencies, many of whom have already left their mates.[6] Women who contact social service agencies have decided that they require expert intervention in their private affairs, and there is good reason to believe that such women differ from women who have *not* sought assistance.

The decision to seek professional help is typically preceded by a complex process of problem definition, and this process is invariably more difficult and of longer duration when the problem involves the behavior of a family member (Goffman, 1969; Schwartz, 1957; Weiss, 1975; Yarrow et al., 1955). Only as a last resort are professional helpers contacted (Emerson and Messinger, 1977; Kadushin, 1969; Mechanic, 1975). Since it is primarily the experiences of women who have reached the end of this help-seeking process which provide evidence for experts' accounts, the generalizability of this evidence is questionable.

Validity

When not simply stating their own perceptions of battered women, experts obtain their evidence in one of two ways. They sometimes question other experts, and they sometimes directly question women. Clearly, others' perceptions, whether expert or not, are of uncertain validity. However, even the evidence based on battered women's responses to the question "Why do you stay?" is of doubtful validity.

To ask a battered woman to respond to this question is to request that she explain her apparently deviant behavior. This leaves her two alternatives. She can either justify her staying ("I love him"; "He's not all bad"; "The kids need him"), or she can excuse her behavior. Since experts have predefined staying as undeniably deviant, it is unlikely that they will honor a justification. Indeed, some experts on battered women have explicitly characterized justifications for staying as "rationalizations," accounts which are self-serving and inaccurate (Ferraro and Johnson, 1983; Waites, 1977–78). Given the experts' presuppositions about the behavior of "staying" and the typical desire of persons to maintain "face" (Goffman, 1955), it is likely that the only accounts the experts will know—excuses—are subtly elicited by the experts who question battered women.[7]

It is hardly surprising, therefore, that the experts on battered women offer remarkably similar accounts of why women stay. This is particularly visible in the evidence which supports the external constraint accounts. By almost exclusively interviewing women who turn to inexpensive or free social service agencies and then constructing an interactional situation which is likely to elicit a particular type of account, experts practically ensure that their presuppositions about external constraints are confirmed.[8] In brief, the validity of the experts' advice is doubtful.

Reliability

Another important question is whether the evidence the experts obtain through interviewing and observation is consistent with evidence obtained using other methods. For example, if the economic dependency (external constraint) excuse is to avoid challenge, it must be supplemented by the additional excuses of unresponsive friends, family members, and social service agencies. Yet, some evidence undermines the excuse that social service agencies and providers discourage battered women from leaving their mates. Pagelow (1981a) found little relationship between her measures of "agency response" and the amount of time battered women had remained with their mates. Hofeller (1982) found that many battered women self-reported being either "completely" or "somewhat" satisfied with the efforts of social service agencies on their behalf.[9]

As with the excuse of unresponsive social service agencies, available evidence conflicts with various internal constraint accounts offered by the experts. For example, available evidence does not support assertions that battered women hold traditional beliefs about "women's proper place," or that these beliefs internally constrain women from leaving their mates. Walker (1983) reports that battered women perceive themselves to be *less* traditional than "other women," and the results of experimental studies conducted by Hofeller (1982) and Rosenbaum and O'Leary (1981) indicate that women who have *not* been victims of wife assault hold more traditional attitudes than women who are victims. Moreover, Pagelow (1981a) reports that her measures of "traditional ideology" did not help explain the length of time battered women remained with their mates.

The experts have also maintained that the low self-esteem assumed to be common to women in general is exacerbated by the process of victimization, producing a powerful internal constraint on the behavior of battered women. Yet in their now classic review of research evidence regarding sex differences in self-esteem, Maccoby and Jacklin (1974:15) labeled as a popular myth the commonsense deduction that "women, knowing that they belong to a sex that is devalued...must have a poor opinion of themselves." Contrary to this commonsense deduction, sex differences in self-esteem have rarely been found in experimental studies, and when they have, women's self-esteem is often higher than men's. In addition, at least two studies contained in the literature on battered women refute the statement that battered women have lower self-esteem than women who have not experienced assault (Walker, 1983; Star, 1978).

In short, the evidence provided to support expert claims about battered women is, by scientific standards, less than convincing. In fact, it appears as if the experts' accounts are presupposed and then implicitly guide both the gathering and interpretation of evidence. In constructing their accounts, the experts have employed the commonsense practice of automatically attributing to individual women (in this case, battered women) sets of traits based on their sex. As females, battered women are automatically assumed to be economically and emotionally dependent upon their mates, to have low self-esteem, and to hold traditional attitudes and beliefs. Methodologies which might yield conflicting evidence are seldom used, and when seemingly conflicting evidence is uncovered it is often explained away. For example, Walker (1983:40) implicitly argues that battered women have an inaccurate perception of themselves. She interprets the finding that battered women consider themselves to be in control of their own behavior as a "lack of acknowledgement that her batterer *really* is in control" (emphasis added). Likewise, Pagelow (1981a) discredits seemingly conflicting evidence by challenging her own measures; the presupposed accounts are not questioned. In other words, the interpretive force of the "master status" of sex "overpowers" evidence to the contrary (Hughes, 1945:357). What the experts on battered women offer in support of their accounts for why women remain is not uncommon knowledge, therefore, but professional "folklore," which, however sophisticated, remains folklore (Zimmerman and Pollner, 1970:44).

The sociologically intriguing issue is not, however, the "truthfulness" of accounts. In a diverse society, a variety of different vocabularies of motive (Mills, 1940) are available for making sense out of the complex interrelationships between actor, biography, situation, and behavior. Under such circumstances, "What is reason for one man is mere rationalization for another" (Mills, 1940:910). Any attempt to ascertain battered women's "true" motives would therefore be an exercise in what Mills termed "motive-mongering." What is of sociological interest is that the experts' accounts are not based upon uncommon knowledge but upon commonsense deductions best described as folklore. Clearly, this should raise questions about both the experts' claim to be speaking on battered women's behalf and their claim to have the right to intervene in such women's private affairs.

Given the experts' claim to be speaking and acting in battered women's "best interests," the sociologically important issue is the relative plausability of the particular vocabulary of motive used by the experts. According to the experts, their primary concerns are the condemnation and elimination of wife assault, tasks which are likely to require specialized expertise. The vocabulary of motive which must be overcome in order to them to behave reasonably—that is, in order for them to leave. But such a vocabulary is not the only plausible way to make sense of women's behavior.

An Alternative Vocabulary of Motive

Prior to the 1970s, the problems of battered women received little attention. In contrast, the contemporary experts have portrayed women as little more than victims. The tendency has been to define both battered women and their relationships with their mates almost exclusively in terms of the occurrence and effects of physical and emotional assault. Battered women are simply defined as assaulted wives who remain with assaultive mates (Ferraro and Johnson, 1983; Pizzey, 1979; Scott, 1974; Walker, 1979), and their relationships are portrayed as no more than victimizing processes. Such a focus leads to what Barry (1979) has termed "victimism," knowing a person only as a victim. One effect of the victimism practiced by the experts on battered women is that possible experiential and behavioral similarities between battered women and other persons are overlooked. However, even a cursory review of the sociological literature on marital stability and instability suggests that, at least in regard to their reluctance to leave their mates, battered women are quite similar both to other women and to men.

This literature consistently indicates that marital stability often outlives marital quality. Goode (1956) found that such stability was only sometimes due to the obvious, objective costs of terminating the relationship ("external constraints"). Contrary to predictions that relationships will terminate when apparent "costs" outweigh apparent "benefits," it is not at all unusual for relationships to be sustained even when outsiders perceive costs to be greater than the benefits. Although experts on battered women have argued that leaving a relationship means that a woman's status will change from "wife" to "divorcee" (Dobash and Dobash, 1979; Truninger, 1971), a variety of family sociologists have noted that terminating a relationship is far more complex than is suggested by the concept of "status change." Over time, marital partners develop an "attachment" to one another (Weiss, 1975), a "crescive bond" (Turner, 1970), a "shared biography" (McLain and Weigart, 1979). As a result, each becomes uniquely irreplaceable in the eyes of the other. Such a personal commitment to a specific mate has been found to persist despite decreases in marital partners' liking, admiration, and/or respect for one another (Rosenblatt, 1977; Weiss, 1975). Battered women who remain in relationships which outsiders consider costly are not, therefore, particularly unusual or deviant.

Moreover, the sociological literature on marital stability and instability suggests that the process of separation and divorce, what Vaughan (1979) terms "uncoupling," is typically difficult. One indication of the difficulty of this process is the considerable time uncoupling often takes (Cherlin, 1981; Goode, 1956; Weiss, 1975). It is also typical for a series of temporary separations to precede a permanent separation (Lewis and Spanier, 1979; Weiss, 1975; Vaughan, 1979). In brief, the lengthy "leaving and returning" cycle said to be characteristic of battered women is a typical feature of the uncoupling process. Further, the guilt, concern, regret, bitterness, disappointment, depression, and lowered perception of self attributed to battered women are labels for emotions often reported by women and men in the process of uncoupling (Spanier and Castro, 1979; Weiss, 1975).

Although the experts attribute unusual characteristics and circumstances to battered women who remain with their mates, the reluctance of battered women to leave can be adequately and commonsensically expressed in the lyrics of a popular song: "Breaking up is hard to do." It can also be expressed in the more sophisticated vocabulary of sociological psychology: Individuals who are terminating intimate relationships "die one of the deaths that is possible" for them (Goffman, 1952). The sociological literature on marital stability and instability does suggest, therefore, an alternative to the vocabulary of battered women's motives provided by the experts on battered women. Because a large portion of an adult's self is typically invested in their relationship with their mate, persons become committed and attached to this mate as a uniquely irreplaceable individual. Despite problems, "internal constraints" are experienced when contemplating the possibility of terminating the relationship with the seemingly irreplaceable other. Again, if this is the case, then women who remain in relationships containing violence are not unusual or deviant; they are typical.

Some experts on battered women have reported evidence which supports this alternative characterization of the motives of women who remain. Gaylord (1975) reports that half of his sample of battered women claimed to be satisfied with their relationships, and Dobash and Dobash (1979) note that, apart from the violence, battered women often express positive feelings toward their mates. Moreover, Ferraro and Johnson (1983) report that battered women typically believe that their mates are the only person they could love, and Walker (1979) reports that battered women often describe their mates as playful, attentive, exciting, sensitive, and affectionate. Yet, because of the victimism they practice, experts on battered women often fail to recognize that such findings demonstrate the multi-dimensionality of battered women's relationships with their mates. Indeed, some of these experts have explicitly advised that battered women's expressions of attachment and commitment to their mates not be believed:

> The statement that abused wives love their husbands need not be taken at face value. It may represent merely a denial of ambivalence or even unmitigated hatred. (Waites, 1977–78:542).
>
> The only reasons the woman does not end the marriage are dependence—emotional or practical—and fear of change and the unknown. These are often masked as love or so the woman devalues herself. (Shainess, 1977:118).

Such expressions of commitment and attachment are *justifications* for why a person might remain with [her] mate. To honor such a justification would be to acknowledge that staying in a relationship which contains violence is not necessarily deviant. In order to sustain their claim to expertise, therefore, the experts on battered women cannot acknowledge the possible validity of this alternative, "justifying" vocabulary of motive even when it is offered by battered women themselves. In other words, the experts discredit battered women's interpretations of their own experiences in order to sustain the claim that such women require their "expert" assistance.

Conclusions

This case study of the social construction of deviance by a group of experts illustrates how members of the knowledge class create a new clientele for their services. In effect, experts discredit the ability of a category of persons to manage their own affairs without interference. The actors in question are portrayed as incapable of either understanding or controlling the factors which govern their behavior. In order for them to understand their experiences and gain control over their behavior, by implication, they require the assistance of specialized experts. Because the category of actors which compose such a clientele are characterized as unreasonable and incompetent, any resistance they offer to the experts' definitions and intervention is easily discredited. For example, battered women's attempts to justify staying with their mates are often interpreted by the experts as further evidence of such women's unreasonableness and incompetence. Experts are able to sustain their claims to be speaking and acting on others behalf, therefore, despite the protests of those on whose behalf they claim to be speaking and acting.

We do not mean to suggest that experts' potential clientele do not benefit from experts' efforts. For example, the experts on battered women have played a major role in focusing public attention on the plight of the victims of wife assault. In doing so, they have helped to dispel the popular myth that these women somehow deserved to be assaulted. In turn, this has undoubtedly encouraged the general public, the police, the courts, and various social service agencies to be more responsive and sensitive to the needs of such women. Yet, battered women may pay a high price for this assistance.

The experts on battered women define leaving one's mate as the normatively expected, reasonable response to the experience of wife assault. By implication, staying with one's mate after such an experience requires explanation. In order to explain this unreasonable response, the experts have provided accounts, that is, ascribed motives to battered women which excuse such deviance. As Blum and McHugh (1971:106) have noted, "observer's ascription of motive serves to formulate...persons." In offering accounts on behalf of battered women who stay, the experts propose a formulation of the type of persons such women are. For example, the experts characterize this type of person as "oversocialized into feminine identity" (Ball and Wyman, 1977–78); "bewildered and helpless" (Ball, 1977), "immature" and lacking clear self-identities (Star et al., 1979), "overwhelmingly passive" and unable to act on their own behalf (Hilberman and Munson, 1977–78), and cognitively, emotionally, and motivationally "deficient" (Walker, 1977–78)." Moreover, these women are described as suffering from the "battered wife syndrome" (Morgan, 1982; Walker, 1983), and, consequently, they are "society's problem" (Martin, 1978). Clearly, the identity of battered women is a deeply discrediting one.

In summary, once a woman admits that she is a victim of wife assault, her competence is called into question if she does not leave. She is defined as a type of person who requires assistance, a person who is unable to manage her own affairs. As a result, the experts on battered women have constructed a situation where victims of wife assault may lose control over their self-definitions, interpretations of experience, and, in some cases, control over their private affairs. In a sense, battered women may now be victimized twice, first by their mates and then by the experts who claim to speak on their behalf.

REFERENCES

Ball, M. 1977. "Issues of Violence in Family Casework." *Social Casework* 58:3–12.

Ball, P.G. & E. Wyman. 1977–78. "Battered Wives and Powerlessness: What Can Consumers Do?" *Victimology* 2:545–52.

Barry, K. 1979. *Female Sexual Slavery.* New York: Avon.

Bass, D. & J. Rice. 1979. "Agency Responses to the Abused Wife." *Social Casework* 60:338–42.

Blum, A. & P. McHugh. 1971. "The Social Ascription of Motives." *American Sociological Review* 36:98–109.

Carlson, B.E. 1977. "Battered Women and Their Assailants." *Social Work* 22:455–60.

Cherlin, A.J. 1981. *Marriage, Divorce, Remarriage.* Cambridge, Massachusetts: Harvard University Press.

Coleman, K.H. 1980. "Conjugal Violence: What 33 Men Report." *Journal of Marital and Family Therapy* 6:207–14.

Davidson, T. 1978. *Conjugal Crime.* New York: Hawthorne.

Denzin, N.K. 1983. "Towards a Phenomenology of Family Violence." Paper presented at the meetings of the American Sociological Association, Detroit, August.

Dobash, R.E. & R. Dobash. 1979. *Violence Against Wives: A Case Against the Patriarchy.* New York: Free Press.

Emerson, R.M. & S.L. Messinger. 1977. "The Micropolitics of Trouble." *Social Problems* 25:121–34.

Erchak, G.M. 1981. "The Escalation and Maintenance of Child Abuse: A Cybernetic Model." *Child Abuse and Neglect* 5:153–57.

Ferraro, K.J. & J.M. Johnson. 1983. "How Women Experience Battering: The Process of Victimization." *Social Problems* 30:325–39.

Fleming, J.B. 1979. *Stopping Wife Abuse.* Garden City, New York: Anchor.

Freeman, M.D.A. 1979. *Violence in the Home.* Westmead, England: Saxon House.

Garfinkel, H. 1967. *Studies in Ethnomethodology.* Englewood Cliffs, New Jersey: Prentice-Hall.

Gaylord, J.J. 1975. "Wife Battering: A Preliminary Survey of 100 Cases." *British Medical Journal* 1:194–97.

Gelles, R.J. 1976. "Abused Wives: Why Do They Stay?" *Journal of Marriage and the Family* 38:659–68.

Giles-Sims, J. 1983. *Wife Battering: A Systems Approach.* New York: Guilford Press.

Goffman, E. 1952. "On Cooling the Mark out: Some Aspects of Adaptation to Failure." *Psychiatry* 15:451–63.

—————.1955. "On Face-Work: An Analysis of Ritual Elements in Social Interaction." *Psychiatry* 18:213–231.

—————.1969. "Insanity of the Place." *Psychiatry* 32:352–88.

Goode, W.J. 1956. *After Divorce.* Glencoe, IL: Free Press.

Hawkins, R. & G. Tiedeman. 1975. *The Creation of Deviance: Interpersonal and Organizational Determinants.* Columbus, OH: Charles E. Merrill.

Hendrix, M.J., G.E. Lagonda, & C.E. Bohen. 1978. "The Battered Wife." *American Journal of Nursing* 78:650–53.

Higgins, J.G. 1978. "Social Services for Abused Wives." *Social Casework* 59:266–71.

Hilberman, E. 1980. "Overview: The 'Wife-Beater's Wife' Reconsidered." *American Journal of Psychiatry* 137:1336–346.

————and K. Munson. 1977–78. "Sixty Battered Women."*Victimology* 2:460–70.

Hofeller, K.H. 1982. *Social, Psychological, and Situational Factors in Wife Abuse.* Palo Alto, California: R. and E. Associates.

Hughes, E. 1945. "Dilemmas and Contradictions of Status." *American Journal of Sociology* 50:353–59.

Kadushin, C. 1969. *Why People Go to Psychiatrists.* New York: Atherton.

Langley, R. & R.C. Levy. 1977. *Wife Beating The Silent Crisis.* New York: Pocket Books.

Lewis, R.A. & G.B. Spainer. 1979. "Theorizing About the Quality and Stability of Marriage." Pp. 268–94. In Wesley R. Burr, Reuben Hill, F. Ivan Nye, and Ira L. Reiss (eds.), *Contemporary Theories About the Family* Vol. 1. New York: Free Press.

Lieberknecht, K. 1978. "Helping the Battered Wife." *American Journal of Nursing* 78:654–56.

Lion, J.R. 1977. "Clinical Aspects of Wifebeating." Pp. 126–36. In Maria Loy (ed.), *Battered Women: A Psychological Study of Domestic Violence.* New York: Van Nostrand Reinhold.

MacCoby, E.E. & C.N. Jacklin. 1974. *The Psychology of Sex Differences.* Stanford, CA: Stanford University Press.

McLain, R. & A. Wiegert. 1979. "Toward a Phenomenological Sociology of Family: A Programmatic Essay." Pp. 160–205. In Wesley R. Burr, Reuben Hill, F. Ivan Nye, and Ira L. Reiss (eds.), *Contemporary Theories About the Family* Vol. 2. New York: Free Press.

McShane, C. 1979. "Community Services for Battered Women." *Social Work* 24:34–39.

Martin, D. 1976. *Battered Wives.* San Francisco: Glide Publications.

————,1978. "Battered Women: Society's Problem," Pp. 111–42 In Jane Roberts Chapman and Margaret Gates (eds.), *The Victimization of Women.* Beverly Hills: Sage Publications.

————,1979. "What Keeps a Woman Captive in a Violent Relationship? The Social Context of Battering." Pp. 33–58 In Donna M. Moore (ed.), *Battered Women.* Beverly Hills: Sage Publications.

Mechanic, D. 1975. "Sociocultural and Social Psychological Factors Affecting Personal Responses to Psychological Disorder." *Journal of Health and Social Behavior* 16:393–404.

Melville, J. 1978. "Women in Refuges." Pp. 293–310 In J.P. Martin, (ed.), *Violence in the Family.* New York: John Wiley.

Mills, C.W. 1940. "Situated Actions and Vocabularies of Motive." *American Sociological Review* 5:904–13.

Moore, D.M. 1979. "An Overview of the Problem." Pp. 7–32 In Donna M. Moore, *Battered Women.* Beverly Hills, CA: Sage.

Morgan, S.M. 1982. *Conjugal Terrorism: A Psychological and Community Treatment Model of Wife Abuse.* Palo Alto, California: R. and E. Associates.

Pagelow, M.D. 1981a. *Women Battering: Victims and Their Experiences* Beverly Hills, California: Sage.

————.1981b. "Factors Affecting Women's Decisions to Leave Violent Relationships." *Journal of Family Issues* 2:391–414.

Pizzey, E. 1979. "Victimology Interview: A Refuge for Battered Women." *Victimology* 4:100–12.

Prescott, S. & C. Letko. 1977. "Battered Women: A Social Psychological Perspective." Pp. 72–96 In Maria Roy (ed.), *Battered Women: A Psychosociological Study of Domestic Violence.* New York: Van Nostrand Reinhold.

Ridington, J. 1977–78. "The Transition Process: A Feminist Environment as Reconstructive Milieu." *Victimology* 2:563–75.

Rosenbaum, A. & K.D. O'Leary. 1981. "Marital Violence: Characteristics of Abusive Couples." *Journal of Consulting and Clinical Psychology* 49:63–71.

Rosenblatt, P.C. 1977. "Needed Research on Commitment in Marriage." Pp. 73–86 In George Levinger and Harold L. Raush (eds.), *Close Relationships: Perspectives on the Meaning of Intimacy.* Amherst: University of Massachusetts.

Rounsaville, B.J. 1978. "Theories in Marital Violence: Evidence from a Study of Battered Women." *Victimology* 21:11–31.

Roy, M. 1977. "A Current Survey on 150 Cases." Pp. 25–44 In Maria Roy (ed.), *Battered Women: A Psychosociological Study of Domestic Violence*. New York: Van Nostrand Reinhold.

Schwartz, C.G. 1957. "Perspectives on Deviance: Wives' Definitions of Their Husbands' Mental Illness." *Psychiatry* 20:275–91.

Scott, M.B. and S.M. Lyman. 1968. "Accounts." *American Sociological Review* 33:46–62.

Scott, P.D. 1974. "Battered Wives." *British Journal of Psychiatry* 125:433–41.

Shainess, N. 1977. "Psychological Aspects of Wifebattering." Pp. 111–18 In Maria Roy (ed.), *Battered Women: A Psychosociological Study of Domestic Violence*. New York: Van Nostrand Reinhold.

Spanier, G. and R.F. Castro. 1979. "Adjustment to Separation and Divorce: An Analysis of 50 Case Studies." *Journal of Divorce* 2:241–53.

Star, B. 1978. "Comparing Battered Women and Non-Battered Women." *Victimology* 3:32–44.

Star, B., C.G. Clark, K.M. Goetz, & L. O'Malia. 1979. "Psychosocial Aspects of Wife Battering." *Social Casework* 60:479–87.

Straus, M.A. 1974. "Forward." Pp. 13–17 In Richard J. Gelles (ed.), *The Violent Home*. Beverly Hills, CA: Sage.

Straus, M.A., R.J. Gelles, and S. Steinmetz. 1980. *Behind Closed Doors: Violence in the American Home*. Garden City, New York: Anchor.

Sykes, G. and D. Matza. 1957. "Techniques of Neutralization: A Theory of Delinquency." *American Sociological Review* 22: 664–69.

Truninger, E. 1971. "Marital Violence: The Legal Solutions." *Hastings Law Journal* 23:259–76.

Turner, R. 1970. *Family Interaction*. New York: John Wiley.

U.S. Department of Justice. 1980. *Intimate Victims: A Study of Violence Among Friends and Relatives*. Washington, D.C.: U.S. Government Printing Office.

Vaughan, D. 1979. "Uncoupling: The Process of Moving from One Lifestyle to Another." *Alternative Lifestyles* 2:415–42.

Waites, E.A. 1977–78. "Female Masochism and the Enforced Restriction of Choice." *Victimology* 2:535–44.

Walker, L.E. 1977–78. "Battered Women and Learned Helplessness." *Victimology* 2:525–34.

——————,1979. *The Battered Woman*. New York: Harper & Row.

——————, 1983. "The Battered Woman Syndrome Study." Pp. 31–48 In David Finkelhor, Richard J. Gelles, Gerald T. Hotaling, and Murray A. Straus (eds.), *The Dark Side of Families*. Beverly Hills, California: Sage.

Weiss, R. 1975. *Marital Separation*. New York: Basic Books.

Yarrow, M.R., C.G. Schwartz, H.S. Murphy, and L.C. Desy. 1955. "The Psychological Meaning of Mental Illness in the Family." *Journal of Social Issues* 11:12–24.

Zimmerman, D. & N. Pollner. 1970. "The Everyday World as a Phenomenon." Pp. 80–104 In Jack Douglas (ed.), *Understanding Everyday Life*. Chicago: Aldine.

NOTES

[1] There has been little systematic study of the possibility of change in relationships. Walker (1979) reports that her pessimism is based on clinical experience. See Coleman (1980) for a more optimistic prognosis.

[2] Of course, this commonsense deduction is also based on the common, although often unspoken, assumption that humans are "rational actors." If the basis of human motivation is a desire to maximize rewards and minimize costs, then why would a battered woman remain in such an obviously "costly" relationship?

[3] A third type of explanation for why victims of wife assault remain with their mates is seldom found in the literature on battered women and, therefore, will not be reviewed here. This type of explanation is based on a systems theory analysis of family interactions. Straus (1974) suggests the empirical applicability of such an approach, and Denzin (1983) provides a phenomenological foundation. Erchak (1981)

used this approach to explain the maintenance of child abuse, and Giles-Sims (2983) had used this to explain the behavior of battered women.

⁴Empirical testing of the association between leaving and childhood experiences has not confirmed this theory (Pagelow, 1981a; Star, 1978; Walker, 1977–78). Likewise, empirical testing of the association between leaving and "severity/frequency" has also not supported theory. See Pagelow (1981b) for a complete discussion.

⁵"Traditional ideology" includes such beliefs as: divorce is a stigma (Dobash and Dobash, 1979; Langley and Levy, 1977; Moore, 1979; Roy, 1977); the children need their father (Dobash and Dobash, 1979); the woman assumes responsibility for the action of her mate (Fleming, 1979; Langley and Levy, 1977; Martin, 1976); or feels embarrassed about the family situation (Ball and Wyman, 1977–78; Fleming, 1979; Hendrix et al., 1978).

⁶Exceptions are Gelles (1976), Hofeller (1981), and Rosenbaum and O'Leary (1981), who included matched samples of persons not receiving services, and Prescott and Letko (1977), who used information from women who responded to an advertisement in *Ms.* magazine.

⁷The situation is more complicated when women who have left are asked why *did* you stay? Or, as Dobash and Dobash (1979:47) asked: "Why do you think you stayed with him as long as you did?" In such situations, the question asks women to retrospectively reconstruct their personal biographies based on their current circumstances and understandings.

⁸However, Rousanville (1978) found that "lack of resources" did not distinguish between women who had left and women who had not left.

⁹The "satisfaction" of victims with social services varies considerably by the type of agency (Hofeller, 1982; Prescott and Letko, 1977).

Chapter 21

THE "DISCOVERY" OF CHILD ABUSE

Stephen J. Pfohl

The Organization of Social Reaction Against the "Battered Child Syndrome"
What organization of social forces gave rise to the discovery of abuse as deviance?
The discovery is not attributable to any escalation of abuse itself. Although some
authors have recently suggested that the increasing nuclearization of the family may
increase the victimization of its offspring (Skolnick & Skolnick,1971), there has
never been any evidence that, aside from reporting inflation due to the impact of new
laws, battering behavior was actually increasing (Eads, 1969). The attention here is
on the organizational matrix encouraging a recognition of abuse as a social problem.
In addressing this issue I will examine factors associated with the organizational
structure of the medical profession leading to the discovery of abuse by pediatric
radiologists rather than by other medical practitioners.

The "discovery" of abuse by pediatric radiology has often been described
chronologically (Radbill, 1968:15; McCoid, 1965:2–5; Thomas, 1972:330). John
Caffey (1946) first linked observed series of long bone fractures in children with what
he termed some "unspecific origin." Although his assumption was that some physical
disturbance would be discovered as the cause of this pattern of "subdural hematoma,"
Caffey's work prompted a series of further investigations into various bone injuries,
skeletal trauma, and multiple fractures in young children. These research efforts led
pediatric radiology gradually to shift its diagnosis away from an internal medical
explication toward the ascription of social cause.

In subsequent years it was suggested that what was showing up on x-rays might
be the results of various childhood accidents (Barmeyer, Anderson, & Cox, 1951), of
"parental carelessness" (Silverman, 1965), of "parental conduct" (Bakwin, 1956),
and, most dramatically, of the "indifference, immaturity and irresponsibility of
parents" (Woolley & Evans, 1955). Surveying the progression of this research and
reviewing his own investigations, Caffey (1957) later specified "misconduct and
deliberant injury" as the primary etiological factors associated with what he had
previously labelled "unspecific trauma." The discovery of abuse was on its way. Both
in scholarly research (McCoid, 1965:7) and journalistic outcry (Radbill, 1968:16),
the last years of the fifties showed dramatically increased concern for the beaten child.

Why did pediatric radiologists and not some other group "see" abuse first? Legal
and social welfare agents were either outside the scene of abusive behavior or inside
the constraining vision of psychoanalytically committed casework. But clinicians,
particularly hospital physicians and pediatricians, who encountered abused children
more immediately, should have discovered "abuse" before the radiologists.

Four factors impeded the recognition of abuse (as it was later labelled). First, some early research maintained that doctors in emergency room settings were simply unaware of the possibilities of "abuse" as a diagnosis (Bain, 1963; Boardman, 1962). While this may be true, the massive symptoms (blood, burns, bruises) emergency room doctors faced far outweighed the lines appearing on the x-ray screens of radiologic specialists. A second line of evidence contends that many doctors were simply psychologically unwilling to believe that parents would inflict such atrocities on their own children (Elmer, 1960; Fontana, Donovan, & Wong, 1963; Kempe *et al.*, 1962). This position is consistent with the existing cultural assumptions pairing parental power with parental wisdom and benevolence. Nonetheless, certain norma-tive and structural elements within professional medicine appear of greater signifi-cance in reinforcing the physician's reluctance to get involved, even diagnostically. These factors are the "norm of confidentiality between doctor and client" and the goal of professional autonomy.

The "norm of confidentiality" gives rise to the third obstacle to a diagnosis of abuse: the possibility of legal liability for violating the confidentiality of the physician-patient relationship (Boardman, 1962). Interestingly, although some re-search connotes doctors' concern over erroneous diagnosis (Braun, Braun, & Simonds, 1963), physicians primarily view the parent rather than the child, as their real patient. On a strictly monetary level, of course, it is the parent who contracts with the doctor. Additional research has indicated that, particularly in the case of pediatricians, the whole family is viewed as one's clinical domain (Bucher & Strauss, 1961:329). It is from this vantage point that the impact of possible liability for a diagnostic disclosure is experienced. Although legal liability for a diagnosis of abuse may or may not have been the risk (Paulsen, 1967:32), the belief in such liability could itself have contributed to the narrowness of a doctor's diagnostic perceptions (McCoid, 1965:37).

A final deterrent to the physician's "seeing" abuse is the reluctance of doctors to become involved in a criminal justice process that would take both their time (Bain, 1963:896) and ability to guide the consequences of a particular diagnosis (Boardman, 1962:46). This deterrent is particularly related to the traditional success of organized medicine in politically controlling the consequences of its own performance, not just for medical practitioners but for all who came in contact with a medical problem (Freidson, 1968:106; Hyde *et al.*, 1954).

The political control over the consequence of one's profession would be jeopar-dized by the medical diagnosis of child abuse. Doctors would be drawn into judicial proceedings and subordinated to a role as witnesses. The outcome of this process would be decided by criminal justice standards rather than those set forth by the medical profession. Combining this relatively unattractive alternative with the obvious and unavoidable drain on a doctor's financial earning time, this fourth obstacle to the clinician's discovery of abuse is substancial.

Factors Conductive to the Discovery of Abuse by Pediatric Radiology

Why didn't the above factors inhibit the discovery of abuse by pediatric radiologists as well as by clinicians? First it must be recognized that the radiologists in question

(Caffey, Barmeyer, Silverman, Woolley, and Evans) were all researchers of children's x-rays. As such, the initial barrier becomes irrelevant. The development of diagnostic categories was a consequence rather than a pre-condition of the medical mission. Regarding the psychological denial of parental responsibility for atrocities, it must be remembered that the dramatic character of a beating is greatly reduced by the time it reaches an x-ray laboratory. Taken by technicians and developed as black and white prints, the radiologic remnants of abuse carry with them little of the horror of the bloody assault.

With a considerable distance from the patient and his or her family, radiologists are removed from the third obstacle concerning legal liabilities entailed in violating the doctor-patient relationship. Unlike pediatricians, radiologists do not routinely regard the whole family as one's clinical domain. Of primary importance is the individual whose name or number is imprinted on the x-ray frames. As such, fears about legal sanctions instigated by a parent whom one has never seen are less likely to deter the recognition of abuse.

Given the irrelevance of the first three obstacles, what about the last? Pediatric radiologists are physicians, and as such would be expected to participate in the "professional control of consequences" ethos. How is it that they negotiate this obstacle in favor of public recognition and labelling of abuse?

The Discovery: An opportunity for Advancement within the Medical Community

To ask why generally the norm of "professional control of consequences" does not apply equally to radiologists as to their clinical counterparts is to confuse the reality of organized medicine with its image. Although the medical profession often appears to outsiders as a separate and unified community within a community (Goode, 1957), and although medical professionals generally favor the maintenance of this image (Glaser, 1960), it is nonetheless more adequately described as an organization of internally competing segments, each striving to advance its own historically derived mission and future importance (Bucher & Strauss, 1961). In analyzing pediatric radiology as one such segment, several key variables facilitated its temporary parting with the dominate norms of the larger medical community. This parting promoted the elevation of its overall status within that community.

The first crucial element is that pediatric radiology was a marginal specialty within organized medicine. It was a research-oriented sub-field in a profession that emphasized face-to-face clinical interaction. It was a safe intellectual endeavor within an overall organization which placed a premium on risky pragmatic enterprise. Studies of value orientations among medical students at the time of the "discovery" of abuse have suggested that those specialties which stress "helping others," "being of service," "being useful," and "working with people" were ranked above those which work "at medical problems that do not require frequent contact with patients" (Cahalan, 1957). On the other hand, intellectual stimulation afforded very little prestige. Supporting this conclusion was research indicating that although forty-three percent of practicing physicians selected "close patient relations" as a mandate of their profession, only twenty-four percent chose "research" as worthy of such an evaluation (Philips, 1964). Pairing this ranking system with the profession's close-knit, "fraternity-like" communication network (Hall, 1946), one would expect research-oriented radiologists to be quite sensitive about their marginal evaluation by colleagues.

Intramedical organizational rankings extend along the lines of risk taking as well as patient encounters. Here, too, pediatric radiologists have traditionally ranked lower than other medical specialties. Becker's (1961) study of medical student culture suggests that the most valued specialties are those which combine wide experiences with risk and responsibility. These are most readily "symbolized by the possibility of killing or disabling patients in the course of making a mistake" (Freidson, 1968:107). From this perspective, it is easy to understand why surgery and internal medicine head this list of the most esteemed specialties. Other research as similarly noted the predominance of surgeons among high elected officials of the American Medical Association (Hall, 1946). Devoid of most risk taking and little involved in life or death decisions, pediatric radiologists are again marginal to this ethos of medical culture.

The "discovery" of child abuse offered pediatric radiologists an alternative to their marginal medical status. By linking themselves to the problem of abuse, radiologists became indirectly tied into the crucial clinical task of patient diagnosis. In addition, they became a direct source of input concerning the risky "life or death" consequences of child beating. This could represent an advance in status, a new basis for recognition within the medical profession. Indeed, after initial documentation of abuse, literature in various journals of radiology, roentgenology and pediatrics, articles on this topic by Woolley and Evans (1955) and Gwinn, Lewin, and Peterson (1961) appeared in the *Journal of the American Medical Association*. These were among the very few radiologic research reports published by that prestigious journal during the time period. Hence, the first factor conducive to the radiological discovery of abuse was a potential for intraorganizational advance in prestige.

The Discovery: An Opportunity for Coalition Within the Medical Community

A second factor encouraging the discovery of abuse by relatively low-status pediatric rediologists concerns the opportunity for a coalition of interests with other more prestigious segments within organized medicine. The two other segments radiologists joined in alliance were pediatrics and psychodynamically oriented psychiatry. By virtue of face-to-face clinical involvements, these specialties were higher ranking than pediatric radiology. Nevertheless each contained a dimension of marginality. Pediatrics had attained valued organizational status several decades prior to the discovery of abuse. Yet, in an age characterized by preventive drugs and treatments for previously dangerous or deadly infant diseases, it was again sliding toward the margins fo the profession (Bucher & Strauss, 1961). Psychodynamic psychiatry (as opposed to its psychosomatic cousin) experienced marginality in dealing with non-physical problems.

For both pediatrics and psychodynamic psychiatry, links with the problem of abuse could partially dissipate the respective marginality of each. Assuming a role in combatting the "deadly" forces of abuse could enlarge the "risky" part of the pediatric mission. A symbolic alliance of psychodynamic psychiatry with other bodily diagnostic and treatment specialties could also function to advance its status. Neither of these specialties was in a position to "see" abuse before the radiologists. Pediatricians were impeded by the obstacles discussed above. Psychiatrists were blocked by the reluctance of abusive parents to admit their behavior as problematic (Steele 7 Pollock, 1968). Nonetheless, the interests of both could perceivably be advanced by a coalition with the efforts of pediatric radiologists. As such, each represented a source of potential support for pediatric radiologists in their discovery of abuse. This potential for coalition served to reinforce pediatric radiology in its movement toward the discovery of abuse.

The Discovery: An Opportunity for the Application of an Acceptable Label

A crucial impediment to the discovery of abuse by the predominant interests in organized medicine was the norm of controlling the consequences of a particular diagnosis. To diagnose abuse as social deviance might curtail the power of organized medicine. The management of its consequences would fall to the extramedical interests of formal agents of social control. How is it then, that such a diagnosis by pediatric radiology and its endorsement by pediatric and psychiatric specialties, is said to have advanced these specialties within the organization of medicine? Wasn't it more likely that they should have received criticism rather than acclaim from the medical profession?

By employing a rather unique labelling process the coalition of discovery interests were able to convert the possible liability into a discernible advantage. The opportunity of generating a medical rather than socio-legal label for abuse provided the radiologists and their allies with a situation in which they could both reap the rewards associated with the diagnosis and avoid the infringement of extramedical controls. What was discovered was no ordinary behavior form but a "syndrome." Instead of departing from the tradition of organized medicine, they were able to idealize its most profound mission. Possessing a repertoire of scientific credibility, they were presented with the opportunity "to label as illness what was not previously labeled at all or what was labeled in some other fashion, under some other institutional jurisdiction" (Freidson, 1971:261).

The symbolic focal point for the acceptable labelling of abuse was the 1962 publication of an article entitled "The Battered Child Syndrome" in the *Journal of the American Medical Association* (Kempe *et al.*, 1962). This report, representing the joint research efforts of a group of radiologic, pediatric, and psychiatric specialists, labelled abuse as a "clinical condition" existing as an "unrecognized trauma" (Kempe *et al.*, 1962:17). It defined the deviance of its "psychopathic" perpetrators as a product of "psychiatric factors" representing "some defect in character structure" (Kempe *et al.*, 1962:24). As an indicator of prestige within organized medicine, it is interesting to note that the position articulated by these labellers was endorsed by the editorial board of the AMA in that same issue of JAMA.

As evidenced by the AMA editorial, the discovery of abuse as a new "illness" reduced drastically the intraorganizational constraints on doctors' "seeing" abuse. A diagnostic category had been invented and publicized. Psychological obstacles in recognizing parents as capable of abuse were eased by the separation of normatively powerful parents from non-normatively pathological individuals. Problems associated with perceiving parents as patients whose confidentiality must be protected were reconstructed by typifying them as patients who needed help. Moreover, the maintenance of professional autonomy was assured by pairing deviance with sickness. This last statement is testimony to the power of medical nomenclature. It was evidenced by the fact that (prior to its publication) the report which coined the label "battered child syndrome" was endorsed by a Children's Bureau conference which included social workers and law enforcement officials as well as doctors (McCoid, 1965:12).

The Generation of the Reporting Movement

The discovery of the "battered child syndrome" was facilitated by the opportunities for various pediatric radiologists to advance in medical prestige, form coalitions with other interests, and invent a professionally acceptable deviant label. The application of this label has been called the child abuse reporting movement. This movement was well underway by the time the 1962 Children's Bureau Conference confirmed the radiological diagnosis of abuse. Besides foreshadowing the acceptance of the sickness label, this meeting was also the basis for a series of articles to be published in *Pediatrics* which would further substantiate the diagnosis of abuse. Soon, however, the reporting movement spread beyond intraorganizational medical maneuvering to incorporate contributions from various voluntary associations, governmental agencies, as well as the media.

Extramedical responses to the newly discovered deviance confirmed the recognition of abuse as an illness. These included reports by various social welfare agencies which underscored the medical roots of the problem. For instance, the earliest investigations of the problem by social service agents resulted in a call for cooperation with the findings of radiologists in deciding the fate of abusers (Elmer 1960:100). Other studies called for "more comprehensive radiological examinations" (Boardman 1962:43). That the problem was medical in its roots as well as consequences was reinforced by the frequent referral of caseworkers to themselves as "battered child therapists" whose mission was the "curing" of "patients" (Davoren, 1968). Social welfare organizations, including the Children's Division of the American Humane Association, the Public Welfare Association, and the Child Welfare League, echoed similar concerns in sponsoring research (Children's Division, 1963; DeFrancis, 1963) and lobbying for "treatment based" legislative provisions (McCoid, 1965).

Not all extramedical interests concurred with treatment of abusers as "sick." Various law enforcement voices argued that the abuse of children was a crime and should be prosecuted. On the other hand, a survey of thirty-one publications in major law journals between 1962–1972 revealed that nearly all legal scholars endorsed treatment rather than punishment to manage abusers. Lawyers disagreed, however, as to whether reports should be mandatory and registered concern over who should report to whom. Yet, all concurred that various forms of immunity should be granted reporters (Paulsen, 1967; DeFrancis, 1967). These are all procedural issues. Neither law enforcers nor legal scholars parted from labelling abuse as a problem to be managed. The impact of the acceptable discovery of abuse by a respected knowledge sector (the medical profession) had generated a stigmatizing scrutiny bypassed in previous eras.

The proliferation of the idea of abuse by the media cannot be underestimated. Though its stories were sensational, its credibility went unchallenged. What was publicized was not some amorphous set of muggings but a "syndrome." Titles such as "Cry rises from beaten babies" (*Life,* June 1963), "Parents who beat children" (*Saturday Evening Post*, October 1962), "The shocking price of parental anger" (*Good Housekeeping*, March 1964), and "Terror struck children" (*New Republic,* May 1964) were all buttressed by an awe of scientific objectivity. The problem had become "real" in the imaginations of professionals and laymen alike. It was rediscovered visually by ABC's "Ben Casey," NBC's "Dr. Kildare," and CBS's "The Nurses," as well as in several other television scripts and documentaries (Paulsen, 1967:488–89).

Discovered by the radiologists, substantiated by their colleagues, and distributed by the media, the label was becoming widespread. Despite this fact, actual reporting laws were said to be the cooperative accomplishments of zealous individuals and voluntary associations (Paulsen, 1967:491). Who exactly, were these "zealous individuals?"

Data on legislative lobbyists reveal that, in almost every state, the civic committee concerned with abuse legislation was chaired by a doctor who "just happened" to be a pediatrician (Paulsen, 1967:491). Moreover, "the medical doctors who most influenced the legislation frequently were associated with academic medicine" (Paulsen, 1967:491). This information provides additional evidence of the collaborative role of pediatricians in guiding social reaction to the deviance discovered by their radiological colleagues.

Lack of Resistance to the Label

In addition to the medical interests discussed above, numerous voluntary associations provided support for the movement against child abuse. These included the League of Women Voters, Veterans of Foreign Wars, the Daughters of the American Republic, the District Attorneys Association, Council of Jewish Women, State Federation of Women Clubs, Public Health Associations, plus various national chapters of social workers (Paulsen, 1967:495). Two characteristics emerge from an examination of these interests. They either have a professional stake in the problem or represent the civic concerns of ceratin upper-middle-class factions. In either case the labellers were socially and politically removed from the abusers, who in all but one early study (Steele & Pollock, 1968), were characterized as lower class and minority group members.

The existence of a wide social distance between those who abuse and those who label, facilitates not only the likelihood of labelling but nullifies any organized resistance to the label by the "deviant" group itself. Research findings which describe abusers as belonging to no outside-the-family association or clubs (Young, 1964) or which portray them as isolates in the community (Giovannoni, 1971) reinforce the conclusion. Labelling was generated by powerful medical interests and perpetuated by organized media, professional and upper-middle-class concerns. Its success was enlarged by the relative powerlessness and isolation of abusers, which prevented the possibility of organized resistance to the labelling.

The Shape of Social Reaction

I have argued that the organizational advantages surrounding the discovery of abuse by pediatric radiology set in motion a process of labelling abuse as deviance and legislating against it. The actual shape of legislative enactments has been discussed elsewhere (DeFrancis, 1967; Paulsen,1967). The passage of the reporting laws encountered virtually no opposition. In Kentucky, for example, no one even appeared to testify for or against the measure (Paulsen, 1967:502). Any potential opposition from the American Medical Association, whose interests in autonomous control of the consequences of a medical diagnosis might have been threatened, had been undercut by the radiologists' success in defining abuse as a new medical problem. The AMA, unlikely to argue against conquering illness, shifted to support reporting legislation which would maximize a physician's diagnostic options.

The consequences of adopting a "sick" label for abusers is mirrored in two findings: the low rate of prosecution afforded offenders and the modification of reporting statutes so as exclusively to channel reporting toward "helping services." Regarding the first factor, Grumet (1970:306) suggests that despite existing laws and reporting statutes, actual prosecution has not increased since the time of abuse's "discovery." In support is Thomas (1972) who contends that the actual percentage of cases processed by family courts has remained constant during the same period. Even when prosecution does occur, convictions are obtained in only five to ten percent of the cases (Paulsen, 1966). And even in these cases, sentences are shorter for abusers than for other offenders convicted under the same laws of aggravated assault (Grumet, 1970:307).

State statutes have shifted on reporting from an initial adoption of the Children's Bureau model of reporting to law enforcement agents, toward one geared at reporting to child welfare or child protection agencies (DeFrancis, 1970). In fact, the attention to abuse in the early sixties has been attributed as a factor in the development of specialized "protective interests" in states which had none since the days of the SPCC crusades (Eads, 1969). This event, like the emphasis on abuser treatment, is evidence of the impact of labelling of abuse as an "illness."

REFERENCES

Bain, Katherine 1963. "The physically abused child." *Pediatrics* 31 (June):895–897.

Bakwin, Harry 1956. "Multiple skeletal lesions in young children due to trauma." *Journal of Pediatrics* 49(July):7–15

Barmeyer, G.H., L.R. Anderson and W.B. Cox, 1951. "Traumatic periostitis in young children." *Journal of Pediatrics* 38(February):184–90.

Becker, Howard S. et al. 1961. *Boys in White*. Chicago: University of Chicago Press.

Boardman, Helen 1962. "A project to rescue children from inflicted injuries." *Journal of Social Work* 7(January):43–51.

Braun, Ida G., Edgar J. Braun and Charlotte Simonds 1963. "The mistreated child." *California Medicine* 99(Augest): 98–103.

Bucher, Rue and Anselm Strauss 1961. "Professions in process". *American Journal of Sociology* 66 (January):325–334.

Caffey, John 1946. "Multiple fractures in the long bones of infants suffering from chronic and radiological features." *British Journal of Radiology* 30 (May):225–238.

Cahalan, Don 1957. "Career interests and expectations of U.S. medical students". 32:557–563.

Children's Division 1963. *Child Abuse-preview of a Nationwide Survey.* Denver: American Humane Association (Children's Division).

Davoren, Elizabeth 1968. "The role of the social worker." Pp. 153–168 IN Ray E. Helfer and Henry C. Kempe (eds.), *The Battered Child.* Chicago: University of Chicago Press.

DeFrancis, Vincent 1963. "Parents who abuse children." *PTA Magazine* 58(November):16–18.

———. 1967. "Child Abuse–the legislative response". *Denver Law Journal* 44 (Winter):3–41.

Eads, William E. 1969. "Observations on the establishment of child protection services in California." *Stanford Law Review* 21 (May):1129–1155.

Elmer, Elizabeth 1960. "Abused young children seen in hospitals." *Journal of Social Work* 3(October):98–102.

Fontana, V., D. Donovan and R. Wong 1963. "The maltreatment syndrome in children." *New England Journal of Medicine* 269 (December):1389–1394.

Freidson, Eliot J. 1968. "Medical personnel: physicians." Pp. 105–114 in David L. Sills (ed.), *International Encyclopedia of the Social Sciences.* Vol. 10. New York: MacMillan.

———. 1971 The Profession of Medicine: A study in the Sociology of Applied Knowledge. New York: Dodd, Mead and Co.

Giovannoni, Jeanne 1971. "Parental mistreatment." *Journal of Marriage and the Family* 33(November):649–657.

Glaser, William A. 1960. "Doctors and politics." *American Journal of Sociology* 66 (November):230–245.

Goode, William J. 1957. "Community within a community: the profession." *American Sociological Review* 22(April):194–200.

Grumet, Barbara R. 1970. "The plaintive plaintiffs: victims of the battered child syndrome." *Family Law Quarterly* 40(September):296–317.

Gwinn, J.J., K.W. Lewin and H.G. Peterson 1961. "Roetenographic manifestations of unsuspected trauma in infancy." *Journal of the American Medical Association* 181 (June):17–24.

Hall, Oswald 1946. "The informal organization of medicine." *Canadian Journal of Economics and Political Science* 12(February.):30–41.

Hyde, D.R., P. Wolff, A. Gross and E.L. Hoffman 1954. "The American Medical Association" Power, Purpose and politics in organized medicine." *Yale Law Journal* 63(May):938–1022.

Kempe, C.H., F.N Silverman, B.F. Steele, W. Droegemuller and H.K. Silver 1962. "The battered-child syndrome." *Journal of the American Medical Association* 181(July):17–24.

McCoid, A.H. 1965. "The battered child syndrome and other assaults upon the family." *Minnesota Law Review* 50 (November):1–58.

Paulsen, Monrad G. 1966. "The legal framework for child protection." *Columbia Law Review* 66(April):679–717.

———. 1967. "Child abuse reporting laws: the shape of the legislation." *Columbia Law Review* 67 (January):1–49.

Philips, Bernard S. 1964. "Expected value deprivation and occupational preference." *Sociometry* 27 (June): 15–160.

Radbill, Samuel X. 1968. "A history of child abuse and infanticide." Pp. 3–17 IN Ray E. Helfer and Henry C. Kempe (eds.), *The Battered Child.* Chicago: University of Chicago Press.

Silverman, F.N. 1965. "The roentgen manifestation of unrecognized skeletal trauma in infants." *American Journal of Roentgenology, Radium and Nuclear Medicine* 69 (March):413–426.

Skolnick, Arlene and Jerome H. Skolnick 1971. *The Family in Transition.* Boston: Little Brown.

Steele, Brandt and Carl F. Pollock 1968. "A psychiatric study of parents who abuse infants and small children." Pp. 103–147 IN Ray E. Helfer and Henry C. Kempe (eds.), *The Battered Child.* Chicago: University of Chicago Press.

Thomas, Mason P. 1972. "Child abuse and neglect: historical overview, legal matrix and social perspectives." *North Carolina Law Review* 50 (February):293–349.

Woolley, P.V. and W.A. Evans Jr. 1955. "Significance of skeletal lesions in infants resembling those of traumatic origin." *Journal of the American Medical Association* 158 (June): 539–543.

Young, Leontine 1964. *Wednesday's Children: A Study of Child Neglect and Abuse.* New York: McGraw-Hill.

Chapter 22

THE LEGISLATION OF MORALITY: CREATING DRUG LAWS

Troy Duster

Introduction

The relationship between law and morality is both complicated and subtle. This is true even in a situation where a society is very homogenous and where one might find a large degree of consensus about moral behavior. Those who argue that law is simply the empirical operation of morality are tempted to use homogenous situations as examples. In discussing this relationship, Selznick asserts that laws are secondary in nature.[1] They are secondary in the sense that they obtain their legitimacy in terms of some other more primary reference point.

> The distinctively legal emerges with the development of secondary rules, that is, rules of authoritative determination. These rules, selectively applied, "raise up" the primary norms and give them a legal status....The appeal from an *asserted* rule, however, coercively enforced, to a justified rule is the elementary legal act. This presumes at least a dim awareness that some reason lies behind the impulse to conform, a reason founded not in conscience, habit, or fear alone, but in the decision to uphold an authoritative order. The rule of legal recognition may be quite blunt and crude: the law is what the king or priest says it is. But this initial reference of a primary norm to a ground of obligation breeds the complex elaboration of authoritative rules that marks a developed legal order.[2]

The most primary of reference points is, of course, the moral order. One can explain why he does something for just so long, before he is driven to a position where he simply must assert that it is "right" or "wrong." With narcotics usage and addiction, the issue in contemporary times is typically raised in the form of a moral directive, irrespective of the physiological and physical aspects of addiction. The laws concerning narcotics usage may now be said to be a secondary set held up against the existing primary or moral view of drugs. However, the drug laws have been on the books for half a century, during which time, as we shall see, this country has undergone a remarkable transformation in its moral interpretation of narcotics usage. Clearly, if we want to understand the ongoing relationship between the law and morality, we are misled by assuming one has some fixed relationship to the other. To put it another way, if a set of laws remains unchanged while the moral order undergoes a drastic transformation, it follows that the relationship of law to morality must be a changing thing, and cannot be static. If narcotics law was simply the empirical element of narcotics morality, a change in the moral judgement of narcotics use should be accompanied by its counterpart in the law, and vice versa. As Selznick points out:

> In recent years, the great social effects of legal change have been too obvious to ignore. The question is no longer *whether* law is a significant vehicle of social change but rather *how* it so functions and what special problems arise.[3]

Selznick goes on to suggest explorations into substantive problems of "change." The connection of law to change is clearly demonstrable. If a society undergoes rapid technological development, new social relationships will emerge, and so too, will a set of laws to handle them. The gradual disintegration of the old caste relationships in India has been and will be largely attributable to the development of new occupations which contain no traditional forms regulating how one caste should respond to another.

The relationship of law to morality is not quite so clear. It is more specific, but more abstract. The sociological study of the narcotics problem is critical to discussion of this relationship, because it provides a specific empirical case where one can observe historically the interplay between the two essential components. More than any other form of deviance, the history of drug use contains an abundance of material on both questions of legislation and morality, and of the relationship between them.

Background and Setting

Despite the public clamor of the 1960s about LSD and marijuana, the drug that has most dominated and colored the American conceptions of narcotics is opium. Among the most effective of painkillers, opium has been known and used in some form for thousands of years. Until the middle of the nineteenth century, opium was taken orally, either smoked or ingested. The Far East monopolized both production and consumption until the hypodermic needle was discovered as an extremely effective way of injecting the drug instantly into the bloodstream. It was soon to become a widely used analgesic. The first hypodermic injections of morphine, an opium derivative used to relieve pain, occurred in this country in 1856.[4]

Medical journals were enthusiastic in endorsing the new therapeutic usages that were possible, and morphine was the suggested remedy for an endless variety of physical sufferings. It was during the Civil War, however, that morphine injection really spread extensively. Then wholesale usage and addiction became sufficiently pronounced so that one could speak of an American problem for the first time.[5] Soldiers were given morphine to deaden the pain from all kinds of battle injuries and illnesses. After the war, ex-soldiers by the thousands continued using the drug, and recommending it to friends and relatives.

Within a decade, medical companies began to include morphine in a vast number of medications that were sold directly to consumers as household remedies. This was the period before governmental regulation, and the layman was subjected to a barrage of newspaper and billboard advertisements claiming cures for everything from the common cold to cholera. "Soothing Syrups" with morphine often contained no mention of their contents, and many men moved along the path to the purer morphine through this route.

> It is not surprising that many persons became dependent on these preparations and later turned to the active drug itself when accidentally or otherwise they learned of its presence in the "medicine" they had been taking.... The peak of the patent medicine industry was reached just prior to the passage of the Pure Food and Drug Act in 1906.[6]

It must be remembered that there were no state or federal laws concerning the sale and distribution of medicinal narcotic drugs during this period under discussion, and pharmacists sold morphine simply when it was requested by a customer. There is no way to accurately assess the extent of addiction at that time, nor is there now, for that matter. However, there are some informed estimates by scholars who have studied many facets of the period. Among the better guesses many will settle for is that from 2 to 4 percent of the population was addicted in 1895.[7] Studies of pharmaceutical dispensaries, druggists, and physicians' records were carried out in the 1880s and 1890s which relate to this problem. The widespread use of morphine was demonstrated by Hartwell's survey of Massachusetts druggists in 1888[8], Hull's study of Iowa druggists in 1885,[9] Earle's work in Chicago in 1880,[10] and Grinnell's survey of Vermont in 1900.[11] The methodological techniques of investigation do not meet present-day standards, but even if certain systematic biases are assumed, the 3 percent figure is an acceptable guess of the extent of addiction.

The large numbers of addicts alarmed a growing number of medical men. The American press, which had been so vocal in its denunciation of the sensational but far less common opium smoking in opium dens in the 1860s and 1870s, was strangely if typically silent on morphine medication and its addicting effects. Just as the present-day press adroitly avoids making news of very newsworthy government proceedings on false advertising (an issue in which there may also be some question of the accomplice), newspapers of that time did not want to alienate the advertisers, because they were a major source of revenue. Nonetheless, the knowledge of the addicting qualities of morphine became more and more common among a sizable minority of physicians.

It was in this setting, in 1898, that a German pharmacological researcher named Dreser produced a new substance from a morphine base, diacetylmorphin, otherwise known as heroin. The medical community was enthusiastic in its reception of the new drug. It had three times the strength of morphine, and it was believed to be free from addicting qualities. The most respectable medical journals of Germany and the United States carried articles and reports lauding heroin as a cure for morphine addiction.[12]

Within five short years, the first definitive serious warnings about the addicting qualities of heroin appeared in an American medical journal.[13] The marvelous success of heroin as a painkiller and sedative, however, made the drug popular with both physician and patient. It should be remembered that one did not need a prescription to buy it. The news of the new warnings traveled slowly, and heroin joined morphine as one the most frequently used pain remedies for the ailing and suffering.

From 1865 to 1900, then, addiction to narcotics was relatively widespread. This is documented in an early survey of material by Terry and Pellens, a treatise which remains the classic work on late nineteenth- and early twentieth-century problems of addiction.[14] In proportion to the population, addiction was probably eight times more prevalent then than now, despite the large increase in the general population.

It is remarkable, therefore, that addiction is regarded today as a problem of far greater moral, legal, and social significance than it was then. As we shall see directly, the problem at the turn of the century was conceived in very different terms, treated in a vastly different manner, and located in opposite places in the social order.

The first task is to illustrate how dramatic and complete was the shift of addicts from one social category to another during a critical twenty-year period. The second task is to examine the legal activity which affected that shift. Finally, the task will be to examine the changing moral judgments that coincided with these developments.

It is now taken for granted that narcotic addicts come primarily from the working and lower classes....This has not always been true. The evidence clearly indicates that the upper and middle classes predominated among narcotic addicts in the period up to 1914. In 1903, the American Pharmaceutical Association conducted a study of selected communities in the United States and Canada. They sent out mailed questionnaires to physicians and druggists, and from the responses concluded that

> while the increase is most effective with the lower classes, the statistics
> of institutes devoted to the cure of habitues show that their patients are
> principally drawn from those in the higher walks of life....[15]

From a report on Massachusetts druggists published in 1889 and cited by Terry and Pellens, the sale of opium derivatives to those of higher incomes exceeded the amount sold to lower-income persons.[16] This is all the more striking if we take into account the fact that the working and lower classes comprised a far greater percentage of the population of the country in 1890 than they do today. (With the 1960 census figures, the population of the United States becomes predominantly white collar for the first time in history.) In view of the fact that the middle class comprised proportionately less of the population, the incidence of its addiction rate can be seen as even more significant.

It was acknowledged in medical journals that a morphine addict could not be detected as an addict so long as he maintained his supply.[17] Some of the most respectable citizens of the community, pillars of the middle-class morality, were addicted. In cases where this was known, the victim was regarded as one afflicted with a physiological problem, in much the same way as we presently regard the need of a diabetic for insulin. Family histories later indicated that many went through their daily tasks, their occupations, completely undetected by friends and relatives.[18]

There are two points of considerable significance that deserve more careful consideration. The first is the fact that some friends and relatives could and did know about an addiction and still did not make a judgement, either moral or psychological, of the person addicted. The second is that the lower classes were not those primarily associated with morphine or heroin usage in 1900.

The moral interpretation of addiction in the twentieth century is especially interesting in view of the larger historical trend. Western man has, on the whole, developed increasing tolerance and compassion for problems that were previously dogmatically treated as moral issues, such as epilepsy, organic and functional mental disorders, polio, diabetes, and so on. There was a time when most were convinced that the afflicted were possessed by devils, were morally evil, and inferior. Both medical opinion and literature of the eighteenth and nineteenth centuries were replete with the moral interpretation of countless physiological problems which have now been reinterpreted in an almost totally nonmoral fashion. The only moral issue now attendant to these questions is whether persons suffering should receive treatment from physicians. Even venereal diseases, which retain a stigma, are unanimously conceived as physiological problems that should be treated physiologically irrespective of the moral conditions under which they were contracted.

The narcotic addict of the 1890s was in a situation almost the reverse of those suffering from the above problems. His acquaintances and his community could know of his addiction, feel somewhat sorry for his dependence upon *medication*, but admit him to a position of respect and authority. If the heroin addict of 1900 was getting a willful thrill out of his injection, no one was talking about either the element of the thrill, not even the drug companies. If the thrill was to be had, there was no reason for manufacturers not to take advantage of this in their advertisements. They had no moral compunctions about patently false claims for a cure, or about including an opium derivative without so stating on the label.

Despite the fact that all social classes had their share of addicts, there was a difference in the way lower-class addicts were regarded. This difference was exacerbated when legislation drove heroin underground, predominantly to the lower classes. Writing in the *American Journal of Clinical Medicine* in 1918, G. Swaine made an arbitrary social classification of addicts, about which he offered the following distinction:

> In Class one, we can include all of the physical, mental, and moral defectives, the tramps, hoboes, idlers, loaders, irresponsibles, criminals, and denizens of the underworld....In these cases, morphine addiction is a vice, as well as a disorder resulting from narcotic poisoning. These are the "drug fiends." In Class two, we have many types of good citizens who have become addicted to the use of the drug innocently, and who are in every sense of the word "victims." Morphine is no respecter of persons, and the victims are doctors, lawyers, ministers, artists, actors, judges, congressmen, senators, priests, authors, women, girls, all of whom realize their conditions and want to be cured. In these cases, morphine-addiction is not a vice, but, an incubus, and, when they are cured they stay cured.[19]

This may seem to jump ahead of the task of this section which is simply to portray as accurately as possible the dramatic shift of addicts from one social category to another during this period. However, the shift itself carried with it more than a description. These were the beginnings of moral interpretations for the meaning of that shift. By 1920, a medical journal reported cases treated at Riverside Hospital in New York City in the following manner:

> Drug addicts may be divided into two general classes. The first class is composed of people who have become addicted to the use of drugs through illness, associated probably with an underlying neurotic temperament. The second class, which is *overwhelmingly in the majority* [italics mine], is at the present time giving municipal authorities the greatest concern. These persons are largely from the underworld, or channels leading directly to it. They have become addicted to the use of narcotic drugs largely through association with habitues and they find in the drug a panacea for the physical and mental ills that are the result of the lives they are leading. Late hours, dance halls, and unwholesome cabarets do much to bring about this condition of body and mind....[20]

Whereas in 1900 the addict population was spread relatively evenly over the social classes (with the higher classes having slightly more), by 1920, medical journals could speak of the "overwhelming" majority from the "unrespectable" parts of society. The same pattern can be seen with the shift from the predominantly middle-aged to the young, and with the shift from a predominance of women to an overwhelming majority of men.

In a study reported in 1880 and cited by Terry and Pellens, addiction to drugs was said to be "a vice of middle life, the larger number, by far, being from 30 to 40 years of age."[21] By 1920, Hubbard's study of New York's clinic could let him conclude that:

> Most, in fact 70 percent of the addicts in our clinic, are young people....the one and only conclusion that we can arrive at, is that acquirements of this practice—drug addiction—is incident to propinquity, bad associates, taken together with weak vacillating dispositions, making a successful combination in favor of the acquirement of such a habit.[22]

A report of a study of addiction to the Michigan State Board of Health in 1878 stated that, of 1,313 addicts, 803 were females, 510 males.[23] This is corroborated by Earle's study of Chicago, reported in 1880:

> Among the 235 habitual opium-eaters, 169 were found to be females, a proportion of about 3-to-1. Of these 169 females, about one-third belong to that class known as prostitutes. Deducting these, we still have among those taking the different kinds of opiates, 2 females to 1 male.[24]

Similarly, a report by Hull in 1885 on addiction in Iowa lists the distribution by sex as two-thirds female, and Terry's research in Florida in 1913 reported that 60 percent of the cases were women.[25] Suddenly, as if in magical correspondence to the trend cited above on social class and age, the sex distribution reversed itself, and in

1914, McIver and Price report[ed] that 70 percent of the addicts at Philadelphia General Hospital were males.[26] A governmental report to the Treasury Department in 1918 found addicts about equally divided between both sexes in this country, but a 1920 report for New York conclusively demonstrated that males were by then the predominant sex among drug addicts. Hubbard's report indicated that almost 80 percent of the New York Clinic's population of addicts were male.[27] The Los Angeles Clinic had a similar distribution for 1920 and 1921. The picture is clear. Taking only the three variables of age, sex, and social class into account, there is a sharp and remarkable transformation to be noticed in the two-decade period at the turn of the century. Let us examine now the legal turn of events of the period.

Prior to 1897, there was no significant legislation in any state concerning the manufacture or distribution of narcotics. As we have seen, the medical profession was becoming increasingly aware of the nature of morphine addiction when heroin was discovered in 1898. The alarm over the common practice of using morphine for a myriad of ills was insufficient to stem the tide of great enthusiasm with which physicians greeted heroin. Nonetheless, a small band of dedicated doctors who had been disturbed by the widespread ignorance of morphine in the profession (warnings about addiction did not appear in medical texts until about 1900) began to agitate for governmental intervention and regulation.[28]

From 1887 to 1908, many states passed individual laws aimed at curbing some aspect of the distribution of narcotics. Opium smoking was a favorite target of most of these laws, a development occasioned by the more concentrated treatment given this issue in the American press. Nonetheless, many of the state legislatures listened to medical men who insisted on the need for more control on the widespread distribution of the medicinally used opium derivatives. New York's state legislature passed the first comprehensive piece of legislation in the country concerning this problem in 1904, the Boylan Act.

As with many other problems of this kind, the lack of uniform state laws meant that control was virtually impossible. There is great variety in the law-making ability of each state, and sometimes it seems as though each state reviews the others carefully in order not to duplicate the provisions of their laws. If New York wanted registration of pharmacists, Massachusetts would want the registration of the central distributing warehouses, Illinois might want only the physician's prescriptions, and so forth. It soon became clear that only national and even international centralized control would be effective.

At the request of the United States, an international conference on opium was called in early 1909. Among countries accepting the invitation to this convention held in Shanghai were China, Great Britain, France, Germany, Italy, Russia, and Japan. Prior to this time, there had been a few attempts at control by individual nations in treaties, but this was the first concerted action on a truly international level. The major purpose of this first conference, as well as two other international conventions that were called within the next four years, was to insure that opium and related drugs be distributed only for expressly medical purposes, and ultimately distributed to the consumer through medical channels. The conferences called for regulation of the traffic at ports of entry, especially, but also tried to deal with the complicated problem of mail traffic. The handful of nations represented at the first Shanghai conference recognized the need for obtaining agreement and compliance from every nation in the world. The United States found itself in the embarrassing position of being the only major power without any control law covering distribution of medicinal narcotics within its borders. (The 1909 federal law was directed at opium smoking.) It was very much as a direct result of participation in the international conventions, then, that this country found itself being pressed for congressional action on the problem.

In this climate of both internal and international concern for the medicinal uses of the opium derivatives, Congress passed the Harrison Narcotic Act, approved December 17, 1914.

The Harrison Act stipulated that anyone engaged in the production or distribution of narcotics must register with the federal government and keep records of all transactions with drugs. This was the first of the three central provisions fo the act. It gave the government precise knowledge of legal traffic, and for the first time, the various uses and avenues of distribution could be traced.

The second major provision required that all parties handling the drugs through either purchase or sale pay a tax. This was the critical portion, because it meant that enforcement would reside with the tax collector, the Treasury Department, and more specifically, its Bureau of Internal Revenue. The Bureau set up a subsidiary organization to deal with affairs related to surveillance of activities covered by the new law. The immediate task was to insure that drugs were registered and passed through legitimate channels, beginning with importation and ending with the consumer. Since everyone was required to keep a record, the Bureau could demand and survey documentary material at every stage of the market operation.

Finally, the third major provision of the Harrison Act was a subtle "sleeper" that was not to obtain importance until the Supreme Court made a critical interpretation in 1919. This was the provision that unregistered persons could purchase drugs only upon the prescription of a physician, and that such a prescription must be for legitimate medical use. It seemed innocent enough a provision, one that was clearly included so that the physician retained the only control over the dispensation of narcotics to the consumer. As such, the bill was designed by its framers to place the addict completely in the hands of the medical profession.

It is one of those ironic twists that this third provision, intended for one purpose, was to be used in such a way as to thwart that purpose. As a direct consequence of it, the medical profession abandoned the drug addict. The key revolved around the stipulation that doctors could issue a prescription only to addicts for *legitimate* medical purposes. The decision about what is legitimate medical practice rests ultimately outside the medical profession in the moral consensus which members of society achieve about legitimacy. Even if the medical profession were to agree that experimental injections of a new drug on a random sample of babies would do most to advance medical science, the moral response against experimentation would be so strong as to destroy its claim to legitimacy. Thus, it is only in arbitrary and confined hypothetical instances that we can cogently argue that the medical profession determines legitimate practice.

So it was that the germ of a moral conception, the difference between good and evil or right and wrong, was to gain a place in the exercise of the new law.

Since the Harrison Act said nothing explicitly about the basis upon which physicians could prescribe narcotics for addicts, the only theoretical change that was foreseeable was the new status of the prescription at the drug counter. All sales were to be registered, and a signed prescription from a physician was required. But when the physician became the only legal source of the drug supply, hundreds of thousands of law-abiding addicts suddenly materialized outside of doctors' offices. It was inconceivable that the relatively small number of doctors in the country could so suddenly handle over half a million new patients in any manner, and certainly it was impossible that they might handle them individually. The doctor's office became little more than a dispensing station for the addict, with only an infinitesimal fraction of addicts receiving personal care. In most cases, this was simply a continuation of the small number who had already been under regular care.

In New York City for example, it was impossible for a doctor with even a small practice to do anything more than sign prescriptions for his suddenly created large clientele. The government agents were alarmed at what they regarded as cavalier treatment of the prescription by the medical profession, and were concerned that the spirit and intent of the new drug law were being violated. They decided to prosecute some physicians who were prescribing to addicts en masse. They succeeded in convicting them, and appeals took the cases up to the Supreme Court. In a remarkable case (*Webb vs. U.S.*, 1919) the Supreme Court made a decision that was to have far-reaching effects on the narcotics traffic, ruling that:

> a prescription of drugs for an addict "not in the course of professional treatment in the attempted cure of the habit, but being issued for the purpose of providing the user with morphine sufficient to keep him comfortable by maintaining his customary use" was not a prescription in the meaning of the law and was not included within the exemption for the doctor-patient relationship.[29]

Doctors who continued to prescribe to addicts on anything but the most personal and individual basis found themselves faced with the real, demonstrated possibility of fines and prison sentences. As I have indicated, there were hundreds of thousands of addicts, and only a few thousand physicians to handle them. If there were thirty or forty addicts outside a doctor's office waiting for prescriptions, *or even waiting for a chance to go through withdrawal*, the Supreme Court decision and the Treasury Department's actions made it almost certain that the doctor would turn them away. A minority of doctors, some for humanitarian reasons, some from the profit-motive of a much higher fee, continued to prescribe. Scores of them were arrested, prosecuted, fined, imprisoned, and set forth as an example to others. The addict found himself being cut off gradually but surely from all legal sources, and he began to turn gradually but surely to the welcome arms of the black marketeers.

And so it was that the law and its interpretation by the Supreme Court provided the final condition and context for a moral reassessment of what had previously been regarded as a physiological problem. The country could begin to connect all addicts with their newfound underworld associates, and could now begin to talk about a different class of men who were consorting with criminals. The step was only a small one to the imputation of criminal intent. The bridge between law and morality was drawn.

NOTES

[1] Philip Selznick, "Sociology of Law" (mimeographed, Center for the Study of Law and Society, University of California, Berkeley), April 1965. Prepared for the *International Encyclopedia of the Social Sciences*.

[2] Ibid.

[3] Ibid., p.23.

[4] Charles E. Terry and Mildred Pellens, *The Opium Problem* (New York: Bureau of Social Hygiene, 1928), p.66.

[5] Ibid., p.69.

[6] Ibid., p.75.

[7] Marie Nyswander, *The Drug Addict as a Patient* (New York: Grune & Stratton, 1956), pp.1–13.

[8] B.H. Hartwell, "The Sale and Use of Opium in Massachusetts," *Annual Report Massachusetts State Board of Health*, 1889.

[9] Terry and Pellens, op. cit., p.17.

[10] C.W. Earle, "The Opium Habit," *Chicago Medical Review*, 2 (1880), 442–90.

[11] A.P. Grinnell, "A Review of Drug Consumption and Alcohol as Found in Proprietary Medicine," *Medical Legal Journal*, 1905, pp.426–589.

[12] A much longer list of references is cited by Terry and Pellens, op. cit., and the following are only a small but representative portion: H. Dreser, the man credited with the discovery of heroin, writing of his own findings in an Abstract to the *Journal of the American Medical Association*, 1898; two reports by M. Manges in the *New York Medical Journal*, November 16, 1898, and January 20, 1900.

[13] G.E. Pettey, "The Heroin Habit, Another Curse," *Alabama Medical Journal*, 15 (1902–1903), 147–80.

[14] Terry and Pellens, op. cit.

[15] E.G. Eberle, "Report of Committee on Acquirement of Drug Habits," *American Journal of Pharmacology*, October, 1903, p.481.

[16] Terry and Pellens, op. cit., p.468.

[17] C.S. Pearson, "A Study of Degeneracy as Seen Among Addicts," *New York Medical Journal*, November 15, 1919, pp.805–8.

[18] For example, cf. T.S. Blair, "Narcotic Drug Addiction as Regulated by a State Department of Health," *Journal of the American Medical Association*, 72 (May 17, 1919), 1442–44.

[19] G.D. Swaine, "Regarding the Luminal Treatment of Morphine Addiction," *American Journal of Clinical Medicine*, 25 (August, 1918), 611.

[20] Terry and Pellens, op. cit., p.499.

[21] Ibid., p.475.

[22] S.D. Hubbard, "The New York City Narcotic Clinic and Differing Points of View on Narcotic Addiction," *Monthly bulletin of the Department of Health, City of New York*, February, 1920.

[23] Terry and Pellens, op. cit., p.11.

[24] Earle, op. cit.

[25] Terry and Pellens, op. cit., pp.470–1.

[26] J. McIver and G.E. Price, "Drug Addiction," *Journal of the American Medical Association*, 66 (February 12, 1916), 477.

[27] Hubbard, op. cit.

[28] Nyswander, op. cit.

[29] Alfred T. Lindesmith, *The Addict and the Law* (Bloomington: Indiana University Press, 1965), p.6.

Chapter 23

MEDICINE AS AN INSTITUTION OF SOCIAL CONTROL: CONSEQUENCES FOR SOCIETY

Peter Conrad
Joseph Schneider

In our society we want to believe in medicine, as we want to believe in religion and our country; it wards off collective fears and reduces public anxieties (see Edelman, 1977). In significant ways medicine, especially psychiatry, has replaced religion as the most powerful extralegal institution of social control. Physicians have been endowed with some of the charisma of shamans. In the 20th century the medical model of deviance has ascended with the glitter of a rising star, expanding medicine's social control function...[We] focus directly on medicine as an agent of social control. First, we illustrate the range and varieties of medical social control. Next, we analyze the consequences of the medicalization of deviance and social control....

Types of Medical Social Control

Medicine was first conceptualized as an agent of social control by Talcott Parsons (1951) in his seminal essay on the "sick role."....Eliot Friedson (1970) and Irving Zola (1972) have elucidated the jurisdictional mandate the medical profession has over anything that can be labeled an illness, regardless of its ability to deal with it effectively. The boundaries of medicine are elastic and increasingly expansive (Ehrenreich and Ehrenreich, 1975), and some analysts have expressed concern at the increasing medicalization of life (Illich, 1976). Although medical social control has been conceptualized in several ways, including professional control of colleagues (Friedson, 1975) and control of the micropolitics of physician-patient interaction (Waitzkin and Stoeckle, 1976), the focus here is narrower. Our concern...is with the medical control of deviant behavior, an aspect of the medicalization of deviance (Conrad, 1975; Pitts, 1968). Thus by medical social control we mean the ways in which medicine functions (wittingly or unwittingly) to secure adherence to social norms—specifically, by using medical means to minimize, eliminate, or normalize deviant behavior. This section illustrates and catalogues the broad range of medical controls of deviance and in so doing conceptualizes three major "ideal types" of medical social control.

On the most abstract level medical social control is the acceptance of a medical perspective as the dominant definition of certain phenomena. When medical perspectives of problems and their solutions become dominant, they diminish competing definitions. This is particularly true of problems related to bodily functioning and in

212

areas where medical technology can demonstrate effectiveness (e.g., immunization, contraception, antibacterial drugs) and is increasingly the case for behavioral and social problems (Mechanic, 1973). This underlies the construction of medical norms (e.g., the definition of what is healthy) and the "enforcement" of both medical and social norms. Medical social control also includes medical advice, counsel, and information that are part of the general stock of knowledge: for example, a well-balanced diet is important, cigarette smoking causes cancer, being overweight increases health risks, exercising regularly is healthy, teeth should be brushed regularly. Such directives, even when unheeded, serve as road signs for desirable behavior. At a more concrete level, medical social control is enacted through professional medical intervention, *qua* medical treatment (although it may include some types of self-treatment such as self-medication or medically oriented self-help groups). This intervention aims at returning sick individuals to compliance with health norms and to their conventional social roles, adjusting them to new (e.g., impaired) roles, or, short of these, making individuals more comfortable with their condition (see Friedson, 1970; Parsons, 1951). Medical social control of deviant behavior is usually a variant of medical intervention that seeks to eliminate, modify, isolate, or regulate behavior socially defined as deviant, with medical means and in the name of health.

Traditionally, psychiatry and public health have served as the clearest examples of medical control. Psychiatry's social control functions with mental illness, especially in terms of institutionalization, have been described clearly (e.g., Miller, 1976; Szasz, 1970). Recently it has been argued that psychotherapy, because it reinforces dominant values and adjusts people to their life situations, is an agent of social control and a supporter of the status quo (Halleck, 1971; Hurvitz, 1973). Public health's mandate, the control and elimination of conditions and diseases that are deemed a threat to the health of the community is more diffuse. It operates as a control agent by setting and enforcing certain "health" standards in the home, workplace, and community (e.g., food, water, sanitation) and by identifying, preventing, and treating, and, if necessary, isolating persons with communicable diseases (Rosen, 1972). A clear example of the latter is the detection of venereal disease. Indeed, public health has exerted considerable coercive power in attempting to prevent the spread of infectious disease.

There are a number of types of medical control of deviance. The most common forms of medical social control include medicalizing deviant behavior—that is, defining the behavior as an illness or a symptom of an illness or underlying disease—and subsequent direct medical intervention. This medical social control takes three general forms: medical technology, medical collaboration, and medical ideology.

Medical Technology

The growth of specialized medicine and the concomitant development of medical technology has produced an armamentarium of medical controls. Psychotechnologies, which include various forms of medical and behavioral technologies (Chorover, 1973), are the most common means of medical control of deviance. Since the emergence of phenothiazine medications in the early 1950s for the treatment and control of mental disorder, there has been a virtual explosion in the development and use of psychoactive medications to control behavioral deviance: tranquilizers such as chlordiazepoxide (Librium) and diazepam (Valium) for anxiety, nervousness, and general malaise; stimulant medications for hyperactive children; amphetamines for overeating and obesity; disulfiram (Antabuse) for alcoholism; methadone for heroin, and many others.[1] These pharmaceutical discoveries, aggressively promoted by a highly profitable and powerful drug industry (Goddard, 1973), often become the treatment of choice for deviant behavior. They are easily administered under professional medical control, quite potent in their effects (i.e., controlling, modifying, and even eliminating behavior), and are generally less expensive than other medical treatments and controls (e.g., hospitalization, altering environments, long-term psychotherapy).

Psychosurgery, surgical procedures meant to correct certain "brain dysfunctions" presumed to cause deviant behavior, was developed in the early 1930s as prefrontal lobotomy, and has been used as a treatment for mental illness. But psychosurgery fell into disrepute in the early 1950s because the "side effects" (general passivity, difficulty with abstract thinking) were deemed too undesirable, and many patients remained institutionalized in spite of such treatments. Furthermore, new psychoactive medications were becoming available to control the mentally ill. By the middle 1950s, however, approximately 40,000 to 50,000 such operations were performed in the United States (Freeman, 1959). In the late 1960s a new and technologically more sophisticated variant of psychosurgery (including laser technology and brain implants) emerged and was heralded by some as a treatment for uncontrollable violent outbursts (Delgado, 1969; Mark and Ervin, 1970). Although psychosurgery for violence has been criticized for both within as well as outside the medical profession (Chorover, 1974), and relatively few such operations have been performed, in 1976 a blueribbon national commission reporting to the Department of Health, Education and Welfare endorsed the use of psychosurgery as having "potential merit" and judged its risks "not excessive." This may encourage an increased use of this form of medical control.[2]

Behavior modification, a psychotechnology based on B.F. Skinner's and other behaviorists' learning theories, has been adopted by some medical professionals as a treatment modality. A variety of types and variations of behavior modification exist (e.g., token economies, tier systems, positive reinforcement schedules, aversive conditioning). While they are not medical technologies per se, they have been used by physicians for the treatment of mental illness, mental retardation, homosexuality, violence, hyperactive children, autism, phobias, alcoholism, drug addiction, eating problems, and other disorders. An irony of the medical use of behavior modification is that behaviorism explicitly denies the medical model (that behavior is a symptom of illness) and adopts an environmental, albeit still individual, solution to the problem. This has not, however, hindered its adoption by medical professionals.

Human genetics is one of the most exciting and rapidly expanding areas of medical knowledge. Genetic screening and genetic counseling are becoming more commonplace. Genetic causes are proposed for such a variety of human problems as alcoholism, hyperactivity, learning disabilities, schizophrenia, manic-depressive psychosis, homosexuality, and mental retardation. At this time, apart from specific genetic disorders such as phenylketonuria (PKU) and certain forms of retardation, genetic explanations tend to be general theories (i.e., at best posting "predispositions"), with only minimal empirical support, and are not at the level at which medical intervention occurs. The most well-publicized genetic theory of deviant behavior is that an XXY chromosome arrangement is a determinant factor in "criminal tendencies." Although this XXY research has been criticized severely (e.g., Fox, 1971), the controversy surrounding it may be a harbinger of things to come. Genetic anomalies may be discovered to have a correlation with deviant behavior and may become a causal explanation for this behavior. Medical control, in the form of genetic counseling (Sorenson, 1974), may discourage parents from having offspring with a high risk (e.g., 25%) of genetic impairment. Clearly the potentials for medical control go far beyond present use; one could imagine the possibility of licensing selected parents (with proper genes) to have children, and further manipulating gene arrangements to produce or eliminate certain traits.

Medical Collaboration

Medicine acts not only as an independent agent of social control (as above), but frequently medical collaboration with other authorities serves social control functions. Such collaboration includes roles as information provider, gatekeeper, institutional agent, and technician. These interdependent medical control functions highlight the extent to which medicine is interwoven in the fabric of society. Historically, medical personnel have reported information on gunshot wounds and venereal disease to state authorities. More recently this has included reporting "child abuse" to child welfare or law enforcement agencies (Pfohl, 1977).

The medical profession is the official designator of the "sick role." This imbues the physician with authority to define particular kinds of deviance as illness and exempt the patient from certain role obligations. These are general gatekeeping and social control tasks. In some instances the physician functions as a specific gatekeeper for special exemptions from conventional norms; here the exemptions are authorized because of illness, disease, or disability. A classic example is the so-called insanity defense in certain crime cases. Other more commonplace examples include competency to stand trial, medical deferment from the draft or a medical discharge from the military; requiring physicians' notes to legitimize missing an examination or excessive absences in school, and, before abortion was legalized, obtaining two psychiatrists' letters testifying to the therapeutic necessity of the abortion. Halleck (1971) has called this "the power of medical excuse." In a slightly different vein, but still forms of gatekeeping and medical excuse, are medical examinations for disability or workman's compensation benefits. Medical reports required for insurance coverage and employment or medical certification of an epileptic as seizure free to obtain a driver's license are also gatekeeping activities.

Physicians in total institutions have one of two roles. In some institutions, such as schools for the retarded or mental hospitals, they are usually the administrative authority; in others, such as in the military or prisons, they are employees of the administration. In total institutions, medicine's role as an agent of social control (for the institution) is more apparent. In both the military and prisons, physicians have the power to confer the sick role and to offer medical excuse for deviance (see Daniels, 1969; Waitzkin and Waterman, 1974). For example, discharges and sick call are available medical designations for deviant behavior. Since physicians are both hired as paid by the institution, it is difficult for them to be fully an agent of the patient, engendering built-in role strains. An extreme example is in wartime when the physician's mandate is to return the soldier to combat duty as soon as possible. Under some circumstances physicians act direct agents of control by prescribing medications to control unruly or disorderly inmates or to help a "neurotic" adjust to the conditions of a total institution. In such cases "captive professionals" (Daniels, 1969) are more likely to become the agent of the institution than the agent of the individual patient (Szasz, 1965; see also Menninger, 1967).

Under rather rare circumstances physicians may become "mere technicians," applying the sanctions of another authority who purchases their medical skills. An extreme example would be the behavior of the experimental and death physicians in Nazi Germany. A less heinous but nevertheless ominous example is provided by physicians who perform court-ordered sterilizations (Kittrie, 1971). Perhaps one could imagine sometime in the future, if the death penalty becomes commonplace again, physicians administering drugs as the "humanitarian" and painless executioners.[3]

Medical Ideology

Medical ideology is a type of social control that involves defining a behavior or condition as an illness primarily because of the social and ideological benefits accrued by conceptualizing it in medical terms. These effects of medical ideology may benefit the individual, the dominant interests in the society, or both. They exist independently of any organic basis for illness or any available treatment. Howard Waitzkin and Barbara Waterman (1974) call one latent function of medicalization "secondary gain," arguing that assumption of the sick role can fulfill personality and individual needs (e.g., gaining nurturance or attention) or legitimize personal failure (Shuval and Antonovsky, 1973).[4] One of the most important functions of the disease model of alcoholism and to a lesser extent drug addiction is the secondary gain of removing blame from, and constructing a shield against condemnation of, individuals for their deviant behavior. Alcoholics Anonymous, a nonmedical quasireligious self-help organization, adopted a variant of the medical model of alcoholism independent of the medical profession. One suspects the secondary gain serves their purposes well.

Disease designations can support dominant social interests and institutions. A poignant example is prominent 19th century New Orleans physician S.W. Cartwright's antebellum conceptualization of the disease drapetomania, a condition that only affected slaves. Its major symptom was running away from their masters (Cartwright, S.W., 1851). Medical conceptions and controls often support dominant social values and morality: the 19th-century Victorian conceptualization of the illness of and addiction to masturbation and the medical treatments developed to control this disease make chilling reading in the 1970s (Comfort, 1967; Englehart, 1974). The recent Soviet labeling of political dissidents as mentally ill is another example of the manipulation of illness designations to support dominant political and social institutions (Conrad, 1977). These examples highlight the sociopolitical nature of illness designations in general (Zola, 1975).

In sum, medicine as an institution of social control has a number of faces. The three types of medical control discussed here do not necessarily exist as discrete entities but are found in combination with one another. For example, court-ordered sterilizations or medical prescribing of drugs to unruly nursing home patients combines both technological and collaborative aspects of medical control; legitimating disability status includes both ideological and collaborative aspects of medical control; and treating Soviet dissidents with drugs for their mental illness combines all three aspects of medical social control. It is clear that the enormous expansion of medicine in the past 50 years has increased the number of possible ways in which problems could be medicalized beyond those discussed [previously]. In the next section we will point out some of the consequences of this medicalization.

Social Consequences of Medicalizing Deviance

Jesse Pitts (1968:391), one of the first sociologists to give attention to the medicalization of deviance, suggests that "medicalization is one of the most effective means of social control and that it is destined to become the main mode of *formal* social control"[5] Although his bold prediction is far-reaching (and, in light of recent developments, perhaps a bit premature), his analysis of a decade ago was curiously optimistic and uncritical of the effects and consequences of medicalization. Nonsociologists, especially psychiatric critic Thomas Szasz (1961, 1963, 1970, 1974) and legal scholar Nicholas Kittrie (1971), are much more critical in their evaluations of the ramifications of medicalization. Szasz's critiques are polemical and although path breaking, insightful, and suggestive, have not been presented in a particularly systematic form. Both he and Kittrie tend to focus on the effects of medicalization on individual civil liberties and judicial processes rather than on social consequences. Their writings, however, reveal that both are aware of sociological consequences.

In this section we discuss some of the more significant consequences and ramifications of defining deviant behavior as a medical problem. We must remind the reader that we are examining the *social* consequences of medicalizing deviance, which can be analyzed separately from the validity of medical definitions or diagnoses, the effectiveness of medical regimens, or their individual consequences. These variously "latent" consequences in inhere in medicalization itself and occur *regardless* of how efficacious the particular medical treatment or social control mechanism. As will be apparent, our sociological analysis has left us skeptical of the social benefits of medical social control. We separate the consequences into the "brighter" and "darker" sides of medicalization. The "brighter" side will be presented first.

Brighter Side

The brighter side of medicalization includes the positive or beneficial qualities that are attributed to medicalization. We review briefly the accepted socially progressive aspects of medicalizing deviance. They are separated more for clarity of presentation than for any intrinsic separation in consequence.

First, medicalization is related to a longtime *humanitarian* trend in the conception and control of deviance. For example, alcoholism is no longer considered a sin or even a moral weakness; it is now a disease. Alcoholics are no longer arrested in many places for "public drunkenness"; they are now somehow "treated," if only to be dried out for a time. Medical treatment for the alcoholic can be seen as a more humanitarian means of social control. It is not retributive or punitive, but at least ideally, therapeutic. Troy Duster (1970:10) suggests that medical definitions increase toleration and compassion for human problems and they "have now been reinterpreted in an almost nonmoral fashion." (We doubt this, but leave the morality issue for a later discussion). Medicine and humanitarianism historically developed concurrently and, as some have observed, the use of medical language and evidence increases the prestige of human proposals and enhances their acceptance (Wooton, 1959; Zola, 1975). Medical definitions are imbued with the prestige of the medical profession and are considered the "scientific" and humane way of viewing a problem....This is especially true if an apparently "successful" treatment for controlling the behavior is available, as with hyperkinesis.

Second, medicalization allows for the extension of the *sick role* to those labeled as deviants...Many of the perceived benefits of the medicalization of deviance stem from the assignment of the sick role. Some have suggested that this is the most significant element of adopting the medical model of deviant behavior (Siegler and Osmond, 1974). By defining deviant behavior as an illness or a result of illness one is absolved of responsibility for one's behavior. It diminishes or *removes blame* from the individual for deviant actions. Alcoholics are no longer held responsible for their uncontrolled drinking, and perhaps hyperactive children are no longer the classroom's "bad boys" but children with a medical disorder. There is some clear secondary gain here for the individual. The label "sick" is free of the moral opprobrium and implied culpability of "criminal" or "sinner." The designation of sickness also may reduce guilt for drinkers and their families and for hyperactive children and their parents. Similarly, it may result in reduced stigma for the deviant. It allows for the development of more acceptable accounts of deviance: a recent film depicted a child witnessing her father's helpless drunken stupor; her mother remarked, "It's okay. Daddy's just sick."[6]

The sick role allows for the "confidential legitimation" of a certain amount of deviance, so long as the individual fulfills the obligations of the sick role.[7]The deviant, in essence, is medically excused for the deviation. But, as Talcott Parsons (1972:108) has pointed out, "the conditional legitimation is bought at a "price," namely, the recognition that illness itself is an undesirable state, to be recovered from as expeditiously as possible." Thus the medical excuse for deviance is only valid when the patient-deviant accepts the medical perspective of the inherent undesirability of his or her sick behavior and submits to a subordinate relationship with an official agent of control (the physician) toward changing it. This, of course, negates any threat the deviant may pose to society's normative structure, for such deviants do not challenge the norm; by accepting deviance as sickness and social control as "treatment," the deviant underscores the validity of the violated norm.

Third, the medical model can be viewed as portraying an *optimistic* outcome for the deviant.[8] Pitts (1968:391) notes, "the possibility that a patient may be exploited is somewhat minimized by therapeutic ideology, which creates an optimistic bias concerning the patient's fate."[9] The therapeutic ideology, accepted in some form by all branches of medicine, suggests that a problem (e.g., deviant behavior) can be changed or alleviated if only the proper treatment is discovered and administered. Defining deviant behavior as an illness may also mobilize hope in the individual patient that with proper treatment a "cure" is possible (Frank, J., 1974). Clearly this could have beneficial results and even become a self-fulfilling prophecy. Although the medical model is interpreted frequently as optimistic about individual change, under some circumstances it may lend itself to pessimistic interpretations. The attribution of physiological cause coupled with the lack of effective treatment engendered a somatic pessimism in the late 19th-century conception of madness....

Fourth, medicalization lends the *prestige of the medical profession* to deviance designations and treatments. The medical profession is the most prestigious and dominant profession in American society (Friedson, 1970). As just noted, medical definitions of deviance become imbued with the prestige of the medical profession and are construed to be the "scientific" way of viewing a problem. The medical mantle of science may serve to deflect definitional challenges. This is especially true if an apparently "successful" treatment for controlling the behavior is available. Medicalization places the problem in the hands of healing physicians. "The therapeutic value of professional dominance, from the patient's point of view, is that it becomes the *doctor's* problem" (Ehrenreich and Ehrenreich, 1975:156, emphasis in original). Physicians are assumed to be beneficent and honorable. "The medical and paramedical professions," (Pitts, 1968:391) contends, "especially in the United States, are probably more immune to corruption than are the judicial and parajudicial professions and relatively immune to political pressure."[10]

Fifth, medical social control is more *flexible* and often more *efficient* than judicial and legal controls. The impact of the flexibility of medicine is most profound on the "deviance of everyday life," since it allows "social pressures on deviance [to] increase without boxing the deviant into as rigid a category as 'criminal'" (Pitts, 1968:391).[11] Medical controls are adjustable to fit the needs of the individual patient, rather than being a response to the deviant act itself. It may be more efficient (and less expensive) to control opiate addiction with methadone maintenance than with long prison terms or mental hospitalization. The behavior of disruptive hyperactive children, who have been immune to all parental and teacher sanctions, may dramatically improve after treatment with medications. Medical controls circumvent complicated legal and judicial procedures and may be applied more informally. This can have a considerable effect on social control structures. For example, it has been noted that defining alcoholism as a disease would reduce arrest rates in some areas up to 50%.

In sum, the social benefits of medicalization include the creation of humanitarian and non-punitive sanctions; the extension of the sick role to some deviants; a reduction of individual responsibility, blame, and possibly a stigma for deviance; an optimistic therapeutic ideology; care and treatment rendered by a prestigious medical profession; and the availability of a more flexible and often more efficient means of social control.

Darker Side

There is, however, another side to the medicalization of deviant behavior. Although it may often seem entirely humanitarian to conceptualize deviance as sickness as opposed to badness, it is not that simple. There is a "darker" side to the medicalization of deviance. In some senses these might be considered as the more clearly latent aspects of medicalization. In an earlier work, Conrad (1975) elucidated four consequences of medicalizing deviance; building on that work, we expand our analysis to seven. Six are discussed here; the seventh is described separately in the next section.

Dislocation of Responsibility

As we have seen, defining behavior as a medical problem removes or profoundly diminishes responsibility from the individual. Although affixing responsibility is always complex, medicalization produces confusion and ambiguity about who is responsible. Responsibility is separated from social action; it is located in the nether world of biophysiology or psyche. Although this takes the individual officially "off the hook," its excuse is only a partial one. The individual, the putative deviant, and the undesirable conduct are still associated. Aside from where such conduct is "seated," the sick deviant is the medium of its expression.

With the removal of responsibility also comes the lowering of status. A dual-class citizenship is created: those who are deemed responsible for their actions and those who are not. The not-completely-responsible sick are placed in a position of dependence on the fully responsible nonsick (Parsons, 1975:108). Kittrie (1971:347) notes in this regard that more than half the American population is no longer subject to the sanctions of criminal law. Such persons, among others, become true "second-class-citizens."

Assumption of the Moral Neutrality of Medicine

Cloaked in the mantle of science, medicine and medical practice are assumed to be objective and value free. But this profoundly misrepresents reality. The very nature of medical practice involves value judgement. To call something a disease is to deem it undesirable. Medicine is influenced by the moral order of society—witness the diagnosis and treatment of masturbation as a disease in Victorian times—yet medical language of disease and treatment is assumed to be morally neutral. It is not, and the very technological-scientific vocabulary of medicine that defines disease obfuscates this fact.

Defining deviance as disease allows behavior to keep its negative judgement, but medical language veils the political and moral nature of this decision in the guise of scientific fact. There was little public clamor for moral definitions of homosexuality as long as it remained defined an illness, but soon after the disease designation was removed, moral crusaders (e.g., Anita Bryant) launched public campaigns condemning the immorality of homosexuality. One only needs to scratch the surface of medical designations for deviant behavior to find overtly moral judgements...Defining deviance as a medical phenomenon involves moral enterprise.

Domination of Expert Control

The medical profession is made up of experts; it has a monopoly on anything that can be conceptualized as an illness. Because of the way the medical profession is organized and the mandate it has from society, decisions related to medical diagnosis and treatment are controlled almost completely by medical professionals.

Conditions that enter the medical domain are not ipso facto medical problems, whether we speak of alcoholism, hyperactivity, or drug addiction. When a problem is defined as medical, it is removed from the public realm, where there can be discussion by ordinary people, and put out on a plane where only medical people can discuss it....The public may have their own conceptions of deviant behavior, but those of the experts are usually dominant. Medical definitions have a high likelihood for dominance and hegemony: they are often taken as the last scientific word. The language of medical experts increases mystification and decreases the accessibility of public debate.

Medical Social Control

Defining deviant behavior as a medical problem, allows certain things to be done that could not otherwise be considered; for example, the body maybe cut open or psychoactive medications given. As we elaborated above, this treatment can be a form of social control.

In regard to drug treatment, Henry Lennard (1971:57) observes: "Psychoactive drugs, especially those legally prescribed, tend to restrain individuals from behavior and experience that are not complementary with the requirements of the dominant value system." These forms of medical social control presume a prior definition of deviance as a medical problem. Psychosurgery on an individual prone to violent outbursts requires a diagnosis that something is wrong with his brain or nervous system. Similarly, prescribing drugs to restless, overactive, and disruptive school-children requires a diagnosis of hyperkinesis. These forms of social control, what Stephan Chorover (1973) has called "psychotechnology," are powerful and often efficient means of controlling deviance. These relatively new and increasingly popular forms of medical control could not be used without the prior medicalization of deviant behavior. As is suggested from the discovery of hyperkinesis and to a lesser extent the development of methadone treatment of opiate addiction, if a mechanism of medical social control seems useful, then the deviant behavior it modifies will be given a medical label or diagnosis. We imply no over malevolence on the part of the medical profession; rather, it is part of a larger process, of which the medical profession is only a part. The larger process might be called the individualization of social problems.

Individualization of Social Problems

The medicalization of deviance is part of a larger phenomenon that is prevalent in our society: the individualization of social problems. We tend to look for causes and solutions to complex social problems in the individual rather than in the social system. William Ryan (1971) has identified this process as "blaming the victim": seeing the causes of the problem in individuals (who are usually of low status) rather than as endemic to the society. We seek to change the "victim" rather than the society. The medical practice of diagnosing an illness in an individual lends itself to the individualization of social problems. Rather than seeing certain deviant behaviors as symptomatic of social conditions, the medical perspective focuses on the individual, diagnosing and treating the illness itself and generally ignoring the social situation.

Hyperkinesis serves as a good example of this. Both the school and parents are concerned with the child's behavior; the child is difficult at home and disruptive in school. No punishments or rewards seem consistently effective in modifying the behavior, and both parents and school are at their wits' end. A medical evaluation is suggested. The diagnosis of hyperkinetic behavior leads to prescribing stimulant medications. The child's behavior seems to become more socially acceptable, reducing problems in school and home. Treatment is considered a medical success.

But there is an alternative perspective. By focusing on the symptoms and defining them as hyperkinesis, we ignore the possibility that the behavior is not an illness but an adaptation to a social situation. It diverts our attention from the family or school and from seriously entertaining the idea that the "problem" could be in the structure of the social system. By giving medications, we are essentially supporting the existing social and political arrangements in that it becomes a "symptom" of an individual disease rather than a possible "comment" on the nature of the present situation. Although the individualization of social problems aligns well with the individualistic ethic of American culture, medical intervention against deviance makes medicine a de facto agent of dominant social and political events.

Depoliticization of Deviant Behavior

Depoliticization of deviant behavior is a result of both the process of medicalization and the individualization of social problems. Probably one of the clearest recent examples of such depoliticization occurred when political dissidents in the Soviet Union were declared mentally ill and confined to mental hospitals (Conrad, 1977).

This strategy served to neutralize the meaning of political protest and dissent, rendering it (officially, at least) symptomatic of mental illness.

The medicalization of deviant behavior depoliticizes deviance in the same manner. By defining the overactive, restless, and disruptive child as hyperkinetic, we ignore the meaning of the behavior in the context of the social system. If we focused our analysis on the school system, we might see the child's behavior as a protest against some aspect of the school or classroom situation, rather than symptomatic of an individual neurological disorder. Similar examples could be drawn of the opiate addict in the ghetto, the alcoholic in the workplace, and others. Medicalizing deviant behavior precludes us from recognizing it as a possible intentional repudiation of existing political arrangements.

There are other related consequences of the medicalization of deviance beyond the six discussed. The medical ideal of early intervention may lead to early labeling and secondary deviance (see Lemert, 1972). The "medical decision rule," which approximates "when in doubt, treat," is nearly the converse of the legal dictum "innocent until proven guilty" and may unnecessarily enlarge the population of deviants (Scheff, 1963). Certain constitutional safeguards of the judicial system that protect individuals' rights are neutralized or bypassed by medicalization (Kittrie, 1971). Social control in the name of benevolence is at once insidious and difficult to confront. Although these are all significant, we wish to expand on still another consequence of considerable social importance, the exclusion of evil.

Exclusion of Evil

Evil has been excluded from the imagery of modern human problems. We are uncomfortable with notions of evil; we regard them as primitive and nonhumanitarian, as residues from a theological era.[12] Medicalization contributes to the exclusion of concepts of evil in our society. Clearly medicalization is not the sole cause of the exclusion of evil, but it shrouds conditions, events, and people and prevents them from being confronted as evil. The roots of the exclusion of evil are in the Enlightenment, the diminution of religious imagery of sin, the rise of determinist theories of human behavior, and the doctrine of cultural relativity. Social scientists as well have excluded the concept of evil from their analytic discourses (Wolff, 1969; for exceptions, see Becker, 1975, and Lyman, 1978).

Although we cannot here presume to identify the forms of evil in modern times, we would like to sensitize the reader to how medical definitions of deviance serve to further exclude evil from our view. It can be argued that regardless of what we construe as evil (e.g., destruction, pain, alienation, exploitation, oppression) there are at least two general types of evil: evil intent and evil consequence. Evil intent is similar to the legal concept mens rea, literally, "evil mind." Some evil is intended by a specific line of action. Evil consequence is, on the other hand, the result of action. No intent or motive to do evil is necessary for evil consequence to prevail; on the contrary, it often resembles the platitude "the road to hell is paved with good intentions." In either case medicalization dilutes or obstructs us from seeing evil. Sickness gives us a vocabulary of motive (Mills, 1940) that obliterates evil intent.

And although it does not automatically render evil consequences good, the allegation that they were products of a "sick" mind or body relegates them to a status similar to that of "accidents."

For example, Hitler orchestrated the greatest mass genocide in modern history, yet some have reduced his motivation for the destruction of the Jews (and others) to a personal pathological condition. To them and to many of us, Hitler was sick. But this portrays the horror of the Holocaust as a product of individual pathology; as Thomas Szasz frequently points out, it prevents us from seeing and confronting man's inhumanity to man. Are Son of Sam, Charles Manson, the assassins of King and the Kennedys, the Richard Nixon of Watergate, Libya's Muammar Kaddafi, or the all-too-common child beater sick? Although many may well be troubled, we argue that there is little to be gained by developing such a medical vocabulary of motives.[13] It only hinders us from comprehending the human element in the decisions we make, the social structures we create, and the actions we take. Hannah Arendt (1963), in her exemplary study of the banality of evil, contends that Nazi war criminal Adolph Eichmann, rather than being sick, was "terribly, terrifyingly normal."

Susan Sontag (1978) has suggested that on a cultural level, we use the metaphor of illness to speak of various kinds of evil. Cancer, in particular, provides such a metaphor: we depict slums and pornography shops as "cancers" in our cities; J. Edgar Hoover's favorite metaphor for communism was "a cancer in our midst"; and Nixon's administration was deemed "cancerous," rotting from within. In our secular culture, where powerful religious connotations of sin and evil have been obscured, cancer (and for that matter, illness in general) is one of the few available images of unmitigated evil and wickedness....Thus we suggest that the medicalization of social problems detracts from our capability to see and confront the evils that face our world.

In sum, the "darker" side of the medicalization of deviance has profound consequences for the putative or alleged deviant and society. We now turn to some policy implications of medicalization.

Medicalization of Deviance and Social Policy

"Social policy" may be characterized as an institutionalized definition of a problem and its solutions. There are many routes for developing social policy in a complex society, but, as John McKnight (1977:85) contends, "There is no greater power than the right to define the question." The definition and designation of the problem itself may be the key to the development of social policy. Problem definitions often take on a life of their own; they tend to resist change and become the accepted manner of defining reality (see Caplan and Nelson, 1973). In a complex society, social policy is only rarely implemented as a direct and self-conscious master plan, as, for example, occurred with the development of community mental health centers....It is far more common for social policies to evolve from the particular definitions and solutions that emerge from various political processes. Individual policies in diverse parts of society may conflict, impinge on, and modify one another. The overall social policy even may be residual to the political process. The medicalization of deviance never has been a formalized social policy;...it has emerged from various combinations of turf battles, court decisions, scientific innovations, political expediencies, medical entrepreneurship, and other influences. The medicalization of deviance has become in effect a de facto social policy....

Criminal Justice:
Decriminalization, Decarceration, and the Therapeutic State

Over the past two decades the percent of officially defined deviants institutionalized in prisons or mental hospitals has decreased. There has been a parallel growth in "community-based" programs for social control. Although this "decarceration" has been most dramatic with the mentally ill, substantial deinstitutionalization has occurred in prison populations and with juvenile delinquents and opiate addicts as well (see Scull, 1977). Many deviants who until recently would have been institution- alized are being "treated" or maintained in community programs—for example, probation, work release, and community correctional programs for criminal offend- ers; counseling, vocational, or residential programs as diversion from juvenile court for delinquents; and methadone maintenance or therapeutic community programs in lieu of prison for opiate addicts.

This emerging social policy of decarceration has already affected medicalization. Assuming that the amount of deviance and number of deviants a society recognizes remains generally constant (see Erikson, 1966), a change in policy in one social control agency affects other social control agents. Thus decarceration of institution- alized deviants will lead to the deployment of other forms of social control. Because medical social control is one of the main types of social control deployed in the community, decarceration increases medicalization. Since the *Robinson* Supreme Court decision and the discovery of methadone maintenance the control of opiate addicts has shifted dramatically from the criminal justice system to the medical system. Control of some criminal offenders may be subtly transferred to the mental health system; one recent study found an increase in the number of males with prior police records admitted to psychiatric facilities and suggested this may be an indication of a medicalization of criminal behavior (Melick, Steadman, and Cocozza, 1979). There is also some evidence that probation officers, in their quest for professional status, adopt a medical model in their treatment of offenders (Chalfant, 1977). Although some observers have suggested that the apparent decarceration of mental patients from mental hospitals and the rise of community mental health facilities has at least partially demedicalized madness,...this is an inaccurate interpre- tation. Moreover, the extent of decarceration has been exaggerated; many of the other former or would-be mental patients are located in other institutions, especially nursing homes (Redlich & Kellert, 1978). Here they remain under medical or quasimedical control. In short, decarceration appears to increase the medicalization of deviance.

Decriminalization also affects medicalization. Decriminalization means that a certain activity is no longer considered to be a criminal offense. But even when criminal sanctions are removed, the act may still maintain its definition as deviance. In this case, other noncriminal sanctions may emerge....[T]he disease model of alcoholism did not begin its rise to prominence until after the repeal of Prohibition, that is, after alcohol use in general was decriminalized. More specifically, we can examine the response to the decriminalization of "public drunkenness" in the 1960s. A recent study has shown that although alcohol and drug psychoses comprised only 4.7% of the mental health population (inpatient and outpatient) in 1950, in 1975 "alcoholism accounted for 46 percent of state hospital patients" and became the largest diagnostic category in mental hospitals (Redlich & Kellert, 1978:26). It is likely that the combination of the declining populations in state mental hospitals and the decriminalization of "public drunkenness" (e.g., police now bring drunks to the mental hospital instead of the drunk tank) is in part reflected in this enormous increase of alcoholics in the mental health system.

Medicalization allows for the decriminalization of certain activities (e.g., public drunkenness, some types of drug use) because (1) they remain defined as deviant (sick) and are not vindicated and (2) an alternative form of social control is available (medicine). If an act is decriminalized and also demedicalized (e.g., homosexuality), there may well be a backlash and a call for recriminalization or at least reaffirmation of its deviant status rather than a vindication. We postulate that if an act is decriminalized and yet not vindicated (i.e., still remains defined as deviant), its control may be transferred from the criminal justice to the medical system.[14]

In the 1960s and early 1970s considerable concern was voiced in some quarters concerning the "social policy" that was leading to the divestment of criminal justice and the rise of the therapeutic state (Kittrie, 1971; Leifer, 1969; Szasz, 1963)....[T]here has been some retreat from the "rehabilitative ideal" in criminal justice. On the other hand, both decarceration and decriminalization have increased medicalization. Thus we would conclude that although the "therapeutic state" is not becoming the dominant social policy as its earlier critics feared, neither is it showing signs of abating. We would suggest that to the extent that decarceration and decriminalization remain social policies, medicalization of deviance can be expected to increase....

Punitive Backlash

Since about 1970 there has been a "backlash" against the increasing "liberalization" of the treatment of deviance and the Supreme Court decision that have granted criminal suspects and offenders greater "rights." This public reaction, coming mostly from the more conservative sectors of society, generally calls for more strict treatment of deviants and a return to more punitive sanctions.

This "punitive backlash" takes many forms. In 1973 New York passed a "get tough" law with mandatory prison sentences for drug dealers. Other legislative attempts have been made to impose mandatory minimum sentences on offenders. There is a considerable public clamor for the return of the death penalty. A current New York state law has allowed juveniles between ages 13 and 15 to be tried as adults for some offenses. The antiabortion crusade has made inroads into the availability of abortions and is aiming for the recriminalization of abortion. Recently antihomosexuality crusades have appeared from Florida to Oregon, defeating anti-discrimination referenda and limiting the rights of homosexuals.

This swell of public reaction may be in part a response to the therapeutic ideology and the perceived "coddling" of deviants. Should this backlash and other recent public reactions such as California's Proposition 13 taxpayer revolt continue to gather strength and grow in popularity, they well may force a retreat from the medicalization of deviance.

Medicalizing Deviance: A Final Note

The potential for medicalizing deviance has increased in the past few decades. The increasing dominance of the medical profession, the discovery of subtle physiological correlates of human behavior, and the creation of medical technologies (promoted by powerful pharmaceutical and medical technology industry interests) have advanced this trend. Although we remain skeptical of the overall social benefits of medicalization and are concerned about its "darker" side, it is much too simplistic to suggest a wholesale condemnation of medicalization. Offering alcoholics medical treatment in lieu of the drunk tank is undoubtedly a more humane response to deviance; methadone maintenance allows a select group of opiate addicts to make successful adaptations to society; some schoolchildren seem to benefit from stimulant medications for hyperkinesis; and the medical discovery of child abuse may well increase therapeutic intervention. Medicalization in general has reduced societal condemnation of deviants. But these benefits do not mean these conditions are in fact diseases or that the same results could not be achieved in another manner. And even in those instances of medical "success," the social consequences indicated...are still evident.

The most difficult consequence of medicalization for us to discuss is the exclusion of evil. In part this is because we are members of a culture that has largely eliminated evil from intellectual and public discourse. But our discomfort also stems for our ambivalence about what can meaningfully be construed as evil in our society. If we are excluding evil, what exactly are we excluding? We have no difficulty depicting such conditions as pain, violence, oppression, exploitation, and abject cruelty as evil. Social scientists of various stripes have been pointing to these evils and their consequences since the dawn of social science. It is also possible for us to conceive of "organizational evils" such as corporate price fixing, false advertising (or even all advertising), promoting life-threatening automobiles, or the wholesale drugging of nursing home patients to facilitate institutional management. We also have little trouble in seeing ideologies such as imperialism, chauvinism, and racial supremacy as evils. Our difficulty comes with seeing individuals as evil. While we would not adopt a Father-Flanagan-of-Boys-Town attitude of "there's no such thins as a bad boy," our own socialization and "liberal" assumptions as well as sociological perspective make it difficult for us to conceive of any individual as "evil." As sociologists we are more likely to see people as products of their psychological and social circumstances: there may be evil social structures, ideologies, or deeds, but not evil people. Yet when we confront a Hitler, an Idi Amin, or a Stalin of the forced labor camps, it is sometimes difficult to reach any other conclusion. We note this dilemma more as clarification of our stance than as a solution. There are both evils in society and people who are "victim" to those evils. Worthwhile social scientific goals include uncovering the evils, understanding and aiding the victims, and ultimately contributing to a more humane existence for all.

228   DEVIANCE

REFERENCES

Arendt, H. 1963. *Eichmann in Jerusalem.* New York: Viking Press.

Becker, E. 1975. *Escape from Evil.* New York: The Free Press.

Caplan, N. & S.D. Nelson. 1973. "On Being Useful: The Nature and Consequences of Psychological Research on Social Problems." *American Psychologist* 28:199–211.

Cartwright, S.W. 1851. "Report on the Diseases and Physical Peculiarities of the Negro Race." *North American Surgical Journal* 7:691–715.

Chorover, S. 1973. "Big Brother and Psychotechnology." *Psychology Today* 7:43–54.

Coe, R.M. 1978. *Sociology of Medicine.* New York: McGraw-Hill Book Co.

Comfort, A. 1967. *The Anxiety Makers.* London: Thomas Nelson & Sons.

Conrad, P. 1975. "The Discovery of Hyperkinesis: Notes on the Medicalization of Deviant Behavior." *Social Problems* 23:12–21.

———. 1977. "Soviet Dissidents, Ideological Deviance, and Mental Hospitalization." Presented at Midwest Sociological Society Meetings, Minneapolis.

Daniels, A.K. 1969. "The Captive Professional: Bureaucratic Limitation in the Practice of Military Psychiatry." *Journal of Social Behavior* 10:255–65.

Delgado, J.M.R. 1969. *Physical Control of the Mind: Toward a Psychocivilized Society.* New York: Harper and Row, Publishers.

Duster, T. 1970. *The Legislation of Morality.* New York: The Free Press.

Edelman, M. 1977. *Political Language: Words That Succeed and Policies That Fail.* New York: Academic Press.

Ehrenreich, B. & J. Ehrenreich. 1975. "Medicine and Social Control." In B.R. Mandell (ed.), *Welfare in America: Controlling the "Dangerous" Classes.* Englewood Cliffs: Prentice-Hall.

Englehardt, H.T., Jr. 1974. "The Disease of Masturbation: Values and the Concept of Disease." *Bulletin of Medical History* 48:234–48.

Erikson, K.T. 1966. *Wayward Puritans.* New York: John Wiley & Sons, Inc.

Fox, R. 1977. "The Medicalization and Demedicalization of American Society." *Daedalus* 106:9–22.

Fox, R.G. 1971. "The XYY Offender: A Modern Myth?" *Journal of Criminology and Police Science* 62:59–73.

Frank, J. 1974. *Persuasion and Healing.* (Rev. ed.). New York: Schocken Books, Inc.

Freeman, W. 1959. "Psychosurgery." In S. Arieti (Ed.), *American Handbook of Psychiatry* (Vol. 2). New York: Basic Books.

Friedson, E. 1970. *Profession of Medicine.* New York: Harper & Row.

———. 1975. *Doctoring Together.* New York: Elsevier North-Holland, Inc.

Goddard, J. "The Medical Business." 1973. *Scientific American* 229:161–8.

Gussow, Z. and G.S. Tracy. 1968. "Status, Ideology, and Adaptation to Stigmatized Illness: A Study of Leprosy." *Human Organization* 27:316–25.

Halleck, S.L. 1971. *The Politics of Therapy.* New York: Science House.

Hurvitz, N. 1973. "Psychotherapy as a Means of Social Control." *Journal of Consulting Clinical Psychology* 40:232–9.

Illich, I. 1976. *Medical Nemesis.* New York: Pantheon Books, Inc.

Kittrie, N. 1971. *The Right to Be Different: Deviance and Enforced Therapy.* Baltimore: Johns Hopkins University Press. Copyright the Johns Hopkins University Press, 1971.

Knowles, J.H. 1977. "The Responsibility of the Individual." *Daedalus* 106:57–80.

Leifer, R. 1969. *In the Name of Health.* New York: Science House.

Lemert, E.M. 1972. *Human Deviance, Social Problems and Social Control* (2nd ed.). Englewood Cliffs, New Jersey: Prentice-Hall.

Lennard, H., Epstein, L.J., Bernstein, A. and Ranson, D.C. 1971. *Mystification and Drug Misuse.* New York: Perennial Library.

Lyman, S. 1978. *The Seven Deadly Sins: Society and Evil.* New York: St. Martin's Press.

Mark, V. and Ervin, F. 1970. *Violence and the Brain.* New York: Harper & Row.

McKnight, J. 1977. "Professionalized Services and Disabling Help." In Illich, et al., *Disabling Professions.* London: Marion Boyars Publisher Ltd.

Mechanic, D. 1973. "Health and Illness in Technological Societies." *Hastings Center Studies* 1(3):7–18.

———. 1974. *Politics, Medicine and Social Science*. New York: John Wiley & Sons.

Melick, M.E., Steadman, H.J., & Cocozza, J.J. 1979. "The Medicalization of Criminal Behavior Among Mental Patients." *Journal of Health and Social Behavior* 20(3):228–37.

Menninger, W.C. 1967. *A Psychiatrist for a Troubled World*. B.H. Hall (ed.), New York: Viking Press.

Miller, K.S. 1976. *Managing Madness*. New York: The Free Press.

Mills, C.W. 1940. "Situated Actions and Vocabularies of Motive." *American Sociological Review* 6:904–13.

Parsons, T. 1951. *The Social System*. New York: The Free Press.

———. 1972. "Definitions of Illness and Health in Light of American Values and Social Structure." In E.G. Jaco (Ed.), *Patients, Physicians and Illness* (2nd ed.). New York: The Free Press.

———. 1975. "The Sick Role and the Role of the Physician Reconsidered." *Health and Society* 53:257–78.

Pfohl, S.J. 1977. "The 'Discovery' of Child Abuse." *Social Problems* 24:310–23 (Feb.).

Phillips, D.L. 1963 "Rejection: a Possible Consequence of Seeking Help for Mental Disorders." *American Sociological Review* 28:963–72.

Pitts, J. 1968. "Social Control: The Concept." In D. Sills (Ed.), *International Encyclopedia of Social Sciences* (Vol. 14). New York: Macmillan Publishing Co., Inc.

Redlich, F. & S.R. Kellert. 1978. "Trends in American Mental Health." *American Journal of Psychiatry* 135:22–28.

Reynolds, J.M. 1973. "The Medical Institution: The Death and Disease-Producing Appendage." In L.T. Reynolds and J.M. Henslin (eds.), *American Society: A Critical Analysis*. New York: David McKay Co., Inc.

Roman, P.M. & H.M. Trice. 1968. "The Sick Role, Labeling Theory and the Deviant Drinker." *Journal of Social Psychiatry* 14:245–51.

Rosen, G. 1972. "The Evolution of Social Medicine." In H.E. Freeman, S. Levine, & L. Reeder (eds.), *Handbook of Medical Sociology*, (2nd ed.). Englewood Cliffs, New Jersey: Prentice-Hall.

Rotenberg, M. 1978. *Damnation and Deviance: The Protestant Ethic and the Spirit of Failure*. New York: The Free Press.

Ryan, W. 1971. *Blaming the Victim*. New York: Vintage Books.

Scheff, T.J. 1963. "Decisions, Rules, Types of Errors, and Their Consequences in Medical Diagnosis." *Behavioral Science* 8:97–107.

Scull, A. 1977. *Decarceration*. Englewood Cliffs, NJ: Prentice-Hall.

Shuval, J.T. and A. Antonovsky. 1973. "Illness: a Mechanism for Coping with Failure." *Social Science Medicine* 7:259–65.

Siegler, M. and H. Osmond. 1974. *Models of Madness, Models of Medicine*. New York: Macmillan Publishing Co., Inc.

Sontag, S. 1978. *Illness as Metaphor*. New York: Farrar, Straus & Giroux.

Sorenson, J. 1974. "Biomedical Intervention, Uncertainty, and Doctor-Patient Interaction." *Journal of Health and Social Behavior* 15:366–74.

Stoll, C.S. 1968. "Images of Man and Social Control." *Social Forces* 47:119–27.

Szasz, T. 1961. *The Myth of Mental Illness*. New York: Hoeber-Harper.

———. 1963. *Law, Liberty and Psychiatry*. New York: Macmillan Publishing Co., Inc.

———. 1965. "Legal and Moral Aspects of Homosexuality." In J. Marmor (ed.), *Sexual Inversion: The Multiple Roots of Homosexuality*. New York: Basic Books, Inc.

———. 1970. *The Manufacture of Madness*. New York: Harper & Row, Publishers, Inc.

1974. *Ceremonial Chemistry*. New York: Anchor Books.

Twaddle, A.C. and R.M. Hessler. 1977. *A Sociology of Health*. St. Louis: The C.V. Mosby Co.

U.S. Department of Health, Education and Welfare. 1974. *The Supply of Health Manpower* (Publication No. [HRA] 75–38). Washington, D.C.: U.S. Government Printing Office.

Veatch, R.M. 1973. "The Medical Model: Its Nature and Problems." *Hastings Center Studies*. 1(3):59–76.

Waitzkin, H. and J. Stockle. 1976. "Information Control and the Micropolitics of Health Care: Summary of an Ongoing Project." *Social Science Medicine* 10:263–76.

Waitzkin, H.K. and B. Waterman. 1974. *The Exploitation of Illness in Capitalist Society*. Indianapolis: The Bobbs-Merrill Co., Inc.

Wolff, K. 1969. "For a Sociology of Evil." *Journal of Social Issues*. 25:111–25.

Wootton, B. 1959. *Social Science and Social Pathology*. London: George Allen & Unwin.

Zola, I.K. 1972. "Medicine as an Institution of Social Control." *Sociological Review* 20:487–504.

———. 1975. "In the Name of Health and Illness: on Some Socio-political Consequences of Medical Influence." *Social Science Medicine* 9:83–7.

NOTES

[1] Another pharmaceutical innovation, birth control pills, also functions as a medical control; in this case, the control of reproduction. There is little doubt that "the pill" has played a significant part in the sexual revolution since the 1960s and the redefinition of what constitutes sexual deviance.

[2] A number of other surgical interventions for deviance have been developed in recent years. Surgery for "gender dysphoria" (transsexuality) and "intestinal bypass" operations for obesity are both examples of surgical intervention for deviance. The legalization of abortions has also medicalized and legitimized an activity that was formerly deviant and brought it under medical-surgical control.

[3] It is worth noting that in the recent Gary Gilmore execution a physician was involved; he designated the spot where the heartbeat was loudest and measured vital signs during the execution ceremony. A few states have actually passed death penalty legislation specifying injection of a lethal drug as the means of execution.

[4] Although Waitzkin and Waterman suggest that such secondary gain functions are latent (i.e., unintended and unrecognized), the cases we have discussed here show that such "gains" are often intentionally pursued.

[5] From Pitts, J. Social Control: the Concept. In D. Sills (Ed.), *International Encyclopedia of Social Sciences* (vol. 14). New York: MacMIllan Publishing Co., Inc., 1968. Copyright 1968 by Crowell Collier and MacMillan, Inc.

[6] It should be noted, however, that little empirical evidence exists for reduced stigmatization. Derek Phillips' (1963) research suggests that people seeking medical help for their personal problems are highly at risk for rejection and stigmatization. Certain illnesses carry their own stigma. Leprosy, epilepsy, and mental illness are all stigmatized illnesses (Gussow & Tracy, 1968); Susan Sontag (1978) proposes that cancer is highly stigmatized in American society. We need further research on the stigma-reducing properties of medical designations of deviance; it is by no means an automatic result of medicalization.

[7] On the other hand, Paul Roman and Harrison Trice (1968:248) contend that the sick role of alcoholic may actually reinforce deviant behavior by removing responsibility for deviant drinking behavior.

[8] For a contrasting viewpoint, see Rotenberg's (1978) work, discussed in [*Deviance and Medicalization: From Badness to Sickness*].

[9] From Pitts, J. Social Control: the concept. In D. Sills (Ed.), *International Encyclopedia of Social Sciences* (Vol. 14). New York: MacMillan Publishing Co., Inc., 1968. Copyright 1968 by Crowell Collier and Macmillan, Inc.

[10] Ibid.

[11] Ibid.

[12] Writing in the early 1970s, Kittrie (1971:347) noted, "Ours is increasingly becoming a society that views punishment as a punitive and vindictive tool and is therefore loth to punish." Some recent scholarship in penology and the controversy about the death penalty has slightly modified this trend.

[13] We *do not* suggest that these individuals or any other deviants discussed...are or should be considered evil. We only wish to point out that medicalization on a societal level contributes to the exclusion of evil. To the extent that evil exists, we would argue that social structures and specific social conditions are the most significant cause of evil.

[14] The decriminalization of abortion has led to its complete medicalization. It is interesting to speculate whether the decriminalization of marijuana, gambling, and prostitution would lead to medicalization. It is likely that with marijuana and gambling, "compulsive" and excessive indulgence would be defined as "sick"; with prostitution, medical certification might be required, as is presently the case in several European countries.

Part VI

ORGANIZATIONAL DEVIANCE—
BEYOND THE INTERPERSONAL LEVEL

In the last section, we examined how some deviant acts and groups of individuals come to be defined as deviant. The very entrepreneurial groups not only create categories of social deviance, but also create the specific rules and corresponding agents and agencies responsible for detecting and processing rule violators.

In this section, we shall explore the formal regulation of deviance—how deviants are detected, officially labelled, processed and treated. In particular, we shall focus on the basic premises underlying the treatment/incarceration of deviants employed by various agencies of social control.

There exist in our society many formal regulatory agencies and institutions whose expressed role is to seek out, identify, and control deviance. Such agencies which include the FBI, the police, the courts, welfare agencies, the FDA—Federal Drug Enforcement Agency, the Department of Treasury, etc., possess a great deal of power as they are legitimized by the State.

The Institutionalization and Bureaucratization of Deviance

Institutionalization of deviance involves the establishment of rules and procedures for seeking out, categorizing and handling individuals adjudged to be deviant. The procedural rules are very detailed, organized and objective in nature. The agencies or organizations are organized in an hierarchical manner, with a formal director at the top, supervisors who report to the director, and various agents who deal directly with the deviant and report to their supervisor. The deviant is placed at the bottom of this hierarchy—with the least amount of power. There exists a highly-developed division of labor within these agencies. Attached to each role is a specified set of duties for dealing with the deviant.

In order for agencies of social control to operate effectively and efficiently, they possess a set of unofficial and official assumptions, defining criteria, specified guidelines for labelling and treating deviants—a perspective that tells agents *who* should be officially labelled, *when* and *how* they should be labelled, *who shouldn't* be labelled, who should be relabelled, *what* action should be taken against the deviant, and *how* they should be processed. This perspective or general body of information and associated techniques is referred to as *the theory of the office*. All of these guidelines aid in the routinization of their official processing and makes things run more smoothly.

The theory of the office defines the characteristics of the clients, specifies the manner by which they will be admitted or processed, the type of agencies and agents that will be responsible for their processing. It involves both formal and informal procedures for labelling and the directives for acting on these rules. By so doing, the theory of the office *orders* and *normalizes* deviance.

Let us examine this notion further. The institutionalization of deviance involves more than merely bureaucratized routines. Agencies and agents are faced with a number of problems in their formal regulatory activities. They may be overworked, understaffed, lack necessary evidence or criteria for booking, etc. The theory of the office attempts to solve their difficulties, perhaps through various shortcuts or procedural violations, thus promoting a smooth and efficient operation and protecting the organization as a whole.

Novices are socialized by more seasoned veterans of the agency into adopting this theory of the office. The neophyte, through observation and participation with oldtimers in the agency learn various ways to make their job easier—they acquire a "recipe knowledge" (Shover, 1984)—the steps that they may skip in their categorization and processing of deviants. Moreover, neophytes also learn "typifications" and "stereotypifications"—standardized categories in which to place deviant cases. Instead of going through the laborious task of gathering in-take information, doing diagnostic tests etc., merely on the basis of criteria, X, Y, and Z, the agent types or labels the deviant "manic depressive," "juvenile delinquent," or "prostitute." The employment of typifications and stereotypifications simplifies the task of the agent, but may have deleterious effects on the individual. Jeffery's (1979) research on emergency rooms, Van Maanen's (1978) study on police work and Sudnow's (1965) research on public defenders all illustrate how those involved in the processing of deviant make use of typifications.

In short then, every deviance regulatory organization or agency possesses a theory of the office, a perspective and set of assumptions for defining and treating deviance—the employment of which aids in the smooth and efficient operation of the workers and the organization as a whole.

The effects of developing and employing a theory of the office are three-fold: firstly, deviance becomes *standardized*—standardized deviance becomes "normal" deviance. It is treated by agents as a standardized entity, a conceptual type. The individual is placed on an assembly-line of sorts and is treated in a systematic manner. Secondly, deviance becomes *objectified* in nature. The individual is conceived of not as John Smith, school teacher, but as Case 3467, Paranoid Schizophrenic. Although objectification enable the agent to process the deviant objectively and efficiently (without letting personal feelings get in the way), this objectification has profound, negative implications for the individual in terms of his self-image and identity (as we shall discuss shortly). Thirdly, it simplifies the job of official agents; in short, it routinizes the entire deviance-processing operation.

Robert Scott in his article, *"The Making of Blind Men,"* discusses the contrasting theories of the office employed by various agencies for the visually impaired and how they deal with their clients.

In surveying the numerous organizations and facilities making up the "blindness system," Scott found that there existed no overall policy for dealing with the visually impaired. Instead, they comprised, "an aggregate of bureaucratic entities that share a common interest in the problems of blindness, but whose activities are not coordinated and integrated to any meaningful degree." Moreover, their services were made only to a small segment of the population.

For those persons who did become clients of agencies, Scott discovered that there was strong pressure to consider themselves as completely "blind" and to adopt views of blindness adopted by agency workers. If a client wished to progress in the agency's program, it was imperative that he or she accept the worker's/agency's conception of his or her problems.

Scott analyzed two major approaches to blindness that may be adopted by agency workers. One he termed, *restorative*, the other *accommodative*. The former aims at maximizing the blind person's capacities for independence and is grounded in the assumption that most visually impaired can lead fairly normal lives. This approach seeks to identify and restore the several kinds of losses associated with blindness—mechanical devices, guide dogs, and communication through braille. The theory of the office of these agencies seeks to reintegrate persons into effectively functioning beings. This focus has a positive effect on the self-conceptions of the clients.

Agencies adopting the accommodative approach, by contrast, possess a theory of the office in which blindness is conceived as posing insurmountable obstacles, making self-sufficiency impossible. The assumption underlying this theory of the office is that "most of their clients will end up organizing their lives around the agency." Scott illustrates how through the context of institutional processing, clients are unable to function in the larger community. According to Scott, this theory of the office was developed not only to aid in the effective treatment of their clients, but also for economic reasons. While most blindness organizations have achieved support from the community, their security depended upon their adopting outlooks and practices in line with the larger community. The perceived needs of the community, in contrast to needs of the blind, shaped the social policies of these agencies.

Just as social welfare agencies operate according to a theory of the office, so too do the police develop their own theory of the office for dealing with deviants.

Albert J. Meehan, in *"Record-keeping Practices in the Policing of Deviants,"* discusses how the police on patrol, through the theory of the office, effectively deal with the difficulties and problems encountered in their job. Specifically, this article focuses on the organizational tensions as they affect, and are expressed in the record-keeping practices of the police. As Meehan illustrates the projected organizational career and its use shapes the form and content of the police record. Police officers are aware of the various prospective uses and careers of the records they create such as to evaluate their productivity and the organization as a whole; thus, they learn how to create the correct record, thus leading to smooth and efficient organizational processing.

The selection by Douglas Thomson deals with the amplification of deviance—the secondary expansion of deviance as a result of societal reactions, including efforts at social control. *"Constructing Probationer Careers: Revocation as Censure Transformation and Tertiary Deviance in the Deviance Amplification Process,"* explores how probation officers negotiate the fates of probationers in light of contingencies of scarce resources, uncertain knowledge, interorganizational relationships, and increased demands on the probation institution. Already certified by courts as deviants, probationers live in a legal limbo. While probation offers a community release status rather than physical confinement, it limits their liberty in multiple ways and threatens incarceration for failure to comply with the restricted personal law that conditions of probation establish. Revocation of probation turns probationers into tertiary deviants, ultra-end products of the deviance amplification process.

Thomson's analysis highlights the significance of this form of censure transformation in light of the growth of probation and the organizational convenience and expanded social control functions it serves. Probation officer responses to alleged violations of probation follow a sequence of discovery, recognition, sanction, expansion, escalation, and closure. These agents have some latitude in choosing among the social control options provided by law and human service technology, but find this discretion constrained by work group norms, exchange relationships, and the structure of the work. The increasing legalization, bureaucratization, and centralization of probation work, together with the general trend toward more surveillant, restrictive, pervasive, and indiscriminant crime control efforts, indicate that we should expect constraints on probation officers and social control of probationers to increase.

Total Institutions and the Effects of Formal Labelling

When an individual adjudged to be deviant comes into contact with a social control agency, the agency may define the person solely in terms of the deviant designation. Such agencies and institutions function to strip the individual of her prior conception of self, her old identities, and to "shape, retool and remold" the individual in the image that the institution has of her.

The extent to which these efforts are engaged in and the effects for an individual's self conception vary greatly from institution to institution. However, suffice it is to say that this process is most apparent in what Goffman (1961:4) refers to as "total institutions" or "people-processing institutions"—organizations that require complete subordination of clients and restrict their interaction with members of the larger society. Examples of total institutions include: psychiatric hospitals, prisons and juvenile detention facilities.

Nancy J. Herman in her article, *"The In-patient Phase in the Moral Career of the Psychiatric Patient: The Context within which Self is Mortified,"* discusses the mental hospital, a total institution and its role in destroying normal identities and self-images and manufacturing deviant identities. Herman describes how the psychiatric hospital functions through a variety of rituals and procedures which serve to eliminate an individual's uniqueness and individuality, reducing him or her to the level of other clients. The author discusses the various admission procedures to which patients are subjected; they are physically stripped of their clothing, their "identity kit" is removed, all belongings are taken from the patient for "safekeeping;" the patient is subjected to a cursory psychiatric examination and a physical examination, and is then issued institutional clothing. From the point of view of the institution's theory of the office, there is a sound rationale for following these procedures. However, from the perspective of the patient however, such rituals are conceived as "a series of abasements, degradations, humiliations and profanations" functioning to strip the individual of his or her prior conception of self—or what Goffman (1961:6) calls *"mortification of self."*

These stripping procedures are not only restricted to the admissions proceedings; in fact, they may be imposed throughout the individual's institutionalization in order to keep or bring the person under control. Verbal, physical abuse, sexual abuse and electric shock treatments—mutilations of the body are involved in identity transformation. Such actions serve as negative sanctions for failure to accept the new identity, corresponding role and status of mental patient offered by the institution. Herman discusses the role of the "privilege system" as the organizational context within which self is reconstituted; patients quickly learn that in order to advance in the privilege system (to be allowed to wear their own clothes, attend more activities, have more freedom), it is imperative to accept the identity, role and status pro-offered by the mental hospital. Failure to do so is equated with non-compliance, results in the negative sanctions indicated above, and forces the individual to remain in the lower levels of the privilege system.

The last article by D.L. Rosenhan, *"Being Sane in Insane Places,"* describes the now classic experiment conducted in the 1970's in which a group of pseudopatients (persons not known to be mentally ill) were hospitalized for "hearing voices" in a variety of psychiatric institutions; their normality remained largely undetected. Staff persistently treated the individuals as if they were "insane"—their aspects of normal behavior were perceived by staff as "symptoms." Despite the fact that the pseudopatients themselves knew they were sane, nevertheless, they felt as if they were on a treadmill trying to resist the process of labelling and depersonalization. Interestingly, although the staff all "saw" mental illness on the part of the pseudopatients, it was the other patients who detected their normalcy.

This study points to the imprecision of deviant categories, the demoralizing nature of becoming a mental patient, and the influence of power relations between definers and those defined. Once individuals are adjudged to be deviant, and are "sucked into" people-processing institutions, staff treat you as if you are deviant, even if you are not—having profound, negative implications for the development and internalization of deviant identities.

REFERENCES

Goffman, Erving, 1961. *Asylums.* New York: Doubleday Anchor.

Jeffery, Roger, 1979. "Rubbish: Deviant Patients in Casualty Departments." *Sociology of Health and Illness* 1:90–107.

Shover, Neal, 1984. "The Official Construction of Deviant Identities." Pp. 66–74 In Jack D. Douglas, ed., *The Sociology of Deviance.* Boston: Allyn and Bacon.

Sudnow, David, 1965. "Normal Crimes." Pp. 174–185 in Earl Rubington and Martin S. Weinberg, eds., *Deviance: The Interactionist Perspective.* New York: MacMillan.

Van Maanen, John, 1978. "The Asshole." Pp. 221–238 in Peter K. Manning and John Van Maanen, eds., *Policing: A View from the Street.* Santa Monica, California: Goodyear.

Chapter 24

THE MAKING OF BLIND MEN

Robert A. Scott

When a blind person first comes to an organization for the blind, he usually has some specific ideas about what his primary problems are and how they can be solved. Most new clients request services that they feel will solve or ameliorate the specific problems they experience because of their visual impairment. Many want only to be able to read better, and therefore request optical aids. Others desire help with mobility problems, or with special problems of dressing, eating, or housekeeping. Some need money or medical care. A few contact agencies for the blind in search of scientific discoveries that will restore their vision. Although the exact type of help sought varies considerably, many clients feel that the substance of their problems is contained in their specific requests....

The personal conceptions that blinded persons have about the nature of their problems are in sharp contrast with beliefs that workers for the blind share about the problems of blindness. The latter regard blindness as one of the most severe of all handicaps, the effects of which are long-lasting, pervasive, and extremely difficult to ameliorate. They believe that if these problems are to be solved, blind persons must understand them and all their manifestations and willingly submit themselves to a prolonged, intensive, and comprehensive program of psychological and restorative services. *Effective socialization of the client largely depends upon changing his views about his problem.* In order to do this, the client's views about the problems of blindness must be discredited. Workers must convince him that simplistic ideas about solving the problems of blindness by means of one or a few services are unrealistic. Workers regard the client's initial definition of his problems as akin to the visible portion of an iceberg. Beneath the surface of awareness lies a tremendously complicated mass of problems that must be dealt with before the surface problems can ever be successfully solved.

Discrediting the client's personal ideas about his problems is achieved in several ways. His initial statements about why he has come to the organization and what he hopes to receive from it are euphemistically termed "the presenting problem," a phrase that implies superficiality in the client's views. During the intake interview and then later with the caseworker or psychologist, the client is encouraged to discuss his feelings and aspirations....However, when concrete plans are formulated, the client learns that his personal views about his problems are largely ignored. A client's request for help with a reading problem produces a recommendation by the worker for a comprehensive psychological work-up. A client's inquiries regarding the availability of financial or medical aid may elicit the suggestion that he enroll in a complicated long-term program of testing, evaluation, and training. In short, blind persons who are acceptable to the agency for the blind will often find that intake workers listen attentively to their views but then dismiss them as superficial or inaccurate....For most persons who have come this far in the process, however, dropping out is not a particularly realistic alternative, since it implies that the blind person has other resources open to him. For the most part, such resources are not available.

...[The] experiences a blind person has before being inducted into an agency make him vulnerable to the wishes and intentions of the workers who deal with them. The ability to withstand the pressure to act, think, and feel in conformity with the workers' concept of a model blind person is further reduced by the fact that the workers have a virtual monopoly on the rewards and punishments in the system. By manipulating these rewards and punishments, workers are able to pressure the client into rejecting personal conceptions of problems in favor of the worker's own definition of them. Much evaluative work, in fact, involves attempts to get the client to understand and accept the agency's conception of the problems of blindness....In face-to-face situations, the blind person is rewarded for showing insight and subtly reprimanded for continuing to adhere to earlier notions about his problems. He is led to think that he "really" understands past and present experiences when he couches them in terms acceptable to his therapist....

Psychological rewards are not the only rewards at stake in this process. A fundamental tenet of work for the blind is that a client must accept the fact of his blindness and everything implied by it before he can be effectively rehabilitated. As a result, a client must show signs of understanding his problem in the therapist's terms before he will be permitted to progress any further in the program. Since most blind persons are anxious to move along in the program as rapidly as possible, the implications of being labeled "uncooperative" are serious. Such a label prevents him from receiving basic restorative services. The uncooperative client is assigned low priority for entering preferred job programs. Workers for the blind are less willing to extend themselves on his behalf. As a result, the alert client quickly learns to become "insightful," to behave as workers expect him to.

Under these circumstances, the assumptions and theories of workers for the blind concerning blindness and rehabilitation take on new significance, for what they do is to create, shape, and mold the attitudes and behavior of the client in his role as a blind person....[It] is in organizations for the blind that theories and explicit and implicit assumptions about blindness and rehabilitation become actualized in the clients' attitudes and behavior. We can therefore gain an understanding about the behavior of clients as blind people by examining the theories and assumptions about blindness and rehabilitation held by workers for the blind.

The Practice Theories of Blindness Workers

The beliefs, ideologies, and assumptions about blindness and rehabilitation that make up practice theories of work for the blind are legion. They include global and limited theories about blindness, ethical principles, common sense ideas, and an array of specific beliefs that are unrelated, and often contradictory, to one another. Contained in this total array of ideas are two basically different approaches to the problems of blindness. The first I will call the "restorative approach"; the most complete and explicit version of this approach is contained in the writings of Father Thomas Carroll.[1] The second I will call the "accommodative approach." This approach has never been formulated into a codified practice theory; rather, it is only apparent in the programs and policies of more orthodox agencies for the blind.

The Restorative Approach

The basic premise of the restorative approach to blindness is that most blind people can be restored to a high level of independence enabling them to lead a reasonably normal life. However, these goals are attainable only if the person accepts completely the fact that he is blind, and only after he has received competent professional counseling and training....

Seven basic kinds of losses resulting from blindness are identified: (1) the losses of psychological security—the losses of physical integrity, confidence in the remaining senses, reality contact with the environment, visual background, and light security; (2) the losses of the skills of mobility and techniques of daily living; (3) the communication losses, such as the loss of ease of written and spoken communication, and of information about daily events in the world; (4) the losses of appreciation, which include the loss of the visual perception of the pleasurable and of the beautiful; (5) the losses of occupational and financial status, which consist of financial security, career, vocational goals, job opportunities, and ordinary recreational activities; (6) the resulting losses to the whole personality, including the loss of personal independence, social adequacy, self-esteem, and total personality organization; and (7) the concomitant losses of sleep, of physical tone of the body, and of decision, and the sense of control over one's life.[2]

Rehabilitation, in this scheme, is the process "whereby adults in varying stages of helplessness, emotional disturbance, and dependence come to gain new understanding of themselves and their handicap, the new skills necessary for their state, and a new control of their emotions and their environment."[3] This process is not a simple one; it involves the pain and recurrent crises that accompany the acceptance of the many "deaths" to sighted life. It consists of "restorations" for each of the losses involved in blindness. The final objective of total rehabilitation involves returning and integrating the blinded person in his society.

...The various restorations in each of these phases correspond to the losses the person has encountered. The loss of confidence in the remaining senses is restored through deliberate training of these senses; the loss of mobility is restored through training in the use of a long cane or guide dog; the loss of ease of written communication is restored through learning braille, and so on. The goal of this process is to reintegrate the components of the restored personality into an effectively functioning whole....

[In] several rehabilitation centers and general agencies...the ideas contained in...[Father Carroll's] book are used as the basis for a formal course taught to blind people while they are obtaining services. The purpose of this course is to clarify for them what they have lost because they are blind, how they must change through the course of rehabilitation, and what their lives will be like when rehabilitation has been completed. These ideas are given added weight by the fact that they are shared by all staff members who deal directly with the client and, in some agencies at least, by other nonservice personnel who have occasional contacts with clients....

We cannot assume that there is a necessary correspondence between the beliefs regarding the limits and potentialities imposed by blindness and the blind client's self-image. The question of the full impact of the former on the latter is an empirical one on which there are no hard data. Our analysis of the client's "set" when he enters an agency for the blind does suggest, however, that such beliefs probably have a profound impact on his self-image.... [When] the client comes to an agency, he is often seeking direction and guidance and, more often than not, he is in a state of crisis. Consequently, the authority of the system makes the client highly suggestible to the attitudes of those whose help he seeks.

There is evidence that some blind people resist the pressures of the environment of agencies and centers that adopt this philosophy by feigning belief in the workers' ideas for the sake of "making out" in the system.[4] In such cases, the impact of the workers on the client's self-image will be attenuated. Despite this, he will learn only those skills made available to him by the agency or center. These skills, which the workers regard as opportunities for individual fulfillment, act also as limits. The choice of compensatory skills around which the theory revolves means the exclusion of a spectrum of other possibilities.

The Accommodative Approach

A basic premise of the restorative approach is that most blind people possess the capacity to function independently enough to lead normal lives. Rehabilitation centers and general service agencies that have embraced this approach therefore gear their entire service programs toward achieving this goal. In other agencies for the blind, no disagreement is voiced about the desirability of blind people's attaining independence, but there is considerable skepticism as to whether this is a feasible goal for more than a small fraction of the client population.[5] According to this view, blindness poses enormous obstacles to independence—obstacles seen as insurmountable by a majority of people....Settings and programs are designed to accommodate the helpless, dependent blind person.

The physical environment in such agencies is often contrived specifically to suit certain limitations inherent in blindness. In some agencies, for example, the elevators have tape recorders that report the floor at which the elevator is stopping and the direction in which it is going, and panels of braille numbers for each floor as well. Other agencies have mounted over their front doors special bells that ring at regular intervals to indicate to blind people that they are approaching the building. Many agencies maintain fleets of cars to pick up clients at their homes and bring them to the agency for services. In the cafeterias of many agencies, special precautions are taken to serve only food that blind people can eat without awkwardness. In one agency cafeteria, for example, the food is cut before it is served, and only spoons are provided.

Recreation programs in agencies that have adopted the accommodative approach consist of games and activities tailored to the disability. For example, bingo, a common activity in many programs, is played with the aid of a corps of volunteers who oversee the game, attending to anything the blind person is unable to do himself.

Employment training for clients in accommodative agencies involves instruction in the use of equipment specifically adapted to the disability. Work tasks, and even the entire method of production, are engineered with this disability in mind, so that there is little resemblance between an average commercial industrial setting and a sheltered workshop. Indeed, the blind person who has been taught to do industrial work in a training facility of an agency for the blind will acquire skills and methods of production that may be unknown in most commercial industries.

The general environment of such agencies is also accommodative in character. Clients are rewarded for trivial things and praised for performing tasks in a mediocre fashion. This superficial and overgenerous reward system makes it impossible for most clients to assess their accomplishments accurately. Eventually, since anything they do is praised as outstanding, many of them come to believe that the underlying assumption must be that blindness makes them incompetent.

The unstated assumption of accommodative agencies is that most of their clients will end up organizing their lives around the agency. Most will become regular participants in the agency's recreation programs, and those who can work will obtain employment in a sheltered workshop or other agency-sponsored employment program. The accommodative approach therefore produces a blind person who can function effectively only within the confines of the agency's contrived environment. He learns skills and behaviors that are necessary for participating in activities and programs of the agency, but which make it more difficult to cope with the environment of the larger community. A blind person who has been fully socialized in an accommodative agency will be maladjusted to the larger community. In most cases, he does not have the resources, the skills, the means, or the opportunity to overcome the maladaptive patterns of behavior he has learned. He has little choice but to remain a part of the environment that has been designed and engineered to accommodate him.

This portrayal of accommodative agencies suggests that the workers in them, like those in restorative agencies, make certain assumptions about the limitations that blindness imposes, and that these assumptions are manifested in expectations about attitudes and behavior that people ought to have because they are blind....

Unfortunately, no hard data are available on socialization outcomes in agencies that adopt either of the two approaches I have described. However, the materials I collected from interviews with blind people suggest that a number of discernably patterned reactions occur.[6] Some clients and trainees behave according to workers' expectations of them deliberately and consciously in order to extract from the system whatever rewards it may have. Others behave according to expectations because they have accepted and internalized them as genuine qualities of character. The former are the "expedient" blind people, and the latter are the "true believers."

Expedient blind people consciously play a part, acting convincingly the way they sense their counselors and instructors want them to act. They develop a keen sense of timing that enables them to be at their best when circumstances call for it. When the circumstances change, the facade is discarded, much as the Negro discards his

"Uncle Tomisms" in the absence of whites. As a rule, the expedient blind person is one who recognizes that few alternatives are open to him in the community; his response is an understandable effort to maximize his gains in a bad situation.

True believers are blind people for whom workers' beliefs and assumptions about blindness are unquestioned ideals toward which they feel impelled earnestly to strive. While this pattern is probably found in all agencies for the blind, it is most obvious in those which embrace the accommodative approach to blindness. Clients who become true believers in such agencies actually experience the emotions that workers believe they must feel. They experience and spontaneously verbalize the proper degree of gratitude, they genuinely believe themselves to be helpless, and they feel that their world must be one of darkness and dependency.

REFERENCES

Barker, R.T., et. al. 1968. *Adjustment of Physical Handicap and Blindness: A Survey of the Social Psychology of Physique and Disability.* New York: Social Science Research Council.

Carroll, T. 1961. *Blindness: What It Is, What It Does, and How to Live with It.* Boston: Little, Brown & Company.

Information Bulletin No. 59. 1968. University of Utah. Salt Lake City: Regional Rehabilitation Research Institute.

NOTES

[1] Carroll, T.J. (1961).
[2] Carroll, T.J., (1961:14–79).
[3] Carroll, T.J, (1961:96).
[4] *Information Bulletin No. 59*, 1968.
[5] Roger G. Barker et al., (1953).
[6] Most of this discussion applies to blind people who have been exposed to agencies that adopt an accommodative approach to rehabilitation. Little information could be gathered on those who have been trainees in restorative agencies, primarily because such agencies are comparatively few in number and recent in origin.

Chapter 25

RECORD-KEEPING PRACTICES IN THE POLICING OF JUVENILES

Albert J. Meehan

"People-processing organizations" (Hasenfeld, 1972) are by necessity involved in information collection and processing through written and oral records that are brought to bear upon decisions about how individual clients are to be treated. However, records used to make decisions are also used to evaluate to productivity of staff and the organization as a whole (Seidman and Couzens, 1974; Manning, 1977). The dual character of records is particularly evident in policing, where institutional demands and expectations make accounting for acts a fundamental consideration (Pepinsky, 1976). In this respect police record work must serve at the same time organizational workers in the provision and control of services for their "clients," and administrators and outsiders such as the courts and the public in their attempts to monitor members of the organization. These conflicting organizational demands affect the sorts of records kept, the type of information created in records, and the practical management of records by police patrol officers.

This article focuses on these organizational tensions as they affect and are expressed in police "record work." By this concept I intend to emphasize two interrelated processes relevant to police record keeping: First, record work highlights the processes affecting how patrol officers *produce* a variety of work- and organization-relevant records. Particularly central here are the ways in which the projected organizational uses and longer-term "careers" of records shape their forms and content. Second, record work references the ways in which police officers *interpret* and infer the meaning, import, and "accuracy" of the various sorts of records they rely upon in carrying out their routine activities. As many officers note, "The record can tell you some things but not others." Describing the process whereby local background knowledge is brought to bear to determine what particular record can "tell you" comprises a second component of record work.

Research Sites and Data Collection

The data used in this discussion are drawn from a one year field study of the police handling of juveniles in two adjoining suburban police departments.[1] This study was part of a larger three-year federally funded project examining the relevance of national standards for the police handling of juveniles in four police departments. I had primary responsibility for the project's relationship with two suburban departments and spent a total of 250 hours on ride alongs in these communities with patrol and youth bureau personnel.

Observation of record-keeping practices provided a major focus for research. I spent two weeks in the records room of each department learning the system, discussing record-keeping procedures with administrative personnel, and collecting arrest and contact records from the previous two years. Over a period of six months I spent an average of four days per week in the field. I recorded field notes of the ride alongs and interviews with administrative personnel directly after leaving the field setting. After this period of active field research, I met more occasionally with police task forces and individual officers in each department during the next four months to discuss the project's findings and to draft recommendations for the department.

The police departments I observed served two small suburban towns located outside a large northeastern city. Grandville's population is almost twice that of Hargrove's 49,000 (as opposed to 26,000), although both occupy five square miles. The residents of both towns are predominantly white-collar professionals, although proportionately more blue-collar workers reside in Grandville than in Hargrove. In Grandville there are more multiple-family dwellings and apartment buildings. Both towns have public housing projects that are perceived as sources of problems with young people. Very few members of racial minorities reside in either community. Each town has one high school and several middle and grammar schools. The towns have a town manager form of government, accountable to elected boards of selectmen. The selectmen exercise control over the police departments in ways equivalent to the police commissions found in larger cities.

The Grandville police department has approximately 80 sworn officers. Two detectives serve as the juvenile officers, investigating cases involving juveniles in addition to an adult caseload (the latter constituting about 35% of their caseload). One works the day shift and the other works the evening shift. These detectives are expected to patrol, especially during the evening, but do not respond to routine calls for service involving juveniles unless additional assistance is needed or requested by patrol officers.

The Hargrove police department has approximately 60 sworn officers. Three officers (two patrol and a detective) serve as the department's juvenile unit. The patrol officers split their time between working the day and the evening shift, while the detective works only days. In contrast to Grandville, these officers only handle cases involving juvenile officers. In both towns, whenever a juvenile is arrested a juvenile officer is called to process the booking and notify parents.

Record Work in the Policing of Juveniles

Each level of police response to an incident (i.e., communications, patrol, detectives) may produce some *paper trace* of that incident. Some of these paper traces are official documents, some are more "informal documents," and others are personal records.[2]

Police officers in both Grandville and Hargrove work with a variety of official forms, including incident/arrest reports, officers' patrol logs, and dispatchers' incident cards. Officers know or assume that the use of official documents routinely extend beyond the individual who produces them. Although it is not possible to specify exactly who might use that document next, or when, or for what purpose, members of the organization can anticipate potential uses and project routine careers for an official document. Police distinguish between two general types of such projected careers: external and internal. That is, some records are assumed likely to be accessible and primarily of interest to external agents (i.e., the courts, the mayor's office), others are assumed likely to be seen and used only or primarily by coworkers. The projection of external as opposed to internal uses of a record, and vice versa, fundamentally shapes the form and content of the resulting documents.

Other paper traces have no formal organizational status and take the form of individual or personal records. Primary examples of such records include an officer's pad, scraps of paper assembled during the course of an investigation, and, in some instances, personal jottings on or additions to official forms. This type of paper trace is a personal system of work-relevant records and an essential source of information immediately available to that individual officer.

Despite the pervasiveness of such written records, much information is "re-corded" without leaving paper traces.[3] Patrol officers acquire a particularly rich stock of local work-relevant knowledge that is an essential and often utilized source of information (Bittner, 1967; Rubinstein, 1973). Such information has a "factual" and authoritative status and for all practical purposes constitutes a record. Each officer accumulates such a stock of knowledge through his or her work experiences and develops his or her own "mental dossier" (Cicourel, 1968:68), which augments the generalized occupational knowledge of the police subculture. In addition, officers share information, and these occasions for revealing information are important interactional events. These interactional exchanges, which I call the "running record," can be conceptually distinguished from both organizational and personal written records, and provide important resources in police decision making.

While creating or producing records makes up one major component of police record work, officer practices for making sense or finding the meaning of the records produced by others provide a second critical component. For officers rarely take a record at "face value," viewing it nonproblematically as a set of objective "facts." Rather, when faced with a formal written account, officers will invoke their mental dossiers and the running record to interpret the significance of the written record for their policing. In effect, officers "read between the lines," treating the record as the product of a set of known decision-making and record-producing practices. Under these circumstances the reading of a record is reflexively informed by an understanding of the work relevancies involved in its production and of the anticipated uses guiding this production.[4]

Organizational Records and Projected External Careers

Records that organizational members assume to be available for *external* consumption (whether on a routine basis or whenever special accounting is required outside the organization) are accorded a projected external career. In policing such records include arrest report, which are routinely forwarded to court to be used by the prosecuting and defense attorneys, and traffic accident and certain other incident reports (i.e., thefts), which are routinely sent or made available to insurance companies for claims purposes.

Records with projected external careers have what Garfinkel and Bittner (1967) call contractual as opposed to actuarial uses. An actuarial use of a record seeks to derive a statistical profile. On the other hand, a record may be read as evidence of a contract between the organization and the person served; in the case of medical clinic records, Garfinkel and Bittner (1967:199) observe, "the contents of clinic folders are assembled with regard for the possibility that the relationship may have to be portrayed as having been in accord with expectations of sanctionable performances by clinicians and patients."

Similarly, in the police context, arrest reports are assembled in ways that portray the actions taken by the police as standing in a "correct" or sanctionable relation with court-honored standards of law enforcement. This assembling process may involve the selection, recasting, and on occasion, even fabrication of "the facts" and the sequence in which they occurred. These dimensions of police record work in constructing an arrest report can be examined by analyzing in close detail the following extended field observations. These field notes describe the decisional contingencies of responding to an emergent street situation, and then turn to the processes by which the arrest report framed this incident in anticipation of its likely contractual uses in the court setting.

A call reporting youths throwing bottles was dispatched to the adjoining sector car. A second call for the same location was then dispatched reporting a possible assault in progress. The officer I was riding with (Bill Brady) was patrolling the sector dividing line, three blocks away from the address, and decided to check it out. Turning up the street where the incident had been reported, the officer stopped and rolled his window down. The sounds of glass breaking, a loud pounding noise, and people yelling could be heard. Speeding toward the direction of these sounds, the officer observed two youths walk out of a driveway, get into their car and leave the scene. The officer turned his spotlight into the driveway, where there were three youths, one of whom had a tire iron in his hand. When the light came on, they immediately ran. The officer leaped out of the car and chased them down the street and into a backyard about seven houses away. At this point, three other patrol cars arrived as Brady reappeared with one youth handcuffed. This youth was then placed in a nearby patrol car.

After this, Brady said to me, "Come on, let's see what they were doing up there. I heard glass breaking." The driveway and yard were searched, but no broken glass was found. Upon leaving the yard, a citizen who had been nearby said that a window on a van down the street was broken. The van was examined and the window was cracked but still intact. "That must be it," said Brady, and took down the license plate number. He then asked the citizen if he knew the owner, but he did not. No victim of an assault was located at the scene either, although another citizen stated to us that someone was definitely getting beaten up in this back yard.

At this point a detective on the scene discussed the incident with Brady. The detective stated the incident was "obviously" drug related: Someone reneged on a drug deal and they were settling the score. According to his "street information," the arrested youth and his friends are known pushers dealing to this side of town: "No one will come forward on this assault, Brady, but you can bet it was drug related." Brady agreed with his assessment and thanked him for the information.

Brady parked in a parking lot several blocks away to write the report that had to be filed at the station. He then said "I'm sure you know I'm gonna have to fudge this one. I violated a lot of procedure back there by not calling in what I was doing or taking my radio with me. But by the time I could have done any of that, those kids would have been gone. There was no way I could have waited for the sector car on the arrest."

In this situation, as in many police incidents, everything happens very quickly. In coming upon and handling this situation, the officer brought to bear a stock of background knowledge to determine what was happening. The officer pursued the youths on the grounds that the available cues on arrival (yelling, glass breaking, the youths running when he saw them) were inferrably the signs of illegal actions. By contrast, Brady did not pursue the youths who were observed walking out of the driveway and getting into the car. In part, I suspect that Brady did not yet know that this driveway was the driveway where the trouble was to be "discovered." Yet their presence leaving the driveway led him to examine it more carefully and thereby locate the other three youths who began running. As Brady mentioned later, "you know they were in the wrong because they blew out of there so fast." Those actions were framed in the context of receiving a call about youths breaking bottles, and a second call for the same location reporting a more serious problem (an assault). (Generally, a second dispatch to a location is assumed by officers to be indicative of more trouble.) Although at this point he did not know what the illegality was, let alone whether anything illegal actually occurred, Brady followed the standard patrol practice of responding immediately and worrying about the law and organizational procedure afterward.

This incident also displayed the use of an officer's stock of knowledge. When the detective told Brady that the person arrested was a known pusher, the incident was provided with an interpretive frame (i.e., a drug vendetta), which made it meaningful in a way that it would not have been otherwise. This interpretive frame resolved ambiguities such as the failure of the van owner to come forward at the scene and the failure to locate someone on the scene who had been beaten as reported by the dispatcher and citizen.

Moreover, for Brady and the detective the incident as originally encountered posed less a legal than a practical problem: Drug deals on this side of town may be entering a violent phase, increasing the need to monitor the neighborhood and persons within it. The information shared at the scene identified drug activity and violence as the real problem and established the interpretation of the incident relevant "for us as police officers."

How the event is reconstructed for the arrest report is another matter: Brady wrote his report and gave it to me saying, "you probably won't recognize this as what you saw, but that's the way it has to be." The report stated,

At 23:05, while on routine patrol, I responded to a call at 27 Rogers Road for youths drinking, throwing bottles, and yelling. When I arrived at the above address, I observed three youths walking down the street yelling and screaming loudly. I further observed the above suspect, Gerald McGee, with a tire iron in his hand, take the iron and smash the right rear window of a Ford van, registration number BK-7538. When the youths see me, all three began to run down Rogers Road. I pursued them to 84 Rogers Road, where they ran into the backyard and the suspect dropped the tire iron. There I apprehended Gerald McGee, aged eighteen, advised him of his rights, and placed him in cruiser number 353, in which he was transported to the station. He is charged with malicious damage to property and being a disorderly person.

The official report on this incident bears a strained resemblance to what I witnessed. The events as they unfolded are retrospectively fitted and, where necessary clearly altered to create the elements of what the law defines as an offense. That the youths were "guilty" was established for all practical purposes when they ran away, and this action provided the officer's grounds for pursuit and arrest. To prove guilt in court, however, requires the reconstruction and transformation of what happened into "facts" that will appear to conform with proper legal procedure. The account is assembled with a set of "facts" that have been inferred from the behaviors of the suspect, which do not in themselves constitute illegal conduct (e.g., running), a set of "facts" indicating evidence that can be produced in court [i.e., the tire iron), and a set of "facts" that are lies (i.e., Brady did not observe the three youths screaming and yelling, nor did he observe McGee break the window).

The process of inferring what happened, and of proving what happened in accordance with the rules of law, is clearly problematic to the officer. Those very inference procedures for acting in the first place are ironically constrained in the official report. Officers see themselves as having few choices in such instances and present such dishonesty as an inevitable occupational hazard and a matter of simple survival (Manning, 1977:179; Van Maanen, 1978:119). As Brady commented during the ride back to the station with his report,

> I said when I came on the job that I'd never fudge a report. I heard about it in school (the academy) and all that but I said "not me." But when it comes right down to it, it's got to be done, otherwise you're liable for false arrest. You know they were in the wrong because they blew out of there so fast. And you can't let them run away like that because then they think they have control, that the cops won't do anything. But when you get in court, if you don't say you saw it, you might as well forget it.

The "drug vendetta" interpretation of the incident was also invoked to explain the subsequent fate of the case in court. The van owner was identified and summoned to court, but testified that the window had been broken two weeks prior to the incident. Indeed, this testimony served to verify the police interpretation. After the case was dismissed, the detective commented, "This is typical in drug cases. They won't testify against each other, they'll settle their scores out of court."

Organizational Records and Projected Internal Careers

Records with envisioned uses primarily or exclusively within an organizational setting may be associated with some projected internal career. Policing juveniles created three types of such records in the two departments studied: (1) the dispatcher's incident cards; (2) patrol officers' log sheets; and (3) field interrogation/observation (FIO) cards.[5] Because the Grandville department did not utilize FIO cards during the period of my field research,[6] a direct comparison of the uses of this document is not possible. Hence, the following analyses will examine only record work practices involving log sheets and incident cards.

Patrol Logs

Accounting for how time is spent on patrol is an age-old problem in policing (Rubinstein, 1973), and the "log" has been an administrative solution to this problem. The patrol log is one example of an internal record that has actuarial uses for the department. Each officer maintains a log sheet for every shift, summarizing activities such as calls for service, patrol area checks, traffic citations, and medical assists. For patrol officers, keeping the log is first and foremost, a matter of displaying their "activity,"[7] performance, and productivity for review by superiors and administrators.

While on patrol, "keeping the log" represents yet another demand on officer time that requires its own forms of creative management. That is, although all calls to which the officer is dispatched will be entered on the log (primarily because the dispatched call has an additional source of verification at headquarters), the problem for the administrator is how to hold officers accountable for how time is spent *between* calls. The "solution" to this problem of accountability from the patrol officer's standpoint involves manipulating "on-view" entries, that is, entries of activity initiated by an officer. There is considerable discretion in defining what constitutes an on-view activity and what entries one "needs" to make for the evening. In the police vernacular, patrol logs for a tour of duty are commonly referred to as "cheat sheets" or "my lies." Instead of recording all "on-view" activities in a manner parallel to the logging of all call responses, only those necessary to fill the time gaps between calls are recorded. Indeed, on evenings on which the officer has a large number of calls for service, there is no need to fill these gaps, even though other work that could be entered onto the log is done (i.e., assisted motorists, wrote parking tickets, conducted area checks). One evening an officer who responded to ten calls for service remarked, "No need to cheat the sheet tonight. I'm already looking like a rate buster!" Indeed, one must "appropriately" manipulate the logs to avoid making coworkers look bad and increasing the administration's expectation of productivity.

One common strategy for managing the logs is "banking" some on-views. For example, areas announced at roll call, especially ones in which citizens have complained that kids are drinking and smoking dope, are ready made "on-view entries." Indeed, officers will record area checks at these locations, even though the checks were done at different times or never checked at all. The log need only show that officers are doing something between calls.

Another tactic is to stretch the definition of an on-view entry. For example, one slow evening we were having coffee at the local coffee shop when a lost motorist asked for directions (this type of service is often rendered during a shift). At the end of the shift, while filling out the log, the officer recalled the encounter and entered it into his log as "assist motorist," a category normally reserved for helping cars that are broken down.

Log entries can also be "traded." One evening an officer stopped a car in another officer's sector for running a stop light. We were meeting this other officer to relieve the boredom of a slow night. The first officer commented, "It was such a blatant and dangerous violation I couldn't let it pass, even though it's an embarrassment to George; I shouldn't be doing this." However, George saw us (he was on his way to meet us) and pulled over. After a quick apology and explanation about the "asshole" motorists who ran the red light, the officer stated, "It's all yours, George." George chuckled, "Great, I need some of this activity." George completed the traffic stop (i.e., he notified the dispatcher of his location, called in the license plate numbers, and issued the citation) and thereby received credit for an "on-view" that had corroborated documentation at headquarters.

Because log entries are known to be the basis upon which a patrol officer's productivity will be judged by higher-ups, one might expect that officers would record all possible incidents, and perhaps even fabricate log entries, at least for those sorts of incidents for which no other record existed. Yet patrol officers are generally constrained from entering everything possible on their logs by at least two considerations: (1) Officers assume they would be held accountable by administrators for higher levels of activity in the future; (2) the apparent incidence of "trouble" in the community would increase, possibly leading to community and political questioning of the department's efforts.

Patrol logs in general can be treated in actuarial ways to assemble an account of the productivity not only of individual officers but also of the department as a whole. Indeed, police administrators have their own concerns with the actuarial summaries that can be produced from log entries, and upon occasion will issue directives to change log-entry practices in order to make certain problems appear and disappear in this actuarial sense. Budget requests for additional funds, for example, often rely upon statistics derived from the logs as an important source for "proving" the department's need; but given administrative directives, those log entries may not in fact have been assembled independently of making such a budgetary showing.

All in all, both patrol officers and police administrators are fully cognizant of the contingent, organizationally propelled character of log entries and of their doubtful correspondence with actual events. To take these records at face value is to draw a naive picture of police activity. Indeed, several officers advised me not to base any research on "these things," chuckling as they filled in the evening's activities.

Incident Cards

In these jurisdictions, the first paper trace in the organizational processing of an incident is the dispatcher's *incident card*. The front of the card records the time of call, the nature of the complaint, the location of the problem, the name and address of complainant (if available), the responding officer(s), and the disposition of the call. The card is time stamped at the time of the phone call, when the dispatch is made, when the officer arrives on the scene, and when the call is cleared.

Incident cards serve a number of routine management functions: They provide a record of the response time of the organization, as well as a quick count of calls for service for which a car is dispatched during the shift. But incident cards also provide critical information for actively working cases. Often this work-relevant information is not that "officially" recorded on the card. As both departments require responding officers to review and sign the incident cards they have investigated during or at the end of the shift, officers may take the opportunity to write additional comments on the backs of the cards. The opportunity to write something on the backs of incident cards is not to be minimized, especially when officers are not filing any other report. If nothing is written on the back of the card, it suggests that nothing about the call is "reportable" from the viewpoint of the officer; that is, it is a "routine" call for this type of problem.

The backs of the cards may contain a short description of "what happened," a name (sometimes a witness or possible suspect), or a "fact," such as the size of a window found broken on the scene. For this reason, they are viewed daily by the detective bureau (which includes the juvenile officers). Detectives, administrators, and other patrol officers use these comments in follow-up investigations of incidents. As one officer observed, "Especially if the incident didn't require a report, this is the only information you have to go on short of tracking down the guy and asking him about it." During an investigation of widespread vandalism, for example, a juvenile officer reviewed incident cards covering a period of about three weeks to see if there were any pattern or additional information responding patrol officers may have noted. While reviewing these cards the officer commented,

> The front of the card tells you nothing. You'd have to read a lot into it to
> figure out what happened on the call, and even then you may not know.
> But if the guy writes something on the back of the card, you have a better
> idea about what went on and you know it means something to him if he
> took the time to put it down.

In a sense, the front of the incident card serves the administration's schema for accountability and control, whereas the back of the card may contain work-relevant information for any interested party within the organization. Put differently, the front of the card contains information on processing time, sector car assigned, and offense category, whereas the back of the card can provide information for "making sense" of the formal information on the front....

Although juvenile officers rely heavily upon incident cards, reviewing them daily for information that has no "official" report status yet might be consequential for their work, incident cards are not limited to such internal uses. For summary information from the shift's composite of incident cards is transferred to the *department blotter* by the officer in charge during or at the end of the shift. The daily blotter, summarizing calls for service and arrest activity, is one of the most public police records, available by law to any member of the public upon request and routinely used by the local newspaper to monitor police activities. In this sense incident cards, while central if unremarkable internal records, are also crucial for the construction of a record that has possible external relevance and contractual uses. The projected external career of incidents that get recorded on the blotter thus shapes both the handling of incident cards and the process of entering information from such cards on the blotter.

Incident cards can be managed in different ways at different points in the police response to keep certain information off the blotter. The dispatcher can simply not fill out a card. In one instance dispatch received repeated calls about youth drinking over several nights from one neighborhood. The dispatcher concluded that neighbors had organized a "call in" program to get the police to patrol the area more frequently and stopped filling out incident cards on such calls.

At the patrol level, I was told that "on occasion" I may see incident cards ripped up by patrol officers to keep incidents off the blotter. And although I never directly observed an instance of this, almost every officer whom I asked to discuss the ins and outs of the blotter recounted how at one time or another they had ripped up cards to "bury" minor incidents (e.g., drinking) "as a favor" to the persons involved or even to another officer. The most serious instance of burying a case was reported by an officer who had investigated the sexual assault of a girl by her boyfriend. Both the girl and the boy were the children of two prominent politicians who were friends of the police chief. He had destroyed the incident card "as a favor to the chief" but showed me several detailed incident reports documenting his investigation, which he kept in his own personal file.

A more common practice for managing the blotter involves defining the nature of the incident. The officer in charge, who transfers information onto the blotter from these cards, has considerable discretion in redefining the nature of the incident for the blotter. For example, a 15-year-old juvenile who had considerable "mental problems" had taken his parents' auto without permission, driven onto the lawn of his ex-girlfriend's house, and sped recklessly through residential areas. The youth reported to his parents (who had informed the police) that he was contemplating suicide. When he was finally apprehended, he was released to his parents, who promised to call the youth's psychiatrist. When it came time to enter the incident card, which had initially been coded, "stolen auto: using without permission," the officer in charge commented to the responding officer, "If we call it a stolen auto, that's not technically true because the parents won't press charges. If we call it a mental case, it'll have the address here and embarrass the parents. Why don't we just call it 'trouble with son'?" This decision reflects a sensitivity to possible legal implications for the organization as well as to the personal circumstances of the parents and youth.

When records have a projected external career, they will be primarily accountable to formal legal and organizational expectations and will be taken at face value. Indeed, they are designed to fulfill these expectations. The attention given to the contractual use of arrest reports is evidenced by the review they are given by a patrol officer's superiors, who will require an officer to rewrite an arrest report in order to "cover one's ass" and/or to make the charge "stick in court" (Manning, 1977:191; Van Maanen, 1978:126–127). Although such a record can be used internally and interpreted "between the lines," this possible interpretation does not define its production. Similarly, records with internal careers differ greatly in form and content. Although these could be used externally, it is questionable what use could be made of them by outsiders as they do not provide an "objective" account to be taken at face value. Rather, they depend upon an interpretive "between the lines" reading and access to the organizational routines and expectations that define their production and are presupposed in such a reading.

Personal Resources: Individual Records

"Official" forms of the organization are not the only written documents that are important records. Personal records, such as officers' pads as well as other "scraps of paper" that are invariably produced over the course of an investigation, are also important sources of information. The officer relies upon these to construct official reports or to trigger his or her memory about individuals and incidents.

For example, the juvenile officer in Hargrove kept a file of all active and closed cases he generated during the month. He offered this explanation of a piece of paper in this file containing only a date and phone number: "[This is] a situation where four kids in a family whose parents are never home have been seen running around the neighborhood at all hours of the night. The neighbors have been complaining. These kids will be a neglect case soon enough." Although the officer did not file an official report on the incident, he did count it at the end of the month as a neglect case in his official departmental report, which is forwarded to the state. Of interest is how the event is and is not a "case" just yet: Officially on record, there is nothing to suggest that the situation exists; yet unofficially, the details of the reported event and the elements of it as a possible case in the future are available and triggered by the notes on the piece of paper.

It is not uncommon to find notes on desks and in the case files of officers. Indeed, they are typically used to construct the "official" report, a copy of which is usually attached in the file. The meaning of these pieces of paper necessarily relies upon the individual officer's interpretation and recounting of the original context of its production. Thus, making sense of them depends upon having direct access either to the event or to the officer's account of the event. However, such accounts, as in the above example, stand as quite "factual" and real matters to the officer. In this sense such personal records, despite their lack of official basis, their brevity, and their often idiosyncratic nature, have significant organizational relevance.

The organizational relevance of such personal records is illustrated by the use of the officer's pad in the court context. While the pad provides a source of information of the officer's own use (in preparing reports, etc.), some officers anticipate its use in court and the potential challenges it might encounter. In this sense, the pad can have both internal and external careers, and entries into it may be made with both possibilities in mind...

Police administrators have long realized the value of officers maintaining their own records. Thus, officers in Grandville were required to carry a pad that the department issued to them. The use of pads was common in both jurisdictions. A new officer assigned to the juvenile bureau showed me his pad, which contained the names of all juveniles he encountered during the first three months of this assignment. This included not only suspects and victims but anyone he encountered in patrol. He justified this practice on the grounds that he needed to know the "population."

The pad is used to document past experiences with youths who have been "given a break" or to assemble information about situations that may require police attention in the future....

Personal Resources: The Running Record and the Mental Dossier

Whereas the courts, the public, and social researchers have relied upon written accounts for information about crime and the police, the police themselves in their routine activities overwhelmingly use verbal exchanges as their critical sources of information. In talk with one another, whether in more formal reports or in fleeting exchanges, officers learn about recent events and individuals as well as about continuing departmental lore. In such common conversational activities as bitching, bantering, complaining, and telling "combat stories" officers assemble, disseminate and hence create a stock of knowledge about local individuals and situations to which I will refer as the *running record*.

The running record is an oral history of persons, places and incidents constructed by virtue of the police officer's access to the everyday activities of individuals. The stock of accumulated knowledge about individuals, the places they inhabit, and events that occur within those places constitute the running record. The running record also includes the ongoing monitoring of events within the department, as the politics of the work environment often has an impact upon the work of officers.

The running record can be conceptually distinguished from an officer's "mental dossier," the term used by Cicourel (1968) to refer to the personal recollection of events or persons. The running record is a collaboratively produced and shared reporting of persons and events. Whereas the mental dossier is particularly important for recalling events, the running record is an occasion for revealing selected aspects of one's mental dossier on an individual, place, or event. In doing so officers share with one another their knowledge, display their expertise with respect to the situation, and effectively present themselves as trustworthy coworkers.

Officers do not share all they know, reveal all their expertise, or care to present themselves as trustworthy all the time. Cliques within the department, whether following patrol/detective, "brass"-front line, or even internal union divisions, all contribute to this. Clearly, information sharing is shaped by political alliances and personal disagreements among officers. Thus, by withholding participation in the running record, officers can reveal their colleagues to be incompetent, not trustworthy, or ignorant of the ways to police the streets. Indeed, the running record attains its legitimacy and authority by virtue of participants' decisions in the first place to share information in an environment in which information is invaluable but not usually shared. Thus, although a written record attains its legitimacy because it is impersonally produced and read (i.e., is available to "anyone", Wheeler, 1969), the running record is valued exactly because it is not available to just anyone.

In the following example, two officers discuss an arrest that had occurred one hour into the evening shift. Neither officer was personally involved in the arrest. Yet one can see how the running record on "Kirkin" is a collaboratively produced history of this youth's prior encounters with the police:

Sgt: Who was that they arrested?

Off: Barry Kirkin.

Sgt: For what?

Off: Driving under [driving under the influence of alcohol].

Sgt: Good ol'Barry, this will mean his license again I'm sure.

Off: He's lucky he didn't kill anybody. There were a lot of kids running around the project at that time.

Sgt: Did he give them a hard time?

Off: No, he was more upset at himself once he realized what might have happened. He was looking like he might try punching a hole in the wall.

Sgt: He should be upset, he just got his license back.

Off: Yeah, he had the green paper. He was coming back from a cousin's wedding. He must have really been crocked. He's not a bad kid though.

Sgt: I know, the parents are just as nice as can be.

Off: Yeah I know them. His mother is a good person.

Sgt: Yeah, they're both nice people. But Barry, I don't know where he went wrong.

Off: Well, he's got that problem.

Sgt: He's got *problems*. It's not just the booze that's doing it to him. Anyone who would jump head first into an empty swimming pool has got more than just a booze problem.

Off:Broke his neck then, didn't he?

Sgt: Yeah, but he's never quite straightened out.

Off: You had him a while back didn't you?

Sgt: January 9 [this is June]. He was quite upset at us then, not himself. Maybe this time he will learn something.

Off: Well, he won't be driving. What do you think will happen to him?

Sgt: This time, they may put him in a special court program for fifteen days. Then he'll be put on probation.

The officers assess the current arrest in light of previous arrests (including the exact date of the last arrest), the youth's demeanor toward the police, his family circumstances, and the apparent incongruence between a good family and a youth with problems. His problems, as manifested by diving in the empty swimming pool, reflect more than just alcohol. Furthermore, his behavior is not explained by "family problems," as the parents are nice people. Rather, Kirkin becomes known on the running record as just plain crazy.[8]...

The running record, in combination with officers' mental dossiers, is also used to assess the meaning and relevance of the information provided in written records or by other officers. The following examples illustrate this process.

Knowledge of the Person

Officers "test" a report's account against their own prior experiences with the person involved; reports that do not mesh with knowledge of that person are treated more skeptically. For example, one evening the juvenile officer was processing Deveau, a juvenile just arrested for drinking in public with whom he had several previous contacts. This juvenile was considered "trouble," and his name was well known in the department.[9] Upon reading the report, which stated that the youth had been observed drinking beer in the park with his girlfriend and had refused to leave the area, the juvenile officer commented, "It didn't sound like something that kid would do; he isn't that dumb to refuse to leave the area when the officer gives him the chance."

The juvenile officer then spoke to the youth, who said he was making out with his girlfriend and had been harassed by the police. During this exchange the officer stood close to the juvenile, and later commented that the youth didn't smell like he had been drinking but had probably taken some drug. The juvenile officer then contacted the arresting officer, who stated that he came upon Deveau and his girlfriend making out (i.e., kissing) while he was responding to a call about youths dumping barrels in the park:

> So I told them they had to leave because the park closes at ten, and Deveau, acting like a big man, says they're not going to because they're not doing anything. Then next to the bench they're on, there is somebody's empty bottles of beer in a six-pack. But some of the bottles have beer in them too. I don't think it was their beer though. So Deveau grabs one of these beers, opens the top, and says, "This ain't mine, but I want it anyway," and takes a sip. So I said, "Screw you," and placed him under arrest.

This account confirmed the juvenile officer's initial suspicion that the report was incongruous with his knowledge of the arrested youth.

Knowledge of the Reporting Officer

Among their colleagues, police officers are known for their specialties. An officer's pattern of law enforcement is typified by coworkers, and these patterns are brought to bear upon the reading of a report generated by that officer. "Some guys are into traffic cites (moving violations); not me," reported one officer. "I'm into house breaks," reported another, "I like to stop suspicious cars acting funny in neighborhoods. Pinched some thieves last week...[I] leave the drinking [arrests] to somebody else." Some officers tolerated no drinking whatsoever, and would arrest regardless of the persons involved (to the surprise of some other officers). One sergeant was described as "a no-bullshit arrest-type officer; if he arrests you, you really had to be doing something wrong!" Another officer was known to his colleagues as a nice guy but a "hothead," who was easily ticked off and made bad arrests.

Records are read in light of such knowledge of the officer involved, a practice that enables officers to reconcile incongruities. For example, if a juvenile not known on the running record as a "troublemaker" is arrested for disorderly conduct by the "hothead," the officer's reputation tends to inform the reading given the incident and to mitigate the guilt attributed to the youth.

In the following example, the juvenile officer met with the parents of one youth who had been arrested with a friend for breaking and entering and larceny earlier in the shift. The officer's report stated that the youths were observed climbing out of the school window and that one of the youths had in his possession the microscope and audio tapes that were taken from the building.

> The mother kept asking, "Which boy had stolen objects in his posses-
> sion?" The juvenile officer could not answer that question except to say,
> "According to the report both youths were observed coming out of the
> building"...The juvenile officer then left the bureau and went to the
> dispatcher and requested that the arresting officer come into the station.
> While at dispatch he commented, "This case stinks, it sounds like a dump
> job to me. Paul [the arresting officer] is not that sloppy." The arresting
> officer came into the juvenile bureau and, after asking the parents to
> describe their son, reported that the other youth had the objects in his
> hands. After the parents left, the juvenile officer instructed the officer to
> write this "fact" into the report. The arresting officer then stated apolo-
> getically, "Look Pete, I just came on duty when I got a call to go up to the
> school. Riley [the veteran day officer, who was just finishing his shift]
> stumbled into these two coming out of the building. So he grabs them and
> dumps them on me saying, 'Arrest these two, I'm going home.' So I didn't
> get all the information. I don't know if their kid had the stuff or not. But
> I could see you were in a tight situation." The juvenile officer thanked
> him for his help and commented to me after the officer left, "I could tell
> it was a dump job by the time of day [i.e., shift change] and the fact that
> Paul is very thorough. We do favors like this, but sometimes it could
> cause trouble."

The juvenile officer's between-the-lines reading of the report takes into account his knowledge of that officer's reputation and aspects of the organization (i.e., shift change) that clearly had an impact on the official record of the incident. Interestingly, when challenged by the parent (i.e., an outsider), he sticks to a face value reading of the report, even though he is certain that the incident could not have happened in that way. He thereby preserves the organization's "front," without exposing the com-plexities of the "backstage."

Conclusion

For many purposes official records are assumed to stand as nonproblematic, objective accounts of events. This view decontexts such records, treating them simplistically as merely accounts of those events, and ignoring the practical organizational and personal circumstances within which they are produced. But records can also be understood as products of the organizational context within which they are generated, including those schemes of accountability enforced in that context. In this case the accounts that records render are seen as part of the very same organizational circumstances they are describing. As Buckholdt and Gubrium have emphasized (1983:249–50), "All accounting schemes produce descriptions that, while they are about clients and what is being done to and for them, are embedded in and reflect practical organizational concerns and realities." In this respect records document (or can be read as documenting) not simply the events and incidents they presumably merely describe, but these very organizational concerns and realities.

In a number of ways, the police recognize and are sensitive to the organizational qualities of their own records and record-keeping practices. Officers are only too aware that in producing records they are creating documents of their own performance as well as of those whom they encounter. As competent organizational actors, they then routinely take care to shape these records in ways that will promote the evaluations of this performance that they desire. In this way, police officers orient as record keepers to the prospective uses of the documents they produce, uses that have their locus both within and without the police department itself.

One implication is that an understanding of the police use of records is indispensable to an interpretation of what any particular record "really" means. This implication holds not only for researchers trying to analyze police records, as Kitsuse and Cicourel (1963) insisted some years ago, but also for police officers themselves when attempting to use and understand the meaning of records in their own routine work.

A second and related implication is that a complete and rich understanding of police work requires attention to the ways in which officers author, use, and read documents. It is not merely that records happen to reflect a range of practical and organizational concerns other than or in addition to "correspondence to what happened." Rather, these concerns explicitly inform and infuse the ways in which police code and decode their records. Indeed, the skillfully deployed knowledge of the organizationally embedded nature of records to write and read documents comprises an important dimension of their competence as organizational actors. This article has sought to make this knowledge and these skills visible.

REFERENCES

Bittner, E. 1967. "The police on skid-row: a study of peace keeping." *American Sociological Review* 32:699–715.

Buckholdt, D., and J. Gubrium 1983. "Practicing accountability in human service institutions." *Urban Life* 12 (3): 249–268.

Cicourel A. 1968. *The Social Organization of Juvenile Justice.* New York: John Wiley.

Garfinkel, H., and E. Bittner 1967. "Good organizational reasons for 'bad' clinic records." Pp. 186–207 IN H. Garfinkel, ed., *Studies in Ethnomethodology.* Englewood Cliffs, New Jersey: Prentice-Hall.

Hasenfeld, Y. 1972. "People processing organizations: an exchange approach." *American Sociological Review* 37: 256–263.

Kitsuse, J., and A. Cicourel 1963. "A note on the use of official statistics." *Social Problems* 11: 131–139.

Manning, P. 1977. *Police Work: The Social Organization of Policing.* Cambridge, MA: MIT Press.

Meehan, A. 1983. "For the record: interactional and organizational practices for producing police records on juveniles." Ph.D. dissertation, Boston University.

Pepinsky, H. 1976. "Police patrolman's offense reporting behavior." *Journal of Research in Crime and Delinquency* 13: 33–47.

Rubinstein, J. 1973. *City Police.* New York: Farrar, Straus, Giroux.

Seidman, D. and M. Couzens 1974. "Getting the crime rate down: political pressure and crime reporting." *Law and Society Review* 8 (3): 457–93.

Van Maanen, J. 1978. "Kinsmen in repose: occupational perspectives of patrolmen." Pp. 41–63 In P. Manning and J. Van Maanen (eds)., *Policing: A View from the Street.* Santa Monica, CA: Goodyear.

Wheeler, S. 1969. *On Record: Files and Dossiers in American Life.* New York: Russell Sage.

NOTES

[1]This research was funded by a grant from the Office of Juvenile Justice and Delinquency Prevention. Access to the police departments was negotiated by full-time project staff, including myself. All of the data collected are subjects to a confidentiality requirement ensuring the anonymity of all participants. Consequently, names of persons and places have been changed.

[2]Although the types of records produced by the police differed slightly in Grandville and Hargrove, I will for the most part ignore these differences in the analyses that follow (but see note 5). For these variations did not fundamentally affect the relationship between the form and content of records and their projected organizational career.

[3]Although the written record has attained a prominence in American society, nonwritten records can still serve as a primary basis for decision making. Yet written records possess a number of characteristics that differentiate them as a type of information from "informal" communication. After Wheeler (1969:5), these characteristics include

"-a legitimacy and authority usually lacking in more informal types of communication;

-a permanence that is generally lacking in informal communication;

-physical transferability that can create a career for the record;

-a capacity for facelessness that is missing from interpersonal communication; and

-a combinatorial capacity in which records from different sources can create a composite profile independent from the original purpose for collection."

[4]Although the data and arguments presented here deal specifically with police record-keeping practices vis-a-vis juveniles, there are strong grounds for suggesting that similar tendencies mark much police work with adults. First, I necessarily observed a number of police work with adults while on ride alongs with patrol officers in Grandville and Hargrove, since only juvenile officers deal more or less exclusively with youth. Many of the record-keeping concerns and practices were similar to those typical of juvenile cases. Second, in prior field research on the policing of juveniles in two larger jurisdiction, and in subsequent study of police handling of the mentally ill in Madison, Wisconsin, I observed processes similar to those described here.

[5]Field interrogation/observation cards (FIO) are used in the Hargrove department for recording the suspicious, but not necessarily illegal, activities of a person whom officers interrogate or observe in the field. These cards document contacts for which, in the normal scheme of paperwork, officers would not be required, or do not have the desire, to write a more lengthy incident report. Those FIOs involving juveniles are routinely forwarded to the juvenile bureau. In this way, the FIOs are used to record with a possible external career is routinely created.

[6]Although the Grandville department did not utilize FIOs during the period of my research, they had been in use five years prior to this time. Approximately one year after my field work, the department reinstituted the use of FIO card. The Grandville juvenile officers did have a "contact" card system. While FIO cards allow the Hargrove police to maintain information an all contacts, whether or not they involved illegal activity, contact cards in Grandville are generated when an official report involving a juvenile is filed (e.g., incident/arrest report). Nevertheless, the cards provided a place to record information such as distinguishing physical features, school, marital status, current offense, and the disposition of the offense

by the court and penciled in notes about a particular juvenile (e.g., "subject is retarded"). In this way, the contact cards serve an important intelligence function. They are filed alphabetically, allowing the juvenile offerers to have their own record of all contact with the juvenile during the past several years. An important use of the contact card was to maintain a record of how many "breaks" a juvenile has been given by the department (i.e., cases in which the juvenile was arrested and formally booked, then released with a warning without forwarding the case to court).

[7] As Rubinstein (1973:440) notes for the Philadelphia police, log entries are read and evaluated for how much "activity" an officer has generated during a particular shift. In Philadelphia the major categories of "activity" include such proactive interventions as "meters" (parking-meter tickets), "parkers" (illegal parking), and "movers" (motor-vehicle code violations). As Rubinstein (1973:44) argues:

"Activity" is the internal product of police work. It is the statistical measure which the sergeant uses to judge the productivity of his men, the lieutenant uses to assure himself that the sergeant is properly directing his men, the captain to assure his superiors that he is capably administering his district the department administrators to assure the public that their tax dollars are not being squandered.

[8] Later that evening Kirkin tried to commit suicide in his cell, an action that confirmed this assessment. Indeed, one of these officers referred to "crazy Kirkin" while instructing a younger officer in techniques for properly searching a prisoner to avoid such problems.

[9] For a police officer, the more often a name is mentioned in the context of police work, the more memorable and significant it becomes. Some officers write down the name of every person they encounter; others pride themselves in just knowing names and the "family" history. One officer, upon stopping a group of juveniles trespassing on town property, asked each to identify himself. He later commented, "I recognized some of the names, but not *as offenders*." Recognizing the name supplies additional information for assessing the report's credibility even if the officer has never had contact with that person. Consequently, names of known trouble makers have a special status independent of any personal experience.

Chapter 26

CONSTRUCTING PROBATIONER CAREERS: REVOCATION AS CENSURE TRANSFORMATION AND TERTIARY DEVIANCE IN THE DEVIANCE AMPLIFICATION PROCESS

Douglas Thomson

How is the amplification of deviance organizationally structured? This paper focuses on a particular type of deviance amplification: censure transformation. As the name suggests, censure transformation is a type of deviance amplification wherein a previously pronounced penalty is changed into another type of penalty by way of processes of escalation (or deescalation). In the present case, the set of censure transformations on which we focus is that consisting of responses to violations of probation as processed in criminal courts and associated agencies in the USA.

Deviance Amplification and Censure Transformation

The concept of deviance amplification has had an estimable history in the societal reaction perspective (or labelling theory) tradition. How do violations of social rules result in sanctions? How do initial acts of deviance escalate? What roles do various social audiences and rule-applying agencies play in imposing sanctions? How and by whom are rules made? How do such sanctions generate further deviance? How much of all of this is behavioral, how much socially constructed? These are the issues of primary and secondary deviance, of Tannenbaum's (1938) "dramatization of evil," Lemert's "societal reaction to primary deviation" (1951, 1967), and Becker's (1963: 9) aphorism: "The deviant is one to whom that label has successfully been applied; deviant behavior is behavior that people so label."

We focus here on the latter stages of this process, even on what lies beyond it, on what might be characterized as tertiary deviance (Kitsuse's (1980) extension of Becker's and Lemert's concepts of primary and secondary deviance). After sanctions (in this case, penal) have been imposed, their control intentions sometimes yield further deviance. In the case of formal legal sanctions, e.g., criminal sentences, the sanction or censure often comes after protracted processing during which there is a complex series of threats, withholding of the threated punishment, lower level control efforts, and the provision or mandating of social services. How does the censure then become transformed into something else, presumably based on its violation?

Censure costs the agency imposing it, and altering it costs even more. Censures are scarce resources for social control agencies. Hence, they are used judiciously. How they are used reveals how the social control network behaves and what functions it serves.

As a sub-set of deviance amplification, censure transformation focuses on what happens toward latter stages of deviance construction. More importantly, especially for current purposes of analyzing organization behavior, it focuses on official behavior. Hence, whether there has actually been a behavioral violation of a rule is not at issue. Rather, we focus on the dynamics of whether or how the previously announced censure is altered.

This seems especially realistic for the subject of probation revocations where the alleged violation may sometimes be a convenient vehicle for punishing or controlling someone in response to some other violation, or even social status or political identity. This occurs when probation is officially revoked for failure to report, but the action is triggered by allegation of a new offense for which the prosecutor may have a weak case. Another instance of censure transformation as a special case of deviance amplification confronts us when probation officers use their discretion with regard to responding to violations to dispose of clients who are troublesome in the sense of being difficult to work with (McCleary, 1978).

Although the concept of censure transformation is most obviously pertinent in the realm of criminal law, it can be significant for other applications in the areas of deviance and sociology of law. Processes which might thus be better understood include: transforming a school suspension into expulsion, escalating denial of privileges in a token economy milieu, and altering the terms of an economic boycott at the international level.

This effort in theory generation derives from several studies of probation in which I have been involved during the past decade. These efforts have been reported elsewhere (e.g., Thomson and Fogel, 1981; Thomson, 1982; McAnany, Thomson, and Fogel, 1984; McAnany and Thomson, 1984; Thomson, 1987a, b) and will not be treated systematically here. Instead I will use the data and materials from the source studies opportunistically to generate and illustrate an organization theory of censure transformation.

For now it should be sufficient to briefly characterize the empirical sources. There are four primary data/materials sources. First, there are survey data on 551 small probation agencies and 1105 of their officers. Second, there are field observation materials derived from visits to 24 such agencies located throughout the USA and operating at local, state, and federal levels of government and in executive and judicial branch settings. These survey and field materials were gathered as part of a national study of probation training provisions and needs, but incorporated a focus on enforcement behaviors including revocations.

The third empirical source consists of field observation materials, recent cases descriptions, and legal environment descriptions, all generated in the course of a year long study of probation revocation practices. This study too was an action research project, directed toward the promulgation of principles and standards for equitable responses to probation violations.

Finally, mostly field observation materials are available from a year long study of intensive probation supervision in Illinois. In addressing a strong version of probation, this research highlighted the dynamics of censure transformation.

All of these primary empirical materials are backed up by correspondence, casual conversations, and occupational literature which have provided opportunities for insights into probation, its networks, and its role in the amplification of deviance. The literature of organization theory and analysis provides the cognitive framework for understanding these phenomena of deviance and social control.

Extent and Significance of Probation Violations and Responses

In the United States of America, probation is a major form of formal social control. For example, in many jurisdictions, most convicted felons are assigned to a term of probation, either alone or in conjunction with a sentence of incarceration. In 1985, 48% of convicted felons in 28 selected jurisdictions were sentenced to probation (Cunniff, 1987: 5). Although it is only recently that the prevalence of felony probation has received much public attention (Petersilia, Turner, Kahan, and Peterson, 1985), it has been a reality for a substantial period of time. Rothman (1980), e.g., in tracing the development of various social control institutions during the Progressive Era, characterizes probation, along with parole and the juvenile court, as a major reform alternative to the asylum. Probation was soon widely used by criminal court judges and prosecutors, albeit primarily in urban and industrialized areas of the cities and generally for guilty plea cases for which charges were often reduced from felonies to misdemeanors.

Another way of measuring probation's social control impact is in terms of its share of the nation's correctional caseload. Since probation terms are generally longer than the average amount of time served in prison, this measure is even more striking. In recent years (1979–1983), the national ratio of probationers to prisoners has hovered around 3.5:1 (Greenfeld, 1984: 2). When parolees are added, probationers still constitute 63% of the nation's adult correctional caseload (Greenfeld, 1984: 6).

While felonies are more serious crimes than are misdemeanors, the latter are more common fare in criminal courts. We should then take them into account if we want adequately to assess the impact of probation as a means of formal social control. Although fines, short jail sentences, and sentences to time served (Feeley, 1979) are frequently applied sentences in misdemeanor courts (Ragona and Ryan, 1983), substantial numbers of convicted misdemeanants are sentenced to probation. In three diverse jurisdictions studied by Ragona and Ryan (1983), the minimum percentages of misdemeanants sentenced to probation ranged from 8% to 64%. The most recent national figures available indicate that in 1976 the number of state and local misdemeanant probationers (467,971) was slightly greater than the number of state and local felony probationers (455,093) (United States Bureau of the Census, 1978: 35).

Despite such impressive numbers, probation does not constitute the severe punishment that incarceration does. There is widespread recognition that the deprivations of liberty, pains, and brutalities associated with incarceration have a painful impact on prisoners. Goffman (1961) painted particularly vivid pictures of the social meanings, constructions, and consequences of being housed in any total institution including prisons. Contemporary analyses of the prospects for prison reform explicitly recognize the need to acknowledge, accept, and plan for the pains of imprisonment (Johnson, 1987).

Probation by contrast is recognized as much less of a sanction. In some states, it is still not even counted as a sentence but rather as an alternative to the more familiar penal sanction of incarceration. While there have been efforts in recent years to make probation more restrictive, more painful, and more accountable (Clear and O'Leary, 1983; Petersilia, 1987), and other attempts to highlight the liberty constraints and control mechanisms which have always been part of probation (Harris, 1984; McAnany, 1984), probation is often viewed popularly as a form of judicial leniency, as a grant of mercy rather than a deserved sanction (Thomson, 1984). This view partially reflects probation's historic justifications in the rhetoric of the rehabilitative ideal (Rothman, 1980; Cullen and Gilbert, 1982).

While such public images form an important part of the cultural environment within which criminal court organizations make probation choices, with our present interest in deviance amplification we are especially concerned with how this type of formal social control is experienced by its recipients, i.e., probationers (Duffee, 1984; McDonald, 1986) and how it is perceived by its crafters, i.e., judges, probation officers, prosecutors, and defense attorneys. While little is known systematically about the views of probationers on this subject, anecdotal evidence and fragmentary and tangential research indicate a mixture of initial relief at "getting probation" followed by chafing resentment over some of the restrictions involved.

A more recent and striking finding has been that more intrusive and surveillant forms of probation, e.g., the contemporary manifestation of intensive supervision (Byrne, 1986), sometimes convince convicted felons to choose to go to prison instead (Thomson, 1987b; Tonry, 1988), in part because they have a keen existential appreciation of the censure transformation process, of their prospects for becoming enmeshed in it, and of its producing even greater pain over the long run. This finding has substantive significance beyond the small number of cases involved, and we shall return to consider at more length what it reveals about the censure transformation process.

Probation's other main "public," the courtroom workgroups for whom it is a resource, share some of the general public and probationer views of this sanction. They perceive it as limited and tend not to ascribe it a great deal of significance. But these views are tempered by their instrumental use of it and the mundane economic value it has come to assume as a mechanism for case processing. And, as we shall see, perhaps through such customary practices, probation has ceremonial and symbolic value for courtroom workgroups. Like many such values, it takes some work to find these and to find those sharing them acknowledging them. By focusing on the censure transformation process in this setting, i.e., on responses to probation violations, we can better appreciate the instrumental, economic, and symbolic identities of probation.

All of this suggests that we need to recognize probation as a contingent sanctioning system and as a product of and source of boundary transactions. That is, probation is not a final sentence; it is conditional and revocable. Also, whether viewed as a criminal sentencing option or as correctional status, probation as sanction and probationers as clients are so defined on the basis of transactions among criminal justice organizations. Leaving probation status similarly requires coordinated legitimation by the criminal justice network.

The Probation Violation Response Process

While there are some important variations and nuances in how it is constructed in the thousands of probation offices around the nation, there is an ideal type of probation violation response process, consisting of six stages: discovery, recognition, sanction, expansion, escalation, and closure. Significantly, we view the process from the perspective of the probation officer, a key audience and agent. Table 1 summarizes the process, with its six stages and resource requirements.

Table 1
Probation Violation Response Sequence

Stage	Resources Required
1) Discovery	Police information
	Jail information
	Probationer information
	Social service agency information
	Probation officer initiative
2) Recognition	Information systems
	Caseload pressures
o recording	Probation officer self-presentation
	capabilities
o confrontation	
o threat	
3) Sanction	Discretionary power available to
	probation officers
o modification of conditions	
4) Expansion	Supervisory relationship
	Workgroup relationship
o supervisor's involvement	Precedent
o staffing	
5) Escalation	Court workload and caseflow
	Court workgroup relationships
o legal professionals	Interest and commitment of legal
	professionals
6) Closure	Intake market unit availabilty

As with any other type of deviant behavior, only a subset of probation violations become known to the pertinent social control agent, in this case, the probation officer.

To discover a violation, the probation offficer is dependent on several parties. Information can be provided by the police, the jailer, or the probationer, or the probation officer can generate it her/himself. Parties outside the criminal justice sector, typically a social service agency to which the probationer had been ordered to report but sometimes a citizen, e.g., a relative who has been victimized, can also cause discovery of a violation.

After discovering a violation, probation officers may choose to recognize in some official or behavioral fashion that it has occurred. From a societal reaction perspective, this stage is critical; making this stage explicit highlights the significance of official perception and action in the deviance amplification process. Recognition may take the form of recording or confrontation. Since probation officers are legal officials, their recording of violations establishes precedent for possible subsequent coercive action. Since they are proactive social control agents, or human service workers, probation officers can use confrontation, sometimes in conjunction with legal threats, to obtain promises of behavioral conformity from probationers who have violated the terms of their probation. Resources on which probation is dependent at the recognition stage are information systems, caseload pressures including caseflow, and officers' self-presentation capabilities.

I have labelled the third stage as sanction because it is here that the probationer may begin to suffer some form of continuing behavioral imposition. At this stage, the interaction remains essentially a two-party game between the probation officer and the probationer. Hence, appropriate discretionary powers to invoke sanctions must be available to the officer. A typical sanction that can be imposed by probation officers in some jurisdictions is modification of probation conditions, e.g., requiring the probation officer to report to the probation office more frequently than originally prescribed or directing the probationer to undergo a particular therapeutic regimen. While the latter may be portrayed by the officer as help and may eventually, or even initially, be so perceived by the probationer, it is typically presented as something with which the probationer must comply or suffer other more dire consequences externally imposed. Since in many jurisdictions, probation officers are not afforded the discretion to impose sanctions such as formal modification of conditions on their own authority, they must often rely on lesser sanctions such as withdrawal of approval and acceptance or by way of other adjustments in the interpersonal relationship of officer and probationer.

This relationship is formally similar to the doctor-patient relationship as analyzed by Parsons (1951: 429–479), but differs in important ways. As the physician's role is associated with death via illness, the probation officer's is associated with the social death of incarceration via revocation. As the patient's role combining helplessness, emotional distress, and an absence of technical competence makes him or her susceptible to the possibility of exploitation by the doctor, so the probationer's analagous circumstances similarly create exploitative temptations for the probation officer. Also, physicians and probation officers alike confront serious problems of inadequate performance due to uncontrollability of client condition and uncertainty of effect of practitioner response. That probation officers lack the autonomous authority, independent work situations, and prestige of the physician and deal with clients severely constrained in their choices by legal disabilities coercively imposed seriously complicate the analogy.

It is these considerations of the impact of interprofessional relationships and the use of law which take on special significance as we move to the final three stages of the probation violation response process. Compared to the physician's, the probation officer's helping role is complicated by a significant coterminous, albeit latent, adversary role which encourages retrospective constructions of client identities conducive to the imposition of greater measures of social control (Cicourel, 1976). Yet, as we shall see, probation officers too find their work substantially shaped by informal controls instead of solely by the more obvious formalizations of law and bureaucracy.

In the fourth stage, expansion, the violation response process becomes a multi-party affair. The probation officer now involves others in the department in sanctioning the violator. In most departments, this is a matter of calling in the probation officer's supervisor. The performance here is designed to reinforce the probation officer's threats by appeal to a concurring higher authority. It can also serve as a kind of role-play tribunal in which it is presumed that the probationer gets a taste of what an actual chastisement by a judge would be like. But it does not require actually drawing on prosecutorial or judicial resources.

A variation on this theme, offering the same resource conservation feature, is a staffing in which the probationer must appear before several of the probation officer's peers. These sessions frequently are confrontational and function as "haircutting" events analagous to Synanon and similar group work strategies for inducing deviance disavowal. The parallel is particularly close in a staffing version which includes former inmates serving as near-peers who are to scare probation violators by graphically describing what awaits them if they continue to deviate and are incarcerated as a result. Judges have been known to make the same case in more formal forums. Availability of the expansion stage is dependent on the nature and strength of the supervisory relationship of officer and superior, workgroup relationships, mechanisms and incentives for including probationer near-peers in those relationships, departmental precedent, and workload pressures.

Escalation, the fifth stage, means going beyond mere quantitative expansion of parties to the violation response process to qualitative expansion. It means appealing to legal authority, involving legal professionals. As a conditional and revocable sentence, probation can ultimately be acted on only by judges (or their executive branch hearing officer counterparts in a few states). Moreover, many states require the involvement of the prosecutor in filing a legal petition for revocation, and almost all require that official's involvement in prosecuting the matter. Significant resource contingencies here include presence of a willing courtroom workgroup, smooth working relationships with it, interest and commitment of legal professionals, and law. The final stage, closure, marks the end of a particular probation violation response process and the final determination of censure transformation. But it may not end the officer's responsibility for the probationer. This situation occurs, for example, when the judge merely admonishes the probationer or modifies the conditions of probation. As indicated in Table 2, this occurs frequently. If a case has proceeded this far, however, that is to the stage of escalation, the officer is often seeking to dispose of the relationship as well as the violation case.

Probation Offense	Violation Type	Allegation Proven	Probation Revoked	Probation Terminated	Probation Extended	Incarcerated
			Table 2			
Legal and Behavioral Outcomes for Recent Cases in Which Revocation Proceedings Were Initiated by Probation Offense and Violation Type (N=205)						

Table 2

Legal and Behavioral Outcomes for Recent Cases in Which Revocation Proceedings Were Initiated by Probation Offense and Violation Type (N=205)

(From Five Probation Departments in Four States in 1982)

Legal and Behavior Outcomes

(percentaged across the rows with probation offense/violation type as the denominator)

Probation Offense	Violation Type	Allegation Proven	Probation Revoked	Probation Terminated	Probation Extended	Incarcerated
Felony	Technical	73%	43%	14%	20%	49%
(N=51)		(37)	(22)	(7)	(10)	(25)
Felony	New Offense	87%	67%	10%	15%	67%
(N=78)		(68)	(52)	(8)	(12)	(52)
Misdemeanor	Technical	93%	55%	17%	38%	52%
(N=42)		(39)	(23)	(7)	(16)	(22)
Misdemeanor	New Offense	91%	50%	24%	35%	50%
(N=34)		(31)	(17)	(8)	(12)	(17)

Source: Probation Revocations Practices Study/Recent Cases Survey (1982)

Escalation means not only an escalation of stakes and greatly increased capacities for embarassment as legal professionals become actors and audience and the courtroom rather than the office becomes the forum, but generally suggests that the case is being defined as a candidate for "last resorts" processing (Emerson, 1981: 1):

> In a variety of social control settings, the use of extreme sanctions is held to be appropriate *only as a last resort*.... Last resorts characteristically claim that there is no alternative but to invoke some dubiously valued sanction, a claim advanced against the backdrop of the "normal remedies" customarily used in a particular setting. Requested last resorts are justified by showing either that all such normal remedies are specifically inappropriate or that they have failed to contain the trouble.
>
> (Emphasis in the original)

That is, practice attends to an ideology of last chances and withdrawn opportunities for those who are viewed as having participated inadequately in previous social control opportunities.

McCleary's (1978) description of parole officers' typification of troublesome parolees as "dangerous men" is apt here as is suggested by the distribution of alleged probation violations shown in Table 3. These allegations are drawn from 208 cases described by probation officers in a 1982 survey in which they were asked to select the three or four most recent cases in which they had initiated revocation proceedings, operationalized as submitting a petition for violation of probation. The most frequent allegation, mentioned in slightly more than half the cases, is failure to report to the probation officer. In only 9% of the cases was the probationer charged with a felony crime against persons, e.g., aggravated battery, armed robbery, and in 22% with a felony property crime, e.g., burglary, grand theft. The pattern of allegations suggests that probation officers may frequently use the revocation option much as McCleary's parole officers did: to remove from their caseload cases which seem unprofitably time-consuming or potentially embarassing, i.e., cases dangerous to the equilibrium of the caseload and office.

Table 3			
Grounds for Initiating Revocation Proceedings			
(From Five Probation Departments in Four States in 1982)			
Allegation	Frequency	Percentage of Allegations)	Percentage of Cases
Technical			
Failure to report to probation officer	109	25%	52%
Failure to pay restitution	58	13%	28%
Moving or otherwise changing status without permission	48	11%	23%
Failure to pay other fees, fines, or costs	41	9%	20%
Failure to pursue substance abuse program	12	3%	6%
Absconding	10	2%	5%
Failure to pursue other counseling or human services	10	2%	5%
New law violation	9	2%	4%
New Offense			
Misdemeanor - public order	27	6%	13%
Misdemeanor - property	25	6%	12%
Misdemeanor - person	16	4%	8%
Felony - public order	15	3%	7%
Felony - property	45	10%	22%
Felony - person	18	4%	9%
Total	443	100%	213%
Source: Probation Revocation Practices Study/Recent Cases Survey (1982)			

In larger scope, McCleary's descriptions and Emerson's (1969) are significant in highlighting how the local ecology of political, enforcement, and social services agencies determines prospects of disposing of the relationship. Thus, both intake market unit (Hasenfeld, 1974; Hasenfeld and Cheung, 1985) availability, in the form of jail and prison space and substance abuse and human services slots, and the recent history of exchange relationships in the courtroom workgroup (Eisenstein and Jacob,

1977) (inclusive of the probation officer) and among the various deviance processing organizations represent critical resources.

Yet, even when officers take some form of action in response to a violation, it often does not result in a revocation. Table 2 illustrates part of the attrition process. In the five departments covered, for example, for felony probationers regarding whom revocation proceedings were initiated for technical violations, most did not result in a revocation. When the violation was for a new crime, as many as one-third of the implicated felony probationers were not revoked. (The incidence of revocation followed by incarceration was inflated by the practice in one department of incarcerating (in prison) all 39 revoked cases (of the 48 in the study sample). That this practice stands in such sharp contrast to court behavior in the other jurisdictions underscores the significance of diversity in this area.)

These findings do not pertain to less formal responses by officers, i.e., responses short of initiating revocation proceedings. Similarly, a 1979 national survey of probation officers found that during the preceding year, they averaged 2.8 technical violation revocations and 4.3 new crime revocations in their caseloads (Thomson, 1982). The value of the revocation process for criminal justice networks lies not so much in the quantity of revocations, but in how the threat shapes the greater number of less formal censure transformations and supervision practices in general. Thus, it operates at this stage of criminal case processing in a way reminiscent of plea bargaining at an earlier stage (Heumann, 1978) and of civil case negotiations (Jacob, 1983b); the law's shadow, the spectre of the court's formal arena, shape the more informal negotiations and case dispositions which never officially become known to them (Mnookin and Kornhauser, 1979).

Revocation Resources for the Technologies of Probation Work

Three characteristics of this process are important. They suggest its significance from the officer's perspective and direct our attention to network functions served by these censure transformation processes.

First, the probation violation response process involves a developmental pattern of negotiations between probationer and officer. When the former allegedly transgresses the boundaries of the behavior space defined by the conditions of probation, the officer may at first ignore or only tacitly acknowledge the event. If other violations come to his or her attention, however, the officer will begin to confront and then threaten the probationer until eventually a third party is included. This third party can be the local jail, the supervisor, the judge, or the prosecutor. In jurisdictions in which the officer has some authority over warrants and petitions, the instruments of legal control, the third party in the form of the jail is a resource which the officer can use with some certainty of outcome.

As legal professionals become involved, however, control of negotiations moves away from the officer due to the greater legal authority available to these officials. When these individuals are called into the transaction, the officer incurs risks such as damaging a working relationship with a probationer who may be returned to the officer's supervision and being embarrassed in court by records inadequacy. The officer also incurs costs such as the additional work of preparing a supplemental presentence investigation report and testifying and the expenditure of drawing on the legal professionals' authority. In return, the officer gains the possibilities of greater control over the probationer through more stringent conditions or the removal of a troublesome case and the work associated with it from one's workload (McCleary, 1978).

The second characteristic concerns how formal responses to violations are enacted sequentially. While they tend to escalate toward more severe sanctions, there are various opportunities for attrition. This yields a differentiated array of paths to identity tranformation or affirmation. Hence, the idea that the conventional probation order itself is the final threat to be followed by revocation and incarceration for the first discovered violation accords poorly with actual violation response practices. Revocation proceedings, findings of violation, and revocations operate according to related but distinct logics. And, as indicated in the preceding pages, such formal actions are greatly outnumbered by probation officers' side bet responses. Even after the formal stage of violation response is attained by filing a petition for revocation, there are several opportunities for imposing sanctions and controls of various levels of formality and legitimacy. Related to this is the marked distinction between new crime and technical violation revocation proceedings and the salience they are accorded by the court's legal professionals. Consequently, the technical violation revocation is a probation officer event. It is more important to her or him than to any other criminal justice functionary and it is initiated by the officer.

This suggests the final characteristic. Revocations, particularly concerning technical violations, are critically important to probation as currently structured. Revocation practices are a hallmark of the occupation even, or perhaps especially, when they do not result in a revocation. It is the threat of such a result that probation officers value. It is not only this compliance function which makes revocation practices central to probation work, however. In addition, it is in such processes that the core technologies of probation work, i.e., investigation and supervision, are synthesized. It is also in these events in their various forms that the probation officer must integrate the human services and legal authority responsibilities of the role (Thomson, 1982: 6–46).

One might wonder at the extent to which this analysis of the probation violation response process focuses on action by probation officers and has relatively little to say about the organizations they represent. This reflects the characteristic of the probation agency as a "make believe bureaucracy" (Klockars, 1976: 403). Klockars argues that probation officers use the probation department and its rules to threaten probationers and gain compliance. This strategic use of rules is thus formally similar, at the practitioner level, to the function which Hilbert (1987) argues has been served, in a broader political fashion, by Competency Based Teacher Education in offering an unachievable level of rationalization which nonetheless energizes proponents and brings an aura of scientific legitimation to sponsoring and adopting organizations.

But in fact, the probation officer is the manifestation of the department to the probationer (Studt, 1973) and has substantial discretion in enforcing the conditions. Klockars concludes that the nature of conditions (all-encompassing, even "silly"), organizational context (norms regarding flexibility in application), structure of the work situation (access, which is both limited and detailed, to information), and officer role (frequently the one ultimately responsible for making the decision to reveal the violation), imply that the department is a "fiction" in the sense of being "the genuine bearer of the authority and control components of the officer role" (Klockar, 1976: 410–411).

This is an important insight and one to which the preceding analysis of the process is attentive. But in the twenty years since Klockars observed his agency, there have been changes in the probation enterprise which appear to have enhanced the role of the department somewhat, and concomitantly diminished the role of the officer, in the revocation process. These changes may be summarized as the legalization (e.g., responsiveness to the due process revolution), professionalization (along dimensions of credentialism, reward, and associational apparatus, if not autonomy, trust, and esoteric knowledge base) and bureaucratization and rationalization of probation (e.g., client classification and caseload management technologies, and centralization efforts). With the invigorated crime control ideology of recent years overlaid on these changes (Gordon, 1990), there is reason to expect greater departmental authority and influence in the censure transformation process.

REFERENCES

Becker, Howard S. 1963. *Outsiders: Studies in the Sociology of Deviance*. New York: Free Press.

Byrne, James M. (ed.) 1986. Special Issue on Intensive Probation Supervision, *Federal Probation* 50 (2).

Cicourel, Aaron V. 1976 (1968). *The Social Organization of Juvenile Justice*. London: Heinemann.

Clear, Todd R. and Vincent O'Leary. 1983. *Controlling the Offender in the Community*. Cambridge, Massachusetts: Lexington.

Cullen, Francis T. and Karen E. Gilbert. 1982. *Reaffirming Rehabilitation*. Cincinnati: Anderson.

Cunniff, Mark. 1987. *Sentencing Outcomes in 28 Felony Courts*. Washington, D.C.: U.S. Department of Justice.

Duffee, David E. 1984. "Client Biography and Probation Organization." Pp. 295–323 in McAnany et al.

Eisenstein, James and Herbert Jacob. 1977. *Felony Justice: An Organizational Analysis of Criminal Courts*. Boston: Little, Brown.

Emerson, Robert M. 1969. *Judging Delinquents: Context and Process in Juvenile Court*. Chicago: Aldine.

———. 1981. "On Last Resorts." *American Journal of Sociology* 87: 1–22.

Feeley, Malcolm. 1979. *The Process Is the Punishment: Handling Cases in a Lower Criminal Court*. New York: Russell Sage.

Goffman, Erving. 1961. *Asylums*. Garden City, New York: Doubleday.

Gordon, Diana. 1990. *The Justice Juggernaut: Fighting Street Crime, Controlling Citizens*. New Brunswick, New Jersey: Rutgers University.

Greenfeld, Lawrence A. 1984. *Probation and Parole 1983*. Bureau of Justice Statistics Bulletin NCJ–94776. Washington, D.C.: U.S. Department of Justice.

Harris, M. Kay. 1984. "Rethinking Probation in the Context of the Justice Model." Pp. 15–37 in McAnany et al.

Hasenfeld, Yeheskel. 1974. "People Processing Organizations: An Exchange Approach." *American Sociological Review* 37: 256–263.

———. and Paul P. L. Cheung. 1985. "The Juvenile Court as a People-processing Organization: A Political Economy Perspective." *American Journal of Sociology* 90: 801–824.

Heumann, Milton. 1978. *Plea Bargaining: The Experiences of Prosecutors, Judges, and Defense Attorneys*. Chicago: University of Chicago.

Hilbert, Richard A. 1987. "Bureaucracy as Belief, Rationalization as Repair: Max Weber in a Post-Functionalist Age." *Sociological Theory* 5: 70–86.

Jacob, Herbert. 1983b. "Trial Courts in the United States: The Travails of Exploration." *Law & Society Review* 17: 407–423.

Johnson, Robert. 1987. *Hard Time: Understanding and Reforming the Prison*. Monterey, California: Brooks/Cole.

Kitsuse, John. 1980. "Coming Out All Over: Deviants and the Politics of Social Problems." *Social Problems* 28 (1): 1–9.

Klockars, Carl B. 1976. "A Theory of Probation Supervision." Pp. 402–414 in *Probation, Parole, and Community Corrections*. Second Edition, edited by Robert M. Carter and Leslie T. Wilkins. Reprinted from *Journal of Criminal Law, Criminology and Police Science* 63 (1972): 550–557.

Lemert, Edwin M. 1951. *Social Pathology: A Systemic Approach to the Theory of Sociopathic Behavior*. New York: McGraw-Hill.

———. 1967. *Human Deviance, Social Problems, and Social Control*. Englewood Cliffs, New Jersey: Prentice-Hall.

McAnany, Patrick D. 1984. "Mission and Justice: Clarifying Probation's Legal Context." Pp. 39–63 in McAnany et al.

McAnany, Patrick D. and Douglas R. Thomson. 1984. *Equitable and Effective Responses to Probation Violations*. Boulder, Colorado: National Institute of Corrections.

McAnany, Patrick D., Douglas R. Thomson. and David Fogel. 1984. *Probation and Justice: Reconsideration of Mission*. Boston: Oelgeschlager, Gunn & Hain.

McCleary, Richard. 1978. *Dangerous Men: The Sociology of Parole*. Beverly Hills: Sage.

McDonald, Douglas Corry. 1986. *Punishment Without Walls: Community Service Sentences in New York City*. New Brunswick, New Jersey: Rutgers.

Mnookin, Robert H. and Lewis Kornhauser. 1979. "Bargaining in the Shadow of the Law: The Case of Divorce." *Yale Law Review* 88: 950.

Parsons, Talcott. 1951. *The Social System*. New York: Free Press.

Petersilia, Joan. 1987. *Expanding Options for Criminal Sentencing*. Santa Monica, California: Rand.

———. Susan Turner, James Kahan, and Joyce Peterson. 1985. *Granting Felons Probation: Public Risks and Alternatives*. Santa Monica, California: Rand.

Ragona, Anthony J. and John Paul Ryan. 1983. "Misdemeanor Courts and the Choice of Sanctions: A Comparative View." *The Justice System Journal* 8: 199–221.

Rothman, David J. 1980. *Conscience and Convenience: The Asylum and its Alternatives in Progressive America*. Boston: Little, Brown.

Studt, Elliot. 1973. *Surveillance and Service in Parole*. Washington, D.C.: National Institute of Corrections.

Tannenbaum, Frank. 1938. *Crime and the Community*. Boston: Ginn.

Thomson, Douglas R. 1982. *The Social Organization of Enforcement Behaviors in Probation Work*. Doctoral dissertation, Department of Sociology, University of Illinois at Chicago.

———. 1984. "Prospects for Justice Model Probation." Pp. 101–135 in McAnany et al.

———. 1987a. "The Changing Face of Probation in the USA." Pp. 100–125 in John K. Harding, editor, *Probation in the Community: a Policy and Practice Reader*. London: Tavistock.

———. 1987b. *Intensive Probation Supervision in Illinois: The First Year Evaluation*. Chicago: Center for Research in Law & Justice, University of Illinois at Chicago.

———. and David Fogel. 1981. *Probation Work in Small Agencies: A National Study of Training Provisions and Needs*. Chicago: Center for Research in Law and Justice, University of Illinois.

Tonry, Michael. 1988. "Structuring Discretion." Pages 267–337 in Michael Tonry and Norval Morris (eds.), *Crime and Justice: A Review of Research*. Volume 10. Chicago: University of Chicago.

U.S. Bureau of the Census. 1978. *State and Local Probation and Parole Systems*. Washington, D.C.: U.S. Department of Justice.

I gratefully acknowledge helpful suggestions offered by Richard Hall, R. Stephen Warner, and James T. Carey. I also appreciate longstanding conceptual and practical contributions by Patrick D. McAnany and important research assistance by Denise Morgan. Some of the underlying research was supported by grants from the National Institute of Corrections (AN-9, AN-9 Supplement Number 1, and CQ-4) and facilitated by the efforts of the Survey Research Laboratory and the Computer Center at the University of Illinois at Chicago.

Chapter 27

THE IN-PATIENT PHASE IN THE CAREER
OF THE PSYCHIATRIC PATIENT

Nancy J. Herman

The Process of Admission: The Context Within Which Self is Mortified

As Goffman (1961:14) emphasizes in his study of total institutions,[1] the individual generally enters the institution with a positive conception of self; however, upon admission and thereafter he/she is stripped of many of his or her accustomed possessions and symbols of identity including clothing. The individual is subjected to a set of mortifying experiences which function to strip him/her of his/her present identity. According to Goffman (1961:14):

> The recruit comes to the establishment with a conception of himself made possible by certain stable social arrangements in his home world. Upon entrance, he is immediately stripped of the support provided by these arrangements. In the accurate language of some of our oldest institutions, he begins a series of abasements, degradations, humiliations and profanations of self. His self is systematically, or often unintentionally mortified. He begins some radical shifts in his moral career, a career composed of the progressive changes that occur in the beliefs that he has concerning himself and others.

In my research, I found that the patients were subjected to certain processes of mortification. Specifically, upon entrance the patient is subjected to certain mortifying experiences or stripping processes that are elaborated in the form of "admission procedures." On entering the hospital, the individual is subjected to a systematic set of procedures: he or she is signed in, assigned to a specific nurse and psychiatrist, asked questions about his/her life history, certain possessions are taken away and stored, the person is given a physical examination, a haircut, instructed in the rules of the ward, assigned to a room, and is issued institutional clothing. In other words, during admission procedures the individual is subjected to a variety of routing operations—in essence, he or she is coded into an object that can be easily processed by administrative mechanisms of the institution.[2] While one might agree that these admission procedures are necessary for the efficient organization and operation of the institution, from the patients' point of view these procedures are seen in a different light. A new admission states:

> When I came in here I felt so mixed up. I was scared. Two female police brought me up here; I had chains on my arms and my feet. They brought

273

me up to the front door and handed me over to the hospital woman. I felt like a piece of garbage you know, not like a human being—they were treating me like a fucking object, that's all. So they handed me over to her and she took me to the ward. We entered the ward and I was signed in. Then they took me down to the sunporch and left me there alone. After about twenty minutes, they came in and got me, asked me a few questions and sent me back there alone again. This time they took me to a room where there was a doctor and a nurse. They were going to give me a physical examination. They told me to strip. I told them that I wasn't going to take my clothes off in front of a woman; she said that it was all right because she was a nurse. I told her to leave but she wouldn't. So I had to stand there nude, right in front of her—she just gawked at me. I felt like a piece of shit I tell you...the doctor examined me and I do mean all over...I felt so damned degraded...they do a lot to us here.

Another patient, recounting his views on the admission procedures says:

When you come in, they take away your possessions, but they also do something that's much worse—they take away your self-respect. You come in here thinking that you are basically a good, decent human being, but they somehow manage to degrade you—make you feel like an inferior, a nothing, a sub-human. Let me tell you how it works: you come in here thinking you are a good person...But from the first minute you come through the front door, things start to happen—they take everything away from you. Then they put you in pajamas...you feel degraded...You feel like you are being pushed down a flight of stairs, each step of the way makes you feel worse. Some patients accept they are nothings, no good; others try to fight it for a while, but in the end the staff finally get you where they want you—to admit that you are a nothing.

Upon admission then, the individual is subjected to a set of procedures which function to curtail or alter the self. The act of physical examination serves to strip the individual in two ways: not only does this procedure force the person to be physically stripped of his clothing, but also symbolically serves to strip him of his self-identity through degradation and humiliation. Moreover, during admission procedures and thereafter, the patient tends to be objectified by the staff. Whereas on the outside the individual is treated as a person and is given respect, upon hospitalization he is accorded an inferior status—he is reduced to the level of an object. In short, he is often treated as a non-person.[3]

The individual undergoes mortification of self in other respects as well. Upon admission the patient is stripped of many of his material possessions such as his wallet, identification, jewelry and other valuables—items that are locked away in storage. Since in Western society material possessions are a significant part of an individual's conception of self, to be stripped of such items represents a major attack on the self. While the institution may rationalize this procedure in terms of protection of the patient's property, the patients however, tend to conceive of this situation in a different manner:

Don:You know what bugs me about this place?

Jane: What?

Don:They won't give me any of my "personals"—you know, like my wallet, ID, and my razor and that kind of stuff...They have it but they just won't give it to me.

Jane:They did that to me, too. They took away all my jewelry and won't give it back to me. They want to seem me beg for it and they still won't give it back.

Don:They make you feel like a piece of garbage—a nothing. When they take all our personals away, *They take away who you are...*

One set of an individual's personal possessions is related to self-conceptions in a special manner. On the outside, an individual possess some control over the personal front which he presents to others. That is, he employs a variety of symbols and tools to create a desired image of self. He employs what Goffman (1961:21) refers to as an "identity kit." However, upon hospitalization the individual is stripped of his usual appearance as well as the equipment used to create and maintain it. In essence, he suffers a personal defacement. A new admission, discussing how his personal appearance was altered shortly after admission states:

> The barber came on the ward last week and dragged me over for a haircut. I didn't want to get it cut off but they (the staff) made me...The barber just plunked me in the chair—didn't even talk to me and just cut off my hair...Shit, I felt awful you know...they were changing so much of me...Where was the old me?

Another patient, complaining about the loss of some items of her identity kit says:

> I hate it in here. They won't give me my razor so I can shave my legs. They even took away my manicure kit. I look like a mess now. I never looked like this before you know...If I want to shave my legs, I have to ask for the "safety razor" at the nursing station.

The loss of certain material possessions and one's identity kit prevent the individual from presenting his usual image of self and presents another instance of how self is altered upon hospitalization.

After admission self-images and identities are assaulted in yet another way—specifically by means of a forced deference pattern. Upon hospitalization the patient soon learns that he must act politely toward the staff or else he will receive negative sanctioning. This very action of required deference functions to attack one's self-conceptions. The self is also mortified by virtue of the fact that the patient is forced to request permission (and is sometimes forced to beg) for small items and activities, such as cigarettes, going for a bath, spending one's own money, going to the canteen, washing one's own clothes—items and activities which the person was able to exercise on his own on the outside. This obligation not only places the patient in an inferior or submissive role, but also leaves him wide open for interruptions from the staff. On the outside if an individual desires something, his requests are readily granted; in contrast, upon institutionalization, his requests may often be denied, questioned or even ignored.

> Last night, I waited and waited at the nursing station. I wanted someone to unlock the door so I could take a bath. The staff all saw me standing there but they just ignored me. After about ten minutes I yelled out to them and told them what I wanted but they just put me off. They told me to come back later and ask again.

In sum, demands for deference and the corresponding implications of inferiority present the individual with a self-image that is incompatible with his prior conception of self.

The self is also mortified in other respects. In Western society there is no more important claim to status, prestige and identity that a person's job (Haas and Shaffir, 1978:33). As Everett Hughes (1958:314) states:

> A man's work is one of the more important parts of his identity, of his self; indeed of his fate in the one life he has to live, for there is something almost as irrevocable about the choice of occupation as there is about the choice of mate.

A person's occupation is an intricate part of his self-identity. However, upon hospitalization the patient is separated from his occupation in the outside world; in its place, he is often given menial work to undertake for which he is paid a small sum of money. So for example, as part of the patient's "therapy," he may be obliged to help in the hospital kitchen clearing tables or scraping plates. For this labor he may be given a few cents or a cigarette. At the Industrial Therapy Workshop of the institution, patients are required to undertake light factory work such as filling packages and cartons with various goods. Others work at the hospital laundry where they wash and iron much of the institutional clothing. For this type of work, the patients are paid menial wages. Being forced to work at such tasks for small sums of money is degrading for the individual and represents yet another instance of how self is assaulted upon hospitalization:

> Working at IT (Industrial Therapy) is fucking awful. You start working for 20 cents an hour and you work your way up to 70 cents an hour and that's doing heavy manual labor, like lifting crates. See that old lady over there? She makes 40 cents an hour stuffing kotex in a box. How degrading!...The money you make in here isn't enough to keep you in cigarettes. It's just token wages, that's all. I used to make over $200.00 a week on the outside, but in here I'm lucky if I make $10.00 a week...It's like a slap in the face, you know.

Two patients, comparing hospital wages to wages in another institution state:

Joe: You know, it's better in prison than in here. In prison the pay is better. Some inmates make 5 or 6 bucks an hour for doing work.

Tom: Yeah, when I was in jail I got paid $1.90 an hour for working in the kitchen. But here in the mental hospital all they pay is 20 cents an hour. Yeah, convicts are treated better than mental patients—even though we have to do a shitty jobs in jail too; at least we're paid a bit better than in this joint!

It is further important to note that another type of mortification occurs upon admission. Essentially, a type of contaminative exposure[4] occurs upon entrance. While in the outside world an individual is able to segregate objects of self-feeling, such as his thoughts, actions, and physical being from certain contaminating items; in the hospital however, the boundaries of the self are violated (Goffman, 1961:23). Specifically, upon entering the hospital, a person's informational preserve relating to self is infringed upon. During entrance procedures information is collected regarding patient's roles, statuses, and his past behaviors (including discreditable information) and is synthesized in the form of a case history of the patient. This file is made readily available to any staff member. The patient has virtually no control over who is allowed to learn certain discreditable facts about himself. In this sense, his territories of self are being violated. Because staff members have access to these case histories, sometimes in the course of group therapy sessions, the therapist forces the patient to reveal certain discreditable facts about himself in front of other group members. A patient recalling his experience in a group therapy session states:

> I hate this place. They (the staff) know everything about us—especially all the bad things we've ever done. Every time I go to one of those sessions they keep bringing up my past. I know I've done a lot of wrong things in my life—things I did a long time ago, right in front of the patients. It makes me feel ashamed when I have to tell bad things about myself and they hear it. I don't want everyone else in the group to know all the things I've done.

While the patient undergoes mortification of self by contaminative exposure of the kind discussed above, he also undergoes mortification of self through interpersonal contamination. As Goffman (1961:28) emphasizes, "when an agency of contamination is another human being, the inmate is in addition contaminated by forced interpersonal contact and, in consequence, a forced social relationship." Many times during a patient's hospitalization his physical being and room may be searched. While the institution rationalizes these actions in terms of the protection of the patients, nevertheless, this very action of searching, along with the person who conducts the search, functions to violate the boundaries of the self. A patient expresses this view:

> You know what bugs me about here? They search our rooms for "junk" (drugs) all the time...There's no privacy at all...Like today my friend Jack came in to visit me and when he left they called me to the office while the others (the staff) went into my room and searched through all my stuff. I saw them do it. Man, we got no privacy at all!

Self is assaulted in yet one final respect—through the enforcement of strict rules and regulations. On the outside, the individual has some control over his world—he is a free, autonomous being. As such, he is free to make choices on his own as well as to act as he pleases with certain prescribed limits. The correctness of his actions is judged only at certain times. The individual is accorded certain civil rights as a Canadian citizen. In contrast, however, upon institutionalization, the mental patient in subjected to a rigorous set of rules and regulations that serve to control *every* aspect of the patient's life.[5] The civil rights he enjoyed on the outside are taken away from him. He no longer has free choices nor is he able to act as he pleases. The patient's actions are constantly being judged by the staff, and negative sanctions result if he violates an institutional norm. A patient aptly describes this situation:

> Did you know that mental patients have no rights?...When you come in here, you lose all the rights you had on the outside. There is no free choice in here—choices are made for you. Like you have to eat at a certain time, wash at a certain time when they tell you, work when they tell you. In here they force you to think and act the way the want...They're always watching what you do and if you goof up, you're punished.

Another patient states:

> When a person is committed into the mental hospital he loses most of the rights he had on the outside as a citizen. For example, we aren't allowed to vote anymore, drive a car or any of those things—we lose all those rights we used to take for granted. With no rights left, we are left to abide by the rules of the hospital or else receive punishments. Taking away all these things is like taking away part of your identity—you lose who you once were.[6]

In sum, the loss of certain rights combined with the vast body of rules and regulations to which the patient is subjected functions to threaten the individual's conception of self. No longer is he a self-sufficient entity; rather, the patient is reduced to a weak, helpless, dependent being.[7]

In short, I have illustrated how a mental institution, in its effort to resocialize and rehabilitate its charges, begins by initially stripping the individual of his old identity through various admission procedures. While the self is curtailed through these mortifying experiences, I would argue that it is largely within the context of the institution's "privilege system" that self is reconstituted.

The Privilege System: The Context Within Which Self is Reconstituted

Examination of the privilege system reveals that it is comprised of three basic components: formal norms, positive sanctions (rewards), and negative sanctions (punishments). In terms of the formal norms, it is evident that the mental institution possesses a rigorous and explicit set of rules and regulations detailing the main requirements and explicit conduct. So for example, such rules prescribe at what time a patient gets up in the morning, what time he/she retires, when he/she is allowed to bathe, whether he/she is allowed to go to the canteen, attend social functions, etc.

A second major component of the privilege system may be termed positive sanctions or rewards. The mental hospital, in exchange for cooperation and compliance, offers the patient a small number of clearly-defined privileges. As I pointed out earlier in this chapter, upon entrance the patient is striped of many of his material possessions. Items and activities which the patient once took for granted on the outside now become privileges upon hospitalization. Through the privilege system, certain possessions, items and activities are held up to the patient as possibilities which he can strive to regain. For example, when the patient becomes obedient in both thought and action, he might be given his identification and wallet back, allowed to go for a walk to the hospital canteen by himself, or even be allowed to venture into the city for a short time. In this sense, the individual feels that he is re-establishing some of the relationships with the outside world which were lost upon hospitalization.

A third and final component of the privilege system may be termed negative sanctions or punishments. When a patient violates one of the institutional norms, he is punished. While corporal punishment is prohibited, punishments may take the form of being placed in the sideroom for a period of time, temporary loss of privileges, or even confinement to pajamas.

Two important points regarding the privilege system should be noted at this point. First, discharge from the hospital is elaborated into the privilege system. As Denzin (1968:349–58) and Hollingshead and Redlich (1958) emphasize, certain patient behaviors and overall presentations of self serve to facilitate the acquisition of more privileges and ultimately, the patient's release, while other types of behavior tend to lengthen his stay:

> ...if the patient presents himself in such a way as to communicate his acceptance of the "psychiatric line," the therapist will act toward him in a way which defines him as a good patient and one who will be easy to treat...It would be predicted that patients defined as holding initial favorable attitudes toward the "psychiatric line" would...remain in the hospital a shorter length of time (Denzin, 1968:350).[8]

Secondly, it is apparent that positive and negative sanctions of the privilege system become elaborated into a residual system. That is, certain places to sleep or interact become clearly-defined as places in which patients with *certain privileges* are allowed to frequent or abide. Basically, patients are moved back and forth from one spatial area to another within the ward as rewards or punishments for their behavior and presentations of self. In this sense then, the system itself remains static while the patients are shifted back and forth within the structure. A patient explains how the privilege system operates:

> When you first come in, you are often put in pajamas. You're not allowed to even wear clothes. You have no privileges at all...They put you on the back part of the ward; you can't go out to the other side of the ward—they

have a locked door between the two sides of the ward. You're confined here for a week or more.

Another patient recounts:

> If you're good and behave like the staff want, you can work your way up and get more benefits...Like when you get semi-privileges you're allowed to go down to the other side of the ward into the music room and listen to the stereo. Also, you no longer have your room on the back part of the ward—the unprivileged side, but you get to move to a room on the front part of the ward with the more privileged people. Later you can work your way up to full-privileges which means that you can go out on your own for walks or to the canteen.

At the official level, the privilege system can be seen to have two functions: (1) as a mechanism of social control, and (2) a therapeutic aim. That is, in terms of the former, the privilege system serves to make the patient obedient and cooperative in terms of the aims of the institution. The privilege system can be viewed as a mechanism of social control utilized to manage a large group of people. In terms of the latter function, the privilege system is also conceptualized by the institutional staff as having some therapeutic value. That is, this system functions to allow the patient to learn responsibility for his own actions as well as the actions of others. It serves to rehabilitate the patient so that he will be able to successfully return to the outside world. A staff member describing the purpose for the privilege system states:

> The way I see the privilege system is this—it essentially has a therapeutic aim in that it provides the patient the opportunity to accept responsibility for himself and other patients...The privilege system also helps us control the patients...It provides the staff with information about a patient's behavior that might otherwise be hidden, so we are able to judge him in this way...

Examination of the privilege system reveals that it is comprised of four levels. These are as follows:

Lowest Level Level I. *WARD PRIVILEGES*—The patient is confined to the back half of the ward, often being forced to remain in pajamas.

Level II. *GROUNDS-ACCOMPANIED*—The patient has semi-privileges which means that he can move freely throughout the ward and is also permitted to go for a walk on the grounds if accompanied by a staff a patient who possesses "full grounds."

Level III. *FULL-GROUNDS*—The patient has full privileges which means that he is allowed to go out of the hospital by himself, go to the canteen by himself, etc.

Highest Level Level IV. *OFF-GROUNDS*—This level of the privilege system entitles the patient to leave the hospital grounds whenever he desires, providing that he returns within a specified time.

Essentially, when a patient enters the hospital, he is placed at Level I and is confined to the ward. After approximately one week's time,[9] the patient can ask permission from the staff to attend a "Privilege Meeting" which is comprised of two staff members and his fellow patients. At this meeting the patient asks permission to advance to the next level in the privilege system and be granted more privileges. The other patients then vote on whether the patient should be granted more privileges, and if a unanimous decision is reached, he is allowed to proceed to the next level. Although one might initially think that the privilege system operates in a democratic manner, closer examination reveals that this is not the case. Although the staff do not take part in the actual voting, they do however, possess the authority to veto any decision if they so desire.

According to the ideology of the institution, the privilege system may be characterized as a resocializing and rehabilitating mechanism—a mechanism that helps the patient learn to "accept responsibility" for his actions. As the patient gradually learns to be more responsible he moves from levels one through four and is eventually discharged back into society as a productive being. In contrast to the ideology of the institution however, when one attempts to make sociological sense of this system, it is seen in a different manner. Specifically, I would argue that the privilege system provides the chief context within which the patient is forced to adopt a redefinition of self as "mentally ill" or "deviant."

From an interactionist perspective, an individual develops a self-identity on the basis of how he or she perceives others are perceiving him/her. A person's conceptions reflect the image he/she believes others have of him/her and is closely tied to the reactions imputed to other individuals. Self is socially-constructed and socially-maintained. When an individual initially enters a mental institution he possesses a conception of self that was made possible by the stable arrangements of society. However, upon admission and thereafter the patient finds that it is virtually impossible to manage his old identity. The patient is separated from individuals and structures on the outside which functioned to validate his behavior. This social separation, combined with the various admission procedures serve to destroy or alter the individual's conception of self. Once stripped to a liminal entry, the hospital offers the patient an alternative identity of self as a "mental patient"—a self-image that is incompatible with his prior conception of self. I would argue that although the patient may not initially agree with this redefinition of self as being mentally ill, nevertheless, through the structure of the privilege system along with the shared definition of himself as being "mentally ill" held by his significant others, the patient is ultimately forced to accept this redefinition. Blake and Moulton (1961:1–2) make the following statement regarding the processes of conformity, resistance to influence, and conversion to a new self-identity:

> An individual requires a stable framework, including salient and firm reference points, in order to orient himself and to regulate his interactions with others. This framework consists of external and internal anchorages available to the individual whether he is aware of them or not. Within an acceptable framework he can resist giving or accepting information that is inconsistent with that framework or that requires him to relinquish it. In the absence of a stable framework he actively seeks to establish one through his own strivings by making use of significant and relevant

information provided him within the context of interaction. By controlling the amount and kind of information available for orientation, he can
be led to embrace conforming attitudes which are entirely foreign to his
earlier ways of thinking.

Further, Thomas Scheff (1966:57) in his discussion of role-playing writes:

Having an audience that acts toward the individual in a uniform way may
lead the actor to play the expected role even if he is not particularly
interested in doing so. The "baby of the family" may come to find this role
obnoxious, but the uniform pattern of cues and actions that confronts him
in the family may lock in with his own vocabulary of responses so that
it is inconvenient and difficult for him not to play the part expected of
him. To the degree that alternative roles are closed off, the pro-offered
role may come to be the only way the individual can cope with the
situation.

In my study, I found that new patients initially respond to their hospitalization by
denying that there is anything wrong with them. They often assert a story proving that
they are not mentally ill, that someone or something else is to blame for their
hospitalization, and that the hospital officials are therefore unjust in forcing this new
label upon them. The following quotations from patients provide illustrations of this
self-respecting tendency:[10]

I've gone through a lot of pain in my life. It's all those people out there
who put me in here, you know...Everyone on the outside is against me.
I'm not sick but they say I am. It's just not true. They forced me to come
in here.

Another patient states:

You know, I'm not crazy like the rest of them in here. I just got fed up with
the working conditions in my home town. The town's dying. There's no
decent jobs anymore. I came to the hospital to rest up, that's all. It's sort
of a retraining program for me.

While most of the time the other patients openly accept the patient's apologia
without question, sometimes however, the patients force each other to view them-
selves as mentally ill. The following conversation aptly illustrates this point:
Bob:There's nothing wrong with me. I don't know why I'm locked up in here.
Dick:There's something wrong with you.
Bob:What?
Dick:You're sick—you're a dangerous mental, Bob. That's why you're in here.
If you don't believe that, you'll never get out.
While fellow patients sometimes play a role in forcing the individual to accept this
redefinition of self as mentally ill, I found that it is the staff, who through context of

the privilege system's rewards and punishments play a significant role in forcing the individual to adopt this redefinition of self.

Scheff, (1966:84) in his study discovered that patients who found evidence for mental illness in both their past and present actions were rewarded by the staff:

> Labeled deviants may be rewarded for playing the stereotyped deviant role. Ordinarily patients who display "insight" are rewarded by psychiatrists and other personnel. That is, patients who manage to find evidence of "their illness" in their past and present behavior, confirming the medical and social diagnoses, receive more benefits.

In my study, I also found that patients, through the context of the institution's privilege system were often rewarded for playing the role of the insane person. As a patient learns to play the role of "being crazy," he is rewarded by the staff members by being allowed to advance to a higher level in the privilege system. A patient states:

> The only way to get out of this place is to "act crazy" and do exactly what the staff want. If you don't give in to the staff, you'll stay in here forever. Like I told you before, the staff all think we are completely insane—they tell us we are. If you disagree with what they say and argue that you're not, then you don't get anywhere. They get mad at you and make it tough. But if you go along with them and "act" mental, then you'll be able to go places and maybe one day will be let out.

Similarly, another patient states:

> The best thing I could do is play along with whatever the staff wants. If the staff think I'm crazy, I should act crazy and not make any trouble. That's the only way to get more privileges around here. That's the only way to ever get out of here. If you don't, then you'll stay down at the bottom of the heap in here—you'll never move up in the privilege system or nothing.

The patient, in his desire to attain more privileges learns to play the role of "mental patient" proffered by the staff.

Just as the patient is rewarded in the context of the privilege system for adopting this redefinition of self and its corresponding role, so too is he punished for refusing to do so:

> If you deny you're mental and saying nothing is wrong with you, you get treated bad by the staff. They can make it tough. They say that you're misbehaving, so they keep you in pj's or put you in the sideroom.

Another patient states:

> If you keep saying that you're not mentally insane, you'll get nowhere. The staff will think that you're really sick then. You keep saying nothing is wrong with you and the staff interpret that as defiance—they will say you are disobeying them and you'll get your privileges taken away.

The patient finds himself in a difficult position. On the one hand he does not want to accept this redefinition of self as "mentally ill." However, due to the shared definitions held by his significant others, coupled with the reward and punishments accorded him in the context of the privilege system the patient comes to "play the role" of mental patient.

I would argue that this situation has serious implications for the patient's identity. Although the symptoms displayed by the patient may begin as a conscious pretense, the constant reinforcement from the staff ultimately causes these behaviors to become involuntary and habitual. In effect, role internalization occurs.[11]

Cain (1964:278–89) in his study on "borderline children" provides evidence in support of this view. That is, he found that institutionalized children "learn" how to play at being crazy. These children possessed images of madness which were constructed from popular conceptions. Similar to my study, these children were also rewarded by the hospital staff for adopting "crazy" symptoms. And although the child may have initially consciously played the role of being "crazy," through the repeated acting out of the role, combined with the reinforcements from the environment, he ultimately internalized this behavior, and thus, it became an unconscious part of his behavioral pattern.

In essence then, both Cain's study and this author's study indicate that the institution's perception of the individual produces a self-fulfilling prophecy whereby the patients come to be shaped in the image that the staff have of them. Just as a teacher's expectations in the classroom can produce brighter or duller students,[12] and the expectations of a researcher can produce his own reality,[13] my study reveals that the expectations of the institutional staff have similar effects.[14]

REFERENCES

Becker, E. 1962. "Socialization, Command of Performance, and Mental Illness." *American Journal of Sociology* 67:494–501.
Bittner, E. 1967. "Police Discretion in Apprehending the Mentally Ill." *Social Problems* 14:278–92.
Blake, R.R. & J.S. Moulton. 1961. "Conformity, Resistance, and Conversion." In I.A. Berg and B.M. Bass, eds., *Conformity and Deviation*. New York: Harper.
Cain, A. 1964. "On the Meaning of 'Playing Crazy' in Borderline Children." *Psychiatry* 27:278–89.
Clausen, J.A. & M. Yarrow. 1955. "Paths to the Mental Hospital." *Journal of Social Issues* 11:25–32.
Cohen, E. 1953. *Human Behavior in a Concentration Camp*. New York: Grosset and Dunlap.
Cumming, J. & E. Cumming. 1957. *Closed Ranks: An Experiment in Mental Health Education*. Mass: Harvard University Press.
Denzin, N.K. 1968. "The Self-Fulfilling Prophecy and Patient-Therapist Interaction." Pp. 349–57 in S. Spitzer and N. Denzin, eds., *The Mental Patient: Studies in the Sociology of Deviance*. New York: McGraw-Hill, 349–57.
Esquirol, J.E., 1867. "A Treatise on Insanity." In C.E. Goshen ed., *Documentary History of Psychiatry: A Source Book on Historical Principles*. New York: Philosophical Library.

Goffman, E. 1961. *Asylums*. Chicago: Aldine Press.

Gough, H.G. 1948. "A Sociological Theory of Psychopathy." *American Journal of Sociology* 53:359–66.

Haas, J. & W. Shaffir. 1978. "Do New Ways of Professional Socialization Make a Difference?" Paper presented at the Ninth World Congress of Sociology, Uppsala, Sweden.

Hollingshead, A.B. & F. Redlich. 1958. *Social Class and Mental Illness*. New York: Wiley.

Johnson, D. McI., & N. Dodds. 1957. *The Plea for the Silent*. London: Christopher Johnson.

Kutner, Luis, 1962. "The Illusion of Due Process in Commitment Proceedings." *Northwestern University Law Review* 57: 383–93.

Laing, R.D. & Esterson, A. 1964. *Sanity, Madness and the Family*. London: Tavistock.

Lemert, E. 1946. "Legal Commitment and Social Control." *Sociology and Social Psychiatry* 9:13–31.

Lewis, Aubrey, 1967. *The State of Psychiatry*. New York: Science House.

Mechanic, D. 1962. "Some Factors in Identifying and Defining Mental Illness." *Mental Hygiene* 46:66–74.

Meyers, J. & L. Schaffer. 1954. "Social Stratification and Psychiatric Practice: A Study of an Outpatient Clinic." *American Sociological Review* XIX:307–10.

Mezer, R.R. & P.D. Rheingold. 1962. "Mental Capacity and Incompetency: A Psycho-Legal Problem." *American Journal of Psychiatry* 118:827–31.

Orne, M.T. 1962. "On the Social Psychology of the Psychological Experiment: With Particular Reference to the Demand Characteristics and Their Implications." *American Psychologist* 17:776–83.

Rosenthal, D. & L. Jacobsen. 1968. "Teacher Expectations for the Disadvantaged." *Scientific American* 218:19–23.

Sampson, H. (et al). 1962. "Family Processes and Becoming a Mental Patient." *American Journal of Sociology* 68:88–96.

Scheff, Thomas, 1964. "The Societal Reaction to Deviance: Ascriptive Elements in the Psychiatric Screening of Mental Patients in a Midwestern State." *Social Problems* 11: 401–413.

——————————, 1966. *Being Mentally Ill*. Chicago: Aldine.

——————————, 1967. *Mental Illness and Social Processes*. New York: Harper.

——————————, 1975. *Labelling Madness*. New Jersey: Prentice-Hall.

Schwartz, C. 1957. "Perspectives on Deviance—Wives' Definitions of Their Husbands' Mental Illness." *Psychiatry* XX:271–91.

Siegler, Miriam, and Humphrey Osmond, 1974. *Models of Madness, Models of Medicine*. New York: MacMillan.

Smith, H. & J. Thrasher. 1968. "Roles, Cliques, and Sanctions: Dimensions of Patient Society." In *The Mental Patient: Studies in the Sociology of Deviance*, S. Spitzer and N. Denzin (eds.). New York: McGraw-Hill.

Smith, K., M. Pumphrey, & J. Hall. 1963. "The 'Last Straw': The Decisive Incident Resulting in the Request for Hospitalization of One Hundred Schizophrenic Patients." *American Journal of Psychiatry* 120:228–33.

Sykes, G. 1958. *The Society of Captives*. New Jersey: Princeton University Press.

Turner, V. 1969. *The Ritual Process*. Chicago: Aldine.

VanGennep, Y., 1969. *Rites of Passage*. Chicago: Aldine.

Yarrow, M., C. Schwartz, H. Murphy, & L. Deasy. 1955. "The Psychological Meaning of Mental Illness in the Family." *Journal of Social Issues* 11:12–24.

Whybrow, P.C., 1972. "The Use and Abuse of the 'Medical Model' as a Conceptual Frame in Psychiatry." *Psychiatry in Medicine* 3:333–342.

NOTES

[1] A total institution may be defined as: "an institution...with encompassing tendencies...Their encompassing or total character is symbolized by the barrier to social intercourse with the outside that is often built right into the physical plant, such as locked doors, high walls, barbed wire, cliffs, forests, or moors" (Goffman, 1961:4).

[2] This is the case in most total institutions. See also, Sykes (1958:68); and Cohen (1953:19).

[3] See also Johnson and Dodds (1957) for a similar example.

[4] This phrase was initially used by Goffman (1961) in his study of total institutions.

[5] For a similar discussion of the prescriptions for behavior in a mental hospital, see Smith and Thrasher (1968:316–24).

[6] Mezer and Rheingold (1962:827–31) discuss the civil/legal implications of being admitted to a mental hospital. Once institutionalized, the patient loses a large number of his civil rights which he/she previously took for granted. Specifically, once hospitalized, the individual is not allowed to make a will, a deed or contract, cannot receive property, loses the right to vote, operate a motor vehicle, cannot get married or divorced, etc. Mezer and Rheingold emphasize that when an individual loses his civil rights, this loss is not selective—it is not assumed that his presumed "illness" has affected certain areas of competency and not others. Because he has been adjudged as mentally ill, this definition strips him of *all* his civil rights despite his actual ability to carry out his rights in certain areas.

[7] See Sykes (1958:73) for a similar discussion concerning the institutionalization of prisoners.

[8] This theme will be fully discussed in the latter part of this paper.

[9] This time is variable depending on the particular patient involved.

[10] This term was initially used by Goffman (1961).

[11] For the patient who remains in hospital for a short period of time, role internalization may not occur, but if he/she is hospitalized for a long time or has been repeatedly institutionalized, the person ultimately internalizes this behavior.

[12] See Rosenthal and Jacobsen (1968:19–23).

[13] See Orne (1962:776–83).

[14] The in-patient phase in the career of the mental patient may be likened to the anthropological notion of "rites of passage." Essentially, this term refers to "rites which accompany every change of place, state, social position, and age" (VanGennep, 1969:95). All rites of passage are comprised of three stages: (1) separation; (2) marginality or liminality; and (3) aggregation. During the first phase, symbolic behavior functions to detach the individual from a fixed point in the social structure, from a set of cultural conditions or from both. That is, this symbolic behavior, in the form of degradations and humiliations serve to strip the individual of his previous status. During the second phase, the liminal phase, the characteristics of the person are unclear. According to Turner (1969:95), "they are neither here nor there; they are betwixt and between the positions assigned and arrayed by law, custom, convention and ceremonial."—individuals possess few if any of the attributes of their past identity. Moreover, they are often even stripped naked to humble themselves. They must obey their superiors implicitly. As Turner (1969:96) states: "*it is as though the subjects are being reduced or ground down to a uniform condition to be fashioned anew...*"

In the third phase, termed as aggregation or reintegration, the individual is reborn as a new being; he is now in a stable social arrangement once more. In short, the individual has been redefined as a clearly-defined structural type, and as such, is expected to behave in terms of this new definition. The reader can clearly see that the in-patient phase in the career of a mental patient has striking similarities with the notion of rites of passage—in symbolic terms, the patient is also stripped of his old status through sometimes degrading rites, he is reduced to a liminal being, then he is reborn with a new identity bestowed upon him by members of society and is obliged to act in accordance with this new status.

Chapter 28

BEING SANE IN INSANE PLACES

D.L. Rosenhan

If sanity and insanity exist, how shall we know them?

The question is neither capricious nor itself insane. However much we may be personally convinced that we can tell the normal from the abnormal, the evidence is simply not compelling. It is commonplace, for example, to read about murder trials wherein eminent psychiatrists for the defense are contradicted by equally prominent psychiatrists for the prosecution on the matter of the defendant's sanity. More generally, there are a great deal of conflicting data on the reliability, utility, and meaning of such terms as "sanity," "insanity," "mental illness," and "schizophrenia."[1] (Ashburn, 1949; Beck, 1962; Boisen, 1938; Kreitman, 1961; Kreitman, et al., 1961; Schmitt and Fonda, 1956; and Seeman, 1953). Finally, as early as 1934, Benedict (1934:10, 59) suggested that normality and abnormality are not universal. What is viewed as normal in one culture may be seen as quite aberrant in another. Thus, notions of normality and abnormality may not be quite as accurate as people believe they are.

To raise questions regarding normality and abnormality is in no way to question the fact that some behaviors are deviant or odd. Murder is deviant. So, too, are hallucinations. Nor does raising such questions deny the existence of the personal anguish that is often associated with "mental illness." Anxiety and depression exist. Psychological suffering exists. But normality and abnormality, sanity and insanity, and the diagnoses that flow from them may be less substantive than many believe them to be.

At its heart, the question of whether the sane can be distinguished from the insane (and whether degrees of insanity can be distinguished from each other) is a simple matter: do the salient characteristics that lead to diagnoses reside in the patients themselves or in the environments and contexts in which observers find them?...[T]he belief has been strong that patients present symptoms, that those symptoms can be categorized, and, implicitly, that the sane are distinguishable from the insane. More recently, however, this belief has been questioned...[T]he view has grown that psychological categorization of mental illness is useless at best and downright harmful, misleading, and pejorative at worst. Psychiatric diagnoses, in this view, are in the minds of the observers and are not valid summaries of characteristics displayed by the observed.[2,3,4]

Gains can be made in deciding which of these is more nearly accurate by getting normal people (that is, people who do not have, and have never suffered, symptoms of serious psychiatric disorders) admitted to psychiatric hospitals and then determining whether they were discovered to be sane and, if so, how. If the sanity of such pseudopatients were always detected, there would be prima facie evidence that a sane individual can be distinguished from the insane context in which he is found...If, on the other hand, the sanity of the pseudopatients were never discovered, serious difficulties would arise for those who support traditional modes of psychiatric diagnosis. Given that the hospital staff was not incompetent, that the pseudopatient had been behaving as sanely as he had been outside of the hospital, and that it had never been previously suggested that he belonged in a psychiatric hospital, such an unlikely outcome would support the view that psychiatric diagnosis betrays little about the patient but much about the environment in which an observer finds him.

This article describes such an experiment. Eight sane people gained secret admission to 12 different hospitals.[5] Their diagnostic experiences constitute the data of the first part of this article; the remainder is devoted to a description of their experiences in psychiatric institutions....

Pseudopatients and Their Settings

The eight pseudopatients were a varied group. One was a psychology graduate student in his 20s. The remaining seven were older and "established." Among them were three psychologists, a pediatrician, a psychiatrist, a painter, and a housewife. Three pseudopatients were women, five were men. All of them employed pseudonyms, lest their alleged diagnoses embarrass them later. Those who were in mental health professions alleged another occupation in order to avoid the special attentions that might be accorded by staff, as a matter of courtesy or caution, to ailing colleagues.[6] With the exception of myself (I was the first pseudopatient and my presence was known to the hospital administrator and chief psychologist and, so far as I can tell, them alone), the presence of pseudopatients and the nature of the research program was not known to the hospital staffs.[7]

The settings were similarly varied. In order to generalize the findings, admission into a variety of hospitals was sought. The 12 hospitals in the sample were located in five different states on the East and West coasts. Some were old and shabby, some were quite new. Some were research-oriented, others were not. Some had good staff-patient ratios, others were quite understaffed. Only one was a strictly private hospital. All of the others were supported by state or federal funds or, in one instance, by university funds.

After calling the hospital for an appointment, the pseudopatient arrived at the admissions office complaining that he had been hearing voices. Asked what the voices said, he replied that they were often unclear, but as far as he could tell they said "empty," "hollow," and "thud." The voices were unfamiliar and were of the same sex as the pseudopatient....

Beyond alleging the symptoms and falsifying name, vocation, and employment, no further alterations of person, history, or circumstances were made. The significant events of the pseudopatient's life history were presented as they had actually occurred. Relationships with parents and siblings, with spouse and children, with people at work and in school, consistent with the aforementioned exceptions, were described as they were or had been. Frustrations and upsets were described along with joys and satisfactions. These facts are important to remember. If anything, they strongly biased the subsequent results in favor of detecting sanity, since none of their histories or current behaviors were seriously pathological in any way.

Immediately upon admission to the psychiatric ward, the pseudopatient ceased simulating *any* symptoms of abnormality. In some cases, there was a brief period of mild nervousness and anxiety, since none of the pseudopatients really believed that they would be admitted so easily. Indeed, their shared fear was that they would be immediately exposed as frauds and greatly embarrassed. Moreover, may of them had never visited a psychiatric ward; even those who had, nevertheless had some genuine fears about what might happen to them. Their nervousness, then, was quite appropriate to the novelty of the hospital setting, and it abated rapidly.

Apart from that short-lived nervousness, the pseudopatient behaved on the ward as he "normally" behaved. The pseudopatient spoke to patients and staff as he might ordinarily. Because there is uncommonly little to do on a psychiatric ward, he attempted to engage others in conversation. When asked by staff how he was feeling, he indicated that he was fine, that he no longer experienced symptoms. He responded to instructions from attendants, to calls for medication (which was not swallowed), and to dining-hall instructions. Beyond such activities as were available to him on the admissions ward, he spent his time writing down his observations about the ward, its patients, and the staff. Initially, these notes were written "secretly," but as it soon became clear that no one much cared, they were subsequently written on standard tablets of paper in such public places as the dayroom. No secret was made of these activities.

The pseudopatient, very much a true psychiatric patient, entered a hospital with no foreknowledge of when he would be discharged. Each was told that he would have to get out by his own devices, essentially by convincing the staff that he was sane. The psychological stresses associated with hospitalization were considerable, and all but one of the pseudopatients desired to be discharged almost immediately after being admitted. They were, therefore, motivated not only to behave sanely, but to be paragons of cooperation. That their behavior was in no way disruptive is confirmed by nursing reports, which have been obtained on most of the patients. These reports uniformly indicate that the patients were "friendly," "cooperative," and "exhibited no abnormal indications."

The Normal Are Not Detectably Sane

Despite their public "show" of sanity, the pseudopatients were never detected. Admitted, except in one case, with a diagnosis of schizophrenia,[8] each was discharged with a diagnosis of schizophrenia "in remission." The label "in remission" should in no way be dismissed as a formality, for at no time during any hospitalization had any question been raised about any pseudopatient's simulation. Nor are there any indication in the hospital records that the pseudopatient's status was suspect. Rather, the evidence is strong that, once labeled schizophrenic, the pseudopatient was stuck with that label. If the pseudopatient was to be discharged, he must naturally be "in remission"; but he was not sane, nor, in the institution's view, had he ever been sane.

The uniform failure to recognize sanity cannot be attributed to the quality of the hospitals....Nor can it be alleged that there was simply not enough time to observe the pseudopatients. Length of hospitalization ranged from 7 to 52 days, with an average of 19 days. The pseudopatients were not, in fact, carefully observed, but this failure clearly speaks more to traditions within psychiatric hospitals than to lack of opportunity.

Finally, it cannot be said that the failure to recognize the pseudopatients' sanity was due to the fact that they were not behaving sanely. While there was clearly some tension present in all of them, their daily visitors could detect no serious behavioral consequences—nor, indeed, could other patients. It was quite common for the patients to "detect" the pseudopatients' sanity...."You're not crazy. You're a journalist, or a professor [referring to the continual note-taking]. You're checking up on the hospital." While most of the patients were reassured by the pseudopatients' insistence that he had been sick before he came in but was fine now, some continued to believe that the pseudopatient was sane throughout his hospitalization.[9] The fact that the patients often recognized normality when staff did not raises important questions.

Failure to detect sanity during the course of hospitalization may be due to the fact that...physicians are more inclined to call a healthy person sick...than a sick person healthy....The reasons for this are not hard to find: it is clearly more dangerous to misdiagnose illness than health. Better to err on the side of caution, to suspect illness even among the healthy.

But what holds for medicine does not hold equally well for psychiatry. Medical illnesses, while unfortunate, are not commonly pejorative. Psychiatric diagnoses, on the contrary, carry with them personal, legal, and social stigmas.[10] It was therefore important to see whether the tendency toward diagnosing the sane insane could be reversed. The following experiment was arranged at a research and teaching hospital whose staff had heard these findings but doubted that such an error could occur in their hospital. The staff was informed that at some time during the following 3 months, one or more pseudopatients would attempt to be admitted into the psychiatric hospital. Each staff member was asked to rate each patient who presented himself at admissions or on the ward according to the likelihood that the patient was a pseudopatient....

Judgements were obtained on 193 patients who were admitted for psychiatric treatment. All staff who had sustained contact with or primary responsibility for the patient—attendants, nurses, psychiatrists, physicians, and psychologists—were asked to make judgements. Forty-one patients were alleged, with high confidence, to be pseudopatients by at least one member of the staff. Twenty-three were considered suspect by at least one psychiatrist. Nineteen were suspected by one psychiatrist *and* one other staff member. Actually, no genuine pseudopatient (at least from my group) presented himself during this period.

The experiment is instructive. It indicates that the tendency to designate sane people as insane can be reversed when the stakes are (in this case, prestige and diagnostic acumen) high. But what can be said of the 19 people who were suspected of being "sane" by one psychiatrist and another staff member? Were these people truly "sane"?...There is no way of knowing. But one thing is certain: any diagnostic process that lends itself so readily to massive errors of this sort cannot be a very reliable one.

The Stickiness of Psychodiagnostic Labels

Beyond the tendency to call the healthy sick—a tendency that accounts better for diagnostic behavior on admission than it does for such behavior after a lengthy period of exposure—the data speak to the massive role of labeling in psychiatric assessment. Having once been labeled schizophrenic, there is nothing the pseudopatient can do to overcome the tag. The tag profoundly colors others' perceptions of him and his behavior.

From one viewpoint, these data are hardly surprising, for it has long been known that elements are given meaning by the context in which they occur....Once a person is designated abnormal, all of his other behaviors and characteristics are colored by that label. Indeed, that label is so powerful that many of the pseudopatients' normal behaviors were overlooked entirely or profoundly misinterpreted. Some examples may clarify this issue.

Earlier I indicated that there were no changes in the pseudopatient's personal history and current status beyond those of name, employment, and, where necessary, vocation. Otherwise, a veridical description of personal history and circumstances was offered. Those circumstances were not psychotic. How were they made consonant with the diagnosis of psychosis? Or were those diagnoses modified in such a way as to bring them into accord with the circumstances of the pseudopatient's life, as described by him?

As far as I can determine, diagnoses were in no way affected by the relative health of the circumstances of a pseudopatient's life. Rather, the reverse occurred: the perception of his circumstances was shaped entirely by the diagnosis. A clear example of such translation is found in the case of a pseudopatient who had a close relationship with his mother but was rather remote from his father during his early childhood. During adolescence and beyond, however, his father became a close friend, while his relationship with his mother cooled. His present relationship with his wife was characteristically close and warm. Apart from occasional angry exchanges, friction was minimal. The children had rarely been spanked. Surely there is nothing especially pathological about such a history....Observe, however, how such a history was translated in the psychopathological context, this from the case summary prepared after the patient was discharged.

> This white 39-year-old male...manifests a long history of considerable ambivalence in close relationships, which began in early childhood. A warm relationship with his mother cools during adolescence. A distant relationship with his father is described as become very intense. Affective stability is absent. His attempts to control emotionality with his wife and children are punctuated by angry outbursts and, in the case of the children, spankings. And while he says that he has several good friends,

one senses considerable ambivalence embedded in those relationships also....

The facts of the case were unintentionally distorted by the staff to achieve consistency with a popular theory of the dynamics of a schizophrenic reaction.[11] Nothing of an ambivalent nature had been described in relations with parents, spouse, or friends....Clearly, the meaning ascribed to his verbalizations (that is, ambivalence, affective instability) was determined by the diagnosis: schizophrenia. An entirely different meaning would have been ascribed if it were known that the man was "normal."

All pseudopatients took extensive notes publicly. Under ordinary circumstances, such behavior would have raised questions in the minds of observers, as, in fact, it did among patients. Indeed, it seemed so certain that the notes would elicit suspicion that elaborate precautions were taken to remove them from the ward each day. But the precautions proved needless. The closest any staff member came to questioning these notes occurred when one pseudopatient asked his physician what kind of medication he was receiving and began to write down the response. "You needn't write it," he was told gently. "If you have trouble remembering, just ask me again."

If no questions were asked of the pseudopatients, how was their writing interpreted. Nursing records for three patients indicate that the writing was seen as an aspect of their pathological behavior....Given that the patient is in the hospital, he must be psychologically disturbed. And given that he is disturbed, continuous writing must be a behavioral manifestation of that disturbance, perhaps a subset of the compulsive behaviors that are sometimes correlated with schizophrenia.

One tacit characteristic of psychiatric diagnosis is that it locates the sources of aberration within the individual and only rarely within the complex of stimuli that surrounds him. Consequently, behaviors that are stimulated by the environment are commonly misattributed to the patient's disorder. For example, one kindly nurse found a pseudopatient pacing the long hospital corridors. "Nervous, Mr. X?" she asked. "No, bored," he said.

The notes kept by pseudopatients are full of patient behaviors that were misinterpreted by well-intentioned staff. Often enough, a patient would go "berserk" because he had, wittingly or unwittingly, been mistreated by, say, an attendant. A nurse coming upon the scene would rarely inquire even cursorily into the environmental stimuli of the patient's behavior. Rather, she assumed that his upset derived from his pathology, not from his present interactions with other staff members....[N]ever were the staff found to assume that one of themselves or the structure of the hospital had anything to do with a patient's behavior. One psychiatrist pointed to a group of patients who were sitting outside the cafeteria entrance half an hour before lunchtime. To a group of young residents he indicated that such behavior was characteristic of the oral-acquisitive nature of the syndrome. It seemed not to occur to him that there were very few things to anticipate in a psychiatric hospital besides eating.

A psychiatric label has a life and an influence of its own. Once the impression has been formed that the patient is schizophrenic, the expectation is that he will continue to be schizophrenic. When a sufficient amount of time has passed, during which the patient has done nothing bizarre, he is considered to be in remission and available for discharge. But the label endures beyond discharge, with the unconfirmed expectation that he will behave as a schizophrenic again. Such labels, conferred by mental health professionals, are as influential on the patient as they are on his relatives and friends, and it should not surprise anyone that the diagnosis acts on all of them as a self-fulfilling prophecy. Eventually, the patient himself accepts the diagnosis, with all of its surplus meanings and expectations, and behaves accordingly (Scheff, 1966)....

Powerlessness and Depersonalization

Eye contact and verbal contact reflect concern and individuation; their absence, avoidance, and depersonalization. The data I have presented do not do justice to the rich daily encounters that grew up around matters of depersonalization and avoidance. I have records of patients who were beaten by staff for the sin of having initiated verbal contact. During my own experience, for example, one patient was beaten in the presence of other patients for having approached an attendant and told him, "I like you." Occasionally, punishment meted out to patients for misdemeanors seemed so excessive that it could not be justified by the most radical interpretations of psychiatric canon. Nevertheless, they appeared to go unquestioned. Tempers were often short. A patient who had not heard a call for medication would be roundly excoriated, and the morning attendants would often wake patients with, "Come on, you m—— f——s, out of bed!"

Neither anecdotal nor "hard" data can convey the overwhelming sense of powerlessness which invades the individual as he is continually exposed to the depersonalization of the psychiatric hospital....

Powerlessness was evident everywhere. The patient is deprived of many of his legal rights by dint of his psychiatric commitment.[12] He is shorn of credibility by virtue of his psychiatric label. His freedom of movement is restricted. He cannot initiate contact with the staff, but may only respond to such overtures as they make. Personal privacy is minimal. Patient quarters and possessions can be entered and examined by any staff member, for whatever reason. His personal history and anguish is available to any staff member (often including the "grey lady" and "candy striper" volunteer) who chooses to read his folder, regardless of their therapeutic relationship to him. His personal hygiene and waste evacuation are often monitored. The [toilets] may have no doors.

At times, depersonalization reached such proportions that pseudopatients had the sense that they were invisible, or at least unworthy of account. Upon being admitted, I and other pseudopatients took the initial physical examinations in a semipublic room, where staff members went about their own business as if we were not there.

On the ward, attendants delivered verbal and occasionally serious physical abuse to patients in the presence of other observing patients, some of whom (the pseudopatients) were writing it all down. Abusive behavior, on the other hand, terminated quite abruptly when other staff members were known to be coming. Staff are credible witnesses. Patients are not.

A nurse unbuttoned her uniform to adjust her brassiere in the presence of an entire ward of viewing men. One did not have the sense that she was being seductive. Rather, she didn't notice us. A group of staff persons might point to a patient in the dayroom and discuss him animately, as if he were not there.

One illuminating instance of depersonalization and invisibility occurred with regard to medications. All told, the pseudopatients were administered nearly 2100 pills....Only two were swallowed. The rest were either pocketed or deposited in the toilet. The pseudopatients were not alone in this. Although I have no precise records on how many patients rejected their medications, the pseudopatients frequently found the medication of other patients in the toilet before they deposited their own. As long as they were cooperative, their behavior and the pseudopatients' own in this matter, as in other important matters, went unnoticed throughout.

Reactions to such depersonalization among pseudopatients were intense. Although they had come to the hospital as participant observers and were fully aware that they did not "belong," they nevertheless found themselves caught up in and fighting the process of depersonalization...

The Consequences of Labeling and Depersonalization

Whenever the ratio of what is known to what needs to be known approaches zero, we tend to invent "knowledge" and assume that we understand more than we actually do. We seem unable to acknowledge that we simply don't know. The needs for diagnosis and remediation of behavioral and emotional problems are enormous. But rather than acknowledge that we are just embarking on understanding, we continue to label patients "schizophrenic," "manic-depressive," and "insane," as if in those words we had captured the essence of understanding. The facts of the matter are that we have known for a long time that diagnoses are often not useful or reliable, but we have nevertheless continued to use them. We know now that we cannot distinguish insanity from sanity. It is depressing to consider how that information will be used.

Not merely depressing, but frightening. How many people, one wonders, are sane but not recognized as such in our psychiatric institutions? How many have been needlessly stripped of their privileges of citizenship, from the right to vote and drive to that of handling their own accounts? How many have feigned insanity in order to avoid the criminal consequences of their behavior, and conversely, how many would rather stand trial than live interminably in a psychiatric hospital—but are wrongly thought to be mentally ill? How many have been stigmatized by well-intentioned, but nevertheless erroneous, diagnoses?...[P]sychiatric diagnoses are rarely found to be in error. The label sticks, a mark of inadequacy forever.

Finally, how many patients might be "sane" outside the psychiatric hospital but seem insane in it—not because craziness resides in them, as it were, but because they are responding to a bizarre setting, one that might be unique to institutions which harbor nether people? Goffman (1961) calls the process of socialization to such institutions "mortification"—an apt metaphor that includes the processes of depersonalization that have been described here. And while it is impossible to know whether the pseudopatients' responses to these processes are characteristic of all inmates—they were, after all, not real patients—it is difficult to believe that these processes of socialization to a psychiatric hospital provide useful attitudes or habits of response for living in the "real world."

REFERENCES

Ash, P. 1949. *Journal of Abnormal Psychology*, 44:272.

Beck, A.T. 1962. *American Journal of Psychiatry*, 119:210.

Becker, H. 1963. *Outsiders: Studies in the Sociology of Deviance.* New York: Free Press.

Benedict, R. 1934. *General Psychology*, 10:59.

Boisen, A.T. 1938. *Psychiatry*, 2:233.

Braginsky, B.M. D.D. Braginsky, and K. Ring. 1969. *Methods of Madness: The Mental Hospital as a Last Resort.* New York: Holt, Rinehart, & Winston.

Crocetti, G.M. and P.V. Lemkau. 1965. *American Sociological Review*, 30:577.

Cumming, J. and E. Cumming. 1965. *Community Mental Health*, 1:135.

Farina, A. and K. Ring. 1965. *Journal of Abnormal Psychology*, 70:47.

Freeman, H. E. and O.G. Simmons. 1963. *The Mental Patient Comes Home.* New York: Wiley.

Goffman, E. 1964. *Behavior in Public Places.* New York: Free Press.

Gove, W.R. 1970. *American Sociological Review*, 35:873.

Hollingshead, A.B. and F.C. Redlich. 1958. *Social Class and Mental Illness: A Community Study.* New York: Wiley.

Johansen, W.J. 1969. *Mental Hygiene*, 53:218.

Kreitman, N. 1961. *Journal of Mental Science*, 107:876.

Kreitman, N., P. Salisbury, J. Towers, J. Scrivner, 1938. *Psychiatry*, 107:887.

Laing, R.D. 1960. *The Divided Self: A Study of Sanity and Madness.* Chicago: Quadrangle.

Lisky, A.S. 1970. *Social Psychiatry*, 5:166.

Phillips, D.L. 1963. *American Sociological Review*, 28:963.

Phillips, L. and J.G. Draguns. 1971. *Annual Review of Psychology*, 22:447.

Rosenthal, R. and L. Jacobson. 1968. *Pygmalian in the Classroom.* New York: Holt, Rinehart, & Winston.

Sarbin, T.R. 1972. *Psychology Today*, 6:18.

Schmitt, H.O. and C.P. Fonda. 1956. *Journal of Abnormal Social Psychology*, 52:262.

Schur, E. 1969. *American Journal of Sociology.* 75:309.

Seeman, W. 1953. *Journal of Nervous and Mental Disorders.* 118:541.

Szasz, T. 1963. *Law, Liberty, and Psychiatry.* New York: MacMillan.

——————.1963. *The Myth of Mental Illness: Foundations of a Theory of Mental Illness.* New York: Hoeber Harper.

Wexler, D.B. and S.E. Scoville. 1971. *Arizona Law Review*, 13:1.

Zubin, J. 1967. *Annual Review of Psychology*, 18:373.

NOTES

[1] For an analysis of these artifacts and summaries of the disputes, see J. Zubin (1967:373); L. Phillips and J.G. Draguns, (1971:447).

[2] See in this regard H. Becker (1963); B.M. Braginsky, D.D. Braginsky, K. Ring, (1969); G.M. Grocetti and P.V. Lemkau, (1965:577); E. Goffman (1964); R.D. Laing (1960); D.L. Philips, (1963:963); T.R. Sarbin, (1972:18); E. Schur, (1969:309); T. Szasz, (1963); For a critique of these views, see W.R. Gove (1970:873).

[3] E. Goffman (1961).

[4] T.J. Scheff, (1966).

[5] Data from a ninth pseudopatient are not incorporated in this report because, although his sanity went undetected, he falsified aspects of his personal history, including his marital status and parental relationships. His experimental behaviors therefore were not identical to those of the other pseudopatients.

⁶Beyond the personal difficulties that the pseudopatient is likely to experience in the hospital, there are legal and social ones that, combined, require considerable attention before entry. For example, once admitted to a psychiatric institution, it is difficult, if not impossible, to be discharged on short notice, state law to the contrary notwithstanding. I was not sensitive to these difficulties at the outset of the project, nor to the personal and situational emergencies that can arise, but later a writ of habeas corpus was prepared for each of the entering pseudopatients and an attorney was kept "on call" during every hospitalization. I am grateful to John Kaplan and Robert Bartels for legal advice and assistance in these matters.

⁷However distasteful such concealment is, it was a necessary first step to examining these questions. Without concealment, there would have been no way to know how valid these experiences were; nor was there any way of knowing whether whatever detections occurred were a tribute to the diagnostic acumen of the staff or to the hospital's rumor network. Obviously, since my concerns are general ones that cut across individual hospitals and staffs, I have respected their anonymity and have eliminated clues that might lead to their identification.

⁸Interestingly, of the 12 admissions, 11 were diagnosed as schizophrenic and one, with identical symptomatology, as manic-depressive psychosis. This diagnosis has a more favorable prognosis and it was given by the only private hospital in our sample. On the relations between social class and psychiatric diagnosis, see A.B. Hollingshead and F.C. Redlich (1958).

⁹It is possible, of course, that patients have quite broad latitudes in diagnosis and therefore are inclined to call many people sane, even those whose behavior is patently aberrant. However, although we have no hard data on this matter, it was our distinct impression that this was not the case. In many instances, patients not only signaled us out for attention, but came to imitate our behaviors and styles.

¹⁰J. Cumming and E. Cumming, (1965:135); A. Farina and K. Ring, 1965:47); H.E. Freeman and O.G. Simmons (1963); W.J. Johannsen, (1969:218); A.S. Linsky, (1970:166).

¹¹For an example of similar self-fulfilling prophecy, in this instance dealing with the "central" trait of intelligence, see R. Rosenthal and L. Jacobson (1968).

¹²D.B. Wexler and S.E. Scoville (1971:1).

Part VII

ORGANIZING DEVIANTS—
SUBCULTURES AND DEVIANT ACTIVITIES

In this section, we shall examine the social worlds and activities of various deviants. It is important to note that in the case of deviant careers, there is no single natural history; rather there exist numerous career histories. One possible career might proceed in the following manner. An individual engages in certain acts which are observed by others and officially labelled as deviant. This person is then processed through one of the various social control agencies discussed in Section VI which function to strip the person of his old identity and social status, and force him to accept a new identity and social status—as a deviant. When the individual is released or discharged from the organization or institution, he may find that normal channels are cut off. The person possesses a stigma which limits his further participation in society. This social processing then, propels the individual underground into an organized deviant lifestyle.

A second possible career path might proceed as follows: the individual interacts with other deviants and is recruited directly into the deviant world where he is resocialized to adopt the ideology or worldview of the group, its norms and values, and a new identity and social status within the group. Moreover, the person learns by virtue of participation in the group the necessary skills to engage in deviant behavior. This is not to imply that deviant careers only fit one of the above patterns; deviant careers vary so much so that an individual might enter his career at a certain stage, exit, re-enter, move forward and backward, or may leave the career altogether.

Deviant Subcultures

A deviant subculture refers to the shared ways of thinking, feeling and acting that members of a group have developed for engaging in deviant behavior, for organizing relations among themselves, and between themselves and "normals," and for defending themselves against social punishments. Members employ these ideas, techniques and stratagems in order to successfully negotiate social situations and identities.

A deviant subculture may share certain majority elements (norms, values) with the larger society, but there may be other elements that they do not share. In the rugby subculture, for example, this group shares certain elements of the dominant culture such as, it is wrong to steal or commit murder. But this subcultural formation is different from the larger culture regarding the treatment of women and their attitudes toward certain acts. For example, this group condones such behaviors as fighting, brawling with opposing teams, public urination, sexual harassment of women, the handling of team members' genitalia, and ostracism of team members. A subculture then, grows out of group membership and defines a set of norms, beliefs and practices. Subcultures specify and define for members what the rules are and what the roles are. In the case of the latter, the prostitution subculture defines four types of customers, the role of the pimp, prostitute and the police.

The various rules specify how to behave, how to execute the deviant act, how to interact with "normals" or "straights" and with other deviants; The subculture also provides members with rules for either avoiding or managing the consequences of deviance (i.e., what to do if caught by the police). Moreover, subcultures provide members with a set of motives or rationales for engaging in deviant acts. In the case of the nudist subculture, their norms include: no unnatural covering of the body, no touching, no staring and no cameras. The rationale for being a nudist is that is a healthy and liberating lifestyle. In Herman's study on subcultures of ex-psychiatric patients entitled, *"The Mixed Nutters and Looney Tuners,"* their norms centered around various socializing activities, therapeutic activities, and activities for "making it on the outside"—stratagems of earning money such as prostitution, and selling their "meds."

Deviant subcultures are highly-varied in nature. They possess various types of boundaries. Some subcultures possess spatial or territorial boundaries. For example, in the case of the nudist subculture, the boundaries are sharply-defined. Individuals can freely walk around nude within the confines of the camp, but not outside. Motorcycle gangs also have sharply-defined territories or turfs in which to carry out their deviant activities.

Boundaries may also be temporal in nature. A subculture can be said to exist at one abstract level and exist continuously, or, it may also exist on another level, only at specified times. Laud Humphrey's and Fred Desroches' studies on "Tearoom" activities—impersonal homosexual behavior in public toilets, illustrates that this subculture exists largely before work, at noon hours, and after work.

Subcultures not only vary spatially and temporally, but also in terms of their elaborateness and scope. For example, in the "Tearoom" there are basically six social roles: (1) the inserter, (2) the insertee, (3) straights, (4) watchers, (5) masturbators and (6) voyeurs. By contrast, other subcultures, such as the Mafia have a highly-developed hierarchy with elaborate social roles.

Subcultures are centered around various interests or patterns of behavior. The skid row subculture or "bottle gang" centers around "booze" or alcohol, and their behavior focuses on this need, looking for a supply to drink, how to cooperate and share it with others, and the manner by which monetary contributions are solicited from others (Rubington, 1982). The behavior of drug addicts similarly centers on obtaining money to purchase the drugs, the procurement of crack, heroin, cocaine etc., and finding a safe place to get high.

Each subculture needs a number of "tools" or "props" in order to carry out their main interests. Skid row alcoholics need such props as inexpensive, fortified wines. When the liquor stores are closed, they may need to enlist the aid of bootleggers in order to supply the booze. When neither option is available, the "skidder" may get his alcohol from paint thinners, vanilla extract, shoe polish or lysol. Similarly, delinquent gangs need such props as guns, knives, chains and lead pipes in order to carry other their deviant activities.

Another characteristic of deviant subcultures is their "argot." Each deviant group develops a special type of language that distinguishes veterans from newcomers, and insiders from outsiders. More importantly, it prescribes symbols for talking and thinking about matters of common interest. For example, *"making the run"* for the bottle gang refers to going off to buy a bottle of booze for the group. The *"runner"* is the person who goes for the bottle. Similarly, in Herman's study of the "Mixed Nutters" and Looney Tuners", *"plucking the rooster"* refers to receiving handouts from clergymen or agents; and *"doing the groceries"* refers to shoplifting activities.

Further, each subculture develops an ideology—an organized set of ideas that suits the interests of the group and justifies their actions. This ideology mitigates their blameworthiness and calls attention to the deviance of seemingly-respectable individuals. For example, the ideology of the bottle gang, provides members with a set of justifications about excessive drinking as a positive, acceptable activity and points to the hidden alcoholism on the part of judges and police officers. The ideology of the "Mixed Nutters" and "Looney Tuners" provides members with a perspective on themselves and their relations with "normal others," a set of ideas repudiating conventional, stereotypical attitudes about the mentally ill, and a set of justifications for engaging in deviant activities.

A final characteristic of deviant subcultures involves providing positive, non-deviant self-images and self-conceptions for its members. Subcultures, through their participation, provide their charges with more respectable, positive self-images, identities and self-conceptions, one that may refute stereotypical conceptions about them. The ex-mental patient subculture, for example, provides such a function for its members.

Why do deviant subcultures come into existence? Subcultures arise when individuals begin interacting with one another, realize that they share similar social fates, social problems, possess the same stigmatizing attribute or merely share the same interests in some deviant activity. Individuals band together in order to avoid further stigma, manage their deviant identities, avoid social punishments, develop definitive solutions to the various problems they are experiencing, or to engage in deviant behavior and not be caught.

In the case of the drug addict subculture, this subcultural formation arose to solve the problem of where to get a supply of drugs, how much to pay for it, where to get high and not be caught. Similarly, the "Mixed Nutters" and "Looney Tuners" arose in order to combat the problems of stigma, exploitation, social isolation, poverty and coping.

The readings by Herman, Tewksbury, Lozano and Foltz, Muzzatti, and Monti, all deal with different deviant subcultures.

As previously mentioned, Herman's paper, "'*Mixed Nutters and Looney Tuners:' The Emergence, Development, Nature and Functions of Two Informal Deviant Subcultures of Chronic Ex-Psychiatric Patients,*" addresses many of the ideas discussed above. Her study focuses on the rise of two subcultures of discharged, ex-psychiatric clients and the various positive and negative functions and these subcultural formations serve for their members.

The second selection by Richard Tewksbury deals with the subculture of female impersonators. In "*Constructing Women and Their World: The Subculture of Female*

Impersonation," the author examines the structure of this subcultural formation, a community that developed as a consequence of stigmatization. Tewksbury provides a detailed, analytic discussion of the characteristics of this subculture, its ideology, norms, attitudes and values—all of which differ widely from those of the cultural mainstream. As the author notes, this subculture of female impersonators is a socially-constructed phenomenon, built as a result of the reactions of both community insiders as well as outsiders. This subculture then develops as a consequence of stigmatization, restricted and patterned relationships, a shared sense of identity and common social fates.

The third selection by Wendy Lozano and Tanice Foltz, "*Into the Darkness: An Ethnographic Study of Witchcraft and Death*" deals with the social world of a subculture of radical, feminist witches. In particular, the authors focus on the beliefs, ideology, values, social activities, norms, roles and various functions that this subcultural formation provides for its members. Lozano and Foltz provide an analytic description of the major elements of the Dianic tradition of Wicca or Witchcraft which interprets death as an integral component of the life cycle.

Our next article deals with the subculture of young, urban motorcyclists. In "*The Urban Speed Gang*," Steve Muzzatti discusses the nature, characteristic traits, norms and values of this subcultural formation—the latter, many of which parallel the larger culture. Moreover, the author discusses the recruitment patterns and entry patterns into this group—how and why riders are attracted to this existing group, and their ideological beliefs and values.

Daniel J. Monti, in "*The Culture of Gangs in the Culture of the School*," explores the relationship between gangs as a subculture within the culture of the school. Monti illustrates how subcultural gangs, their norms, values, ideological beliefs, activities and roles can function within the *limits* imposed by the official school culture. The gang subculture in schools parallel the culture endorsed by adults who are officially in control of the setting. As Monti notes, the two cultures do not directly clash but rather "bump"—a bumping that allows the adults to continue their routines and ignore the influence of the gangs. The gang subculture is an expression of the dialectic existing between the school and the community in which it is entrenched.

Deviant Activities

Just as we may learn a great deal from an examination of the social organization of deviants, we may also profit by focussing on the behaviors and activities themselves. Deviant acts vary widely as you can probably well imagine. Some acts may be carried out over a period of several years or even over a lifetime; others, may be engaged in for several months; and still others, may only be carried out one time.

Certain deviant activities can be carried out by a solitary individual, that is, without the presence or assistance of another. Examples of individual deviance include: check forging, committing suicide, baby snatching, drug addiction, and body piercing.

By contrast, other deviant activities require the presence and assistance of two or more individuals. Such cooperative activity may involve providing deviant services to others, the transfer of various deviant items such as drugs or firearms, and the exchange of money. In other cases, various items or goods are exchanged. Sometimes, individuals engaging in these deviant activities may earn a living through such means.

Craig J. Forsyth's *"Parade Strippers: A Note on Being Naked in Public"* provides an excellent illustration of cooperative deviant activities not involving the transfer of monetary funds. Rather, females expose their breasts in exchange for glass beads, trinkets or "throws" thrown from parade floats during Mardi Gras. Forsyth obtained data from 54 men who rode parade floats and from 51 women who exposed themselves. Conceived of as "creative deviance," parade stripping has become so commonplace in New Orleans that those who expose themselves are referred to as "beadwhores." The author compares this phenomenon to other exhibitionist practices such as: nudism, mooning, nude sunbathing and streaking. The motives for engaging in such behavior, and the functions it provides for the participants are addressed.

A second example of cooperative deviance not involving money can be found in Frederick Desroches' *"Policing Morality: Impersonal Sex in Public Places."* In this paper, the author presents an update of Laud T. Humphrey's famous study on impersonal sex in "tearooms," which was conducted in the late 1960's. While Humphrey conducted his study in the United States, Desroches gathered data in Canada. Desroches' paper is illustrative of the territoriality and temporality of deviant subcultures. He begins by discussing the nature and characteristics of the participants who frequent tearooms, the norms of the group, the various roles, and the stratagems used by participants. Similar to Humphrey's study, the author found that participants took one of six roles in the tearoom: inserter, insertee, straight, watcher, masturbator, or voyeur. In contrast to Humphrey's sample, teenagers did not participate in these activities. Those participating abided by a number of strictly enforced norms which include: (1) not undressing or engaging in anal sex; (2) ceasing sex when someone enters the tearoom; (3) not ordinarily approaching straight men; (4) communicating with others largely through non-verbal cues; (5) reading and writing of homosexual graffiti; (6) no interaction with participants outside of the tearoom; (7) no violation of anonymity; (9) brief sexual encounters; (10) individuals departing the tearoom separately, with the inserter leaving first.

Further, Desroches addresses the motives of individuals to participate in these activities in such a setting. For closet gays or bisexual, this activity proves to be exciting and stimulating, when still remaining hidden. Tearooms, thus, allow them to keep their gay urges private and lead "normal" straight lives on the outside. For primarily heterosexual men, the impersonal nature of this behavior, allows individuals to protect their self-concept; such acts involve no emotional commitment, and very limited physical involvement on the part of participants. For certain others, the tearoom is the only source of sexual gratification or an alternative source of gratification for them.

The article by Steven Worden and Donna Darden entitled, *"Knives and Gaffs: Definitions in the Deviant World of Cockfighting,"* centers on the cooperative activity of cockfighting. The authors discuss the social meanings that participants give to the artificial spurs or heels—social objects with meanings, typifications and lines of action. Worden and Darden address the differences in belief systems between the "traditional cockers" and the "knife fighters," and how joint action in a cockfight unfolds within the larger context defined by various participants.

REFERENCES

Rubington, Earl, 1982. "Deviant Subcultures." Pp. 42–70 In M. Michael Rosenberg, R. Stebbins, and A. Turowetz, eds., *The Sociology of Deviance*. New York: St. Martin's.

Chapter 29

"MIXED NUTTERS" AND "LOONEY TUNERS:"
THE EMERGENCE, DEVELOPMENT, NATURE, AND FUNCTIONS
OF TWO INFORMAL, DEVIANT SUBCULTURES OF CHRONIC,
EX-PSYCHIATRIC PATIENTS

Nancy J. Herman

INTRODUCTION

In the sociological literature on deviant subcultures, much attention has been devoted to the drug subculture (Burr, 1984; Johnson, 1980; Lipton and Johnson, 1980; Ray, 1961), the gay subculture (Humphreys and Miller, 1980; Partridge, 1972), the motorcycle gang subculture (Hopper and Moore, 1980), the delinquent subculture (Cohen, 1979: Demotte, 1984; Yablonsky, 1959), the skid row subculture (Rubington, 1968; Wallace, 1965), the inmate subculture (Webb, 1984); religious subcultures (Lofland, 1966; Melville, 1972), and even the suicide subculture (Platt, 1981) among others.

Despite the preponderance of sociological research on such diverse, deviant groups, and the concomitant theoretical approaches[1] used to explain such phenomena little if any use has been made of such works in the examination of discharged/ deinstitutionalized psychiatric patients.[2]

Over the past twenty-five years, with the movement toward deinstitutionalization and development of community psychiatry, there has been a marked shift *away* from the hospital *to* the community.[3] As a result of the movement toward deinstitutionalization, hundreds of thousands of persons once institutionalized for long periods of time in mental hospitals in the United States, Canada, and Great Britain, have been released into the community. Moreover, with this shift in policy and treatment of the mentally ill, newly-diagnosed or defined psychiatric patients, are no longer being sent directly to government or state institutions. Rather, they are being treated primarily on an out-patient basis in community mental health centers or are admitted on a short-term basis to psychiatric wards in general hospital facilities, and are only admitted to mental institutions or "tertiary care facilities" as a *last resort*.

Since the advent of the movement toward deinstitutionalization and development of community psychiatry, abounding in the literature are studies examining its ideological foundations, background philosophies, treatment programs, and the medical psychological consequences of such treatment and aftercare programs for the ex-psychiatric patients.[4] Although a multitude of research studies exist on various aspects of the deinstitutionalization phenomenon and development of community psychiatry, the majority of such works have been conducted from an objectivist standpoint largely employing medical, psychiatric, psychological or social work models, with only a dearth of ethnographically-based research (Cheadle et al., 1978; Dear et al., 1980; Estroff, 1981; Reynolds and Farberow, 1977) focussing on the effects of deinstitutionalization/discharge from the perspectives of the ex-patients themselves. Moreover, no published work has been located documenting the origins and development of an informal deviant subculture of chronic[5] ex-psychiatric patients.

It is the purpose of this paper then, to explore the effects of deinstitutionalization from the perspectives of chronic discharged psychiatric patients, individuals who are directly affected by this shift in treatment, housing and policies. Adopting a symbolic interactionist perspective, this study seeks to discover the social meanings that the ex-patients define and determine to be important and real. Specifically, this paper examines the ex-patient subculture[6]—one major organizational adaptive response former chronic ex-patients develop and utilize to deal with their "deviantness", the structural and interactional factors giving rise to this formation, its characteristic traits, and the functions it serves for its members.

The Effects of Deinstitutionalization on Chronic Ex-Psychiatric Patients: The Stigma of Mental Illness, Deviant Identities and Adaptive Responses

In other papers, this author (Herman, 1993, 1986a, 1986b) systematically examined the post-hospital social worlds of 285 non-chronic[7] and chronic ex-psychiatric patients. Specifically, this research examined the relationship among the concepts of stigma, deviant identities, stigma management strategies/adaptive responses, and identity transformation as they related to non-chronic and chronic cases. The data indicated that, in the case of the former group, namely, the non-chronics, upon discharge, such persons actively sought to return to a life of normality. Such persons conceived of their acquired deviant identities as "temporary fixtures," a perception of self influenced not only by the nature, duration and type of psychiatric treatment received, but also, by the type of psychiatric label bestowed on them, and the minimal numbers and dosages of medications they were taking. Moreover, the data suggested that non-chronic ex-patients employed five major "offensive" stratagems or adaptive responses to mitigate the stigma potential of mental illness on their daily rounds: selective concealment, preventive telling, therapeutic telling, normalization and political activism—strategies having positive implications for identity transformation. By contrast, in the case of the latter group, the chronics, the data indicated that, such persons, upon completion of their hospitalization, made little or no attempt to return to a life of normality. Given that such persons had been hospitalized for a number of years,[8] or on a multitude of occasions[9], they had fully internalized the role of mental patient and its corresponding status. Such a perception of self as possessing a permanent deviant identity was reinforced by the types of deviant labels bestowed on them while institutionalized, the great number and dosages of medications they were receiving (and their associated side-effects), and the "disability" cheques they were receiving. In contrast to many non-chronics in the research, who received positive support from family and friends, most chronics interviewed were stigmatized by such persons. The only social ties chronic ex-patients had were with one or two other ex-patients. In an attempt to avoid further or potential stigma from others, such persons adopted the following "defensive" stratagems or adaptive responses: "institutional retreatism," "societal retreatism," capitulation and passing—strategies having negative implications for identity transformation. Just as the chronic ex-patients made use of the above individual stigma management techniques, so too, did they develop and utilize one other such technique, specifically an organizational stratagem of stigma management. It is this stratagem or organizational adaptive response[10] to which this paper will now turn.

Methodology, Sample and Settings

Data were collected from December, 1981 to June, 1984 by means of participant observation and informal interviewing with ninety-seven chronic ex-psychiatric patients living in two cities in Southern Ontario, Canada.

As part of a larger, ongoing study, the researcher initially obtained a disproportionate, stratified random sample[11] of two hundred and eighty-five chronic and non-chronic ex-psychiatric patients living in eight communities in Southern Ontario. Through semi-formal and informal interviewing with the respondents, this researcher came upon, quite by accident, the discovery of two informal ex-psychiatric patient subcultures, referred to here as the "Mixed Nutters" and "Looney Tuners."

In terms of the former, this cultural formation is comprised of forty-nine members (thirty-six males and thirteen females) living in rooming houses, boarding homes and cheap hotels in the Southwest section of a large metropolitan city of 2.5 million. Subjects ranged in age from twenty-one to forty-two years of age, were predominantly from working-class backgrounds and were poorly-educated with a mean level of educational attainment being grade seven.

In terms of the latter group, this subculture is comprised of forty-eight members (twenty-six males and twenty-two females) living in boarding homes, rooming houses, in missions, or simply on the streets in the northern section of a smaller city of 300,000 in Southern Ontario. Similar to the Mixed Nutters, the Looney Tuners were also poorly-educated with a mean level of educational attainment being grade eight, were from working and middle-class backgrounds and ranged in age from twenty-two to forty-five.

The Emergence of Two Informal Ex-Psychiatric Patient Subcultures

Early subcultural theorists (Gans, 1962; Gillen, 1955; Lewis, 1961) contended that deviant subcultures emerge largely in response to particular problems or social situations. Speaking on the subculture of poverty, Lewis (1961:27) argues that:

> Many of the traits of the subculture of poverty can be viewed as attempts
> at local solutions for problems not met by existing institutions and
> agencies because the people are not eligible for them, cannot afford them,
> or are suspicious of them.

In a similar vein, Gans (1962:248) argues:

> Each subculture is an organized set of related responses that has developed out of people's efforts to cope with the opportunities, incentives, and rewards, as well as the deprivations, prohibitions, and pressures which the natural environment and society—that complex of coexisting and competing subcultures—offer to them.

Reacting against this primary emphasis on *response* to the neglect of secondary role of interaction as having importance for the development of subcultures, other theorists (Becker, 1963; Cohen, 1955; Hughes, 1961; Shibutani, 1955; and Wallace, 1965), proposed an alternative explanation that places equal importance on *both* factors for subcultural development. Wallace (1965:149); speaking on the emergence of the skid row subculture, for example, states:

> One effect of the self and community imposed isolation [of skid row persons] has been the emergence of skid row subculture. Skid rowers share similar problems of adjustment to their deviance and are in effective interaction with one another.

Cohen (1955), in his systematic attempt to develop a theory of subcultures, states that the following conditions are important in the development of this cultural form: (1) experiencing a problem or set of problems; (2) communicating such problems; (3) effectively interacting over an extended period of time with like others on the basis of such problems; and (4) developing solutions to these common problems.

In the case of the Mixed Nutters and Looney Tuners, the data suggest that these ex-psychiatric patient subcultures emerged in 1978 and 1980 respectively.[12] Prior to their formation, chronic ex-psychiatric patients were experiencing a number of post-hospital problems. These problems included: the stigma of mental illness, social isolation, poverty, exploitation, and coping. Speaking on the problems of isolation and poverty, a male ex-patient states:

> It's been the shits ever since I got out [of the hospital]. They plunk you in this room. . . you're all alone with no friends in the world, and you get this disability cheque every month most of which goes for rent. You hardly get enough left over to buy a cup of coffee or some smokes.

Another ex-patient, speaking of the stigma of mental illness and problems of exploitation says:

> Since I was let out, I've had nothing but heartache. Having mental illness is like having the Black Plague. People who know me have abandoned me—my family and friends. And the people who find out that I was in the mental center. . .treat me the same way. . .And at the boarding home where I was placed, I hardly get enough to eat. For lunch and supper today, all we got was a half a sardine sandwich and a cup of coffee. And

they take three-hundred and fifty dollars a month for that kind of meals and lousy, overcrowded, bug-infested rooms to live in.

● The ex-psychiatric patient subcultures came into being when the individuals began communicating with one another and realizing that they had a number of problems in common, they shared a common fate of being "in the same boat." Speaking on his discovery of others experiencing the same problems in the community, an ex-patient says:

> It was really by accident that I came to realize that I wasn't the only one but there with these horrid problems. For the longest time, I just kept it inside, but then one day when I was so down in the dumps, so low, that I opened up to "Cliff," this patient I met in the park, and we started talking. I took a chance and opened up, and to my surprise, I found that he was also going through the same problems.

Analysis of the data indicates that, subsequent to this initial communication of their problem(s) with others, individuals began interacting with one another over an extended period of time on the basis of their newly-discovered shared fate:

> The four of us girls came clean with each other in October. I mean that this day outside the drop-in center we opened up and told our true feelings about some of the problems we faced every day since being discharged. . .From that time on, us girls, and later more people, made a pact to meet every Tuesday and Thursday outside "Lacey's" Department Store where we'd gab and bitch, and just plain listen to each other's problems.

Out of this semi-regular interaction with others of their own kind, chronic ex-psychiatric patients attempt to develop solutions to the various problems they are collectively experiencing. Speaking of their initial efforts to come up with a solution to the problems of the stigma of mental illness, two middle-aged males state:

> At first, we thought that we should buy a gun, load it, and blast anyone who reacted meanly to us because of our sickness. But we knew that we'd only wind up in jail. We also thought about suicide as an answer to our problem, but that's the coward's way out. So we kept thinking and thinking until we figured out something less drastic!

In a similar vein, three young males, discussing their attempts to develop solutions to the problem of poverty, remark:

> We wanted to rob a Brink's truck or some big department store but that would be too risky. We were just tossing around ideas trying to come up with some solution to give us some cash. Eventually, we came up with a better and easier way to make a buck that is a lot less risky, by selling our meds to guys on the streets.

In short then, the data analysis reveals that certain interactional and structural factors contribute to the rise of the ex-mental patient subculture. This subcultural formation arises essentially in response to the various problems and negative post-hospital situations collectively faced by a number of chronic ex-patients, insofar as they are able to effectively communicate and interact with one another over an extended period of time. Given that, upon discharge, these ex-psychiatric patients are "placed" in rooming houses, boarding homes and "approved homes" in specific geographical sections of the city, such concentrated placement in specific neighborhoods increases the probability of social interaction among ex-patients. When ex-psychiatric patients have the opportunity to interact with one another, they are more likely to develop a subculture to deal with such specific problems as poverty , exploitation, stigma, social isolation, and in general, with problems developing out of the discrepancies between their personal perceptions of mental illness and mental patients, and the stereotypical perceptions held by society.

The Social Characteristics of The Mixed Nutters and Looney Tuners

As noted earlier, chronic ex-psychiatric patients have one thing in common: their deviant attribute (and the problems associated with it). Such things give chronic ex-patients a sense of a common fate. It is from this feeling of a shared fate that the Mixed Nutters and Looney Tuners have developed subcultures consisting of: a set of perspectives or world-view about the nature of society, its members, and how to deal with them, and a body of activities based on this world-view, some of which are specifically centered on providing solutions to the problems associated with the attribute of mental illness. These deviant subcultures possess five major characteristics to which attention will now turn.

1. Behavioral Patterns

The ex-mental patient subculture centers its attention, interests and activities around their deviant attribute, and the problems associated with it. Specifically, the Mixed Nutters and Looney Tuners participate in three major activities referred to by the subjects as: (1) "Hanging Around"; (2) "Shrink Sessions"; (3) "Schooling". The data indicate that a major portion of the chronic ex-patients' day is spent usually at a specified location such as a park, shopping center, street corner, donut shop or hospital canteen:

> Every day, after I get kicked out the boarding home, I go up town to a bench in front of "Meadville" Shopping Center and meet a few of the "boys." We're "regulars" you might say. We usually hang around four or five hours watching the people go by, cracking jokes, and rolling our smokes. The day goes by quick when you got someone to share it with.

Similarly, another ex-patient, discussing the activity of "hanging around" remarks:

> There's three, four or sometimes even six of us that meet every day. It's not always the same crowd though. Each day, different faces show up at the "Delicious" Donut Shop...It's our second home and that's why we do our hanging around there. We scrape up our money and drink coffee until we got no more left and Gus, the owner "invites" us to leave.

In order to be allowed to "hang around" in such locations as donut shops or hospital canteens, it is a prerequisite that ex-patients purchase (and continue to purchase) food and/or drink. For those ex-patients unable to purchase items on their own, other group member make contributions, thus enabling them to remain with the others:

> When people don't have enough money to pay for a cup of coffee, or a donut, we chip in to make up the difference. I may give a nickel, another guy may give two cents, but little by little, it all adds up. We give whatever we got. And I know that if I am short of cash next week that the guys would do the same for me!

The activity of "hanging around" or being in the company of other ex-psychiatric patients serves to combat feelings of alienation, social isolation and fear experienced by such persons. As one middle-aged male put it:

> We don't really do anything constructive when hanging around on Elm Street; I mean, we don't have intellectual debates about Regan or Russia, but meeting with people at a certain place every day and having them just sit next to me helps me not to feel so alone in the world.

Similarly, a second chronic ex-patient adds:

> When we're together, it really boosts me up! We support each other. I feel comfortable with them and they really care about what happens in my life. That makes all the difference in the world. They're my friends.

A second major activity in which chronic ex-psychiatric patients engage are "Shrink Sessions." Shrink sessions or primitive, informal self-help meetings, usually occur (in case of the Mixed Nutters) at the hospital canteen where ex-patients frequent or at a drop-in center for discharged patients (in case of the Looney Tuners). Such meetings vary in duration from a half an hour up to three hours with members coming and going throughout. The data indicate that the sessions begin when an individual initiates the topic of conversation and petitions others for advice. During these sessions, members of the subculture complain about such problems as anxiety, stress, depression and poor follow-up care by psychiatric professionals. So too, do ex-patients "experts" supportively respond. Speaking of post-hospital anxiety and stress in his life and the helpful suggestions proposed by the group, one chronic male remarks:

When we sit down and start "shrinking" each other, I sometimes talk about how tense and nervous I get being out [discharged]. Everything is moving at such a fast pace that it freaks me out. There's too much stress for me...When I talked about it to the other guys, it felt so good to let it all out, and the guys really helped me get a handle on it...They really know about these things, because, after all, they've been through it themselves a hundred times before.

Another ex-patient, speaking of airing, to the group, the problems he was experiencing with stigma, states:

One day, I brought up the fact that we've all got the mark of Cain on us because of our sickness. I poured my guts out about how my wife and even my parents turned away from me, and how no one wants anything to do with me now...Talking about it made me feel better. They hammered into me the idea that having mental illness isn't nothing to be ashamed of. They made me think more highly of myself, and they showed me how to avoid people who are biggotted about mental illness!

These "shrink sessions" then, serve a three-fold function for the ex-psychiatric patients: disclosure of concerns and complaints in a cathartic fashion, serves to alleviate a portion of the burden of their loads; ex-patients are given social support and helpful suggestions to deal with various problems; and they are presented with an ideology and positive self-image of ex-psychiatric patient that refutes stereotypical beliefs about mental patients held by conventional society, thereby elevating their self-esteem.

Just as chronic ex-psychiatric patients frequently engage in the activities of "hanging around" and "shrink sessions", so too do they participate in one other activity referred to by the subjects as "schooling." Schooling involves ex-patients teaching each other various methods for "making it on the outside" or how to capitalize[13] on their deviant identities. By making it on the outside, ex-patients, through informal interaction with other subcultural members, learn how to make the most of their deviant identities. They are taught such things as where, how, and when they can pick up "quick cash," "free eats," and where to get a "free place to crash." So, for example, the neophyte entering the ex-patient subculture is taught that he/she can pick up "quick cash" by: selling their "meds" for money, and selling their bodies (not only where to sell these commodities, but for how much), and a set of rationalizations justifying such actions:

When I first started hanging around with those guys, they showed me the ropes. I was pretty green about things, and I never had any money. But they told me that if I ran short of bucks, I could pick up an extra twenty or fifty by selling my meds. They even pointed out this group of young boys who would be willing to but the stuff.

A female chronic ex-patient adds:

I sell my "wares" when I need to. I'm not a prostitute, don't get me wrong. But when I need money for cigarettes, something important, then I don't mind doing it once in a while. The other patients I know do it too. Kerry and Jean were the ones who taught me to do it and how much to charge...I make five or ten bucks a shot.

Moreover, in the context of the ex-patient subculture, members learn which religious and social agencies give "hand-outs"—where such agencies are located, how much they may give, and how to approach them:

Dave and Bill took me to this agency that gives out hand-outs. There's one church down the street. If you ask for the pastor, and tell them this heart-sob story that you've practiced before-hand, he's usually good for ten bucks. Then there's the welfare people, and this other community service place. The other guys taught me when's the best time to hit these places, the story to give them which makes things go a lot smoother.

Another chronic ex-patient, discussing the skills and knowledge about various agencies she acquired through interaction with others in the subculture, remarks:

If it wasn't for my friends, I would be out in the cold. I wouldn't know nothing about where to get a hand-out when I really needed it. They took me by the hand when I met then and pointed out each and every one of them in the area, and not only that, they teached me to dress poorly, muss up my hair and cry a lot when I went to them.

Further, ex-patients learn through participation in their subculture, which agencies, missions and restaurants provide such things as free food, clothing and shelter:

At first, I didn't know nothing. But my friends taught me where I could get free food whenever I wanted it, like down at the "Lakeside Mission." You gotta put up with their praying and singing, but that's O.K. They also showed me where to do to this church if I needed new threads and some lady will give you whatever you want.

Speaking on his major source of free food from one fast-food restaurant, a middle-aged male says:

Moe was the one who wised me up about the free eats from "Burger Town". A couple of times the manager caught us snatching left-overs from the garbage and we told him how hungry we were and really laid it on thick to him. He felt sorry for us, I guess, so he told me to come back near closing and we get a lot of the hamburgers and fries that they don't sell.

Through participation in the Mixed Nutters and Looney Tuners, persons not only learn the "in's and out's" of the system and how to use it to their advantage, but also learn how to capitalize on their deviant identities by becoming "professional crazies:"

> I learned that if I want to make some real money, I just have to act pitiful on a certain street where lots of people go by, and hold out my hand and say, "I need money to help with my treatment. I have mental problems. Please help me." Sometimes, I get booed, sometimes I get a quarter. Sometimes, a businessman will throw a dollar or two. On a good day, in a good location, I can make twenty bucks.

A second ex-patient, speaking on the capitalization of his deviant identity says:

> I usually go down the subway at rush hour and act all confused, saying that I'm sick and I'm trying to get back to the hospital but I have no money. Usually someone will give me the money to buy a token, but I just pocket the money and start the act all over again. Last night, I made six bucks...This is the one time when being mental works to my advantage!

In short then, these three behavioral patterns serve to combat the social isolation ex-patients are experiencing, provide a therapeutic function, enhance their self-esteem, provide pragmatic solutions to various problems, and equip ex-patients with important knowledge and skills for "making it on the outside".

2. Subcultural Norms

All cultures and subcultures, for that matter, develop norms, and the ex-psychiatric patient subcultures are no exceptions. In contrast to some subcultures, such as religious sects (Lofland, 1966) and prison inmates (Irwin, 1970) which have fairly elaborate sets of subcultural rules, the ex-mental patient subculture, by contrast, has established a rather simple code specifying beliefs and actions. One such set of norms centers upon the activity of "hanging around". So, for example, in the context of this activity, ex-patients make and adhere to, rules requiring all participants to share their tobacco, contribute money to buy others' coffee if they are unable to buy it for themselves, and to reciprocate generosity. As one male ex-patient put it:

> When us guys meet at the donut shop, it's expected that if a guy has a whole pack of tobacco and the others have run out that he shares it with everyone. And next time, if he don't have any, and we got some tobacco, we naturally share it with him.

In a similar vein, another adds:

> Last night, we were hanging around at this joint and I run out of dough (money). But my friends didn't let me down. They pitched in and bought

me coffee the rest of the night...Next time, when they're out of dough, I'll buy their coffee. That's how we work it.

Another set of norms centers on the activities in which the chronic ex-patients engage in order to "make it on the outside" or capitalize on their deviant identities. Such norms[14] specify the conditions under which it is appropriate to engage in acts of prostitution, and what type of sexual acts are appropriate. Speaking of necessity as a prime prerequisite for selling her body, one woman states:

The only time that it's O.K. to screw for money is when I'm absolutely broke. That's the only time that my friends, Sarah and Rhoda-Sue do it...I'm not a whore and neither are they. I'm a decent person and don't do any of those dirty, kinky things, just straight, plain sex.

Similarly, other norms specify the conditions under which it is appropriate to engage in the selling of their maintenance medications and shoplifting. In the case of the former, necessity again being the major prerequisite, ex-patients follow rules regarding to whom they should sell their meds:

We never sell them to young boys or even teenagers. No way. We have morals too, you know. We only sell the meds if absolutely necessary— like when we're dying for a smoke or we need to buy something. And we only sell it to adults and if they blow their minds, that's their problem. They're old enough to know better.

In the case of shoplifting activities, that data indicate that such behavior is only deemed appropriate in emergency situations, with only certain articles defined as "acceptable merchandise":

We only take things from stores when we really need them. Like when we don't have nothing to eat, so we rip off a can of pork and beans. But we don't steal big things like radios or televisions—that would be wrong. We just take food and essential things like that!

One final set of norms have been created in the context of the ex-psychiatric patient subculture, norms centering on the "shrink sessions" in which ex-patients frequently participate. Such norms include not interrupting others disclosing their problems, maintaining confidentiality, and non-ridicule. Speaking of adherence to these rules, one female states:

When we first began getting together, people used to talk all at once, so we made this rule that when one person is talking, the others shut up. And even if the person is talking stupid, you don't laugh, because laughing can be a deadly weapon—it can hurt someone deeply...Whatever we talk about, nobody goes out and gossips to someone else. It's kept under our hats.

The set of norms to which the Mixed Nutters and Looney Tuners have created and adhere function to regulate the conduct of their groups. Their prescriptions contribute to a form of social order and not only protect but dignify their members. In this latter regard, the strict norms regarding the commission of deviant/illegal acts and the concomitant set of justifications, enable members to maintain a positive image of self and high self-esteem.

For those members who breached a subcultural norm, depending upon the norm, and the circumstances surrounding the breach, they would receive some sort of negative sanctioning. Such sanctioning included verbal abuse, physical abuse, temporary and permanent expulsion from the group. Recounting the negative sanctions he received for violating the rule of non-ridicule during a "shrink session," an ex-patient says:

> Millie was talking about some problem she was having and it sounded so trivial and stupid to me that I blurted out laughing. Everyone got real upset though and told me to get lost. They didn't have nothing to do with me for two months. When I returned, I watched my step; I sure learned my lesson.

For those who breached norms regarding the commission of deviant/illegal acts, the penalties are more severe:

> Joe got himself into a lot of trouble. He knew that it was wrong to sell his meds to little kids on the corner and we called him on it. He didn't like our warning him and he turned on us and went to the cops and gave them our names saying we was the ones selling the dope. He caused a lot of trouble for us...But we got even. One night we got him and beat the shit out of him. After that, he towed the line.

3. Argot

The Mixed Nutters and Looney Tuners communicate with their respective members be means of an argot (still in its developmental stage), a distinctive vocabulary that demarcates not only outsiders from insiders, but also, neophytes from veterans. Speaking on the role of argot, one Mixed Nutter remarks:

> The lingo we use is really useful because we can be sitting in a coffee shop talking about some ways to pick up quick cash, and some of these ways are illegal. The people who are sitting right beside us may be eaves-dropping, but they won't be able to understand what we're saying.

In a similar vein, a member of the Looney Tuners adds:

> The words we make up and use describe certain things and they protect us from enemies...It's like we're this club and we share things that no one

else understands...The way we speak also lets you know up front who is one of us and who ain't, and who may be a green-horn wanting to be one of us.

Moreover, their argot prescribes symbols for cognition and communication regarding matters of interest to chronic ex-psychiatric patients. So, for example, "plucking the rooster" refers to receiving handouts from clergy or social agency members. "Going to a banquet" refers to individuals discovering a place giving out large amounts of free food. "Doing the groceries" refers to shop-lifting various foodstuffs.

All groups make evaluations of its members in an effort to maintain some sense of order and stability. So for example, in the case of the Looney Tuners, at certain times, usually when "hanging around," members will talk about "cheapers," those ex-patients who violated the norm of reciprocity. So too, do they speak about "dozers," those individuals who were caught committing a deviant act. The Mixed Nutters, also refer to members being "turncoats" or "fruitcakes." The former term refers to those ex-patients who have violated norms of trust and confidentiality. The latter term refers to individuals with little common sense. Moreover, they use the terms, "oldies" and "shit-kid" to make distinction between veterans and novices.

In their demarcation between themselves and outsiders, the Mixed Nutters use the such terms as "Nazi," referring to individuals who reject or stigmatize them; the term "moron" refers to unacceptable ex-patients who do not meet the standards for acceptance into the group. Similarly, the Looney Tuners use such terms as "head shrinkers" and "cop patrols" to refer to psychiatric professionals and social workers respectively.

4. Boundaries

Similar to the nudist (Weinberg, 1966) and motorcycle gang (Hopper and Moore, 1980) subcultures, the data indicate that the ex-psychiatric patient subcultures also have sharply-defined territorial boundaries, within which they carry out their activities. In the case of the Looney Tuners, members live and carry out their daily activities in a territorial area of approximately 2.5–3.0 square miles. This territory contains a mixture of residential housing, commercial and service-oriented properties. The Mixed Nutters live and carry out their activities in a somewhat larger territorial area of approximately 3.0-4.0 square miles. This territory contains a mixture of commercial and service-oriented properties, residential housing, and some light industries.

During the three years this researcher studied these two groups, individuals rarely stepped outside their respective territories. The territories of these two subcultures provide ex-patients with everything they need to "get by on." They bring the world down to size and make life more manageable for the ex-patients. By remaining inside these imaginary boundaries, the individuals come to know every inch of their territory—a knowledge that gives them a sense of security:

In all the time I've been discharged, I've always stayed right here in this area. Most of us do. It's rare to hear that so and so took a bus to Buffalo or Ottawa. You can walk to anywhere you have to. It's like a small town in this neighborhood. At first I was scared, but now I know every street and store and restaurant. I'm more at ease now.

5. Ideology

Similar to other deviant subcultures, the ex-psychiatric subcultures develop an ideology: a perspective on themselves and on their relations with other societal members, a set of ideas repudiating conventional, stereotypical attitudes about their deviant attribute, and a set of justifications for engaging in deviant/illegal activities.

The ideology of the Mixed Nutters and Looney Tuners provides their members with a set of ideas about "normals" in society, and the relations between themselves and such persons. Normals are generally perceived as cruel, untrustworthy, uncaring, dangerous and unknowledgeable about mental illness, an ideology prescribing avoidance on the part of ex-patients. As one ex-patient, speaking on this subject, puts it:

> People out there are just plain mean most of the time. Or they just don't give a damn about us. Some of them wouldn't care if we vanished off the face of this earth. Most are so stupid. They don't have any true idea about what mental illness is...The best thing we can do is try to avoid them when we can. They don't want us, and we don't want or need them.

Moreover, the ideology of these ex-psychiatric patient sub-cultures refutes stereotypical perceptions about mental patients and mental illness generally held by conventional society. Members are provided with a set of rationalizations and justifications for their illnesses mitigating their blameworthiness[15], thereby enabling ex-patients to redefine themselves in a more positive, although still deviant light. According to one male ex-patient:

> Since I met these people, they reminded me of the fact that I wasn't some crazy lunatic on the loose—the vision that others seemed to have of me. My fellow patients made me realize that I was a person, someone with psychological problems, an illness that was not my fault. It was all beyond my own control...Since they've been telling me this, I think more highly of myself now.

Similarly, another ex-patient remarks:

> My friend told me that I wasn't responsible for my situation. How could I be? It's not my own fault...They helped me to see that my sickness was caused by others, and that's what I try to convince other (ex-patients) of. It makes them feel less guilt and really picks them up mentally.

Just as the ideology of the subculture provides ex-patients with ideas about normal others and a set of justifications holding others accountable for their deviant attribute, so too, does it function in one final respect: specifically, it provides members with a set of justifications for carrying out deviant/illegal acts. This self-justifying rationale then, furnishes ex-patients with "sound" reasons for engaging in such activities as prostitution, selling their medication, and shoplifting:

> We're not doing anything that's really wrong. We don't murder or rob or things like that. We only take a few groceries once in a while from the A & P store. And we only do that when it's absolutely necessary. Other people who have lots of money do it all the time, and they take things much bigger than we do. We do it for medical reasons—our health, but they just do it for greed.

In a similar vein, another ex-patient discussing her rationale for engaging in prostitution, says:

> The world is against us patients and we got to get by somehow. And we can't make ends meet on a disability pension. The boarding home takes most of the monthly cheque and we're only left with a few bucks for the whole month. So, what the hell, we "work under the covers" once in a while. It's not that we do it for pleasure, it's necessary. No one will give me a "normal" job because of my sickness, so this is my only option. You look down the big streets and avenues and see lots of girls doing it anyway. It's just another way to make a buck!

In short then, the chronic ex-patients in this study develop and utilize an ideology: a set of ideas that suit their own interests, justify their post-hospital actions, and holds others accountable for their mental illness. Moreover, this ideology contains a set of ideas and judgements about others in society and provides ex-patients with specific prescriptions for action.

Summary and Discussion

This sociological study on the subcultures of chronic ex-psychiatric patients was stimulated by the observation that despite the wealth of sociological research on various deviant subcultures, and the concomitant theoretical approaches utilized to explain such phenomena, little, if any use was made in the examination of discharged/ deinstitutionalized chronic psychiatric patients. Moreover, what research had been conducted on ex-patients, had been done either form a psychiatric, social work or psychological perspective. Little research had focussed on the effects of deinstitutionalization from the perspectives of the ex-patients themselves. Further, no published work (at the time of the study) had been located which documented the origins, nature, and functions of a deviant subculture of chronic ex-psychiatric patients. Therefore, this paper was concerned with the effects of deinstitutionalization from the subjective standpoints of chronic ex-patients. In specific, this paper has focussed on the subcultures that these deviants have developed and utilize, their characteristics, and the role that they serve their members.

According to Simmons (1969:88):

> In response to society's disapproval and harassment, deviants usually band together with others in the same plight. Beyond the ties of similar interests and views...deviants find that establishing fairly stable relationships with other deviants does much to ease procurement and coping problems and to provide a more stable and reliable source of direct support and interaction. In these indirect ways, society's condemnation "creates" the deviant subculture.

The results of this study have indicated that this subcultural formation emerged when ex-patients began experiencing a number of problems (created by the deinstitutionalization of mental health services and societal attitudes toward the mentally ill), communicating such problems to other discharged chronic ex-patients, subsequently interacting with like others on the basis of their problems, and attempting to provide solutions to their difficulties. Ex-psychiatric patient subcultures were characterized by: crystallized patterns of behavior centered around their social plights, a set of clearly-defined norms and values, and an idealogy: a set of ideas developed to suit their own interests and justify their actions. Analysis of the data revealed that the ex-psychiatric patient subcultures provided a number of functions for their members. Firstly, through subcultural participation, ex-patients established social relationships with understanding others—a relationship that was supportive in nature and served to combat feelings of fear and social isolation. Secondly, group activities, in particular, "Shrink Sessions," allowed members to discuss problems of anxiety, stress, depression, stigma, and alike, and ask fellow group members for advice on how to deal with such problems. Through such "Shrink Sessions," ex-patients were able to disclose various concerns and dilemmas in a cathartic fashion; by so doing, they were able to alleviate a portion of the burden of their loads, thereby elevating their self-esteem. Moreover, in the context of their daily interactions, in general, and during "Shrink Sessions" specifically, fellow members provided "expert advice" and practical strategies for mitigating the stigma potential of mental illness on their daily rounds. Given that others in the subculture had experienced the stigma of mental illness on numerous occasions during the post-patient phase of their careers, such persons had indeed become "expert managers"—they had a great deal of advice on the "do's and don'ts" of avoiding stigma associated with their discreditable attribute. In the context of this subcultural formation, various stigma management strategies were imparted upon new charges. Fourthly, in the context of participating in the ex-mental patient subcultures, members were provided with an ideology, a set of justifications or "sound" rationales about their deviant attribute. The ideology of the Mixed Nutters and Looney Tuners provided ex-patients with a set of rationalizations which mitigated their blameworthiness; instead, blame was placed upon various others, ranging from spouses, children, teachers, parents, to society, in general. By placing blame on others for their discreditable attribute, this enables ex-patients to re-define themselves in a more positive, although still deviant light. Further, the ideology of that normals were untrustworthy, callous, and uneducated about mental illness—an ideology that prescribed "avoidance of normals" to members of the subculture. Fifthly, the ideology of the ex-patient subcultures furnished members with a self-justifying rationale for engaging in various deviant/illegal activities. Ex-patients, through subcultural participation, were provided with a set of "sound" reasons for engaging in such activities as selling drugs, shoplifting and prostitution, enabling them to maintain positive self-images. A final function of the ex-psychiatric patient subcultures was that they provided members with various practical stratagems for "making formal sense," how to capitalize on their deviant identities, specifically, by selling their bodies, selling their medication, locations where to get "free eats" or a "free place to crash." In short, in the context of this subcultural form, individuals were taught how to make the most of their attributes by becoming "professional crazies."

This is not to say, however, that ex-psychiatric patients experienced only positive consequences from participation in the subcultures. In fact, the author observed on a number of occasions, situations of conflict surrounding authority, verbal abuse among members, stolen wallets, tobacco, cigarettes and various articles of clothing. However, the positive consequences of subcultural participation far outweighed the negative effects:

> There is good and bad with everything and this is true of the "Looney Tuners" group. In the last couple of years, there has been a few fist fights over some cigarettes and cash that went missing, but all in all, it's this group that really helped us to make it on the outside. We would have been totally lost without each others help and support.

According to the ideology behind the movement toward deinstitutionalization of mental health services, individuals would be released or discharge from the institution. However, "stone walls do not a prison make, nor iron bars a cage." Many chronic ex-psychiatric patients, even though discharged, remain imprisoned in a metaphorical sense with their guards and wardens being the family, friends, potential employers, and society in general who are unable to tolerate mental illness. The term, "deinstitutionalization" is defined by chronic ex-patients as a from of "social segregation and reinstitutionalization in *certain* areas in the community." Such persons are *in* but certainly not *of* the community. Ex-patients, for the most part, are confined in "institutions without walls, bars of locks" living lives of frustration, disappointment, fear, exploitation and poverty. In response to their undesirable social situations, these persons, [similar to other stigmatized deviants in society], have developed and entered into deviant subcultures or "informal self-help groups"—an "expressive group" (cf. Gordon and Babchuk, 1959:25) "exist(ing) primarily to furnish activities for members," including evading stigma.

REFERENCES

Anspach, Renee 1975."From Stigma to Identity Politics: Political Activism among the Physically Disabled and Former Mental Patients". *Social Science and Medicine* 13A: 765–773.

Bassuk, Ellen. L., and Samuel Gerson 1978."Deinstitutionalization and Mental Health Services". *Scientific American* 238: 46–53.

Becker, Howard S. 1963. *Outsiders: Studies in the Sociology of Deviance*. New York: Free Press.

Bellak, Leopold, 1964. "Community Psychiatry: The Third Psychiatric Revolution". In L. Bellak, (ed.), *Handbook of Community Psychiatry and Community Mental Health*. New York: Grune and Stratton.

Brown, Philip, 1979. "The Transfer to Care: U.S. Mental Health Policy Since World War II". *International Journal of Health Services* 9: 645–662.

Burr, Angela, 1984."The Illicit Non-Pharmaceutical Heroin Market and Drug Scene in Kensington Market". *British Journal of Addiction* 79 (3): 337–343.

Cheadle, A.J., H. Freeman and J. Korer, 1978. "Chronic Schizophrenics in the Community". *British Journal of Psychiatry* 132: 221–227.

Chu, F.D. and S. Trotter,1974.*The Madness Establishment: Ralph Nader's Study Group Report on the National Institute of Mental Health*. New York: Grossman.

Cloward, R.A., and L.E. Ohlin, 1964.*Delinquency and Opportunity*. New York: Free Press.

Cohen, Albert, 1955. *Delinquent Boys*. Glencoe, Illinois: Free Press.

Cohen, Jere, 1979."High-School Subcultures and the Adult World". *Adolescence* 14 (55): 491–502.

Dear, Michael, L. Bayne, G. Boyd, E. Callaghan and E. Goldstein

1980. *Coping in the Community: The Needs of Ex-Psychiatric Patients*. Mental Health Hamilton Project.

Demotte, Charles, 1984."Conflicting worlds of Meaning: Juvenile Delinquency in 19th century Manchester". *Deviant Behavior* 5: 193–215.

Estroff, Sue E, 1981. *Making it Crazy: An Ethnography of Psychiatric Clients in an American Community*. Community. Berkeley: University of California Press.

Gans, Herbert, 1962. *The Urban Villagers*. New York: Free Press.

Gillen, John, 1955."National and Regional Cultural Values in the United States". *Social Forces* (Dec.): 110–115.

Goffman, Erving, 1963.*Stigma*. Englewood Cliffs, New Jersey. Prentice-Hall.

Gordon, C. Wayne and Nicholas Babchuk, 1959."A Typology of Voluntary Associations". *American Sociological Review* 24 (February): 22–29.

Gordon, Milton M., 1964. *Assimilation in American Life*. London: Oxford University Press.

Herman, Nancy J.,1993. "Return to Sender: The Reintegrative Stigma-Management Strategies of Ex-Psychiatric Patients." *Journal of Contemporary Ethnography* vol. 22 #3: 295–330.

———. 1986a. *Crazies in the Community: An Ethnographic Study of Ex-Psychiatric Clients in Canadian Society*. Unpublished Ph.D. dissertation, McMaster University, Hamilton, Ontario, Canada.

———. 1986b."The Chronically Mentally Ill in Canada". Pp.111–123 In B. Havens and E. Rathbone-McCuan, eds., *The North American Elders: A Comparison of U.S.and Canadian Issues*. New Hampshire: Greenwood.

Hopper, Columbus and J. Moore, 1980."Hell on Wheels: the Outlaw Motorcycle Gang". Paper presented at the Mid-South Sociological Association Annual Meetings.

Hughes, Everett Cherington, 1961. *Students' Culture and Perspectives: Lectures on Medical and General Education*. Lawrence, Kansas: University of Kansas Law School.

Humphreys, L. and B. Miller, 1980. "Identities in the Emerging Gay Culture". In J. Marmor (ed.), *Homosexual Behavior: A Modern Reappraisal*. New York: Basic Books.

Irwin, John, 1970. *The Felon*. Englewood Cliffs, New Jersey: Prentice-Hall.

Johnson, Bruce, 1980. "Towards a Theory of Drug Subculture". Paper presented at the annual meetings of the Society for the Study of Social Problems.

Kitsuse, J.I. and D.C. Dietrick, 1959. "Delinquent Boys: A Critique". *American Sociological Review* 24: 213–215.

Leifer, Rod,1959. "Community Psychiatry and Social Power". *Social Problems* 14: 16–22.

Lewis, Oscar,1961. *The Children of Sanchez*. New York: Vintage Books.

Landy, David and Sara Singer, 1961. "The Social Organization and Culture of a Club for Former Mental Patients". *Human Relations* 14: 31–40.

Lipton, D.S. and B.D. Johnson, 1980. "Control at the Subcultural Interface: Heroin vs. Methadone". Paper presented at the annual meetings of the Society for the Study of Social Problems.

Lofland, John, 1966. *Doomsday Cult*. Englewood Cliffs, New Jersey: Prentice-Hall.

Matza, David, 1964.*Delinquency and Drift*. New York: Wiley.

Melville, K., 1972. *Communes in the Counter Culture*. New York: Morrow.

Partridge, W.L.,1973. *The Hippie Ghetto. The Natural History of a Subculture*. New York: Holt, Rinehart and Winston.

Platt, Stephen D.,1985. "A Subculture of Parasuicide"? *Human Relations* 38 (4): 257–297.

Ralph, Diana, 1980. Where Did Community Psychiatry Come From?: The Labour Theory of Community Psychiatry. Mimeo. University of Regina, Saskatchewan, Canada.

Ray, Marsh B.,1961. "Abstinence Cycles and Heroin Addicts". *Social Problems* 9: 132–140.

Reynolds, David K. and Norman Farberow, 1977. *Endangered Hope: Experiences in Psychiatric Aftercare Facilities*. Berkeley: University of California Press.

Rubington, Earl,1968. "The Bottle Gang:" *Quarterly Journal of Studies on Alcohol* 29: 943–955.

———. 1982. Deviant Subcultures. Pp. 42–70 In M. Michael Rosenberg, R. Stebbins and A. Turowetz (eds.), *The Sociology of Deviance*. New York: St. Martin's.

Scott, Robert,1969. *The Making of Blind Men: A Study of Adult Socialization*. Russell Sage Foundation.

Scull, Andrew, 1977. *Decarceration: Community Treatment and the Deviant: A Radical View*. New Jersey: Prentice-Hall.

Simmons, J.L., 1969. *Deviants*. Berkeley: The Gendessary Press.

Shibutani, Tamotsu, 1955. "Reference Groups as Perspectives": *American Journal of Sociology* (May): 565–566.

Sykes, G.M. and D. Matza, 1957. "Techniques of Neutralization: A Theory of Delinquency". *American Sociological Review* 22: 124–136.

Wallace, Samuel E., 1965. *Skid Row as a Way of Life*. New York: Harper Torchbook.

Webb, Gary, 1984. "The Inmate Subculture: A Case Study". Paper presented at the Western Social Science Association Meetings.

Weinberg, Martin S., 1966. "Becoming a Nudist". Psychiatry: *Journal for the Study of Interpersonal Processes* 29 (1): 15–24.

Wolfgang, Marvin and Franco Ferracuti, 1967. *The Subculture of Violence*. London: Tavistock.

Yablonsky, Lewis, 1959. "The Delinquent Gang as a Near Group". *Social Problems* 7 (2): 108–117.

NOTES

[1] Cloward and Ohlin (1964); Cohen (1955); Gorden (1964); Kitsuse and Dietrick (1959); Matza (1964); Sykes and Matza (1957); Wallace (1965); and Wolfgang and Ferracuti (1967).

[2] See Anspach (1979) and Landy and Singer (1961) for discussions of *formal* social organizations for ex-mental patients.

[3] For detailed discussions concerning the origins and development of the movement toward deinstitutionalization of psychiatric services, consult: Bassuk and Gerson (1978); Bellak (1964); Brown (1979); Chu and Trotter (1974); Herman (1986a); Leifer (1967); Ralph 1980); and Scull (1977).

[4] For an extensive review of the literature, consult Herman (1986a).

[5] For the purposes of this research, the term "chronic" is defined *not* in diagnostic terms, i.e., "chronic schizophrenic"; rather it is defined in terms of duration, continuity and frequency of hospitalizations. Specifically, this term refers to those individuals institutionalized on a continual basis, or those institutionalized on five or more occasions.

[6] Following Rubington (1982), the concept of deviant subculture is defined in this paper as: "the shared ways of thinking, feeling, and acting that members of a deviant group have developed for engaging in deviant behavior, organizing relations among themselves, and defending themselves against social punishment".

[7] The term "non-chronic" is defined by the researcher in terms of duration, continuity, and frequency of hospitalizations. Specifically, it refers to those hospitalized for time-periods of less than two years, those hospitalized on a discontinuous basis, and those hospitalized on less than five occasions.

[8] The mean number of years these respondents were institutionalized was 7.5 years.

[9] The mean number of occasions upon which such persons were institutionalized was six.

[10] This response is, by no means, exclusive to ex-patients in light of the movement toward deinstitutionalization. Such a collective response has been well-documented among skid row alcoholics (Rubington, 1968; Wallace, 1965); homosexuals (Humphreys and Miller, 1980); delinquents (Cohen, 1955; Yablonsky, 1959), among countless others.

[11] For specific details concerning the sample, consult Herman (1986a).

[12] In contrast to the Mixed Nutters who had been in existence for three years prior to the beginning of this research project, the researcher was able to directly follow the development of the Looney Tuners shortly following their inception.

[13] See Goffman (1963) and Scott (1969) for discussions on the capitalization of blind persons.

[14] These norms have as their underlying assumption the idea of confidentiality.

[15] See Sykes and Matza (1957) for a discussion of similar neutralizing techniques employed by juvenile delinquents.

Chapter 30

CONSTRUCTING WOMEN AND THEIR WORLD: THE SUBCULTURE OF FEMALE IMPERSONATION

Richard Tewksbury

"Female impersonator," "illusionist," "performer," or simply "entertainer." But, never a "drag queen," at least not if you're a stranger. These are the proper and acceptable forms of address for men who present professional entertainment routines, appearing *as* female performers (Tewksbury, 1993a). More common, however, are labels such as "pervert," "weirdo" and "one sick individual." These are the labels that are commonly given to all men who crossdress, not just female impersonators (see Tewksbury and Gagné, 1994). What we have then, is a group of professional entertainers who perceive (apparently correctly) that they are socially stigmatized.

Stigmas can have several types of effects on both individuals and social groups. First of all, stigmas can drive individuals underground, minimizing the visibility that such undesirable persons have. Second, stigmas may have positive consequences (Herman and Miall, 1990). The positive consequences that stigmas may produce are that they may provide for therapeutic opportunities, encourage personal growth or stigmas may facilitate new and additional interpersonal opportunities as stigmatized individuals redirect their social activities (most probably toward interactions with similarly stigmatized others). It may also follow that aspects of these three positive consequences will combine to produce an additional consequence, which either may or may not have positive long term consequences, the development of a subcultural community.

It is my intent in this paper to examine the structure of one subcultural community of female impersonators, a subculture that is a consequence of the experience of stigmatization, and its accompanying development. This work also contributes to our small, but growing, body of knowledge regarding the world of female impersonators (see Miller, 1978; Newton, 1972; Tewksbury, 1993a, 1994).

The world of the majority of female impersonators is confined almost entirely to urban gay communities.[1] However, even here, within the confines of a relatively distinct subcultural community, female impersonators stand as stigmatized outsiders (Newton, 1972; Tewksbury, 1993a). This is not to say that female impersonators are shunned or driven from their communities, instead they are supported (socially and financially) by gay audiences. However, this support is confined to the context of the nightclub performance; outside the performance arena the female impersonator is often viewed as a "freak." Impersonators organize and present benefit shows for gay community organizations, stand as political spokespersons and often bear the brunt of homophobic attacks. Regardless, it is the belief of most female impersonators that they receive little if any respect, even from within the gay community (Newton, 1972; Tewksbury, 1993a).

The impersonator is usually viewed not as a person, but rather simply judged on her appearance. Such appearance based judgements (of both ascribed value and rights of access to locations) are not unique to female impersonators. Instead, this is the common way that people assess others (Stone, 1975). However, these appearance-based judgements may be more pronounced for members of stigmatized groups (Gardner, 1991). With stigmatized others our assessments of appearance serve as gate-keeping mechanisms that determine the social and physical realms to which we (mainstream society) will grant individuals access. Such assessments take on special relevance in potential interactions between strangers. In these instances, "communication between the unacquainted rests on a symbolism of individual appearance, dress, and gesture" (Gardner, 1991). In other words, we look at others to decide whether they will "fit" or "blend" with "our world" to which they are seeking access. For the female impersonator, this means that when a man presents himself as a female the assessment conducted is not just of his appearance, but of how others present are likely to respond. The assessment is not just of the illusionist, it is of the context to which the illusionist presents herself. When gatekeepers determine that the context is not likely to accept the illusionist's presence, stigmas are strengthened.

The female impersonator is not a naturally occurring phenomena; rather, these are performers who consciously choose to pursue an entertainment career, with full knowledge of how they will be received within their communities. Even with this in mind, many men do elect to subject themselves to the arduous work of transforming their bodies and social interactions to those of women. Within the world of female illusion there are three basic varieties of performers. Most well-known is the celebrity impersonator, a man who performs impersonations of well-known female entertainers (Madonna, Whitney Houston, Cher, Marilyn Monroe). A second, and most commonly encountered variety is what Newton (1972) calls the "glamour" performer. These entertainers present images of highly sophisticated, very fashionable women that supposedly represent ideals of feminine beauty. Finally, and least commonly encountered, is the comedic performer. The comedy queen dresses and speaks as a woman, but will frequently step out of character while telling jokes and sarcastically harassing audience members. The work involved in creating a successful illusion (especially for celebrity or glamour impersonators) is time consuming, expensive and often difficult to master (Tewksbury, 1994). Yet, in exchange for the opportunity to perform for their peers, and to compete for the affections of admiring others, men continue to enter the world of female impersonation.

In this paper, the concepts and processes which have previously been established in the literature are approached from a new angle, the perspective of social organization. Female impersonators are commonly viewed as social deviants, if not mentally ill individuals. As such, those men who work in the world of female impersonation find their primary support providers are either others in the industry or those who have an affinity for the art of female illusion. As we might expect, this is a rather restricted set of persons. Consequently, communities of female impersonators can be expected to create an insular community where mutual support and encouragement proliferate. In other words, a subculture of female impersonators can be expected to develop.

My work draws on interviews conducted with ten professional female imperson-ators and several months of participant observation with performers in one midwestern city. All interviews were conducted during the spring and summer of 1991 by a team of interviewers consisting of the author and producers of an educational videotape about female impersonation. Eight of the ten interviews were videotaped with performers appearing as their characters.[2] Interviews followed an open-ended, structured schedule and lasted an average of one hour. All interviews were tran-scribed in full. All interviewed impersonators were observed during nightclub performances between 1990 and 1992; dozens of other female impersonators have also been observed and conversed with during dressing room preparations and in nightclub audiences over the period spanning 1988 to 1992.[3]

Interviewed performers have professional experience as female impersonators ranging from one month to more than 16 years, with an average of 5.5 years of experience. The sample ranges in age from 22 to 36, with an average age of 28.7. Nine of the 10 interviewed performers are employed or attend school full time. All interviewees are white and 9 of the 10 self-identify as gay while one identifies as bisexual.

Throughout this discussion performers are referred to with feminine names, all of which are pseudonyms. Feminine names are used to reflect the fact that 8 of the 10 interviewees conducted their interviews in character, "as" their female personas.[4] Therefore, in reporting the accounts of these individuals it is necessary to see these comments and reported experiences as originating from the individual's feminine, not masculine, identity presentation.

Critical Concepts in the Construction of a Subculture of Female Impersonators

The insular world of female illusionists is a socially constructed entity which develops from the intersection of three primary forces: experiences of stigmatization, patterns of relationships among a stigmatized group and shared identities.

As already introduced, female impersonators believe they are viewed as "among the lowest of the low," even within gay communities. Regardless of whether or not this is in fact how urban gay men and lesbians perceive entertainers, the fact that this perception is shared and accepted as true is significant in leading illusionists to believe there is a need for insulation from non-performers.

Relationships among performers develop into a network of both positively and negatively connotated exchanges. The important point here, though, is that there are networks of relationships. For most female illusionists these networks exist only within the particular city where she performs; for others, those who are most successful professionally, networks may form on a regional or national level. In response to their perceptions of stigmatization, illusionists look to similarly situated others for interactions. Even when relationships with these similarly situated others are not highly rewarding, they remain "safe." Even your most despised colleague remains someone who understands the rules and dynamics of the impersonator world. While performers may do battle with one another, they do not stigmatize one another.

Finally, the subculture of female impersonators is drawn together by individuals' recognition of their shared identities. There are two primary identities that are significant in drawing female impersonators together into a subcultural community. First is the shared identity as a "performer." In part, this identity is a response to the negative external evaluations of illusionists. The performer identity also arises from these individuals' desires and commitment to achieve success and renown for their entertainment productions. Second, the identity as a member of the gay community serves to bond performers. Despite the political and social advances of the past twenty-five years, gay men and lesbians remain stigmatized and often despised by mainstream society (Gallagher, 1992). Recognition of such public reactions leads gay men and lesbians, and especially those seen as the "lowest of the low" to turn their interactional energies toward similarly situated others. Hence, shared identities can be reinforced by stigmatization, which in turn intensifies the desire for an insular community structure.

Stigmas

The fact that female impersonators are socially stigmatized is generally accepted in our society, and to many makes sense. After all, these are *men* who present themselves as *women*. Why would a man consciously elect to be something that he is not? For most observers the answer is clear: obviously there must be something wrong with, or missing from, the individual. However, what is it that is not quite right? As experienced by female impersonators, there are three basic explanations that appear to guide the thinking of those who apply stigmas to illusionists. These explanations are that the man who presents himself as a woman must be devoid of masculinity, impersonators are simply unable to do anything more challenging (or normative), or as considered most commonly, these are "freaks" whose behavior is most probably indicative of other, perhaps more serious, flaws of personality or biology.

An assumption that the female impersonator is lacking in masculinity is not something that comes as a surprise to most impersonators, yet it remains disheartening. What such an assumption shows is the fact that observers are unable to understand the differences across the variety of men that wear women's clothing. Female impersonators are only one group of men who crossdress (see Tewksbury and Gagn_, 1995); each set of crossdressers is differently motivated. The professional female impersonator is motivated by strictly utilitarian drives, most notably to establish a career and to make money. However, this is not recognized by observers who assess the illusionist solely on their appearance. As Paula argues,

> People think that if you paint up to be a female illusionist, with all the hair and everything that goes with it, they think that you're an automatic sissy.... They just think that because you put on a wig and make-up and pair of pumps and all that they think that you're an automatic sissy. I'm here to tell you that that's not true!

Of course, two of the assumed qualities that accompany masculinity in our society are intelligence and skill. Therefore, when a man is perceived to lack masculinity, he is naturally assumed to lack in the qualities that are assumed to accompany masculinity. Therefore, most illusionists report being treated by others as if they are lacking in intelligence. Often this takes the form of treating the impersonator as a child. Infantilizing the female impersonator, treating her as if she were a small child incapable of complex thought or activity, could be viewed as a natural outgrowth of her "child-like behavior" of "playing dress-up." However, such a perception is exceedingly narrow, and ignores the degree of skill that is necessary to successfully transform a male to a female (both physically and socially).[5] Once again, appearance alone determines interactions. Cherise, a highly successful celebrity impersonator, expresses her frustrations with her audiences when she says observers almost always act as if:

> we're stupid, that we're ignorant. That we don't know anything except how to do make-up, or how to look like a woman. That's not true at all....that's probably the biggest misperception.

While being viewed by others as not very masculine or not very intelligent can be hurtful, these are perceptions that most men face at least once in their lives. These are also the types of stigmas that potentially can be overcome, perhaps with as little as one public display of "manliness" or intelligence. Other forms of stigmas, however, can be more permanent and present a wider range of implications for individuals.

Among female illusionists the stigma that appears to be the most damaging (both emotionally and socially) is the labeling of performers as "freaks." As Cherise explains the reactions she sees from most observers, "general America sees us as freaks, they're not sure what we want to do with out lives, and they think this is an excuse." Coupled with the assumption that the impersonator is stupid, a label as a freak effectively relegates the impersonator to the realm of the socially useless. While it may be that a "freak show" is entertaining to watch, the performers themselves are considered dispensable, because they have little if any value outside the brief periods of entertainment they provide. Said slightly differently, Paula tells us that "personally, I think society thinks of it that we should be traveling with Ringling Brothers' circus!" Female impersonators are attributed about as much value as the sideshows of the circus: they're funny to look at, so long as they don't stay in town and present themselves as "normal."

The fact that illusionists are viewed so negatively by mainstream society is not nearly as distressing to performers as is the fact that performers perceive equally strong condemnations from within their own gay communities. For centuries gay men (and usually lesbians) have been denigrated and devalued by heterosexual society. Consequently, gay subcultures have sprung up in most urban areas, so as to address the stigmatization of homosexuality, the need for social outlets of lesbians and gays and as a way to reaffirm a shared sense of identity. However, in the 1990s there has been an increasing tendency to see internal distinctions arise in gay communities, as hierarchies of value and political correctness have been established.

Among those gay community groups that have received additional layers of stigma have been leather enthusiasts, pedophiles and exceptionally effeminate men. We can also add female impersonators to this list, as their experiences show they have been consistently ostracized and denigrated by their gay brothers and sisters.

"We're the worst of the gay community, much less the straight community! You can't get any lower than us!" This is quite a strong statement, as spoken by Mary, which tells us that the impersonator recognizes where she has been placed in the hierarchy of value that structures our society. Even within gay communities, nobody loves a drag queen.[6] The illusionist is perceived to be a negative image that can be exploited by political foes for purposes of swinging public opinion against the gay rights movement. What occurs in this instance is a failure to understand motivations and identities, on the part of both gay community outsiders and insiders. Janice, a 16 year veteran of female impersonation explains how she sees gay community reactions.

> There are an awful lot of, right inside our own gay community, there are an awful lot of men that believe that being an entertainer, a female entertainer, is wrong. They feel that we're setting gay rights back, setting the clock back on gay rights....I think with the gay community they don't understand. Most of the men just don't understand why another man would want to put on a dress.

Stigmas, then, both from inside and outside the gay community, appear to be a product of misunderstanding and a lack of information. Female impersonators denounce the content of these stigmas based on misinformation, or simple falsehoods. However, not all stigmatized groups form insulating subcultures to protect themselves from the harmful effects of stigmatizing labels. There must be additional factors that stimulate the emergence of such a form of social organization. One of these additional factors is the form and variety of relationships among such similarly situated individuals.

Relationships Among Female Impersonators

Due to the lack of general acceptance from others, and the fact that learning and practicing one's presentation can be a very time consuming activity, plus the mere fact that preparations, rehearsals and performances compel interactions, a large portion of the female impersonator's time and energies are devoted to relationships with other performers. These relationships may include other members of the gay entertainment industry, such as male strippers, singers and management and technical support staff, but the primary others with whom female impersonators develop relationships are other female impersonators.

The structure of these relationships are plagued with contradictions. On the one hand performers speak very highly of their colleagues, often crediting other illusionists with the degree of success an individual has achieved. However, and often within moments of praising her colleagues performers are likely to speak of the fierce competitiveness that exists between performers. While many performers will be-friend and work with other illusionists, many (sometimes the exact same individuals) will also engage in near warfare with these same colleagues. In the end, however, it is the unity among the performers that distinguishes the female impersonators' subculture from the broader gay community (and mainstream society).

When impersonators are asked how they have developed their current appearance and character, almost all will name several other performers who have "taken me under her wing and shown me the way." A willingness to work with one another and share techniques of presentation, as well as make-up, clothing, jewelry and perfor-mance suggestions is a hallmark of a community of female impersonators. Dana, a relative newcomer to professional female impersonation explains that,

> I've been inspired by a number of performers. By that what I mean is they've told me "just keep trying, just keep trying, you look good, you're going to get better." That's nice to hear. There has been one performer that has taken me literally by the hand and sat me down and said "here's what you're doing wrong. You've got a great start, but you've got to fix this and this and this." I had lots to fix, and she's really teaching.

This performer who has been so instrumental in Dana's professional development, Elaine, is also credited with "discovering" Paula, another relatively new face on the local impersonation stage. As Paula explains it, she had never seriously considered entering female impersonation, as her previous experiences in the entertainment world were stereotypically masculine endeavors. Two years prior to taking the stage as a female impersonator Paula was crowned Mr. Gay (city), and prior to that time was the emcee for a regional male strip troupe. However, Paula has been significantly influenced by Elaine, and in a short span of time has achieved local renown as a top quality female impersonator. In reflecting on her relationship with Elaine, Paula explains that,

> Elaine is my idol, she is my "drag mother." She helps me with a lot of things. There was one of those times when we were playing around and she says "well, honey you'd be kind of cute as a little girl." I thought, okay, so she's kind of helped along with it....Elaine is the one that really helped me do this. I don't intend on letting her down.

Others, such as Cherise, also credit other performers (although in this instance others who perform the same celebrity impersonations) with providing them the skills and tools to develop a quality presentation. Cherise thoroughly enjoys attending shows by others who do the same celebrity impersonation because such instances provide opportunities to critique others, and then apply these criticisms to her own performances.

The settings in which performers learn from one another can be either a formal, structured teaching situation, such as Elaine has done with Paula and Dana, or more informal. Informal learning is more common, and in many ways much easier than actual instruction. If other performers are the professors of impersonation, the laboratories are nightclub dressing rooms. Almost universally, performers claim that they have learned the majority of their skills and tricks by watching other performers in dressing rooms. In simple terms, as Cherise says, "I've learned more in dressing rooms than anywhere else."

The fact that essentially all performers (subtly) watch and study each other is widely accepted among performers. Most performers are proud of the fact that others respect them enough to try to learn from them. Those performers who are actively involved in instructing others in the tricks of the trade proudly list their proteges. However, in most instances the fact that they have helped others is viewed as simply something that is naturally done, not something for which their is an expectation of reciprocity. Elaine, the "drag mother" of several performers explains that she enjoys helping others, although a few of her students have later turned on her.

> I've helped a few people that really needed it and they were then ungrateful, that's how I like to say it. I've never been one to be too good to help someone, even if they were prettier than me, or had more talent. I'm more than willing to help them.

The apparent reason for the lack of gratefulness that performers like Elaine speak of is the high level of competition evident among performers. The rewards for which illusionists compete are partially financial, but primarily intangible. To be a success in the female impersonator community is to have fans that attend your shows, to be invited to more and better parties and social events, and to gather more compliments and applause (as well as, of course, tips) during performances. The ultimate reward is to win a title and a crown in a pageant. To be crowned Miss Gay (city), or Miss Gay (state) is a high honor. The ultimate honor for a female impersonator is to win a national title. However, most competition occurs on the local level, as illusionists compete for annual Miss (nightclub) titles. A title and crown are endorsements for the quality of a performer's illusion. More importantly, a title is a ticket into nightclub bookings. When asked if she currently held a crown, Elaine quickly listed her current title and explained that, "I have a local title, and since I've gotten it, well I've always worked before it, but it's now like constant. It's very important." Titles then, while usually not being accompanied by more than a symbolic financial prize, are the key to long term financial success.

The competition for crowns can be intense. Winners are adored by their fans, and despised by their competitors. Legends abound about performers who sabotage others' dresses, make-up and wigs. When a losing competitor, or one of their devoted fans believes that the results of a pageant are undeserved, violence and retaliatory strikes are always a possibility. Cherise, also a local title holder, relates the following story as evidence of the degree to which competitors value such rewards.

> Right after I won Miss _____, I was crowned not even two minutes, and this queen from NorthTown walks up to me and she shakes my hand and I thought she was going to say "congratulations." She said, "for the life of me, I cannot figure out why in the world they would given this to you." I thought, okay, how do you handle this? So I just walked away

from her, I just moved over on the stage.....Later we ended up going to (a different nightclub) and I wore my crown and my sash and that kind of thing. Well, I'm the type of person that wants to know why somebody says something....So, she was there and we were at the bar, and she would not go more than five feet away from me. So I looked at her and finally walked up to her and said "excuse me," very nicely, and then said to her "I don't quite understand what you mean by your comment that you made over at the other bar." She looks at me and this evil rage comes over her face. "You didn't deserve this!" And she snatches the tiara off my head and we proceed to rumble on the floor of the bar....the bartender comes flying over the bar and breaks us up. I didn't do anything to provoke her, at least I don't think I did. She got thrown out of course. The manager did come over and apologize and asked "So, can I buy you a shot?" So me and the manager of the bar did a shot, you know.

While Cherise's experience may not be the norm for pageant winners, it is not surprising, considering the fact that pageant audiences are almost always filled with other performers and competitors' fans, friends and others. Most of the illusionists interviewed reported going to pageants, yet almost never agreeing with the outcome. As Paula says, "It's a lot of favoritism and it's who you know and all that." With both emotional rewards and long-term financial rewards on the line, such responses should not come as much of a surprise.

Impersonators are usually happy to help other performers improve their appearance and performance, especially when those being assisted are new or fresh faces. However, this does not impede the development of personal and professional jealousies between entertainers. Sometimes jealousies are overt and directly evident, such as in Cherise's story above. Other times, and as is most typical, jealousies are evident only in "backstabbing," "bitchiness" and "hatefulness" which characterizes conversations and behind-the-scenes politics of nightclubs and bookings. Sometimes it's even more subtle, and evident only in what is missing from individuals' interactions and relationships. Jeri, another seasoned veteran of the local female impersonation scene, and who claims to know everyone involved with the subculture, says jealousies can be seen in instances when,

I can go out with another, well there's a lot of times when my drag sisters, I guess that's what we would call them. I can go out with them and they kind of don't want to go out with me because all the men will hit on me.

The important thing to realize about both the personal and professional jealousies, however, is that to be successful (i.e. to get bookings) an entertainer may have to overcome, or at least not display, her jealousies. The booking of performers for shows is often handled by veteran performers in a particular community. Therefore, these performers hold a great deal of discretionary power over which other entertainers will be allowed opportunities to perform. When an illusionist is not getting booked for shows she is not being seen in the community, and is not making any money. Therefore, not only does the new performer need to hone her skills with make-up, clothing and accessories, as well as her social presentation skills, but she must also make certain she stays in the good graces of the senior members of the subculture. Or, as Elaine warns her proteges, "you have to be patient, you have to be nice, you have to kiss ass a lot, especially with the girls who have been around for a long time."

The subcultural world is not only hierarchically low within the already stigmatized gay/lesbian subculture, but this is an internally hierarchical world as well. The factors that determine one's placement within the illusionist hierarchy are seniority, public recognition, crowns and the number and strength of positive interpersonal relations with other illusionists. Cherise says that being liked by other performers is a crucial matter, for

> If they don't like you they ain't going to give you the time of day. Or, they're going to want to fight with you in the parking lot!

While this discussion may make it appear that impersonators are an untrustworthy and vicious set of persons who are disliked by society, disliked by their own community and consequently are willing to strike out at anyone (including their similarly situated others), this is an erroneous, superficial conclusion. In fact, despite the political and personal conflicts that run throughout the impersonator community, there is a sense of unity and shared identity among illusionists. Yes, there is competition, but it need not be seen as negative. Cassandra, a performer who competes at the top level of national pageants suggests that,

> The competition, actually it's healthy....Sometimes it can get vicious, but pretty much it's real mild...and it keeps you on your toes....If you mess with one though, you've got them all! They are pretty close knit when it comes down to it. They don't want to admit it, but we'll back each other up and protect each other. Then we'll turn around and knock each other down so we can get that next crown!

Shared Identities

The identities that are shared across the female impersonator community are of two general forms. First, as has been elaborated elsewhere (Tewksbury, 1993a, 1994) all performers share an identity as a professional entertainer, not a sexual deviant or mental patient. Second, the identity as a member of the gay community serves to initially draw individuals together. The identity as a gay community member is an identity of the first order, with an identity as a performer serving to segment and distinguish this collection of individuals within that larger community.

The relationship between one's sexuality and their career as a female impersonator may or may not be viewed by performers as an important (or even existent) relationship. Most illusionists believe that there is some relationship, but not necessarily a very strong or significant one. It is important to note that no female impersonators believe that they are gay because they are illusionists, nor do any believe that the primary reason for their career is the fact that they are gay. There are heterosexual men who perform female illusion, although their numbers are believed to be small. Instead of the relationship being based on sexuality, some believe the relationship reflects a correlation of values from both the gay community and the world of female impersonation. For example, Mary suggests that,

> The only real relationship between my persona and my gay identity is the way I look. I like to look good, I like for other people to see me that way, whether I be as I am right now (as a man), or as Mary. That's the one similarity between the two. I want to look my best.

For some illusionists there is a small part of the experience that may, on occasion, be sexually arousing. This is not to say that female impersonators are transvestites though. The motivation for the impersonator is strictly financial and professional, not sexual. Even so, due to the setting and the attraction that is created for audience members, there may be occasions when sexual opportunities arise. For most performers sexual propositions are seen as distractions and bothersome. Most sexual propositions come from men who want the performer to maintain her feminine appearance and performance while in bed. According to most illusionists, these requests are highly unlikely to be granted. As explained by Jeri and Mary,

> A lot of men they pick you up in drag because they think they're going home with a woman. I'm like, no, when I get home this stuff comes off and you're enjoying me, you're not going to go to bed with Jeri. I'm not going to bed with some man and leave all this make-up on and a fake identity. That's not me. If you're going to go to bed with me it's with what you're seeing! It's not going to be with the make-up and heels.

In simple terms, to be asked to have sex while maintaining the illusion is an insult to most performers. To receive such a request is to be viewed as an object, as nothing more than a fantasy or play thing. In other words, propositions such as these are seen as further evidence of stigmatization: the impersonator is not a real person (or man), but simply a freak who thinks he is a woman.

Among the most common misconceptions about female impersonators is the idea that these are actually transsexuals, or men who want to be a woman. Not true. There are a small minority of performers who admit they wouldn't mind being a woman, or as Dana says, "If I could snap my fingers and be a woman, yes, I would do it." However, the great majority of performers share an identity as a man, a gay man. Accompanying this is a strong sense of masculinity and respect for women. Again, this is directly contrary to the stereotypes and stigmatized views that society appears to have regarding female impersonators.

One of the things about which female impersonators wish they could educate mainstream society is that they perform as illusionists not to ridicule or denigrate women, but as Cassandra says,

> I think women should consider this art form the highest compliment. For a man to go through the torture that they go through in these pumps, they should consider it a compliment!

Female illusion is viewed by performers and enthusiasts alike as an art form, as a way of paying homage to things of beauty. Even among comedic performers, there are rarely negative things said about women, rather, most of the comedy is directed towards men. Even so, because these are men *acting like* women, they are commonly thought to be acting out a hatred toward women. This is distressing to impersonators. Elaine says it simply, "If I hated women I wouldn't be doing this! I'm not making fun of them by a longshot!" Elaine, as with almost all entertainers, firmly believes this.

Conceptual Intersections Leading to the Formation of a Subculture

What we see then, is that female impersonators do have a common set of values and shared identities. Some of these values and identities are drawn from the larger gay community in which illusionists live, and some are unique products of the subculture. What is most striking though, is the fact that these values and shared identities are, in most instances, contrary to common perceptions. It is that body of mainstream society's perceptions that create and maintain the stigmas that are so freely and frequently applied to female impersonators.

These stigmas, in turn, are the forces that draw similarly situated individuals together into persistent and confined patterns of behaviors and relationships. All three forces — stigmatization, restricted relationships and shared identities — serve to reinforce the existence of each other. As a consequence there is created an internally perceived need to maintain the insular nature of the profession. This insulation from outside forces has the immediate consequence of shielding insiders from stigmas (or at least from the harmful impacts of stigmas). More powerfully, however, the long-term consequences of maintaining an insular stance, against both mainstream and general gay culture, are to restrict insiders' primary relationships to one another and to magnify the similarities among insiders and their differences (in values and identities) from outsiders.

A subculture — a group of persons whose perspective and life style significantly differs from those of the cultural mainstream and who identify themselves as different based on shared norms, attitudes and values — exists among female impersonators. This subculture is not a naturally occurring entity. Rather, as has been shown in this discussion, a subculture of female impersonators is socially constructed, built from the responses of both community insiders and outsiders. It is in the intersection of stigmatization, restricted and patterned relationships and a shared sense of identity that the subculture develops. These are the necessary factors to fuel the creation of a subculture of social deviants.

REFERENCES

Gallagher, John. 1992. "What America Thinks of You." *The Advocate*, 613, (October 6): 91–94.

Gardner, Carol Brooks. 1991. "Stigma and the Public Self: Notes on Communication, Self and Others." *Journal of Contemporary Ethnography*, 20, (3):251–262.

Herman, Nancy and Charlene Miall. 1990. "The Positive Consequences of Stigma: Two Case Studies in Mental and Physical Disability." *Qualitative Sociology*, 13, (3): 251–269.

Miller, Gale. *Odd Jobs*. Englewood Cliffs, N.J.: Prentice-Hall.

Newton, Esther. 1972. *Mother Camp: Female Impersonators in America*. Chicago: University of Chicago Press.

Stone, Gregory. 1975. "Appearance and the Self." In Dennis Brissett and Charles Edgley eds., *Life as Theatre: A Dramaturgical Sourcebook*. Chicago: Aldine.

Tewksbury, Richard. 1993a. "Men Performing as Women: Explorations in the World of Female Impersonators." *Sociological Spectrum*, 13, (4):465–486.

Tewksbury, Richard. 1993b. "Male Strippers: Men Objectifying Men." Pp. 168–181 In Christine L. Williams, editor, *Doing 'Women's Work': Men in Nontraditional Occupations*. Beverly Hills: Sage.

Tewksbury, Richard. 1994. "Gender Construction and the Female Impersonator: The Process of Transforming 'He' to 'She'." *Deviant Behavior*, 15, (1):27–43.

Tewksbury, Richard and Patricia Gagné. 1996. "Transgenderists: Products of Non-Normative Intersections of Sex, Gender and Sexuality." In Nancy Herman and Larry Reynolds (eds.), *Symbolic Interaction: An Introduction to Social Psychology*, Second Edition. Dix Hills, New York: General Hall, forthcoming.

NOTES

[1] There are also a number of female impersonators that have become integrated to top level entertainment circles in Las Vegas, Atlantic City and occasionally Hollywood or the world of music. However, the vast majority of female impersonators live and work almost entirely within the parameters of gay culture.

[2] One interview was conducted in the interviewee's home using a modified version of the interview guide and with the interviewee not crossdressed. One interviewee declined to dress for the interview.

[3] During all observations I openly recorded notes, whether in the public or backstage nightclub areas. My recognized status as a researcher in the female impersonator and male stripper (where I observed dozens of impersonators; see Tewksbury, 1993b) industries afforded me the luxury of openly recording notes without being questioned.

[4] The two interviewees who did not appear dressed as their characters did, however, frequently preface their comments with statements such as "well, speaking for Sandy" or "the way Mary sees it is..."

[5] See Tewksbury (1994) for a discussion of the skills involved in physical and social transformations undertaken by men who perform as female impersonators.

[6] To even be called a drag queen is to be insulted. Although used by performers to refer to themselves or each other, the term is considered a political statement, and when used by an unqualified other, taken as an insult. Similar use of terminology is seen in some African-American communities where individuals may refer to each other as "boy" or "nigger." This same dynamic is may be found among adult women who may refer to "the girls," but will quickly correct a man who uses such a form of address.

Chapter 31

INTO THE DARKNESS:
AN ETHNOGRAPHIC STUDY OF WITCHCRAFT AND DEATH

Wendy G. Lozano and Tanice G. Foltz

Introduction

This paper is part of a larger study of a coven of radical feminist witches, a group whose religious or spiritual base derives from what is known as the Old Religion, the Craft, or Wicca and is informed by the second wave of feminism. Contemporary witches believe that the roots of their religion predate Judeo-Christian tradition, drawing from the Goddess-centered cultures believed to have been located in and around Europe, the Mediterranean, and Aegean. They freely admit, however, that they practice the old Religion in new ways (Starhawk, 1988). They believe these new ways fit societal changes and their own perceived needs. Wicca, in both its radical feminist and more traditional forms, is an example of what Ellwood (1979) call an "emergent religion" or "alternative spirituality" existing alongside mainline religions, although often suppressed. It possesses a rich system of symbols and a growing community of believers, who are brought together by participating in ritual and magic.[1]

Religion and Death

All viable religions allocate an important position in their constitutive symbolism to the experienc: and event of death, according to functional sociologists Parsons and Lidz. Death has such disorienting effect that a religion

> ...must provide a framework for interpreting death that is meaningful and appropriate, in relation to other elements of the culture, for defining attitudes regarding both the deaths of others and the prospect of one's own death (Parsons and Lidz, 1967:135)

Yinger (1957) also emphasizes that one of the fundamental effects of religion is to rescue individuals and communities from the destructiveness of death.

Integration theories show how religion helps to maintain a state of homeostasis in a community when certain events threaten its stability. Through death and funeral rites, religion provides a potent means of reintegration of the group's "shaken solidarity" and reestablishes its morale (Geertz, 1973; Malinowski, 1948: Vernon, 1970). Funeral behavior thus serves an important social function.

336

Nevertheless, Lofland (1978) suggests that old ways of dealing with death do not effectively address current experience. Dying is increasingly being prolonged, while the experience of dying occurs in a context that is more and more bureaucratized and secularized. The unique capacity of humans to create and use complex symbols allows us to conceive of own mortality, and the possibility of immortality. Lofland argues that contemporary culture and social organization of death offer few clues as to teleological meaning.

> In the face of meaninglessness, we construct for ourselves a new set of
> beliefs, new orientations, new ways of looking or feeling that will fill the
> void (Lofland, 1978:33).

In stressing the importance of religion to social solidarity, Durkheim observed that religion is ultimately collective, expressing shared meanings and social ideals that unite participants into one moral community (Durkheim, 1915). Collective representation and social rituals are essential to religion precisely because language and symbols depend upon shared meanings. To examine shared meanings reveals a shared reality. By examining the worldview of radical witches, their rituals and their symbols, we can better understand their shared subjective reality.

This paper presents an historical overview of radical feminist Wicca, known as the Dianic tradition. It then focuses on the major religious symbols of Wicca that relate to death and describes a funeral in which one of the authors was able to participate.[2] Through the use of a case study, we will demonstrate how religion gives meaning to death for both the living and the dying.

Methodology

Data were collected through what Denzin (1970) calls a "triangulation" of qualitative methods. Primary source of data were fieldnotes written independently by both researchers. Observations covered all ritual activities, planning sessions, and mountain retreats we attended, as well as a wedding and a funeral. After several months in the setting, when we had gained some understanding of appropriate questions, we conducted in depth interviews with all coven members. Our interviews were semistructured, making use of a topical guide (see Gorden, 1969). We employed team research in order to increase perspectives on the setting (see Douglas, 1976). One of us was less experienced in ethnographic methods, but more familiar with feminist theory and some of the group's beliefs about mythology and goddesses. The other was an ethnographer with previous research and publication on a para-religious healing group. We each interviewed witches with whom we felt some affinity. We interviewed the core coven members more than once to cross-validate our data and ask newly formulated questions. Our team fieldwork extended form March 1988 through Summer 1989, when Foltz moved out of the area for job reasons. Lozano continued to attend rituals occasionally and maintain relations with the coven. In addition to fieldwork and interviewing, we sought out literature artifacts, workshops, and festivals on feminist spirituality, neo-paganism and goddess-worship. We then employed a modified form of "indefinite triangulation" as a validity check (see Cicourel, 1964).

Coven Members

The coven we call the Circle of the Redwood Moon[3] was composed of seven core members during the period of our research. The seven included three women defined as Priestesses, one Initiate, and three Apprentices.[4] The women ranged in age form 28 to 48 and came form working class and lower middle class backgrounds. They came to witchcraft at widely different ages— one in her early teens and the latest in her 40s. They came from a variety of Western religions. Yet a common thread was that all but one can be classified as a spiritual "seeker" (see Lofland and Skonovd, 1981) who had actively sought out and explored other religions and spiritual traditions before settling on Wicca. The exception is a core coven member who, at age 11, reported hearing a voice inform her that "she belonged to the Lady." She says she had no idea what that meant at the time, but became a self-avowed pagan by the age of 17 and now has been one for 22 years. Out of respect for her long history and experiences with the Craft, she was given the title of Elder Priestess by the coven.

By the time of this study, most of the women had taken some college courses. Two had completed four-year degrees, with one then taking some post-graduate study and the other working on a Master's Degree. Three women held clerical jobs, one was a salesclerk, one a "psych-tech" on a mental ward, and two were unemployed. Five of the seven women were Caucasian, the oldest women was an African-American, and one woman was a Latina. Only the Elder Priestess, who had been with the coven almost since its start in 1971, was involved in a heterosexual relationship at the time of our research. She and her husband were married by Spiderwoman, Priestess of Ritual and Magic, during the Spring of 1989. All other members were self-identified lesbians, most of whom had held romantic relationships with men in the past. Two of them were previously married, and one has adult children.[5]

The Setting

Most of the ritual activities took place in the home of two of the witches, Aletheia and Spiderwoman. They had been partners for three years by the time we entered the setting. Their condominium was located in a working-class neighborhood on the outskirts of Los Angeles. The decor consisted of soft lighting, a variety of goddess figurines, and numerous "witchy" artifacts, including a pentacle door harp, a frosted glass light in the shape of a crescent moon, and a crystal ball. During rituals, the glass-topped coffee table in the living room was often moved to the side and a small round table was used as an altar in the center of the room. The dining area held bookcases filled with books on philosophy, feminism, lesbianism, witchcraft, and goodness-worship. The large heavy table in the dining area served as a place for the women to gather and plan future rituals and other coven activities. Sometimes this area was used for the ritual, and the large table would be moved outside to a small patio for sharing potluck items afterward. The patio was rimmed by a foot of dirt in which a few abundant rose bushes grew. In the corner was a jacuzzi where the witches sometimes bathed after ceremonies.

Rituals that were open to other women took place at a campsite in a nearby mountain range. The death rituals took place at a funeral home and cemetery described later in this paper.

Gaining Entree

We gained entree to the Circle of the Redwood Moon when an opportunity presented itself near the end of Spring Semester, 1988. One of Lozano's students invited her class to attend a Spring Equinox ritual sponsored by her coven. (We later found that "open ritual" is one way the coven recruits new members, if not to the coven itself, to the religion.) We gained access to the coven by making use of what Reimer (1977) calls an "opportunistic" research strategy. Lozano was informed that everyone attending the ritual was expected to participate actively; no one would be allowed to simply observe. Given the stereotype of witchcraft and its practitioners, we entered the setting with some trepidation about what we might encounter and what might be expected of us during the ritual. We quickly discovered we had nothing to fear.

The ritual was a spring celebration in which every person was to make a personal commitment to the earth and to the women's community. Members of the coven "raised energy and cast a circle," which is done at the beginning of every ritual as a means of "creating sacred space" (see Sparhawk,1979:55), and various priestesses led visualizations, meditations, dancing, and chanting for the next hour or so. The ritual closed with a potluck "feast," womens' music, and informal socializing. We left earlier than the others, saturated and exhausted by what we had seen, heard, and felt. Our first experience with Wiccan ritual and our debriefing session on the way home left one of the author's feeling hesitant about pursuing the research, while the other felt the group provided a fascinating setting to explore sociologically. Within a few days, we both had decided to pursue this unique research opportunity.

Lozano contacted the coven to discuss the possibility of our conducting team research. Her student served as "gatekeeper" and lobbied for the project. The other coven members were extremely protective. In a long interview, however, Lozano apparently answered their questions satisfactorily and gained permission on a tentative basis. A bargain was made that the witches would not have editorial control over what we wrote, but could control our access to the ritual settings. We agreed that, while we would not do anything to violate our personal ethics, we would *actively* participate at some level during the rituals.

Research Roles

In keeping with our epistemological ideal of gaining understanding from a "member's perspective" (Jules-Rosette, 1975), we engaged in participant observation using a phenomenological approach. Similar to Damrell (1977, 1978), Rochford (1985), and

Forrest (1986), we felt it important to experience the subjective meanings that are integral to witchcraft, rather than simply to document what we saw from an "objective" point of view. Since experiencing an altered state of consciousness was deemed critical in grasping the meaning of the coven's worldview, we found it important to immerse ourselves in the ritual experience over time, thereby "becoming the phenomenon" (Mehan and Wood, 1975). This process was limited, however, by the fact that we did not undergo apprenticeship training with the coven.[6]

A central issue in ethnographic research is the role the participant observer adopts. For example, Gold (1958) located four roles that field researchers adopt on a continuum between the "complete observer" and the "complete participant." Adler and Adler (1987) discussed three "membership roles" that sociologists "carve out" for themselves in fieldwork settings: peripheral-, active-, and complete-member researcher roles. Using the Adlers' terminology, we began our research on the coven in a "peripheral-membership-researcher role." Upon gaining permission to conduct the study, we agreed to participate in rituals to the extent that were relatively comfortable with them. We were comfortable with being required to express personal commitments to the planet or environment, to the women's community, and to ourselves as part of each ritual, and were not required to take on central roles. Although our agreement to participate was made in order to attend and do research, we did not feel that we had to adopt the witches' worldview, beliefs, and practices as our own in order to conduct the study. We did not "hang out" with the women outside of ritual settings, we debated their beliefs with them, and we asked many questions.

As we attended more rituals, we were greeted more warmly and we felt more comfortable. It became clear to us that, even though we attended coven activities as sociologists, we were viewed as potential converts and friends. Similar to other researchers' experiences in religiously-orientated groups (see Damrell, 1977; Rochford, 1985; Snow, 1980), the witches welcomed us in part because of the possibility of recruiting us to their belief system if not their group.[7] Almost without our recognition, our researcher roles shifted. While attending the Mountain Retreat at the end of the Summer of 1988, we were asked to play functional roles in the coven's activities. We had planned to retreat to our tent on occasion to record our fieldnotes and to interview people in our spare time, but it turned out that we had *no* "spare time." As often happens, informants find roles for researchers to take. We were asked to help lead groups, help make food, and be present for and give input into planning and preparation for rituals. Being thrust into these new roles came as a surprise. They were time-consuming and required energy and active participation, limiting our time for observation and fieldnote writing. At the funeral in mid Fall, the author present was introduced as the "coven auxiliary," a term subsequently applied to both authors and used during the rest of our fieldwork, indicating our status as a part of the coven, but not quite real members....

Eventually, we were moved by the philosophy and worldview of the radical witches as well as touched by the experiential aspects of ritual in the group. Although Gold (1958) has cautioned fieldworkers not to become too involved subjectively and then lose objectivity, other fieldworkers, such as Johnson (1975), Douglas (1976) and Adler and Adler (1987), dispute the notion that the researcher is unable to observe effectively as the participant role increases....

As a result of our change in perspective to that of observing participants, we began to understand phenomena in ways that we had not before. We eventually carved out membership roles that were something more than novitiates and yet less than full apprentices. We thus acquired the subjective meanings essential to coven activities and yet maintained what Douglas (1970:199) calls the "theoretic stance." Although we adopted active membership-researcher roles, we did not become complete members. We achieved a "member's perspective" by participating in and experiencing the effects of the rituals as fully as possible, but remained different from members. We made no attempt formally to apprentice ourselves, and our sexual orientation was clearly different from that of most others. Even though we were welcome to do so, we did not regularly attend planning sessions, volunteer to take on central roles during rituals, nor socialize regularly with witches....

History and Worldview

....All Wiccan covens consider the primary divinity to be female, and refer to "the Goddess." Almost all of the covens also believe in and incorporate into their rituals the male principle, represented as the "Horned God," her son and consort. Because of the emphasis on female creativity, divinity, and authority, as well as the leadership of female witches within the group, all covens support feminist ideology to some degree. Nevertheless, as Adler (1986:217) informs us,

> The traditional Craft is solidly based on the idea of male-female polarity,
> which is basic to most Craft magical working and ritual symbology.

Radical feminist witches are known within the Wiccan community as Dianics, after the goddess Diana. Unlike traditional witches, most Dianics celebrate an autonomous female principle as divine, excluding both the male principle and men. They have incorporated feminist concepts of sex, gender, and power relationships into their understanding of the divine. Thus, their religion has become political and their politics religious. This has created controversy in the larger pagan community, where Dianics have been accused of being "too Dianic," a phrase they take to mean too feminist, too separatist, and far too political.[8] The beginning of the Dianic tradition is credited to Z. Budapest, who, with a few other women, started the first Dianic coven in Los Angeles in 1971.[9] Over the years, this coven split or "hived" into several covens, one of which is now known as Circle of the Redwood Moon.

For Dianic witches, the spiritual and the personal are viewed as political. The "work" accomplished through magic and ritual is perceived as leaning toward an elimination of the patriarchal mindframe (Collins, 1974; Spretnak, 1982). The Dianic tradition deconstructs patriarchal ideas about religions, society, and human nature, replacing them with a belief system that values women, their creativity, nurturing qualities, and love for and connection with nature. All of this is subsumed in the concept of the Goddess. Newcomers are cautioned that the symbolism of the Goddess should not be seen as "Yaweh with a skirt,",...since the patriarchal God is viewed as "...a distant, judgmental, manipulative figure of power who holds us all in a state of terror" (Spretnak, 1982:vii). The Dianic notion of the Goddess stands in sharp contrast, as described by Starhawk, a well-known politically active witch and licensed psychotherapist:

> The Goddess does not rule the world, she *is* the world. The importance of the Goddess inspires women to see ourselves as divine, our bodies as sacred, the changing phases of our lives as holy, our aggression as healthy, our anger as purifying, and our power to nurture and create, but also to limit and destroy when necessary, as the very force that sustains all life. Through the Goddess, we can discover our strength, enlighten our minds, own our bodies, and celebrate our emotions....(Starhawk, 1979:9).

The emphasis on personal growth and experience is similar to that found in feminist conscious-raising (CR) groups in the late 60s and early 70s, a period which coincided with the growth of neo-paganism. In CR, women met to share experiential truths in an environment which excluded men. For some, this led to a recognition of widespread and systematic oppression of women. Self-identified "radical feminists" originally used this label to signify their commitment to uncovering and destroying the causes of this oppression, which they believed to be at the root of all other systems of oppression. Radical feminists have since explored feminist alternatives in fields such as music, literature, health, sexuality and spirituality. Thus, it is not surprising that the Wiccan movement should have attracted radical feminists among others looking for community and meaning during a period of rapid social change. According to Spiderwoman, the "dethroning of the Goddess" and the development of patriarchal religions are at the root of women's oppression. As Adler (1986) argues, feminism has had an enormous impact on the Craft.

In an attempt to differentiate their religious traditions from mainstream religions, Wiccans claim to have no dogma, doctrine, or sacred book. This idea was reiterated frequently in the Circle of the Redwood Moon. Yet it represents a claim that, in sociological terms, cannot be taken at face value, but must be interpreted.[10] It is more accurate to state that the key emphasis in Wicca, especially in the Dianic tradition, is on *experience*. The stress falls on engaging in practices that witches believe change consciousness and awaken what Starhawk (1988) calls the "power within.".....

The power within is achieved through ritual, meditation, and other techniques. It is also considered to *be* the Goddess, regarded as immanent in nature, human beings, and personal relationships. As such, the Goddess represents "the normative image of immanence" (Starhawk, 1988:9), the interconnectedness of all things. Magic is believed to be possible because the forces of energy are connected, even if they appear to be separate...During our discussions, the witches of Redwood Moon also described magic as, first, "perceiving" that the energy from one thing flows into another and, then, using that understanding as the basis for a visualization in which that energy flow is altered.

Thus Wicca stresses linking or relinking the divine within us and the divine around us in the natural world. Besides this concept of immanence as manifested by the Goddess, Budapest (1980:16) claims that an "important cornerstone philosophy" of Dianic Wicca is the concept of trinity, rather than duality...The concept of the trinity is syncretic rather than oppositional. It refers to the dynamic an continuous cycle of birth, life, death, and rebirth represented by the Goddess' three aspects of Maiden, Mother, and Crone.

Symbols of the Darkness: Death and Regeneration

The Crone

The third aspect of the Goddess, the Crone, is the Dianic symbol that best represents how the religion gives meaning to death and dying. The Crone if often portrayed as the third Fury who cuts the thread of life. She is seen by Dianics as a natural and necessary part of the life cycle. Her season is late fall and winter, when the earth moves toward darkness with the shortening of the days. As Spiderwoman says, "This is the time of turning crops under into the soil, the dying time of year." She stresses that the Crone is the only aspect of the goddess that has been passed down through the ages:

> ...unsanitized by Christian tradition. The Maiden and the Mother were adopted, sterilized, and rendered impotent. The Crone was diabolized...and survived with her powers intact.

Her special ritual or sabbat is Hallowmas on October 31.[11] This is the night that the Crone, as the Sacred Hag, Destroyer of Life, is believed to return to offer protection and vengeance. Hallowmas is a rite of passage wherein witches symbolically "pass through the veil between the worlds," enter the darkness, and meet the Crone. Her sabbat is the last one of the year and is referred to as "Women's New Year" (Budapest, 1986). It is a reminder that endings are always followed by beginnings.

There is a more gentle aspect to the Crone as well. Sometimes death is a welcomed friend. As the bringer of death, the Crone also ends pain. Some Dianics believe that, at some unspecified time in the past, terminally ill people went to "dying houses" and were gently guided in dying by women who served the Crone. She is often seen as the loving, protective grandmother. Having passed menopause, the Crone is believed to "withhold her wise blood" and so be immensely knowing. She watches out for her grandchildren, especially the female ones. In this aspect, she is not the Death Bringer, but a figure so ancient that her very visage is a reminder that death is near.

As Dianics reject the form of polarities, they do not conceive of death and darkness as separate and apart from life and light. One cannot exist without the other. The female principle is not only the Death Bringer but also the Life Giver (Walker, 1985). The Crone, as death, is integral to the life cycle. The same dialectics also apply to the first aspect of the Goddess that of the Maiden.

The Kore/Persephone Myth

A central symbol of Dianic Wicca is the maiden Kore, daughter of Demeter, goddess of fertility and vegetation. In the classical myth, Kore was kidnapped and carried off by Hades, Lord of the Dead. In her grief, Demeter refused to let the Earth produce. Zeus ordered Hades to return the maiden, but the Lord of the Dead secretly tricked Kore into eating part of a pomegranate, so that she would be forced to return to him several months each year. Out of this conception grew the Eleusinian mysteries and the doctrine of immortality.

In Dianic tradition, Kore descends, not because she is carried off, but because she hears the lost and confused cries of the dead. Nete, Elder Priestess of Song and Ritual, informed us that Kore walked of her own free will into the darkness. She passed beyond the veil and came to the Land of the Dead, where she comforted the dead, explained the reason for death to them, and helped ready them for rebirth. When at last she returned to the world of the living, she was forever marked by her experience. Having eaten seven pomegranate seeds, she "...can never again be wholly severed from the dark, the earth, the flesh" (Starhawk, 1988:91). Kore then took the name Persephone, and her story became a continual one of life, death, and rebirth, a reminder that Spring must be preceded by Winter. In her acceptance and understanding of death, Kore/Persephone affirms the cycle of life.

The Serpent

An important Wiccan symbol of rebirth and regeneration is the serpent. Snake jewelry is popular and live pet boas can be seen at almost any large pagan gathering. Although all witches use the snake to symbolize rebirth, it is a particularly powerful symbol for Dianics. The association of woman and snake goes back far beyond the book of Genesis: at 3500 b.c.e., the serpent and the Mother Goddess could be seen on Sumerian seals (Campbell, 1987). According to Joseph Campbell (1987:45), the serpent represents the power of life. It sheds its skin, its past, and is reborn... The symbol of the serpent eating its own tail is a powerful image of life, according to Campbell. One Dianic coven in Southern California uses this symbol for its name and for the sacred cord that members wear in Ritual.

The Cauldron

A last important symbol of the cycle of life and death is the small iron cauldron that is often placed on the alter during Dianic Rituals. It represents the womb, the site of transformation, of birth and rebirth. According to Barbara Walker (1985:103), it is a symbol of vast antiquity:

Always the cauldron was understood to signify the cosmic womb, source of regeneration and rebirth. All life, mind, matter, and energy arose in various forms from the ever-boiling vessel, only to return thereto, when each form came to its destined end.

The cauldron is used, among other things, to burn incense. It also represents the West, which is water. Thus, in burning incense and turning matter into energy, it is water turning earth into fire and then air, thus combining the four elements and four directions. Personal conversations with members of COG in California reveal that some covens use their spas during ritual to represent "the bubbling cauldron of regeneration."

Music

Much of the music sung by witches also reflects their worldview concerning death as an integral part of the life cycle. The feeling of the naturalness of death can be seen in one of their chants.

Darkness is the place of birth
Darkness is the womb
Darkness is the place of death
Darkness is the tomb
Death belongs to life
Half of day is night

Their songs also contain frequent references to the rebirth of light and to fresh growth sprouting from decay, or "black December's sadness." The songs emphasize the necessity of darkness, winter, and death.

Now the green blade riseth from the buried grain,
Wheat that in the dark Earth many days has lain.
Love comes again, that with the dead has been.
Love is come again like wheat that springeth green.
In the Earth they laid them in a barren place,
Witches from the burning nameless and erased.
Rising again, their ashes feed the grain.
We are come again like wheat that springeth green.

Personal Beliefs

As can be seen in the lyrics of the second song, a literal belief is reincarnation or survival of the soul is not necessary to accept the idea that death is an important part of life. When asked if they believe whether that which is unique in the individual survives death, most members of Redwood Moon answered no. One who disagreed stressed that it is an option that the essence of self may exercise, not a given nor a necessity assigned to the individual. Author Robin Morgan (1977:306) explores an alternate concept:

> ....reincarnation is seen by some as a metaphor for mystically cellular transition in which the dancers DNA and RNA immortally twine themselves.

Starhawk (1979) reminds us that in a worldview that views everything cyclical, death will not be seen as the final ending. The title of her fine book, *The Spiral Dance*, is the name of a winding dance of celebration sometimes performed during Wiccan rituals. Its symbolism evokes both snakes and DNA and thus death, rebirth, and life.

The Funeral Rites

The importance of symbols as metaphors for a worldview and hence a shared subjective reality becomes even clearer when one examines how the symbols are used in times of crisis. During crises, issues concerning the nature of life and death become especially important and religion is called upon to interpret the personal experiences. The sense of community created by shared meanings also becomes particularly valuable.

In the summer of 1988, the father of a member of Redwood Moon was diagnosed as having lung cancer. His daughter Aletheia at first tried solitary magic to effect a cure. The coven, however, decided that the disease had progressed to a point where too much damage had been done. The members believe that dying, like living, can be prolonged. But they decided that the most effective magic would be to send the man energy to help deal with pain. Spiderwoman put it succinctly when she told us, "You can't stop death. You can postpone and prolong it, but you can't stop it."

The death occurred in November. Aletheia's father Sep had remarried years after the death of her mother. He left behind Aletheia and her brother, who rejected his sister because of her sexual orientation. Sep was also survived by his Catholic widow and her adult children from her first marriage. There had been considerable strain between the two families during his lifetime.

Although nominally a Unitarian, Sep had developed considerable interest in Celtic lore and had written a long poem to the Goddess during his illness. Aletheia was the only family member aware of this aspect of his life. Sep had apparently attended Sunday Mass with his wife on a regular basis, told his son, Aletheia's brother, that he was an atheist, and allowed his daughter to believe he was a pagan with Druidic leanings. Not surprisingly, the deeply divided family was confused over the form the death rites should take. Sep's son, who flew in alone from across the country, was vehemently opposed to any kind of religious ceremony at all. He was also furious with his sister for making even minor arrangements without his approval. After a great deal of argument and difficult negotiation, the family decided that Sep's wife and her children would arrange one service and his adult children by his first marriage another. The outcome was a Catholic mass for the deceased on Friday night, followed by a Wiccan ceremony that the Circle of the Redwood Moon performed in the funeral home on Saturday morning. The coven, family members, and guests then accompanied the body to the Catholic Cemetery, where the coven performed another Dianic ritual over the open grave. Incidentally, this was not the first funeral conducted by the witches, three of whom are empowered by COG and the State of California to "marry and bury."

As the initial arrangements were being made with the undertaker, Aletheia reported experiencing a lack of connection, a lack of meaning. The Christian symbols in the funeral home alienated her. She accordingly asked that a large stained glass window of Jesus in the memorial chapel be covered for the ceremony. She and

Spiderwoman were shown row after row of coffins that, according to the latter, were designed to preserve the deceased's remains intact "even in event of nuclear holocaust." At last, they came upon a fairly plain oak coffin. Oak is a sacred wood in Wicca, a Celtic symbol of rebirth and regeneration. Aletheia's reaction upon seeing the oak coffin was that,"....all of a sudden something had meaning. Dad had to be oak." As a symbol of both mortality and immortality, the oak coffin revitalized for her the framework through which Wicca interprets death and gives it meaning.

The funeral director had serious misgivings about the religious service, especially when informed that the witches were going to "priestess" the ceremony themselves...When he asked what religion the ceremony represented he was told "neo-pagan." When he balked at that, Spiderwoman told him that it was "non-denominational." Although he finally agreed, he appeared uncomfortable about the ceremony. He frequently peeked in at the service and later complained about the smell of incense. The arrangements for the interment were made through him, so it is unclear what the officials of the Catholic cemetery were told would occur.

The rites in the funeral home began before any of the guests arrived. One of the coven's apprentices performed a ritual cleansing of the room with a cauldron of burning sage, which is believed to purify everything it touches, and by sprinkling oil, dedicated to Diana, to help create "sacred space." The closed coffin had been aligned with the body's head in the East, the direction which, for Dianics, represents new beginnings, and therefore endings, the closing of the circle. The coffin was placed in the front of the memorial chapel under an arch painted with a quote from *John* that promises eternal life through belief in Jesus. The stained glass window had not been covered. The flower arrangements chosen by the coven were seasonal, deep rusts, oranges, and yellows. Each display included oak leaves and shafts of wheat, symbolizing rebirth and regeneration. Wicker baskets filled with evergreen needles and pine cones were on the floor under the casket, repeating the same theme. Later it was disclosed that the needles and cones had been picked that morning from a tree where Sep liked to go when considering issues of life and death. All of the witches, except for Aletheia, wore conservative dark dresses, highlighting the pentacles, moons, and snake jewelry they wore. Aletheia, a large woman who always wears pants, had chosen an expensive man's suit, shirt, and necktie, all black. Around her waist, she had knotted her witch's cord, a red braid. She wore snake and pentacle rings, a pentacle medallion the size of her fist over her necktie, and a silver crescent moon on a copper band around her forehead.

Dianic rituals tend to vary from coven to coven and even within the same coven over time. Rituals of the Circle of the Redwood Moon are usually improvisational, but there was a written agenda for the funeral. Nevertheless, at the last moment, Aletheia decided that she wanted the coven, and its auxiliary, to perform a self-blessing before beginning the service. We stood in a circle in front of the coffin and each of us, in turn, using the same oil that had been sprinkled around the room, anointed the forehead, eyes, nostrils, mouth, breasts, abdomen, genitals, and feet of the woman to our left. Each woman using whatever words came to her while doing this, said in essence as follows:

Blessed be thy mind that thou mayst partake of her wisdom, thy eyes that
share her vision, thy nostrils that smell her essence, thy mouth to speak
her truth, thy breasts to nurture her children, thy womb the source of her
creativity, thy yoni the source of her pleasure and energy, and thy feet that
they may walk her path. (See Budapest, 1980:96–100).

The blessing was sealed with a light kiss on the mouth. Several members and
friends of Sep's Catholic family walked in during this part of the ceremony. Seeing
the anointing and the kiss, they demanded loudly to know just what was going on. An
apprentice was sent to reassure them as well as accompany the widow to her pew.

Another apprentice tended a tape recorder playing Sep's favorite music, sea
chanties, as the rest of the guests filed in. Spiderwoman took the podium and
welcomed everyone. She lit a white tapered candle. One of the apprentices began to
burn copal, a resin-based incense she had chosen because it intuitively "felt right."
The apprentice discreetly tended the burning incense during the entire ceremony,
sprinkling fresh rein on the charcoal block in the small iron cauldron near the coffin
and gently fanning the smoke. Nete sounded a small gong and performed a dramatic
reading about beginning a new day. She referred to the Goddess as "the Lady" and
specifically mentioned "the Lord," her consort. She said later that she had done this
with the intention of accommodating "those who believe in a patriarchal religion."
Spiderwoman sang, "Morning Has Broken" and the coven joined in. She then read
the poem that Sep had written to the Goddess, a long ballad-like piece that spoke about
Diana's bow and her sacred woods. Individuals were invited to get up and share
personal memories about Sep. None of the guests seemed prepared to do this.

The initiate became concerned at the lack of audience participation, which was
clearly not what Aletheia had planned. Taking the podium, the initiate said she had
met Sep only once, but through Aletheia's talking about him and loving him so much
she felt that he had influenced her life through his influence on his daughter. It was
a generous, loving thing for Aletheia's "coven sister" to do at a critical point. It pulled
the service out of the embarrassed silence it had fallen into. When the initiate finished,
she rang the gong and Aletheia took the podium. She shared memories of her father,
things he had said, things they had done together. It was difficult for her; sometimes
she laughed and sometimes she cried as she spoke. When she was done, she rang the
gong and lit a green candle to represent rebirth.

Aletheia then called the coven up to stand in a semi-circle around the coffin. She
raised a ceramic chalice that she had used in doing solitary magic for her father and
announced that she had placed her wishes for Sep's freedom from pain within the
chalice. Then she handed the chalice to the woman on her right. (The insistence on
improvisational abilities in the Redwood Moon was important here, since the author
present had no idea she was going to be called on to perform in this manner). The
chalice was passed around the circle counterclock-wise or "widdershins" to represent
dispersal. As each woman accepted the chalice, she announced her wish for the
deceased. The wishes ranged from eternal peace to being remembered with joy. The
audience was invited to participate in this ritual magic, either silently or out loud.
Only Sep's son chose to join the ceremony verbally, announcing tearfully a wish that
his father could see and hear the beautiful things that had been said about him.

Then Sep was "cut free of his earthly ties." Spiderwoman, in the West, pulled Aletheia's long broadsword from under the flowers on the coffin and waved it over the lid. As she did so, she called on the powers or goddesses of the West to free Sep. The sword was passed to the priestesses at the South and East, then finally to Aletheia in the North, the direction which represents the body, earth, and darkness. At each point of the compass, the priestesses called in free verse upon Water, Fire, Air, and Earth respectively to set the deceased free. Spiderwoman then began a chant. She sang one line and the coven members repeated it. Phrases involving "deep peace" were chanted over and over, as initiated witches at the four corners placed their hands on the coffin and visualized peace flowing through their bodies and into the body in the coffin.

Aletheia asked us to take our seats and listen to a brief tape of a Celtic autoharp. After a few minutes, Spiderwoman requested that the audience regroup at the cemetery and announced that maps were available in the outer lobby.

Aletheia asked the coven to remain after the rest of the mourners had departed. She raised the coffin lid and tucked the ceramic chalice in the crook of her father's arm. She placed some personal items in his inside coat pocket, including a "charm," a braid made of the hair of some witches who had performed magic for him. She took a small branch from his evergreen tree and laid it on his breast. With Diana oil, she began to bless him. When she came to his genitals, she paused. Dianics are familiar with the word "yoni," but the word "lingham," the male counterpart, was unknown to the separatists in Redwood Moon. After a little shared laughter, Aletheia shrugged and blessed her father's yoni. The funeral director came in and asked us to get a couple of "strong men" for the coffin. Several of the women immediately volunteered to carry it. The rest of us joined the procession to the cemetery.

Near the open grave, everyone lined up behind the coven. We followed the coffin singing a hymn Dianics claim was sung by Italian women who linked arms and walked into the sea to welcome death, rather than be tortured and burned for witchcraft during the witch purges several centuries ago. Nete stood at one end of the coffin and Aletheia at the other, as Nete read from her Book of Shadows about the meaning of the evergreen. She stressed that death precedes life, which always follows death. An apprentice passed through the crowd of family and friends of the deceased, handing out the sprigs of evergreen from the baskets that had been under the coffin during the memorial service. Many people accepted the sprigs, others refused to touch them. Spiderwoman spoke briefly about the debt that was owed to the widow, who had been so loving and caring toward Sep during his illness. Aletheia and her brother laid large pine branches on the coffin and those of us who had taken sprigs followed suit. Spiderwoman blessed the coffin and the grave, then announced that Sep was at rest.

A woman's voice rang out loudly, "And may Jesus Christ have mercy on your soul." One of the widow's daughters had created immediate tension in a small gathering with what appeared to be both a declaration of faith and a challenge to the witches.

An entirely unexpected thing then happened. Aletheia's brother, who had initially been the most angry and argumentative, refusing to attend any religious ceremony, stepped forward to heal the breach. He said that his father had taught him that the true meaning of Jesus Christ was that good lives were led by good people, regardless of their religions. The crowd seemed mollified and slowly dispersed for the reception.[12]

It is important to note that Sep's funeral was not typical. Dianics do not have a typical funeral rite. What is meaningful to individual witches and their families is worked into the service. Symbols of rebirth and regeneration, however, are used consistently, even though reincarnation in a literal sense was not mentioned that day.

Discussion

Attempts at achieving reintegration of the surviving family occurred in the rituals at both the chapel and graveside. The invitations to the mourners to share memories of the deceased and to join in the ritual magic of placing wishes (or spells) in the chalice were obvious attempts to establish a sense of community, as was the passing out of the evergreen sprigs. The attention paid to the widow by the coven, especially the praise and thanks offered to her at the graveside, helped somewhat to reestablish family solidarity. That these efforts were not more successful is only partially due to the deep divisions in the family and its lack of solidarity during Sep's lifetime. Geertz (1973:167) has demonstrated that conflict can occur when a particular funeral rite becomes both "a paean to God" and an affirmation of political belief. In spite of their attempt to be inclusive, when they called on the goddess, the radical feminist witches of Redwood Moon were symbolically challenging all social institutions based on patriarchal relationships.

It is significant that Sep's homophobic and sexist son, the most alienated individual present, and the only one without the immediate support of a community, was the one who attempted to heal the breach caused by conflicting religions. Although he professed to be an atheist, the Wiccan funeral and the symbolism it contained held meaning for him. Aletheia reported that the two of them were closer that weekend than they had been in their entire adult lives. She and Sep's widow, who had been estranged from each other during Sep's life, also appeared to renegotiate their relationship, at least on a temporary basis. We were later told that this relationship became strained again over the deceased's financial affairs.

It is also obvious that witchcraft provides a framework for interpreting and giving meaning to death, even in today's society where pain and dying are often prolonged. In so doing, Dianic Wicca also gives greater meaning to life. As Joseph Campbell (1987:152) has written, death and life are two aspects of the same thing, which is being, becoming:

> One can experience an unconditional affirmation of life only when one
> has accepted death, not as contrary to life but as an aspect of life.

Although she claimed not to have a personal belief in literal reincarnation, Aletheia found comfort in using the Dianic symbols of rebirth in dealing with her father's death. This, then, was an affirmation of belief in the life cycle.

Contemporary witchcraft, with its acceptance of death and emphasis on imma-nence, the interconnectedness of all things, and natural cycles rather than polarities, is a joyous, life-affirming religion, even in death. Spiderwoman epitomized this outlook in a powerful image when she and Aletheia were at the funeral home, wandering among the lead-lined steel coffins with rubber gaskets and special locking devices. As the mortician reminded them that they had to bring underwear to dress the corpse, Spiderwoman turned to him and announced, "When I die, I want to be buried naked, standing up, with a tree planted on my head." Aletheia told us later that she thought this was wonderful....

REFERENCES

Adler, Margot, 1986. *Drawing Down the Moon*. 2nd edition, 1976; rpt: Boston: Beacon.

Adler, Patricia, and Pater Adler, 1987. *Membership Roles in Field Research*. Beverly Hills: Sage.

Benjamin, Jessica, 1980. "The Bonds of Love: Rational Violence and Erotic Domination." *Feminist Studies* 6(1) Spring:144–174.

Budapest, Zsuzsanna, 1986. *The Holy Book of Women's Mysteries*, vol. 1, 2nd edition, 1979 rpt. Oakland, CA: Susan B. Anthony Coven No. 1.

————. 1980. *The Hold Book of Women's Mysteries*, Part II. Berkeley: Susan B. Anthony Books.

Campbell, Joseph, 1987. *The Power of Myth*. New York: Doubleday.

Cicourel, Aaron, 1964. *Method and Measurement in Sociology*. New York: Free Press.

Collins, Sheila D., 1982. "The Personal is Political." Pp. 362–367 IN C. Spretnak, editor, *The Politics of Women's Spirituality*. Garden City, New York: Anchor Press.

Damrell, Joseph, 1977. *Seeking Spiritual Meaning*. Beverly Hills: Sage.

————. 1988. *Search for Identity*. Beverly Hills: Sage.

Denzin, Norman K., 1970 *The Research Act*. Chicago: Aldine.

Douglas, Jack D., 1970 "The Relevance of Sociology." Pp. `185–233 IN J. Douglas, editor, *The Relevance of Sociology*. New York: Appleton-Century-Crofts.

————. 1976. *Investigative Social Research*. Newbury Park, California: Sage.

Douglas, Jack D., and J. M. Johnson, 1977. *Existential Sociology*. New York: Cambridge University Press.

Durkheim, Emile, 1915. *The Elementary Forms of Religious Life*. Translated by J.W. Swain. London: George Allen and Unwin Ltd.

Ellwood, Robert, 1979. *Alternative Altars: Unconventional and Eastern Spirituality in America*. Chicago: University of Chicago Press.

Forrest, Burke, 1986. "Apprentice-participation: Methodology and the study of subjective reality." *Urban Life* 14: 431–453.

Geertz, Clifford, 1973. *The Interpretation of Cultures*. New York: Basic Books.

Gold, R. L. 1958. "Roles in sociological field observations." *Social Forces* 36: 217–223.

Gordon, Raymond, 1969. *Interviewing, Strategy, Techniques, and Tactics*. Homewood, IL: Dorsey Press.

Hartsock, Nancy, 1985. *Money, Sex, and Power*. Boston: Northeastern University Press.

Jagger, Alison, 1983. *Feminist Politics and Human Nature*. Totowa, New Jersey: Rowman and Allanheld.

Johnson, John M., 1975. *Doing Field Research*. New York: Free Press.

Jorgensen, Danny L., 1989. *Participant Observation: A Methodology for Human Studies*. Newbury Park, California: Sage.

Jules-Rosette, Bennetta, 1975. *African Apostles*. Ithaca: Cornell University Press.

————. 1976. "The conversion experience: The apostles of John Maranke." *Journal of Religion in Africa* 7: 132–164.

Keller, Evelyn Fox, 1985. *Reflections of Gender and Science*. New Haven: Yale University Press.

Lofland, John, and Norman Skonovd, 1981. "Conversion Motifs." *Journal for the Scientific Study of Religion* 20(4): 373–385.

Malinowski. Bronislaw, 1948. *Magic, Science, and Religion*. Glencoe, Illinois: The Free Press.

Mehan, Hugh, and H. Wood, 1975. *The Reality of Ethnomethodology*. New York: John Wiley.

Morgan, Robin, 1977. *Going Too Far*. New York: Random House.

Parsons, Talcott, and V. Lidz, 1967. "Death in American Society." Pp. 133–170 IN E. Shneidman, editor, *Essays in Self-Destruction*. New York: Science House.

Reimer, Jeffrey, W., 1977. "Varieties of opportunistic research." *Urban Life* 5(4): 467–477.

Rochford, E. B., Jr., 1985. *Hare Krishna in America*. New Brunswick, New Jersey, Rutgers University Press.

Snow, David A, 1980. "The disengagement process: a neglected problem in participant observation research." *Qualitative Sociology* 3: 100–22.

Spretnak, Charlene, 1982. *The Politics of Women's Spirituality*. Garden City, New York: Anchor Press.

Starhawk, 1979. *The Spiral Dance*. San Francisco, California: Harper and Row.

———. 1980. *Dreaming the Dark*. 2nd edition, 1982, rpt. Boston: Beacon Press.

Vernon, G., 1970 *Sociology of Death: An Analysis of Death-Related Behavior*. New York: Ronald Press.

Walker, Barbara, 1985. *The Crone: Woman of Age, Wisdom, and Power*. San Francisco, California: Harper and Row.

Yinger, Milton, 1957. *Religion, Society, and the Individual*. New York: MacMillan.

NOTES

[1]Durkheim's assertion that "There is no Church of Magic" (Durkheim, 1915:60) was based on an idea of magicians as lone, instrumental practitioners who shunned the openness of shared ritual and direct involvement in a community bound together by common beliefs. This does not apply to Wiccan covens, where both are profoundly important.

[2]The word "participate is stressed because Wicca, especially for radical witches, is as experiential religion with strong performative aspects. Only on rare occasions is one allowed passively to observe a religious ceremony or ritual.

[3]Although the coven originally requested that its true name and real names of its members be used, pseudonyms were agreed upon and appear in this paper. Legislation was proposed in both the House and Senate in 1985 to mandate specific discrimination against witches and practitioners of the Craft. Although this failed to pass, it is not impossible that witches will be persecuted again in the future. The authors thus felt that pseudonyms were necessary to protect individuals who make this research possible.

[4]According to tradition, any women may call herself a witch if she "knows" herself to be one. Apprentices are considered witches who have not been initiated. An Initiate is a coven member who has studied for a year and a day, demonstrated to the satisfaction of all initiated coven members her understanding of Dianic traditions, and been initiated herself, usually during the ritual known as candlemas in February. Initiates may them choose to engage in further study in a particular area of expertise, such as ritual, chants, or herbology. The study must again last a year and a day, and the consensus of all initiated witches in Redwood Moon determine whether or not one will be advanced to priestess of ritual, Chants, or Herbs.

[5]In her chapter on feminist witchcraft, Adler (1986) argues that lesbianism is as much or more of a political and cultural phenomenon as it is a sexual orientation. She refers to asexual and/or celibate women who call themselves lesbians. In Redwood Moon, one self-identified lesbian was celibate, another said she believed most people were really bisexual, and another said she made "a political choice to become a lesbian." Regardless of sexual orientation, all Dianics learn a radical feminist analysis of religion and the roots of women's oppression.

[6]Lozano opted not to request apprenticeship training for professional reasons. Foltz was not aware that as a researcher she might have been permitted to become an apprentice until late into the research, when she was planning to relocate.

[7]The distinction between the two is made because one must request to become an apprentice. As Redwood Moon is governed by consensus, we may only surmise that our petition would have been granted unanimously. On at least two occasions during our research, consensus was lacking on the advancement of members within the coven, so candidates were held back. As several witches later informed us, joining a coven has much of the intensity of a group marriage. The commitment between members is a profound one and must be made "in perfect love and perfect trust."

⁸Upon hearing this accusation for the first time, the witches of Redwood Moon immediately went out and had T-shirts printed that read, "Too Dianic!"

⁹In 1968, WITCH (Women's International Terrorist Conspiracy from Hell) was formed in New York with the intention of using guerilla theater to be the "striking arm of the Women's Liberation Movement." Within a few weeks, covens had sprung up in major cities across the United States united by common style—theatricality, humor, irreverence and feminist activism (Morgan, 1970). Although they performed public rituals and hexings and wrote of spell-casting, their focus was political action rather than religious practice. Budapest lived in New York at this time and appears to have been influenced by WITCH's theatricality and feminist politics.

¹⁰We spent over a year learning the doctrine of this particular group of witches. To claim to have neither dogma nor doctrine is a misstatement; rather each group creates its own, taking what it likes from certain reference and "how-to" books, and passing these teachings on to new recruits. The basic Craft Law is "As and ye harm none, do what thou wilt." Other than this, Wiccan traditions and the individual covens tend to make their own, often highly creative, decisions in these areas. As one priestess told us, "You want to know the answers, but we haven't finished making them up yet!" Even then, the results are often highly idiosyncratic. Each witch in Redwood Moon is expected to keep a "Book of Shadows," where she details the magic and rituals she engages in, what seems to work for her, and her thoughts about her personal growth. One witch shared her beautifully bound antique-leather book filled with copious notes, another told us she wrote things down on scraps of paper and threw them into a dresser drawer.

¹¹There are eight "sabbats" or holy days in the Dianic calendar, celebrated at the solstices, equinoxes, and the "cross points" between them. Sabbats celebrate the wheel of the year and are used to reaffirm the connections among the individual, the community, and nature. Dianic sabbats share things with, but are not the same as, the sabbats in other Wiccan traditions. See Budapest (1986) for a detailed discussion.

¹²The reception, basically a family gathering, had not been mentioned to the author present until that very moment. Thus, a prior commitment prevented attendance. This was unfortunate, as rich data on the interaction of family members and verbal impressions of the Wiccan ceremonies were obviously missed.

Chapter 32

THE URBAN SPEED GANG:
AN EXAMINATION OF THE SUBCULTURE
OF YOUNG MOTORCYCLISTS

Stephen L. Muzzatti

Introduction

Living near Main Street in a major North America urban center like Gotham City, you may be rudely awakened late one night by screeching tires spinning on asphalt followed by an onslaught of police sirens. Driving on one of the highways in or around the city, you may be alarmed to notice the rapidly advancing headlights of a dozen, to as many as 70 brightly-colored high performance Japanese made motorcycles (sport-bikes).

Contrary to popular belief, this group is not a criminal/outlaw club but rather an example of the subculture of young motorcyclists that I have deemed the "Urban Speed Gang."[1] The following is an endeavor to illustrate that this group's existence is fostered and maintained by the structures of capitalist political economy in a large industrial-urban setting. While viewed by many as rebels and deviants, investigation illustrates that this group embodies many of the same beliefs and values of the "wider culture" but manifests them in a different form.

Methodology

Because the Urban Speed Gang is a small subculture, Symbolic Interactionism/ Participant Observation is extremely conducive to affording one access to the group. Even in the earliest steps of the complex interaction that exists between researcher and host, the Urban Speed Gang members were willing to speak to me, as I approached them in a "familiar way" (Wax, 1980: 273)[2]. Being accepted as part of the in-group was necessary to obtain the first-hand knowledge necessary to understand the subculture and the intricate definitions of the situation shared by it's members[3]. Informal, unstructured interviews were conducted with Urban Speed Gang members while hanging out on the street or in the numerous coffee shops that they frequented. While I occasionally decided on common questions which were posed to everyone, it was usually the members whom I allowed to control the content and length in both private and group discussions. My initial contacts among the Urban Speed Gang members were helpful in alerting me to other members who would be the most approachable, facilitating a form of "snowball sampling" (Weppner, 1977:25).

This methodology has allowed me to build on some general theories of subcultures, leisure, and deviance so as to formulate the field data in a fashion which guided my research toward consequential factors in the epistemology of the Urban Speed Gang.

Pre-Entry Experiences

There appears to be a greater emphasis on structural "pull" factors such as the media, and the importance of leisure than personal "push" factors, preceding the individual's participation in this subculture. This is to say that unlike some "deviant" groups who felt "pushed" out of conventional society due to school or family problems, Urban Speed Gang members were "pulled" away from traditional leisure pursuits through media-generated images which allowed for a fragmented social totality to be grasped (Hebdige, 1985:85).

It is the ownership of the sport-bike and the view of it as more than a means of transportation that brings these individuals together. All the members stated that their initial interest in motorcycles was leisure, or recreationally-based. The Urban Speed gang members have appropriated motorcycle riding through the living myth of leisure. Sport-bike ownership was a product of a pre-existing set of values and provided a focus for the elaboration of the subculture (Stratton, 1985:210). If viewed in terms of traditional deviance models, participation in the gang occurs only after the outbreak of delinquency on the part of the individual actor (Glueck, 1968). For the sake of argument, the "deviance" in this case is the use of a transportation medium as a recreational tool, thereby violating not only the normative understanding of the vehicle but as well that of "appropriate leisure".

Making The Connection

Attracted by the lure of downtown glitter and the collectivity of a larger group, individual motorcycle riders begin to interact with an existing organization. Identifying with a large group of sport-bike riders offers an identity for one to embrace and hold up to other dominant identities[4] in the system (Irwin, 1973:146). The members participate in interactions that validate their sense of well-being (Nash, 1979:200). In this case, the members embodied beliefs of themselves as the cool, rebellious types, largely dictated by the media, and sought collective actions which reinforced these images. An analogy to Lemert's Theory of Primary and Secondary Deviance can be seen. If someone is labelled "deviant," the individual may begin to engage in "more serious deviant behavior." Thus the cultural and ideological spheres of the motorcycling subculture are colonized, resulting in meanings not only being bestowed on "others," but as well ideas, representations, and images of oneself. Participation in the Urban Speed Gang is also largely attributable to individuals attempting to further bridge the disjuncture between what they are and what the media, as an ideological state apparatus, tells them they are.

Becoming Part Of The Scene

Due to the fact that leisure is a marketable commodity, great importance is placed on the use of one's "free time." The degree to which one is involved in a given activity in her/his "free time" serves to create and recreate the particular activity and its environment as meaningful and eventful (Nash, 1979: 216). The coming together of numerous individuals who share the penchant for an activity allows for the creation of a "scene" (Irwin, 1977). The very nature of the Urban Speed Gang fosters the establishment of a community by regularly bringing individuals together for extended periods of time.

Truly becoming part of the scene requires a pro-active assiduousness on the part of the individual motorcyclist to seek out the other sport-bike riders in what Oldenburg (1980) referred to as a "third place." In these informal gatherings sport-bike ownership is embellished with specific meanings, rules, symbols, and subsidiary meanings emerging out of the interaction with other participants. Through congregation at these third places, "articulation" (Irwin, 1973:134) takes place through which the individuals piece together a lifestyle, in this case, based on their use of free time and the sport-bike .

Unlike the typical "American Gang" studied by Thraser, Cohen, or the "outlaw motorcycle gangs" studied by Thompson, Hill, Lavigne, or Wolf, there is no attempt by the Urban Speed Gang to duplicate the straight world of business or the family. There are no specific initiation rites or role allocation (Campbell, Munce & Galea, 1989:80). Instead, what takes the place of formalized rules is an ideology penetrating that which is inscribed in mundane rituals and social encounters. This results in the lack of a comprehensive role map for incoming participants. The lack of formally-defined rules opens the door to a hegemonic order which seeks to secure consent among the subordinate members (new or otherwise) by setting up accessible ways by which negotiated compromises between the full rejection and full acceptance of the hegemonic order can be reached (Williams, 1989:315). To take part in the negotiations, let alone be aware of them, individuals gravitate toward these third places, immersing themselves in pre-existing social relations.

The Street As A Playground

Access to sport and leisure is often blocked by lack of money, time, or facilities (Eitzen & Sage, 1978:62). These, as well as additional, constraints are placed on the members of the sport-bike subculture. Since these individuals enjoy racing on their motorcycles, the logical location would be a racetrack. However, this obvious choice of location is, blocked due to the aforementioned reasons.[5] Because of this blockage the Urban Speed Gang uses the streets and highways in and around Gotham City as its personal racetrack. The use of public roads, however, presents additional difficulties to contend with. In addition to the obvious dangers posed by other motorists and pedestrians, there is also the police presence. It is for these reasons that Urban Speed Gang members choose locations and times for racing that circumvent, or at least minimize, their chances of encountering any of these problems.

Time

The majority of the riding activity takes place late at night, often spilling over into the early morning hours when traffic in the downtown core and surrounding arteries is light and is most conducive to high-speed riding and motorcycle stunts[6]. Furthermore, the absence of observers decreases the likelihood that someone might be inconvenienced by the Urban Speed Gang and call the police.

Barben Road

Barben is an industrial road where the Urban Speed Gang engage in these forms of plays. As it is lined by factories and industrial/commercial units, it is a perfect example of blind-eyed turf (Jacobs, 1961:57); i.e., it is devoid of traffic and pedestrians late at night. Furthermore, the group does not have to deal with what they view as a police intrusion, as this excerpt illustrates:

> We've managed to pull a fast one on the cops. Once last summer, some guys got nailed for dragging by some cops coming in to check out the units to see that nobody had broken in. P.S. has checked it out, and they come here every night between 12:15 a.m. and 12:30 a.m. So we just come here after 12:30 a.m.
> (D.F., conversational interview, June 12, 1992)

The "Hooker Corner"

Located in Gotham's downtown core the name "Hooker" refers to the fact that many female sex trade workers congregate on the corner and along part of the strip. The various other activities that take place in and around the "Hooker Corner" allows for a degree of anonymity for the Urban Speed Gang. Because it is located in the downtown core and has a variety of uses and users even late at night, it is less likely that the Gang's presence would draw the attention, or at least the sole attention, of the police. The members are aware of this and use it to their advantage, as this excerpt illustrates:

> It's beautiful here. There's so much else going on that nobody notices us, and nobody bothers us. The cops are so busy dealing with the hookers over there and the pushers in the alley, that we're the least of their worries.
> (K.P., conversational interview, June 12, 1992)

Urban Speed Gang members choose sites for socialization and play that serve their basic needs and are viewed as "safe," both pragmatically (in terms of minimizing the likelihood of collisions and injury) and socially (in terms of isolation from those who may find their activities deviant or criminal) so that they can adequately articulate and transmit their ideology, procure support, and validate their sense of self.

Street Relations: Reinforcement of Subcultural Identification

Urban Speed Gang members establish links and continue interaction based on their collective experience as sport-bike riders. This affiliation is purposive and rational. The choice of the solitary motorcyclist or small "cluster" of motorcyclists to proceed and continue with the subcultural affiliation is a conscious decision made from numerous eligible options. In this case, it is the myth of the good life through fetishized leisure. By continuing their subcultural associations, members build an identity with others and themselves through equation to their sport-bike (Barandese, 1983:16). The actors engage in face-to-face interaction through which sets of values are fit together into a new subcultural configuration (Irwin, 1973:158). The sport-bike rider must not only have knowledge of the cultural items; some measure of identification with the group associated with this knowledge is necessary for the acceptance and usage of this cultural form (Fine & Kleinman, 1979:12).

As Althusser suggests, each "locale" imposes its own structure through rules, meanings, and hierarchies of values (Hebdige, 1979:12). Extended network boundaries provide parameters of knowledge characterizing the subculture. In this case, it is the sport-bike rider's identification with the Urban Speed Gang that serves to motivate her/him to adopt artifacts, norms, and behaviors (Fine & Kleinman, 1979:1). The Urban Speed Gang is not a formal organization but a loose peer association in a state of constant flux through which negotiations of meaning result in the continual production of socially-constructed realities (Fine & Kleinman, 1979:6). This "information" reaches only those who are perceived as receptive by established Gang members. This information includes the ideological realm (values and norms) and the visible physical realm (artifacts and practices) that delineates the subculture (Fine & Kleinman 1979:7). As this excerpt illustrates:

> I'd never shoot my mouth off about what I do with these guys [Urban
> Speed Gang] to other people. They'd think I'm an idiot. Man, if my dad
> knew what I did down here, he'd snap. If he knew I hung out and raced
> the ramps,... I don't know. He doesn't know anything. All he knows is
> what he sees on the news, like kids getting killed in crashes and stuff. If
> he saw us here, he'd think we're a gang or something, like Hell's Angels.
>
> (D.D., conversational interview, July 10, 1992)

Tipping the Scales of Justice

Access to - and control of - knowledge is yet another tool of domination through which the dialectic of power realizes itself. Like the general public, Urban Speed Gang members feel intimidated when confronted by the police. This feeling of helplessness stems not only from an unfamiliarity with the law and their civil rights, but as well from the predominant social beliefs that are scripted onto the subculture which signify an accosting by a police officer as the articulation of "trouble."

Certain Gang members have connections which have allowed them easier access to information about the law and the rights, resulting in their empowerment as citizens and an elevated standing within the subcultural hierarchy. In this study only four individuals had even a cursory enough understanding of the law and their rights to demonstrate some degree of confidence in their exchanges with the police. This group of individuals was comprised of three members whose intimates were connected to the legal/law enforcement profession, and one individual whose only qualifications were an extensive history of run-ins with the police so that he was well-versed in legal procedures. As can be expected, these individuals were highly sought for their "legal advice." They were well known, and their information promulgated among the other members, as this excerpt illustrates:

> If we ever get pulled over in a group, stay near P.S. He knows how to talk to these cock-suckers [the police]; he doesn't take any bullshit. His mom and dad used to be cops. If they [the police] nail you with a ticket, go to court and fight it. J.S. can help you; she's a para-legal. Or talk to R.J.; his mom's a lawyer, he knows the tricks. Thanks to these guys, I've only had one ticket stick in the past three years. Thank God I know them; I've probably gotten almost 20 tickets in the last three years. That's not too bad; R.S. - 19, cops - 1.
>
> (R.S., private interview, April 10, 1992)

Due to the complex web of social influence patterns that simultaneously exhault and marginalize individuals, it can be concluded that there is no real leader in the Urban Speed Gang. Groups of prominent individuals have emerged, and while perhaps appearing to pull the group apart may in fact only be testing its resilience and their power in a reification of subcultural cohesiveness. The lack of clearly-defined leaders is likely beneficial to the Urban Speed Gang as it nullifies the possibility of an effacious power struggle which would ultimately be detrimental to the subculture's existence. It creates a balance of power that serves to integrate an individual well enough to serve her/his needs, yet it is not oppressive or cumbersome.

Embodiment of the Gang: Taking on the Subcultural Perspective

By establishing a link between the sport-bike and one's identity, a powerful cultural message is transmitted through the style, imagery, and suggestive symbolism expressive of wider social values (Chambers, 1983:301). Urban Speed Gang members struggle for the possession and manipulation of the motorcycle to bolster their threatened identity and self-esteem (Loftus, 1977:393). While the Urban Speed Gang's riding habits undermine the discourse of conscientious driving, thereby challenging to a degree the attitudes of safety and sanctity of property, they are really only part of the middle-class fantasy (Stratton, 1985:204). This refers specifically to dominant cultural myths about leisure and rebellion as the middle-class fantasy.

The Re-Definition

Urban Speed Gang members find meaning through ritual drama in which there is a symbolic flaunting of social discipline (Barandese, 1983:18). The Gang attempts to monopolize the concept of sport-bike riding, transforming it from a means of transportation into an intense and cohesive group ritual. Thus they have transformed a mass produced commodity into a menacing symbol of group solidarity. The object is diverted from its ends, coupled to a new name and signed (Hebdige, 1979:105). As subcultural bricoleurs, the Gang juxtapositions two apparently unrelated realities (the street as playground; the helmet as a disguise from the police, etc.) to disrupt and reorganize meaning. Like the American delinquent gangs studied by Cohen as well as Cloward and Ohlin, these sport-bike riders come together with like-minded others, withdrawing legitimacy from, and inverting dominant values (Campbell, Munce, & Galea, 1982:82). As this excerpt illustrates:

> In high school, they tell you to socialize, participate in extra-curricular activities, become a well-rounded person. Well, this is what we're doing, but I know it freaks people out. I see their faces when we ride by.
>
> (A.B., private interview, June 20, 1992)

The subculture is derived from the wider culture. In the case of the Urban Speed Gang, it is not only leisure and the establishment of social relations, but also technology as power over nature and the capacity to seek freedom and adventure (Williams, 1989:317). The wider cultural norms are readily absorbed by the Gang if they are viewed as appropriate and functional by its members (Fine & Kleinman, 1979:17). In this sense, the Gang is seen as a social pariah. Through their appropriation of values and objects, they form imaginary solutions to real problems. These individuals violate dominant cultural norms from within. As with all "subversives," it is not the damage that they do, but rather the perception held by the dominant group regarding the amount of damage that they are capable of, that results in the labelling as deviant and subsequently the perpetuation of crime/deviance as a marketable commodity.

The Hegemonic Order

Unlike "outlaw motorcycle gangs" such as Satan's Choice or the Hell's Angels, there are no formally-defined positions with the group hierarchy. There is no formal commitment to the Urban Speed Gang because it is not a formal organization. However, there exists an unwritten standard of commitment, based upon one's willingness and frequency of group participation. There exists an ideology concerning the benefits/responsibilities of group participation that operates and thrives at a "common-sense" level. There is rarely dissent because the understanding of group participation has been fostered in an atmosphere isolated from competing viewpoints and has been internalized by the members. Deviation from group consensus usually takes the form of an individual opting out of participation rather than the dissemination of an oppositional ideology seeking to procure its own support.

The ideological beliefs which exist within the Urban Speed Gang are consequences of past accomplishments. A continually growing list is incorporated, resulting in the emergence of the "crotch rocket hero" as a negotiated accomplishment.

The Crotch Rocket Hero: An Attitude

Word ... We are the standard by which all motorcyclists should be measured. We're crotch rocket heroes.
> (P.H., conversational interview, August 18, 1991)

Viewing themselves as the epitome of "real motorcyclists," the members of the Urban Speed Gang learn to project an image appropriate to the management of this role. The content of their ideology serves to justify their behavior (Williams, 1989:319). By thinking of oneself as a participant in the Urban Speed Gang, the creation of the crotch rocket hero's self-identity take place. By imitating the behaviours and values of hegemonic opinion leaders, the participant strengthens her/his identification with the group and subsequently enhances her/his own self-identity. If one wishes to conceptualize this in terms of traditional deviance models Glueck's (1968) theory could be applied. He argues that participation in a gang only takes place after an outbreak of delinquency on the part of the individual actor. He goes on to state that once "inside," the gang reinforces the actor's confidence in the rationality of the choice. Opinion leaders with the group, and outside influences such as the special interest media, reinforce the identification with the image of "real motorcyclists." While not to suggest that one's identification with the image of a crotch rocket hero is their sole identity, based on the frequency of participation in group activities and exposure to the media influencing, it becomes increasingly important in their definition of self (Nash, 1979: 213). The predominance of one's identity as a "real motorcyclist" is greatly influenced by the fact that this identity is voluntarily accepted or, perhaps more accurately, voluntarily sought as a means of overcoming problems that an individual experiences as a result of the political economy of values in capitalist society. As this excerpt illustrates:

I'm a sport-biker, an [Urban Speed Gang] boy first and foremost. Everything else that I do,... I do because I have to. I don't have a choice. I've got to go to school, I've got to work part-time, I've got to go to my girlfriend's stupid parents' house. I do this 'cause I want to. J.R. the student, J.R. the employee, J.R. the future son-in-law is all forced on me. J.R. the sport-bike rider "extraordinaire" is my choice. I like it, and I'm going to keep doing it. I'll probably even do it when I'm old.
> (J.R., private interview, May 25, 1992)

The plenary importance placed on one's identity as a "real motorcyclist" manifests itself in many ways including denying the illegality or ignoring the dangers inherent in group participation, claiming ownership of public spaces and engaging in identity politics.

Concentration of Ownership

The greater a member's identification with the Urban Speed Gang, the greater the likelihood that s/he will claim ownership of a public/private resource or an object on behalf of the subculture. Commodities are "repossessed" and seen as the property of the group. Motorcyclists who are not participants in the Gang, and thus not "real motorcyclists," are constantly criticized, marginalized, and seen as illegitimate users of commodities that the group has appropriated and converted into subcultural symbols.

Much of the struggle for ownership is spatial in nature. The Urban Speed Gang goes to great lengths to use areas of the city at times when they will not have to endure "intrusion" by others. Thus, when their "property" is trespassed upon, members become visibly agitated. As this excerpt illustrates:

—"Get the hell out of the way!"
—"Move, can't you see what we're trying to do?"
—"Get that piece of shit [car] off the road!"

(various members shouting at a passing motorist; Everston and Hwy.#5, September 12, 1992)

Deny Illegality / Ignore Danger

By ardently clinging to the identity of the crotch rocket hero members deny the illegality and the consequences of possible injury. Likewise by claiming that their riding activities are just a form of play, they portray it as a victimless crime and therefore legitimate. Many members attempt to talk their way out of traffic violations by asserting that they "were not doing anything wrong" despite the fact that they were aware that they were well in excess of the posted speed limit.

Members often claim that no one is seriously hurt when riding, despite the fact that there have been instances of fallen riders breaking collarbones and bruising ribs. The crotch rocket hero shows a flippant disregard for danger:

> Yeah, I went down hard once coming off of the ramps. I was going about 120–130 [km/hr]. At least, I fell riding hard. I must've slid about 60–70 feet along the pavement. I got up and was worried about my bike. I did some big-time damage to it.
>
> (J.R., private interview, June 8, 1992)

This cavalier attitude towards one's personal safety was simply an example of the perceived advantages of gaining status through the successful completion of this racing outweighing the possible consequences of an accident. In the event that one did crash and walk away uninjured, this could be interpreted as a status-enhancer. This is likely due to the fact that televised motorcycle races place great emphasis on images of the fallen rider picking up her/his motorcycle and rejoining the race. It is also fundamental to recognize it as part of a wider continuum of societal values which emphasizes daringness and sublime excitement as the epitome of "really living."

From roller coaster rides on one end of the spectrum to sky diving and motorcycle racing at the other, the transformation of "cognito ergo sum" to "I have crashed and burned therefore I have truly lived" is embodied, promulgated and embellished.

Essentialism

As a "real motorcyclist," the Urban Speed Gang member often feels that s/he holds a monopoly of knowledge on issues regarding motorcycles, motorcycling, racing, mechanics, the laws of physics (as they relate to speed, trajectory, and ergonomics), and the *Highway Traffic Act*. Some members feel that their personal experience as "real motorcyclists" gives them sacrosanct authority to conduct a diatribe on any of the aforementioned topics. Thus, as Fuss states, these identity politics authorize the crotch rocket hero's speech while marginalizing others. Using experience as the essential truth, ontology becomes epistemology (1989:113). Though extreme, I submit this excerpt to illustrate how far the "real motorcyclist" will take this. Following a bitter exchange in a donut shop that began as an innocent inquiry by a non-motorcyclist:

> I don't care if he goes to university. What does he know? All he knows
> is a bunch of formulas. Let him drag his knee around the Everston ramp
> at 130 [km/hr], and I'll show him centrifugal force in action. He's full of
> it. He didn't know what he was talking about.
> (J.C., private interview, April 28, 1992)

Feeling maligned and discounted as criminals or delinquents, it is clear why members use their authority of experience and affiliation to a larger group to achieve self-worth through the marginalization of those who they feel are responsible. If the traditional vehicles for the discussion of one's thoughts and feelings are blocked in the social settings, the classroom, or the workplace, it is logical that the Urban Speed Gang member should so vehemently cling to the street as her/his critical space.

The Urban Speed Gang As "Deviance"

Angela Davis states that crime is both a protest against society and an attempt to partake in its exploitive nature (Pfohl, 1985:335). While Urban Speed Gang members do engage in routine law breaking (speeding, careless driving, failing to stop for a police officer), it is more their violation of social norms that have caused them to fall into disrepute among Gotham City's citizens and police. It is the symbolic violation of the social order which attracts attention to and provokes the censure of them (Hebdige, 1979:19). Regardless of whether it is the violation of formalized laws or social norms, Davis' comment carries much currency. The Gang embodies many of the values of the political economy of capitalism such as the myth of leisure, competition, and conspicuous consumption. However, the means by which they embody and transmit these values violate the normative understanding and resulting in their labelling as rebels. While old school criminologists may argue that the Gang member is not a "rebel" but rather an "innovator" accepting cultural goals, but rejecting the institutionalized means of achieving them (Merton, 1968:132), it is the wider society's perceptions reflected through agents of social control that results in the label of "rebel." It is the dominant class' perception of the subalterns as a threat, more so than any intrinsic threat that they pose which results in forces being mobilized in an effort to further suppress them. In the following sections, I discuss both examples and ramifications of this deviantizing.

Motorists

Automobile drivers are possibly the most vocal opponents of motorcyclists in general and the Urban Speed Gang specifically. The roads and highways in and around Gotham City as desired resources are the sites of the symbolic (and occasionally literal) battles between the Gang and other motorists. Automobile-drivers share no collectivity among themselves; i.e., for the most part, there is no sense of group cohesion. With the exception of state regulation (traffic signals, highway dividers, etc.), there is no shared identity among automobile drivers. By contrast, Urban Speed Gang members share a common identity as a minority group of road-users. This, coupled with the fact that the sport-bikes favoured by the Gang, will out-perform even the best sportscars, resulting in the automobile driver "losing" in a struggle for optimum positioning in traffic serves as an irritant.

The Urban Speed Gang can be said to control the road. The Gang member realizes this and regularly asserts her/his authority in traffic by weaving between the slower-moving and less manoeuvrable cars in the city and easily passing even the fastest-moving cars on the highway. That which has been routinized in practice becomes part of their ideology and institutionalized in conflict, as this excerpt illustrates:

> Motorcyclists have the right of way at all times. Considering that people
> in cars are all daft and probably don't realize this, I just let them know by
> taking it. Next time, maybe they'll think twice about fuckin' with me.
> (R.B., conversational interview, July 12, 1992)

As a menacing symbol of group solidarity, it is little wonder why many motorists cringe (both out of intimidation and contempt) at the sight of the approaching Urban Speed Gang.

Inciting/Manifesting Conflict

Aware both of his/her advantages on the road and the public's fear and loathing, the Urban Speed Gang member often deliberately antagonizes other motorists[7].

While the majority of the automobile drivers' dislike for the Urban Speed Gang is channelled into horn-honking, vulgar gestures, and cursing, there have been instances of more direct and dangerous conflicts including instances of physical altercations with other motorists. (field notes, August 11, 1992 - 12:30 a.m)

Medical Concerns

Within the wider culture, there exists a strange myth regarding motorcycles and traffic accident fatalities. While motorcyclists are unarguably at greater risk of injury than automobile drivers in the event of a motor vehicle accident, popular myth seems to transcend even this. The myth has two parts. Firstly, the motorcycle rider is always at fault when s/he is involved in an accident. Secondly, all motorcycle accidents result in the rider being killed, paralyzed, or in some other way horribly injured[8]. As further evidence of the widespread nature of these beliefs, I submit the following examples:

> When I told my dad that I wanted to get a motorcycle, he told me that if I wanted to kill myself, I should get a gun instead.
>
> (K.A., conversational interview, September 1, 1992)
>
> AND
>
> My mom was really against me getting a motorcycle. She told me all these stories about people getting killed in motorcycle accidents. Then she told me that her and my dad would pitch in some extra money so that I could buy a used car.
>
> (D.D., conversational interview, September 1, 1992)

As discursive texts, the comments by these member's parents transmit the convoluted logic symptomatic of wider cultural views. K.A.'s father assumed that as a motorcyclist, she will certainly (1) be incompetent and cause an accident, and (2) die as a result of injuries sustained in the accident. Similarly, D.D.'s mother also assumed that he will be involved in an accident. She rationalized her opposition to him regarding purchasing a motorcycle, citing examples of individuals being killed in motorcycle accidents. She was not, however, opposed to him purchasing a car and was even willing to financially assist him, apparently unaware of the fact that far greater numbers (in total, as well as proportionately) of people die annually in automobile accidents than in motorcycle accidents. While motorcycling requires a greater degree of skill and caution on the rider's part, it is the rife belief of it as a form of certain death which leads to the societal view of its participants as foolish and their labelling as deviant.

Medical Staff

Embodying the above-mentioned normative understanding of motorcycling, medical personnel are often unsympathetic to Urban Speed Gang members who have been injured while riding:

> This one night, I fell and banged up my shoulder. At the hospital, the
> doctor gave me one of these "I told you so" speeches.
>
> (C.S., private interview, May 18, 1992)

Similar to Jeffrey's examination of "rubbish" in the hospital emergency ward, the medical staff appeared - if not openly hostile to the injured Urban Speed Gang member - then certainly unsympathetic. According to Jeffrey's findings, the medical staff appeared to be displeased with the rubbish because they were directly responsible for their illness, and they did not fully co-operate in getting well ((Rubington & Weinberg, 1987: 118–119). This attitude is mirrored in the instances that I observed. S.T. was chastised for breaking his shoulder while riding and then further belittled in addition for protesting when the staff wanted to cut his leather jacket off.

Another example of this deviantizing of the Urban Speed Gang and their subsequent mistreatment at the hands of medical personnel include ambulance drivers, referring to sport-bikes as "donorcycles" and tauntingly reminding members to "sign the back of your driver's licence." In emphasizing the fatal consequences of Gang activities, a moral regulation of one's body, and the discourse of "appropriate" leisure is established under the auspices of health and safety.

The Police

As a repressive state apparatus entrusted to enforce formalized laws and societal norms in the public domain, the police represent the most visible and powerful agents of the deviantizing /criminalizing process directed against the Urban Speed Gang. The police characterize the Gang as roving groups of motorcyclists who violate speed limits, ignore traffic signals, drive improperly-equipped vehicles, and commit various other reckless driving offenses (Loftus, 1977:385). In terms of general law enforcement, the police are reactive; i.e., they react to citizens complaints. Observations and the self-reporting of participants indicates that in the case of the Gang, as with any individual or group that is designated as "troublesome," the police are pro-active. The police are vigilant in attempts to seek out pockets of sport-bike riders and disperse them. They embark on intense patrols designed to break up the group before they congregate. This type of law enforcement is more than a legal victory for the police; it is a victory over the control of social reality (Quinney, 1979:304). Through attempts to control leisure activities, the police further the contempt that Urban Speed Gang members feel toward them. As this excerpt illustrates:

> The worst is when they pull you over for nothing. They say it's just a
> routine check, and they try to get chatty with you ... you know, Where are
> you fellas headed? ... that sort of stuff. You know they're just stopping
> you to break your balls.
>
> (T.D., conversational interview, June 5, 1992)

The Urban Speed Gang is well known among the police. As this excerpt illustrates:

OFFICER: So, you're in with that [Urban Speed Gang] race crowd, are you?
S.M.: No, sir.
OFFICER: No, eh? Sure, sure, fuckhead. I see you jokers all lined up, leather on, ready to go. You losers are always going like hell. One day you're gonna be sorry.
(Gotham Police Officer, September 6, 1992)

The harassment experienced by Gang members enhances an already strong anti-police sentiment within the subculture. The animosity between all types of motorcyclists and the police is long-standing and well-documented. From their historical examination of motorcycle magazines, Cuneen and Lynch cite examples of the notion that motorcyclists were unfairly harassed by the police as far back as 1936 (1988:7). The result is the development of an extensive folklore based on harassment and subcultural responses. In the case of Gotham's Urban Speed Gang, police harassment acts as a unifying force, enhancing group solidarity:

> Sure, some of these guys [participants] are goofs, but when it comes to
> the cops, I'll stick by them. It's us against the cops. We can't let the pigs
> push us around.
> (P.P., conversational interview, August 9, 1992)

The disdain for the police, and enhanced subcultural identification, result in the Urban Speed Gang mounting a symbolic challenge in the form of ritualized play (Cuneen & Lynch, 1988:11). Often too intimidated by the police to consider making these challenges on their own, the Gang member is reassured of the validity of the ritual as well as the safety and anonymity the group setting can offer. As this excerpt illustrates:

> I rarely try to outrun the cops when I'm alone. When there's a group of
> us, though, the bigger the better; that's when to do it. One cop car can't
> chase down 30 guys.
> (J.R., conversational interview, July 11, 1992)

Leading by example, the opinion leaders illustrate not only the symbolic but as well the practical benefits of challenging police authority. In addition to increasing self-esteem, the symbolic challenge offers pragmatic dividends such as escaping the police and avoiding a ticket.

Conclusion

While I termed the group that I have studied the "Urban Speed Gang," I have - throughout this work - referred to it as the "subculture." Similarly, I have alternated between "members" and "participants" when referring to the individuals who were the focal point of my street relations. These apparent contradictions were, in fact, a contrived attempt to avoid falling into what I view as little more than a discursive battle of semantics. While some researchers might have devoted considerable time and effort in an attempt to sort this social action into one of the two rigidly-defined categories, it quickly became evident to me that it had no currency.

While exhibiting some characteristics of the traditional gang model such as the members' frequent face-to-face interaction and a degree of territoriality, equally strong characteristics of subcultures were discernable such as informal relations and the absence of a formally-defined hierarchy. Similarly, in some aspects, it resembled a commodity-oriented youth subculture through the structuring of relations around ownership of a particular object while in others, the intersection of its form with the dominant cultural form pointed to it as a spectacular youth subculture.

The view of the Urban Speed Gang as a deviant group stems from the public's normative understanding of leisure. While embodying many of the values of the political economy of capitalism, including that of leisure, the group imbues different and occasionally directly-oppositional meanings to objects. The subculture is labelled as deviant because they are an extreme manifestation of an economy of values which emphasizes fetishized leisure. Action against the member of this subculture is primarily motivated out of a normative perception of her/his potential as "trouble." These findings encourage a critical interrogation of the designation "deviant subculture". Notions of deviance/criminality are contextualized within wider social formations and generic social processes that indict prevailing ideologies.

REFERENCES

Barandese, M.A. 1983. "Individualism, Technology and Sport: The Speedway Nexus." *Journal of Sport and Social Issues* 7(1):15–23.
Blumer, H. 1969. *Symbolic Interactionism*. Englewood Cliffs: Prentice Hall.
Campbell, A. and S. Munce and J. Galea. 1982. "American Gangs and British Subcultures: A Comparison." *International Journal of Offender Therapy and Comparative Criminology* 26(1):76–89.
Chambers, D.A. 1983. "Symbolic Equipment and the Objects of Leisure Images." *Leisure Studies* 2(3):301–315.
Cunneen, C. and R. Lynch. 1988. "The Socio-historical Roots of Conflict in the Riots at the Bathurst Bike Races." *Australian and New Zealand Journal of Sociology* 24(1):5–31.
Eitzen,D. and G.H. Sage. 1978. *Sociology of American Sport*. Dubuque: Wm. C. Brown Company Publishers.
Fine,G. and S.Klienman. 1979. "Re-Thinking Subcultures:An Interactionist Analysis." *American Journal of Sociology* 85(1): 1–20.
Fuss, D. 1989. *Essentially Speaking*. London: Routledge.
Glueck, S. 1968. *Delinquents and Non-Delinquents in Perspective*. Cambridge: Harvard University Press.
Hebdige, D. 1979. *Subculture: The Meaning of Style*. London: Routledge.
Irwin, J. 1977. *Scenes*. Beverly Hills: Sage Publications.
Irwin, J. Surfing: 1973. "The Natural History of the Urban Scene." *Urban Life and Culture* 2(2):131–160.
Itwaru, A. 1989. *Critiques of Power*. Toronto: Terebi.
Jacobs, J. 1961. *The Death and Life of Great American Cities*. New York: Vintage Books.
Loftus, R.P. 1977. "The Idioms of Contemporary Japan:Bosozoku." *Japan Interpreter* 17(11):384–395.
Merton, R.K. 1969. *Social Theory and Social Structure*. New York: The Free Press.
Nash, J.E. 1979. "Weekend Racing as an Eventful Experience." *Urban Life* 8(2):199–218.
Oldenburg, R. 1989. *The Great Good Place*. New York: Paragon House.
Pfohl, S.J. 1985. *Images of Deviance and Social Control*. Toronto: McGraw Hill.
Rubington, E. and M. Weinberg. 1987. *Deviance: The Interactionist Perspective*. New York: MacMillan Publishing Company.

Stratton, J. 1985. "Youth Cultures and their Cultural Context." *Australian and New Zealand Journal of Sociology* 21(2):194–218.

Visano, L.A. 1987. *This Idle Trade*. Toronto: Vitasana Books.

Wax, M. 1980. "Paradoxes of Consent to the Practice of Fieldwork." *Social Problems* 27(3):272–283.

Williams, T. 1989. "Sport Hegemony and Subcultural Reproduction:The Process of Accomodation in Bicycle Road Racing." *International Review for the Sociology of Sport* 24(4):315–333.

NOTES

[1] Taking this name from the figurative translation of a group of young male motorcycle riders in Japan studied by Loftus (1977:384). "Bosozoiku" is literally translated in two parts. The prefix "boso" means "wild or reckless motion;" "out of control at high speed." The suffix "zoiku" means "tribe" or "kin-group."

[2] As a long time motorcyclist I was able to ride up to the group on a sport-bike attired in racing leathers and signal to them my authenticity as a motorcyclist and potential as an Urban Speed Gang participant.

[3] The full understanding of a subculture can only be achieved by participation in the daily routines of its members (Blumer, 1969: 61). Pearson referred to this as "naturalism" in which the willing researcher unobtrusively studies the actor's real-live settings, outside of the research context (Visano, 1987:47). Working within the Symbolic Interactionist tradition, the researcher must carefully tread the line between observer and participant. One of the most salient concerns that a researcher immersed in participant observation must consider is one of not being exploitive (Visano, 1987:54). In my research, there was no deliberate deception of the subjects. The members in the Urban Speed Gang were aware of my presence as participant observer. As a participant observer, the Urban Speed Gang Members expected me to fully participate in their endeavours. This included "hanging out" until 2 a.m or 3 a.m, as well as riding in a fashion, and at speeds that at times I felt to be unsafe. Connected with this was the question of legality. Although relatively minor, these "illegal" activities such as speeding - and other traffic violations - wee an integral part of the group's activities. It was absolutely necesary for me to participate in such activities, more so for pragmatic reasons such as not losing visual contact with the group as they moved from one location to another, than to reinforce my credibility as a capable sport-bike rider.

The researcher has a responsibility to the group under study in so far as the quest for data and academic recognition must not disrupt its functioning during or following the study (Visano, 1987:57). I carefully concealed my notes and maps from anyone not directly involved in the Urban Speed Gang. In addition, I made up the names of the streets and the City (Main Street, Gotham City), and used only Members' initials who I mention in my notes (Stephen Muzzatti is "S.M."). I also made a conscious effort to further maintain confidentiality by not having detailed descriptions of members' riding apparel or motorcycles. It is not inconceivable that given the amount of attention the Urban Speed Gang draws from the police, and officer could conceivably confiscate my notes and maps and use them in a "crackdown."

[4] These other dominant identities include other leisure activities that young males participate in, from recreational sports teams to the nightclub scene. The Urban Speed Gang is an overwhelmingly male endeavour. Of the 70 individuals that I came into contact with during the course of my field research there were only five female participants. The noticeable absence of women from the group is due to the wider cultural differentiation of appropriate leisure pursuits based on gender and not to any active exclusionary practices undertaken on the part of the male participants. The male members are at worse complicit in perpetuating the gendered division of leisure by not actively encouraging female participation. For a more comprehensive analysis of women and their relationship to motorcycling see D.A. Chambers (1983).

[5] The closest racetracks to Gotham City are located over one hour away. In addition, these tracks restrict admission to those who have a special racing permit and who can pay a substantial registration fee.

[6] These include drag racing, high speed cornering, and doing "wheelies."

[7] A favourite trick of the Gang is to race up behind an automobile on th ehighway with their headlights turned off. When they are literally inches away from the car's rear bumper, they switch on their high beams on and startle the unsuspecting motorist. Others include "boxing" motorists in by surrounding the automobile and then racing off.

[8] Patricia Zonker's best-seller *Murdercycles* (1978) is an excellent testimony to the predominance of these beliefs.

Chapter 33

THE CULTURE OF GANGS IN THE CULTURE OF THE SCHOOL

Daniel J. Monti

The picture of tough young men swaggering down school corridors, intimidating their teachers and fellow students, fighting with dangerous weapons, and selling drugs is compelling and scary stuff. It has spilled across the airways and through the print media and arises frequently in discussions about the sorry state of public education. Notwithstanding the publicity and furor over gangs in schools, we do not know much about the subject beyond the mounds of frightening testimony built by school teachers, administrators, and students. We do not know how far gangs have spread throughout public school systems. Nor are we at all clear on how big a problem they really pose in the schools where they appear.

As to the first issue, the present paper will provide no insight or comfort. No data exist that can pinpoint with any accuracy the number and types of schools in which gangs are found. No study since Walter Miller's 1975 report to the National Institute of Juvenile Justice and Delinquency Prevention has offered a clue as to how many schools have gangs and where those schools are located.

We also do not know much about what gangs do in schools. Research on gangs undertaken before and after Miller's survey has provided little information on this matter. One finds predictable references to the poor performance of boy and girl gang members in school and allusions to gangs as a kind of "shadow government" in schools where they are found (Vigil and Long, 1990; Campbell, 1990; Fagan, 1990; Sanchez Jankowski, 1991, Vigil, 1990). There is a little information about the way school routines and staff encourage young persons to take on a gang identity (Padilla, 1992). There also are understandable pleas for money to reach gang members in school and surprising revelations about the role of school desegregation programs in spreading gangs to new schools (Spergel and Curry, 1990; Hagedorn, 1988; Monti, 1991).

Nowhere until recently, however, could one find a treatment of how substantially school routines and programs are affected by gangs (Hutchison and Kyle, 1993). Gangs may set themselves up as some quasi-institutional competitor to the schools. Yet it is not clear to what extent this challenge is acknowledged or carried out in the schools.

This is a modest but far from trivial goal, given the significance of the phenomenon and how little we know about it. One can understand the desire of academic researchers, school administrators, law enforcement officials, and policy makers to bring some closure to ongoing debates about the character and purpose of contemporary gang behavior. On the other hand, it is silly and potentially dangerous to offer generalizations about a complex phenomenon whose broad outline we are only now

370

beginning to make out. In our search for answers to tough questions, we run the risk of applying poorly tested treatments to problems for which they are not applicable (Goldstein and Huff, 1993) or offering up autobiographical accounts of experiences with gangs as if such musings meant that the author had really become part of the gang member's world (Sanchez Jankowski, 1991). I do not intend to contribute here to the growing body of self-aggrandizing cant that has passed as scholarship on this subject.

Presented here is a summary of information collected largely, but not entirely, from semi-structured interviews with approximately 400 schoolaged children who were between ten and nineteen years old at the time of the study. These interviews and my analysis of them are presented in great detail in my forthcoming book entitled *Wannabe: The Making and Unmaking of Gang Members in Suburbs and School*. The material is rich and substantial. It reveals the impact of gang life on children in elementary, junior high, and senior high school....

The information conveyed by the youngsters consisted of much more than their perceptions about gangs. Indeed, many youngsters made an explicit distinction between what they knew about gangs through their own experience or observations and what they thought or had heard about gangs. Those students who did not make clear such a distinction on their own were asked to distinguish their perceptions from their experiences. Much of what they talked about could be observed by adults in the schools and on the streets. The author looked for and found examples of situations and conditions described by the students. He had worked for sixteen years in the communities where these students lived and attended school.

While familiar with virtually all of the available literature on contemporary youth gangs, I did not have a pet hypothesis or much expectation about what I would observe and be told. Based on what I learned, however, it became clear that David Matza (1964) had much to say about youth gangs that was useful. His ideas about the way young persons drift in and out of delinquent activities and constitute a subculture of delinquency that stands simultaneously in and in opposition to a more conventional world (Matza, 1964: 27–42) helped to make sense of much that I discovered about gangs.

Much heated discussion about gangs revolves around the issue of how well or poorly these groups are integrated into the conventional world (Horowitz, 1990). The position taken here is that gangs and their members do not stand apart from the larger culture but are trying to find a way to fit in it (Katz, 1988). Who they are and what they do complements what is going on in the larger society, even though it may not flatter that society. The culture of the school, marked as it is by bureaucratic procedures and meritocratic principles, has become more susceptible to challenges from gangs, communal groups whose members draw on the strength of their ascribed status as part of a fictive brotherhood. How representatives of these different, yet complementary, cultures manage to coexist is the subject of this paper.

Gangs in Schools

The first published study of gangs in schools (Hutchison and Kyle, 1993) was conducted during the early 1980s in two Chicago high schools that served a largely

Hispanic population. The research was based on extensive field work and interviews with many of the young persons whose gangs were studied. Some data also were acquired through a survey of students attending the schools where the gangs were found.

The Chicago neighborhoods studied by Hutchinson are on the city's northwest side. Their population was about 50,000 in the early 1980s and it had been predominantly poor and ethnically mixed for decades. Approximately 60 percent of the population at the time of the study was Hispanic, and the same portion of these people were of Puerto Rican descent. There were several white ethnic neighborhoods interspersed among the Hispanic peoples; but the area otherwise was a patchwork of neighborhoods that had undergone a great deal of change during the 1970s. Two high schools served these neighborhoods. Each had approximately 2,000 students, and their student bodies were overwhelmingly Hispanic.

The 14 gangs operating in the neighborhoods and two high schools varied in size, but the larger ones probably had up to 100 members. These groups, like the neighborhood schools, were largely Hispanic. They allied themselves with one of two gang confederations in Chicago.

It was apparent to Hutchison and Kyle that gangs were a big problem in the two Chicago high schools. They were able to dictate who could use certain parts of the school, conducted their drug trade openly, intimidated other students, recruited new members, and generally did most anything they wanted to do within the school, on the school grounds, and on the blocks surrounding the school.

School personnel, according to Hutchison and Kyle, acquiesced to the control exercised by the gangs. They did not interfere in the drug dealing, intimidation, and recruitment activities of gang members, even though such behavior violated district policies and state law. Staff were willing to transfer members of gangs that did not "control" a particular school to a building where their friends had more power when conditions at the first school became too dangerous for them. On the other hand, they showed little sympathy for students who cut classes in order to avoid being recruited or intimidated by gangs. These youngsters sometimes were suspended because of their truant behavior. Large numbers of students dropped out of school, and gang activity was a frequently cited reason for their leaving.

Much of what Hutchison and Kyle found conforms to our conventional images of how gangs are organized and behave in school. In a private communication, Hutchison indicated that gang activity first revealed itself in the junior high schools. It did not decline once youngsters entered the high schools, even though some gang members had dropped out of school by then. If anything, he observed that gang activity became more intense at the high schools.

Insofar as their work conveys ideas that reflect our conventional view of gangs in schools, it will provide a basis of comparison for the information provided in the present paper. At no point in his paper, it must be noted, does Hutchison portray his work as the definitive treatment of gangs in schools. Indeed, he knows full well that some schools have little or no gang activity. His research nonetheless makes an important contribution because it offers a good summary of how gangs were organized and behaved in high schools found in a particular type of community.

Gangs in a Suburban School District

The present study was conducted during 1989 and 1990 in a school district outside a major United States city. Several administrators from the Fairview School District were certain that there was some gang activity in their schools, but they had no idea how much. They asked the author to conduct a study of gangs in the district's schools in order to determine the nature and extent of gang activity. The present paper is derived from that study.

The research was based on observations and interviews conducted at nine elementary schools and the district's sole junior and senior high school. Approximately 200 students from the elementary schools were interviewed. Another 100 students were interviewed at each of the other schools. Several teachers, counselors and principals were interviewed more informally at each site.

The youngsters who were interviewed at the elementary schools were selected by school staff. Only a quarter of the students interviewed at the junior and senior high schools were suggested by the school staff. The remaining youngsters were suggested by their fellow students. Boys and girls were interviewed at each school.

Youngsters at the elementary schools were interviewed in the presence of a school counselor. Interviews with junior and senior high school students were conducted without another adult in the room. All students were informed that they did not have to answer any questions, would remain anonymous, and were not to divulge the name of any child who might be engaged in illegal activities.

Most youngsters were candid and shared what information they had. Some shared information but also kept details from the interviewer. Most students were willing to talk. Only a few students at each school refused to cooperate once the interview began. An even smaller number obviously misrepresented their involvement in gang activity or knowledge of it.

Gangs from smaller towns in the Fairview School District probably had no more than one or two dozen members. Gangs from the larger municipalities may have had no more than 100 members. All gangs could count on the support of an indefinite but substantial number of young persons from their town during a fight with gangs from other municipalities. This was the case for fights in schools, but it was especially true of fights prompted by the "invasion" of youngsters from different towns into one's home "turf."

Recruitment of would-be gang members was done informally. Family and friendship ties, students said, were terribly important in this regard. The primary base for gang activity in the Fairview School District was the township and the interpersonal ties bred there. What happened to students in school did not seem to be crucial to the creation of gangs. What happened to students in school, however, affected the gang identity of individual youngsters and the behavior of the group as a whole.

Many young children indicated that they played at being gang members during the regular school day. While much of this play and imitative behavior had a game-like quality to it, the children took it seriously. They also appreciated the significance of what it meant to become a gang member by "trying on" the gang role. It was through often rough group play, the wearing of colors, and flashing of signs that young children explored the role of "gang member" and identified themselves as potential recruits.

The term "recruitment" was too strong and formal a term to describe how young persons became gang members in the Fairview School District. They became active members in a fairly natural and non-threatening way, youngsters said. They were introduced to it during the course of their everyday life and, having found it a source of fellowship and self-identity, simply slid into gang membership as easily as adults might slide into the local church. Children avoided becoming active gang members in much the same way. There was not much, if any, pressure put on young persons to become gang members. The municipally-based gangs provided most youngsters with their first exposure to a real "voluntary organization" intended only for them (Sanchez Jankowski, 1991). As such, the gangs introduced children to a type of organization that their elders count on for fellowship and mutual support.

The schools were a logical and convenient site where the process of identifying oneself as a gang member could be pursued in a relatively safe and predictable way. The self-selection process continued at the junior and senior high schools. Membership was not mandatory, but some status was conferred upon persons who did become active members. The degree of involvement exhibited by individual members varied considerably. At a bare minimum, persons claiming some affiliation with any gang were expected to "go down" with their fellow members in fights with other groups.

There were exceptions even to this requirement, however. Students said that a gang member could find ways to avoid a particular fight in school or in the community without losing any credibility with his peers. This was particularly apparent when relatives or former neighbors living in a different town had become members of a new municipal gang. It also worked for young men whose girl friends had brothers in another gang. An individual could be excused from participating in a fight under such circumstances.

Most gang members were male and of African American descent. There were some white members of the municipally-based groups and some whites who would be considered affiliates of specific gangs. Black gang members took considerable care not to expose their white comrades to their enemies. This was particularly true in school where the number of black students was far greater than the number of white students. There were female gangs as well. Students told me that these groups were not as numerous or large as the male gangs. Nor were they as involved with drug dealing or fighting as were the male gangs. None of their members was white.

Gangs had their start in the community. The schools provided a forum through which gang allegiances were reinforced and conflicts among gangs were fomented. Students said that there were long standing rivalries among the towns comprising the Fairview School District that predated the migration of blacks into the area. Fights had often occurred among youngsters from these different towns. The introduction of gangs provided a more organized medium through which the traditional rivalries were carried on and elaborated upon. Gangs also provided a means through which some criminal activities such as burglary, car theft, and drug sales were conducted.

Most students observed that schools became sites where both the social and economic functions of gangs were played out and reinforced. Lingering disagreements between gangs or their individual members were voiced routinely in the schools. New challenges and old scores were settled. In the junior and senior high schools, gang members took advantage of the setting in order to plan or carry out criminal activities.

There appeared to be little criminal activity in the elementary schools. Extortion occasionally took place, I was told, and youngsters sometimes brought weapons or drugs to school. Fighting and intimidation were far more common in these schools.

Students in the junior high school talked openly about intimidation and fighting in and around the school. Most of it was initiated by black students and directed against other black students. Some students acknowledged that members of several black gangs had intimidated and assaulted white students and extorted money from them on occasion.

Most of the municipal gangs had ties to the Crips or Bloods, but few if any of the individuals with whom I spoke expressed any sense of being part of a larger organization. Relations between larger, non-local gangs and local municipal gangs were based on business considerations rather than personal loyalties. It was from representatives of those larger gangs that local groups bought their "product." Some local gangs were better organized than others and sold more drugs. Only one appeared to have been so well organized and profitable, however, that its senior members had invested their profits in more conventional enterprises such as real estate.

Gangs whose members sold drugs, and all gangs apparently had members who did, differed in several important ways. None so far as the author was able to determine condoned drug sales to children for the purpose of consumption. Some gangs even prohibited the involvement of children in the drug trade altogether until youngsters turned thirteen. Other gangs integrated children as young as eight years old into their operation. Most gangs condoned the selling of drugs to any adult. Only one or two would sell drugs only to white persons.

Female gangs were not known for selling drugs, though individual girls did sell or assisted boys who sold. By the time youngsters entered junior high school, it was the boys who went out to work and earned money. The girls by and large waited to be courted with the proceeds from drug sales. They took "presents" from the boys and often exchanged sexual favors for cash and gifts. Some girls did this with several boys simultaneously. Some boys had at least two "girl friends" on the string at the same time. All of them acquired status in the eyes of many peers for successful conquests. Schools became an important site for displaying the goods or girls won through these conquests.

Formal alliances between gangs were rare. Students said that it was common for some gangs to be "close" to others or to be viewed as traditional rivals. The views of which gangs were close to each other or terrible enemies depended, in part, on the age of the children providing the information.

It was apparent from the students' descriptions of gang "alliances" that relations between gangs were brittle and fluid. The municipally-based gang was the organizational building block for the different combinations or unions identified by all the youngsters. Individual friendships and family ties could draw whole groups into fairly stable unions. The physical proximity of towns had the same effect. Disagreements between members of two groups were not likely to rupture such unions. Disagreements between members of rival groups, on the other hand, kept traditional animosities heated. Interpersonal disputes were an important factor in starting fights between groups with no prior history of animosity.

The distribution and sale of illegal drugs added another dimension to contacts among gangs. Representatives of the Crips and Bloods were the primary source of drugs sold by individual gang members. Gangs aligned with the Crips bought most of their drugs from individual Crips, though some persons had independent sources for their "product." The same was true for gangs connected with Bloods. It was possible that one or more members of a municipally-based gang also were members of the Crips or Bloods.

The Crip and Blood identity was important, students indicated, but not so important as the identity that came from one's community attachment. This caused some interesting conflicts for individual members with Crip or Blood ties when their town fought persons from their Los Angeles-based gang. In general, the member avoided becoming involved in the fight if at all possible. Had avoidance not been a viable option, the member in question would "go down" with his neighborhood gang. Gang members from several municipalities went so far as to push Los Angeles gang members out of their towns for a time just to limit the amount of violence that their big-city "brothers" or "cousins" seemed to provoke. The expelled persons were said to have moved into the city.

In light of the failure of the Crips and Bloods to successfully take over the territories of municipally-based gangs, it was most unlikely that a strong union of local gangs could be fashioned. The local groups would continue to serve as wholesale distribution outlets for drugs pushed by Crips and Bloods. Individual members of the local gangs would continue to seek and hold a companion membership in either the Crips or Bloods. Their primary allegiance, though, would remain with the neighborhood group.

The fragmented character of the Fairview School District also militated against the creation of a strong union or a permanent hierarchy among different township gangs. The boundaries for each gang's territory were fixed by virtue of being identical to those of the township. This made it all but inevitable that some degree of animosity would persist among different gangs. On the other hand, it made the massing of large gang "nations" most unlikely. Oddly enough, the very fragmented structure of the school district probably helped to keep gang violence and drug dealing more restrained than it might otherwise have been.

The significance of this should not be ignored and can be illustrated by comparing what happened in Fairview's one high school to what Hutchison and Kyle found in the two Chicago high schools they studied. Gang members in Fairview High School made little effort to mask their identity and often moved in small groups through the school. Yet none of the gangs controlled particular parts of the school. The cafeteria was the one spot where students from different gangs had the greatest opportunity to mix and confront each other; and occasionally persons did act out there. Most of the time, however, gang members stayed pretty much to themselves and ate at different tables. No such tolerance was exhibited by rival gang members in the Chicago high schools.

Gang members attending Fairview High School who sold drugs ordinarily did not do so in the school. They arranged transactions that would be made away from the school somewhat later in the day. Little money or "product" was exchanged in the school or on school grounds. There were severe penalties for selling drugs on or near school buildings in this state. It was the same in Illinois; but Hutchison and Kyle found widespread drug dealing going on in the two high schools that they studied.

It is interesting to note that marijuana, considered to be a light recreational drug by the youngsters, was sold regularly for $1 in cigarette form and smoked in different spots throughout Fairview High School by a number of students. Some students also consumed alcohol on a regular basis both before and during the school day and showed various signs of being drunk. The point is that these acts were no less a violation of school rules and state laws than the selling of crack cocaine, but gang members constrained themselves and did not treat the school as an open marketplace for their drug dealing. They also did not bring to school the violence one usually associates with drug dealing.

Gang members at Fairview High School did not recruit actively in or around the school. There was some intimidation and fighting in the school and on school grounds, but it was confined almost exclusively to known gang members who were freshmen. These youngsters tried to establish a reputation for themselves at the school during the first few months after their arrival and started most of the trouble. Older gang members usually stayed out of these fights unless their involvement could not be avoided. Other students participated only when they chose to help a gang member who happened to be from their town. The vast majority of students did not elect to join a gang, and they were not harassed in school. This, again, was quite a different situation from the one described by Hutchison and Kyle.

Students did drop out of school, but it is unlikely that gang activity was the cause of this at the Fairview High School. Most white parents removed their children from district schools before they reached the high school. The decline was particularly obvious after children graduated from elementary school and then again after they finished attending the junior high school. A perceived drop in the quality of education and friction among black youngsters or between them and white students contributed to the abandonment of the district by white parents. These factors no doubt had an impact on black parents as well, but a number of black youngsters were removed from school for a time or left altogether because of disciplinary problems they created. An unknown portion of these students were gang members.

District administrators believed that gangs were active in Fairview High School, but the principal did not attribute much significance to the gangs and did little to deal explicitly with difficulties they caused. He started two groups consisting of "good kids" that were to serve as positive role models for students. He also had a reputation among students as a firm but fair administrator which no doubt helped him. Equally important, however, was the fact that students could not transfer to another school in order to avoid unpleasant peer or adult relations. Gang members begin to learn the significance of this while in the junior high school.

Students in the Fairview School District first came into routine contact at the junior high school. Established or would-be gang members responded to this situation with an upsurge in organized fighting, intimidation, and drug dealing both in and around the school. This behavior persisted throughout the two years they spent at the school, but it declined markedly at the high school after a few months. One might have been surprised by this. Given the apparent naivete or tolerance exhibited by the high school staff, one easily could have expected more, not less, overt gang activity. Yet this did not happen. Some of the reasons why this did not happen are explored below.

The Subculture of Gangs in the Culture of the School

Gangs create a subculture in schools that parallels the culture endorsed by adults who are supposed to operate the site. The two cultures do not clash so much as bump; and the bumping occurs in ways that allow adults to carry on many of their routines and to ignore the influence that gangs have acquired. The gang subculture is an exaggerated and better organized version of the "peer culture" that operates in all schools to varying degrees. It serves as a powerful device for socializing youngsters and is every bit a part of the school's "hidden curriculum" as are the racial, class, and gender biases that some observers find lurking in almost every school routine (Anyon, 1989; Lubeck, 1989). The gang subculture has another source of strength and legitimacy. It is as an expression of the tension that frequently exists between the school and the community in which it is embedded.

The "peer culture" in schools is noteworthy because it can be simultaneously maddening and silly and because it ordinarily can be accommodated within the officially endorsed culture of the school. Indeed, the adults who operate schools often try to capture that peer culture and channel its energy into age and sex segregated clubs or teams that somehow complement the school culture. The gang subculture is far more intrusive and disruptive than the broader peer culture of which it is part. The gang culture is remarkable for the degree to which it is organized and sets itself up as a challenge to the official culture administered by adults.

The subculture of gangs is not expressed in a single way, however. It can vary from one to another school setting. It even can be accommodated within the school's officially endorsed culture under many circumstances. There are occasions when gangs and school officials coexist quite nicely and find ingenious, if somewhat tortured, ways to ignore or avoid offending the other party. This ability and wish not to offend the other party too openly is the key to understanding how the subculture of gangs existed so well in the Fairview School District.

Mention already has been made of the willingness of school staff to transfer gang members to other buildings, an action that both "protects" the students and rids the school of a troublemaker. School personnel also offer outright denials about the presence of gangs and often fail to report incidents involving gang members for fear that it will reflect badly on their management skills. Such actions, however, are not reserved only for gang members. These are rather standard administrative practices. Their application in matters involving gangs becomes altogether too common to avoid detection and throw both the receiving schools and bureaucratic machinery used to process transfer students into an overheated mess.

Gang members, for their part, also can work to soften their appearance at school without jeopardizing their effectiveness outside of school. They can refrain, at least at the high school level, from provocative displays of intimidation and violence. Gang members attending Fairview High School certainly did this. They also offered school personnel satisfactory explanations for those fights that could not be avoided. The confrontations, it was suggested, are just about "he-say-she-say" stuff (i.e., rumors or unkind comments about a person) or disagreements between students from different towns. Students first used this explanation in the junior high school and found that it worked rather well. School officials readily accepted and/or passed along such explanations in reports about even substantial fights among numerous students. There was a measure of truth to both explanations; but carefully overlooked was the fact that these exchanges ordinarily involved persons associated with different gangs.

Gang members also masked their involvement in such "illegitimate groups" by participating in regular school activities and by doing at least passable academic work. Some gang members at Fairview High School did considerably better than that. They avoided more overt forms of drug dealing and wore clothing that did not immediately identify them as gang members. Finally, they acquire the grudging admiration of a sizable portion of the non-gang student body by purchasing items that others could not afford and by providing a measure of protection for youngsters from their respective municipalities.

In these and other ways, then, gangs and school staff were able to find a basis for mutual tolerance, if not respect. The culture of the gang could be accommodated in the culture of the school by defining and treating it as similar to the broader peer or "teen culture." In its more exaggerated and intimidating forms, the gang culture rendered the officially endorsed school culture ineffective and toothless. It did so while allowing most of the school's bureaucratic routines to stand, if only as a feeble memorial to the vacant claims of a more conventional world on the lives of many youths.

It is in this latter way that most persons see the gang culture affecting schools; and there are many instances when this view is warranted. On such occasions, gangs might be seen as establishing a "counter culture" that lays out codes of conduct, beliefs, and routines which compete with those promoted by school staff (Yinger, 1960). However, gangs ordinarily do not supplant the regular school culture. They merely nudge it aside.

The gang culture is reactionary in that local customs are extolled and defended against the encroachment of persons and ways of behaving considered to be alien (Tilly, 1979). In its most extreme forms, the gang culture actively resists conventional models and myths of success and discourages many students from endorsing them. It also promotes the introduction of illegal activities into school routines. Its support for these acts transform the school from a haven into a sanctuary, from a place of safety into a place immune to the law.

This view of the gang culture is appealing on several levels. It is consistent with much popular and scientific speculation about gangs and it feeds commonly held prejudices about the public schools. Were schools more effective, one would expect less gang activity to take place there. Gangs also might be seen, therefore, as doing little more than filling a vacuum created by the absence or ineffectiveness of a more conventional culture in the school. Gangs may not present the best face that a local community can offer, but they do represent a parochial alternative to the more cosmopolitan world view offered in the school. They implicitly challenge the values and work of more conventional community groups and reject as unrealistic the idea that youngsters like themselves might grow into more conventional adult roles. Schools are seen and are treated as being largely irrelevant and not worthy of respect. Gang members act out against the school instead of passively accepting what it has to offer.

The idea that gangs fill a big social and moral hole in schools implies that they perform an important service. It would be inaccurate to portray this service as benefiting only the members of gangs. Historically, gangs have given expression to feelings held by many community residents toward outsiders (Thrasher, 1927). Within the culture of the school, then, gangs might be viewed as reinforcing or laying the groundwork for some important, perhaps even conventional, values. Among the strongest of these values would be loyalty to real and fictive kin, attachment to a place, and collaborative economic ventures.

Many observers have commented on the family-like quality of life within gangs and ties among gang members (Horowitz, 1990; Vigil and Yun, 1990). The notion of gangs as a "substitute family" speaks to the continuing importance of the family as an institution and the impoverished state of that institution in communities where gangs are found. It is important to bear in mind, however, that the uprooted members of many immigrant populations often created families for themselves from persons in the same rooming house, fraternal lodge, or church (Hohenberg and Lees, 1985). This helped them to survive in an otherwise ill-defined and sometimes hostile urban setting.

Gang members have accomplished this to varying degrees, but school officials are understandably reluctant to encourage them to build on that success within the school building. Some merely spend a great deal of their spare time together, but others have been known to share a common dwelling. Included in this second category would be youngsters, interviewed by the author, who sold drugs in order to pay rent on a house they shared because living at home had become too painful.

The place to which most gang members show loyalty and for which they express warm feelings is their territory or "turf." Not all gangs exhibit the same degree of attachment to a territory (Moti, 1993). No matter how thin that attachment might be, however, it is nonetheless critical to any effort to build a permanent community. Observers have noted that some gangs are enmeshed in a stable community and some gangs exist almost as a tiny island, free from much contact with many other people or groups that might be near them. In either case, it is the fact of being rooted to a place that makes more credible any group's claim to being part of a community with it own routines, rituals, and folklore. Theorists have long held that such ties are vital to any group's successful integration in an unsettled urban world (Wirth, 1938; Suttles, 1968).

Another prominent feature of successful group and community life, of course, is the ability to earn a living. The degree to which gangs or gang members engage in ventures to acquire money varies quite substantially. Individual gang members sometimes hold marginal jobs in the regular economy even as they are involved in illicit enterprises. Most of the moneymaking opportunities pursued by gangs as groups are fixed firmly on the illegal margins of the irregular economy (Monti, 1993; Skolnick, 1993; Padilla, 1993). This is not surprising, given the history of entrepreneurial activities inside some minority communities and the African American community in particular (Lane, 1986). Nevertheless, contemporary youth gangs have reproduced some collaborative techniques for making and investing money that have served different ethnic groups for generations.

Foremost among these strategies are rotating credit associations and mutual trade associations (Cummings, 1980; Velez-Ibanez, 1983; Light, 1972). The former requires persons, usually of modest means, to commit a portion of their disposable income to a common fund whose proceeds are given to a single contributor for some useful purpose. The fund is replenished and reallocated to other contributors until it has been "rotated" through the entire group. In essence, members of the group advance credit to each other under the assumption that persons will contribute to the fund even after they have enjoyed their turn at the trough. Mutual trade associations require the collaboration of individual entrepreneurs who compete fiercely but share some expenses and preserve the integrity of their market against would-be rivals. They are intended to restrain both the number of traders or producers in an area and the tactics that members use to capture clients.

The illicit ventures engaged in by gangs combine important features of rotating credit associations and mutual trade associations. Gang leaders often extend other members credit to buy their first supplies of drugs and assign them sales territories, better established groups also create a common "defense fund" that is intended to be used by members who are arrested or need legal assistance. Gang members who become more deeply involved in the drug trade frequently reduce their expenses by using the same wholesale distributor. They also go to great lengths to protect each other when competitors attempt to encroach upon their trading territory. The collaborative strategies attached to the drug trade also find expression in other illegal ventures such as extortion, burglary, and car stealing. Furthermore, older gang members take seriously their roles as teachers and patrons of younger members. In this way, the social and economic benefits of gang membership come to reinforce each other.

The youngsters who sell drugs on a retail basis do not earn a great deal and move in and out of the trade as their need for spending money rises and falls. They may even come to view themselves as being exploited (Padilla, 1992). Nevertheless, they establish a precedent for successful retail trades that capture a healthy share of a white middle-class market. This is an achievement for any ethnic enterprise, and it has historical roots in illicit businesses created by earlier generations of minorities with few conventional alternatives available to them (Lame, 1986).

However valid and real the parallel between organized drug dealing by gangs and more conventional ethnic enterprises may be, there are practical barriers to realizing the full benefit of such enterprises for youth gangs that sell drugs. First, the purveyors work exceedingly hard to conjure up dreadful adult images for themselves, but they are unmistakably children and cannot participate more fully or effectively in a conventional adult world (Katz, 1988: 129). Second, most pass in and out of the trade (Padilla, 1992,1993) and, more generally, drift in and out of delinquency until they become adults (Matza, 1964). Third, and finally, their work and violence are confined exclusively to the fringes of the irregular economy. They cannot easily translate their successful work into more conventional activities leading to other careers, or at least that they have not shown much inclination to do so, in part because so much of their energy is spent on activities that stand in opposition to conventional standards (Katz, 1988: 145–147). That is why the presence and impact of gangs in schools is so troubling.

It was known well before the present study that much of what gangs do in and out of schools is destructive and cannot be dismissed casually. The fact that gang activity often is tolerated in schools speaks to the ineffectiveness of school personnel, the irrelevance of the standards they support, and the persistent tension between the school and the community in which gangs are found. It is equally apparent that the relation between the culture of the gang and the culture of schools is far more complex than is commonly supposed. Educational routines and administrators' practices in some schools encourage more severe gang activity or can discourage it. The object of the author in this paper has been to describe and to account for some of the complexity in the relation between gang activity and the culture of schools.

REFERENCES

Anyon, J. (1989). "Social Class and the Hidden Curriculum of Work." Pp. 257–279 In J. H. Ballantine, (ed.), *Schools and Society*. Mountain View, CA: Mayfield Publishing Company.

Campbell, A (1990). "Female Participation in Gangs." Pp. 163–182 In C.R. Huff, (ed.), *Gangs in America*, Newbury Park, CA: Sage publications.

Chin, Ko-Lin. (1990). "Chinese Gang and Extortion." Pp. 129–145 In C. R. Huff, (ed.), *Gangs in America*. Newbury Park, CA: Sage Publications.

Chubb, J.E. and Moe, T.M. (1990). *Politics, Markets & America's School*. Washington, D.C.: The Brookings Institute.

Cummings, S.ed. (1980). *Self-Help in Urban America*. Port Washington, NY: Kennikat Press Corporation.

———. (1993). "The Wilding Gang." Pp. 49–74 In S. Cummings and D, Monti (eds.), *Gangs: The Origins and Impact of Contemporary Youth Gangs in the United States*, Albany: State University of New York Press.

Fagan, J. (1990). "Social Processes of Delinquency and Drug use Among Urban Gangs." Pp. 183–222 In C. Huff (ed.), *Gangs in America*. Newbury Park, CA: Sage Publications.

Goldstein, A.,and Kyle, C. (1993). *The Gang Intervention Handbook*. Champaign, IL.: Research Press.

Hagedorn, J. (1985). *People and Folks: Gangs, Crime and the Underclass in a Rustbelt City*. Chicago: Lakeview Press.

Hohenberg, P.M.,and Lees, L.H. (1985). *The Making of Urban Europe 1000–1950*. Cambridge: Harvard University Press.

Horowitz, R.(1990). "Sociological Perspectives on Gangs: Conflicting Definitions and Concepts." Pp. 37–54 In C. Huff (ed.), *Gangs in America*, Newbury Park, CA:Sage Publications.

Hutchison, R.,and Huff, C. (1993). "Gangs in Schools." Pp. 137–172 In S. Cummings and D. Monti (eds.), *Gangs: The Origins and Impact of Contemporary Youth Gangs in the United States*, Albany: State University of New York Press.

Katz, J. (1988). *Seductions of Crime*. New York: Basic Books.

Lane, R. (1986). *Roots of Violence in Black Philadelphia 1860–1900*. Cambridge: Harvard University Press.

Light, I. (1972). *Ethnic Enterprise in America*. Berkeley: University of California Press.

Lubeck, S. (1989). "Sandbox Society: Summary Analysis." Pp. 280–292 In J. H. Ballantine (ed.), *Schools and Society*. Mountain View, CA: Mayfield Publishing Company.

Matza, D. (1964). *Delinquency and Drift*. New York: John Wiley & Sons Inc.

Miller, W.B. (1975). *Violence by Youth Gangs and Youth Groups as a Crime Problem in Major American Cities*. Report to the National Institute for Juvenile Justice and Delinquency Prevention. Washington, D.C.

Monti, D. (1991). "The Practice of Gang Research." *Sociological Practice Review* 2:29–39.

Monti, D. (1993). "Gangs in More- and Less-Settled Communities," Pp. 219–256 In S. Cummings and D. Monti (eds.), *Gangs: The Origins and Impact of Contemporary Youth Gangs in the United States*. Albany: State University of New York Press.

Moore, J. (1985). "Isolation and Stigmatization in the Development of an Underclass: The Case of Chicano Gangs in East Los Angeles." *Social Problems* 33:1–10.

Padilla, F. (1992. *The Gang as an American Enterprise*. New Brunswick: Rutgers University Press.

———. (1993). "The Working Gang." Pp. 173–192 In S. Cummings and D. Monti (eds.), *Gangs: The Origins and Impact of Contemporary Youth Gangs in the United States*. Albany: State University of New York Press.

Pinderhughes, C. (1993). "Down with the Program': Racial Attitudes and Group Violence Among Youth in Bensonhurst and Gravesend," Pp. 75–94 In S. Cummings and D. Monti (eds.), *Gangs: The Origins and Impact of Contemporary Youth Gangs in the United States*. Albany: State University of New York Press.

Sanchez, J., Martin (1991). *Islands in the Street: Gangs and American Urban Society*. Berkeley: University of California Press.

Skolnick, J.H., Blumenthal, R., and Correl, T. (1993). "Gang Organization and Migration." Pp. 193–218 In S. Cummings and D. Monti (eds.), *Gangs: The Origins and Impact of Contemporary Youth Gangs in the United States*. Albany: State University of New York Press.

Spergel, I., and Curry, G.D., (1990) "Strategies and Perceived Agency Effectiveness in Dealing with the Youth Gang Problem." Pp. 288–309 IN C.R. Huff (ed.), *Gangs in America*. Newbury Park, CA: Sage Publications.

Suttles, G. (1968). *The Social Order of the Slum*. Chicago: University of Chicago Press.

Thrasher, F.M., (1927). *The Gang: A Study of 1,313 Gangs in Chicago*. Chicago: University of Chicago Press.

Tilly, C. (1979). "Collective Violence in European Perspective." Pp. 83–118 In H.D. Graham and T.R. Gurr, (eds.), *Violence in America*. Beverly Hills, CA: Sage Publications.

Velez-Ibanez, C.G. (1983). *Bonds of Mutual Trust*. New Brunswick: Rutgers University Press.

Vigil, J.D., (1990) "Cholos and Gangs: Culture Change and Street Youth in Los Angeles." Pp. 116–128 In C. Huff (ed.), *Gangs in America*. Newbury Park, CA: Sage Publications.

Vigil, J.D., and Long, J.M. (1990) "Emic and Etic Perspectives on Gang Culture: The Chicano Case." Pp. 55–70 In C.R. Huff (ed.), *Gangs in America*. Newbury Park, CA: Sage.

Wirth, L. (1938). "Urbanism as a Way of Life." *American Journal of Sociology* 44:1–24.

Yinger, J.M. (1960). "Contraculture and Subculture." *American Sociological Review* October: 625–635.

Chapter 34

PARADE STRIPPERS:
A NOTE ON BEING NAKED IN PUBLIC

Craig J. Forsyth

This article is concerned with the practice of exposing the female breasts in exchange for "throws" (trinkets and glass beads thrown from floats) from Mardi Gras parade floats in the New Orleans area. It has become so commonplace that the term "beadwhore" has emerged to describe women who participate in this activity. This phenomenon is compared to other related practices: nude sunbathing (Douglas, Ramussen, and Flanagan, 1977), nudism (Weinberg 1981a, 1981b), mooning (Bryant, 1977, 1982), and streaking (Toolan, Elkins, and D'Encarnacao, 1974; Anderson, 1977; Bryant, 1982).

Being Naked in Public

As a topic for research, being naked in public can be discussed under the broad umbrella of exhibitionism or within the narrow frame of fads or nudity (Bryant, 1977). In general, exhibitionism involves flaunting oneself in order to draw attention. In the field of deviance the term exhibitionism may also refer to behavior involving nudity for which the public shows little tolerance (Bryant, 1977:100; Bartol, 1991:280). This research, however, focuses on a form of public nudity that has a degree of social acceptance.

An extensive sociological study of public nudity was *The Nude Beach* (Douglas, et al., 1977). Weinberg's (1981a, 1981b) study of nudists represents another type and degree of public nakedness. Other research has addressed the topics of streaking (running nude in a public area) (Toolan et al., 1974; Anderson, 1977; Bryant, 1982) and mooning (the practice of baring one's buttocks and prominently displaying the naked buttocks out of an automobile or a building window or at a public event) (Bryant, 1977, 1982). Both streaking and mooning were considered fads. One question considered by sociological research on nakedness is when and why it is permissible, appropriate, or acceptable to be naked in public (Aday, 1990). Researchers have also addressed some possible motivations or rationales for public nudity. Toolan et al. (1974:157), for example, explain motivations for streaking as follows:

> While streaking is not in itself a sex act, it is at least a more-than-subtle assault upon social values. Its defiance serves as a clarion call for others to follow suit, to show "the squares" that their "old hat" conventions, like love, marriage, and the family, are antiquated.

384

Both Bryant (1982) and Anderson (1977) say that streaking began as a college prank that spread quickly to many campuses. As a fad, it still retained parameters of time and place. Bryant (1982:136) contended that it was one generation flaunting their liberated values in the faces of the older, more conservative generation. Anderson (1977:232) said that it embodied the new morality and thus was "perceived by many to be a challenge to traditional values and laws."

Mooning, like streaking, was considered a prank and an insult to conformity and normative standards of behavior. Neither streaking nor mooning had any erotic value (Bryant, 1982). Unlike streaking, mooning is still not uncommon on college campuses.

Nudism in nudist camps has had little erotic value. Indeed, nudity at nudist camps has been purposively antierotic. Weinberg (1981b:337) believes that the nudist camp would "anesthetize any relationship between nudity and sexuality." One strategy used by nudist camps to ensure this was to exclude unmarried people.

> Most camps, for example, regard unmarried people, especially single men, as a threat to the nudist morality. They suspect that singles may indeed see nudity as something sexual. Thus, most camps either exclude unmarried people (especially men), or allow only a small quota of them (Weinberg, 1981b:337).

Nudity, in this setting, was seen as being pursued in the interest of vitality and health and incorporated in lifestyle.

> In the nudist camp, nudity becomes routinized; its attention-provoking qualities recede, and nudity becomes a taken-for-granted state of affairs (Weinberg, 1981b:341).

Nude sunbathing incorporates many rationales from voyeurism to lifestyle and in many cases has a degree of erotic value. The sexuality of the nude beach has been evaluated as situational.

> Voyeurism...poses a dilemma for the nude beach naturalists, those who share in some vague way the hip or casual vision of the nude beach....voyeurs have become the plague of the nude scene....The abstract casual vision of the beach does not see it as in any way a sex trip, but the casual vision of life in general certainly does not exclude or downgrade sex (Douglas et al., 1977:126–7).

Similar to the nudist in the nudist camp, nude beachers expressed contempt for the "straight" voyeur.

> Sometimes I really feel hostile to the lookers. Obviously you can't look at people that way even if they are dressed... it really depends on your attitude in looking. I've even told a couple of people to fuck off...and some people to leave. I was thinking this would be the last time I would

come down here... there were too many sightseers...it sort of wrecks your time to have someone staring at you (Douglas et al., 1977:130).

But there were those on the beach who mixed pity and pleasure from being peeped at.

A group of boys had apparently entered [the nude beach] with the intention of peeking at some nudes. Since I was the only woman there, they congregated around me. This wouldn't have bothered me at all if they had been nude, too. But they remained clothed in their surfer suits. At first, this seemed a prostitution of the purpose of the Beach—they were being "dirty" about it and it almost made me feel that way. But after a while I realized that if I gave them pleasure by looking at me, then that was a fine thing. If their thing is to look at nude women for a charge, I certainly am not one to stop them from doing their thing (Douglas et al., 1977:128).

The concern of this paper is now to describe the method used to analyze the most recent phenomenon of being naked in public: parade stripping.

Methodology

Data for this research were obtained in two ways: interviews and observations in the field. Interview data were gotten from an available sample of men who ride parade floats (N=54) and from women who expose themselves (N=51). These interviews ranged in length from 15 to 45 minutes. In the interviews with both float riders and parade strippers an interview guide was used to direct the dialogue. The guide was intended to be used as a probing mechanism rather than as a generator of specific responses. Respondents were located first through friendship networks and then by snowballing. Snowball sampling is a method through which the researcher develops an ever-increasing set of observations (Babbie, 1992). Respondents in the study were asked to recommend others for interviewing, and each of the subsequently interviewed participants was asked for further recommendations. Additional informal interviews were carried out with other viewers of Mardi Gras.

Observations were made at Mardi Gras parades in the city of New Orleans over two carnival seasons: 1990 and 1991.[1] Altogether, 42 parades were observed. The author assumed the role of "complete observer" for this part of the project (Babbie, 1992:289). This strategy allows the researcher to be unobtrusive and not affect what is going on. The author has lived a total of 24 years in New Orleans and has been a complete participant in Mardi Gras many times. Observations were made at several different locations within the city.

Mardi Gras: Deviance Becomes Normal

On Mardi Gras day in New Orleans many things normally forbidden are permitted. People walk around virtually nude, women expose themselves from balconies, and the gay community gives new meaning to the term outrageous. Laws that attempt to legislate morality are informally suspended. It is a sheer numbers game for the police; they do not have the resources to enforce such laws.

> The greatest tradition of Mardi Gras was what is known in the old days as "promiscuous" masking. In the 1830s, 40s, and 50s every Mardi Gras saw masqueraders in the street—some on foot and the better heeled in carriages and wagons. There were even some organized groups such as the Bedouin Company and although Mardi Gras almost came to a halt in the 1850s, because of the outrageous behavior of its participants, the custom of putting on a costume and mask on Shrove Tuesday continues to this day (Huber, 1972:37).

Although masking is allowed only on Mardi Gras day, the idea of masking pervades the season. In a sense, the season becomes a mask for any outrageous behavior. What one does during Mardi Gras does not count as a mark on one's character.

Another of the traditions of Mardi Gras is the tossing of beads and trinkets.

> This custom began in the 1830s when masqueraders in carriages tossed bonbons and dragees (sugar coated almonds) for extra fun. They also tossed little bags of flour which broke upon striking a person, showering him with a coating of white. But onlookers also armed themselves with bags of flour to be tossed at maskers, and one writer described certain streets in New Orleans on Ash Wednesday morning as presenting the aspect of a snow blanket (Huber, 1972:37).

This began an active relationship between the float rider and viewer. As participants became more active, behavior became more outrageous and many residents called for an end to the festival. One offended viewer said:

> Boys with bags of flour paraded the streets, and painted Jezebels exhibited themselves in public carriages, and that is about all. We are not sorry that this miserable annual exhibition is rapidly becoming extinct. It originated in a barbarous age and is worthy of only such (Huber, 1972:46).

As Mardi Gras continued, the behavior of the day started to spread to any time there was a parade. As behavior became more offensive to some, particularly in the late 1960s and early 1970s, other "family celebrations" spread into the suburbs. This had the effect of removing the "censors" from the scene and both concentrating and attracting the "norm violators." Now anyone who comes into the city for parades during the Mardi Gras season experiences a different celebration.

Parade Stripping

The celebration of carnival or Mardi Gras as it occurs in New Orleans and surrounding areas primarily involves balls and parades. These balls and parades are produced by carnival clubs called "Krewes." Parades consist of several floats, usually between

15 and 25, and several marching bands that follow each float. There are riders on the floats. Depending on the size of the float, the number of riders can vary from 4 to 15. The floats roll through the streets of New Orleans on predetermined routes. People line up on both sides of the streets on the routes. The float riders and the viewers on the street engage in a sort of game. The riders have bags full of beads and other trinkets that they throw out to the viewers along the route. The crowds scream at the riders to throw them something. Traditionally, the scream has been "throw me something mister." Parents put their children on their shoulders or have ladders with seats constructed on the top in order to gain some advantage in catching some of these throws. These "advantages" have become fixtures, and Mardi Gras ladders are sold at most local hardware stores. It is also advantageous if the viewer knows someone on the float or is physically closer to the float. Another technique is to be located in temporary stands constructed along the parade route that "seat" members of the other carnival krewes in the city or other members of the parading krewe.

In recent years another technique has emerged. Women have started to expose their breasts in exchange for throws. The practice has added another permanent slogan to the parade route. Many float riders carry signs that say "show me your tits"; others merely motion to the women to expose themselves. In some cases, women initiate the encounter by exposing their breasts without any prompting on the part of the float rider.

The author became aware of the term "beadwhore" while viewing a Mardi Gras parade. There were several women exposing their breasts to float riders. I had my 3–year-old son on my shoulders and I was standing in front of the crowd next to the floats. I am also a tall person. All of these factors usually meant that we caught a lot of throws from the float riders, but we caught nothing. Instead, the float riders were rewarding the parade strippers. As we moved away to find a better location, a well-dressed older woman, who had been standing behind the crowd, said to me:

> You can't catch anything with those beadwhores around. Even cute kids
> on the shoulders of their fathers can't compete with boobs. When the
> beadwhores are here, you just need to find another spot.

The term was also used by some of the interviewees as indicated below.

Findings

The practice of parade stripping began in the late 1970s but its occurrence sharply increased from 1987 to 1991. During this study, no stripping occurred in the daytime. It always occurred in the dark, at night parades. Strippers were always with males. Those interviewed ranged in age from 21 to 48; the median age was 22. Most of them were college students. Many began stripping during their senior year in high school, particularly if they were from the New Orleans area. If from another area, they usually began in college. All of the strippers interviewed were in one location, a middle-class white area near two universities. Both riders and strippers said it was a New Orleans activity not found in the suburbs, and they said it was restricted to only certain areas of the city. One float rider said:

In Metairie [the suburbs] they do it rarely if at all, but in New Orleans they have been doing it for the last ten years. Mostly I see it in the university section of the city during the night parades.

Parade strippers often attributed their first performances to alcohol, to the coaxing of the float riders, to other strippers in the group, or to a boyfriend. This is consistent with the opinion of Bryant (1982:141–2), who contended that when females expose themselves it is usually while drinking. Alcohol also seemed to be involved with the float riders' requests for women to expose themselves. One rider stated:

> Depending on how much I have had to drink, yes, I will provoke women to expose themselves. Sometimes I use hand signals. Sometimes I carry a sign which says "show me your tits." If I am real drunk I will either stick the sign in their face or just scream at them "show me your tits."

Data gained through both interviews and observation indicated that parade stripping is usually initiated by the float riders. But many of the women indicated that they were always aware of the possibility of stripping at a night parade. Indeed, some females came well prepared for the events. An experienced stripper said:

> I wear an elastic top. I practice before I go to the parade. Sometimes I practice between floats at parades. I always try to convince other girls with us to show 'em their tits. I pull up my top with my left hand and catch beads with my right hand. I get on my boyfriend's shoulder. I do it for every float.....I'll show my breasts longer for more stuff and I'll show both breasts for more stuff.

Other parade strippers gave the following responses when asked, "Why do you expose yourself at parades?"
I'm just a beadwhore. What else can I say?
For beads. It's a challenge.
I expose myself because I'm drunk and I'm encouraged by friends and strangers on the floats.
I get drunk and like to show off my breasts. And yes, they are real.
For beads or cups.
Basically for beads. I do not get any sexual gratification from it.
I only did it once. I did it because a float rider was promising a pair of glass beads.
When I drink too much at a night parade, I turn into a beadwhore.
It's fun.
I expose myself for pairs of long beads only.
Shock value.
I exposed myself once on a dare. Once I did it, I was embarrassed.
I exposed myself because I was drunk.
Only one woman admitted that she did it for sexual reasons. At 48, she was the oldest respondent. When asked why she exposed her breasts at parades, she said:

> Sexual satisfaction. Makes me feel young and seductive. My breasts are the best feature I have.

One woman who had never exposed herself at parades commented on her husband's efforts to have her participate during the excitement of a parade.

> We were watching a parade one night and there were several women exposing their breasts. They were catching a lot of stuff. My husband asked me to show the people on the float my breasts so that we could catch something. He asked me several times. I never did it and we got into an argument. It seemed so unlike him, asking me to do that.

Float riders often look upon bead tossing as a reward for a good pair of breasts, as the following comments show:
The best boobs get the best rewards.
Ugly women get nothing.
Large boobs get large rewards.
When parade strippers exposed themselves they were not as visible to people not on the float as one would think. Strippers were usually on the shoulders of their companions and very close to the float. For a bystander to get a "good look" at the breasts of the stripper was not a casual act. A person had to commit a very deliberate act in order to view the event. Those who tried to catch a peek but who were either not riding the floats or not among the group of friends at the parade were shown both pity and contempt.

> I hate those fuckers [on the ground] who try to see my boobs. If I'm with some people they can look. That's ok. But those guys who sneak a look they are disgusting. I bet they can't get any. They probably go home and jerk off. I guess I feel sorry for them too. But I still don't like them. You know it's so obvious, they get right next to the float and then turn around. Their back is to the float. They are not watching the parade. We tell them to "get the fuck out of here asshole" and they leave.

Like a small minority of nude sunbathers who like to be peeped at (Douglas et al., 1977:128), there are strippers who like the leering of bystanders. Our oldest respondent, mentioned earlier, said she enjoyed it. "I love it when they look. The more they look the more I show them," she remarked.

Parade strippers most often perform in the same areas. Although parade stripping usually involves only exposing breasts, three of the interviewees said they had exposed other parts of their bodies in public situations.

Strippers and their male companions tried to separate themselves from the crowds; they developed a sense of privacy needed to perform undisturbed (Sommer, 1969; Palmer, 1977). Uninvited "peepers" disturbed the scene and were usually removed through verbal confrontation.

Most strippers and others in attendance apparently compartmentalized their behavior (Schur, 1979:319; Forsyth and Fournet, 1987). It seemed to inflict no disfavor on the participants, or if it did they seemed to manage the stigma successfully (Grambling and Forsyth, 1987).

Discussion

There are alternative explanations of public nudity of individuals or groups.

> Individuals go naked or expose portions of their anatomy in the presence of others, and especially others of the opposite sex, in violation of social proscription for a number of reasons, and may even justify their actions with various rationales. People may exhibit their bare anatomy out of pride, for economic purposes, or to frighten, disgust, or even interest members of the opposite sex. Public nudity, partial or total, may be fashionable, or it may be an act of defiance....Persons may exhibit themselves...to sexually stimulate the observer or as a means of sexually arousing themselves. Nudity may be pursued in the interest of health and vitality, to be more comfortable, or constituent to entertaining. Depending on the social context, anatomical exposure may be conceptualized as artistic, erotic, healthful, or even cute, or it may also be defined and labeled as pathological, perverted, and/or criminal (Bryant, 1977:99–100).

One goal of research on deviant behavior is to fit the behavior within a larger social classification. This paper has attempted to describe parade stripping within the larger frame of public nudity. It has also examined the individual motivations for this behavior, within an existent list of "excuses" for nudity (sexual, defiance, shock value, lifestyle).

The rationales of parade strippers did not fit neatly into any of the above. Parade stripping seemed to exist because trinkets and beads were given; for those interviewed, there was no apparent sexuality attached except in one case.

Parade stripping is probably best understood as "creative deviance" (Douglas et al., 1977:238), deviance that functions to solve problems or to create pressure for the individual. Many forms of deviance, however, do not work in such simplistic ways.

> Most people who go to a nude beach, or commit any other serious rule violation, do not find that it *works* [emphasis added] for them. They discover that they are too ashamed of themselves or that the risk of shaming by others is too great, so they do not continue. Other people find it hurts them more (or threatens them) or, at the very least, does not do anything good for them. So most forms of deviance do not spread (Douglas et al., 1977:239).

Some forms of deviance apparently do "work," and parade stripping is one of them. The beadwhore engages in a playful form of exhibitionism. She and the float rider both flirt with norm violation. The stripper gets beads and trinkets and the float rider gets to see naked breasts. Both receive pleasure in the party atmosphere of Mardi Gras, and neither suffers the condemnation of less creative and less esoteric deviants.

REFERENCES

Aday, D.P. 1990. *Social Control at the Margins*. Belmont, CA: Wadsworth.
Anderson, W.A. 1977. "The Social Organization and Social Control of a Fad." *Urban Life* 6:221–40.
Babbie, E. 1992. *The Practice of Social Research*. Belmont, CA: Wadsworth.
Bartol, C.R. 1991. *Criminal Behavior: A Psychological Approach*. Englewood Cliffs, NJ: Prentice-Hall.
Bryant, C.D. 1977. *Sexual Deviancy in Social Context*. New York: New Viewpoints.
———. 1982. *Sexual Deviancy and Social Proscription: The Social Context of Carnal Behavior*. New York: Human Sciences Press.
Douglas, J.D., P.K. Rasmussen, and C.A. Flanagan. 1977. *The Nude Beach*. Beverly Hills, CA: Sage.
Forsyth, C.J. and L. Fournet. 1987. "A Typology of Office Harlots: Party Girls, Mistresses and Career Climbers." *Deviant Behavior* 8:319–28.
Grambling, R. and C.J. Forsyth. 1987. "Exploiting Stigma." *Sociological Forum* 2:401–15.
Huber, L. 1972. "The Great Traditions of Mardi Gras." *New Orleans Magazine* 6:36, 37, 46, 48, 50, 52, 54, 56, 59, 60–5.
Palmer, C.E. 1977. "Microecology and Labeling Theory: A Proposed Merger." Pp. 12–17 in *Sociological Stuff*, edited by H.P. Chalfant, E.W. Curry, and C.E. Palmer. Dubuque, IA: Kendall/Hunt.
Schur, E.M. 1979. *Interpreting Deviance*. New York: Harper & Row.
Sommer, R. 1969. *Personal Space*. Englewood Cliffs: Prentice-Hall.
Toolan, J.M., M. Elkins, and P. D'Encarnacao. 1974. "The Significance of Streaking." *Medical Aspects of Human Sexuality* 8:152–65.
Weinberg, M.S. 1981a. "Becoming a Nudist." Pp. 291–304 IN E. Rubington and M.S. Weinberg (eds.),*Deviance: An Interactionist Perspective*. New York: Macmillan.
———. 1981b. "The Nudist Management of Respectability." Pp. 336–45 IN E. Rubington and M.S. Weinberg (eds.), *Deviance: An Interactionist Perspective*. New York: Macmillan.

NOTES

[1]The Mardi Gras parade season is between 2 and 3 weeks long between mid-January and early March. Its exact date each year varies with the beginning of Lent. The last day of Mardi Gras season, Mardi Gras Day, Shrove Tuesday, is the day before the first day of Lent, Ash Wednesday.

Chapter 35

KNIVES AND GAFFS:
DEFINITIONS IN THE DEVIANT WORLD OF COCKFIGHTING

Steven Worden
Donna Darden

It was about 10:00 on a Sunday morning, and Bobby had borrowed his parents' big late-model Buick to go to the fight because it had air-conditioning. In the back seat six roosters peered excitedly out of the windows of their varnished wooden cases. In the front seat, the three of us were squeezed in together, arguing over who had to sit in the middle. About ten miles out of town, Bobby realized that he had forgotten to bring the tarpaper.

At the next town, we pulled into a lumberyard and paid for a roll of tarpaper. As we drove across the lumberyard to pick up the roll, several employees watched us. The roosters sensed the excitement and began crowing for all they were worth. As they hit full cry, the workers pointedly stared at us, snickering and shaking their heads.

We looked at each other sheepishly and Bobby shook his head, "You can just tell what they're thinking: nothin' sorrier than a bunch of rooster fighters goin' to a chicken fight on a Sunday morning." We just looked at each other and laughed.

In recent years, we have gained much valuable insight into various "social worlds," including those of concert musicians (Gilmore, 1987), artists (Becker, 1982), computer users (Kling and Gearson, 1978), car collectors (Dennefer, 1980), fantasy game players (Fine, 1983), and gun collectors (Olmstead, 1988).

Although supporters argue that cockfighting is the oldest and most universal sport in the world, the study of it as a complex and diffuse social world seems to have been somewhat neglected. Of the workers who have looked at cockfighting (or "cocking" as many participants prefer to call it), many have analyzed it as a "pariah group" encountering society's disapproval and harassment (Bryant, 1982; Hawley, 1989; McCaghy and Neal, 1972; Ritzer and Walczak, 1986). Any attempt to view cocking and cockers as anything other than an undifferentiated mass of deviants has been muddled in the claims and counterclaims that surround any stigma contest (Schur, 1980). We will explore the complex internal dynamics of this unique social world, bracketing external issues of legitimacy and morality. Following traditional symbolic interactionist theory, we believe it more useful to study cocking by examining the social objects used within the subculture rather than by dwelling on the controversy surrounding the violation of the norms of the larger society. As Hewitt (1991:180) pointed out:

...people ordinarily focus their attention on social objects rather than social norms. They are concerned with their goals, with finding and using the right recipe knowledge for pursuing and attaining them, and with making sense of others' activities so that they can participate in social acts with them and carry out their own acts.

The basic object of a cockfight is to pit two roosters against each other in a fight to the finish, which usually means the death of one—or both—of the birds. Gambling is usually a very important component of the activity; depending on the setting, as explained below, very large sums of money may exchange hands. Bird owners and spectators bet. Most often, the birds are specially bred and raised strains of cocks. Although some cockers fight their roosters with their natural or "naked" heels, most cockers arm their roosters with some type of metal spur, or "heel," that adds to the violence and bloodshed for which the sport is generally disvalued by outsiders.

Therefore, we will begin by examining the meanings associated with these metal spurs. Heels, sometimes called "steels," strongly differentiate and divide the social world of cocking. When cockers meet, the first question they ask each other is, "What kind of chickens do you have?" This question qualifies or disqualifies one as a member of the "fraternity of cockers." If a person seems to be a member, the second question might be, "What kind of heels do you fight in?" As we shall see, the answer to this second question is crucial because it reveals the expectations and assumptions that people use in acting toward one another in specific situations.

Setting and Methods

This paper is based upon ongoing research that began in the spring of 1989. The data were obtained through participant observation, intensive interviewing, and analysis of secondary materials. The naturalistic study took place along the border region of eastern Oklahoma and western Arkansas. Worden did the primary research and observation, while Darden's role was limited to locating respondents and secondary research. This is not a world in which the principal figures would easily accept a middle-class female college professor as an interviewer-participant.

Observation took place at 12 formal cockfights or "derbies" and six informal cockfights or "hack fights." Settings varied from relatively posh legal "major circuit" private clubs to small rural game clubs and to apparently illegal "brush pits" in a corner of a farmer's barn. Numbers of participants at these events ranged from 400 to 500 for a major circuit club, 25 to 30 for a small derby at a brush pit, and 2 or 3 for an informal brush fight.

Interviews with main informants and informal conversations with many different participants were carried out over a period of 19 months. The number of informants is limited by the illegal nature of cocking in the states in which the interviews occurred. A purposive sample was deliberately undertaken to enable casual interviewing of a cross section of rooster breeders, handlers, gamblers, pit owners, referees, sew-up girls, and other ancillary personnel. Furthermore, for the purposes of interviewing participants in a clearly illegal activity, information from those living in "illegal" states was emphasized.

As a check on the validity of the interview responses and observations, we carefully studied 24 issues of one national cocking publication, *The Gamecock*. We also looked at issues of other national magazines such as *Feathered Warrior* and *Grit and Steel* for negative cases. Finally, an informant read and commented on this paper and corroborated its major conclusions as well as our interpretations of supporting data.

The participant phase of this research involved feeding, working with, and transporting game fowl for a period of 23 months. In keeping with Blumer's (1969) insistence on getting a close familiarity with the empirical world, Worden helped take care of chickens, attached wing bands to stags and cocks, and helped "dub" or trim roosters' combs. Ongoing discussions of gamecock and cockfighting accompanied these activities. Discussions with informants or a group of informants lasted anywhere from 15 minutes to 5 hours. Worden engaged in almost weekly discussions or activities having to do with the raising and fighting of game fowl with cockfighters.

A particular problem for this study involved gaining access to the social world. Participants in cocking refer to themselves as members of the "fraternity of cocking." Entry into the brotherhood proceeds by degrees and is particularly difficult because cockfighting is illegal in 44 states and controversial in the others.

At first, the interviews and observations were only partially successful in entering into the cockfighting network. During an attempt at an interview with one taciturn informant, for example, Worden was cut off abruptly. "Talkin' doesn't have much to do with fightin' roosters. You do it, you don't talk about it," the cocker told him. It was only after his active involvement by transporting roosters and helping prepare for a gamecock fight that Worden could even pass as a semipartisan.

Many cockfighters still refuse to discuss cocking in any detail with anyone who does not own and actively fight roosters in the arenas or "pits." Until then, the researcher may be suspected, especially by older cockers, of being "an agent for the humane society." As one older cocker commented, "Until he raises and fights some of his own roosters, I'm not going to talk to him."

However, several informants felt that it was a good thing that "finally someone would tell our side of the story." Most cockers whom we studied approved of our research because it focused on the interpretive and subjective experiences of cockers. We were aware that researchers who use this technique have been accused of romanticizing the subject matter (Merton, 1972; Thio, 1988) and we made a special effort to remain objective.

Despite the vagaries associated with studying a controversial, defensive, and generally illegal sport, we have found that the social world is naturally divided up into distinct orientations based on the use of some social objects. We explore these ideas more fully below.

Heels as Social Objects

One of the first choices a cocker has to make is the kind of heel (artificial spur) in which he fights his roosters. To underestimate the importance of the type of spurs a person uses on his roosters is to disregard the importance of a central object. The heel is probably the fundamental indicator of the meanings of cocking for a participant. The following discussion shows some of the practical as well as symbolic aspects of using one type of heel: the gaff.

Fighting the Gaff

The gaff is a 1- to 2 1/2-inch long, slightly curved steel spur, perfectly round and tapering to an extremely sharp point. Gaffs come in different shapes such as "bayonets," "jaggers," and "regulation" and may be pointed at various angles termed as "full-drop," "high," or "medium" points. Cockers may pay as much as $130 a pair, although most gaffs cost around $75 a pair. Generally gaffs are made out of extremely light, tempered, high carbon/tungsten steel and may be nickel-chromium or even gold plated. A cocker often carries his entire set of gaffs in a polished walnut case lined with velvet, which seldom leaves his side in a cockfight.

Heeling the Gaff

The gaff is affixed to a socket embedded in soft calfskin that is designed to fit over the rooster's spur. The rooster's leg and the natural heel are carefully padded with moleskin to cushion the gaff as it is fitted onto the rooster's leg. The person tying on the gaffs, the heeler, wraps the leather carefully around the rooster's leg so that the gaff fits down solidly over the trimmed-off natural spur.

In the act of heeling some of the "recipe knowledge" associated with the gaff is evident. Esoteric ritual usually surrounds this secretive act, which often takes place in seclusion behind a closed door, behind a barn, or out in the brush. As one observer noted,

> There is much mystique connected with all phases of cocking. Almost every aspect has its full share of secrets and voodooism. Many budding cockers are led to believe if only they had the key to certain of these mysteries their success was secure forever....But nowhere was the mystery deeper or darker than in the realm of heeling (Narrangansett, 1982).

A heeler may stand a certain way or use special kinds of waxed strings. It often takes a yard or more of string to tie a gaff securely to the leg of a rooster. Other heelers show some disregard for the ceremony: "I just use dental floss, I just tie the gaffs on good and tight, but not too tight, and that's it," one heeler commented.

At one fight a heeler working with a rooster happened to say in an offhand way, "You know, I have never seen one of these actually come off. I guess I make too big a deal of it. But, I sure don't want to have one come off, either." Onlooking heelers agreed.

Part of the mystery of the ritual may stem from the necessity for two people to complete the heeling. Two people stand facing each other; one holds the bird and places its feet on the heeler's chest. The heeler, the one with the bird's feet on his chest, can feel the feet contract or relax as he ties the gaffs. Thus, he can judge the proper fit of the heels when he feels the muscles or toes of the bird tightening. Heeling must be done very carefully to ensure that the toes and muscles of the bird have full flexibility and circulation. The heeler then pops the knuckles of the bird to loosen up its toes.

In another style of heeling, one person holds a rooster tightly against himself and holds out one leg for heeling. Then the rooster is turned around for the fitting of the gaff on the other leg.

A properly fitted and tied set of gaffs will enable the bird to fly up into the air, hold its legs out in front of itself, and repeatedly strike its opponent in the head or body. The cocker hopes the gaffs have been properly tied so they will not come loose or break. Either possibility would almost certainly mean the death of the rooster and loss of the fight.

Fighting in the Gaff

Specific rules governing cockfights vary from somewhat arbitrary house rules to the standardized Worthman's rules (Worthman, 1965). Particularly in brush pits, with a volunteer referee, there may not be any final authority on the rules, since many people may be uncertain about the details. Often spectators are asked to referee, and there may not be much consistency. As one older cocker said, "That's why when I referee, I always carry a copy of Worthman's rules in my back pocket. I can just pull it out at any time and show people what it says in black and white."

Usually a fight begins when the referee tells the handlers holding the roosters to "flirt them" or "bill them." In this process, the two handlers stand side by side, next to each other, holding the gamecocks so that they can peck at each other.

When the roosters become angry at each other they begin to show their aggressiveness and energy. It is at this point that the handlers and the people in the crowd make wagers on their favorites. The wagering may stop after the roosters begin to fight or, depending on the rules, spectators can continue to make wagers as the fight progresses, and the odds change as the audience revalues the merits of the roosters and their handlers.

After the billing, the referee says, "Fly 'em," and the two handlers stand facing each other and hold their roosters, by the legs, out in front of them. As the roosters lunge at each other and flap their wings, their hackle feathers generally stand out from their necks, indicating readiness to fight. If, however, in the billing a rooster refuses to peck at another or refuses to demonstrate willingness to fight when flown, it will not be fought.

At the last stage of the preparation for battle, the referee tells the handlers to go to the score lines approximately 8 feet apart in the dirt. The handlers get ready by putting the roosters on the line. At the verbal command "Pit!" the roosters are released.

When the roosters see each other they run toward each other and either begin to attack or to calculate through feints and dodges the other's moves. Then, when they meet, it is usually as Geertz (1972:8) described it: "the cocks fly almost immediately at one another in a wing-beating, head-thrusting, leg-kicking explosion of animal fury so pure, so absolute, and in its own way so beautiful as to be almost abstract, a Platonic concept of hate."

Handling in the Gaff Fight

When the roosters become entangled with each other or "hung" with spurs tangled up in each other, as they generally do in the gaff fight, the referee calls "handle," and each rooster's handler runs to disentangle his gamecock. But they do not run too fast to help them because the birds may become disentangled and attack the handler. A combination of speed and discretion is required. An inviolate rule stipulates that the handler whose rooster has been hurt by a gaff pulls out the gaff: "You always remove the gaff from your own bird. Otherwise, the other handler may twist it around and make the injury worse."

In removing a gaff from your own bird, you use one open hand to hold your opponent's rooster in place while you wait for the other handler. Although it is considered very unfair, if the referee is not looking, a person can press down too hard on the other bird, "mashing" it and thereby injuring it further. If a person is caught mashing another bird, he may be required to forfeit the match. Beyond that, as one person said, "It is just bad sportsmanship. It is cheating like that which gives the sport a bad name because it appears that the only important thing is winning money."

After untangling the birds, each handler retreats to his end of the pit with his bird and begins to try to minister to its injuries. Depending on the injury, the handler will stroke its back to warm up the spinal cord, breathe on its neck to warm it, and even put its beak in his mouth to try to pull up material that may be clogging the bird's throat. Onlookers and supporters in the audience will call advice to the handler as to how to care for the rooster. Generally, if the bird is in pretty good shape, it needs only to walk around in order to "adjust itself." This requires that the handler stand between his bird and the opposing rooster so that they cannot see each other as they rest for 20 seconds.

Several handlers insisted that you can tell by the feel of the rooster when it will or will not fight: "It is as if there is a current of electricity running through his body. You can feel it in your hands and when you feel that, all you do is just be as gentle as possible in handling the bird and he will feel your confidence in him and he will win for you." Another handler agreed: "It must be the tension in their muscles or something but when you feel that, you know that no matter how badly hurt, he will continue to fight. On the other hand, I had one rooster that wasn't really hurt at all, but when I put him down, he didn't have that electricity and he just sat there and wished that he was somewhere else."

"Draggin'" the Roosters

Roosters fighting with gaffs may batter at each other for anywhere from a few minutes to an hour or longer. As one cocker put it, "There's a lot of noise from the wing flappin' but if they are not cutting, it's all show. They may not be doing any damage to one another at all. But the crowd gets all excited at the noise and action." Some cockers say that they get bored if the roosters are not aggressively fighting. If the roosters simply settle down and wrestle with each other's beaks, onlookers will begin to yell at the rooster, "Hit him, don't kiss him" or "Now you've got him, finish him off!"

Although cockers regard the better birds as those that are able to finish off their opponents in the first few minutes of the fight, at the first buckle (when the birds first engage), many times the winner will not be decided until the birds are exhausted. As the fighting slows, the referee may decide that the fight is slowing down the momentum of the cockpit and order the handlers to "drag 'em."

On this command, the two birds are moved out of the main pit to a smaller pit called the "drag pit." The fight in the drag pit can last as long as 2 hours or more until a winner is decided. In the smaller pit, the bird that is able to peck last at its opponent wins. This rule is to ensure that the bird with the most determination or strength, or "gameness," wins. No bird that refuses to fight can win the match.

An observer looking for gruesomeness in the gaff fight would most likely find it in the drag pit, where the fowl are fighting injured or exhausted. However, gamecocks rarely make a noise of complaint about their injuries and rarely try to get away from their opponents. It is this refusal to run and the fowl's constant effort to try to kill its opponent that cockers who fight in the gaff value most highly. They call it gameness, and gaff-fighting cockers say that it is only by fighting in the gaff fight that true gameness can be measured.

Gaffs and Gameness

This willingness of gamecocks to fight regardless of their chances of victory is probably the most prized element in the social world of cocking. A great rooster can "break high" and hold its head back with its feet out in front of its body. A great rooster is also a "good cutter," a bird that carefully points its spurs and hits deeply and rapidly in the vulnerable areas of the opponent, and it is smart and uses judgement in feinting and timing blows.

However, the most admired roosters are the ones that defiantly try with their last dying gasps to reach and kill their opponents. Such a cock is then awarded the highest compliment: it is "deep" game, "bitterly" game, or "dead" game. As one person described it, "I guess I really like the courage, or what we think of as courage, of the gamecock." The main point, argue cockers, is that gameness can be measured only in the longer gaff fight.

A rooster's gameness is tested by his willingness to attack his opponent repeatedly in a fight that may last from 5 minutes to several hours. A rooster may be exhausted and almost unable to move, but, owing to the relative simplicity of its biology and its rapid metabolism, it often will recover, regain its strength, and come back from almost impossible odds to win the fight.

According to the majority of gaff fighters, "true" cockers fight with only gaffs and disdain the knife (explained below), calling the knife the "slasher." As one gaff-fighting cocker related:

You will never see me attending a slasher fight as a spectator or a participant. I will never knowingly sell fowl that are to be used in the slasher; if the day comes that only slashers are the weapons of combat, that is the day I will leave the sport.

Fighting the Knife

The knife is a 1- to 3-inch long, razor sharp steel blade, carefully affixed to one leg of the rooster. Since cockers consider chickens to be "left-legged," they attach the knife to the left leg. Although much ritual surrounds heeling the gaff, cockers deem heeling the knife to be a particularly arcane art because of the versatility of the knife. They discuss and debate the placing and pointing of the blade. Heelers learn from other heelers how to accomplish this task, although some video training tapes are available. The crucial role of heeling is such that often in recording in a magazine the winner of a particular match, the owner, the handler, and the heeler of the particular entry all get credit.

Knives can be either fork knives or socket knives. Socket knives are generally just fitted over the rooster's trimmed-down natural spur and tied; fork knives can be fitted on the leg of the rooster with a fork of steel straddling the spur. Thus the fork knife can be adjusted or aimed with great flexibility according to the capabilities of the bird. It is crucial when heeling a knife to keep a scabbard on the knife at all times because of the likelihood of serious injury if the rooster becomes excited and decides to attack its handler or become a "man-fighter."

Handling in the Knife Fight

Although it is not uncommon for a handler in a gaff fight to receive several puncture wounds in his hands or arms or even a gaff run through his hand, a rooster with a knife can be more dangerous. Many handlers carry long scars, and we heard one anecdote:

> One handler was attacked by his own rooster and received a gash in a main artery near his groin area. He bled to death in the pit before anyone could help him.

Because of the knife's extraordinary sharpness and deadliness, matches between fowl with these weapons may be over in a matter of seconds. The two birds' handlers "flirt 'em" and "fly 'em" just as in the gaff fights. Then they remove the scabbards. In the knife fight, when the birds attack, often one bird climbs higher in the air or "breaks higher" than its opponent. If one bird is above the other, it can slash and kill its opponent with one quick swipe. As one cocker put it, "This one will break higher and cross over the other one. When he does that, he kills the other one with one quick slash across the throat. That's why I call him Cut-throat."

Because of the nature of the blades and their destructiveness, the birds do not often become entangled with each other as they do in gaff fights. When the birds do become "hung" and the referee signals the handlers to untangle their charges, they do it very carefully. Drag pits are unnecessary in knife fighting because of the lethality of the fight. Fights typically do not even slow down because the birds rarely become exhausted. One usually kills the other in a matter of a few minutes, if not seconds.

The ministrations of the handler play a much smaller role in the knife fight. For knife fighters, this may be a positive benefit, as one said:

> It is in the drag pit that the real cheatin' can go on. Depending upon whether you have the count or not, you can set the rooster down on the line so as to make him move or to make him stay. You put him down one foot at a time and he'll move. That's where the real cheatin' can go on: in the drag.

For gaff fighters, the handling of the birds may be the real point of the cockfight: the rapport between the rooster and his handler. As one handler explained, "If you show confidence in your rooster and show him you believe in him, he will go out there and give his all for you." Another handler explained his technique: "You have to be as gentle as possible with a rooster. You can't just sling 'em around." One onlooker at a gaff fight was actually scratching his arms, saying, "I want to handle a rooster so bad sometimes, it even makes my arms itch." For many skilled handlers, it is their interaction with the bird that is the rewarding part of the sport.

Cockers' Definition of the Gaff Versus the Knife

Although using the knife or the gaff has considerable implications for equipment, handling, heeling, and the length of the cockfight, it is clear that the choice of heels has a central role in indicating a major division within the social world of cockfighting.

Cockers who use gaffs often regard the knife as extremely detrimental to the sport for three reasons. First is the high mortality rate of the roosters in the knife fight, even those that win. As one said, "It's simply a waste of good chickens." Another said, "In the knife, even the winner usually dies or is so injured as to be only good for brood stock." Not only do many breeders not want to see 2 years of breeding and feeding lost in a manner of seconds, but also the quick death and high mortality have implications for whether this is still a sport for the "little guy."

Second, because of the high rate of attrition, it takes many fowl for a cocker to enter knife fights consistently. Some breeders simply do not have enough chickens to be able to fight in knife fights. "You may need several hundred chickens in your yard just to have enough cocks and stags to fight one season. Only the biggest breeders can have that many chickens. It's not for the little guy," a veteran cocker explained.

In addition, some cockers suspect that the more fowl that are killed in knife fights, the greater the market will be for battle cocks supplied by professional breeders or "phony chicken peddlers" who simply want to sell chickens to anyone who wants to fight them and do not care about anything other than their market.

Third, other cockers argue that knife fights are a threat to the core values of cocking. Because of the importance of one bird's breaking higher than another, it may be that luck and accident determine the winner. The most sacred of all qualities, "gameness," does not enter as a factor. It is no longer a sport of courage. As one cocker said, "You can take an ordinary Leghorn out of the barnyard [what cockers refer to as "dunghill"], put a knife on him and the dunghill can go out and maybe kill a good gamecock before he turns and runs."

Supporters of knife fighting disagree. They contend that "In a short knife [less than 1 inch long] fight, a fight may last 30 to 45 minutes and a bird will have to prove that he is game in order to win." Even supporters of the knife concede that luck has a lot to do with which bird wins, compared to the situation in gaff fighting. Many knife fighters appeal to other values in favoring their fights. One knife fighter believed that Southerners especially like to fight the knife: "I guess it's just because us Southerner boys don't have the patience of the Yankees, we want to get it over in a hurry. Maybe it is the hot weather or something."[1]

The popularity of knife fighting is growing, and there are several reasons. The knife season lasts longer; during warm weather, roosters molt and may be too sore or too stressed for a long fight but may still be able to fight the shorter knife fight. The shortness of the bouts is one of the main reasons for the growing popularity of knife fights. The knife fight may take only seconds or at least a few moments, so that the wagering that accompanies the match can take place rapidly and the spectacle can be more exciting for the audience. In the knife fight, the victor can be decided in a few seconds, compared to the longer time in the drag pit at the gaff fight.

The difference between knife and gaff fights can be felt tangibly in the different arenas. A medium-sized club in which gaff fights are fought has the leisurely feel of a livestock barn at a county fair. For $6, spectators sit on wooden bleachers, with the smell of animals and fresh dirt in the air. Women, children, and old men in the crowd visit each other and drink soft drinks. The excitement is low-key, and entries are frequently late in arriving. The greatest excitement in the gaff derby centers on the last fight, in which the winner of the overall prize money is determined.

In contrast, in an arena where knife fights are held, the admission is usually $20 and middle-aged and older men predominate. With the faster pace of fighting and with beer sold on the premises, an atmosphere of a western bar prevails. As one cocker said about knife fighting, "The gamblers like it more. It keeps the action moving faster."

Because of the speed of the fights and perhaps because of the larger size of the wagers, different "feeling rules" (Hochschild, 1979) seem to apply at knife fights: there is more shouting, more clustering of groups, and more agitation. An interviewee agreed, "It's real excitin'. Little groups of men are hustlin' back and forth from the ring to the cockhouses, takin' birds in and carryin' 'em out. Everyone seems like they will bet on anythin' just for the excitement of it."

The type of wagering that accompanies the knife fight represents a difference in the styles of cockfighting, too. In a gaff fight, one person may lay a personal wager with a person standing next to him just as a person may make an informal bet with a person sitting next to him on a bar stool watching a basketball game in a tavern. The wager in cocking may be informed by knowledge about the particular handler, his age, his skill, and the type of rooster he is fighting. Gaff fighting in particular demands more skill in caring for and handling a rooster over a longer period of fighting.

In contrast to the gaff fights, in a knife fight the breed, the handler, and the skill in handling the bird count less because of the increased importance of luck. One cocker said:

> I can take an ol' Leghorn out of the barnyard and put a knife on him and he may kill a good rooster just because of his luck in getting off the ground first. But he would not be game enough to fight for more than a few seconds.

Many gamblers may be less concerned with backing a particular handler or a particular strain of rooster and more concerned with just "getting some action." This results in a particular type of wager, the "Call 10–40."[2] For this bet, the major factor is luck. As one purist said in disgust:

> The guy doesn't care anything about the birds or the sport. He is just playing the percentages; he figures that just by the law of averages he can come out ahead even if he loses three times for every time that he wins.

This conspicuous disdain for the traditions of the breeding and raising of gamefowl, in addition to the inability of many smaller cockers to raise enough roosters to fight in the knife arenas, feeds the controversy within the social world of cocking. As one cocker complained, "The knife is the gambler's tool." He urged other cockers not to fight with the knife, pleading, "Don't let the sport go to gamblers, dope dealers, and 'money men.'"

Other cockers argue that knife fighting is ruining the sport as they know it: "We seem to be losing the family atmosphere and drifting into a high-rolling, semi-pro type sport. My feelings are that the big money events are being played up too much. Big money attracts an element we don't need or want."

One informant did not like raising roosters to fight in the knife: "I've taken care of these roosters, fed 'em and doctored 'em, for over two years. And then I am supposed to let them get killed in a matter of seconds just because of luck?" However, that particular breeder's "backer," a physician in Chicago who helped finance the breeder's operation and put up money for entries, insisted that they enter their fowl in knife fights. The informant reluctantly complied, but he said that he still hated it. He finally concluded:

> This is going to be illegal everywhere in ten years and it's because of the knife. It attracts the dopers, the big money gambles, and the wrong type of people. Because of that it attracts bad publicity, too, from TV.

Supporters of the knife argue that gaff fights are more painful for roosters than knife fights and that fighting in the knife is more humane. They insist that the "humaniacs" were after the sport long before there was widespread fighting in the knife. They note that public disapproval of the sport does not distinguish between the types of heels used. However, other cockers argue that as the larger and more conspicuous knife-fighting clubs attract more attention and alarm from the average person, as well as the "animal rights fanatics," it is likely that stiffer laws against cocking will be passed and enforced. Ironically, some people see such an outcome as positive for the sport: it could cause the sport to go back to the informal low stakes of the brush pit fighting conducted for the conviviality of the sport rather than the money.

Summary

As Simmons (1969) noted, deviant social worlds are not cohesive, tightly knit, clearly structured entities but are rife with internal shifts and factionalism. Deviant social worlds have their own subworlds, each with its own traditions, ideologies, prestige systems, and codes.

We have explored the various meanings of two segments of a deviant social world by looking at the definitions of specific objects as they entered into the cockfight. We have analyzed the importance of the heel as a social object associated with specific typifications, meanings, and lines of action. We have seen that the more traditional cockers who fight with the gaff believe that the knife fighters endanger the future of the sport because they care more about money than gameness and breeding of the birds. We have seen how the knife fighters feel equal disdain for the old-fashioned gaff fighters, and we have noted their more defensive postures in this ideological dispute. We have seen how joint action in a cockfight unfolds in a larger context defined by various participants such as breeders, handlers, and heelers, each with its own line of action understandable only within his particular subworld.

The various meanings of the tools, participants, and different settings serve to illustrate that cocking is a complex, multilayered process, with different orientations and intentions among the various participants. Involved in the carrying out of this form of joint action are rooster merchants, gamblers, breeders and feeders, heelers, handlers, pit owners, and proponents and opponents of styles of fighting. Crucial distinctions clarifying segments of this social order revolve around the use of the knife or the gaff. On the one hand we have the typification of the "good ol' boy" with his traditional populist values and the old-time country sportsmanship; on the other, we see the typification of commercialized breeding operations, greedy chicken peddlers, big money gamblers, and a fast lifestyle.

People use these typifications to fit together lines of action in which they are continually taking into account other people and situations and reacting to them. With the increased interest being paid to cocking because of the growing publicity that the more conspicuous pits attract, it seems reasonable to anticipate increased hostility to cocking, which will drive it further underground.

More research is needed on unconventional or offensive social worlds that can be viewed in terms of social objects. We suggest that if cocking becomes less formally organized, it will be seen as a limited or regionalized threat only and thus be tolerated, as are rattlesnake roundups, frog gigging, and jumping mules.

REFERENCES

Becker, H.S. 1982. *Art Worlds*. Berkeley: University of California Press.

Blumer, H. 1969. *Symbolic Interactionism*. Englewood Cliffs, NJ: Prentice-Hall.

Bryant, C.D. 1982. "Cockfighting in Socio-Historical Context: Some Sociological Observations on a Socially Devalued Sport." *The Gamecock* 45:80–5.

Dennefer, D. 1980. "Rationality and Passion in Private Experience: Modern Consciousness and the Social World of Old Car Collectors." *Social Problems* 27:392–412.

Fine, G.A. 1983. *Shared Fantasy: Role Playing Games as Social Worlds*. Chicago: University of Chicago Press.

Geertz, C. 1972. "Deep Play: Notes on the Balinese Cockfight." *Daedalus* 101:1–27.

Gilmore, S. 1987. "Coordination and Convention: The Organization of the Concert World." *Symbolic Interaction* 10:209–27.

Hawley, F.F. 1989. "Cockfight in the Cotton: A Moral Crusade in Microcosm." *Contemporary Crises* 13:129–44.

Hewitt, J.P. 1991. *Self and Society: A Symbolic Interactionist Social Psychology* (5th ed.). Boston: Allyn & Bacon.

Hochschild, A.R. 1979. "Emotion Work, Feeling Rules, and Social Structure." *American Journal of Sociology* 85:551–75.

McCaghy, C. & A.C. Neal. 1974. "The Fraternity of Cockfighters: Ethical Embellishments of an Illegal Sport." *Journal of Popular Culture* 8:557–69.

Merton, R.K. 1972. "Insiders and Outsiders: A Chapter in the Sociology of Knowledge." *American Journal of Sociology* 78:24–43.

Narragansett, F.S. 1982. *The Best of Narragansett*. Hartford, AR:Marburger Publishers.

Olmstead, A.D. 1988. "Morally Controversial Leisure: The Social World of Gun Collectors." *Symbolic Interaction* 11:277–87.

Ritzer, G. & D. Walczak. 1986. *Working: Conflict and Change* (3rd ed.). Englewood Cliffs, NJ: Prentice-Hall.

Schur, E.M. 1980. *The Politics of Deviance: Stigma Contests and the Uses of Power*. Englewood Cliffs, NJ: Prentice-Hall.

Simmons, J.L. 1969. *Deviant Behavior* (3rd ed.). New York: Harper & Row.

Wortham, D.H. 1965. *Wortham's Rules*. Hartford, AR: Marburger Publishers.

NOTES

[1]Knife fighting is also the most popular form of fighting in Latin America, Mexico, and the Pacific Islands.

[2]The "Call 10–40" indicates that the caller is willing to put up $10 against anyone else's $40. The person wagering the $40 then can pick his favorite. The person wagering the $10 takes the other. The person who calls 10–40 is indifferent to the type of bird or its holder.

Chapter 36

POLICING MORALITY: IMPERSONAL SEX IN PUBLIC PLACES

Frederick J. Desroches

In recent years, police forces across Canada have conducted major investigations in response to a minor criminal offense common to urban areas—the use of public washrooms ("tearooms") by men for impersonal sex. The mass arrests have resulted in local and national publicity and severe criticism of the police. This study analyzes tearoom activity and the characteristics of participants using police-generated data.

The Data and Research Methodology

The data for this study are gathered from police case materials and through interviews with law enforcement personnel in five Canadian urban areas ranging in size from 24,000 to 600,000. Based on direct observations of sexual behavior in seven public toilets, police in these communities arrested 190 men charging them with committing an indecent act. The washrooms under surveillance included: (1) a park washroom, (2) a washroom in the basement of a town theater, (3) three washrooms located in shopping malls, (4) a washroom in a large department store located in a shopping center, and (5) a restaurant washroom located in the basement of a shopping mall. Police in three communities gathered evidence with the use of a video camera, whereas police in the other two cities made direct observations through air vents installed in the ceiling and wall. Surveillance was maintained from six days to eight weeks and players were found to visit tearooms an average 2 1/2 times per week.

The only other study of this activity is Laud Humphreys' (1970) *Tearoom Trade: Impersonal Sex in Public Places.* Based on surreptitious observations of sexual encounters as a voyeur-lookout ("watchqueen"), in-depth interviews with selected players, and disguised interviews with others, Humphreys' research is a detailed sociological analysis of the activities of men who frequent public washrooms in search of fast and anonymous sex. The origin of the term "tearoom" is unknown but it is used to refer to isolated public toilets that are frequented by men for sexual encounters. From April 1966 to April 1967, Humphreys observed 120 sexual acts in 19 different men's washrooms, located in five parks in a city of two million people. He discovered that the fear and suspicion encountered by tearoom participants produced a voyeur-lookout role whereby one man would situate himself at a door or window and alert participants of anyone approaching. By serving as a "watchqueen" Humphreys was able to observe the action without alarming or disrupting the participants. In addition, Humphreys gained the trust and cooperation of twelve participants whom he interviewed. He also recorded the license plate numbers of 50 participants, changed his appearance, and interviewed these men a year later in their homes under the pretense of conducting a social health survey. His varied but controversial (Von Hoffman, 1970) research strategies provided him with detailed, intimate, and comprehensive data on the behavior, lifestyles, and social characteristics of tearoom participants. This paper will compare and contrast Humphreys' observations with the data generated by police surveillance in five Canadian urban areas.

The Location of Tearooms

Sexual activities in this sample took place in one park washroom and six washrooms located in shopping malls. It appears that shopping malls have usurped parks as the favorite meeting place of tearoom participants because malls provide an increasing number of locales that remain open year round and are easily accessible by car. Shopping centers devote heavily traveled areas to retail ventures and relegate public washrooms to out-of-the-way corridors. Located in basements and other isolated areas of the mall, these facilities are seldom used by shoppers, making them ideal for tearoom play. Humphreys noted that the women's side of the park restrooms was seldom used. Investigating officers in this study similarly observed that women seldom visit these facilities, preferring to use the washrooms provided by restaurants and taverns located in the malls. They also note that 85-90% of male visitors either participate in tearoom sex or appear to be looking for action.

Participants who frequent shopping plaza tearooms are less conspicuous than men who use park washrooms because their vehicles are not as obvious. In addition, there are many legitimate reasons for visiting a shopping center whereas one's presence in a park is likely to arouse suspicion. Many police forces also deter sexual encounters in park washrooms by patrolling these areas to protect children who use recreational facilities. Shopping malls, on the other hand, are privately run and plaza owners normally contract security firms to discourage undesirables. Private security is less of a deterrent to tearoom participants than the police who are better trained, equipped, and legally empowered.

Discovering the Tearoom

As noted by Humphreys, certain washrooms gain a reputation in the gay community as a place where homosexual encounters occur. This does not explain how tearoom participants learn about the popularity of a washroom, since most do not participate in the gay community. In addition, both Humphreys' research and this study indicate that most players are strangers to one another, hide their deviance from others, remain silent during sex play, and avoid outside homosexual contacts. How does the uninitiated discover the existence and location of these facilities? One possibility is through the media. Police in one community were curious as to why men gravitated to the Hudson Bay Department Store washroom since there is a more isolated public washroom in the basement of this shopping center. Surprisingly, the majority of men explained that they had interpreted the store's advertisement sexually—"Meet me at the Bay"—and correctly assumed that others would do likewise. This suggests that media publicity given to tearoom arrests may deter some men from involvement, but at the same time inform others who were previously unaware that such locales exist. Tearooms may also be discovered accidentally by observing what is happening or through the explicit homosexual graffiti found in most active washrooms. Police in several communities observed men seated in washroom stalls move into sex play by following instructions written on the stall door.

The Players

The median age of 41 years for tearoom participants in the present study is higher than the 34 years in Humphreys' sample. The occupational status of tearoom participants in both samples vary widely and most appear to be mainly working, lower-middle, or middle-class men whose occupational statuses cover a broad spectrum. Of the 50 men interviewed by Humphreys, 54% were married, 38% single, 6% divorced, and 2% separated. In this sample, 58% are known to be married and living with their wives, 29% are single, 6% are separated or divorced, and 3% are living common-law. Significantly, both studies reveal that the majority of tearoom participants are married and on the surface, lead "normal" heterosexual lives. Although a few men admitted to the police to being gay or bisexual, most presented themselves as heterosexual. The majority of players appear to fall into the category Humphreys (1970:111) refers to as "trade"—married or once married men with dependent occupations, masculine in appearance, and heterosexual in their orientation. These men do not seek homosexual contact as such, do not involve themselves in the gay community, and hide their deviance from family and others. They are emotionally devastated at arrest and express extreme concern over the possibility that they may be publically identified.

The Breastplate of Righteousness

Because they have so much to lose, Humphreys suggests that these covert deviants attempt to protect themselves by creating an image of superpropriety. From visiting them in their homes, he noticed that they drive clean, late model cars, maintain exceptionally manicured yards, and are impeccably groomed and dressed. He suggests that these covert deviants physically and morally create a presentation of self that is neat, clean, proper, conscientious, moral, conservative, righteous, and religious. Investigating officers in the present study similarly note the neat and conservative appearance of tearoom participants. As a case in point, a subject who committed suicide shortly after his arrest was described in the local newspaper as "an exemplary husband and father...who was a victim of his secret life. His friends and family are shocked because he was a model citizen, a dedicated family man married for about 15 years, active in his church and well-liked by everyone who knew him. He taught Sunday school and coached children's soccer. On public holidays he flew the Canadian flag on his front lawn." The meticulous and scrupulous image cultivated by this man was about to be destroyed by his arrest for tearoom activities and he no doubt anticipated the loss of his family, community respect, self-respect, and perhaps even his job.

Humphreys suggests that tearoom participants adopt a respectable lifestyle in order to shield themselves from suspicion and possible exposure. But why would anyone ever suspect they were involved in this type of activity and how does this breastplate protect the offender from police surveillance, arrest, and public disgrace? The public display of propriety is not only an ineffective shield, it can also create a horrible backlash from persons who view their actions as a form of betrayal and/or hypocrisy. The pillar of the community topples from a greater height because he has publically proclaimed this higher status.

Three alternative hypotheses are offered to help explain this phenomenon: (1) Reaction Formation: Psychiatrists describe an exaggerated or intense reaction to something that is threatening as "reaction formation." This over-reaction functions to reassure the subject against the inner and/or external threat. It can be hypothesized that the excessive concern with neatness and propriety that tearoom participants exhibit result from the anxiety brought on by their sexual deviance. The donning of the breastplate of righteousness may have a psychological cleansing effect—an emotional catharsis—in which the "clean" lifestyle washes away the "stains" that have been picked up at play; (2) Self Validation: The public definition of tearoom behavior as "perverted" threatens the self-concept of participants. The breastplate of righteousness may function to validate a view of oneself as "normal" and reassure players that they are not perverts. The actor encapsulates the deviant activity forgetting about it for the time being and denying that this is "really him." Instead, he takes seriously the clean image that is fostered. He is indeed this person whom everyone knows him to be—a husband, a father, a faithful employee, a good neighbor, and an upstanding citizen in the community. The mask of propriety represents the view that these men have or wish to have of themselves. By playing a conforming role, they convince themselves (and others) that this is their true self. The successful performance validates their identity; (3) Cause or Effect?: Each of the above hypotheses assumes that tearoom participation precedes the concern with an image or lifestyle that is clean, conservative, and righteous. But neither Humphreys' nor this study have sufficient evidence to indicate which comes first. Humphreys' (1970:137) tearoom sample included a disproportionately high representation of Roman Catholics and Episcopalians.

Obviously their religious upbringing precedes tearoom participation. It may be that an overly conservative and sexually repressive childhood influences sexual behavior later in life. Perhaps the breastplate of righteousness is merely their acquiescence to society's definition of how their lives should be led—a home, family, career, church, and all the other trappings of a socially conservative and respectable person. But clearly, participation in this sexual activity indicates that something is lacking in their lives. Unfulfilled but unable or unwilling to reject the values and roles acquired, they seek release in the furtive and impersonal sex offered in men's washrooms.

Rules, Roles, and Sexual Behavior

Humphreys' detailed analysis of tearoom behavior makes clear how the norms within the washroom function to keep the sexual encounter impersonal and preserve anonymity. Both his and the present study indicate that participants avoid the exchange of biographical data, stay away from teenagers and children, and do not force their intentions on others. Police observations in all five communities reveal that young persons are not involved in sex play, the action is noncoercive, and sexual encounters are contracted and performed in silence. Although regular patrons occasionally nod to one another in recognition, no conversations occur within the washrooms. Participants often signal a willingness to play by lingering at the stalls and urinals and by looking about.

The behavior or strategies of tearoom participants in this study varies somewhat from washroom to washroom and appears to be influenced by the physical character-istics of each room. Specifically, sexual encounters usually take place in the area of the room hidden from view, allowing participants time to disengage when intruded upon. In one washroom, for example, the sexual activity took place mainly at the urinals situated behind a partition and out of view of the entrance. The action typically began with one man lingering at the urinal until another arrives. The two stand there for a few moments, look about, one or both will fondle and display an erection and looks for a response. Sex play begins by one man reaching over and stroking his neighbor's penis or fellating him. Although mutual masturbation is common, fellatio is not reciprocated. A squeaky door warns participants of intruders, allowing each man sufficient time to zip up and depart.

In the other four communities, sexual contact usually took place in the toilet stalls hidden from view. In two washrooms, an opening in the metal divider separating the stalls was strategic in sex play. In one, a fist size "glory hole" had been punctured three feet above the floor; in the other, the toilet paper dispenser opened to allow the occupants to peer in on one another. With the stalls occupied, sex play begins with casual masturbation. This activity is visible through the opening and appears to be the cue for action. Police observed that some men engage in sex immediately, while others seem to enjoy the flirtation as a type of foreplay. Still others appear shy and nervous, perhaps needing the time to build up their courage before making contact. Sex normally includes masturbation, mutual masturbation, and fellatio, and most of the activity takes place through the opening or underneath the stalls.

In two other communities in this study, sexual activities were observed in shopping mall washrooms with most of the action taking place between adjacent stalls. Normally a player arrives, waits in the stall, engages in casual masturbation, and spends time reading and/or writing messages on the wall. When the adjacent booth becomes occupied, contact begins by one man gradually moving his foot into the other's stall eventually touching his neighbor's foot. Sexual activity takes place when one man kneels beneath the partition or extends his lower torso (much like a limbo dancer) under the partition in order to be masturbated or fellated. Fellatio is not reciprocated and the recipient leaves first while the insertee waits in his stall for a moment before departing. Participants rarely see one another's face.

Since there are no windows in these washrooms, the lookout role that Humphreys assumed is seldom observed by police in the present study. A squeaky door is the first sign of an intrusion, giving participants little time to disengage. This necessitates the use of different strategies and accounts for the fact that most participants commit their acts out of sight of the entrance—at the urinals where they can quickly disengage, or in separate stalls where they can sit up and look innocent. Despite the danger of being caught in the act, some players engage in sexual encounters in open areas of the washroom. Police also observed men masturbating alone and/or attending the washroom simply to watch others. Participants were charged only if they engaged in sexual acts with one another or in open view of someone. Police also observed men who were unsuccessful in their search for a sexual partner. These men would enter the washroom, linger for long periods, sit in the stall, play with themselves, read and write graffiti, and leave often without using the facilities. Some are discriminating and will enter the washroom up to a dozen times a day without meeting someone to their liking. Most, however, respond to whomever happens to be willing. Frequent tearoom visitors generally do not have sex with another, apparently preferring someone new. In both studies, players waited outside the tearoom and watched for others to arrive.

The Motivation

Why do men, many of whom are married and presumably heterosexual, participate in sexual activities with other men in public washrooms? Why do they risk criminal prosecution and serious damage to family relations, reputations, and careers? Participants who are closet gays or bisexuals may find this type of sexual activity arousing because they are attracted to other men yet do not wish to be known as homosexual. Because they value their marriages, careers, and reputations, open involvement in the gay community is ruled out. Tearooms allow them to keep their homosexual urges private and lead publically respectable lives as long as they are not exposed.

For men who are gay, the attraction to tearoom sex is perhaps easier to understand given their sexual orientation. Yet most gays avoid tearooms. It can be hypothesized that they do so because they are unconcerned about having a gay reputation, thus allowing them the freedom to frequent locales that offer personal and impersonal sex in a less dangerous setting. In addition, some men are involved in monogamous relationships and spurn impersonal sexual encounters.

For men who are primarily heterosexual, involvement in tearoom sex is theoretically difficult to explain because the behavior conflicts with a heterosexual self-concept. Humphreys' research indicates that such men are unlikely to take the insertee role in fellatio, telling themselves that they are not "queer" if they are on the receiving end. Other studies similarly note the use of this rationalization in male to male sex (Reiss, 1961). Several men in the present study emphasized their limited role in the sexual encounter telling the police, "No, I'm not gay! I never gave blow jobs." It appears that the impersonal nature of their contact in conjunction with the self-imposed constrictions on sexual behavior, allow them to participate in tearoom sex yet still protect their self-concept as heterosexual. There is, after all, minimal physical involvement and no emotional commitment.

Married men who find their sex lives inadequate may also turn to tearooms as an alternative means of sexual gratification. Humphreys describes the married lives of several of the men whom he interviewed as woefully lacking in affect and physical pleasure. Tearoom sex fulfills a need that is not met in the context of their conjugal relationships. Police in this sample report that although a few men complain that their wives have put on weight or are no longer interested in sex, many more claim to be happily married and do not have serious marital problems. They are at a loss to explain their actions and often say no more than, "I have this urge."

If heterosexual men have an urge for illicit sex, then why don't they have an affair or visit a prostitute? Even if they are bisexual or gay, why participate in furtive impersonal sex in a public washroom with so much risk? What are the factors that make tearoom sex attractive? As Humphreys tells us, tearoom sex is impersonal, anonymous, and does not lead to problem entanglements. Ironically, it may be considered a safer alternative than having an affair. Tearoom sex involves minimal effort, commitment, obligation, expectation, resources, or demands on one's time. Prostitution is impersonal, anonymous, and free of entanglements and obligations, but can become expensive if used on a regular basis. No money is exchanged for tearoom sex.

Another feature of tearoom encounters is the fact that they typically take place in ten to twenty minutes. Players do not have to be away from family for extended periods of time or explain lengthy absences. In addition, the risk factor may itself be an attraction since players make contact with a variety of partners, all of whom are strangers. Thus, for men who are attracted to other men or for whom heterosexual outlets are unavailable, tearoom sex provides fast, inexpensive, impersonal, relatively safe, exciting sex with a variety of partners.

One final question must still be addressed. Even if one is inclined to participate in tearoom sex, why does the possibility of arrest and exposure not act as a powerful deterrent? Although some men are surveillance conscious, most are not. Given the fact that the majority participate regularly in tearooms, they have perhaps been lulled into a false sense of security because they have experienced no problems. Since there is no coercion, no victim, and the behavior is discreet, participants may believe that law enforcement agencies care and/or know little about their activities. Consistent with this hypothesis is the fact that most men are not surveillance conscious. Some are, however, and search for cameras, leave quickly if disturbed, and take evasive actions when leaving the washroom. These men knowingly take risks, but ignorance of police capabilities perhaps leads them to believe that they can detect surveillance and are safe in this criminal conduct. We can also hypothesize that most offenders simply fail to consider the possibility or consequences for themselves and their families. Finally, some men may be naively unaware that their behavior constitutes a criminal offense.

Summary

The present research largely substantiates the picture drawn by Humphreys in his classic study. Consistent with his observations, most tearoom participants (a) are primarily heterosexual and married, (b) communicate through non-verbal gestures and seldom speak, (c) do not associate outside the tearoom or attempt to learn one another's identity or exchange biographical information, (d) depart separately with the inserter leaving first, (e) do not undress or engage in anal sex, (f) break off sexual contact when someone enters the washroom, (g) rarely approach straight men, (h) read and write sexually explicit homosexual graffiti, and (i) linger inside and outside the washroom for someone to appear. In addition, (j) fellatio is generally not reciprocated and fellators are usually older men; (k) most offenders are neat in appearance; (l) some engage in series and simultaneous encounters; (m) encounters are brief, usually not exceeding twenty minutes; and (n) few have criminal records with the exception of those previously convicted of similar offenses. In view of the fact that tearoom participants normally commit their sex acts out of sight of the entrance and accidental exposure, do not use force or coercion, and do not involve adolescents or children, they are more aptly classified as nuisance offenders rather than as serious threats to the community.

REFERENCES

Desroches, F.J. 1991. "Tearoom Trade: A Law Enforcement Problem." *Canadian Journal of Criminology* 33:1–21.

———. 1990. "Tearoom Trade: A Research Update." *Qualitative Sociology* 13:39–61.

Hagan, J. 1984. *The Disreputable Pleasures: Crime and Deviance in Canada*. Toronto: McGraw-Hill Ryerson.

———. 1985. *Crime, Criminal Behavior, and Its Control*. Toronto: McGraw-Hill Book Company.

Humphreys, L. 1970. *Tearoom Trade: Impersonal Sex in Public Places*. New York: Aldine Publishing Company.

Pfohl, S.J. 1985. *Images of Deviance and Social Control*. Toronto: McGraw-Hill Book Company.

Reiss, A.J. 1961. "The Social Integration of Queers and Peers." *Social Problems* 9: 102–120.

Sacco, V.F. 1988. *Deviance, Conformity, and Control in Canadian Society*. Scarborough: Prentice-Hall Canada Inc.

Stebbins, R.A. 1988. *Deviance: Tolerable Differences*. Toronto: McGraw-Hill Ryerson Limited.

Von Hoffman, N. 1970. "Sociological Snoopers and Journalistic Moralizers." In Laud Humphreys (ed.), *Tearoom Trade: Impersonal Sex in Public Places*. New York: Aldine.

Wilson, J.Q. 1968. "The Police and the Delinquent in Two Cities." Pp. 9–30 In S. Wheeler (ed.), *Controlling Delinquents*. New York: John Wiley and Sons.

Part VIII

Becoming Deviant

Deviant Careers, Statuses and Identities

The concept of career involves three related notions. As Goffman (1961:127–28) notes:

> Traditionally the term *career* has been reserved for those who expect to enjoy the rises laid out within a respectable profession. The term is coming to be used, however, in a broadened sense to refer to any social strand of any person's course through life...One value of the concept of career is its two-sidedness. One side is linked to internal matters held dearly and closely...the other side concerns public position, jural relations and style of life...The concept of career, then, allows one to move back and forth between the personal and the public, between the self and its significant society...The main concern will be with the moral aspects of career—that is, the regular sequence of changes that career entails in the person's self and in his framework of imagery for judging himself and others.

The concept of career then, involves three elements. Objectively, it refers to the movement of individuals through a social structure. In this sense, it refers to alterations in social statuses and roles. Subjectively, it refers to changes in self-images, identities and self-conceptions as the individual moves through the institution or organization. As Everett C. Hughes (1958) contends, the changes in an objective career lead to alterations in a person's self-identity. The objective and subjective elements of the career are important as they set the stage for redefinition of self.

Sociologists are interested in studying *moral* aspects of careers—that is, regular sequences of alterations in careers, the effect on a person's self, and his/her framework for judging self and others (Goffman, 1961). Any moral career is a temporal process that flows through a person's life. Some careers are short-lived; others are more long-term. Careers do not always follow a straight trajectory path; some paths are, in fact, zig zag in nature, such as an alcoholic jumping on and off the wagon, or the drug addict going straight for awhile or moving from hard to soft drugs. Careers have certain peak points when involvement is intense—a time when the individual fully adopts the role, identity and consequences of the involvement; at other times, the involvement may be flitting in nature.

Deviant careers (similar to their non-deviant counterparts) are not produced in isolation; rather they are the product of interactions with individuals and organizations/institutions. These individuals and structures often influence the direction that

414

a person's career will take. Other persons then, can either positively or negatively influence a person's moral career.

Career Entrance

Some deviant careers may be entered into voluntarily such as beginning to use drugs or alcohol, or becoming a nudist; other careers may be entered into involuntarily— that is, as a result of unofficial and/or official labelling of the individual and their subsequent incarceration/institutionalization. Examples of involuntary careers would be incarceration in a federal prison or institutionalization in a psychiatric hospital. Still other deviant careers commence through recruitment by others. Examples include gangs recruiting new members, or the Moonies recruiting new religious charges.

The consequences of such recruitment can be examined in terms of a *gradual* process of conversion or identity transformation wherein the individual is stripped of his/her former identities and social statuses, and is proffered new identities and social statuses—as a deviant.

Once an individual is unofficially and/ or officially defined as deviant, therein begins the first stage in his/her moral career. The person's life begins to change drastically in several manners. People not only begin to conceive of the individual as "different," but alter their behavior toward him/her.

Placing deviant labels upon individuals then, discredits their social identities— *past, present,* and *future.* Such labels can have a serious effect on all future encounters between the deviant and others—the latter accepting the "truth" of the person so labelled. Specifically, others may gradually *exclude* the adjudged deviant from normal, routinized social interaction. This exclusionary process, the first stage in the development of a deviant identity, is illustrated in Edwin Lemert's classic piece, "*Paranoia and the Dynamics of Exclusion.*" The author contends that paranoia is not a feature of individual personality, but rather, it is more accurately perceived as a social relationship wherein difficulties, problems or failure on the part of one individual leads to a breakdown in communication. Despite the cause, other "normals" react by restricting interaction with the adjudged deviant, and the strategies they employ are often collusive and conspiratorial in nature. Exclusion of the deviant limits feedback necessary for him/her to correct the behavior. Moreover, the person who is cut off from interaction with the group, may become defensive and aggressive in nature. The person may make desperate, inappropriate attempts to elicit a response from those who are excluding him/her. This behavior, in turn, functions to further exclude the individual from the group. As a result, the relationship only deteriorates.

The selection by Nancy J. Herman, "*Creating Crazies/Making Mentals: The Pre-Patient Phase in the Career of the Psychiatric Patient,*" also deals with the initial stage in the involuntary career of the deviant. Specifically, the author illustrates how family members and various agencies of social control collaborate, unofficially and officially define, and take action against the individual adjudged to be "mentally ill." Herman points out that defining an individual as mentally ill is *not* an automatic process. Whether a person is so labelled depends on several factors, including the tolerance limits of the group. Many families tolerate much bizarre behavior—it is optimized, neutralized, normalized, or otherwise explained away. It is only in a crisis situation, that family members move toward labelling the individual as mentally ill. As Herman notes, a number of agents and agencies play a role in the definitional process and subsequent institutionalization of the individual. These include: (1) the individual him/herself; (2) the legal system; (3) family and friends; and (4) psychiatric officials. Similar to Lemert's study, wherein the adjudged individual felt that others were conspiring against him/her, Herman's subjects also felt that others around them were colluding and conspiring. Moreover, they felt an unforgivable feeling of betrayal on the part of family and friends.

Turning to voluntary moral careers and identity transformation, the third piece by Richard Troiden, *"A Model of Homosexual Identity Formation,"* examines how a person develops a homosexual identity—an organized perception of self as homosexual in relation to sexual and romantic settings. Troiden asserts that individuals are not born with perceptions of themselves as homosexual, bisexual or heterosexual. Prior to identifying themselves in terms of a certain social category, they must first learn that a category representing their feelings and actions exists; they must discover that others occupy this social category; and they must perceive that their own interests and needs are similar to others occupying this category. Moreover, such persons must begin to identify with those members of the social category and begin to self-label as gay. Finally, they must gradually incorporate this identity into their self-concept. The result of these subjective processes is an identity transformation wherein individuals change their perceived sexual orientation from heterosexual or bisexual to homosexual. Becoming gay or homosexual then, involves formation of new self-perceptions as homosexual and the decision to adopt homosexuality as a way of life. In this article, Troiden discusses a four-stage ideal-type model of homosexual identity formation and the variables influencing its rates.

The piece by Jack Haas *"Acquiring the Addict/Alcoholic Identity,"* also addresses the processual dimensions of identity formation. Specifically, the author illustrates that the pathway to addiction begins with childhood alienation. A child is born into a family and is completely dependent upon them to fulfill their physical and psychological needs. Children develop their self-perceptions on the basis of how they perceive others are perceiving them. A child reared in a dysfunctional family, one in which he/she is abused, neglected and or abandoned, who lives life in emotional turmoil and fear, develops self-feelings of hatred and worthlessness. These negative self-feelings combined with attitudes of "not belonging" or "not fitting in," are internalized and become the basis of self-concept. Such familial alienation then produces the pre-addict phase of the persons's identity. When others reject the individual, life becomes so unbearable that he/she attempts to dissociate so as not to experience such negative feelings. The individual, according to Haas, abandons him/herself. The abandonment of self is carried out insofar as the child develops a "false self" or "disconnected self"—a self-protective mechanism utilized to mitigate further pain and to separate the individual from authenticity and self-acceptance. The problem of repressed emotions may manifest itself in depression, anger or to seek alternative ways to escape—the individual begins to abuse sex, drugs, alcohol or food. Individuals come to adopt the identity of addict in an effort to create a self-induced, dissociate state which provides *temporary* relief from their problems and fears, enabling them to "transcend their reality" and "move to a higher level of consciousness." However, these addictive processes are themselves isolating and alienating—the rituals involved may provide a temporary "fix" but they concomitantly exacerbate their negative feelings of self-hatred. In short, such addictive behaviors perpetuate the addiction cycle.

The next piece by Murphy et al., *"Drifting into Dealing: Becoming a Cocaine Seller,"* focuses on the voluntary career of the drug dealer. Specifically, this article centers on the subtle process of identity transformation that occurs when people move from a user identity to a dealer identity. Interviewing 80 ex-cocaine dealers, the authors suggest that entry into the social world of selling cocaine is a "fluid process akin to [David] Matza's notion of drift." Murphy et al., discuss the five major ways in which individual begin to sell cocaine: (1) by becoming a go-between seller who buys only for friends, later envisioning the profits; (2) by becoming a stash dealer— an individual who sells small amounts in order to better afford his own; (3) by becoming a connoisseur—the individual's desire to buy high quality drugs wholesale; (4) through apprenticeship activities wherein the individual lives with an established seller, learns the ropes, and eventually takes over part of the business; and (5) through product line expansion wherein dealers start out selling other drugs and then move into cocaine.

The final selection in this section by Ken Levi entitled, *"Becoming a Hit Man: Neutralization in a Very Deviant Career,"* deals with another voluntary deviant career—that of the professional murderer. Specifically, the article deals with the manner by which individuals are socialized to become hit men and how they effectively neutralize their potentially discreditable identities and behaviors. The author asserts that, in contrast to the professional murderer, the novice does not possess techniques of neutralization or "neutralizers" that are provided by the profession. The novice is faced with two basic problems: (1) overcoming his fears and inhibitions; and (2) maintaining a positive self-image. In this paper, Levi discusses how these problems are managed differentially by the organized killer versus the independent killer. The former type belongs to an organized crime group, is not given financial remuneration for the job, and frequently kills out of revenge. The organized murderer rationalizes his behavior by employing a number of rationalizations *learned* from others in the group. The latter type, in contrast, does not have support from others, is not socialized to accept various justifications to neutralize their activities; rather, the independent murderer draws upon other sources. Levi discusses how the characteristics of the role of the independent killer can aid in the maintenance of a positive self-image and identity, and effectively neutralize their deviant activities.

REFERENCES

Goffman, Erving. 1961. *Asylums.* New York: Anchor.
Hughes, Everett C., 1958. *Men and their Work.* New York: The Free Press.

Chapter 37

PARANOIA AND THE DYNAMICS OF EXCLUSION

Edwin M. Lemert

One of the few generalizations about psychotic behavior which sociologists have been able to make with a modicum of agreement and assurance is that such behavior is a result or manifestation of a disorder in communication between the individual and society. The generalization, of course, is a large one, and, while it can be illustrated easily with case history materials, the need for its conceptual refinement and detailing of the process by which disruption of communication occurs in the dynamics of mental disorder has for some time been apparent. Among the more carefully reasoned attacks upon this problem is Cameron's (1943) formulation of the paranoid pseudocommunity.

In essence, the conception of the paranoid pseudocommunity can be stated as follows:[1]

Paranoid persons are those whose inadequate, social learning leads them in situations of unusual stress to incompetent social reactions. Out of the fragments of the social behavior of others the paranoid person symbolically organizes a pseudocommunity whose functions he perceives as focused on him. His reactions to this *supposed community* of response which he sees loaded with threat to himself bring him into open conflict with the actual community and lead to his temporary or permanent isolation from its affairs. The "real" community, which is unable to share in his attitudes and reactions, takes action through forcible restraint or retaliation *after* the paranoid person "bursts into defensive or vengeful activity" (Cameron, 1943).

That the community to which the paranoid reacts is "pseudo" or without existential reality is made unequivocal by Cameron (1943) when he says:

> As he (the paranoid person) begins attributing to others the attitudes which he has towards himself, he unintentionally organizes these others into a functional community, a group unified in their supposed reactions, attitudes and plans with respect to him. He in this way organizes individuals, some of whom are actual persons and some only inferred or imagined, into a whole which satisfies for the time being his immediate need for explanation but which brings no assurance with it, and usually serves to increase his tensions. The community he forms not only fails to correspond to any organization shared by others but actually contradicts this consensus. More than this, the actions ascribed by him to its personnel are not actually performed or maintained by them; *they are united in no common undertaking against him.*

418

The general insightfulness of Cameron's analysis cannot be gainedsaid and the usefulness of some of his concepts is easily granted. Yet a serious question must be raised, based upon empirical inquiry, as to whether in actuality the insidious qualities of the community to which the paranoid reacts are pseudo or a symbolic fabrication. There is an alternative point of view, which is the burden of this paper, namely that, while the paranoid person reacts differently to his social environment, it is also true that "others" react differentially to him and this reaction commonly if not typically involves covertly organized action and conspiratorial behavior in a very real sense. A further extension of our thesis is that these differential reactions are reciprocals of one another, being interwoven and concatenated at each and all phases of a process of exclusion which arises in a special kind of relationship. Delusions and associated behavior must be understood in a context of exclusion which attentuates this relationship and disrupts communication...

From what has been said thus far, it should be clear that our formulation and analysis will deal primarily with what Tyhurst (1957) calls paranoid patterns of behavior rather than with a clinical entity in the classical Kraepelinian sense. Paranoid reactions, paranoid states, paranoid personality disturbances, as well as the seldom-diagnosed "true paranoia," which are found superimposed or associated with a wide variety of individual behavior or "symptoms," all provide a body of data for study so long as they assume priority over other behavior in meaningful social interaction. The elements of behavior upon which paranoid diagnoses are based— delusions, hostility, aggressiveness, suspicion, envy, stubbornness, jealousy, and ideas of reference—are readily comprehended and to some extent empathized by others as social reactions, in contrast to the bizarre, manneristic behavior of schizophrenia or the tempo and affect changes stressed in manic-depressive diagnoses. It is for this reason that paranoia suggests, more than any other forms of mental disorder, the possibility of fruitful sociological analysis....

The Generic Processes of Exclusion

The paranoid process begins with persistent interpersonal difficulties between the individual and his family, or his work associates and superiors, or neighbors, or other persons in the community. These frequently or even typically arise out of bona fide or recognizable issues centering upon some actual or threatened loss of status for the individual. This is related to such things as the death of relatives, loss of a position, loss of professional certification, failure to be promoted, age and physiological life cycle changes, mutilations, and changes in family and marital relationships. The status changes are distinguished by the fact that they leave no alternative acceptable to the individual, from whence comes their "intolerable" or "unendurable" quality. For example: the man trained to be a teacher who loses his certificate, which means he can never teach; or the man of 50 years of age who is faced with loss of promotion which is a regular order of upward mobility in an organization, who knows that he can't "start over"; or the wife undergoing hysterectomy, which mutilates her image as a woman.

In cases where no dramatic status loss can be discovered, a series of failures often is present, failures which may have been accepted or adjusted to, but with progressive tension as each new status situation is entered. The unendurability of the current status loss, which may appear unimportant to others, is a function of an intensified commitment, in some cases born of an awareness that there is a quota placed on failures in our society. Under some such circumstances, failures have followed the person, and his reputation as a "difficult person" has preceded him. This means that he often has the status of a stranger on trial in each new group he enters, and that the groups or organizations willing to take a chance on him are marginal from the standpoint of their probable tolerance for his actions.

The behavior of the individual—arrogance, insults, presumption of privilege and exploitation of weakness in others—initially has a segmental or checkered pattern in that it is confined to status-committing interactions. Outside of these, the person's behavior may be quite acceptable—courteous, considerable, kind, even indulgent. Likewise, other persons and members of groups vary considerably in their tolerance for the relevant behavior, depending on the extent to which it threatens individual and organizational values, impedes functions, or sets in motion embarrassing sequences of social actions. In the early generic period, tolerance by others for the individual's aggressive behavior generally speaking is broad, and it is very likely to be interpreted as a variation of normal behavior, particularly in the absence of biographical knowledge of the person. At most, people observe that "there is something odd about him," or "he must be upset," or "he is just ornery," or "I don't quite understand him" (Cumming and Cumming, 1957).

At some point in the chain of interactions, a new configuration takes place in perceptions others have of the individual, with shifts in figure-ground relations. The individual, as we have already indicated, is an ambiguous figure, comparable to textbook figures of stairs or outlines cubes which reverse themselves when studied intently. From a normal variant the person becomes "unreliable," "untrustworthy," "dangerous," or someone with whom others "do not wish to be involved." An illustration nicely apropos of this came out in the reaction of the head of a music department in a university when he granted an interview to a man who had worked for years on a theory to compose music mathematically:

> When he asked to be placed on the staff so that he could use the electronic computers of the University *I shifted my ground*...when I offered an objection to his theory, he became disturbed, so I changed my reaction to "yes and no."

As is clear from this, once the perceptual reorientation takes place, either as the outcome of continuous interaction or through the receipt of biographical information, interaction changes qualitatively. In our words it becomes *spurious*, distinguished by patronizing, evasion, "humoring," guiding conversation onto selected topics, underreaction, and silence, all calculated either to prevent intense interaction or to protect individual and group values by restricting access to them. When the interaction is between two or more persons it is cued by a whole repertoire or subtle expressive signs which are meaningful only to them.

The net effects of spurious interaction are to:

1.stop the flow of information to ego;

2. create a discrepancy between expressed ideas and affect among those with whom he interacts;

3.make the situation or the group image an ambiguous one for ego, much as he is for others.

Needless to say this kind of spurious interaction is one of the most difficult for an adult in our society to cope with, because it complicates or makes decisions impossible for him and also because it is morally invidious.[2]

The process from inclusion to exclusion is by no means an even one. Both individuals and members of groups change their perceptions and reactions, and vacillation is common, depending upon the interplay of values, anxieties and guilt on both sides. Members of an excluding group may decide they have been unfair and seek to bring the individual back into their confidence. This overture may be rejected or used by ego as a means of further attack. We have also found that ego may capitulate, sometimes abjectly, to others and seek group reentry, only to be rejected. In some cases compromises are struck and a partial reintegration of ego into informal social relations is achieved. The direction which informal exclusion takes depends upon ego's reactions, the degree of communication between his interactors, the composition and structure of the informal groups, and the perceptions of "key others" at points of interaction which directly affect ego's status.

Organizational Crisis and Formal Exclusion

Thus far we have discussed exclusion as an informal process. Informal exclusion may take place but leave ego's formal status in an organization intact. So long as this status is preserved and rewards are sufficient to validate it on his terms, an uneasy peace between him and others may prevail. Yet ego's social isolation and his strong commitments make him an unpredictable factor; furthermore the rate of change and internal power struggles, especially in large and complex organizations, means that preconditions of stability may be short lived.

Organizational crises involving a paranoid relationship arise in several ways. The individual may act in ways which arouse intolerable anxieties in others, who demand that "something be done." Again, by going to higher authority or making appeals outside the organization, he may set in motion procedures which leave those in power no other choice than to take action. In some situations ego remains relatively quiescent and does not openly attack the organization. Action against him is set off by growing anxieties or calculated motives of associates—in some cases his immediate superiors. Finally, regular organizational procedures incidental to promotion, retirement or reassignment may precipitate the crises.

Assuming a critical situation in which the conflict between the individual and members of the organization leads to action to formally exclude him, several possibilities exist. One is the transfer of ego from one department, branch or division of the organization to another, a device frequently resorted to in the armed services or in large corporations. This requires that the individual be persuaded to make the change and that some department will accept him. While this may be accomplished in different ways, not infrequently artifice, withholding information, bribery, or thinly disguised threats figure conspicuously among the means by which the transfer is brought about. Needless to say, there is a limit to which transfers can be employed as a solution to the problem, contingent upon the size of the organization and the previous diffusion of knowledge about the transferee.

Solution number two we call encapsulation, which, in brief, is a reorganization and redefinition of ego's status. This has the effect of isolating him from the organization and making him directly responsible to one or two superiors who act as his intermediator. The change is often made palatable to ego by enhancing some of the material rewards of his status. He may be nominally promoted or "kicked upstairs," given a larger office, or a separate secretary, or relieved of onerous duties. Sometimes a special status is created for him.

This type of solution often works because it is a kind of formal recognition by the organization of ego's intense commitment to his status and in part a victory for him over his enemies. It bypasses them and puts him into direct communication with higher authority who may communicate with him in a more direct manner. It also relieves his associates of further need to connive against him. This solution is sometimes used to dispose of troublesome corporation executives, high-ranking military officers, and academic *personae non gratae* in universities.

A third variety of solutions to the problem of paranoia in an organization is outright discharge, forced resignation or non-renewal of appointment. Finally, there may be an organized move to have the individual in the paranoid relationship placed on sick leave, or to compel him to take psychiatric treatment. The extreme expression of this is pressure (as on the family) or direct action to have the person committed to a mental hospital.

The order of the enumerated solutions to the paranoid problem in a rough way reflects the amount of risk associated with the alternatives, both as to the probabilities of failure and of damaging repercussions to the organization. Generally, organizations seem to show a good deal of resistance to making or carrying out decisions which require expulsion of the individual or forcing hospitalization, regardless of his mental condition. One reason for this is that the person may have power within the organization, based upon his position, or monopolized skills and information,[3] and unless there is a strong coalition against him the general conservatism of administrative judgments will run in him favor. Herman Wouk's novel of *The Caine Mutiny* dramatizes some of the difficulties of cashiering a person from a position of power in an essentially conservative military organization. An extreme of this conservatism is illustrated by one case in which we found a department head retained in his position in an organization even though he was actively hallucinating as well as expressing paranoid delusions.[4] Another factor working on the individual's side is that discharge of a person in a position of power reflects unfavorably upon those who placed him there. Ingroup solidarity of administrators may be involved, and the methods of the opposition may create sympathy for ego at higher levels.

Even when the person is almost totally excluded and informally isolated within an organization, he may have power outside. This weighs heavily when the external power can be invoked in some way, or when it automatically leads to raising questions as to the internal workings of the organization. This touches upon the more salient reasons for reluctance to eject an uncooperative and retaliatory person, even when he is relatively unimportant to the organization. We refer to a kind of negative power derived from the vulnerability of organizations to unfavorable publicity and exposure of their private lives that are likely if the crises proceeds to formal hearings, case review or litigation. This is an imminent possibility where paranoia exists. If hospital commitment is attempted, there is a possibility that a jury trial will be demanded, which will force leaders of the organization to defend their actions. If the crisis turns into a legal contest of this sort, it is not easy to prove insanity, and there may be damage suits. Even if the facts heavily support the petitioners, such contests can only throw unfavorable light upon the organization.

The Conspiratorial Nature of Exclusion

A conclusion from the foregoing is that organizational vulnerability as well as anticipations or retaliations from the paranoid person lay a functional basis for conspiracy among those seeking to contain or oust him. Probabilities are strong that a coalition will appear within the organization, integrated by a common commitment to oppose the paranoid person. This, the exclusionist group, demands loyalty, solidarity and secrecy from its members; it acts in accord with a common scheme and in varying degrees utilitizes techniques of manipulation and misrepresentation.

Conspiracy in rudimentary form can be detected in informal exclusion apart from an organizational crisis. This was illustrated in an office research team in which staff members huddled around a water cooler to discuss the unwanted associate. They also used office telephones to arrange coffee breaks without him and employed symbolic cues in his presence, such as humming the Dragnet theme song when he approached the group. An office rule against extraneous conversation was introduced with the collusion of supervisors, ostensibly for everyone, actually to restrict the behavior of the isolated worker. In another case an interview schedule designed by a researcher was changed at a conference arranged without him. When he sought an explanation at a subsequent conference, his associates pretended to have no knowledge of the changes.

Conspiratorial behavior comes into sharpest focus during organizational crises in which the exclusionists who initiate action become an embattled group. There is a concerted effort to gain consensus for this view, to solidify the group and to halt close interaction with those unwilling to completely join the coalition. Efforts are also made to neutralize those who remain uncommitted but who can't be kept ignorant of the plans afoot. Thus an external appearance of unanimity is given even if it doesn't exist.

Much of the behavior of the group at this time is strategic in nature, with determined calculations as to "what we will do if he does this or that." In one of our cases, a member on a board of trustees spoke of the "game being played" with the person in controversy with them. Planned action may be carried to the length of agreeing upon the exact words to be used when confronted or challenged by the paranoid individual. Above all there is continuous, precise communication among exclusionists, exemplified in one case by mutual exchanging of copies of all letters sent and received from ego.

Concern about secrecy in such groups is revealed by such things as carefully closing doors and lowering of voices when ego is brought under discussion. Meeting places and times may be varied from normal procedures; documents may be filed in unusual places and certain telephones may not be used during a paranoid crisis.

The visibility of the individual's behavior is greatly magnified during this period; often he is the main topic of conversation among the exclusionists, while rumors of the difficulties spread to other groups, which in some cases may be drawn into the controversy. At a certain juncture steps are taken to keep the members of the ingroup continually informed of the individual's movements and, if possible, of his plans. In effect, if not in form, this amounts to spying. Members of one embattled group, for example, hired an outside person unknown to their accuser to take notes on a speech he delivered to enlist a community organization on his side. In another case, a person having an office opening onto that of a department head was persuaded to act as an informant for the nucleus of persons working to depose the head from his position of authority. This group also seriously debated placing an all-night watch in front of their perceived malefactor's home.

Concomitant with the magnified visibility of the paranoid individual, come distortions of his image, most pronounced in the inner coterie of exclusionists. His size, physical strength, cunning, and anecdotes of his outrages are exaggerated, with a central thematic emphasis on the fact that he is dangerous. Some individuals give cause for such beliefs in that previously they have engaged in violence or threats, others do not. One encounters characteristic contradictions in interviews on this point, such as: "No, he has never struck anyone around here-just fought with the policeman at the State Capitol," or "No, I am not afraid of him, but one of these days he will explode."

It can be said parenthetically that the alleged dangerousness of paranoid persons storied in fiction and drama has never been systematically demonstrated. As a matter of fact, the only substantial data on this, from a study of delayed admissions, largely paranoid, to a mental hospital in Norway, disclosed that "neither the paranoiacs nor paranoids have been dangerous, and most not particular troublesome" (Odesard, 1958). Our interpretation of this, as suggested earlier, is that the imputed dangerousness of the paranoid individual does not come from physical fear but from the organizational threat he presents and the need to justify collective action against him.[5]

However, this is not entirely tactical behavior—as is demonstrated by anxieties and tensions which mount among those in the coalition during the more critical phases of their interaction. Participants may develop fears quite analogous to those of classic conspirators. One leader in such a group spoke of the period of the paranoid crisis as a "week of terror," during which he was wracked with insomnia and "had to take his stomach pills." Projection was revealed by a trustee who, during a school crisis occasioned by discharge of an aggressive teacher, stated that he "watched his shadows," and "wondered if all would be well when he returned home at night." Such tensional states, working along with a kind of closure of communication within the group, are both a cause and an effect of amplified group interaction which distorts or symbolically rearranges the image of the person against whom they act.

Once the battle is won by the exclusionists, their version of the individual as dangerous becomes a crystallized rationale for official action. At this point misrepresentation becomes part of a more deliberate manipulation of ego. Gross misstatements, most frequently called "pretexts," become justifiable ways of getting his cooperation, for example, to get him to submit to psychiatric examination or detention preliminary to hospital commitment. This aspect of the process has been effectively detailed by Goffman (1959), with his concept of a "betrayal funnel" through which a patient enters a hospital. We need not elaborate on this, other than to confirm its occurrence in the exclusion process, complicated in our cases by legal strictures and the ubiquitous risk of litigation.

The Growth of Delusion

The general idea that the paranoid person symbolically fabricates the conspiracy against him is in our estimation incorrect or incomplete. Nor can we agree that he lacks insight, as is so frequently claimed. To the contrary, many paranoid persons properly realize that they are being isolated and excluded by concerted interaction, or that they are being manipulated. However, they are at a loss to estimate accurately or realistically the dimensions and form of the coalition arrayed against them.

As channels of communication are closed to the paranoid person, he has no means of getting feedback on consequences of behavior, which is essential for correcting his interpretations of the social relationships and organization which he must rely on to define his status and give him identity. He can only read overt behavior without the informal context. Although he may properly infer that people are organized against him, he can only use confrontation or formal inquisitorial procedures to try to prove this. The paranoid person must provoke strong feelings in order to receive any kind of meaningful communication from others—hence the accusations, his bluntness, his insults. Ordinarily this is nondeliberate; nevertheless, in one complex case we found the person consciously provoking discussions to get readings from others on his behavior. This man said of himself: "Some people would describe me as very perceptive, others would describe me as very imperceptive."

The need for communication and the identity which goes with it does a good deal to explain the preference of paranoid persons for formal, legalistic, written communications, and the care with which many of them preserve records of their contracts with others. In some ways the resort to litigation is best interpreted as the effort of the individual to compel selected others to interact directly with him as equals, to engineer a situation in which evasion is impossible. The fact that the person is seldom satisfied with the outcome of his letters, his petitions, complaints and writs testifies to their function as devices for establishing contact and interaction with others, as well as "setting the record straight." The wide professional tolerance of lawyers for aggressive behavior in court and the nature of Anglo-Saxon legal institutions, which grew out of a revolt against conspiratorial or star-chamber justice, mean that the individual will be heard. Furthermore his charges must be answered; otherwise he wins by default. Sometimes he wins small victories, even if he loses the big ones. He may earn grudging respect as an adversary, and sometimes shares a kind of legal camaraderie with others in the courts. He gains an indemnity through notoriety....

REFERENCES

Cameron, N. (1943). "The Paranoid Pseudocommunity." *American Journal of Sociology* 46: 33–38.

———. (1959). "The Paranoid Pseudocommunity Revisited." *American Journal of Sociology* 65:52–58.

Cumming, E. and J. Cumming. (1957). *Closed Ranks*. Cambridge, Mass: Harvard Press.

Goffman, E. (1959). "The Moral Career of the Mental Patient." *Psychiatry* 22:127.

Levenson, B. (1961). "Bureaucratic Succession." Pp. 362–395 IN A. Etzioni, (ed.), *Complex Organization*. New York: Holt, Rinehart and Winston.

Odegard, O. (1958). "A Clinical Study of Delayed Admissions to a Mental Hospital". *Mental Hygiene* 42:66–67.

Sapir, E. (1915). "Abnormal Types of Speech in Nootka." *Canada Department of Mines,* Memoir 62, No. 5.

Tyhurst, J. S. (1957). "Paranoid Patterns." Ch II *Explorations in Social Psychiatry*. New York: Basic Books.

NOTES

[1] In a subsequent article Cameron (2) modified his original conception, but not of the social aspects of paranoia, which mainly concern us.

[2] The interaction in some ways is similar to that used with children, particularly the *"enfant terrible"*. The function of language in such interactions was studied by Sapir (7) years ago.

[3] For a systematic analysis of the organizational difficulties in removing an "unpromotable" person from a position see (5).

[4] One of the cases in the first study.

[5] *Spura*, p.3.

Chapter 38

CREATING CRAZIES/MAKING MENTALS:
THE PRE-PATIENT PHASE IN THE MORAL
CAREER OF THE PSYCHIATRIC PATIENT

Nancy J. Herman

Introduction

Who can tell where health ends and disease begins? When disease is found to have shed its blighting influence over the system, is it possible, after establishing the fact, to decide what amount or kind is necessary to occasion aberration of mind, and when this amount or quality is developed? When developed, does it at once manifest its baleful influence upon the brain, by producing insanity; or does it not rather brood over the delicate organ of the mind, and gradually fulfill its dread commission? When again the mind begins to totter, and reason to sit insecurely upon her throne, do the friends and acquaintances of the unhappy sufferer recognize these first monitions? Or do they not rather behold—if indeed they observe anything—a simple change of habit, slightly perverted moral feelings, or trifling eccentricities of character? (Esquirol, 1845, in Goshen, 1967:316).

The study of insanity has been approached from a variety of perspectives. Traditionally, psychiatrists and psychologists (Siegler and Osmond, 1974; Lewis, 1967; and Whybrow, 1972) advocating a medical model stance have conceptualized mental disorders as disease entities located within the individual. Adopting an objective theoretical and nosological classification scheme, such persons have focused on the examination, classification, etiology and treatment of observable, pathological behavior of the patient. In this perspective, mental disorders are comprehended from an objective point of view and treated in a manner similar to other illnesses. Humans are conceived as "diseased" psychological or physiological entities—no attempt is made to understand the patients from their perspectives.

In reaction against the premise that mental disorders are intrinsic defects located within the individual, sociologists and social psychologists developed an alternative conceptual framework that places emphasis on the social aspects of mental illness. Conceiving of mental illness as subjectively problematic, proponents (Goffman, 1961; Kutner, 1962; Sampson et al., 1955; Scheff, 1964, 1966, 1967, 1975) of this perspective examine the social processes by which an individual comes to be labelled and treated as mentally ill, and how such a definition impinges upon the actor. The majority of these sociological studies on mental patients were conducted in the 1950's

427

and 1960's. I would argue that institutional life and ideology are not static, but rather dynamic in nature; therefore it is useful to re-examine the social worlds of psychiatric patients and they subjectively experience it some twenty years later.

The purpose of this paper then, is to present a description and analysis of social worlds of psychiatric patients as they subjectively experience it. Adopting a symbolic interactionist approach, specifically a labelling approach to the study of mental illness, this paper examines one phase in their "moral careers"—the pre-patient. Objectively, this study focuses on the processes by which individuals are set apart, labelled and subsequently treated as mentally ill. Subjectively, it focuses on the effect of labelling upon the individual.

Pathways Leading to the Mental Hospital:
The Pre-patient Phase in the Career of the Psychiatric Patient

Mental illness, according to the social-role model is *not* an inherent feature that characterizes the mentally ill; however, it is a *social definition* bestowed by members of society upon individuals exhibiting certain types of behavior.

Seen from this perspective, the career of the mental patient begins when societal members *react*—express discontent and/or take action against behavior by the actor and subsequently define him/her as "mentally ill." Specifically, individuals are judged to be mentally ill when they exhibit a special type of culturally-inappropriate behavior—behavior Scheff (1966:33) refers to as "residual rule violations":

> The culture of the group provides a vocabulary of terms for categorizing many norm violations: crime, perversion, drunkenness and bad manners...Each of these terms is derived from the type of behavior involved. After exhausting these categories, however, there is always a residue of the most diverse kinds of violations for which the culture applies no explicit label...Although there is great cultural variation in what is defined as decent or real; each culture tends to reify its definition of decency or reality, and so provides no way of handling violations of its expectations in these areas. The typical norm governing decency or reality, therefore, literally 'goes without saying' and its violation is unthinkable for most of its members. For the convenience of the society in construing those instances of unnameable rule-breaking which are called to attention, these violations may be lumped together into a residual category: witchcraft, spirit possession, or, in our own society, mental illness.

Mental illness then, according to this perspective, is conceived as a residual category of deviant behavior—violations for which society provides no explicit label.

In my study, the majority of the subjects began their careers as mental patients when members of society reacted to such residual rule violations as: (1) throwing dishes at a family member, (b) breaking a window in the house, (c) engaging in repeated urinating and defecating on oneself, (d) refusal to maintain habits of cleanliness, (e) providing unacceptable responses to others in the context of social interaction, etc.

A large proportion of residual rule violations frequently go undetected—the behavior remains unrecognized, or if it is acknowledged, it is rationalized or 'normalized' by the social audience.[1] While various residual rule violations are ignored or rationalized away, in some instances, individuals exhibiting similar violations are reacted to by societal members and are labeled as mentally ill. Goffman (1961:134), taking as problematic the application of the label "mentally ill," states:

> For every offense that leads to an effective complaint, there are many
> psychiatrically similar ones that never do. No action is taken which leads
> to other extrusory outcomes; or ineffective action is taken, leading to a
> mere pacifying or putting off of the person who complains.

In other words, defining an individual as mentally ill is not an *automatic* process. Whether a person is so labelled is contingent upon several factors, including the tolerance level of the community, the severity of the rule violation, and/or the social status of the rule breaker relative to the audience reacting to his/her behavior (Scheff, 1975:10).[2]

A number of studies focusing on the tolerance limits of the family have documented the capacity of family members to minimize, overlook, and rationalize evidence of mental illness.[3] It is only in the event of a shift in the tolerance of the family members—when the individual's behavior becomes unmanageable, when a crisis situation develops,[4] that others define him/her as being in need of psychiatric help. The data from this study suggest that family members adopted similar patterns of accommodation—suspicions of mental illness were rationalized or normalized. Such accommodative mechanisms collapsed when family members were confronted with an unmanageable emergency. As the mother of a young woman, hospitalized for exhibiting 'bizarre' behavior recalls:

> My daughter wasn't quite 'right' for a long time. But it took me a long
> time to realize that. You see, at first I refused to face that anything was
> wrong with her. Her grades started getting worse when she entered high
> school. But I thought she was just not trying hard enough. Then she
> started to get worse—I mean by being violent. Initially, I thought that she
> was just letting off steam—I didn't realize that she was "sick." But
> gradually I came to the conclusion that she was sick when one day she got
> so mad at me that she went "berserk" and started throwing things. I was
> so afraid that I called the police.

Not only do accommodative patterns break down in crisis situations, but also result when the individual repeatedly exhibits culturally-inappropriate responses in the context of social interaction with others. As Mechanic (1962:68) states:

> Mental illness and other forms of deviancy become visible when persons
> in the participant's group *recognize his inability and reluctance to make*
> *proper responses in his network of interpersonal relations.*

Similar to Laing and Esterson (1964), the data indicate that individuals were adjudged by significant others to be mentally ill as a consequence of their inability to accurately respond to interpersonal demands of others in the situation.[5] As one family member recalls:

> I gradually realized that something was wrong. When I would ask Joe a question, he would answer in a strange way. I mean, if I asked him a question about "apples" he would answer and tell me about "oranges." Our conversations just didn't click! That's when I realized that he must be sick.

Similarly, a friend of an individual hospitalized in a mental facility states:

> Before she was hospitalized, it was just like she was on another wavelength. I would be talking about a certain thing and she would answer me with a statement that was completely alien to the conversation. Sometimes she didn't answer at all. At first, I just shrugged it off, but when it persisted, I realized that she must be mentally ill and desperately in need of psychiatric help.

A third individual, recalling his wife's behavior prior to hospitalization states:

> My wife started acting "funny" a few years ago. I mean, she went into this depression and wouldn't talk to anyone. No matter what anyone said, she just wouldn't answer. Then, after a while when she did answer, she would say things that didn't make any sense whatsoever. That's when I decided to get her psychiatric help.

In short then, the career of the mental patient begins when societal members notice that the behavior exhibited by the person is strange or peculiar. Although the social audience may initially deny or minimize the peculiarity, if the individual repeatedly fails to respond to the interpersonal demands of the other in the situation, or if his behavior becomes unmanageable, societal members move toward defining him as mentally ill.

A number of agents and agencies participate in the definitional process and subsequent hospitalization of the individual. As Goffman (1961:135) notes, these "circuit of agents—and agencies—participate faithfully in his passage from civilian to patient status." Essentially, in my research, four agents reacted to residual rule violations exhibited by individuals, thereby activating commitment proceedings into the mental hospital: (1) self as agent; (2) the legal system as agent; (3) family and friends as agents; and (4) psychiatric officials in a general hospital as agents.[6]

(1) Self as Agent

One possible pathway leading to psychiatric hospitalization is through self-referral. A small number,[7] upon self-examination find themselves to be acting in strange and incomprehensible manners. Such behavior often frightens the person and leads him/ her to believe that he/she is "going nuts" or "losing his mind." This threatening view of self as being potentially mentally ill impels the individual to admit him/herself willingly to a psychiatric facility. One patient, discussing his experiences as a pre-patient states:

> I kept hearing voices before I came to the hospital. I didn't know what was happening to me. It was so frightening. I thought that I was losing my mind—going bananas. That's when I decided to admit myself to the hospital and get help.

Similarly, another patient states:

> It all started about four years ago—things happened to the family—my mother dies; my two uncles died; my aunt died. I was very close to my aunt. My son and I used to live with my aunt in her house. I used to look after her. I saw that she was gradually going down hill and I knew that she was going to die. It was very hard on me. When she did die, I became very depressed...It was really depressing and my nerves got bad. To make things worse, my son decided that he would like to go out on his own. It was such a big shock and it depressed me further. I didn't want to eat or take care of myself. I knew that something was wrong with me. I wasn't "normal." That's when I decided to get help for my nervous breakdown and came to the hospital.

Concomitant with the self-realization that he/she is in need of psychiatric help, the pre-patient is also faced with the sometimes arduous and anxiety-provoking task of attempting to conceal from others his/her newly discovered discreditable image of self. The individual struggles to maintain his/her role as a "normal" person in the context of social interaction with others while constantly fearful that he/she will be "found out." When the social situation becomes too stressful for the pre-patient to manage, he/she often feels relief by admitting himself/herself into the mental institution. As Goffman (1961:132–33) notes, "instead of being himself a questionable person trying to maintain a role as a full one, he can become an officially questioned person known to himself to be not so questionable at that." A person, describing his stressful experiences prior to hospitalization states:

> In my heart I knew that there was something mentally wrong with me, but I tried to hide it. I tried to hide it from myself but I eventually realized— I faced the fact that I needed help...I couldn't concentrate—I felt so mixed up—I thought that everyone was against me. And these feelings got progressively worse as time went on. As well as trying to hide my illness from myself, I also tried to hide it from my friends and other employees at work. Sometimes, it was quite difficult to pretend everything was ok. I kept wondering if they thought I was "going mental"—whether they knew or not. I tried to hide it for a time, but that created more pressures

on me until I couldn't take it anymore...It was a relief to go to the hospital. I didn't have to hide it anymore. Now I could get some help for my sickness.

For individuals who were either frightened by the strange behavior they were exhibiting, or were no longer able to manage the stressful experiences of attempting to conceal certain discreditable aspects of their selves from others, admission to the psychiatric hospital is seen in a positive light.

Despite the fact that some pre-patients admit themselves willingly to the mental hospital for treatment, the majority of individuals are admitted involuntarily, their social experiences as pre-patients are generally seen in a negative manner (Goffman, 1961). Since the majority of persons in my study were admitted in this latter manner,[8] this discussion will now focus on the various agents that participate in committing the individual involuntarily and the individual's reaction to such action.

(2) The Legal System as Agent

A number of individuals mark the beginning of their careers as mental patients when legal authorities interpret their behavior as evidence of mental illness and consequently admit them to a psychiatric facility.[9] Specifically, legal authorities participate in the individual's passage from civilian to patient status in two ways: (1) a person exhibiting "bizarre" behavior on the outside is apprehended by the police and admitted directly to a psychiatric hospital for treatment; and (2) an individual committing a legal offense is apprehended by the police and imprisoned. At a subsequent hearing, the court decides to send the person to a mental hospital for psychiatric evaluation.

In terms of the former path, some individuals, although not breaking the law are apprehended by the police. That is, according to a provision in the legal mandate, police officers ar given the authority to apprehend and hospitalize individuals acting in a strange manner—persons committing rule violations. From the standpoint of the police officer, psychiatric hospitalization for the individual is conceived as a necessary step in order to ensure that he does not injure himself/herself or others. However, from the point of view of the person himself/herself, his/her apprehension and involuntary hospitalization are events which he/she sees in a negative light. Specifically, most individuals apprehended and hospitalized by the police cannot comprehend why such action was taken against them. For these persons, hospitalization is unjust—they adamantly deny that anything is wrong with them. An individual, expressing the moral outrage of his social situation as a pre-patient states:

I just can't understand it. One minute I was out there minding my own business—not bothering anyone, then the next minute, I find myself being brought to the hospital by the cops. I never did anything. I'm not sick. There is no way that they should have done that to me! I demand to be let free!

Similarly, another person states:

> I was on a highway and the police just picked me up and brought me here.
> I never asked them why they picked me up. I was too scared. I can't
> understand why they brought me to this place. To this day, I still don't
> know why!

In short, individuals that I interviewed who were admitted to the psychiatric hospital
by the police as a result of committing some residual rule violation felt that such action
was totally unjust and demanded to be released immediately. These individuals felt
that they were the victims of a gross misjudgment on the part of the police.

In contrast to individuals admitted to the psychiatric facility by the police as a
consequence of exhibiting strange or incomprehensible behavior, others are admitted
by the legal authorities as a result of committing a legal offense. Persons breaking
such laws as arson, burglary, murder, rape, etc., are apprehended by the police and
taken into custody. During a subsequent court hearing, the details of the case are
discussed; if the motive behind the crime appears to be irrational in the eyes of the
judge and/or the defense attorney, the individual's sanity may be called into question.
Hence, the court may decide to send the offender to a mental hospital for a psychiatric
assessment in order to ascertain whether he/she is "psychiatrically fit" to stand trial.[10]

The legal offender, wearing handcuffs is transported over to the hospital by the
police at which time he is handed over to the hospital staff and becomes the property
of the psychiatric institution.

For such individuals, their moral experiences as pre-patients are generally
conceived of in a negative manner. That is, most persons admitted to the hospital in
this manner express indignation regarding the objectification[11] of their selves by both
legal authorities and hospital staff. One patient, recalling his social situation as a pre-
patient states:

> They treated me like an object, that's all! Right from the moment I was
> caught by the police, in the courtroom, right up until the time they handed
> me over to the ward staff of the hospital. No one talked to me like I was
> a person—they just talked about me as if I wasn't there. They treated me
> just like a piece of cargo that needed to be moved from one place to
> another.

Similarly, another patient recalls:

> When I was brought up from the jail by the cops, everyone handled me
> like some piece of trash—something without feelings. They talked about
> me as if I wasn't capable of understanding what they were saying about
> me. It made me so mad.

In contrast to persons admitted to the mental hospital by the police as a result of
committing a residual rule violation—individuals who generally express moral
outrage for such action taken against them, others committed via the court reacted to

their incarcerations in a somewhat acquiescent manner. Although such pre-patients may not be in accordance with the adjudgement of their selves as potentially mentally ill, they are informed of the rationale behind the judgement, the course of action that will be taken, and the length of time they will be required to remain in the hospital— knowledge which makes their social situations more tolerable. Conceiving of his situation as "doing time," one patient states:

> They (the court officials) don't know what they're talking about—trying to say that I'm crazy. I know that there's nothing wrong with me. Oh, I don't care what they think anyways. I'll just do my time. I only have to be here for thirty days for some kind of assessment, then I'll be out.

Another patient states:

> There's nothing wrong with me. I'll be out of here pretty soon. I just have to be on my best behavior and do my time and I'll soon be out. You just have to learn to bear it.

While some pre-patients processed by the court do not think that they are mentally ill, others[12] however, prior to being sent for psychiatric examination, have come to see themselves as mentally imbalanced. For these individuals, admission (even involuntary admission) to a mental facility is often seen as a welcome relief to their problems. As one person explains:

> I went to jail for break and entry. But you know, I never knew that I committed the crime until after it happened, and the police picked me up and told me what I did. I knew I needed psychiatric help...I didn't object to coming here.

For persons, who prior to hospitalization were already questioning their sanity, their entire experiences as pre-patients are generally conceived as a positive step toward the alleviation of their problems.

(3) Family and Friends as Agents

A third group of agents who frequently play a role in the individual's passage from person to patient are his/her family and friends—a group of persons with whom the pre-patient most frequently interacts, and in whom he/she places complete trust.

During the pre-patient phase of his/her moral career, the individual gradually discovers that although he/she has placed reliance on family and friends to be supportive in times of trouble, these are often the very individuals who are the first to doubt the pre-patient's sanity and take action against him/her. When the individual repeatedly fails to correctly respond to the interpersonal demands of the others in the situation, the others react to such behavior and adjudge the individual to be mentally ill. Subsequent to interpreting the pre-patient's behavior as evidence of mental illness, friends or family of the person frequently enlist the help of the family physician, mental health official, justice of the peace, or other official third parties in committing the individual to the psychiatric facility—action which the pre-patient views as traitorous and conspiratorial in nature.

In some cases, the process of commitment begins when family members or friends attempt to persuade the individual into visiting a family physician or mental health counselor for what they are repeatedly told is "consultation purposes only." As one patient recalls:

> My mother told me that nothing was going to happen to me. No one was going to take me anywhere. She said that the doctor just wanted to talk with me—we were just going to talk—that's all!

Similarly, another individual states:

> My cousin came over and tried to talk me into seeing the doctor—just to "talk things over." She said that he would just talk about how I was doing and that would be the end of it.

If the individual refuses to oblige, he is often threatened by his significant others with desertion, legal action, or disfellowship. One person recalling his social experiences as a pre-patient states:

> My wife told me if I wouldn't go to see the doctor then she was going to leave me. She said that she'd take the kids and get as far away from me as possible...

Another patient recalls:

> I was told that if I refused to keep the appointment with the family doctor, I would have to get out of my father's house and never show my face around there again.

Generally, a family member or friend, prior to attempting to persuade the pre-patient to "consult" a professional, will have already set up the appointment. Moreover, he/she will have "filled in" the official third party regarding the case history of the adjudged individual. Such action, according to Goffman (1961:137), "tends to establish the next-of-relation as the responsible person to whom pertinent findings can be divulged, while effectively establishing the other as the patient."

Prior to arriving for the appointment, friends or family members engage in polite small talk with the pre-patient—no mention is made of the pre-patient's pending fate. The pre-patient's significant others emphasize repeatedly that they will not let anything happen to him. However, during the course of the interview, the pre-patient gradually discovers that a coalition has been formed against him in an attempt to commit him to a psychiatric institution. That is, upon arrival for the appointment, the pre-patient finds out that he has been accorded the role of "patient" by the professional and his significant others. Moreover, from the nature of the conversation and the types of questions asked during the consultation, the pre-patient realizes that he has been "informed on" or betrayed. The pre-patient finds out that his significant others—those individuals who prior to the appointment stressed that they were "on his side" and would not let anything happen to him, turn against him and take the side of the professional who emphasizes the need for hospitalization. In short, the pre-patient sadly finds out that his friends or relations, the ones on whom he thought he could depend, have betrayed him.[13] A patient, discussing his feelings of embitterment and betrayal toward his family states:

> All the time, they kept telling me that they weren't going to let anything happen to me. That's what they told me. They never mentioned one word about putting me in this hospital. Then we go to Dr. ____'s office and I saw what was really going on. My whole family and the doctor were plotting against me behind my back. My mother told the doctor all kinds of things about me even before I showed up. They were trying to get me committed to this place. They're all traitors and I hate them!

(4) Psychiatric Officials of a General Hospital as Agents

A fourth and final route leading to hospitalization in a psychiatric facility is via psychiatric officials of a general hospital. Specifically, a number of individuals exhibiting symptoms of mental illness are reacted against by various social audiences and are admitted to the psychiatric ward of a general hospital for treatment.[14] If a person fails to respond to treatment, or is diagnosed as being in need of extended psychiatric care, psychiatric officials subsequently transfer him/her to a mental hospital. Some individuals respond to such action taken against their selves in a positive manner:

> When I didn't get any better after the shock treatments, they transferred me to Meadowdale. I didn't really mind going there. I thought that I might get treated better than in the ordinary hospital. I thought they could help me get better.

Similarly, another individual states:

> At first in ____ (general hospital) they tried all kinds of drugs on me but it didn't make me feel much better. Dr. ____ thought that it would be best for me to go to the psychiatric hospital...I agreed because I wanted to feel better and get well.

Others, however, respond to the action of transfer in a negative manner. These individuals expressed fear and anxiety regarding their fates:

I was scared, I mean, really scared when I found out that they were transferring me to this place. When I was on the psychiatric ward in the general hospital, I thought that they would just keep me there for a few days and then let me out, but I never thought I'd end up here. I didn't know how long they planned to keep me at this place and it scared me.

While admission to a psychiatric ward of a general hospital against the pre-patient's will brings a loss of freedom, the action of transfer to the psychiatric facility proper presents yet a further loss:

It was bad enough in Oakridge (the general hospital). When they admitted me in there, they took away a lot of my things—they kept watching me all the time. I couldn't do anything freely on my own. But being sent here to Meadowdale was much worse. It was like becoming a lower being...You see, you lost most, if not all your freedom that you used to have when you come in. It's like going down a flight of stairs—you were once at the top, but when you got admitted, you quickly fall to the bottom.

Another person states:

It was worse once I got to Meadowdale. They took all my personals away...I couldn't even have my wallet and my money. You lose all your freedom. They lock you up like animals.

In general, most patients conceive of the pre-patient experience of transfer with animosity. While involuntary admission to the psychiatric ward of a general hospital is viewed by these individuals as a gross misjudgment, they conceive of the action of transfer as yet a further and more serious error on the part of others—a mistake that is unforgivable. A patient, expressing contempt toward a psychiatric official's decision to transfer him to a mental hospital states:

I hate that doctor for sending me in here. How could he do this to me? He had no right. I feel like killing him. I hated it when they admitted me to the psych. ward in the ordinary hospital—there was nothing wrong with me. They made a big mistake. But when that doctor said that I needed "therapy" so he was sending me to Meadowdale, I nearly hit the roof. They were making a worse mistake—there was nothing wrong with me and they were sending me to the nut house.

REFERENCES

Becker, E. 1962. "Socialization, Command of Performance, and Mental Illness." *American Journal of Sociology* 67:494–501.

Bittner, E. 1967. "Police Discretion in Apprehending the Mentally Ill." *Social Problems* 14:278–92.

Blake, R.R. & J.S. Moulton. 1961. "Conformity, Resistance, and Conversion." Pp. 111–125. In I.A. Berg and B.M. Bass, eds., *Conformity and Deviation*. New York: Harper.

Cain, A. 1964. "On the Meaning of 'Playing Crazy' in Borderline Children." *Psychiatry* 27:278–89.

Clausen, J.A. & M. Yarrow. 1955. "Paths to the Mental Hospital." *Journal of Social Issues* 11:25–32.

Cohen, E. 1953. *Human Behavior in a Concentration Camp*. New York: Grosset and Dunlap.

Cumming, J. & E. Cumming. 1957. *Closed Ranks: An Experiment in Mental Health Education*. Mass: Harvard University Press.

Denzin, N.K. 1968. "The Self-Fulfilling Prophecy and Patient-Therapist Interaction." Pp. 349–57 IN S. Spitzer and N. Denzin, eds., *The Mental Patient: Studies in the Sociology of Deviance*. New York: McGraw-Hill.

Esquirol, J.E., 1867. "A Treatise on Insanity." Pp. 10–32. In C.E. Goshen ed., *Documentary History of Psychiatry: A Source Book on Historical Principles*. New York: Philosophical Library.

Goffman, E. 1961. *Asylums*. Chicago: Aldine Press.

Gough, H.G. 1948. "A Sociological Theory of Psychopathy." *American Journal of Sociology* 53:359–66.

Haas, J. & W. Shaffir. 1978. "Do New Ways of Professional Socialization Make a Difference?" Paper presented at the Ninth World Congress of Sociology, Uppsala, Sweden.

Hollingshead, A.B. & F. Redlich. 1958. *Social Class and Mental Illness*. New York: Wiley.

Johnson, D. Mc I., & N. Dodds. 1957. *The Plea for the Silent*. London: Christopher Johnson.

Kutner, Luis, 1962. "The Illusion of Due Process in Commitment Proceedings." *Northwestern University Law Review* 57: 383–93.

Laing, R.D. & Esterson, A. 1964. *Sanity, Madness and the Family*. London: Tavistock.

Lemert, E. 1946. "Legal Commitment and Social Control." *Sociology and Social Psychiatry* 9:13–31.

Lewis, Aubrey, 1967. *The State of Psychiatry*. New York: Science House.

Mechanic, D. 1962. "Some Factors in Identifying and Defining Mental Illness." *Mental Hygiene* 46:66–74.

Meyers, J. & L. Schaffer. 1954. "Social Stratification and Psychiatric Practice: A Study of an Outpatient Clinic." *American Sociological Review* XIX:307–10.

Mezer, R.R. & P.D. Rheingold. 1962. "Mental Capacity and Incompetency: A Psycho-Legal Problem." *American Journal of Psychiatry* 118:827–31.

Orne, M.T. 1962. "On the Social Psychology of the Psychological Experiment: With Particular Reference to the Demand Characteristics and Their Implications." *American Psychologist* 17:776–83.

Rosenthal, D. & L. Jacobsen. 1968. "Teacher Expectations for the Disadvantaged." *Scientific American* 218:19–23.

Sampson, H. (et al). 1962. "Family Processes and Becoming a Mental Patient." *American Journal of Sociology* 68:88–96.

Scheff, Thomas, 1964. "The Societal Reaction to Deviance: Ascriptive Elements in the Psychiatric Screening of Mental Patients in a Midwestern State." *Social Problems* 11: 401–413.

———. 1966. *Being Mentally Ill*. Chicago: Aldine.

———. 1967. *Mental Illness and Social Processes*. New York: Harper.

———. 1975. *Labelling Madness*. New Jersey: Prentice-Hall.

Schwartz, C. 1957. "Perspectives on Deviance—Wives' Definitions of Their Husbands' Mental Illness." *Psychiatry* XX:271–91.

Siegler, Miriam, and Humphrey Osmond, 1974. *Models of Madness, Models of Medicine*. New York: MacMillan.

Smith, H. & J. Thrasher. 1968. "Roles, Cliques, and Sanctions: Dimensions of Patient Society." Pp. 235–62. In *The Mental Patient: Studies in the Sociology of Deviance*, S. Spitzer and N. Denzin (eds.). New York: McGraw-Hill.

Smith, K., M. Pumphrey, & J. Hall. 1963. "The 'Last Straw': The Decisive Incident Resulting in the Request for Hospitalization of One Hundred Schizophrenic Patients." *American Journal of Psychiatry* 120:228–33.

Sykes, G. 1958. *The Society of Captives*. New Jersey: Princeton University Press.

Turner, V. 1969. *The Ritual Process*. Chicago: Aldine.

VanGennep, Y., 1969. *Rites of Passage*. Chicago: Aldine.

Yarrow, M., C. Schwartz, H. Murphy, & L. Deasy. 1955. "The Psychological Meaning of Mental Illness in the Family." *Journal of Social Issues* 11:12–24.

Whybrow,P.C., 1972. "The Use and Abuse of the 'Medical Model' as a Conceptual Frame in Psychiatry." *Psychiatry in Medicine* 3:333–342.

NOTES

[1] This stage of rationalization is referred to as "denial" by Cumming and Cumming (1957:92–103). See also, Clausen and Yarrow (1955:25–33) and Hollingshead and Redlich (1958:170–76).

[2] For a discussion of some of the career contingencies that may affect hospitalization in a mental facility, see: Lemert (1946:370–78); and Meyers and Schaffer (1954:307–10).

[3] See, for example, Sampson et al. (1962); Yarrow et al. (1955); Schwartz (1957); Hollingshead and Redlich (1958); Laing and Esterson (1964).

[4] Smith et al. (1963:228–33) in their research on the tolerance limits of the family found that accommodative patterns broke down when a "last straw" type incident occurred.

[5] See also Becker (1962:494–501); Gough (1948:359–66) for a somewhat similar discussion regarding the definitional process of an individual as mentally ill.

[6] For the purposes of this paper, an analytical separation has been made between the four routes leading to hospitalization. However, in reality, there exists an interplay between the various agents' reactions to the residual rule violation and the individual—an interplay which is beyond the scope of this paper.

[7] In this case, five subjects (or 25% of the sample).

[8] In this case, fifteen subjects (or 75% of the sample).

[9] See also, Bittner (1967:278–92) for a discussion of police discretion in the apprehension of the mentally ill.

[10] Psychiatric assessments ranged from 30–60 days during which time forensic staff evaluated patients by means of observation, interviews and psychological testing.

[11] This theme continues, and is intensified during the in-patient phase of the person's career as a mental patient.

[12] In my study, such individuals were in a minority, specifically only 5% of the sample.

[13] The individual discovers that his family members are actually serving as "double agents"—on the one hand they pretend to be loyal and supportive, and yet, such persons turn against the individual and realign themselves with the professional.

[14] While some pre-patients are admitted directly to the psychiatric hospital for treatment, others are sent first to a psychiatric ward of a general hospital. The reason for such action is two-fold: (1) in some cases, the individuals are living in a region that does not contain a mental hospital; (2) with the trend toward deinstitutionalization of the mental health facilities, individuals are admitted to a psychiatric ward in a general hospital for short-term treatment and then are released back into the community. Only when such treatment fails are patients transferred for further treatment to a psychiatric institution.

Chapter 39

A MODEL OF HOMOSEXUAL IDENTITY FORMATION

Richard Troiden

This paper develops an ideal-typical model that describes how committed homosexuals—men and women who have defined themselves as homosexual and adopted homosexuality as a way of life—recall their arrival at perceptions of self as homosexual in relation to romantic and sexual settings. More specifically, the paper describes ideal types,...presents a four-stage ideal-typical model of homosexual identity formation in both lesbians and gay males, and calls attention to the variables that influence rates of homosexual identity formation.

Ideal Types

Ideal types represent abstractions based on concrete observations of the phenomena under investigation. They are heuristic devices—ways of organizing materials for analytical and comparative purposes. These types are not real; nothing and nobody fits them exactly (Theodorson and Theodorson, 1969).

Ideal types are used as benchmarks against which to describe, compare, and test hypotheses relating to empirical reality (Theodorson and Theodorson, 1969); they are frameworks for ordering observations logically. Ideal types are similar to stereotypes except that they are examined and refined continuously to correspond more closely to the empirical reality that they try to represent. At best, ideal models capture general patterns encountered by many individuals; variations are expected and explained, and often lead to revisions of ideal types.

The four-stage model of homosexual identity formation outlined here describes only general patterns encountered by committed homosexuals—women and men who see themselves as homosexual and adopt corresponding lifestyles. Often-repeated themes in the life histories of lesbians and gay males, clustered according to life stages, provide the content and characteristics of each stage. Progress through the various stages increases the probability of homosexual identity formation, but does not determine it fully. A shifting effect is involved; some men and women "drift away" at various points before the fourth and final stage and never adopt homosexual identities or lead homosexual lifestyles.

Themes of Models

During the past decade, several investigators have proposed theoretical models that attempt to explain the formation of homosexual identities (Cass, 1979, 1984; Coleman, 1982; Lee, 1977; Minton and McDonald 1983/1984; Plummer, 1975;

Ponse, 1978; Schafer, 1976; Sophie, 1985/1986; Troiden, 1977, 1979; Weinberg, 1977, 1978). Although the various models suggest different numbers of stages to explain homosexual identity formation, they describe strikingly similar patterns of growth and change as major hallmarks of homosexual identity formation.

First, nearly all models view homosexual identity formation as taking place against a backdrop of stigma. The stigma surrounding homosexuality affects both the formation and management of homosexual identities. Second, homosexual identities are described as developing over a protracted period and involving a number of "growth points or changes" that may be ordered into a series of stages (Cass, 1984). Third, homosexual identity formation involves increasing acceptance of the label "homosexual" as applied to the self. Fourth, although "coming out" begins when individuals define themselves to themselves as homosexual, lesbians and gay males typically report an increased desire over time to disclose their homosexual identity to at least some members of an expanding series of audiences. Thus, coming out, or identity disclosure, takes place at a number of levels: to self, to other homosexual, to heterosexual friends and family, to co-workers, and to the public at large (Coleman, 1982; Lee, 1977). Finally, lesbians and gays develop "increasingly personalized and frequent" social contacts with other homosexuals over time (Cass, 1984)....

An Ideal-Typical Model

....Sociological analysis of homosexual identity formation begins with an examination of the social contexts and patterns of interaction that lead individuals to accumulate a series of sexual meanings, which predispose them to identify themselves subsequently as homosexual (Plummer, 1975). The meanings of feelings or activities, sexual or otherwise, are not self-evident. Before people can identify themselves in terms of a social condition or category, they must learn that a social category representing the activity or feelings exists (e.g., homosexual preferences or behavior); learn that other people occupy the social category (e.g., that homosexuals exist as a group); begin to identify with those included in the social category; decide that they qualify for membership in the social category, on the basis of activity and feelings in various settings; elect to label themselves in terms of the social category, that is, define themselves as "being" the social category in contexts where category membership is relevant; and incorporate and absorb these situationally linked identities into their self-concepts over time (Lofland, 1969; McCall and Simmons, 1966; Simmons, 1965).

A word of warning: From an interactionist perspective, although identities develop over time in a series of stages, identity formation is not conceptualized as a linear, step-by-step process, in which one stage follows and builds on another, with fluctuations written off as regressions. Instead, the process of homosexual identity formation resembles a horizontal spiral, like a spring lying on its side. Progress through the stages occurs in a back-and-forth, up-and-down fashion; the stages overlap and recur in somewhat different ways for different people (McWhirter and Mattison, 1984). In many instances, stages are encountered in consecutive order, but sometimes they are merged, glossed over, bypassed, or realized simultaneously. In particular, the approximate ages outlined for each stage are rough guidelines. Because these ages are based on averages, variations are to be expected and should not be treated as regressions. People also vary somewhat in the order in which they encounter homosexual events (e.g., age at first homosexual activity).

Stage 1: Sensitization

The *sensitization* stage occurs before puberty. At this time, most lesbians and gay males do not see homosexuality as personally relevant; that is, they assume they are heterosexual, if they think about their sexual status at all. Lesbians and gay males, however, typically acquire social experiences during their childhoods that serve later as bases for seeing homosexuality as personally relevant, lending support to emerging perceptions of themselves as possibly homosexual. In short, childhood experiences sensitize lesbians and gays to subsequent self-definition as homosexual. Sensitization parallels Minton and McDonald's (1983/1984) "egocentric" stage.

Sensitization is characterized by generalized feelings of marginality, perceptions of being different from same-sex peers. The following comments illustrate the forms these childhood feelings of difference assumed for lesbians: "I wasn't interested in boys"; "I was very shy and unaggressive"; "I felt different: unfeminine, ungraceful, not very pretty, kind of a mess"; "I was becoming aware of my homosexuality. It's a staggering thing for a kid at that age to live with"; "I was more masculine, more independent, more aggressive, more outdoorish"; "I didn't express myself the way other girls would. For example, I never showed my feelings. I wasn't emotional" (Bell, Weinberg, and Hammersmith, 1981a:148, 156).

Similar themes of childhood marginality are echoed in the comments of gay males: "I had a keener interest in the arts"; "I couldn't stand sports, so naturally that made me different. A ball thrown at me was like a bomb"; "I never learned to fight"; "I wasn't interested in laying girls in the cornfields. It turned me off completely"; "I just didn't feel I was like other boys. I was very fond of pretty things like ribbons and flowers and music"; "I began to get feelings I was gay. I'd notice other boys' bodies in the gym and masturbate excessively"; "I was indifferent to boys' games, like cops and robbers. I was more interested in watching insects and reflecting on certain things"; and "I was called the sissy of the family. I had been very pointedly told that I was effeminate" (Bell, Weinberg, and Hammersmith, 1981a:74, 86).

Research by Bell, Weinberg and Hammersmith (1981a) found that homosexual males (N=573) were almost twice as likely (72% vs. 39%) as heterosexual controls (N=284) to report feeling "very much or somewhat" different from other boys during grade school (grades 1–8). Lesbians (N=229) were also more likely than heterosexual controls (N=101) to have felt "somewhat or very much" different from other girls during grade school (72% vs. 54%).

During sensitization, childhood social experiences play a larger role than emotional or genital events in generating perceptions of difference. Both lesbians and gay males in the Bell, Weinberg and Hammersmith sample saw gender-neutral or gender-inappropriate interests or behaviors as generating their feelings of marginality (the social realm). Only a minority of the lesbians and gay males felt different because of same-sex attractions (the emotional realm) or sexual activities (the genital realm).

More specifically, lesbians in the Bell, Weinberg and Hammersmith study were more likely than heterosexual controls to say they felt different because they were more "masculine" than other girls (34% vs. 9%), because they were more interested in sports (20% vs. 2%), or because they had homosexual interests or lacked heterosexual interests (15% vs. 2%). Moreover, fewer lesbians than heterosexual controls (13% vs. 55%) reported having enjoyed typical girls' activities (e.g, hopscotch, jacks, playing house), but lesbians were much more likely (71% vs. 28%) to say they enjoyed typical boys' activities (e.g., baseball, football).

In a similar vein, homosexual males were more likely than heterosexual controls to report that they felt odd because they did not like sports (48% vs. 21%), because they were "feminine" (23% vs. 1%), or because they were not sexually interested in other boys (18% vs. 1%). Gay males were also significantly more likely than heterosexual controls (68% vs. 34%) to report having enjoyed solitary activities associated only indirectly with gender (e.g., reading, drawing, music). Moreover, homosexual males were much less likely than heterosexual controls (11% vs. 70%) to report having enjoyed boys' activities (e.g., football, baseball) "very much" during childhood.

Although a sense of being different and set apart from same-sex age mates is a persistent theme in the childhood experiences of lesbians and gay males, research indicates that only a minority of gay males (20%) and lesbians (20%) begin to see themselves as *sexually* different before age twelve, and fewer still—only 4 percent of the females and 4 percent of the males—label this difference as "homosexual" while they are children (Bell, Weinberg and Hammersmith, 1981b:82–3). It is not surprising that "prehomosexuals" used gender metaphors rather than sexual metaphors to interpret and explain their childhood feelings of difference; the mastery of gender roles rather than sexual scripts is emphasized during childhood (Doyle, 1983; Tavris and Wade, 1984). Although they may have engaged in heterosexual and/or homosexual sex play, children do not appear to define their sexual experimentation in heterosexual or homosexual terms. The socially created categories of homosexual, heterosexual, and bisexual hold little or no significance for them. Physical acts become meaningful only when they are embedded in sexual scripts, which are acquired during adolescence (Gagnon and Simon, 1973). For these reasons, prehomosexuals rarely wonder, "Am I a homosexual?" or believe that homosexuality has anything to do with them personally while they are children.

The significance of sensitization resides in the meanings attached *subsequently* to childhood experiences, rather than the experiences themselves. Because sociocultural arrangements in American society articulate linkages between gender-inappropriate behavior and homosexuality, gender-neutral or gender-atypical activities and interests during childhood provide many women and men with a potential basis for subsequent interpretations of self as possibly homosexual. Childhood experiences gained in social, emotional, and genital realms come to be invested with homosexual significance during adolescence. The reinterpretation of past events as indicating a homosexual potential appears to be a necessary (but not sufficient) condition for the eventual adoption of homosexual identities.

Stage 2: Identity Confusion

Lesbians and gay males typically begin to personalize homosexuality during adolescence, when they begin to reflect upon the idea that their feelings or behaviors could be regarded as homosexual. The thought that they are potentially homosexual is dissonant with previously held self-images. The hallmark of this stage is *identity confusion*—inner turmoil and uncertainty surrounding their ambiguous sexual status. The sexual identities of lesbians and gay males are in limbo; they can no longer take their heterosexual identities as given, but they have yet to develop perceptions of themselves as homosexual. Minton and McDonald (1983/1984) draw a similar portrait in their "sociocentric" stage, and Sophie (1985/1986) calls this the "first awareness" stage of lesbian identity formation.

Cass (1984:156) describes the early phase of identity confusion in the following way:

> You are not sure who you are. You are confused about what sort of person you are and where your life is going. You ask yourself the questions "Who am I?," "Am I a homosexual?" "Am I really a heterosexual?"

By middle or late adolescence, a perception of self as "probably" homosexual begins to emerge. In retrospective studies involving adults, gay males begin to suspect that they "might" be homosexual at an average age of seventeen (Troiden, 1979; Troiden and Goode, 1980), lesbians at an average age of eighteen (Schafer, 1976).

Cass (1984:156) describes the later phase of identity confusion as follows:

> You feel that you *probably* are a homosexual, although you're not definitely sure. You feel distant of cut off from [other people]. You are beginning to think that it might help to meet other homosexuals but you're not sure whether you really want to or not. You prefer to put on a front of being completely heterosexual.

Several factors are responsible for the identity confusion experienced during this phase: altered perceptions of self, the experience of heterosexual and homosexual behavior, the stigma attached to homosexuality, and inaccurate knowledge about homosexuals and homosexuality.

Altered perceptions of self are partly responsible for the identity confusion experienced during this phase. Childhood perceptions of self as different crystallize into perceptions of self as sexually different after the onset of adolescence. Whereas only 20 percent of the lesbians and gay males in the Bell, Weinberg and Hammersmith (1981a) study saw themselves as sexually different before age twelve, 74 percent of the lesbians and 84 percent of the gay males felt sexually different by age nineteen, as compared to only 10 percent of the heterosexual female and 11 percent of the heterosexual male controls. For both homosexual women and men, the most frequently cited reasons for feeling sexually different were homosexual interests and/or the lack of heterosexual interests. Gender atypicality was mentioned, but not as frequently. Thus genital and emotional experiences, more than social experiences, seem to precipitate perceptions of self as sexually different during the stage of identity confusion.

Another source of identity confusion is found in sexual experience itself. Recent investigations of homosexuality have revealed consistently that homosexuals exhibit greater variability in their childhood and adolescent sexual feelings and behaviors than heterosexuals (Bell and Weinberg, 1978; Bell, Weinberg and Hammersmith, 1981b; Saghir and Robins, 1973; Schafer, 1976; Weinberg and Williams, 1974). By early to middle adolescence, most lesbians and gay males have experienced both heterosexual and homosexual arousal and behavior. Only a minority of the Bell, Weinberg and Hammersmith sample, for example—28 percent of the gay males and 21 percent of lesbians—were *never* sexually aroused by the opposite sex, and only 21 percent of the males and 12 percent of the females reported ever having an opposite-sex encounter that they or others considered sexual. Thus significant majorities of lesbians and gay males experience heterosexual and homosexual arousal and behavior before age nineteen. Since American society portrays people as either homosexual or heterosexual, it is not surprising that adolescent lesbians and gay males are uncertain and confused regarding their sexual orientations.

As a general rule, gay males are aware of their same-sex attractions at earlier ages than lesbians. Males report awareness of their same-sex feelings at an average age of thirteen (Bell, Weinberg and Hammersmith, 1981a; Dank, 1971; Kooden et al., 1979; McDonald, 1982). The corresponding average age for lesbians is between fourteen and sixteen (Bell, Weinberg and Hammersmith, 1981a; Kooden et al., 1979; McDonald, 1982; Riddle and Morin, 1977; Troiden, 1979; Troiden and Goode, 1980); Gay males first act on their sexual feelings at an average age of fifteen (Bell, Weinberg and Hammersmith, 1981a), whereas lesbians first act on their sexual feelings at an average age of twenty, four to six years after first awareness of their same-sex attractions (Bell, Weinberg and Hammersmith, 1981a; Riddle and Morin, 1977; Schafer, 1976).

The stigma surrounding homosexuality also contributes to identity confusion because it discourages adolescent (and some adult) lesbians and gay males from discussing their emerging sexual desires and/or activities with either age mates or families. As Plummer (1975) has noted, the societal condemnation of homosexuality creates problems of guilt, secrecy, and difficulty in gaining access to other homosexuals. Moreover, the emphasis placed on gender roles and the privatization of sexuality compounds identity confusion and aloneness.

Ignorance and inaccurate knowledge about homosexuality also contribute to identity confusion. People are unlikely to identify themselves in terms of a social category as long as they are unaware that the category exists, lack accurate information about the kinds of people who occupy the category, or believe they have nothing in common with category members (Lofland, 1969). In other words, before they can see themselves as homosexuals, people must realize that homosexuality and homosexuals exist, learn what homosexuals are actually like as people, and be able to perceive similarities between their own desires and behaviors and those of people labeled socially as homosexual. Today, accurate information about homosexuality has been circulated and distributed throughout society, making it easier to identify homosexual elements in feelings and activities (Dank, 1971; Troiden, 1979; Troiden and Goode, 1980). Lesbians and gay males first understand what the term homosexual means at approximately the same time, at the average age of sixteen or seventeen respectively (Riddle and Morin, 1977). Knowledge about the term homosexual may be acquired more rapidly in urban areas than in rural areas, where homosexuality is less likely to be discussed.

Lesbians and gay males typically respond to identity confusion by adopting one or more of the following strategies: denial (Goode, 1984; Troiden, 1977); repair (Humphreys, 1972); avoidance (Cass, 1979); redefinition (Cass, 1979; Troiden, 1977); and acceptance (Cass, 1979; Troiden, 1977).

Gay males and lesbians who use *denial* disclaim the homosexual component to their feelings, fantasies, or activities. *Repair* involves wholesale attempts to eradicate homosexual feelings and behaviors. Professional help is sought to eliminate the sexual feelings, fantasies, or activities considered unacceptable.

Avoidance is a third overall strategy for dealing with identity confusion (Cass, 1979). Although avoidant women and men recognize that their behavior, thoughts, or fantasies are homosexual, they regard them as unacceptable, something to be avoided.

Avoidance may assume at least one of several forms. Some teenaged (and adult) men and women *inhibit* their behaviors or interests they have learned to associate with homosexuality: "I thought my sexual interest in other girls would go away if I paid more attention to boys and concentrated more on being feminine"; "I figured I'd go straight and develop more of an interest in girls if I got even more involved in sports and didn't spend as much time on my art" (author's files).

Some adolescent men and women *limit* their *opposite-sex exposure* to prevent peers or family from learning about their relative lack of heterosexual responsiveness: "I hated dating. I was always afraid I wouldn't get erect when we petted and made out and that the girls would find out I was probably gay." "I felt really weird compared to the other girls. I couldn't understand why they thought guys were so great. I dated only to keep my parents off my back" (author's files).

Other gay males and lesbians *limit* their *exposure to information* about homosexuality during adolescence because they fear that the information may confirm their suspected homosexuality: "Your first lecture on homosexuality awakened my fears of being homosexual. I cut class during the homosexuality section and skipped the assigned readings. I just couldn't accept the idea of being a lesbian" (author's files); "One ingenious defense was to remain as ignorant as possible on the subject of homosexuality. No one would ever catch *me* at the 'Ho' drawer of the New York Public Library Card Catalog" (Reid, 1973:40).

Another avoidance strategy is to assume *antihomosexual postures*. Some teenaged (and adult) men and women distance themselves from their own homoerotic feelings by attacking and ridiculing homosexuals: "At one time I hated myself because of sexual feelings for men. I'm ashamed to admit that I made a nellie guy's life miserable because of it"; "I really put down masculine acting women until I came out and realized that not all lesbians act that way and that many straight women do" (author's files).

Heterosexual immersion is another strategy for avoidance. Some adolescent lesbians and gay males establish heterosexual involvements at varying levels of intimacy in order to eliminate their "inappropriate" sexual interests: "I thought my homosexual feelings would go away if I dated a lot and had sex with as many women as possible"; "I thought my attraction to women was a passing phase and would go away once I started having intercourse with my boyfriend" (author's files). In some instances, an adolescent girl may purposely become pregnant as a means of "proving" that she could not possibly be homosexual.

Another avoidance strategy is *escapism*. Some adolescent lesbians and gay males avoid confronting their homosexual erotic feelings through the use and abuse of chemical substance. Getting high on drugs provides temporary relief from feelings of identity confusion and may be used to justify sexual feelings and behaviors ordinarily viewed as unacceptable.

A fourth general means of reducing identity confusion is to *redefine* behavior, feelings, or context along more conventional lines. (Plummer [1984] calls redefinition "neutralization.") Redefinition is reflected in the use of special-case, ambisexual, temporary-identity (Cass, 1979), or situational strategies.

In the *special-case* strategy, homosexual behavior and feelings are seen as an isolated case, a one-time occurrence, part of a special, never-to-be-repeated relationship: "I never thought of my feelings and our lovemaking as lesbian. The whole experience was too beautiful for it to be something so ugly. I didn't think I could ever have those feelings for another woman" (author's files).

Defining the self as *ambisexual* (bisexual) is another redefinitional strategy: "I guess I'm attracted to both women and men" (author's files). People who adopt *temporary-identity* strategies see their homosexual feelings and behaviors as stages or phases of development that will pass in time: "I'm just passing through a phase, I'm not really homosexual" (author's files). Finally, those who adopt *situational* strategies define the situation, rather than themselves, as responsible for the homosexual activity or feelings: "It only happened because I was drunk"; "It never would have happened if I hadn't been sent to prison."

A fifth overall strategy is *acceptance*. With acceptance, men and women acknowledge that their behavior, feelings, or fantasies may be homosexual, and seek out additional sources of information to determine the nature of their sexual preferences. For adolescent men and women who always felt different because they felt that their thoughts, feelings, and behaviors were at odds with others of their sex, their sense of isolation is diminished by the gradual realization that homosexuals exist as a social category and that they are "probably" homosexual. The homosexual category provides them with a label for their difference. "From the time I was quite young I felt different from other girls and I felt more masculine than feminine. When I learned that lesbians existed I had a word that explained why I was different from other girls" (author's files). "The first name I had for what I was, was 'cocksucker.' 'Cocksucker' was an awful word the way they used it, but it meant that my condition was nameable. I finally had a name for all those feelings. I wasn't nothing (Reinhart, 1982:26).

Perceptions of self anchored in the strategies of denial, repair, avoidance, or redefinition may be sustained for months or years or permanently. Ambisexual perceptions of self, for example—a redefinitional strategy—may be maintained or undermined by a person's social roles, social structures, and relationships, and by the perceived strength, persistence, and salience of the homosexual feelings. Although individuals may use several different strategies for stigma management, they characteristically use some more than others.

Whether the etiology of homosexuality is anchored in biological predispositions or social learning, "the evidence now available suggests that, at least for some individuals, childhood and adolescent experiences may serve as the basis for adult homosexual identity" (Minton and McDonald, 1983/1984:97).

Stage 3: Identity Assumption

Despite differences in stigma-management strategies, a significant number of men and women progress to *identity assumption*, the third stage of homosexual identity formation, during or after late adolescence. In this stage, the homosexual identity becomes both a self-identity and a presented identity—at least to other homosexuals. Defining the self as homosexual and presenting the self as homosexual to other homosexuals are the first stages in a larger process of identity disclosure called *coming out* (Coleman, 1982; Lee, 1977). The hallmarks of this stage are self-definition as homosexual, identity tolerance and acceptance, regular association with other homosexuals, sexual experimentation, and exploration of the homosexual subculture.

Homosexual self-definition occurs in contexts that vary between the sexes. Lesbians typically arrive at homosexual self-definitions in contexts of intense affectional involvements with other women (Cronin, 1974; Schafer, 1976). Seventy-six percent of the lesbians interviewed by Cronin, for example, defined themselves in contexts of meaningful emotional involvements with other women. Gay males, in contrast, are more likely to arrive at homosexual self-definitions in social/sexual contexts where men are reputed to gather for sexual purposes—gay bars, parties, parks, YMCAs, and men's rooms (Dank, 1971; Troiden, 1979; Warren, 1974). Only a minority of males appear to define themselves in contexts of same-sex love relationships (Dank, 1971; McDonald, 1982; Troiden, 1979). Today, I suspect that young men are more likely to arrive at homosexual self-definitions in romantic or fantasized contexts than in sexual settings. For many men, the possibility of contracting AIDS has reduced the perceived desirability of sexual experimentation.

Patterns laid down during sex-role socialization explain why lesbians define themselves in emotional contexts, gay males in social/sexual contexts. "Male sexuality is seen as active, initiatory, demanding of immediate gratification, and divorce from emotional attachment; female sexuality emphasizes feelings and minimizes the importance of immediate sexual activity" (deMonteflores and Schultz, 1978). For males, admitting a desire for homosexual activity implies the label of homosexual; for females, intense emotional involvement with the same sex has similar implications.

Lesbians and gay males also typically define themselves as homosexual at different ages. Retrospective studies of adult homosexuals suggest that gay males arrive at homosexual self-definitions between the ages of nineteen and twenty-one, on the average (Dank, 1971; Harry and Devall, 1978; Kooden et al., 1979; McDonald,

1982; Troiden, 1979). Retrospective studies involving small samples of adolescent gay males indicate a younger age at the time of self-identification as homosexual: age fourteen, on the average (Remafedi, 1987). Adult lesbians recall reaching homosexual self-definitions slightly later, between the average ages of twenty-one and twenty-three (Califia, 1979; Riddle and Morin, 1977; Schafer, 1976; Smith, 1980).

Self-definition as homosexual may occur just before, at the same time as, or shortly after first social contact with other homosexuals (Cronin, 1974; Dank, 1971; Ponse, 1978; Troiden, 1979). Initial contacts may have been engineered consciously (e.g., by deciding to go to a homosexual bar) or accidentally (e.g., by learning that a friend is homosexual). Only a minority of lesbians and gay males appear to define themselves as homosexual without having direct contact with one or more homosexuals. Self-designation as homosexual in the absence of affiliation with other homosexuals (e.g., as a consequence of reading about homosexuality) has been referred to as *disembodied affiliation* (Ponse, 1978).

Although homosexual identities are assumed during this stage, initially they are tolerated rather than accepted. Cass (1984:156) describes people who tolerate their homosexual identities as follows:

> You feel sure you're a homosexual and you put up with, or tolerate this. You see yourself as a homosexual for now but are not sure about how you will be in the future. You usually take care to put across a heterosexual image. You sometimes mix socially with homosexuals, or would like to do this. You feel a need to meet others like yourself.

Sophie (1985/1986) describes this period as the "testing and exploration" phase of lesbian identity formation.

The quality of a person's initial contacts with homosexuals is extremely important (Cass, 1979). If initial contacts are negative, further contact with homosexuals may be avoided and nonhomosexual perceptions of self will persist, maintained through the strategies of denial, repair, self-definition as ambisexual, or temporary identity described earlier. Perceptions of the increased risks of living as a homosexual in a homophobic society, such as blackmail or fear of AIDS, may also encourage individuals to cling to nonhomosexual perceptions of self.

Positive contacts with other homosexuals, on the other hand, facilitate homosexual identity formation. Favorable contacts provide lesbians and gay males with the opportunity to obtain information about homosexuality at first hand. Direct positive exposure provides a basis for re-examining and re-evaluating their own ideas about homosexuality and for seeing similarities between themselves and those labeled "homosexual," the meanings attributed to the homosexual label begin to change in a more favorable direction.

Personally meaningful contacts with experienced homosexuals also enable neophytes to see that homosexuality is socially organized and that a group exists to which they may belong, which diminishes feelings of solitariness and alienation. Other homosexuals provide neophytes with role models from whom they learn strategies for stigma management, rationalizations that legitimize homosexuality and neutralize guilt feelings, the range of identities and roles available to homosexuals, and the norms governing homosexual conduct.

Once they adopt homosexual identities, lesbians and gay males are confronted with the issue of stigma and its management. They may adopt one or several stigma-evasion strategies during identity assumption: capitulation, minstrelization (Levine, 1987), passing, or group alignment (Humphreys, 1972).

Women and men who *capitulate* avoid homosexual activity because they have internalized a stigmatizing view of homosexuality. The persistence of homosexual feelings in the absence of homosexual activity, however, may lead them to experience self-hatred and despair. In *minstrelization*, individuals express their homosexuality along lines etched out by the popular culture. They behave as the wider culture expects them to behave—in highly stereotyped, gender-inappropriate fashions.

Passing as heterosexual is probably the most common stigma-evasion strategy (Humphreys, 1972), especially among recently self-defined homosexuals. Women and men who pass as heterosexual define themselves as homosexual, but conceal their sexual preferences and behavior from heterosexuals—family, friends, and colleagues—"by careful, even torturous, control of information" (Humphreys, 1972:138). Passers lead "double lives;" they segregate their social worlds into heterosexual and homosexual spheres and hope the two never collide.

Group alignment is also adopted commonly by neophyte homosexuals to evade stigma. Men and women who evade stigma through affiliation become actively involved in the homosexual community. The perception of "belonging" to a world of others situated similarly eases the pain of stigma. They look upon other homosexuals as sources of social and emotional support, as well as sexual gratification. Yet an awareness of "belonging" to the homosexual subculture also fosters an awareness of "not belonging," perceptions of being excluded from the world of opposite-sex dating, marriage, and parenthood. People may deal with this alienation by *immersing* themselves completely in the homosexual subculture; by *avoiding* heterosexual settings that remind them of their stigma; by *normalizing* their behaviors, that is, minimizing the differences between heterosexuals and homosexuals (Ponse, 1978); by *aristocratizing* homosexual behavior, that is, attaching a special significance to homosexual experience (Ponse, 1980); or by *nihilizing* heterosexual experience, that is, viewing heterosexual patterns as deviant (Warren, 1980).

To recapitulate, positive homosexual experiences facilitate homosexual self-definition, whereas unrewarding experiences reinforce negative attitudes toward homosexuality. Undesirable homosexual experiences may prompt people to reject the identity ("I am really heterosexual"), abandon the behavior ("I want sex with others of the same sex but can get by without it"), or reject both identity and behavior ("I am not homosexual. I can learn to desire the opposite sex").

By the end of the identity assumption stage, people begin to accept themselves as homosexual. Cass (1984:156) describes *acceptance* of the homosexual identity as follows:

> You are quite sure you are a homosexual and you accept this fairly
> happily. You are prepared to tell a few people about being a homosexual
> but you carefully select whom you will tell. You adopt an attitude of

fitting in where you live and work. You can't see any point in confronting people with your homosexuality if it's going to embarrass all concerned.

Sophie (1985/1986) also uses the term "identity acceptance" to describe this stage of lesbian identity development.

Stage 4: Commitment

A *commitment* is a feeling of obligation to follow a particular course of action (Theodorson and Theodorson, 1969). In the homosexual context, it involves adopting homosexuality as a way of life. For the committed homosexual, "it becomes easier, more attractive, less costly to remain a homosexual" than to try to function as a heterosexual (Plummer, 1975:150). Entering a same-sex love relationship marks the onset of commitment (Coleman, 1982; Troiden, 1979). The identity assumption and commitment stages described here are incorporated in Minton and McDonald's (1983/1984) "universalistic" stage. Following Cass (1979), Sophie (1985/1986) labels the fourth stage of lesbian identity formation "identity integration."

The hallmarks of the commitment stage are self-acceptance and comfort with the homosexual identity and role. Commitment has both internal and external dimensions. It is indicated *internally* by the fusion of sexuality and emotionality into a significant whole, a shift in the meanings attached to homosexual identities, a perception of the homosexual identity as a valid self-identity, expressed satisfaction with the homosexual identity, and increased happiness following self-definition as homosexual. It is indicated *externally* by same-sex love relationships, disclosure of the homosexual identity to nonhomosexual audiences, and a shift in the kinds of stigma-management strategies.

Internal Indicators. The fusion of same-sex sexuality and emotionality into a meaningful whole is one internal measure of a person's commitment to homosexuality as a way of life (Coleman, 1982; Troiden, 1979; Warren, 1974). The same sex is redefined as a legitimate source of love and romance, as well as sexual gratification. Homosexuals themselves see same-sex romantic preferences as differentiating "true" homosexuals from those who are merely experimenting (Warren, 1974).

Another internal measure of commitment to homosexuality as a way of life is reflected by the meanings attached by homosexuals to the homosexual identity. The homosexual subculture encourages both lesbians and gay males (Ponse, 1978, 1980; Warren, 1974, 1980; Warren and Ponse, 1977) to perceive the homosexual identity as an "essential" identity—a state of being and a way of life—rather than merely a form of behavior or sexual orientation. Lesbian feminists are especially likely to view lesbianism as all-encompassing: "A lesbian's entire sense of self centers on women. While sexual energies are not discounted, alone they do not create the lesbian feminist" (Faderman, 1984/1985:87).

The perception of the homosexual identity as a valid self-identity is another measure of internal commitment. Homosexual expression is reconceptualized as "natural" and "normal" for the self. Committed homosexuals find the homosexual identity "a more valid expression of the human condition than that afforded by a heterosexual one" (Humphreys, 1979:242).

The degree of satisfaction that people express about their present identities is another measure of internal commitment (Hammersmith and Weinberg, 1973). When Bell and Weinberg (1978) asked their sample of homosexuals whether they would remain homosexual even if a magic pill would enable them to become heterosexual, 95 percent of the lesbians and 86 percent of the gay males claimed they would *not* take the magic pill. In addition, 73 percent of the gay males and 84 percent of the lesbians indicated they had "very little or no" regret about their homosexuality. Only 6 percent of the male and 2 percent of the female homosexuals felt "a great deal" of regret. Societal rejection and punitiveness and the inability to have children were the most frequently mentioned sources of regret.

Increased happiness is another indication of an internal commitment to homosexuality. When asked, "At this time would you say you are more, less, or about as happy as you were prior to arriving at a homosexual self-definition?," 91 percent of the gay males I interviewed indicated they were more happy, 8 percent stated they were about as happy, and only one person said he was less happy (Troiden, 1979).

External Indicators. A same-sex love relationship is one external sign of a commitment to homosexuality as a way of life (Coleman, 1979; Troiden, 1979; Warren, 1974), a concrete manifestation of a synthesis of same-sex emotionality and sexuality into a meaningful whole. Lesbians appear to enter their first same-sex love relationships between the ages of twenty-two and twenty-three (Bell and Weinberg, 1978; Riddle and Morin, 1977), a year or less after they define themselves as lesbians. Gay males typically have their first love affairs between the ages of twenty-one and twenty-four (Bell and Weinberg, 1978; McDonald, 1982; Troiden, 1979), roughly two to five years after they define themselves as homosexual. In keeping with their gender-role training, males are much more likely than lesbians to gain sexual experiences with a variety of partners before focusing their attentions on one special person (Troiden, 1979). Lesbians are more likely to explore the homosexual community and gain sexual experiences in the context of an emotional relationship with one other woman, or a series of "special" women (Cronin, 1974; Smith, 1980).

Disclosure of the homosexual identity to heterosexual audiences is another external measure of commitment to homosexuality as a way of life. As mentioned earlier, coming out involves disclosure of the homosexual identity to some members of an expanding series of audiences ranging from self to other homosexuals, to heterosexual friends and/or family, to co-workers, to employers, and to the general public by self-identification as homosexual through the media (Coleman, 1982; Hencken and O'Dowd, 1977, Lee, 1977).

Homosexual identity formation is characterized over time by an increasing desire to disclose the homosexual identity to nonhomosexual audiences (Cass, 1984). Few people, however, disclose their homosexual identities to everybody in their social environments. Instead, they fluctuate "back and forth in degrees of openness, depending on personal, social, and professional factors" (deMontflores and Schultz, 1978). Lesbians and gay males appear more likely to come out to siblings, close heterosexual friends. or parents than to co-workers or employers. Fifty percent of the gay males and 62 percent of the lesbians interviewed by Bell and Weinberg (1978) said they had told "some or all" of their siblings about their homosexuality. Regarding disclosure to heterosexual friends, 54 percent of the lesbians and 53 percent of the gay males claimed that "some or most" of their heterosexual friends knew about their homosexuality. Fewer had told their parents about their homosexuality. Forty-two percent of the gay males and 49 percent of the lesbians said they had come out to their mothers, and 37 percent of the females and 31 percent of the males said they had told their fathers.

Bell and Weinberg's (1978) respondents exercised even greater discretion in disclosing their homosexual identities to co-workers and employers. Sixty-two percent of the gay males and 76 percent of the lesbians stated that "few or none" of their co-workers knew they were homosexual, and 85 percent of the lesbians and 71 percent of the gay males claimed that their employers were unaware of their homosexuality. Lesbians and gay males appear reluctant to come out in the workplace for two reasons: fear of endangering job credibility or effectiveness, and fear of job or income loss (Kooden et al., 1979; Riddle and Morin, 1977).

Those lesbians who disclose their homosexual identities to nonhomosexual friends begin to do so at an average age of twenty-eight (Riddle and Morin, 1977); gay males begin to disclose their identities between the average ages of twenty-three and twenty-eight (Mc Donald, 1982; Riddle and Morin, 1977). Gay males who disclose their homosexual identities to their parents do so at age twenty-eight, on the average; lesbians at an average age of thirty (Riddle and Morin, 1977). Those who come out in professional settings do so at even later average ages—thirty-two for lesbians and thirty-one for gay males (Riddle and Morin, 1977). The AIDS epidemic has increased the stigma attached to homosexuality. As a result, younger (and older) gay males and lesbians may be less willing today than in the past to disclose their homosexual identities to nonhomosexual audiences.

A third external indicator of commitment is a shift in stigma-management strategies. Covering (Humphreys, 1972) and blending appear to replace passing and group alignment as the most common strategies, with a minority opting for conversion (Humphreys, 1972).

Women and men who *cover* are ready to admit that they are homosexual (often because it is obvious or known), but nonetheless take great pains to keep their homosexuality from looming large. They manage their homosexuality in ways meant to demonstrate that although they may be homosexual, they are nonetheless respectable. "Imitation of heterosexual marriage, along with other roles and lifestyles designed to elicit praise from the straight segments of society" typifies this form of stigma evasion (Humphreys, 1972:139). Like people who blend, people who cover turn to other homosexuals for social and emotional support as well as sexual gratification, and disclose their homosexual identities selectively to significant heterosexuals.

People who *blend* act in gender-appropriate ways and neither announce nor deny their homosexual identities to nonhomosexual others. They perceive their sexual preferences as irrelevant to the kinds of activities they undertake with heterosexuals, and cloak their private lives and sexuality in silence. When quizzed or challenged about their sexual preferences or behavior, they are likely to respond: "What's it to you?" or "It's none of your business." Women and men who blend affiliate with the homosexual subculture and present themselves as homosexual to other gay males and lesbians and to carefully selected nonhomosexuals. As used here, blending is similar to Warren's (1974:94) "avoidance without hiding."

Lesbians and gay males who *convert* acquire an ideology or world view that not only destigmatizes homosexuality but transforms it from a vice to a virtue, from a mark of shame to a mark of pride. People who convert confront rather than evade the homosexual. Formally or informally, they attempt to inform the general public about the realities of homosexuality and the special contributions made to society by homosexuals in hopes of eliminating oppression through education and political change (e.g., equal rights in jobs and housing). A few lesbians and gay males adopt conversionist strategies during the identity assumption stage when they define themselves as homosexual.

Stigma-evasion strategies are situational rather than constant—that is, personal, social, or professional factors may prompt individuals to blend or cover in some situations, disclose their homosexual identity openly in others, and switch to conversionist modes in yet other contexts. Selective and relatively nonselective self-disclosure have important consequences for the self. Identity disclosure enables the homosexual identity to be realized more fully—that is, brought into concrete existence—in a wider range of contexts. A more complete integration between homosexuals' identities and their social worlds is made possible when they can see and present themselves as homosexual and can be viewed as such by others. *Identity synthesis*, associated with identity disclosure, is described by Cass (1984:156) in the following way:

> You are prepared to tell [almost] *anyone* that you are a homosexual. You are happy about the way you are but feel that being a homosexual is not the most important part of you. You mix socially with homosexuals and heterosexuals [with whom] you are open about your homosexuality.

The passage of time also forges links between many social situations and identities, which accounts partly for the stability of adult identities. By the time individuals reach middle age, the people with whom they routinely interact have a huge backlog of evidence about what they are like, and should be like, in a variety of roles and situations (Atchley, 1982). It becomes increasingly difficult to misrepresent oneself to intimates and co-workers. Moreover, as time passes,

> people tend to conclude that they know themselves as well and probably better than anyone else does or could. This can lead us to assign more weight to what we think about ourselves than to what others say about us. We may also feel that stereotypes about some category we might be assigned to are irrelevant to our own self images (Atchley, 1982:383).

Commitment to the homosexual identity and role is a matter of degree. Homosexuals span a continuum from low to high levels of commitment on both internal and external dimensions, which may vary across time and place. For this reason, commitment is always somewhat inconsistent, strengthened or weakened at various points and contexts by personal, social, or professional factors.

Conclusions

In the final analysis, homosexual identity is emergent—never fully determined in a fixed or absolute sense, but always subject to modification and further change. Homosexual identity formation is continuous, a process of "becoming" that spans a lifetime, a process of "striving but never arriving" (Plummer, 1975). The rates of homosexual identity formation, however, may be influenced by a number of factors, which serve as qualifications to the model.

Homosexual events are well defined, clearly recognizable occurrences in the lives of women and men who define themselves as homosexual and adopt homosexuality as a way of life. As indicated earlier, these events or components of homosexual experience are often clustered with the various stages. Examples of homosexual events include first awareness of same-sex attraction, first homosexual activity, self-definition as homosexual, first association with other homosexuals, and first same-sex love relationship.

The average ages for the homosexual events reported here were obtained from only a few studies; further replications are necessary. Until more investigations have been conducted, these average ages should be viewed as educated guesses.

Sample characteristics have been shown to influence rates of homosexual identity formation and the reported ages for the homosexual events; the mean ages of respondents in the studies cited here vary, for example. In samples consisting of relatively older lesbians and gay males, the respondents recall that they encountered the various events at relatively higher averages than younger informants, thus raising the averages ages at which the events seem to occur. Older informants grew up during a time when homosexuality was rarely discussed, and then only in highly stereotypical terms.

Research conducted in the 1970s and 1980s indicates that adolescent lesbians and gay males in the United States may encounter the events and acquire their homosexual identities at earlier ages than did their older counterparts. More specifically, homosexuals under twenty-five may encounter the various components of homosexual identity at significantly lower average ages than those reported here. Increased openness, tolerance, and accurate information about homosexuality in the United States may have made it easier to perceive similarities between self and "homosexuals" (Dank, 1971; Remafedi, 1987; Troiden, 1977, 1979; Troiden and Goode, 1980).

On the other hand, the onset of the AIDS epidemic may have the opposite effect on homosexual identity formation; it may delay the process (at least among males) because AIDS has increased the stigma attached to homosexuality. The possibility of contracting AIDS may motivate people defensively to deny their erotic feelings, to delay acting on them, or to express them only in the context of a committed love relationship. In addition, the AIDS crisis may undermine identity integration and a positive sense of homosexual identity. To avoid being seen as potential disease carriers, lesbians and gay males may choose not to disclose their homosexual identities to nonhomosexual audiences. Identity fear may replace identity pride; fears of infection my promote erotophobia—the fear of sexual relations—and cause people to avoid homosexual behavior completely or reduce their sexual experimentation.

Gender-inappropriate behavior (Harry, 1982), adolescent homosexual arousal and activity, and an absence of heterosexual experiences (Troiden and Goode, 1980) may also facilitate progress through the events and stages. Gender-atypical, homosexually active, heterosexually inexperienced lesbians and gay males may experience less identity confusion than other homosexuals to the extent that gender conventions in American society articulate linkages between adult homosexuality and all three of these characteristics. Conversely, gay males and lesbians who are gender-typical, heterosexually active, and homosexually inexperienced may experience more confusion regarding their sexual identities because their characteristics are at variance with prevailing homosexual stereotypes.

Supportive family and friends may also facilitate homosexual identity formation. Individuals may feel more comfortable in acting upon their sexual feelings when they believe that those close to them will accept them as they are. Conversely, lesbians and gay males with nonsupportive families and friends may find it much more difficult to acknowledge and act upon their sexual feelings. Fears of rejection appear to inhibit homosexual identity formation to various degrees.

Educational level and the prevailing atmosphere of the workplace may also facilitate or hinder homosexual identity formation. Highly educated lesbians and gay males in homophobic professions may fear that they have more to lose by acknowledging and acting upon their sexual feelings than their less highly educated counterparts. Fears of job or income loss, or concerns about endangering professional credibility, appear to inhibit homosexual identity formation (Kooden et al., 1979; Riddle and Morin, 1977; Troiden, 1977). Less educationally specialized lesbians and gay males and those who work in more supportive occupations may not perceive themselves as occupationally at risk by acting upon and integrating their sexual feelings into their overall lives.

REFERENCES

Atchley, R.C. 1982. "The Aging Self." *Psychotherapy: Theory, Research, and Practice.* 19:388–96.
Bell, A.P. and M.S. Weinberg. 1978. *Homosexualities: A Study of Diversity among Men and Women.*New York: Simon & Schuster.
Bell, A.P., M.S. Weinberg, & S.K. Hammersmith. 1981a. *Sexual Preference: Its Development in Men and Women.* Bloomington: Indiana University Press.
———. 1981b. *Sexual Preference: Its Development in Men and Women: Statistical Appendix.*Bloomington: Indiana University Press.
Blumstein, P.E. & P. Schwartz. 1974. "Lesbianism and Bisexuality." Pp. 278–95 in E. Goode and R.R. Troiden, (eds.), *Sexual Deviance and Sexual Deviants.* New York: Morrow.
Califia, P. 1979. "Lesbian Sexuality." *Journal of Homosexuality* 4:255–66.
Cass, V.C. 1979. "Homosexual Identity Formation: A Theoretical Model." *Journal of Homosexuality* 4:219–35.
———. 1983/1984. "Homosexuality Identity: A Concept in Need of Definition." *Journal of Homosexuality* 9:102–26.

————. 1984. "Homosexual Identity Formation: Testing a Theoretical Model." *Journal of Sex Research* 20:143–67.

Coleman, E. 1982. "Developmental Stages of the Coming-out Process." Pp. 149–58 in W. Paul, J.D. Weinrich, J.C. Gonsiorek, and M.E. Hotvedt, (eds.), *Homosexuality: Social, Psychological, and Biological Issues.* Beverly Hills: Sage.

Cronin, D.M. 1974. "Coming out Among Lesbians." Pp. 268–77 in E.Goode and R.R. Troiden (eds.), *Sexual Deviance and Sexual Deviants.* New York: Morrow.

Dank, B.M. 1971. "Coming out in the Gay World." *Psychiatry* 34:180–97.

Demonteflores, C. & S.J. Schultz. 1978. "Coming out: Similarities and Differences for Lesbians and Gay Men." *Journal of Social Issues* 34:59–72.

Doyle, J.A. 1983. *The Male Experience.* Dubuque, Iowa: Wm. C. Brown.

Faderman, L. 1984/1985. "The 'New Gay' Lesbians." *Journal of Homosexuality* 10:85–95.

Gagnon, J.H. & W. Simon. 1973. *Sexual Conduct: The Social Sources of Human Sexuality.* Chicago: Aldine.

Hammersmith, S.K. & M.S. Weinberg. 1973. "Homosexual Identity. Commitment, Adjustments, and Significant Others." *Sociometry* 36:56–78.

Harry, J. 1982. *Gay Children Grown up: Gender Culture and Gender Deviance.* New York: Praeger.

Harry, J. and W. Devall. 1978. *The Social Organization of Gay Males.* New York: Praeger.

Hencken, J.D. and W.T O'Dowd. 1977. "Coming out as an Aspect of Identity Formation." *Gai Saber* 1:18–26.

Humphreys, L. 1972. *Out of the Closets: The Sociology of Homosexual Liberation.* Englewood Cliffs, New Jersey: Prentice-Hall.

————. 1979. "Being Odd Against all Odds." In R.C. Frederico, (ed.),*Sociology* 2nd ed. Reading, Mass: Addison-Wesley.

Kooden, H.D., S.F. Morin, D.I. Riddle, M. Rogers, B.E. Strang, & F. Strassburger. 1979. *Removing the Stigma: Final Report of the Board of Social and Ethical Responsibility for Psychology's Task Force on the Status of Lesbian and Gay Male Psychologists.* Washington, D.C.: American Psychological Association.

Lee, J.A. 1977. "Going Public: A Study in the Sociology of Homosexual Liberation." *Journal of Homosexuality* 3:49–78.

Levine, M.P. 1987. "Gay Macho: Ethnography of the Homosexual Clone." Doctoral dissertation, New York University.

Lofland, J. 1969. *Deviance and Identity.* Englewood Cliffs, New Jersey: Prentice-Hall.

McCall, G.J. & J.L. Simmons. 1966. *Identities and Interactions: An Examination of Human Associations in Everyday Life.* New York: Free Press.

McDonald, G.J. 1982. "Individual Differences in the Coming out Process for Gay Men: Implications for Theoretical Models." *Journal of Homosexuality* 8:47–60.

McWhither, D.P. & A.M. Mattison. 1984. *The Male Couple: How Relationships Develop.* Englewood Cliffs, New Jersey: Prentice-Hall.

Mills, C.W. 1940. "Situated Actions and Vocabularies of Motive." *American Sociological Review* 5:904–13.

Minton, H.L. & G.J. McDonald. 1983/1984. "Homosexual Identity Formation as a Developmental Process." *Journal of Homosexuality* 9:91–104.

Plummer, K. 1975. *Sexual Stigma: An Interactionist Account.* London: Routledge & Kegan Paul.

Ponse, B. 1978. *Identities in the Lesbian World: The Social Construction of Self.* Westport, Connecticut: Greenwood Press.

Reid, J. 1973. *The Best Little Boy in the World.* New York: Putnam.

Reinhart, R.C. 1982. *A History of Shadows.* New York: Avon Books.

Remafeldi, G. 1987. "Male Homosexuality: The Adolescent's Perspective." *Pediatrics* 79:326–30.

Riddle, D.I. & S.F. Morin. 1977."Removing the Stigma: Data from Individuals." *APA Monitor* (November):16, 28.

Saghir, M.T. & E. Robins. 1973. *Male and Female Homosexuality: A Comprehensive Investigation.* Baltimore: Williams & Wilkins.

Schafer, S. 1976. "Sexual and Social Problems among Lesbians." *Journal of Sex Research* 12:50–69.

Simmons, J.L. 1965. "Pubic Stereotypes of Deviants." *Social Problems* 13:233–32.

Smith, K.S. 1980. "Socialization, Identity and Commitment: The Case of Female Homosexuals." Master's thesis, Miami University.

Sophie, J. 1985/1986. "A Critical Examination of Stage Theories of Lesbian Identity Development." *Journal of Homosexuality* 12:39–51.

Tavris, C. & C. Wade. 1984. *The Longest War: Sex Differences in Perspective* 2nd ed. New York: Harcourt Brace Jovanovich.

Theodorson, G.A. & A.G. Theodorson. 1969. *A Modern Dictionary of Sociology.* New York: Crowell.

Troiden, R.R. 1977. "Becoming Homosexual: Research on Acquiring a Gay Identity." Doctoral dissertation, SUNY-Stony Brook.

———. 1979. "Becoming Homosexual: A Model of Gay Identity Acquisition." *Psychiatry* 42:362–73.

Troiden, R.R. & E. Goode. 1980. "Variables Related to the Acquisition of a Gay Identity." *Journal of Homosexuality* 5:383–92.

Warren, C.A B. 1974. *Identity and Community in the Gay World.* New York: Wiley.

———. 1980. "Homosexuality and Stigma." Pp. 123–41 in J. Marmor, (ed.), *Homosexual Behavior: A Modern Reappraisal.* New York: Basic Books.

Warren, C.A.B. & B. Ponse. 1977. "The Existential Self in the Gay World." Pp. 273–89 in J.D. Douglas and J.M. Johnson, (ed.), *Existential Sociology.* New York: Cambridge University Press.

Weinberg, T.S. 1977. "Becoming Homosexual: Self-Disclosure, Self-Identity, and Self-Maintenance." Doctoral dissertation, University of Connecticut.

———. 1978. "On 'Doing' and 'Being' Gay: Sexual Behavior and Homosexual Male Self-Identity." *Journal of Homosexuality* 4:143–56.

Weinberg, M.S. & C. Williams. 1974. *Male Homosexuals: Their Problems and Adaptations.* New York: Oxford University Press.

Chapter 40

BECOMING AN ADDICT/ALCOHOLIC

Jack Haas

Introduction

This paper describes addict/alcoholics perceptions of their childhood that resulted in a set of feelings and beliefs about themselves which they later sought to alter or relieve through an addictive solution. Throughout is an attempt to understand the path to the addictive "fix" from the point of view of the participants themselves. What becomes clear in the analysis of personal accounts is the precondition of feelings of alienation[1] or dis-ease related to perceptions of childhood abuse, neglect, and/or abandonment.

The methodology of participant observation best provides for a first-hand and intimate glimpse of addicts/alcoholics and this research involved extensive participant observation and informal interviewing of addicts in twelve-step groups over a ten year period. The main participants of the study have been alcoholics belonging to Alcoholics Anonymous, including members in Belgium, Canada, Germany, Great Britain, Scotland, and the United States. Other addicts in Narcotics Anonymous, Overeaters Anonymous, Sex and Love Addicts Anonymous, Sexaholics Anonymous, Emotions Anonymous, and co-dependents in Al Anon and Adult Children of Alcoholics have also been observed and informally interviewed. Additionally, published accounts and personal stories of these and other addictions, have been read and analyzed in the continuing search for a more general and theoretically enriched understanding of the processes of addiction and recovery.

Though the process of "becoming" is an interactive process, the inability to actively observe the process has required a methodology dependent upon retrospective accounts of "what happened." Using this self-report approach I've come to understand, from their point of view, "what it was like, what happened, and what it is like now," and I've noted some shared perceptions and concomitant beliefs and attitudes about their childhood and themselves which provide the framework for an understanding of why people become addict/alcoholics.

Childhood Alienation

At birth a child is born solely dependent both physically and psychologically, in terms of a developing self-concept or view of self (Becker, 1962). This complete psychological vulnerability and powerlessness makes young children ready and willing candidates to conform and accept others' attitudes and expectations. In order to receive warmth, affection and attention the child absorbs and imitates parental roles and gestures, as well as their attitudes about themselves and life in general. Most important is their perception of how the parents feel about them as this forms the core about how the child feels about themself. The child's mirror of who s/he is and whether s/he is worth loving is reflected to the child and is internalized and becomes one's own. These internalized attitudes become the basis of self-concept and their primary nature makes them lasting and difficult to change.

In describing the relationship between alienation and addiction, the focus is on those relationships that promote the development of fear and emotional turmoil, feelings of being different, not belonging or fitting in, which characterize addicts' stories.[2] Most of these feelings reflect problems between parent(s) and child. Growing up in contexts where the parents are addicts or abusive, neglectful, inconsistent, or shame producers, provides fertile ground for producing co-dependents and addicts. Generally, though all co-dependents do not become addicts, most addicts are co-dependents who come from dysfunctional families.[3]

Generally, it is the perception of unmet needs of childhood which create the self-reported feelings of being "different" and "not belonging." The attendant fears, low self-image and self-hatred, the "isms" or feelings of dis-ease, prompt the creation of an alien self and attempts to escape through mood changing, mind altering substances and processes. Dysfunctional families are the breeding grounds of the alienation that is a pre-condition of addiction.[4] The families are described and characterized by addicts as rigid emotionally, having unrealistic expectations, and enforcing denial, the rule of silence, isolation, and shame. They may also include qualities of physical and psychological abuse and violence, including sexual abuse and mental illness. Family life usually involves parental neglect which plays a crucial role in the child's developing identity, core beliefs, and concept of self-worth.

Brenda Schaeffer, in her book, *Is It Love or Is It Addiction?*, describes the typical pattern of familial alienation that produces the pre-addict when she writes:

> Sometimes, for any number of reasons, parental care is inadequate — needs are not met and discomfort escalates. Parents could not always be there as needs arose. Sometimes we were separated from our parents, and we were cared for by people who seemed strange to us. Infants seem to know instinctively that if certain needs are not met, they will die. As a result, panic sets in. (1987:15)

If childhood is perceived as deprived, neglectful or abusive, the scar tissue of one's feelings handicaps the adult's ability to relate to others, to be intimate with them and to participate satisfactorily in social life. The effects of an unhappy childhood are very directly related to later dysfunction. As adults, these formative attitudes persist, and even in the parent's absence, adults use them as a basis for evaluating and criticizing themselves. The old attitudes, irrespective of present conditions and successes, may cripple ambition and satisfactions, as the lessons of the "critical parent(s)," or significant others of the past maintain their dominance over perceptions of self. The core self of childhood lives on, exerting its influence.

When parents and other adults reject, shame, abandon or abuse children, the pain is often so unbearable that s/he dissociates so as to not experience these feelings. Thus the individual abandons him/herself. The loneliness of this abandonment often leads to alternative ways to escape. The abandonment of self goes further as the child develops a false self, a disconnected self, to protect oneself from the pain of loneliness and as an attempt to get desperately sought approval and love. Fears of the pain of aloneness and loneliness, those imprinted feelings of childhood, are the driving force for all the ego protections, including the loss of self through the development of a protective false self that further separates oneself from feelings, authenticity and acceptance of self.

The problem of repressed emotions which, we note, characterizes addict's biographies may never disappear but continue to manifest themselves in depression, panic attacks, "free-floating" anxiety, angry outbursts, and the unconscious search for the fix of mood-changing addictions.

A precondition of addiction then is a childhood marked by deep feelings of inadequacy, inferiority and low self-esteem, and a pervasive sense of rejection by parents and significant others. These feelings and beliefs about oneself stimulate the search for behaviour and activities that produce relief from this distress.

Alienation and the Pre-addict Career

The basic thesis that evolves from the analysis of the self-reports of addicts is that addictions, of whatever kind, can best be understood as symptomatic of underlying feelings of dis-ease or discomfort caused by alienation (Haas, 1989). Ray Hoskins in his excellent book *Rational Madness: The Paradox of Addiction* well describes the symptomatic nature of addiction when he writes:

> Addiction is a false path to meaning, based on false beliefs, inept coping behaviors, and a basic self-centeredness which treats symptoms instead of coping with reality (1989: 10).

Personal accounts about recovering addicts' childhoods, no matter what the addiction, generally emphasize characteristics of a "dysfunctional" family and the child's perception of separation or alienation. Some examples of accounts written by recovering "sex and love addicts," found in their basic twelve step text *Sex and Love Addicts Anonymous* (1986), reinforces these themes.

> We were one of those families that seemed to "work." But because I was the youngest, I always felt left out, like I didn't belong. (p. 185).
>
> I was raised in a relatively "normal" family. There was no substance abuse, no physical abuse, no sexual abuse. Yet the feelings I grew up with are very similar to those of the people I have heard in *S.L.A.A.* who grew up in a much more obviously troubled environment. My mother was a strong-willed, hot-tempered woman who found it easy to criticize but difficult to offer praise or reassurance. As I entered adolescence, I was already experiencing strange feelings of self-doubt, self-hate and insecurity...I felt unlistened to, judged, and unaccepted. Those deeply embedded feelings became the foundation of my addictive patterns, and my relationship with people, men in particular, grew out of an endless inner sense of neediness. (pp. 210, 211)

I will pass up the litany of my deprived childhood; I had screwed up parents who offered neither role models nor affection so necessary to healthy growth. My desperate need for love/approval, and my denial of this need, led to thirty years of frenetic behaviour in a number of areas. (p. 216)

My parents abused me, both physically and emotionally, and I looked for anything to avoid feeling the constant pain. We rarely hugged or kissed in my family, and we never talked about our feelings. (p. 225)

I never suffered any broken bones, but no part of my body was safe and I was often hit about the face and head. I wanted desperately to love and be loved by my parents, and I decided that I must deserve abuse since they had to be right...(p. 257)

I was born to very sick parents. I was hated and constantly told how no-good and sub-human I was. I was sexually molested by many adults in my life - this included parents, aunts, physicians, a deacon of the church, a psychiatrist, neighbours, and even my mother "sold" me in the hopes of getting rid of me. (p. 274)

Narcotic addicts, indeed addicts of all types, report similar sources of alienation contributing to feelings of low self-worth. Personal stories in the book *Narcotics Anonymous* describe pre-addict feelings:

I think that I was predisposed to addiction. Deep inside, I had feelings of inadequacy and inferiority (1982:194)

Loneliness is something that I've lived with for years. From the time I was a child, people always let me know that I was different (1982:110)

From the time I was a little girl, I can remember feeling like I didn't quite belong. I thought I must be an alien from another planet. It seemed that I always said and did the wrong things at the wrong time. I felt a big empty hole inside of me, and I spent the next twenty years trying to fill it.

I always wanted desperately to fit in somewhere. I always seemed to feel better being one of the guys, so I usually stayed around them. I didn't really understand or trust girls.

I had a very low self-image. I realize now that I hated myself, I wished I would be somebody, anybody, other than me (1982:121).

I grew up on the wrong side of the tracks, poor, deprived, during the depression, in a broken home. The words of love were never spoken in my household...

I just remember going through life feeling different, feeling deprived. I never felt quite comfortable with who I was, with whatever I had at any given time. I grew up in a fantasy world (1982:147).

From a very early age I had an intense feeling and belief that I was different! While other girls my age were trying on mom's clothes and playing with Barbie dolls, I was playing football with the guys, smoking pot, and pondering the mysteries of the universe (1982:164).

As I was growing up, I remember wanting to belong or be a part of other groups of people. I was a loner and did not know how to belong. Fear and inferiority feelings were a part of me since childhood. I was unable to participate in sports and other activities because of the fear that I could not do it. I had a fear of people, especially in groups, so I lived in a fantasy world where I was somebody (1982:171).

Accounts from people with problems of food addiction, as reported in the text, *Overeaters Anonymous* (1980), present a similar perception of alienation:

...And that was how I found the world to be. I never quite fit in. I was always scared, or awkward, or superior. But different; always different...Cooking showed love.

Love wasn't expressed otherwise. It was an embarrassing subject. No one touched or hugged (p. 45).

When I was lonely, food was my friend. It soothed and comforted me and filled the hole that was there when I felt unloved, which was most of the time (p. 56).

My compulsive overeating may have had something to do with my older brother's chronic illness. He spent his entire childhood in an out of hospitals and my parents were preoccupied with his health. Just as his disease was brought under control and I was struggling through adolescence, my younger brother developed schizophrenia, and my parents' concern shifted to him. Somehow, in the midst of all this, food became my reward and punishment, love and companionship (p. 102).

In *Workaholics: The Respectable Addicts*, (1991), Barbara Killinger describes the roots of workaholism and distorted perfectionism as also lying in childhood perceptions when she says:

Some children, for many different reasons, feel they must perform in order to be loved and appreciated. Such children are rewarded for what they do, rather than for who they are. Future workaholics learn early that praise is attached to performance, and that acting responsibly brings rewards. Their emotional stability is dependent on their parents' reactions to what they do (p. 21).

As these descriptions of childhood help demonstrate, future addicts are, if anything, preoccupied with self and, for most, the roots of the self-absorption and narcissism rest in the perception of the mixed or hostile messages of significant others. Whether their perception is correct or not, they as W.I. Thomas wrote, "are real in their consequences."

Charles H. Cooley nicely summarizes three chief elements of the development of the self-idea; imagining how we appear to the other person; imagining his judgment of that appearance; and, as a result, experiencing some sort of self-conception and feeling — pride, embarrassment, unease, shame, etc. (1902:20–21). For most future addicts the emotional malise or dis-ease develops at an early time when they are denied their feelings and they learn others' contempt, which becomes their internalized self-hatred. The young victim becomes his/her own victimizer, as he/she carries the lessons others have taught as literal truth. The child begins to live a life with a distorted sense of self and self-worth.

Stanton Peele describes the typical self conception of the addict when he writes:

> He is anxious in the face of a world he fears, and his feelings about himself are likewise unhappy. Yearning to escape from a distasteful consciousness of his life, and having no abiding purpose to check his desire for unconsciousness, the addict welcomes oblivion. He finds it in any experience that can temporarily erase his painful awareness of himself and his situation (1975:56).

Alienation and the False Self

Carl Rogers in his book, *On Becoming a Person* indicates his agreement with Danish philosopher, Soren Kierkegaard, who pointed out that the most common despair is not choosing, or not willing, to be oneself; but that the deepest despair is to choose "to be another than himself" (1961:10).

When the pre-addict child is not effectively nurtured and made to feel safe and secure, a false or "co-dependent" self emerges. This concept, of a "child within," has a long history in the psychotherapeutic literature. Such notables as Erikson, (1964) Horney, (1937) Sullivan, (1953) and Winnicott (1957) have all contributed to our understanding that a "real self" or "inner child" is stifled or denied when not nurtured and allowed freedom to develop in a secure environment and, concomitantly, a false or co-dependent self emerges (Whitfield, 1987:7–9).

John Bradshaw in his book *Healing the Shame that Binds You* (1988) describes how toxic shame (shame that becomes internalized as an identity where individuals believe themselves flawed and defective) leads to the development of a false self or what Alice Miller calls "social murder" (1981). Gershen Kaufman in her book *Shame: The Power of Caring* writes:

> Shame is the affect which is the source of many complex and disturbing inner states: depression, alienation, self-doubt, isolating loneliness, paranoid and schizoid phenomena, compulsive disorders, splitting of the self, perfectionism, a deep sense of inferiority; inadequacy or failure, the so-called borderline conditions and disorders of narcissism. (1980:60)

Experiencing alienation from the real self (the trusting, loving, creative and freely expressing self) the damaged child (adult) feels unauthentic, controlling, other-directed, uncomfortable and empty. When addicts describe their youth as one in which they always felt "different" or that "they didn't belong," they are essentially describing their alienation or separateness from society and others, and their development of the protective "other self."

The other self develops through the repression of the true self. The true self is repressed in its observations, feelings and reactions as they have come to be invalidated by significant others. The child begins to create an alternative self and reality in the struggle to resist the pain and uncertainty of the perceived reality. Out of this struggle, the child develops a set of protective escapes or denials which move him/her further and further from reality. As real feelings get stuffed, denied, replaced and ignored, the child becomes increasingly separated from a trusting and real sense of self and others, thus also contributing to the creating of an artificial world through fantasy and/or compulsive behaviour. As expressed by Marion Woodman in her book *Addiction to Perfection: The Still Unravished Bride,* "Aloneness is a crucial component in compulsive syndromes.... Real compulsives carry out their rituals alone" (1982:27). The natural desire for transcendent experience, for ritual, is perverted into addictive behaviour in the desperate attempt to escape loneliness, alter feelings, and hold the world together. Ray Hoskins (1989:11) sums it up well when he writes: "The addict tries to replace uncomfortable feelings with as much security, sensation, and power feelings as possible."

Alienation, Alien Self and Core Beliefs

In describing the early socialization of the sexual addict Patrick Carnes, in his excellent book *Out of the Shadows: Understanding Sexual Addiction,* describes four factors in a child's development which ultimately contribute to their addiction; self-image, or how they perceive themselves; relationships, or how children perceive their relationships with others; needs, or how they perceive their own needs; and sexuality, or how they perceive their own sexual feelings and needs. Carnes argues that these perceptions ultimately become "core beliefs" central to the process of addiction (1983:66–67).

Carnes also points out that the fear of abandonment is a strong theme in the lives and childhoods of addicts. This is fairly characteristic of the dysfunctional family with its contradictory, conflicting, negative, and sometimes violent reactions and controls. The fear of abandonment of the child in a dysfunctional family contributes to the child's interpretation or core belief that he/she is unwanted and, relatedly, "unworthy" and/or "bad." The child who views him/herself as unworthy and/or bad also is likely to develop a correlative core belief that no one would "love me as I am." This critical appraisal of self, based on the child's interpretations of others' reactions contributes to a denial and self-hatred of self which goes to the heart of the addict's self-perception and self-image. Damaged by others' negativity and desiring social acceptance and approval, a basic human need, the child neurotically tries to alter others' perceptions by repressing the "bad" and "unworthy" self.

The despised and wounded pre-addict and addict have, as I've described, a public and private self. S/he has powerful feelings of inadequacy, anxiety, fear, self-doubt and hate which are often cloaked by a public false front of confidence, pride and control. For some this false front goes to extreme characterizations of grandiosity, where the hidden fear-filled self enacts a role of the "big-shot" full of self.[5]

This pride-filled caricature is the extreme denial of the fear-laden, insecure and troubled self it is meant to hide. In this regard, alcoholics are described and describe themselves as "egomaniacs with an inferiority complex." The fragility of the addict's view of self often leads to such extreme ways of denial, but also to an exaggerated self-consciousness which contributes to egocentricism and narcissism.

Carnes (1983:83) points out how the fear of abandonment also feeds a fear of intimacy, while desiring it, and fear of dependence on others, while afraid of isolation and rejection. The addict's fear of abandonment, a fear typically learned at an early age, produces these paradoxical fears of closeness and rejection which feed each other and put the addict in a hopeless internal struggle. Fearing rejection and the pain that comes with it the addict is generally unable to move in a trusting way to create intimate relationships. This resistance to closeness is confounded by a desire for closeness, but to become dependent emotionally is to risk pain. To not get closer, however, is to contribute to still greater feelings of alienation, isolation and rejection.

Most importantly, any addiction is an avoidance of intimacy with the self, and thus fundamentally contributes to the alienation which, as I have described, precipitates and reinforces the move from pre-addiction to addiction. Alienation is implicit in the process because "addiction is the chronic neglect of yourself in favor of someone or something else" (Covington and Beckett, 1988:5). The alienation that precedes, prompts, sustains, and reinforces addictive behavior involves both the separation from others and the dissection of the self. These two processes reinforce each other and fire the pre-addicts search for release and nirvana.

The addict comes to believe that because of earlier traumas, e.g., perceived rejections (abandonment, inconsistency, contempt by others, etc.) that others can't be depended upon and that the addict's needs will not be met. Expressions of love are distrusted. Rejection is often anticipated. One consequence of this core belief, that needs will never be met because others can't be depended upon, is strong feelings of anger and rage about not having these needs met. The anger often is directed inward in the form of depression and resentments. Self-pity and suicide are common reflections of this belief (Carnes, 1983:84). The damaged individual who comes to believe in their inadequacy loses confidence in their perceptions, actions, and thought processes. Their everyday lives are characterized by uncertainty. They sometimes become immobilized by fear, untrusting in their perceptions, feelings, needs and wants. Many become frozen in their ability to make decisions because they have lost trust in their world and themselves. Any possible decision or action faces their ingrained critical eyes raising problems and scenarios foretelling disaster and failure. The pre-addicts/addicts becomes their own worst critics and doomsdayers. The practice of self-deprecation becomes so automatic as to paralyze the individual from the notion that they could act appropriately without fear of criticism.

The "Fix" or Addictive Solution

The development of a particular addiction or set of addictions is contingent upon the pattern of behavior meeting three attributes: 1) It blurs reality testing by diverting one's attention from a chronic aversive state; 2) It lowers self-criticism and self-consciousness, deflecting preoccupation from one's perceived inadequacies; and 3) it permits complimentary daydreams and wish-fulfilling fantasies about oneself (Jacobs, 1989: 46–47).

If we accept the stories of addicts at face value, as ones in which they perceive and experience much fear and pain, and thus have strong motivation for mood change, we can appreciate their move toward addictive behavior. The addict seeks and finds ways to create a self-induced, dissociative condition which provides them temporary relief from their angst. When they find processes or substances that distort or alter reality, a reality that imprisons them and keeps them unhappy and suffering, they can be understood for seeking such relief and release. Their quest is for some freedom from their feelings, and obsessive-compulsive behavior and mind-altering substances or processes provide the release they desire. Once they experience the euphoria of freedom from the crippling feelings of their perceived reality and environment they begin an insatiable quest to return to or heighten their release. The desire for an altered consciousness, and the experience of changed perceptions and feelings creates the lust for satiation and the next "fix," even in the face of harmful or disastrous consequences.

The pre-addict is necessarily predisposed to seek and find ways of changing their uncomfortable, virtually intolerable, feelings. Experiencing pain and emotional turmoil, the pre-addict and addict attempt to transcend their discomforting reality in order to reach an escape and, more ideally, a nirvana of good feelings. This desire for transcendence is magnified for the pre-addict and addict and the addiction process contains within it a set of rituals which assist transcendence from reality. Seeking peace, the addict uses substances or activity to escape the here and now and move to a higher level of consciousness. As Ernest Kurtz in his book *Not-God: A History of Alcoholics Anonymous* points out:

> ...it was this thirst for transcendence that expressed itself in the alcoholic's
> addictive, obsessive-compulsive drinking. The thirst for transcendence
> had been perverted into a thirst for alcohol (1979:205).

Similarly, Stanton Peele writes of love addiction as "a consequence of seeing love as a life solution, a transcendent experience...."(1977:121).

The process begins with the underlying feeling of dis-ease or discomfort which stimulate the addict to seek ritual, sometimes sacramental, relief. Although the pattern of addiction may have produced "baleful results" the addict is compelled by the ritual relief of his addiction to obsess about using or abusing. When the addictive ritual process is in full motion, the stimuli of discomfort or dis-ease gives way to the excitation of the ritualized release process. Reality flies out the window as the excitation about and the obsession to use or abuse takes over. Planning and acting out the process of use is paramount in giving sacred form to the compulsion to transcend reality. During the process, excitation shuts out other matters in the developing addict's quest for nirvana. The addict reaches an out of control phase where seemingly nothing will stop the pursuit of release or ecstasy. The excitement becomes overwhelming until satiation - where transcendent escape may or may not be realized (Haas, 1990).

The transcendental quality of the ritual "fix" is graphically described by a sex addict when he writes:

> ...one night I started playing with myself and experienced strong genital sensations for the first time. When they crescended into orgasm the effect was so startling and unexpected that I was caught completely off guard. It was as if there were swirling lights in front of my eyes, as the power of it swept through my body. The experience was transcendental. I felt that I had tapped some secret, tabooed power which really ran the universe, but which was never acknowledged in the world. Orgasm via masturbation became a daily staple for me right away. (Augustine Fellowship, 1986:3)

As the addictive process takes hold and the addict seeks relief through some obsessive-compulsive activity, the addict becomes fixated on the process or object of their addiction.

As Carnes (1983:86) points out the fourth core belief is that a "fix" is their most important need. For the sex addict, sex is their most important need. Addicts of other kinds get similarly obsessed with an addiction or addictions which dominates their thinking and lives. Increasingly their ordinary lives and routines are taken over by their addiction(s) which contributes to a greater need to hide and deny their behavior and lifestyle from others and themselves. Lies and deception, including self-deception and denial, characterize the addict's perceptions and adaptations. The crutch of addiction begins to cripple, the user becomes an abuser and life revolves around the next "fix."

Conclusion

Addiction is thus understood as symptomatic behavior—a temporary and problem-filled solution to the problems of emotional turmoil, low self-esteem and perceptions of alienation, e.g. "not belonging," "feeling different," etc, which typically are family based and develop during childhood. Given this premise, recovery is not complete with abstinence, which only eliminates a symptom. Emotional sobriety, peace of mind, and relief from the inner turmoil of self-hatred and inadequacy also requires a reconstitution of self through the theraputic healing of the scars of childhood.

The dis-ease of addiction is largely rooted in the addict's desire to transcend the "inner newsreel" of negativity learned from others. This self-fulfilling prophecy, where others are the "cracked mirror" for the child's self-perception and developing self-image, helps shape an identity that provides the basis for the individual's attitude toward self, and the pre-addict "sees" a contemptible self. Addiction thus involves an extreme example of self-alienation wherein the individual uses addictive processes to prevent intimacy with the self and others, a self that evolves out of the perceived appraisal of others.

Childhood perceptions of alienation thus set the stage for individuals to seek relief from the emotional turmoil of personal discomfort through mood altering, ritual processes of addiction. These addictive processes are, themselves, essentially isolating and alienating rituals which may temporarily provide a "fix" to the addict's feelings of unease but they concomitantly exacerbate and reinforce negative feelings of remorse, shame, guilt, and self-loathing. Consequently, they encourage and perpetuate an addictive cycle because of the unrelieved, even heightened, desire for release from negative feelings.

Most importantly, any addiction is an avoidance of intimacy with the self, and thus fundamentally contributes to the alienation which, as I have described, precipitates and reinforces the move from pre-addiction to addiction. Given this premise, recovery is not complete with abstinence, which only eliminates a symptom. Emotional sobriety, peace of mind, and relief from the inner turmoil of self-hatred and inadequacy also requires a reconstitution of self through the theraputic healing of childhood.

REFERENCES

Augustine Fellowship, 1986. *Sex and Love Addicts Anonymous* Boston: The Augustine Fellowship Press.

Becker, Ernest, 1962. *The Birth and Death of Meaning*, 2nd. ed.,New York: The Free Press.

Bradshaw, John, 1988. *Healing the Shame That Binds You*, Deerfield Beach, Florida: Health Communications, Inc.

Carnes, Patrick, 1983. *Out of the Shadows: Understanding Sexual Addiction*. Minneapolis, Minnesota: Comp Care Publications.

Cooley, C.H., 1902. *Human Nature and the Social Order* New York: Scribner's.

Covington, Stephanie and Liane Beckett, 1988. *Leaving the Enchanted Forest: The Path From Relationship Addiction to Intimacy*. New York: Harper & Row.

Csicsai, Rose, 1983. "From Alienation to Integration in Alcoholics Anonymous: A Descriptive Analysis Using Dialectical Sociology of Religion." Unpublished Master's thesis., McMaster University, Hamilton, Ontario, Canada.

Erikson, Erik H., 1964. *Childhood and Society*, 2nd ed. New York: Norton.

Haas, Jack, 1990. "Addiction and Recovery as Ritual Processes of Transcendence," International Sociological Association, Madrid, Spain, July.

Haas, Jack, 1989. "Alienation and Addiction: Addiction as Symptomatic of Dis-ease," Midwest Sociological Association, St. Louis, Missouri, April.

Haas, Jack, 1991. "How It Works: Self-help Changing Self," Qualitative Research Conference, Carleton University, Ottawa, May.

Horney, Karen, 1937. *The Neurotic Personality of Our Time*. New York: W.W. Norton & Co.

Hoskins, Ray, 1989. *Rational Madness: The Paradox of Addiction*. Blue Ridge: Summit, P.A.

Jacobs, David F. 1989., "A General Theory of Addictions: Rationale for and Evidence Supporting a New Approach for Understanding and Treating Addictive Behaviors," Pp. 35–64 In Howard S. Shaffer, Sharon A. Stein, Blase Gambino and Thomas N. Cummings, eds., *Compulsive Gambling*, Lexington, Kentucky: Lexington Books.

Kaufman, Gershen, 1980 *Shame: The Power of Caring*, Cambridge, Massachusetts: Schenkman.

Kurtz, Ernest. 1979. *Not-God: A History of Alcoholics Anonymous*. Center City, Minnesota: Hazelden.

McCord, William and Joan McCord. 1960. *Origins of Alcoholism*, Stanford, California: Stanford University Press.

Narcotics Anonymous. 1982. Van Nuys, Calif: World Service Office, Inc.

Peele, Stanton with Archie Brodsky., 1976. *Love and Addiction*. New York: New American Library.

Rogers, Carl R., 1961. *On Becoming a Person*. Boston, Massachusetts: Houghton Miffin Co.

Rose, Arnold., 1962. "A Social Psychological Theory of Neurosis" in A. Rose, ed. *Human Behavior and Social Process*. pp. 537–549. Boston: Houghton Mifflin Co.

Rudy, David R., 1986. *Becoming Alcoholic*. Carbondale and Edwardsville, Illinois: Southern Illinois University Press.

Schaef, Anne Wilson, 1987. *When Society Becomes an Addict*, Toronto: Fitzhenry and Whiteside.

Shaeffer, Brenda, 1987. *Is it Love Or Is It Addiction?* New York: Harper/Hazelden.

Sullivan, H.S., 1953. *The Interpersonal Theory of Psychiatry*. New York: Norton.

Whitfield, Charles, 1987. *Healing the Child Within*. Deerfield Beach, Florida: Health Communications, Inc.

Winnicott, O.W., 1957. *The Child and the Outside World: Studies in Developing Relationships*. London: Tavistock.

NOTES

[1] I am indebted to Rose Csicsai for her analysis of alcoholism and alienation found in her MA thesis, "From Alienation to Integration in Alcoholics Anonymous: A Descriptive Analysis Using Dialectical Sociology of Religion," (1983).

[2] In an interesting longitudinal and comparative study of pre-alchoholic children and adult alcoholics McCord and McCord describe the existence of an "alcoholism-prone" character which includes intensified dependency longings which were outwardly suppressed and their socialization in conflictful, antagonistic homes. The authors conclude by writing:

The findings suggest the 'pre-disposition' to alcoholism is established rather early in life, through the person's intimate experiences within his family. (1960:164).

Jacobs (1989) also posits a general theory of addictions which is supportive of this analysis. He notes that on the basis of his research and the analysis of a host of studies of addicts that there are two predisposing factors that determine whether an individual risks an addiction pattern of behaviour: an abnormal physiological resting state that is chemically or expressively either depressed or excited, and childhood experiences that have produced a deep sense of personal inadequacy and rejection.

[3] For most addicts the process leading to addiction begins, as I emphasize, early in life. Though it is disputable as to the relative significance of environment *vis à vis* genetics, it is safe to say that the probability of addiction increases if there is a familial background of addiction and if the family is dysfunctional. There is not single cause but I want to emphasize that the addicts I've listened to, read about, and talked with number in the thousands and, with very few exceptions, are people who have suffered difficult upbringing. This fact makes me secure in this analysis. The few exceptions also support the analysis because "late bloomer" addicts generally report some profound experience of alienation, such as the loss of a loved one, in their adult years, which prompts them to seek relief through some addictive process. Individuals who repeatedly and excessively ingest addictive substances may become physically and/or psychologically dependent but are not necessarily addicts whose addiction is symptomatic of disease.

[4] The alienation experienced by the pre-addict is not the alienation described by Karl Marx and his followers involving man's separation from the product of his labor. Rather, the alienation involves the separation from others and the dissection of the self. These two processes, though analytically distinguishable, feed and reinforce each other. What should not be overlooked in the study of addiction, but which we do not have space for, is an examination of the cultural supports that contribute to and help legitimize obsessive behavior. In North American society we note how members would get confused about appropriate drug and alcohol use, work and sexual activity, physical fitness, eating, etc. In these examples, and others, the media, and other socializing institutions, present a confusing picture about correct attitudes and behaviour. Thus, we observe that dysfunctional belief systems can create confusion and conflict. On the one hand, the process or object of addiction (food, sex, alcohol) may be culturally idealized and made desirable. On the other hand, cultural standards of excess may be condemned and the addict stigmatized and made to feel guilty and worthless.

Anne Wilson Schaef, in her book *When Society Becomes an Addict*, 1987, makes the argument that there exists an addictive process that underlies an addictive system that the individual selects. Society and its organizations, she argues, promote addictive behaviour to numb us from the reality of our lives.

[5] Alcoholism has been referred to as the disease of "big-shotism." See David Rudy, *Becoming Alcoholic*, 1986.

Chapter 41

DRIFTING INTO DEALING: BECOMING A COCAINE SELLER

Sheigla Murphy
Dan Waldorf
Craig Reinarman

Introduction

No American who watched television news in the 1980s could have avoided images of violent drug dealers who brandished bullets while driving BMW's before being hauled off in handcuffs. This new stereotype of a drug dealer has become a staple of popular culture, the very embodiment of evil. He works for the still more vile villains of the "Columbian cartel," who make billions on the suffering of millions. Such men are portrayed as driven by greed and utterly indifferent to the pain from which they profit.

We have no doubt that some of such characters exist. Nor do we doubt that there may be a new viciousness among some of the crack cocaine dealers who have emerged in ghettos and barrios already savaged by rising social problems and falling social programs. We have grave doubts, however, that such characterizations tell us anything about cocaine sellers more generally. If our interviews are any guide, beneath every big-time dealer who may approximate the stereotype there are hundreds of smaller sellers who do not.

This paper describes such sellers, not so much as a way of debunking a new devil but rather as a way of illuminating how deviant careers develop and how the identities of the individuals who move into this work are transformed. Along with the many routine normative strictures against drug use in our culture, there has been a mobilization in recent years for a "war on drugs" which targets cocaine dealers in particular. Many armaments in the arsenal of social control from propaganda to prisons have been employed in efforts to dissuade people form using/selling such substances. In such a context it is curious that ostensibly ordinary people not only continue to use illicit drugs but also take the significant additional step of becoming drug sellers. To explore how this happens, we offer an analysis of eighty in-depth interviews with former cocaine sellers. We sought to learn something about how it is that otherwise conventional people—some legally employed, many well edu-cated—end up engaging in a sustained pattern of behavior that their neighbors might think of as very deviant indeed.

Deviant Careers and Drift

Our reading of this data was informed by two outside classic theoretical works in the deviance literature. First, in *Outsiders*, Howard Becker (1963:102) observed that,

471

"The career lines characteristic of an occupation take their shape from the problems to that occupation. These, in turn, are a function of the occupation's position vis-a-vis other groups in society." He illustrated the point with the dance musician, caught between the jazz artist's desire to maintain creative control and a structure of opportunities for earning a living that demanded the subordination of this desire to mainstream musical tastes. Musicians' careers were largely a function of how they managed this problem. When the need to make a living predominated, the basis of their self conceptions shifted from art to craft.

Of course, Becker applied the same proposition to more deviant occupations. In the next section, we describe five discrete modes of becoming a cocaine seller which center on "the problems peculiar to" the world of illicit drug use and which entail a similar shift in self conception. For example, when a drug such as cocaine is criminalized, its cost is often greatly increased while its availability and quality are somewhat limited. Users are thus faced with the problems of avoiding detection, reducing costs, and improving availability and quality. By becoming involved in sales, users solve many of these problems and may also find that they can make some money in the bargain. As we will show, the type of entree and the level at which it occurs are functions of the individual's relationship to networks of other uses and suppliers. At the point where one has moved from being a person who *has* a good connection for cocaine to a person who *is* a good connection for cocaine, a subtle shift in self conception and identity occurs.

Becker's model of deviant careers entails four basic steps, three of which our cocaine sellers took. First, the deviant must somehow avoid the impact of conventional commitments that keep most people away from intentional non-conformity. Our cocaine sellers passed this stage by ingesting illegal substances with enough regularity that the practice became normalized in their social world. Second, deviant motives and interests must develop. These are usually learned in the process of the deviant activity and from interaction with other deviants. Here too our cocaine sellers had learned the pleasures of cocaine by using, and typically were moved toward involvement in distribution to solve one or more problems entailed in such use. Once involved, they discovered additional motivations which we will describe in detail below.

Becker's third step in the development of deviant careers entails public labeling. The person is caught, the rule is enforced, and his or her public identity is transformed. The new master status of "deviant," Becker argues, can be self fulfilling when it shapes others' perceptions of the person and limits his or her possibilities for resuming conventional roles and activities. Few of our respondents had been publicly labeled deviant, but they did describe a gradual change in identity which may be likened to self-labeling. This typically occurred when they deepened their deviance by dealing on top of using cocaine. This shift in self conception for our subjects was more closely linked to Becker's fourth step—movement into an organized deviant group in which people with a common fate and similar problems form subcultures. There they learn more about solving problems and ideologies which provide rationales for continuing the behavior, weakening the hold of conventional norms and institutions and solidifying deviant identities. In the case of our other subjects, becoming sellers further immersed them into deviant groups and practices to the point where many came to face the problems of, and to see themselves as, "dealers."

The fact that these processes of deeper immersion into deviant worlds and shifts in self conception were typically gradual and subtle brought us to a second set of theoretical reference points in the work of David Matza (1964; 1969).[1] In his research on delinquency, Matza discovered that most so-called delinquents were not self-consciously committed to deviant values or lifestyles, but on the contrary continued to hold conventional beliefs. Most of the time they were law abiding, but because the situation of "youth" left them free from various restraints, they often *drifted* in and out of deviance. Matza found that even when caught being delinquent, young people tended to justify or rationalize their acts through "techniques of neutralization" (Sykes and Matza, 1957) rooted in conventional codes of morality. Although we focus on entering selling careers we found that Matza's concept of drift (1964) provided us with a useful sensibility for making sense of our respondents' accounts. The modes of entree they described were as fluid and non-committal as the drift into and out of delinquency that he described.

None of the career paths recounted by our subjects bear much resemblance to the stereotypes of "drug dealers."[2] For decades the predominant image of the illicit drug dealer was an older male reprobate sporting a long, shabby overcoat within which he had secreted a cornucopia of dangerous consciousness-altering substances. This proverbial "pusher" worked school yards, targeting innocent children who would soon be chemically enslaved repeat customers. The newer villains have been depicted as equally vile but more violent. Old or new, the ideal-typical "drug dealer" is motivated by perverse greed and/or his own addiction, and has crossed a clearly marked moral boundary, severing most ties to the conventional world.

The cocaine sellers we interviewed, on the other hand, had more varied and complex motives for selling cocaine. Moreover at least within their subcultures, the moral boundaries were both rather blurry and as often wandered along as actually crossed. Their life histories reminded us of Matza's (1969:68) later but related discussion of the *overlap* between deviance and conventionality:

> Overlap refers to...the marginal rather than gross differentiation between deviant and conventional folk and the considerable though variable interpenetration of deviant and conventional culture. Both themes sensitize us to the regular exchange, traffic, and flow—of persons as well as styles and precepts—that occur among deviant and conventional worlds.

Our subjects were already seasoned users of illicit drugs. For years their drug use coexisted comfortably with their conventional roles and activities; having a deviant dimension to their identities appeared to cause them little strain. In fact, because their use of illicit drugs had gone on for so long, was so common in their social worlds, and had not significantly affected their otherwise normal lives, they hardly considered it deviant at all.

Thus, when they began to sell cocaine as well as use it, they did not consider it a major leap down an unknown road but rather a series of short steps down a familiar path. It was not as if ministers had become mobsters; no sharp break in values, motives, world views, or identities was required. Indeed, few woke up one morning and made a conscious decision to become sellers. They did not break sharply with the conventional world and actively choose a deviant career path; most simply drifted into dealing by virtue of their strategies for solving the problems entailed in using a criminalized substance, and only then developed additional deviant motives centering on money.

To judge from our respondents, then, dealers are not from a different gene pool. Since the substances they enjoy are illegal, most regular users of such drugs become involved in some aspect of distribution. There is also a growing body of research on cocaine selling and distribution that has replaced the simplistic stereotype of the pusher with complex empirical evidence about underground economies and deviant careers (e.g., Langer, 1977; Waldorf et al., 1977, 1991; Adler, 1985; Plasket and Quillen, 1985; Morales, 1986a, 1986b; Sanchez and Johnson, 1987; Sanabria, 1988; and Williams, 1989). Several features of underground economies or black markets in drugs contribute to widespread user participation in distribution. For example, some user who could obtain cocaine had other user-friends who wanted it. Moreover, the idea of keeping such traffic among friends offered both sociability and safety. For others, cocaine's high cost inspired many users to become involved in purchasing larger amounts to take advantage of volume discounts. They then sold part of their supply to friends in order to reduce the cost of personal use. The limited supply of cocaine in the late seventies and early eighties made for a sellers' market, providing possibilities for profits along with steady supplies. For most of our subjects, it was not so much that they learned they could make money and thus decided to become dealers but rather, being involved in distribution anyway, they learned they could make money from it. As Becker's model suggests, deviant motives are learned in the course of deviant activities; motivation follows behavior, not the other way around....

[We will now] describe in more detail: 1) the various modes and levels of entree into cocaine sales; 2) some of the practices, rights and responsibilities entailed in dealing; 3) the subtle transformation of identity that occurred when people who consider themselves rather conventional moved into careers considered rather deviant.

Dealers

Dealers are people who are "fronted" (given drugs on consignment to be paid for upon sale) and/or who buy quantities of drugs for sale. Further, in order to be considered a dealer by users or other sellers a person must: 1) have one or more reliable connections (suppliers); 2) make regular cocaine purchases in amounts greater than a single gram (usually an eighth of an ounce or greater) to be sold in smaller units; 3) maintain some consistent supplies for sale; and 4) have a network of customers who make purchases on a regular basis. Although the stereotype of a dealer holds that illicit drug sales are a full-time occupation, many dealers, including members of our sample, operate part-time and supplement income from a legal job.

As we noted in the introduction, the rather average, ordinary character of the respondents who fit this definition was striking. In general, without prior knowledge or direct observation of drug sales, one would be unable to distinguish our respondents from other, non-dealer citizens. When telling their career histories, many of our respondents invoked very conventional middle-class American values to explain their involvement in dealing (e.g., having children to support, mortgages or rent to pay in a high-cost urban area, difficulty finding jobs which paid enough to support a family). Similarly, their profits from drug sales were used in "normal" ways—to buy children's clothes, to make house or car payments, to remodel a room. Moreover, like Matza's delinquents, most of our respondents were quite law-abiding, with the obvious exception of their use and sales of an illicit substance.

When they were not dealing, our respondents engaged in activities that can only be described as mainstream American. For example, one of our dealers, a single mother of two, found herself with a number of friends who used cocaine and a good connection. She needed extra income to pay her mortgage and to support her children so she sold small amounts of cocaine within her friendship network. Yet while she sold cocaine, she worked a full-time job, led a Girl Scout troop, volunteered as a teacher of cardio-pulmonary resuscitation (CPR) classes for young people, and went to Jazzercize classes. Although she may have been a bit more civic-minded than many others, her case served to remind us that cocaine sellers do not come from another planet.

Modes of Entree into Dealing

Once they began selling cocaine, many of our respondents moved back and forth between levels in the distribution hierarchy. Some people dealt for short periods of time and then quit, only to return several months later at another level of sales.[3] The same person may act as a broker on one deal, sell a quarter gram at a profit to a friend or another, and then pick up an ounce from an associate and pass it on to another dealer in return for some marijuana in a third transaction. In a few instances each of these roles were played by the same person within the same twenty-four hour period.

But whether or not a dealer/respondent moved back and forth in this way, s/he usually began selling in one of five distinct ways. All five of these modes of entree pre-suppose an existing demand for cocaine from people known to the potential dealers. A person selling any line of products needs two things, a group of customers and a product these customers are interested in purchasing. Cocaine sellers are no different. In addition to be able and willing to pay, however, cocaine customers must also be trustworthy because these transactions are illegal.

The first mode of entree, *the go-between*, is fairly straightforward. The potential seller has a good cocaine connection and a group of friends who place orders for cocaine with him/her. If the go-between's friends use cocaine regularly enough and do not develop their own connections, then a period of months or even years might go by when the go-between begins to spend more and more time and energy purchasing for them. Such sellers generally do not make formal decisions to begin dealing; rather, opportunities regularly present themselves and go-betweens gradually take advantage of them. For example, one 30 year-old, African-American who became a gram dealer offered this simple account of his passage from go-between to seller:

> Basically, I first started because friends pressured me to get the good coke I could get. I wasn't even making any money off of it. They'd come to me and I'd call up my friend who had gotten pretty big selling a lot of coke.

This went on for six months before he began to charge his friends money for it. Then his connection started fronting him eighths of ounces at a time, and he gradually became an official dealer, regularly selling drugs for a profit. Others who began in this way often took only commission-in-kind (a free snort) for some months before beginning to charge customers a cash mark-up.

Another African-American male began selling powdered cocaine to snorters in 1978, and by the mid-eighties had begun selling rock cocaine (crack) to smokers. He described his move from go-between to dealer as follows:

> Around the time I started indulging [in cocaine] myself, people would come up and say, "God, do you know where I can get some myself?" I would just say, "Sure, just give me your money," I would come back and either indulge with them or just give it to them depending on my mood. I think that's how I originally set up my clientele. I just had a certain group of people who would come to me because of they felt that I knew the type of people who could get them a real quality product.
>
> And pretty soon I just got tired of, you know, being taken out of situations or being imposed upon...I said that it would be a lot easier to just do it myself. And one time in particular, and I didn't consider myself a dealer or anything, but I had a situation one night where 5 different people called me to try to get cocaine...not from me but it was like, "Do you know where I can get some good cocaine from?"

Not all go-betweens-cum-dealers start out so altruistically. Some astute business-men and women spot the profit potential early on and immediately realize a profit, either in-kind (a share of the drugs purchased) or by tacking on a surcharge to the purchase price. The following respondent, a 39 year old African-American male, described this more profit-motivated move from go-between to a formal seller:

> Well, the first time that I started it was like I knew where to get good stuff...and I had friends that didn't know where to get good stuff. And I knew where to get them really good stuff and so I would always put a couple of dollars on it, you know, if I got it for $20 I would sell it to them for $25 or $30 or whatever.
>
> It got to be where more and more people were coming to me and I was going to my man more and I would be there 5 or 6 times a day, you know. So he would tell me, "Here, why don't you take this, you know, and bring me x-amount of dollars for it." So that's how it really started. I got fronted

and I was doing all the business instead of going to his house all the time, because he had other people that were coming to his house and he didn't want the traffic.

The second mode of entree is the *stash dealer*, or a person who becomes involved in distribution and/or sales simply to support or subsidize personal use. The name is taken from the term "stash," meaning a personal supply of marijuana (see Fields, 1985, on stash dealers in the marijuana trade). This forty-one year-old white woman who sold along with her husband described her start as a stash dealer this way:

(Q) So what was your motivation for the sales?

(A) To help pay for my use, because the stuff wasn't cheap and I had the means and the money at the time in order to purchase it, where our friends didn't have that amount of money without having to sell something...Yeah, friendship, it wasn't anything to make money off of, I mean we made a few dollars...

The respondents who entered the dealing world as stash dealers typically started out small (selling quarter and half grams) and taking their profits in product. However, this motivation contributed to the undoing of some stash dealers in that it led to greater use, which led to the need for greater selling, and so on. Unless they then developed a high-volume business that allowed them to escalate their cocaine use and still make profits, the reinforcing nature of cocaine tempted many of them to use more product than was good for business.

Many stash dealers were forced out of business fairly early on in their careers because they spent so much money on their own use they were financially unable to "re-cop" (buy new supplies). Stash dealers often want to keep only a small number of customers in order to minimize both the "hassle" of late-night phone calls and the risk of police detection, and they do not need many customers since they only want to sell enough to earn free cocaine. Problems arise, however, when their small group of customers do not buy the product promptly. The longer stash dealers had cocaine in their possession, the more opportunities they had for their own use (i.e., for profits to "go up your nose"). One stash dealer had an axiom about avoiding this: "It ain't good to get high on your own supply." The predicament of using rather than selling their product often afflicts high-level "weight dealers" as well, but they are better able to manage for longer periods of time due to larger volumes and profit margins.

The third mode of entry into cocaine selling had to do with users' desire for high-quality, unadulterated cocaine. We call this type the *connoisseur*. Ironically, the motivation for moving toward dealing in this way is often health-related. People who described this mode of entree described their concerns, as users, about the possible dangers of ingesting the various adulterants or "cuts" commonly used by dealers to increase profits. User folklore holds that the larger the quantity purchased, the purer the product. This has been substantiated by laboratory analysis of the quality of small amounts of street drugs (typically lower) as opposed to larger police seizures (typically higher).

The connoisseur type of entry, then, begins with the purchase of larger quantities of cocaine than they intend to use in order to maximize purity. Then they give portions of the cocaine to close friends at a good price. If the members of the network start to use more cocaine, the connoisseurs begin to make bigger purchases with greater regularity. At some point they begin to feel that all this takes effort and that it makes sense to buy large quantities not only to get purer cocaine but to make some money for their efforts. The following 51 year-old, white business executive illustrated the connoisseur route as follows:

> I think the first reason I started to sell was not to make money or even to pay for my coke, because I could afford it. It was to get good coke and not be snorting a lot of impurities and junk that people were putting into it by cutting it so much. So I really think that I started to sell it or to get it wholesale so that I would get the good stuff. And I guess my first,...what I did with it in the beginning, because I couldn't use all that I had to buy to get good stuff. I sold it to some of my friends for them to sell it, retail it.

Connoisseurs, who begin by selling unneeded quantities, often found they unlearned certain attitudes when they moved from being volume buyers looking for quality toward becoming dealers looking for profit. It was often a subtle shift, but once their primary motivation gradually changed from buying-for-purity to buying-to-sell they found themselves beginning to think and act like dealers. The shift usually occurred when connoisseurs realized that the friends with whom they had shared were in fact customers who were eager for their high quality cocaine and who often made demands on their time (e.g., friends seeking supplies not merely for themselves, but for other friends a step or two removed from the original connoisseur). Some connoisseurs also became aware of the amount of money that could be made by becoming business-like about what had been formerly friendly favors. At such points in the process they began to buy-to-sell, for a profit, as well as for the purpose of obtaining high-quality cocaine for personal use. This often meant that, rather than buying sporadically, they had to make more regular buys; for a successful businessperson must have supplies when customers want to buy or they will seek another supplier.

The fourth mode of entree into cocaine selling is an *apprenticeship*. Like other types, apprentices typically were users who had already had loosened conventional normative strictures and learned deviant motives by interacting with other users and with dealers; and they, too, drifted into dealing. However, in contrast to the first three types, apprentices moved toward dealing less to solve problems inherent in using a criminalized substance than to solve the problems of the master dealer. Apprenticeships begin in a personal relationship where, for example, the potential seller is the lover or intimate of a dealer. This mode was most often the route of entry for women, although one young man we interviewed learned to deal from his father. Couples often start out with the man doing the dealing—picking up the product, handling the money, weighing and packaging, etc. The woman gradually finds herself acting as an unofficial assistant—taking phone messages, sometimes giving people pre-packaged cocaine and collecting money. Apprentices frequently benefit from being involved with the experienced dealer in that they enjoy both supplies of high-quality cocaine and indirect financial rewards of dealing.

Some of our apprentices moved into official roles or deepened their involvement when the experienced dealer began to use too much cocaine to function effectively as a seller. In some such cases the abuse of the product led to an end of the relationship. Some apprentices then left dealing altogether while others began dealing on their own. One thirty-two year-old African American woman lived with a pound dealer in Los Angeles in 1982. Both were freebasers (cocaine smokers) who sold to other basers. She described her evolution from apprentice to dealer this way:

> I was helping him with like weighing stuff and packaging it and I sort of got to know some of the people that were buying because his own use kept going up. He was getting more out of it, so I just fell into taking care of it partly because I like having the money and it also gave me more control over the situation, too, for awhile, you know, until we both got too out of it.

The fifth mode of entree into cocaine selling entailed the *expansion of an existing product line*. A number of the sellers we interviewed started out as marijuana salespersons and learned many aspects of the dealers' craft before they ever moved to cocaine. Unlike in the other modes, in this one an existing marijuana seller already had developed selling skills and established a network of active customers for illicit drugs. Expansion of product line (in business jargon, horizontal integration) was the route of entry for many of the multiple-ounce and kilo cocaine dealers we interviewed. The combination of the availability of cocaine through their marijuana connection and their marijuana customers' interest in purchasing cocaine, led many marijuana sellers to add cocaine to their product line.

Others who entered dealing this way often found that expanding from marijuana to cocaine solved some problems inherent in marijuana dealing. For example, cocaine is far less bulky and odoriferous than marijuana and thus did not present the risky and costly shipping and storage problems of multiple pounds of marijuana. Those who entered cocaine selling via this product line expansion route also recognized, of course, that there was the potential for higher profits with cocaine. They seemed to suggest that as long as they were already taking the risk, why shouldn't they maximize the reward? Some such dealers discontinued marijuana sales altogether and others merely added cocaine to their line. One white, 47 year-old mother of three grown children described how she came to expand her product line:

(Q) How did you folks [she and her husband] get started dealing?

(A) The opportunity just fell into our lap. We were already dealing weed and one of our customers got this great coke connection and started us onto dealing his product. We were selling him marijuana and he was selling us cocaine.

(Q) So you had a network of week buyers, right? So you could sell to those...?

(A) There was a shift in the market. Yeah, because weed was becoming harder [to find] and more expensive and a bulkier product. The economics of doing a smaller, less bulkier product and more financially rewarding product like cocaine had a certain financial appeal to the merchant mentality.

Conscious Decision to Sell

... The majority of our sample were middle class wholesalers who, in the various ways just described, drifted into dealing careers. The few street sellers we interviewed did not drift into sales in the same way. We are obliged to note again that the five modes of entry into cocaine selling we have identified should not be taken as exhaustive. We have every reason to believe that for groups and settings other than those we have studied there are other types of entree and career trajectories. The five cases of street sellers we did examine suggest that entree into street-level sales was more of a conscious decision of a poor person who decided to enter an underground economy, not an effort to solve a user's problems. Our interviews with street sellers suggest that they chose to participate in an illicit profit-generating activity largely because licit economic opportunities were scarce or nonexistent. Unlike other types, such sellers sold to strangers as well as friends, and their place of business was more likely to be the street corner rather than homes, bars, or nightclubs. For example, one 30 year-old Native American ex-prostitute described how she became a street crack dealer this way:

> I had seen in the past friends that were selling and stuff and I needed extra money so I just one day told one of my friends, you know, if he could help me, you know, show me more or less how it goes. So I just went down by what I seen. So I just started selling it.

A few higher level dealers also made conscious decisions to sell (see Adler, 1985), particularly when faced with limited opportunity structures. Cocaine selling, as an occupation, offers the promise of lavish lifestyles otherwise unattainable to most ghetto youth and other impoverished groups. Dealing also provides an alternative to the low paying, dead-end jobs typically available to those with little education and few skills. A 55 year-old African-American man who made his way up from grams to ounce sales described his motivation succinctly: "The chance presented itself to avoid the 9 to 5."

Street sellers and even some higher-level dealers are often already participating in quasi-criminal lifestyles; drug sales are simply added to their repertoire of illicit activities. The perceived opportunity to earn enormous profits, live "the good life," and set your own work schedule are powerful enticements to sell. From the perspective of people with few life chances, dealing cocaine may be seen as their only real chance to achieve the "American Dream" (i.e., financial security and disposable income). Most of our sample were not ghetto dwellers and/or economically disadvantaged. But for those who were, there were different motivations and conscious decisions regarding beginning sales. Popular press descriptions of cocaine sellers predominantly portray just such street sellers. Although street sellers are the most visible, our data suggest that they represent what might be called the tip of the cocaine dealing iceberg.

Levels of Entry

The levels at which a potential dealer's friends/connections were selling helped determine the level at which the new dealer entered the business. If the novitiate was moving in social scenes where "big dealers" are found, then s/he is likely to begin by selling grams and parts of grams. When supplies were not fronted, new dealers' personal finances, i.e., available capital, also influenced how much they could buy at one time.

Sellers move up and down the cocaine sales ladder as well as in and out of the occupation (see Adler, 1985). Some of our sellers were content to remain part-ounce dealers selling between a quarter and a half ounce a week. Other sellers were more ambitious and eventually sought to become bigger dealers in order to increase profits. One interviewee reported that her unusually well organized suppliers had sales quotas, price fixing, and minimum purchase expectations which pushed her toward expansion. The levels of sales and selling styles of the new dealer's suppliers, then, interacted with personal ambitions to influence eventual sales careers.

Another important aspect of beginning to sell cocaine is whether the connection is willing to "front" the cocaine (willing to risk consignment arrangement) rather than requiring the beginner to pay in full. Having to pay "up front" for one's inventory sometimes slowed sales by tying up capital, or even deterred some potential dealers from entering the business. Fronted cocaine allowed people with limited resources to enter the occupation. Decisions to front or not to front, were based primarily on the connection's evaluation of the new seller's ability to "move" the product. This was seen as a function of the potential volume of business the beginning seller could generate among his/her networks of friends and/or customers. The connection/ fronter also evaluates the trustworthiness of the potential dealer, as well as their own capability of absorbing the loss should the deal "go bad" and the frontee be unable to pay. The judgement of the fronter is crucial, for a mistake can be very costly and there is no legal recourse.

Learning to Deal

In the go-between, stash and connoisseur modes of entree, novices gradually learn the tricks of the trade by observing the selling styles of active dealers, and ultimately by doing. Weighing, packaging, and pricing the product are basic techniques. A scale, preferably a triple-beam type which are accurate to the tenth of a gram, is a necessary tool. In the last ten years answering machines, beepers, and even cellular phones have become important tools as well. Learning how to manage customers, and to establish selling routines and rules of procedure are all essential skills that successful dealers must master.

The dealers who enter sales through the apprenticeship and product line expansion modes have the advantage of their own or their partner/seller's experience. Active marijuana sellers already have a network of customers, scales, familiarity with metric measures, and, most important, a connection to help them move into a new product line. Apprentices have lived with and/or observed the selling styles of their dealer/mentors and have access to their equipment, connections and customers. Both apprentices and marijuana dealers who have expanded into cocaine also know how to "maintain a low profile" and avoid any kind of attention that might culminate in arrest. In this way they were able to reduce or manage the paranoia that often inheres in drug dealing circles.

Many sellers learn by making mistakes, often expensive mistakes. These include: using too much cocaine themselves, fronting drugs to people who do not pay for them, and adding too much "cut" (usually an inactive adulterant such as vitamin B) to their product so they develop a reputation for selling inferior cocaine and sometimes have difficulty selling the diluted product. One thirty-two year-old African-American male made one such error in judgement by fronting to too many people who did not "come through." It ended up costing him $15,000:

> It was because of my own recklessness that I allowed myself to get into that position. There was a period of time where I had a lot of weight that I just took it and just shipped it out to people I shouldn't have shipped it out to...I did this with 10 people and a lot of them were women to be exact. I had a lot of women coming over to my house and I just gave them an ounce apiece at a time...So when maybe 6 of those people didn't come through...there was a severe cramp in my cash flow. This made me go to one of the family members to get the money to re-cop.

Business Sense/People Sense

Many people have a connection, the money to make the initial buy, a reputation for being reliable, and a group of friends interested in buying drugs, but still lack the business sense to be a successful dealer. Just because a person drifts into dealing does not mean that he or she will prosper and stay in dealing. We found a variety of ways in which people initially become dealers, few of which hinged on profits. But what determined whether they continued dealing was their business sense. Thus even though a profit orientation had little to do with becoming a dealer, the ability to consistently realize profits had a major influence over who remained a dealer. In this sense, cocaine selling was like any other capitalist endeavor.

According to our respondents, one's ability to be a competent dealer depended on being able to separate business from pleasure. Success or failure at making this separation over time determined whether a profit was realized. Certain business practices were adopted by prosperous dealers to assist them in making this important distinction. For example, prepackaging both improves quality control and helps keep inventory straight; establishing rules for customers concerning when they can purchase and at what prices reduces the level of hassle; limiting the amount of fronting can reduce gross sales volume, but it also reduces financial risk and minimizes the amount of debt collection work; and limiting their own personal use keeps profits from disappearing up one's nose or in one's pipe.

Being a keen judge of character was seen as another important component of being a skilled dealer. Having the "people skills" to judge whether a person could be trusted to return with the money for fronted supplies, to convince people to pay debts that the dealer had no legal mechanisms for collecting, and to engender the trust of a connection when considerable amounts of money were at stake, are just a few of the sophisticated interpersonal skills required of a competent dealer.

Adler (1985:100) also discusses the importance of a "good personal reputation" among upper level dealers and smugglers:

> One of the first requirements for success, whether in drug trafficking, business enterprise broadly, or any life undertaking, is the establishment of a good personal reputation. To make it in the drug world, dealers and smugglers had to generate trust and likability.

Adler's general point applies to our respondents as well, although the experiences of some of our middle and lower level dealers suggested a slight amendment: A likeable person with a good reputation could sell a less than high quality product, but an unlikable person, even one with a bad reputation, could still do a considerable amount of business if s/he had an excellent product. One forty-seven year-old white woman described her "difficult" husband/partner, "powder keg Paul":

> He would be so difficult, you couldn't believe it. Somebody [this difficult] better have a super primo product to make all this worthwhile...He's the kind of guy you don't mind buying from because you know you'll get a good product, but he's the kind of guy you never want to sell to...he was that difficult. (Case# E–1)

High quality cocaine, in other words, is always at a premium in this subculture, so even without good people skills' a dealer or connection with "good product" was tolerated.

From User to Dealer: The Transformation of the Identity

In each of our respondents' deviant careers there occurred what Becker referred to as a change in self conception. Among our respondents, this took the form of a subtle shift in identity from a person who *has* a good connection for cocaine to a person who *is* a good connection for cocaine. There is a corresponding change in the meaning of, and the motives for, selling. The relationship between the seller and the customers undergoes a related transformation, from "picking up something for a friend" to conducting a commercial transaction. In essence, dealing becomes a business quite like most others, and the dealer gradually takes on the professional identity of a business person. Everett Hughes (1951:313), writing on the sociology of work, urged social scientists to remember that when we look at work,

> We need to rid ourselves of any concepts which keep us from seeing that the essential problems of men at work are the same whether they do their work in the laboratories or some famous institution or in the messiest vat of a pickle factory.

When they had fully entered the dealer role, our respondents came to see selling cocaine as a job—work, just like other kinds of work save for its illegality. For most, selling cocaine did not mean throwing out conventional values and norms. In fact, many of our respondents actively maintained their conventional identities (see Broadhead, 1983). Such identities included those of parents, legally employed workers, neighbors, church-goers and softball players, to list just a few. Dealer identities tended not to replace former, "legitimate" identities but were added to a person's repertoire of more conventional identities.

Like everyone else in modern life, sellers emphasized one or another dimension of their identities as appropriate to the situation. In his study of heroin addicts Biernacki (1986:23) notes that, "The arrangement of identities must continuously be managed in such a way as to stress some identities at certain points in particular social worlds and situations and at the same time to de-emphasize others." Our sellers, too, had to become adept at articulating the proper identity at the proper time. By day, one woman dealer was a concerned mother at her daughter's kindergarten field trip, and that same evening she was an astute judge of cocaine quality when picking up an ounce from her connection. At least for our interviewees, selling cocaine rarely entailed entirely terminating other social roles and obligations.

Yet, at some point in all of our sellers' careers, they found themselves transformed from someone who has a good connection to someone who is a good connection, and they gradually came to accept the identity of dealer as a part of their selves. Customers began to treat them like a salesperson, expecting them to be available to take calls and do business and even for services such as special off-hour pick-ups and deliveries or reduced rates for volume purchases. When dealers found themselves faced with such demands, they typically began to feel *entitled* to receive profits from selling. They came to be seen as dealers by others, and in part for this reason, came to see themselves as dealers. As Becker's (1963) model suggests, selling *behavior* usually preceded not only motivation but also changes in attitude and identity. As one 38 year-old white woman put it,

> I took over the business and paid all my husband' debts and started to
> make some money. One day I realized I was a coke dealer...It was scary,
> but the money was good.

Acceptance of the dealer identity brings with it some expectations and values shared by dealers and customers alike. Customers have the expectation that the dealer will have a consistent supply of cocaine for sale. Customers also expect that the dealer will report in a fairly accurate manner the quality of his/her present batch of drugs within the confines of the *caveat emptor* philosophy that informs virtually all commercial activities in market societies. Buyers do not expect sellers to denigrate their product, but they do not expect the dealer to claim that their product is "excellent" if it is merely "good." Customers assume the dealer will make a profit, but dealers should not be "too greedy." A greedy dealer is one who makes what is estimated by the buyer to be excessive profits. Such estimations of excessiveness vary widely among customers and between sellers and buyers. But the fact that virtually all respondents spoke of some unwritten code of fairness in fact suggest that there is, in E.P. Thompson's (1971) phrase, a "moral economy" of drug dealing that constrains the drive for profit maximization even within an illicit market.[4]

For their part, dealers expect that customers will act in a fashion that will minimize their chances of being arrested by being circumspect about revealing their dealer status. One simply did not, for example, bring to a dealer's house friends whom the dealer had not met. Dealers want customers to appreciate the risks undertaken to provide them with cocaine. And dealers come to feel that such risks deserve profits. After all, the seller is the one who takes the greater risks; s/he could conceivably receive a stiff jail sentence for a sales conviction. While drifting into dealing and selling mostly to friends and acquaintances mitigated the risks of arrest and reduced their paranoia, such risks remained omnipresent.

In fact, the growing realization of such risks—and the rationalization it provided for dealing on a for-profit basis—was an integral part of becoming a cocaine seller. As our 38 year-old white woman dealer put it, "When it's all said and done, I'm the one behind bars, and I had better have made some money while I was selling or why in the hell take the risk?"

REFERENCES

Adler, P. 1985. *Wheeling and Dealing: An Ethnography of an Upper-Level Drug Dealing Community*. New York: Columbia University Press.

Becker, H.S. 1953. "Becoming a Marijuana User." *American Journal of Sociology* 59:235–42.

———. 1986. *Pathways from Heroin Addiction*. Philadelphia: Temple University Press.

Biernacki, P. & Waldorf, D. 1981. "Snowball Sampling: Problems and Techniques of Chain Referral Sampling." *Sociological Methods and Research* 10:141–63.

Broadhead, R. 1983. *The Private Lives and Professional Identity of Medical Students*. New Brunswick, NJ: Transaction Books.

Feldman, H.W. 1968. "Ideological Supports to Becoming and Remaining a Heroin Addict." *Journal of Health and Human Behavior* 9:131–39.

Fields, A. 1985. "Weedslingers: A Study of Young Black Marijuana Dealers." *Urban Life* 13:247–70.

Goldstein, P,, Brownstein, H., Ryan, P., & Belucci, P. 1989. "Crack and Homicide in New York City, 1988." *Contemporary Drug Problems* 16:651–87.

Grinspoon, L. & Bakalar, J. 1976. *Cocaine: A Drug and Its Social Evolution*. New York: Basic Books.

Hughes, E. 1951. "Work and the Self." Pp. 313–23 In John Rohrer and Muzafer Sherif (eds.), *Social Work at the Crossroads*, New York: Harper and Brothers.

Langer, J. 1977. "Drug Entrepreneurs and Dealing Culture." *Social Problems* 24:377–86.

Lindesmith, A. 1947. *Addiction to Opiates*. Chicago: Aldine Press.

Macdonald, P., Waldorf, D., Reinarman, C. & Murphy, S. 1988. "Heavy Cocaine Use and Sexual Behavior." *Journal of Drug Issues* 18:437–55.

Matza, D. 1964. *Delinquency and Drift*. New York: Wiley.

———. 1969. *Becoming Deviant*. Englewood Cliffs, NJ: Prentice-Hall.

Morales, E. 1986a. "Coca Culture: The White Gold of Peru." *Graduate School Magazine of City University of New York* 1:4–11.

———. 1986b. "Coca and Cocaine Economy and Social Change in the Andes in Peru." *Economic Development and Social Change* 35:143–61.

Murphy, S., Reinarman, C., & Waldorf, D. 1989. "An Eleven Year Follow-up of a Network of Cocaine Users." *British Journal of the Addictions* 84:427–36.

Plasket, B. & Quillen, E. 1985. *The White Stuff*. New York: The Dell Publishing Company.

Preble, E. & Casey, J.H.Jr. 1969. "Taking Care of Business: The Heroin User's Life on the Streets." *The International Journal of the Addictions* 4:1–24.

Reinarman, C., Waldorf, D., & Murphy, S. 1988. "Scapegoating and Social Control in the Construction of a Public Problem: Empirical and Critical Findings on Cocaine and Work." *Research in Law, Deviance, and Social Control* 9:37–62.

Reuter, P. 1990. *Money from Crime: The Economics of Drug Dealing*. Santa Monica, CA: Rand Corporation.

Rosenbaum, M. 1981. *Women on Heroin*. New Brunswick, NJ: Rutgers University Press.

Sanabria, H. 1988. *Coca, Migration, and Socio-Economic Change in a Bolivian Highland Peasant Community*. Ph.D. thesis, University of Wisconsin.

Sanchez, J. & Johnson, B. 1987. "Women and the Drug Crime Connection: Crime Rates Among Drug Abusing Women at Riker's Island." *Journal of Psychoactive Drugs* 19:205–15.

Sykes, G. & Matza, D. 1957. "Techniques of Neutralization." *American Sociological Review* 2:664–70.

Thompson, E.P. 1971. "The Moral Economy of the English Crowd in the Eighteenth Century." *Past and Present* 50:76–136.

Waldorf, D. Reinarman, C. Murphy, S., & Joyce, B. 1977. *Doing Coke: An Ethnography of Cocaine Snorters and Sellers*. Washington, D.C.: Drug Abuse Council.

Waldorf, D., Reinarman, C., & Murphy, S. 1991. *Cocaine Changes*. Philadelphia: Temple University Press.

Watters, J.K. & Biernacki, P. 1989. "Targeted Sampling: Options for the Study of Hidden Populations." *Social Problems* 36:416–30.

Williams, T. 1989. *The Cocaine Kids*. New York: Addison Wesley.

NOTES

[1] Adler (1985:127–28) also refers briefly to Matza's formulations within her discussion of becoming a dealer.

[2] It must be noted at the outset that the predominantly white, working and middle class cocaine sellers we interviewed are very likely to differ from inner-city crack dealers depicted in the media. While there is now good reason to believe that both the profits and the violence reported to be endemic in the crack trade have been exaggerated (e.g., Reuter, 1990; Goldstein et al., 1989, respectively), our data are drawn from a different population, selling a different form of the drug, who were typically drawn from a different population. Thus the exigencies they faced and their responses to them are also likely to differ from those of inner-city crack sellers.

[3] These movements back and forth among different levels of involvement in dealing were different from the "shifts and oscillations" found among the cocaine dealers studied by Adler (1985:133–41). She studied a circle of high-level dealers over an extended period of field work and found that the stresses and strains of dealing at the top of the pyramid often led her participants to attempt to get out of the business. While many of our interviewees felt similar pressures later in their careers and subsequently quit, our focus here is on becoming a cocaine seller.

[4] In addition to the lore about "righteous" and "rip off" dealers, there were present other norms that suggested the existence of such an unwritten code or moral economy, e.g., refusing to sell to children or to adults who "couldn't handle it" (i.e., had physical, financial, familial, or work-related problems because of cocaine use).

Chapter 42

BECOMING A HIT MAN:
NEUTRALIZATION IN A VERY DEVIANT CAREER

Ken Levi

Our knowledge about deviance management is based primarily on behavior that is easily mitigated. The literature dwells on unwed fathers (Pfuhl, 1978), and childless mothers (Veevers, 1975), pilfering bread salesman (Ditton, 1977), and conniving shoe salesmen (Friedman, 1974), bridge pros (Holtz, 1975), and poker pros (Hayano, 1977), marijuana smokers (Langer, 1976), massage parlor prostitutes (Verlarde, 1975), and other minor offenders (see, for example, Berk, 1977; Farrell and Nelson, 1976; Gross, 1977). There is a dearth of deviance management articles on serious offenders, and no scholarly articles at all about one of the (legally) most serious offenders of all, the professional murderer. Drift may be possible for the minor offender exploiting society's *ambivalence* toward his relatively unserious behavior (Sykes and Matza, 1957). However, excuses for the more inexcusable forms of deviant behavior are, by definition, less easily come by, and the very serious offender may enter his career with few of the usual defenses.

This article will focus on ways that one type of serious offender, the professional hit man, neutralizes stigma in the early stages of his career. As we shall see, the social organization of the profession provides "neutralizers" which distance its members from the shameful aspects of their careers. But for the novice, without professional insulation, the problem is more acute. With very little outside help, he must negate his feelings, neutralize them, and adopt a "framework" (Goffman, 1974) appropriate to his chosen career. This process, called "reframing," is the main focus of the present article. Cognitively, the novice must *reframe his experience* in order to enter his profession.

The Social Organization of Murder

Murder, the unlawful killing of a person, is considered a serious criminal offense in the United States, and it is punished by extreme penalties. In addition, most Americans do not feel that the penalties are extreme enough (Reid, 1976:482). In overcoming the intense stigma associated with murder, the hit man lacks the supports available to more ordinary types of killers.

Some cultures allow special circumstances or sanction special organizations wherein people who kill are insulated from the taint of murder. Soldiers at war, or police in the line of duty or citizens protecting their property operate under what are considered justifiable or excusable conditions. They receive so much informal

487

support from the general public and from members of their own group that it may protect even a sadistic member from blame (Westley, 1966).

Subcultures (Wolfgang and Ferracuti, 1967), organizations (Maas, 1968), and gangs (Yablonsky, 1962) that unlawfully promote killing can at least provide their members with an "appeal to higher loyalties" (Skyes and Matza, 1957), if not a fully developed set of deviance justifying norms.

Individuals acting on their own, who kill in a spontaneous, "irrational" outburst of violence can also mitigate the stigma of their behavior.

> I mean, people will go ape for one minute and shoot, but there are very
> few people who are capable of thinking about, planning, and then doing
> it (Joey, 1974:56).

Individuals who kill in a hot-blooded burst of passion can retrospectively draw comfort from the law which provides a lighter ban against killings performed without premeditation or malice or intent (Lester and Lester, 1975:35). At one extreme, the spontaneous killing may seem the result of mental disease (Lester and Lester, 1975:39) or dissociative reaction (Tanay, 1972), and excused entirely as insanity.

But when an individual who generally shares society's ban against murder, is fully aware that his act of homicide is (1) unlawful, (2) self-serving, and (3) intentional, he does not have the usual defenses to fall back on. How does such an individual manage to *overcome his inhibitions and avoid serious damage to his self-image* (assuming that he does not share society's ban)? This is the special dilemma of the professional hit man who hires himself out for murder.

Research Methods

Information for this article comes primarily from a series of intensive interviews with one self-styled "hit man." The interviews were spread over seven, tape-recorded sessions during a four-month period. The respondent was one of fifty prison inmates randomly sampled from a population of people convicted of murder in Metropolitan Detroit. The respondent told about an "accidental" killing, involving a drunken bar patron who badgered the respondent and finally forced his hand by pulling a knife on him. In court he claimed self-defense, but the witnesses at the bar claimed otherwise, so they sent him to prison. During the first two interview sessions, the respondent acted progressively ashamed of this particular killing, not on moral grounds, but because of its "sloppiness" of "amateurishness." Finally, he indicated there was more he would like to say. So, I stopped the tape recorder. I asked him if he was a hit man. He said he was.

He had already been given certain guarantees, including no names in the interview, a private conference room, and a signed contract promising his anonymity. Now, as a further guarantee, we agreed to talk about him in the third person, as a fictitious character named "Pete," so that none of his statements would sound like a personal confession. With these assurances, future interviews were devoted to his career as a professional murderer, with particular emphasis on his entry into the career and his orientation toward his victims.

Was he reliable? Since we did not use names, I have no way of checking the veracity of the individual cases he reported. Nevertheless, I was able to compare his account of the hit man's career with information from other convicted murderers, with police experts, and with accounts from the available literature (Gage, 1972; Joey, 1974; Maas, 1968). Pete's information was generally supported by these other sources. As to his motive for submitting to the interview, it is hard to gauge. He apparently was ashamed of the one "accidental" killing that had landed him in prison, and he desired to set the record straight concerning what he deemed an illustrious career, now that he had arrived, as he said, at the end of it. Hit men pride themselves on not "falling" (going to jail) for murder, and Pete's incarceration hastened a decision to retire-that he had already been contemplating, anyway.

A question might arise about the ethics of researching self-confessed "hit men" and granting them anonymity. Legally, since Pete never mentioned specific names or specific dates or possible future crimes, there does not seem to be a problem. Morally, if confidentiality is a necessary condition to obtaining information about serious offenders, then we have to ask: Is it worth it? Pete insisted that he had retired from the profession. Therefore, there seems to be no "clear and imminent danger" that would justify the violation of confidentiality, in the terms set forth by the American Psychological Association (1978:40). On the other hand, the *possibility* of danger does exist, and future researchers will have to exercise their judgement.

Finally, hit men are hard to come by. Unlike more lawful killers, such as judges of night watchmen, and unlike run-of-the-mill murderers, the hit man (usually) takes infinite care to conceal his identity. Therefore, while it is regrettable that this paper has only one case to report on, and while it would be ideal to perform a comparative analysis of a number of hit men, it would be very difficult to obtain such a sample. Instead, Pete's responses will be compared to similar accounts from the available literature. While such a method can never produce verified findings, it can point to suggestive hypotheses.

The Social Organization of Professional Murder

There are two types of professional murderers: the organized and the independent. The killer who belongs to an organized syndicate does not usually get paid on a contract basis, and performs his job out of loyalty and obedience to the organization (Maas, 1968:81). The independent professional killer is a freelance agent who hires himself out for a fee (Pete). It is the career organization of the second type of killer that will be discussed.

The organized killer can mitigate his behavior through an "appeal to higher loyalties" (Sykes and Matza, 1957). He also can view his victim as an enemy of the group and then choose from a variety of techniques available for neutralizing an offense against an enemy (see, for example, Hirschi, 1969; Rogers and Buffalo, 1974). But the independent professional murderer lacks most of these defenses.

Nevertheless, built into his role are certain structural features that help him avoid deviance ascription. These features include:

(1) *Contract.* A contract is an unwritten agreement to provide a sum of money to a second party who agrees, in return, to commit a designated murder (Joey, 1974:9). It is most often arranged over the phone, between people who have never had personal contact. And the victim, or "hit," is usually unknown to the killer (Gage, 1972:57; Joey, 1974:61–62). This arrangement is meant to protect both parties from the law. But it also helps the killer "deny the victim" (Sykes and Matza, 1957) by keeping him relatively anonymous.

In arranging the contract, the hired killer will try to find out the difficulty of the hit and how much the customer wants the killing done. According to Pete, these considerations determine his price. He does not ask about the motive for the killing, treating it as none of his concern. Not knowing the motive may hamper the killer from morally justifying his behavior, but it also enables him to further deny the victim by maintaining his distance and reserve. Finally, the contract is backed up by a further understanding.

> Like this guy who left here (prison) last summer; he was out two months before he got killed. Made a mistake somewhere. The way I heard it, he didn't finish filling a contract (Pete).

If the killer fails to live up to his part of the bargain, the penalties could be extreme (Gage, 1972:53; Joey, 1974:9). This has the ironic effect that after the contract is arranged, the killer can somewhat "deny responsibility" (Sykes and Matza, 1957), by pleading self-defense.

(2) *Reputation and Money.* Reputation is especially important in an area where killers are unknown to their customers, and where the less written the better (Joey, 1974:58). Reputation, in turn, reflects how much money the hit man has commanded in the past.

> And that was the first time that I ever got 30 grand...it's based on his reputation....Yeah, how good he really is. To be so-so, you get so-so money. If you're good, you get good money (Pete).

Pete, who could not recall the exact number of people he had killed, did like other hit men, keep an accounting of his highest fees (Joey, 1974:58,62). To him big money meant not only a way to earn a living, but also a way to maintain his professional reputation.

People who accept low fees can also find work as hired killers. Heroin addicts are the usual example. But, as Pete says, they often receive a bullet for their pains. It is believed that people who would kill for so little would also require little persuasion to make them talk to the police (Joey, 1974:63). This further reinforces the single-minded emphasis on making big money. As a result, killing is conceptualized as a "business" or as "just a job." Framing the hit in a normal businesslike context enables the hit man to deny wrongfulness, or "deny injury" (Sykes and Matza, 1957).

In addition to the economic motive, Pete, and hit men discussed by other authors, refer to excitement, fun, game-playing, power, and impressing women as incentives for murder (Joey, 1974:81–82). However, none of these motives are mentioned by all sources. None are as necessary to the career as money. And, after awhile, these other motives diminish and killing becomes only "just a job" (Joey, 1974:20). The primacy of the economic motive has been aptly expressed in the case of another deviant profession.

> Women who enjoy sex with their customers do not make good prostitutes, according to those who are acquainted with this institution first hand. Instead of thinking about the most effective way of making money at the job, they would be doing things for their own pleasure and enjoyment (Goode, 1978:342).

(3) *Skill.* Most of the hit man's training focuses on acquiring skill in the use of weapons.

> Then he met these two guys, these two white guys...them two, them two was the best. And but they stayed around over there and they got together, and Pete told (them) that he really wanted to be good. He said, if (I) got to do something, I want to be good at it. So they, they got together, showed him, showed him *how to shoot*....And gradually, he became good....Like he told me, like when he shoots somebody, he always goes for the head; he said, that's about the best shot. I mean, if you want him dead then and there....And these two guys showed him, and to him, I mean, hey, I mean, he don't believe nobody could really outshoot these two guys, you know what I mean. *They know everything you want to know about guns, knives, and stuff like that* (Pete).

The hit man's reputation, and the amount of money he makes depends on his skill, his effective ability to serve as a means to *someone else's ends*. The result is a focus on technique.

> Like anything you do, when you do it, you want to do it just right....On your target and you hit it, how you feel: I hit it! I hit it! (Pete).

This focus on technique, on means, helps the hit man to "deny responsibility" and intent(Sykes and Matza, 1957). In frame-analytic terms, the hit man separates his morally responsible, or "principal" self from the rest of himself, and performs the killing mainly as a "strategist" (Goffman, 1974:523). In other words, he sees himself as a "hired gun." The saying, "If I didn't do it, they'd find someone else who would," reflects this narrowly technical orientation.

To sum up thus far, the contract, based as it is on the hit man's reputation for profit and skill, provides the hit man with opportunities for denying the victim, denying injury, and denying responsibility. But this is not enough. To point out the defenses of the professional hit man is one thing, but it is unlikely that the *novice* hit man would have a totally professional attitude so early in his career. The novice is at a point where he both lacks the conventional defense against the stigma of murder, *and* he has not yet fully acquired the exceptional defenses of the professional. How, then, does he cope?

The First Time: Negative Experience

Goffman (1974:378–379) defines "negative experience" as a feeling of disorientation:

> Expecting to take up a position in a well-framed realm, he finds that no particular frame is immediately applicable, or the frame that he thought was applicable no longer seems to be, or he cannot bind himself within the frame that does apparently apply. He loses command over the formulation of viable response. He flounders. Experience, the meld of what the current scene brings to him and what he brings to it—meant to settle into a form even while it is beginning, finds no form and is therefore no experience. Reality anomically flutters. He has a "negative experience"—negative in the sense that it takes its character from what it is not, and what it is not is an organized and organizationally affirmed response (1974:378–379).

Negative experience can occur when a person finds himself lapsing into an old understanding of the situation, only to suddenly awaken to the fact that it no longer applies. In this regard, we should expect negative experience to be a special problem for the novice. For example, the first time he killed a man for money, Pete supposedly became violently ill:

> When he (Pete), you know, hit the guy, when he shot the guy, the guy said, "You Killed me"...something like that, cause he struck him all up here. And what he said, it was just, I mean, *the look right in the guy's eye*, you know. I mean he looked like: *Why me?* Yeah? And (Pete) couldn't shake that. Cause he remembered a time or two when he got cut, and all he wanted to do was get back and cut this guy that cut him. And this here....No, he just could not shake it. And then he said that at night-time he'll start thinking about the guy: like he shouldn't have looked at him like that....I mean actually (Pete) was sick....He couldn't keep his food down, I mean, or nothing like that....(It lasted) I'd say about two months....Like he said that he has feelings...that he never did kill nobody before (Pete).

Pete's account conforms to the definition of negative experience. He had never killed anyone for money before. It started when a member of the Detroit drug world had spotted Pete in a knife fight outside an inner city bar, was apparently impressed with the young man's style, and offered him fifty dollars to do a "job." Pete accepted.

He wanted the money. But when the first hit came about, Pete of course knew that he was doing it for money, but yet his orientation was revenge. Thus, he stared his victim in the *face*, a characteristic gesture of people who kill enemies for revenge (Levi, 1975:190). Expecting to see defiance turn into a look of defeat, they attempt to gain "face" at the loser's expense.

But when Pete stared his victim in the face, he saw not an enemy, but an innocent man. He saw a look of: "Why me?" And this *discordant* image is what remained in his mind during the weeks and months to follow and made him sick. As Pete says, "He shouldn't have looked at him like that." The victim's look of innocence brought about what Goffman (1974:347) refers to as a "frame break":

> Given that the frame applied to an activity is expected to enable us to come to terms with all events in that activity (informing and regulating many of them) it is understandable that the unmanageable might occur, an occurrence which cannot be effectively ignored and to which the frame cannot be applied, with resulting bewilderment and chagrin on the part of the participants. In brief, a break can occur in the applicability of the frame, a break in its governance.

When such a frame break occurs, it produces negative experience. Pete's extremely uncomfortable disorientation may reflect the extreme dissonance between the revenge frame, that he expected to apply, and the unexpected look of innocence that he encountered and continued to recall.

Subsequent Time: Reframing The Hit

According to Goffman (1974:319), a structural feature of frames of experience is that they are divided into different "tracks" of types of information. These include, "a main track of story line and ancillary tracks of various kinds." The ancillary tracks are the directional track, the overlay track, the concealment tracks, and the disattend track. The disattend track contains the information that is perceived but supposed to be *ignored*. For example, the prostitute manages the distasteful necessity of having sex with "tricks" by remaining "absolutely...detached. Removed. Miles and miles away" (1974:344). The existence of different tracks allows an individual to define and redefine his experience by the strategic placement of information.

Sometimes, the individual receives outside help. For example, when Milgram in 1963 placed a barrier between people administering electric shocks, and the bogus "subjects" who were supposedly receiving the shocks, he made it easier for the shockers to "disattend" signs of human distress from their hapless victims. Surgeons provide another example. Having their patients completely covered, except for the part to be operated on, helps them work in a more impersonal manner. In both examples, certain crucial information is stored away in the "concealment track" (Goffman, 1974:218).

In other cases help can come from guides who direct the novice on what to experience and what to block out. Beginning marijuana smokers are cautioned to ignore feelings of nausea (Becker, 1953:240). On the other hand, novice hit men like Pete are reluctant to share their "experience" with anyone else. It would be a sign of weakness.

In still other cases, however, it is possible that the subject can do the reframing *on his own*. And this is what appears to have happened to Pete.

> And when the second one (the second hit) came up, (Pete) was still thinking about the first one....Yeah, when he got ready to go, he was thinking about it. *Something changed.* I don't know how to put it right. Up to the moment that he killed the second guy now, he waited, you know. Going through his mind was the first guy he killed. He still seeing him, still see the *expression on his face.* Soon, the second guy walked up; I mean, it was like just his mind just *blanked out* for a minute, everything just blanked out....Next thing he know, he had killed the second guy....*He knew what he was doing,* but what I mean, he just didn't have nothing on his mind. Everything was wiped out (Pete).

And when the second victim approached, Pete says that he noticed the victim's approach, he was aware of the man's presence. But he noticed none of the victim's personal features. He did not see the victim's face or its expression. Thus, he did not see the very thing that gave him so much trouble the first time. It is as if Pete had *negatively conditioned* himself to avoid certain cues. Since he shot the victim in the head, it is probable that Pete saw him in one sense; this is not the same kind of experience as a "dissociative reaction," which has been likened to sleepwalking (Tanay, 1972). Pete says that, "he knew what he was doing." But he either did not pay attention to his victim's personal features at the time of the killing, or he blocked them out immediately afterward, so that now the only aspect of his victim he recalls is the victim's approach (if we are to believe him).

After that, Pete says that killing became *routine*. He learned to view his victims as "targets," rather than as people. Thus, he believes that the second experience is the crucial one, and that the disattendence of the victim's personal features made it so.

Support from other accounts of hit men is scant, due to a lack of data. Furthermore, not everything in Pete's account supports the "reframing" hypothesis. In talking about later killings, it is clear that he not only attends to his victims' personal features, on occasion, but he also derives a certain grim pleasure in doing so.

> (The victim was) a nice looking woman....She started weeping, and (she cried), "I ain't did this, I ain't did that"....and (Pete) said that he shot her. Like it wasn't nothing....he didn't feeling nothing. It was just money (Pete).

In a parallel story, Joey (1974:56) the narrator of the *Killer*, also observes his victim in personal terms.

> (The victim) began to beg. He went so far as to tell us where he had stashed his money. Finally, he realized there was absolutely nothing he

could do. He sat there quietly. Then, he started crying. I didn't feel a thing for him (1974:56).

It may be that this evidence contradicts what I have said about reframing; but perhaps another interpretation is possible. Reframing may play a more crucial role in the original redefinition of an experience than in the continued maintenance of that redefinition. Once Pete has accustomed himself to viewing his victims as merely targets, as "just money," then it may be less threatening to look upon them as persons, once again. Once the "main story line" has been established, discordant information can be presented in the "overlay track" (Goffman, 1974:215), without doing too much damage. Indeed, this seems to be *the point* that both hit men are trying to make in the above excerpts.

The Heart of The Hit Man

For what I have been referring to as "disattendance" Pete used the term "heart," which he defined as a "coldness." When asked what he would look for in an aspiring hit man, Pete replied,

> See if he's got a whole lot of heart....you got to be cold...you got to build a coldness in yourself. It's not something that comes automatically, cause, see, I don't care who he is, first, you've got feelings (Pete).

In contrast to his view, Joey (1974:56) said,

> There are three things you need to kill a man: the gun, the bullets, and the balls. A lot of people will point a gun at you, but they haven't got the courage to pull the trigger. It's as simple as that. It may be that some are born with "heart," while others acquire it in the way I have described.

However, the "made rather than born" thesis does explain one perplexing feature of hit men and other "evil" men whose banality has sometimes seemed discordant. In other aspects of their lives they all seem perfectly capable of feeling ordinary human emotions. Their inhumanity, their coldness, seems narrowly restricted to their jobs. Pete, for example, talked about his "love" for little children. Eddie "The Hawk" Ruppolo meekly allowed his mistress to openly insult him in a public bar (Gage, 1972). And Joey (1974:55) has this to say about himself:

> Believe it or not, I'm a human being. I laugh at funny jokes, I love children around the house, and I can spend hours playing with my mutt.

All of these examples of human warmth indicate that the cold heart of the hit man may be less a characteristic of the killer's individual personality, than a feature of the professional framework of experience which the hit man has learned to adapt himself to, when he is on the job.

Discussion

This article is meant as a contribution to the study of deviance neutralization. The freelance hit man is an example of an individual who, relatively alone, must deal with a profound and unambiguous stigma in order to enter his career. Both Pete and Joey emphasize "heart" as a determining factor in becoming a professional. And Pete's experience, after the first hit, further indicates that the inhibitions against murder-for-money are real.

In this article "heart"—or the ability to adapt to a rationalized framework for killing—had been portrayed as the outcome of an initial process of reframing, in addition to other neutralization techniques established during the further stages of professionalization. As several theorists (see, for example, Becker, 1953; Douglas *et al.*, 1977 Matza, 1969) have noted, people often enter into deviant acts first, and then develop rationales for their behavior later on. This was also the case with Pete, who began his career by first, (1) "being willing" (Matza, 1969), (2) encountering a frame break, (3) undergoing negative experience, (4) being willing to try again (also known as "getting back on the horse"), (5) reframing the experience, and (6) having future, routine experiences wherein his professionalization increasingly enabled him to "deny the victim," "deny injury," and "deny responsibility." Through the process of reframing, the experience of victim-as-target emerged as the "main story line," and the experience of victim-as-person was downgraded from the main track to the disattend track to the overlay track. Ironically, the intensity of the negative experience seemed to make the process all the more successful. Thus, it may be possible for a person with "ordinary human feelings" to both pass through the novice stage, and to continue "normal relations" thereafter. The reframing hypothesis has implications for other people who knowingly perform stigmatized behaviors. It may be particularly useful in explaining a personal conversion experience that occurs despite the relative absence of deviant peer groups, deviant norms, extenuating circumstances, and neutralization rationales.

REFERENCES

American Psychological Association. (1978). *Directory of the American Psychological Association.* Washington, DC: Author.

Becker, H. (1953). "Becoming a Marijuana User." *American Journal of Sociology* 59:235–243.

Berk, B. (1977). "Face-Saving at the Singles Dance." *Social Problems* 24, 5:530–544.

Ditton, J. (1977). Alibis and Aliases: Some Notes on Motives of Fiddling Breas Salesman." *Sociology* 11, 2:33–255.

Douglas, J., P. Rasmussen, and C. Flagagan. (1977). *The Nude Beach.* Beverly Hills: Sage.

Farrell, R., and J. Nelson. (1976). "A Casual Model of Secondary Deviance; The Case of Homosexuality." *Sociological Quarterly* 17:109–120.

Friedman, N.L. (1974). "Cookies and Contests: Notes on Ordinary Occupational Deviance and its Neutralization." *Sociological Symposium* (Spring):1–9.

Gage, N.(1972). *Mafia, U.S.A.* New York: Dell.

Goffman, E. (1974). *Frame Analysis.* Cambridge, MA: Harvard University Press.

Goode, E. (1978). *Deviant Behavior: An Interactionist Approach.* Englewood Cliffs, New Jersey: Prentice-Hall.

Gross, H.(1977). "Micro and Macro Level Implications for a Sociology of Virtue-Case of Draft Protests to Vietnam War." *Sociological Quarterly*. 18, 3:319–339.

Hayano, D. (1977). "The Professional Poker Player: Career Identification and the Problem of Respectability." *Social Problems* 24 (June):556–564.

Hirschi, T.(1969). *Causes of Delinquency*. Berkeley: University of California Press.

Holtz, J. (1975). "The Professional Duplicate Bridge Player: Conflict Management in a Free, Legal, Quasi-Deviant Occupation." *Urban Life* 4,2:131–160.

Joey.(1974). *Killer: Autobiography of a Mafia Hit Man*. New York: Pocket Books.

Langer, J. (1976). "Drug Entrepreneurs and The Dealing Culture." *Australian and New Zealand Journal of Sociology* 12, 2:82–90.

Lester, D., and G. Lester. (1975). *Crime and Passion: Murder and The Murderer*. Chicago: Nelson-Hall.

Levi, K. (1975). *Iceman*. Ann Arbor, MI: University Microfilms.

Maas, P. (1968). *The Valachi Papers*. New York: G. P. Putnam.

Matza, D. (1969). *Becoming Deviant*. Englewood Cliffs. N.J.: Prentice-Hall.

Pfuhl, E. (1978). "The unwed father: a non-deviant rule breaker." *Sociological Quarterly* 19:113–128.

Reid, S.(1976). *Crime and Criminology*. Hinsdale, Illinois: Dryden Press.

Rogers, J., and M. Buffalo. (1974). "Neutralization Techniques: Toward a Simplified Measurement Scale." *Pacific Sociological Review* 17,3: 313.

Sykes, G., and D. Matza. (1957). "Techniques of Neutralization: A Theory of Delinquency." *American Sociological Review* 22:664–670.

Tanay, E. (1972). "Psychiatric Aspects of Homicide Prevention." *American Journal of Psychology* 128:814–817.

Veevers, J. (1975). "The Moral Careers of Voluntarily Childless Wives: Notes on the Defense of a Variant World View." *Family Coordinator* 24, 4:473–487.

Verlarde, A. (1975). "Becoming Prostituted: The Decline of the Massage Parlor Profession and the Masseuse." *British Journal of Criminology* 15, 3:251–263.

Westley, W. (1966). "The Esclation of Violence Through Legitimation." *Annals of the American Association of Political and Social Science* 364 (March) 120–126.

Wolfgang, M., and F. Ferracuti. (1967). *The Subculture of Violence*. London: Tavistock.

Yablonsky, L. (1962). *The Violent Gang*. New York: Macmillan.

Part IX

MANAGING STIGMA/MANAGING DEVIANT IDENTITIES

Placing deviant labels on individuals "marks" them in the eyes of others. Social stigmas are uncomfortable accoutrements to persons. Despite how they are acquired, the associated redefinitions and social statuses rarely fair well for the bearers of this mark. Stigmata then, refer to attributes or characteristics that are deeply discrediting in nature.

To be sure, not all stigmata are similar in nature. In the classic selection by Erving Goffman, "*Stigma and Social Identity*," he states that there are three basic types: abominations of the body, which include various physical deformities; secondly, there are blemishes of character, qualities or actions influentially based on the individual having engaged in acts such as drug use, swinging, homosexuality, having been labelled mentally ill, etc. Thirdly, there are what Goffman terms, tribal stigmas—stigmas of race, religion and nation. By virtue of one's skin pigmentation or religious affiliation, he or she may be stigmatized by others.

Despite the type, all stigmata denote individuals' "spoiled identities;" they are disvalued and conceived of as undesirable in the eyes of others.

A discussion of stigma may benefit from noting the variation in the nature of stigma. In certain cases, individuals possess stigmas that are readily known or apparent to others. It is obvious from looking at individuals that they are obese; by observing the man with the seeing eye dog, it is evident that he is visually impaired; by observing the woman in the wheelchair, it is apparent that she is a paraplegic. These persons possess what Goffman terms *discredited* deviant identities.

In other cases, individuals possess stigmas that are not readily known or apparent to others. Consider the cases of the infertile woman, the former mental patient, the ex-con—their "deviantness" is not readily apparent to others. Such persons possess what Goffman refers to as *discreditable* deviant identities.

Goffman argues that it is a constant effort on the part of those who possess discredited/discreditable identities to attempt to manage and control social information about themselves. Deviants spend a great deal of time and energy at this never-ending task. In this view, deviants are portrayed as strategists, expert managers, and negotatiators who engage in a number of stratagems and techniques in order to mitigate the stigma of their "failing" on their daily rounds.

Deviants develop and employ various defensive and offensive stratagems based upon the specific deviant situations, and they may be employed singly or in combination with each other.

The Discredited: Techniques of Stigma Management

When persons cannot conceal their stigma, they frequently engage in a technique referred to as disavowal or normalization. The aim of those who possess a discredited

498

deviant identity centers on seeking to reduce the relevance of their stigmatized status by attempting to maintain a positive, non-deviant self-image and public identity.

In the selection by Fred Davis, *"Deviance Disavowal: The Management of Strained Interaction by the Visibly Handicapped,"* the author discusses this tactic of *deviance disavowal*—denial or repudiation of their deviant identity and corresponding status, denial that they are abnormal or different from others. Also referred to as *normalization*, this strategy seeks to normalize that which has been otherwise regarded as deviant.

Davis states that the disavowal process consists of three stages. The first involves a fictional acceptance of the deviant as normal and equal to others. During this stage, interaction between normals and the deviant is characterized by curiosity, privacy and politeness. Although normals tend to be curious, norms regarding the value of privacy constrain individuals from reacting too obviously to certain aspects of the deviant person. Individuals avoid conversing about the very thing that is on their minds, amounting to civil inattention.

Feigning equality and normalcy allows for the fictional acceptance that there is no difference between the two parties. It also prolongs interaction between them so that normals may begin to relate to the deviant in relation to terms other than those associated with the deviant attribute. It is at this juncture, Davis argues that the second stage of deviance disavowal begins: the facilitating of normal roles by the deviant. This second stage is reached when individuals are able to interact with the deviant in terms of the latter's non-deviant social statuses, not his or her master status as "deviant." At this point, normals can begin to use terms such as cripple or peg-leg when talking to the deviant. Davis states that during this stage the deviant begins to actively project a positive, non-deviant self-image to others. While the deviant makes an active attempt to disavow his or her deviance and pro-offers to others a positive redefinition of self, others do not always respond in a positive manner. It may be an arduous series of negotiations before the deviant is no longer seen in the eyes of others as deviant, handicapped, etc. It is at this level that interaction is no longer strained, but is natural. Success may not always be achieved. In his research on polio victims and their families, Davis noted that sometimes disavowal does not work—others are frequently unable or unwilling to accept the deviant's redefinition of self as normal.

Breaking through interactional limitations leads to the third stage in this process, institutionalized normal relationships with others. This refers to the process whereby others acknowledge prevailing conditions and work them into their normal relationship. The boss makes reservations in a restaurant that he is sure is wheelchair accessible and asks for a table to accommodate them.

The Discreditable: Strategies of Information and Stigma Management

In contrast to the problem of the discredited, the discreditable possess certain other problems. As Goffman (1963:42) suggests, such persons are often faced with the dilemma of whether to disclose or not to disclose, should they tell anyone, if so who? Deviants spend a great deal of time anguishing over these questions.

In her article, "*Return to Sender: Reintegrate Stigma-Management Strategies of Ex-Psychiatric Patients*", Nancy J. Herman details the problems encountered by ex-psychiatric patients with respect to stigma—those who possess discreditable deviant identities. Her research focuses on the various techniques and strategies such persons employ in order to lessen or mitigate the stigma potential of their failing, and the concomitant consequences for identity transformation (which we shall deal with in Section X). Mental patients adopted and employed four stratagems of information control: selective concealment, therapeutic disclosure; preventive disclosure; and political activism. We shall now turn to a brief discussion of each.

Concealment and Selective Concealment

On the basis of their own socialization, past experiences, or fear of rejection, many individuals who possess a discreditable identity attempt to actively conceal it from others. As scholars note, being a closet or secret deviant is much more complicated than either choosing to be in the closet or out, or disclosing or not. Research studies suggest that deviants selectively conceal information about their deviant attributes from certain individuals, at certain times, in certain settings, but will freely disclose to others, at other times, in other settings. As Herman indicates, "concealment and disclosure then, are contingent upon a complex interaction of one's learned perceptions of the stigma [of their attribute], actual 'test' experiences with others before/or after disclosure, and the nature of the particular relationship involved."

In her research, Herman found that employment of concealment on the part of ex-psychiatric patients took a number of forms. As strategists and managers ex-patients often avoided selected "normals" who they deemed to be "untrustworthy." Ex-patients also redirected conversations so as to avoid detection. A third technique involved the use of disidentifiers (Goffman, 1963:44)—symbols used to prevent a person from being conceived of as a deviant. Further, ex-patients attempted to control information about themselves by avoiding contact with stigma symbols (Goffman, 1963:43)—signs that may call attention to or reveal their true identity.

While concealment' as a stratagem of information and stigma management, may be used solely by many deviants, research by Herman and others indicates that the strong desire for secrecy on the part of deviants is often gradually replaced by alternative strategies of information and stigma management to which we will now turn.

Therapeutic Disclosure

Therapeutic disclosure may be defined as selecting disclosure on the part of the deviant to certain trusted individuals in order to renegotiate personal perceptions of their deviant attributes. Disclosure to supportive others allows deviants to release feelings of frustration and anxiety, it is cathartic, it functions to elevate their self-esteem and allows for the renegotiation for more positive non-deviant perceptions of self.

Preventive Disclosure

Preventive disclosure refers to selective telling to certain normal others in an effort to influence others' perceptions about the deviant and about his or her deviant attribute in general. As Herman indicates, mental patients often used this technique in situations where they anticipated future rejection by normals and also to influence normals' attitudes about themselves and about mental illness in general.

Political Activism

In contrast to the above individualized stigma management techniques, deviants also employ collective management strategies in order to control information, deal with the stigma potential of their deviant attribute, and alter deviant identities. (We shall discuss these organizations more fully in Section X). Many such voluntary associations exists in our society, such as the National Stuttering Project, the Gray Panthers, and COYOTE (Call Off Your Old Tired Ethics). In Herman's study, she found that ex-psychiatric patients join and participate in ex-mental patient activist groups. This social organization with its goal of self-affirmation provides three important functions for the ex-patient: it rejects societal standards of normalcy—standards by which ex-patients could not measure up; it provides individuals with a new non-deviant conception of self; and it serves to propagate this new identity, and positive self-image to other individuals, groups and institutions in society.

The selection by Mark Kowalewski entitled, "*Double Stigma and Boundary Maintenance*," deals with the reactions that 'normal' members of the gay community (a stigmatized group) have toward other gays who possess a second, discredited characteristic—those who have the AIDS virus.

Persons part of the gay community, in an effort to avoid the stereotypes attached to their stigma, attempt to detach themselves from others who they perceive to be *more* stigmatized. Kowalewski indicates that gays define themselves as 'normal' in relation to others who are gay and possess AIDS—persons who possess a "double stigma." One manner of stigma management involves distancing themselves from gays with AIDS. This tactic may be achieved by joining an out-group in their chastisement of promiscuity. Moreover, gays have also maintained their separateness from those with a double stigma by distancing themselves physically, emotionally and through their self-concept.

Our final selection by Mark Nagler, "*Ostomates: Negotiating an Involuntary Identity*," deals with the social processes by which those who have undergone ostomy surgery attempt to manage their stigma. Having a bowel and/or urinary tract removed and replaced with a bag to collect waste material is extremely upsetting for individuals. Ostomates are continually forced to be involved with and worried about the evacuation of their bodily wastes; in many cases, spillage occurs, gas seeps out, and ostomates have a number of accidents. Ostomates perceive of themselves as possessing a stigmatizing status; in an effort to pass, they will attempt to employ the strategy of concealment from others. Others, after experimentation, will find it operant to disclose their spoiled identities. As Nagler points out, many feel that they have no choice but to disclose; they find camouflage to be difficult. Similar to Herman's study on ex-psychiatric patients, ostomates make decisions to disclose or conceal based on a complex interaction of various social factors. For ostomates, the career of renegotiating a new identity commences when individuals realize the physical transformation that has been accomplished. Confronted with the notion that the individual is now a different kind of person, he or she has two options: to fight the label or accept it. Acceptance denotes living up (or down) to the expectations that others have for them. Nagler indicates that most ostomates conceive of themselves as occupying a devalued position with reduced life chances. The problematic character of their acceptance leads to a renegotiation of new identities. The aim of identity renegotiation is to both maintain and establish relationships with others that would probably otherwise be negatively affected.

REFERENCES

Goffman, Erving, 1963. *Stigma: Notes on the Management of Spoiled Identities*. Englewood Cliffs, New Jersey: Prentice-Hall.

Chapter 43

STIGMA AND SOCIAL IDENTITY

Erving Goffman

Society establishes the means of categorizing persons and the complement of attributes felt to be ordinary and natural for members of each of these categories. Social settings establish the categories of persons likely to be encountered there. The routines of social intercourse in established settings allow us to deal with anticipated others without special attention or thought. When a stranger comes into our presence, then, first appearances are likely to enable us to anticipate his category and attributes, his "social identity"—to use a term that is better than "social status" because personal attributes such as "honesty" are involved, as well as structured ones, like, "occupation."

We lean on these anticipations that we have, transforming them into normative expectations, into righteously presented demands.

Typically, we do not become aware that we have made these demands or aware of what they are until an active question arises as to whether or not they will be fulfilled. It is then that we are likely to realize that all along we had been making certain assumptions as to what the individual before us ought to be. Thus, the demands we make might better be called demands made "in effect, " and the character we impute to the individual might better be seen as an imputation made in potential retrospect-a characterization "in effect," a *virtual social identity*. The category and attributes he could in fact be proved to possess will be called his *actual social identity*.

While the stranger is present before us, evidence can arise of his possessing an attribute that makes him different from others in the category of persons available for him to be, and of a less desirable kind—in the extreme, a person who is quite thoroughly bad, or dangerous, or weak. He is thus reduced in our minds from a whole and usual person to a tainted, discounted one. Such an attribute is a stigma, especially when its discrediting effect is very extensive; sometimes it is also called a failing, a shortcoming, a handicap. It constitutes a special discrepancy between virtual and actual social identity. Note that there are other types of discrepancy between virtual and actual social identity, for example, the kind that causes us to reclassify an individual from one socially anticipated category to a different but equally well anticipated one, and the kind that causes us to alter our estimation of the individual upward. Note, too, that not all undesirable attributes are at issue, but only those which are incongruous with our stereotype of what a given type of individual should be.

The term *stigma*, then, will be used to refer to an attribute that is deeply discrediting, but it should be seen that a language of relationships, not attributes, is really needed. An attribute that stigmatizes one type of possessor can confirm the usualness of another, and therefore is neither creditable nor discreditable as a thing in itself. For example, some jobs in America cause holders without the expected college education to conceal this fact; other jobs, however, can lead the few of their holders who have a higher education to keep this a secret, lest they be marked as failures and outsiders. Similarly, a middle-class boy may feel no compunction in being seen going to the library; a professional criminal, however, writes:

> I can remember before how on more than one occasion, for instance, going into a public library near where I was living, and looking over my shoulder a couple of times before I actually went in just to make sure no one who knew me was standing about and seeing me do it.[1]

So, too, an individual who desires to fight for his country may conceal a physical defect, less his claimed physical status be discredited; later, the same individual, embittered and trying to get out of the army, may succeed in gaining admission to the army hospital, where he would be discredited in not really having an acute sickness[2]. A stigma, then, is really a special kind of relationship between attribute and stereotype, although I don't propose to continue to say so, in part because there are important attributes that almost everywhere in our society are discrediting.

The term *stigma* and its synonyms conceal a double perspective: Does the stigmatized individual assume his differentness is known about already or is evident on the spot, or does he assume it is neither known about by those present nor immediately perceivable by them? In the first case one deals with the plight of the *discredited*, in the second with that of the *discreditable*. This is an important difference, even though a particular stigmatized individual is likely to have experience with both situations. I will be begin with the situation of the discredited and move on to the discreditable but not always separate the two.

Three grossly different types of stigma may be mentioned. First there are abominations of the body—the various physical deformities. Next there are blemishes of individual character perceived as weak will, domineering or unnatural passions, treacherous and rigid beliefs, and dishonesty, these being inferred from a known record of, for example, mental disorder, imprisonment, addiction, alcoholism, homosexuality, unemployment, suicidal attempts, and radical political behavior. Finally there are the tribal stigmas of race, nation, and religion, these being stigmas that can be transmitted through lineages and equally contaminate all members of a family[3]. In all of these various instances of stigma, however...the same sociological features are found: An individual who might have been received easily in ordinary social intercourse possesses a trait that can obtrude itself upon attention and turn those of us whom he meets away from him, breaking the claim that his other attributes have on us. He possess a stigma, an undesired differentness from what we had anticipated. We and those who do not depart negatively from the particular expectations at issue I shall call the *normals*.

The attitudes we normals have toward a person with a stigma, and the actions we take in regard to him, are well known, since these responses are what benevolent social action is designed to soften and ameliorate. By definition, of course, we believe the person with a stigma is not quite human. On this assumption we exercise varieties of discrimination, through which we effectively, if often unthinkingly, reduce his life chances. We construct a stigma-theory, an ideology to explain his inferiority and account for the danger he represents, sometimes rationalizing an animosity based on other differences, such as those of social class.[4] We use specific stigma terms such as cripple, bastard, moron in our daily discourse as a source of metaphor and imagery, typically without giving thought to the original meaning.[5] We tend to impute a wide range of imperfections on the basis of the original one,[6] and at the same time to impute some desirable but undesired attributes, often of a supernatural cast, such as "sixth sense," or "understanding":[7]

> For some, there may be a hesitancy about touching or steering the blind, while for others, the perceived failure to see may be generalized into a gestalt of disability, so that the individual shouts at the blind as if they were deaf or attempts to lift them as if they were crippled. Those confronting the blind may have a whole range of belief that is anchored in the stereotype. For instance, they may think they are subject to unique judgment, assuming the blinded individual draws on special channels of information unavailable to others.[8]

Further, we may perceive his defensive response to his situation as a direct expression of his defect, and then see both defect and response as just retribution for something he or his parents or his tribe did, and hence a justification of the way we treat him.[9]

Now turn from the normal to the person he is normal against. It seems generally true that members of a social category may strongly support a standard of judgment that they and others agree does not directly apply to them. Thus, it is that a businessman may demand womanly behavior from females or ascetic behavior from monks, and not construe himself as someone who ought to realize either of these styles of conduct. The distinction is between realizing a norm and merely supporting it. The issue of stigma does not arise here, but only where there is some expectation on all sides that those in a given category should not only support a particular norm but also realize it.

Also, it seems possible for an individual to fail to live up to what we effectively demand of him, and yet be relatively untouched by this failure; insulated by his alienation, protected by identity beliefs of his own, he feels that he is a full-fledged normal human being, and that we are the ones who are not quite human. He bears a stigma but does not seem to be impressed or repentant about doing so. This possibility is celebrated in exemplary tales about Mennonites, Gypsies, shameless scoundrels, and very orthodox Jews.

In America at present, however, separate systems of honor seem to be on the decline. The stigmatized individual tends to hold the same beliefs about identity that we do; this is a pivotal fact. His deepest feelings about what he is may be his sense of being a "normal person," a human being like anyone else, a person, therefore, who deserves a fair chance and a fair break.[10] (Actually, however phrased, he bases his claims not on what he thinks is due *everyone*, but only everyone of a selected social category into which he unquestionably fits, for example, anyone of his age, sex, profession, and so forth). Yet he may perceive, usually quite correctly, that whatever others profess, they do not really "accept" him and are not ready to make contact with him on "equal grounds."[11] Further, the standards he has incorporated from the wider society equip him to be intimately alive to what others see as his failing, inevitably causing him, if only for moments, to agree that he does indeed fall short of what he really ought to be. Shame becomes a central possibility, arising from the individual's perception of one of his own attributes as being a defiling thing to possess, and one he can readily see himself as not possessing.

The immediate presence of normals is likely to reinforce this split between self-demands and self, but in fact self-hate and self-derogation can also occur when only he and a mirror are about.

> When I got up at last...and had learned to walk again, one day I took a hand glass and went to a long mirror to look at myself, and I went alone. I didn't want anyone...to know how I felt when I saw myself for the first time. But there was no noise, no out cry; I didn't scream with rage when I saw myself. I just felt numb. That person in the mirror couldn't be me. I felt inside like a healthy, ordinary, lucky person—oh, not like the one in the mirror! Yet when I turned my face to the mirror there were my own eyes looking back, hot with shame...when I did not cry or make any sound, it became impossible that I should speak of it to anyone, and the confusion and the panic of my discovery were locked inside me then and there, to be faced alone, for a very long time to come.[12]

> Over and over I forgot what I had seen in the mirror. It could not penetrate into the interior of my mind and become an integral part of me. I felt as if it had nothing to do with me; it was only a disguise. But it was not the kind the of disguise which is put on voluntarily by the person who wears it, and which is intended to confuse other people as to one's identity. My disguise had been put on me without my consent of knowledge like the ones in fairy tails, and it was I myself who was confused by it, as to my own identity. I looked in the mirror, and was horror-struck because I did not recognize myself. In the place where I was standing, with that persistent romantic elation in me, as if I were a favored fortunate person to whom everything was possible, I saw a stranger, a little pitiable, hideous figure, and a face that became, as I stared at it, painful and blushing with shame. It was only a disguise, but it was on me, for life. It was there, it was there, it was real. Everyone of those encounters was like a blow on the head, They left me dazed and dumb and senseless every time, until slowly and stubbornly my robust persistent illusion of well-being and of personal beauty spread all through me again, and I forgot the irrelevant reality and was all unprepared and vulnerable again.[13]

The central feature of the stigmatized individual's situation in life can now be stated. It is a question of what is often, if vaguely, called "acceptance." Those who have dealings with him fail to accord him the respect and regard which the uncontaminated aspects of his social identity have led them to anticipate extending, and have led him to anticipate receiving; he echoes this denial by finding that some of his own attributes warrant it.

Notes

[1] T. Parker and R. Allerton, 1962. *The Courage of His Convictions.* London: Hutchinson and Company:109.

[2] In this connection see the review by M Meltzer, "Countermanipulation through Malingering," in A. Biderman and H. Zimmer, eds., *The Manipulation of Human Behavior.* (New York: John Wiley & Sons, 1961): 277–304.

[3] In recent history, especially in Britain, low class status functioned as an important tribal stigma, the sins of the parents, or at least their milieu, being visited on the child, should the child rise improperly far above his initial station. The management of class stigma is of course a central theme in the English novel.

[4] D. Riesman, "Some Observations Concerning Marginally," *Phylon,* Second Quarter, 1951: 122.

[5] The case regarding the mental patients is presented by T.J. Scheff in a forthcoming paper.

[6] In regard to the blind, see E. Henrich and L. Kriegel, eds., *Experiments in Survival* (New York: Association for the Aid of Crippled Children, 1961): 152 and 186; and H. Chevigny, *My Eyes Have a Cold Nose* (New Haven, Conn: Yale University Press, paperbound, 1962): 201.

[7] In the words of one blind woman, "I was asked to endorse a perfume, presumably because being sightless my sense of smell was super-discriminating." See T. Keitlen (with N. Lobsenz), *Farewell to Fear.* (New York: Avon, 1962): 10.

[8] A. G. Gowman, *The War Blind in American Social Structure.* (New York: American Foundation for the Blind, 1957): 198.

[9] For examples, see F. Macgregor *et al., Facial Deformities and Plastic Surgery* (Springfield, Ill.: Charles C. Thomas, 1953).

[10] The notion of "normal human being" may have its source in the medical approach to humanity or in the tendency of largescale bureaucratic organizations, such as the nation state, to treat all members in some respects as equal. Whatever its origins, it seems to provide the basic imagery through which laymen currently conceive of themselves. Interestingly, a convention seems to have emerged in popular life-story writing where a questionable person proves his claim to normalcy by citing his acquisition of a spouse and children, and, oddly, by attesting to his spending Christmas and Thanksgiving with them.

[11] A criminal's view of this nonacceptance is presented in Parker and Allerton, op cit.: 110–111.

[12] K. B. Hathaway, *The Little Locksmith* (New York: Coward-McCann, 1943): in B Wright, *Physical Disability-A Psychological Approach.* (New York: Harper & Row, 1960):157.

[13] Ibid.: 46–47. For general treatments of the self-disliking sentiments, see K. Lewin, *Resolving Social Conflicts,* Part III (New York: Harper & Row, 1948); A. Kardiner and L. Ovesey, *The Mark of Oppression: A Psychosocial Study of the American Negro* (New York: W. W. Norton & Company, 1951); and E. H. Erikson, *Childhood and Society* (New York: W. W. Norton & Company, 1950).

Chapter 44

DEVIANCE DISAVOWAL:
MANAGEMENT OF STRAINED INTERACTION
BY THE VISIBLY HANDICAPPED

Fred Davis

Interviews I conducted with a small number of very articulate and socially skilled informants who were visibly handicapped. I inquired into their handling of the imputation that they were not "normal, like everyone else." This imputaion usually expresses itself in a pronounced stickiness of interactional flow and in the embarrassment of the normal, by which he conveys the all too obvious message that he is having more difficulty in relating to the handicapped person[1] than he would to "just an ordinary man or woman." Frequently he will make faux pas, slips of the tongue, revealing gestures, and inadvertent remarks which overtly betray this attitude and place the handicapped person in an even more delicate situation (see Goffman, 1956; 1957; 1959). The triggering of such a chain of interpersonal incidents is more likely with new persons than with those with whom the handicapped have well-established and continuing relations. Hence, the focus here is on more or less sociable occasions, it being these in which interactional discomfort is felt most acutely and coping behavior is brought into relief most sharply....

[T]he analysis will attempt to delineate in transactional terms the stages through which a sociable relationship with a normal typically passes, assuming of course, that the confrontation takes place and that both parties possess sufficient social skill to sustain a more than momentary engagement.

For present purposes we shall designate these stages as: (1) fictional acceptance, (2) the facilitation of reciprocal role-taking around a normalized projection of self, and (3) the institutionalization in the relationship of a definition of self that is normal in its moral dimension, however qualified it may be with respect to its situational contexts. As we shall indicate, the unfolding of these stages comprises what may be thought of as a process of deviance disavowal or normalization[2] depending on whether one views the process from the vantage point of the "deviant" actor or his alters.[3]

Fictional Acceptance

In Western society the overture phases of a sociable encounter are to a pronounced degree regulated by highly elastic fictions of equality and normalcy. In meeting those with whom we are neither close nor familiar, manners dictate that we refrain from remarking on or otherwise reacting too obviously to those aspects of their persons

508

which in the privacy of our thoughts betoken important differences between ourselves. In America at least, these fictions tend to encompass sometimes marked
divergences in social status as well as a great variety of expressive styles; and, it is
perhaps the extreme flexibility of such fictions in our culture rather than, as is
mistakenly assumed by many foreign observers, their absence that accounts for the
seeming lack of punctiliousness in American manners. The point is nicely illustrated
in the following news item:

NUDE TAKES A STROLL IN MIAMI

Miami, Fla., Nov, 13 (UPI)-A shapely brunette slowed traffic to a snail's pace
here yesterday with a 20-minute nude stroll through downtown Miami...

"The first thing I knew something was wrong," said Biscayne Bay bridgetender
E.E. Currey, who was working at his post about one block away, "was when I saw
traffic was going unusually slow."

Currey said he looked out and called police. They told him to stop the woman, he
said.

Curry said he walked out of his little bridge house, approached the woman
nervously, and asked, "Say, girl, are you lost?"

"Yes," she replied. "I am looking for my hotel."

Currey offered help and asked, "Say, did you lose your clothes?"

"No," he said the woman replied, "Why?"

Currey said that he had to step away for a moment to raise the bridge for a ship
and the woman walked away....(San Francisco Chronicle, November 14, 1960)

Unlike earlier societies and some present-day ones in which a visible handicap
automatically relagates the person to a castelike, inferior status like that of mendicant,
clown, or thief—or more rarely to an elevated one like that of oracle or healer—in our
society the visibly handicapped are customarily accorded, save by children,[4] the
surface acceptance that democratic manners guarantee to nearly all. But, as regards
sociability, this proves a mixed blessing for many. Although the polite fictions do
afford certain entree rights, as fictions they can too easily come to serve as substitutes
for "the real thing" in the minds of their perpetrators. The interaction is kept starved
at a bare subsistence level of sociability. As with the poor relation at the wedding
party, so is the reception given the handicapped person in many social situations:
Sufficient that he is here, he should not expect to dance with the bride.

At this stage of the encounter, the interactional problem confronting the visibly
handicapped person is the delicate one of not permitting his identity to be circumscribed by the fiction while at the same time playing along with it and showing
appropriate regard for its social legitimacy. For, as transparent and confining as the
fiction is, it frequently is the only basis upon which the contact can develop into
something more genuinely sociable. In those instances in which the normal fails or
refuses to render even so small a gesture toward normalizing the situation, there exists
almost no basis for the handicapped person to successfully disavow his deviance.[5]
The following occurrence related by a young female informant is an apt, if somewhat
extreme illustration:

> I was visiting my girlfriend's house and I was sitting in the lobby waiting
> for her when this woman comes out of her apartment and starts asking me

questions. She just walked right up. I didn't know her from Adam, I never saw her before in my life. "Gee, what do you have? How long have you been that way? Oh gee, that's terrible." And so I answered her questions, but I got very annoyed and wanted to say, "Lady, mind your own business."

"Breaking Through"-Facilitating Normalized Role-Taking

In moving beyond fictional acceptance, what takes place essentially is a redefinitional process in which the handicapped person projects images, attitudes, and concepts of self which encourage the normal to identify with him (i.e., "take his role") in terms other than those associated with imputations of deviance (Mead, 1934; Strauss, 1959:44–88). Coincidentally, in broadening the area of minor verbal involvements, this also functions to drain away some of the stifling burden of unspoken awareness that, as we have seen, so taxes ease of interaction. The normal is cued into a larger repertoire of appropriate responses, and even when making what he, perhaps mistakenly, regards as an inappropriate response (for example, catching himself in the use of such a word as *cripple* or *blind*) the handicapped person can by his response relieve him of his embarrassment. One young informant insightfully termed the process "breaking through":

> The first reaction a normal individual or good-legger had is, "Oh gee, there's a fellow in a wheelchair," or "there's a fellow with a brace." And they don't' say, "Oh gee, there is so-and-so, he's handsome," or "he's intelligent," or "he's a bore," or what have you. And then as the relationship develops they don't see the handicap. It doesn't exist any more. And that's the point that you as a handicapped individual become sensitive to. You know after talking with someone for a while when they don't see the handicap any more. That's when you've broken through.

What this process signifies from a social-psychological standpoint is that as the handicapped person expands the interactional nexus he simultaneously disavows the deviancy latent in his status; concurrently, to the degree to which the normal is led to reciprocally assume the redefining (and perhaps unanticipated) self-attitudes proffered by the handicapped person, he comes to normalize (i.e., view as more like himself) those aspects of the other which at first connoted deviance for him. (Sometimes, as we shall see, the normal's normalizing is so complete that it is unwittingly applied to situations in which the handicapped person cannot possibly function "normally" due to sheer physical limitations). These dynamics might also be termed a process of identification. The term is immaterial, except that in "identifying" or "taking the role of the other" much more is implicated sociologically than a mere subjective congruence of responses. The fashioning of shared perspectives also implies a progressively more binding legitimation of the altered self-representations enacted in the encounter; that is, having once normalized his perception of the handicapped person, it becomes increasingly more compromising—self-discrediting, as it were—for the normal to revert to treating him as a deviant again.

The ways in which the visibly handicapped person can go about disavowing deviance are, as we have stated, many and varied. These range from relatively straightforward conversational offerings in which he alludes in passing to his involvement in a normal round of activities to such forms of indirection as interjecting taboo or privatized references by way of letting the normal know that he does not take offense at the latter's uneasiness or regard it as a fixed obstacle toward achieving rapport. In the above quote, for example, the informant speaks of "good-leggers," an ingroup term from his rehabilitation hospital days, which along with "dirty normals" he sometimes uses with new acquaintances "because it has a humorous connotation...and lots of times it puts people at their ease."[6]

Still other approaches to disavowing deviance and bridging fictional acceptance include: an especially attentive and sympathetic stance with respect to topics introduced by the normal, showing oneself to be a comic, wit, or other kind of gifted participant, and, for some, utilizing the normalization potential inherent in being seen in the company of a highly presentable normal companion (Gowman, 1956). These, and others too numerous to mention, are not of course invariably or equally successful in all cases; neither are such resources equally available to all handicapped persons, nor are the handicapped equally adept at exploiting them. As a class of corrective strategies however, they have the common aim of overcoming the interactional barrier that lies between narrow fictional acceptance and more spontaneous forms of relatedness.

Inextricably tied in with the matter of approach are considerations of setting, activity, and social category of participants, certain constellations of which are generally regarded as favorable for successful deviance disavowal and normalization while others are thought unfavorable. Again, the ruling contingencies appear to be the extent to which the situation is seen as containing elements in it which: (1) contextually reduce the threat posed by the visible handicap to the rules and assumptions of the particular sociable occasion, and (2) afford the handicapped person opportunities for "breaking through" beyond fictional acceptance.

The relevance of one or both of these is apparent in the following social situations and settings about which my informants expressed considerable agreement as regards their preferences, aversions, and inner reactions. To begin with, mention might again be made of the interactional rule violations frequently experienced at the hands of small children. Many of the informants were quite open in stating that a small child at a social occasion caused them much uneasiness and cramped their style because they were concerned with how, with other adults present, they would handle some bare-faced question from the child. Another category of persons with whom many claimed to have difficulty is the elderly. Here the problem was felt to be the tendency of old people to indulge in patronizing sympathy, an attitude which peculiarly resists redefinition because of the fulsome virtue it attributes to itself. In another context several of the informants laid great stress on the importance of maintaining a calm exterior whenever the physical setting unavoidably exposed them to considerable bodily awkwardness. (At the same time, of course, they spoke of the wisdom of avoiding, whenever possible, such occasions altogether). Their attitude was that to expressively reflect gracelessness and a loss of control would result in further interactional obstacles toward assimilating the handicapped person to a normal status.

> It makes me uncomfortable to watch anyone struggling, so I try to do what I must as inconspicuously as possible. In new situations or in strange places, even though I may be very anxious, I will maintain a deadly calm. For example, if people have to lift the chair and I'm scared that they are going to do it wrong, I remain perfectly calm and am very direct in the instructions I give.

As a final example, there is the unanimity with which the informants expressed a strong preference for the small, as against the large or semipublic social gathering. Not only do they believe that, as one handicapped person among the nonhandicapped, they stand out more at large social gatherings, but also that in the anonymity which numbers further there resides a heightened structural tendency for normals to practice avoidance relations with them. The easy assumption on such occasions is that "some other good soul" will take responsibility for socializing with the handicapped person. Even in the case of the handicapped person who is forward and quite prepared to take the initiative in talking to others, the organization and ecology of the large social gathering is usually such as to frustrate his attempts to achieve a natural, nondeviant place for himself in the group. As one young man, a paraplegic, explained:

> The large social gathering presents a special problem. It's a matter of repetition. When you're in a very large group of people whom you don't know, you don't have an opportunity of talking to three, four, or five at a time. Maybe you'll talk to one or two usually. After you've gone through a whole basic breakdown in making a relationship with one— after all, it's only a cocktail party—to do it again, and again, and again, it's wearing and it's no good. You don't get the opportunity to really develop something.

Institutionalization of the Normalized Relationship

In "breaking through" many of the handicapped are confronted by a delicate paradox, particularly in those of their relationships which continue beyond the immediate occasion. Having disavowed deviance and induced the other to respond to him as he would to a normal, the problem then becomes one of sustaining the normalized definition in the face of the many small amendments and qualifications that must frequently be made to it. The person confined to a wheelchair, for example, must brief a new acquaintance on what to do and how to help when they come to stairs, doorways, vehicle entrances etc. Further briefings and rehearsals may be required for social obstructions as well: for example, how to act in an encounter with—to cite some typical situations at random—an overly helpful person, a waitress who communicates to the handicapped person only through his companion, a person who stares in morbid fascination (Gowman, 1956).

Generally, such amendments and special considerations are as much as possible underplayed in the early stages of the relationship because, as in the case of much minority group protest, the fundamental demand of the handicapped is that they first be granted an irreducibly equal and normal status, it being only then regarded as fitting and safe to admit to certain incidental incapacities, limitations, and needs. At some point, however, the latter must be broached if the relationship to the normal is to endure in viable form. But to integrate effectively a major claim to "normalcy" with numerous minor waivers of the same claim is a tricky feat and one which exposes the relationship to the many situational and psychic hazards of apparent duplicity: the tension of transferring the special arrangements and understandings worked out between the two to situations and settings in which everyone else is "behaving normally"; the sometimes lurking suspicion of the one that it is only guilt or pity that cements the relationship, of the other that the infirmity is being used exploitatively, and of onlookers that there is something "neurotic" and "unhealthy" about it all.[7]

From my informants' descriptions it appears that this third, "normal, but..." stage of the relationship, if it endures, is institutionalized mainly in either one of two ways. In the first, the normal normalizes his perceptions to such an extent as to suppress his effective awareness of many of the areas in which the handicapped person's behavior unavoidably deviates from the normal standard. In this connection several of the informants complained that a recurring problem they have with close friends is that the latter frequently overlook the fact of the handicap and the restrictions it imposes on them. The friends thoughtlessly make arrangements and involve them in activities in which they, the handicapped, cannot participate conveniently or comfortably.

The other major direction in which the relationship is sometimes institutionalized is for the normal to surrender some of his normalcy by joining the handicapped person in a marginal, half-alienated, half-tolerant, outsider's orientation to "the Philistine world of normals."[8] Gowman (1956) nicely describes the tenor and style of this relationship and its possibilities for sharply disabusing normals of their stereotyped approaches to the handicapped. E'pater le bourgeois behavior is often prominently associated with it, as is a certain strictly ingroup license to lampoon and mock the handicap in a way which would be regarded as highly offensive were it to come from an uninitiated normal. Thus, a blind girl relates how a sighted friend sometimes chides her by calling her "a silly blink." A paraplegic tells of the old friend who tries to revive his flagging spirits by telling him not to act "like a helpless cripple." Unlike that based on overnormalization, the peculiar strength of this relationship is perhaps its very capacity to give expressive scope to the negative reality of the larger world of which it is inescapably a part while simultaneously removing itself from a primary identification with it.

REFERENCES

Goffman, Erving (1956). "Embarrassment and Social Organization." Pp. 264–71. *American Journal of Sociology* 62:264–71.

Goffman, Erving (1957). "Alienation from Interaction. "*Human Relations* 10:47–60.

Goffman, Erving (1959). *Presentation of Self in Everyday Life*. New York: Doubleday and Co.

Gowman, Alan G. (1956). "Blindness and the Role of the Companion. *Social Problems* 4:1–6.

Mead, George H. (1934). *Mind, Self and Society*. Chicago: University of Chicago Press.

Schwartz, Charlotte G. (1957). "Perspectives on Deviance—Wives' Definitions of their Husbands' Mental Illness." Pp.275–*Psychiatry* 20:275–91.

Strauss, Anselm (1959). *Mirrors and Masks*. Glencoe, Illinois: The Free Press.

Strong, Samuel M. (1946). "Negro-White Relations as Reflected in Social Types." *American Journal of Sociology* 52:24.

NOTES

[1] Throughout this paper, whether or not the term "handicap" or "handicapped" is joined by the qualifier "visible," it should be read in this way. Unfortunately, it will not be possible to discuss here that which sociologically distinguishes the situation of the visibly handicapped from that of persons whose physical handicaps are not visible or readily apparent, and how both differ from what is termed the "sick role." These are thought important distinctions whose analysis might illuminate key questions in the study of deviance.

[2] As used here the term "normalization" denotes a process whereby alter for whatever reason comes to view as normal and morally acceptable that which initially strikes him as odd, unnatural, "crazy," deviant, etc., irrespective of whether his perception was in the first instance reasonable, accurate or justifiable. Cf. Schwartz, 1957.

[3] 3.Because of the paper's focus on the visible handicapped person, in what follows his interactional work is highlighted to the relative glossing over of that of the normal. Actually, the work of normalization calls for perhaps as much empathic expenditure as that of deviance disavowal and is, obviously, fully as essential for repairing the interactional breach occasioned by the encounter.

[4] The blunt questions and stares of small children are typically of the "Emperor's Clothes" variety. "Mister, why is your face like that?" "Lady, what are you riding around in that for? Can't you walk?" Nearly all of my informants spoke of how unnerving such incidents were for them, particularly when other adults were present. Nonetheless, some claimed to value the child's forthrightness a good deal more than they did the genteel hypocrisy of many adults.

[5] On the other side of the coin there are of course some handicapped persons who are equally given to undermining sociable relations by intentionally flaunting the handicap so that the fiction becomes extremely difficult to sustain. An equivalent of the "bad nigger" type described by Strong (1946), such persons were (as in Strong's study)regarded with a mixture of admiration and censure by a number of my informants. Admiration, because the cruel stripping away of pretenses and forcing os issues was thought morally refreshing, especially since, as the informants themselves recognized, many normals refuse to grant anything more than fictional acceptance while at the some time imagining themselves ennobled for having make the small sacrifice. Censure, because of the conviction that such behavior could hardly improve matters in the long run and would make acceptance even more difficult for other handicapped persons who late came into contact with a normal who had received such treatment.

[6] Parallel instances can easily be cited from minority group relations as, for example, when a Jew in conversation with a non-Jew might introduce a Yiddish phrase by way of suggesting that the other's covert identification of him as a Jew need not inhibit the interaction unduly. In some situations this serves as a subtle means of declaring, "O.K., I know what's bothering you. Now that I've said it, let's forget about it and move on to something else."

[7] The rhetoric of race relations reflects almost identical rationalizations and "insights" which are meant among other things to serve as cautions for would-be transgressors. "Personally I have nothing against Negroes" (the handicapped), but it would be bad for my reputation if I were seen socializing with them." "She acts nice now, but with the first argument she'll call you a dirty Jew (good-for-nothing cripple)." Regardless of how sympathetic you are toward Negroes (the disabled), the way society feels about them you'd have to be a masochist to marry one.

[8] Students of race relations will recognize in this a phenomenon closely akin to "inverse passing," as when a white becomes closely identified with Negroes and passes into a Negro subculture.

Chapter 45

RETURN TO SENDER:
THE REINTEGRATIVE STIGMA-MANAGEMENT STRATEGIES
OF EX-PSYCHIATRIC PATIENTS

Nancy J. Herman

Although scholars have addressed the exit phase of deviant careers (cf. Adler and Adler (1983); Faupel (1991); Frazier (1976); Harris (1973); Glasser et al. (1983); Inciardi (1970); Irwin (1970); Luckenbill and Best (1981); Meisenhelder (1977); and Ray (1961), the issue of reintegrating deviants back into society has received little sociological attention. So too has little attention been given to the wide array of factors affecting role exit and reintegration.

Brown (1991) focused on the reintegration of deviants who became "professional ex's"—individuals who capitalized on their deviant identity and status by moving into therapeutic counselling careers. Similarly, Braithwaite (1989) studied the effects of shaming individuals into role exit. Only a few studies (Chambliss 1984); Shover (1983, 1985); Snodgrass (1982) centered on the lives of ex-deviants in order to document their post-deviant worlds These studies focused on the effects of former (prior) attributes, activities, or processing on their subsequent lives. Another notable exception is Adler (1992), who conducted a follow up study of upper-level drug dealers and smugglers and the factors affecting reintegration into society. She found that individuals returned to the mainstream due to certain structural factors, and when trafficking was no longer considered enjoyable but anxiety-provoking. Moreover, Adler documented the problems ex-traffickers faced in attempting to secure or return to mainstream, legitimate, occupational realms and the career-based factors which aided or inhibited reintegration.

With respect to the sociological literature on the stigma of the mentally retarded and social reintegration, scholars have addressed: (1) public attitudes toward the mentally ill (Bord 1970; Cochrane and Nieradzik 1985; D'Arcy and Brockman 1977; Farina and Ring 1965; Lamy 1966; Nunnally 1961; Taylor et al. 1979; Trute and Loewen 1978; and Whatley 1959); (2) correlates of societal acceptance or rejection of ex-psychiatric patients (Rabinowitz, 1982); (3) family acceptance or stigmatization of former mental patients (Clausen 1981; Doll et al. 1976; Kreisman and Joy 1974; (4) stigma experienced by relatives of former patients (Freeman and Simmons 1961; Segal et al. 1980); (5) the stigma of mental illness and available housing (Goldmeir et al. 1977); (6) the stigma of seeing a psychiatrist (Bar-Levav 1976); and (7) employer responses to psychiatric stigmata (Miller and Dawson 1965; Webber and Orcutt 1982).

Despite the preponderance of sociological research on the mentally ill, there is a dearth of ethnographically-based studies dealing with the post-hospital lives of ex-psychiatric patients Such studies, as they do exist, deal largely with chronic ex-patients living in halfway houses or boarding homes, or involved in specific aftercare treatment programs (Cheadle et al. 1978; Estroff 1981; Lamb and Goertzel, 1977; Reynolds and Farberow 1977). Little systematic attention has been given to ex-patients' perceptions of mental illness as a stigmatizable/stigmatizing attribute,[1] the numerous problems they face on the outside, the ways such persons manage discreditable information about themselves in the context of social interaction with others, and the consequences of employing these strategies for altering their deviant identities and social reintegration. In this paper I address these deficits in the sociological literature by presenting ethnographic evidence from a study of 146 non-chronic,[2] ex-psychiatric patients. First, I begin with a discussion of the setting and methods used in this study. Second, I illustrate how ex-patients came to perceive their attribute as potentially-stigmatizing. Third, I analyze the five strategies these persons developed and employed in their "management work." Finally, I address the implications of adopting such stratagems for identity transformation and social reintegration. In this paper I hope to contribute to the existing literature on stigma, deviant career exit, management work, and the reintegration of deviants.

Setting and Methods

My interest in mental illness and psychiatric patients has been a longstanding one. My father was employed as an occupational therapist for twenty-five years at a large psychiatric institution in a metropolitan city in Ontario, Canada. Throughout my childhood and adolescent years, I made frequent trips to the institution interacting with many of the patients on the "admission" and "back" wards, in the hospital canteen, in the occupational therapy workshop, and on the grounds. Moreover, during those years, my father often brought a number of his patients into our home (those, in particular whose families had abandoned them or who did not have any relatives) to spend Easter, Thanksgiving, and Christmas holidays with our family.

My childhood interest in mental patients sparked my initial involvement in this topic, and I began to study mental patients in 1980 as a graduate student at McMaster University. Having a father who was highly-esteemed by the institutional gatekeepers greatly facilitated my access [although I encountered numerous gatekeeper problems during the course of the study in their effort to secure control over "constructions of reality" (Berger and Luckmann 1966) and "definitions of the situation" (Thomas 1931); [see Herman (1981a) for details]. I spent eight months ethnographically studying the institutionalization of psychiatric patients (Herman, 1981a). After completing this study on the pre- and in-patient phases of the patients' careers, I became interested in learning about the post-patient phase of their careers. As a result of the movement toward deinstitutionalization, chronic patients, once institutional-ized for periods of years, were being released into the community. Moreover, newly-diagnosed patients were being hospitalized for brief periods of time and shortly released. I became interested in examining the post-hospital social worlds and experiences of these ex-psychiatric clients.

I began a four year research project on this topic in January, 1981 (see Herman, 1986). In contrast to my earlier study on institutionalized mental patients, where I encountered numerous problems with institutional gatekeepers, this time I encountered relatively few such problems. Rather than dealing with the same provincial institution to obtain a list of discharged patients, I contacted the Director of Psychiatric Services and Professor of Psychiatry at the Medical School affiliated with my university. After hearing about my research proposal he granted his support for the project and served as my sponsor to the Ethics Committee of the hospital. Approximately one month later, I was given access to a listing of discharged (chronic[3] and non-chronic) ex-psychiatric patients who had been released from the psychiatric wards of seven general hospitals and from two psychiatric institutions in the Southern Ontario area between 1975 and including 1981. In order to protect the identities of those ex-patients not wishing to participate in my study, and to avoid litigation against the hospital for violating rights of confidentiality, I agreed to only be given access to the names of those individuals who agreed to participate. A stratified random sample of 300 ex-patients was formed from the overall discharge list. Upon drawing this sample, the hospitals sent out a letter to each potential subject on my behalf, outlining the general nature of the study, my identity, and my affiliation. Two weeks later, hospital officials made follow-up telephone calls asking potential subjects if they were willing to participate in the study. I was subsequently given a list containing the names of 285 willing participants, 146 non-chronic and 139 chronic ex-patients.[4]

I initially conducted informal interviews with each of the ex-patients in coffee shops, their homes, in malls, or at their places of work. The interviews lasted from three to five and one half hours. These interviews not only provided me with a wealth of information about the social worlds of ex-patients, but many subjects invited me to subsequently attend and participate with them in various social settings, including self-help group meetings, activist group meetings and protest marches, and therapy sessions. In addition, I frequently met ex-patients where they worked during coffee and lunch breaks and was able to observe them interacting with co-workers. I ate lunches and dinners in their homes (as they did in mine) watched them interacting with family members, friends, and neighbors. Each Wednesday afternoon, I met a group of six ex-patients at a local donut shop where they would discuss the problems they were facing "on the outside" and collectively search for possible remedies.

Perceptions of Mental Illness as Stigma

In his classic work, *Stigma*, Goffman (1963:4) distinguished between stigmata that are "discrediting" are those that are "discreditable;" the former refer to attributes that are immediately apparent to others, such as obesity, physical abnormalities, and blindness; the latter refer to attributes that are not visible or readily apparent to others, such as being a secret homosexual or ex-prisoner. Mental illness, is conceptualized, for the most part, as a discreditable or potentially-stigmatizing attribute in that it is not readily apparent to others. It is equally important to note however, that for some ex-psychiatric patients, mental illness is a deeply discrediting attribute. Many ex-patients, especially the chronic ones, were rendered discredited by inappropriate patterns of social interaction and the side-effects of medication, which took the forms of twitching, swaying, jerking and other bizarre mannerisms (see Herman 1986).[5] When ex-patients made voluntary disclosures of personal information about their psychiatric histories or other people somehow became aware of their histories, ex-patients were categorized in negative terms, as representing some sort of personal failure to "measure up" to the rest of society. Tom, a 45 year old male, summed it up for most of the ex-patients:

> Having been diagnosed as a psychiatric patient with psychotic tenden-
> cies is the worst thing that has ever happened to me. It's shitty to be
> mentally ill; it's not something to be proud of. It makes you realize just
> how different you are from everybody else—they're normal and you're
> not. Things are easy for them; things are hard for you. Life's a ball for
> them; life's a bitch for you! I'm like a mental cripple! I'm a failure at life!

The ex-psychiatric patients learned the social meaning of their "failing," that they possessed a potentially-stigmatizing attribute, in the following manners: (1) through formal societal reaction, official labeling and institutional processing; (2) through direct, negative, disvaluing post-treatment experiences with others; (3) through a combination of (1) and (2); or (4) through self-labeling.

Societal Reaction, Official Labeling, and Institutional Processing

One of the major means by which ex-psychiatric patients learned that they possessed a stigmatizable attribute was through societal reaction, official labeling of their behavior as "mental illness," and subsequent institutional processing. In the context of the pre- and in-patient phases of their "moral careers" (Goffman 1961), these persons not only acquired a new conception of self as mental patient, but also learned about the stigma attached to this label. In the pre-patient phase, 25 percent of those studied learned this information through official labeling by such persons as the clergy, the police, and the family physician, etc., while others learned, through unofficial, informal labeling by family, friends and co-workers. Billy, a 26 year old ex-patient, discussing the role of official labeling in "educating" him about his identity and the stigma associated with it, stated:

> They watched me for a time, thought I was acting weird, stepped in and
> called me "crazy." From that moment on, things changed. Before I was
> considered a fairly normal fellow—that's how I saw myself. From the
> time that they pinned that new name on me—"mental patient"—"men-
> tally sick" they made everyone see me differently. And it even got me to
> thinking about me as being "sick" too....I soon learned what I was in for—
> I mean what came along with the name-tag. I found that mental illness is
> a disgrace—your family and the doctors and even the attendants treat you
> like you got leprosy—why they call you mental and put you in the

hospital, you realize now you have a *pock* that makes people act weird toward you.

Moreover, much of what mental patients learned about their stigma was transmitted to them during prolonged forced interaction with others in an institution who were also being transformed into mental patients by the institutional staff. Calling attention to the role of hospitalization in educating him that he possessed a discreditable attribute, Mario, a middle-aged non-chronic, expressed:

> I learned that I had a defiling trait—that's what mental illness is. I learned this information from the moment I was hospitalized at "Sunnybrook." When you go into a place like that, you really learn the ropes. I mean, they not only want you to believe you're sick, in order that you get better, but by virtue of the fact that you're on the ward every day with fifty other "mentals"—they're the ones who teach you what it means to be mentally ill—you know have a *mark of Cain*—a blight that will affect the way everyone acts towards you.

Post-Hospital Experiences with "Normals"

A second means through which ex-psychiatric patients came to see their condition as discreditable or potentially-stigmatizing was through direct post-hospital exposure to members of society who rejected or disapproved of them. Approximately 32 percent of the ex-patients in this study learned the social meaning of their "failing" in this manner. Joan, an elderly female released from the hospital three weeks before, indicated that she learned that she possessed a stigmatizable attribute through negative experiences with her family:

> When I was released, I presumed that I could resume with the "good times" once again. I was treated—I paid my dues. But I was wrong. From the first moment I set foot back onto the streets of "Wilsonville" and I tried to return to my kids, but they didn't want me...I learned the hard way that my kids didn't want nothing to do with me—they were scared to let me near the grandkids—that I might do something to them. They told me this right to my face...Having mental illness is like having any other illness like heart troubles, but people sure do treat you different. If you have heart troubles, you get treated, and then you come out good as new and your family still loves you. But that's not so with mental illness...you come out and people treat you worse than a dog!

Just as family members sometimes "taught" ex-psychiatric patients that they possessed a stigmatizable attribute, so too, did co-workers, neighbors and friends sometimes provide such information. As Art stated:

I worked as a chartered accountant for several years with this firm. After seven months of hospitalization, I was released and I felt pretty good— that I could cope with things again. However, to my amazement, my colleagues treated me differently. We all used to go to lunch together, but after my release, they said they no longer eat lunch; neither do they play golf or go out for a few drinks after work—the things we used to do together. They used to huddle in the doorway near the water cooler whispering and when I came along they clammed up....After a number of these incidents, I realized the stigma attached to being a discharged patient.

Societal Reaction, Official Labeling, Institutional Processing and Post-Hospital Experience with "Normals"

A third group of ex-psychiatric patients reported discovering the social meaning of their failing through a combination of institutional and interpersonal means. Approximately 18 percent of the ex-patients in this study reported that they came to regard mental illness as a discreditable attribute through a combination of official labeling and negative post-hospital experiences with family, friends, and others. Don, a 34 year old ex-patient, recently released for the fourth time, remarked:

The first time I got out, I was so naive, I thought things would be like they once were. How wrong I was. I now know the truth. You first learn about what it means to be a mental patient right there in the hospital—the attendants, the nurses and even the cleaners get this message through to you that you are somehow "sub-human" or "dirty" with your illness. And even the old-timers on the ward get you to thinking along these lines too....And each time I was let out, friends or people I thought were friends treated me like I had the plague or made cruel jokes. I finally got it into my head that I really did have something that was disgraceful!

In a similar vein, Charlene, a 39 year old ex-patient of Italian descent, spoke of the manner by which she learned the social meaning of her failing:

I learned what it means to have mental illness—I mean that it is something like a curse or a scar. First of all, after being discharged, my landlady and some of my neighbors would stare at me, or if they saw me coming, would run the other way. That was the first indication that I had something—a condition that was worse than having A.I.D.S. People treat you with fear....Also, this idea was pounded into me right there in the hospital by the staff. You get the feeling that you should be ashamed of what you've got. Being a mental patient really sucks!

Self-Labeling

One final means by which non-chronic ex-patients came to view themselves as possessing a potentially-stigmatizing attribute was through self-labeling (cf. Lorber 1967; Robins 1980; Schur 1979; Sagarin and Kelly 1980; Thoits 1985). Schneider and Conrad (1980:35) described the importance of self-labeling when they said:

> Most sociological work on stigma assumes that the stigmatized learn the meaning of their attribute or performance primarily through direct exposure to rejection and disapproval from others. Less understood is the place of the perception of stigma—of what the putatively stigmatized think others think of them and 'their kind' and about how these others might react to disclosure.

Approximately seven percent of the ex-patients in this study indicated that they subjectively perceived mental illness to be personally stigmatizing, that is, likely to lead to personal debasement if discovered by others. Such persons labeled themselves as possessing some sort of "mental illness" or "psychological sickness" above and apart from any formal or informal reaction and official labeling. Similar to Scheff's (1984) findings, ex-patients learned and internalized, early in life, stereotypical imagery of mental illness and insanity—imagery that was constantly reaffirmed throughout their adult lives in the context of social interaction with others and through the mass media. So too did such persons learn and internalize stereotypical images of normality early in life—images that were constantly reaffirmed in ordinary social discourse. In short, by incorporating the stereotypes of "normal" and "crazy," some individuals self-labeled their behavior as "mental illness;" moreover, upon making such self-definitions, the ex-patients also realized the discreditable nature of the attribute of mental illness. Mabel, a 32 year old woman, hospitalized on four occasions in a psychiatric institution, recalled the manner by which she defined herself as being mentally ill and her perception of mental illness as personally stigmatizing:

> For me, I knew about mental illness and the stigma or negative effects that goes with it, before anyone had to hospitalize me, or even say that I might be "sick." You see, I've lived in the world for many years before going to the hospital; during that time I learned from the kids on the block, my friends, and on TV, and even from my folks what is healthy normal behavior and what ain't—like what is OK and what ain't. I watched so much TV in my time—the movies and the soaps about people having nervous breakdowns—so I knew in my heart of hearts that I was getting sick. I judged myself....And no one had to shun me to make me realize about the results of being mentally ill. I knew that my friends would treat me badly if they knew. You just know!

In short then, through internalization of stereotypical images of normality and insanity, some ex-patients (prior to official or unofficial labeling), defined themselves as being mentally ill; moreover, such stereotypes provided ex-patients with self-definitions of discreditability.

Mental Illness and Strategies of Information Management

Some studies on the discreditable (Edgerton 1967; Humphreys 1972; Ponse 1976) have suggested that individuals either disclose their attribute to others *or* make attempts to actively conceal such information about their selves. Other studies (Bell and Weinberg 1978; Miall 1986; Schneider and Conrad 1980; Veevers 1980) have suggested that being a "secret deviant" is far more complex than either choosing to disclose or not disclose one's "failing." These studies suggest that individuals *selectively* conceal such information about themselves at certain times, in certain situations, with certain individuals, and freely disclose the same information at other times, in other situations, with other individuals. Concealment and disclosure then, are contingent upon a "complex interaction of one's learned perceptions of the stigma [of their attribute], actual 'test' experiences with others before/or after disclosure, and the nature of the particular relationship involved" (Schneider and Conrad 1980:39).

The complex reality of how individuals selectively conceal and disclose information was evident in the case of non-chronic ex-psychiatric patients. Examination of their post-hospital worlds revealed that many ex-patients not only faced economic hardships, had problems coping in the community, and experienced adverse side-effects from their "meds,"[6] but also, that their perception of mental illness as a potentially-stigmatizing attribute presented severe problems in their lives. Many lived their lives in states of emotional turmoil, afraid and frustrated—deciding who to tell or not tell, when to tell and when not to tell, and how to tell. Joan, a 56 year old waitress, aptly summed it up for most non-chronics:

> It's a very difficult thing. It's not easy to distinguish the good ones from the bad ones . . . You've gotta figure out who you can tell about your illness and who you better not tell. It is a tremendous stress and strain that you have to live with 24 hours a day!

Ex-psychiatric patients learned how, with whom, and under which circumstances to disclose or conceal their discreditable aspects of self, largely through a process of trial and error, committing numerous *faux pas* along the way. Frank, a 60 year old factory worker, spoke of the number of mistakes he made in his "management work:"

> I was released over two years now. And since then, I've developed an ulcer trying to figure out how to deal with my "sickness"—that is, how or whether others could handle it or not. I screwed up things a few times when I told a couple of guys on the bowling team. I made a mistake and thought that they were my buddies and would accept it.

In fact, even if no *faux pas* were committed, there was no guarantee that others would accept proffered meanings and definitions of self. As Charlie, a 29 year old graduate student, hospitalized on three occasions, remarked:

> I'm not a stupid person. I learned how to handle effectively the negative
> aspects of my sickness—I mean how others view it. I've been doing OK
> now since my discharge, but still, each time I'm entering a new situation,
> I get anxious; I'm not always a hundred percent sure of whether to tell or
> not to—especially in the case of dating relationships. Even if you've had
> success in telling certain types of people, there's always the chance—and
> it happens more than you think, that people will just not "buy" what
> you're trying so desperately to "sell" them.

Nearly 80 percent of the non-chronics in this study engaged in some form of information control about their illnesses and past hospitalizations. Specifically, the stratagems adopted and employed by the ex-patients, resembling those observed in other deviant groups (cf. Davis 1961; Hewitt and Stokes 1975; Levitin 1975; Miall 1986; Schneider and Conrad 1980), included (1) selective concealment; (2) therapeutic disclosure; (3) preventive disclosure; and (4) political activism—stratagems adopted by ex-patients in their effort to lessen or avoid the stigma potential of mental illness, elevate self-esteem, renegotiate societal conceptions of mental illness as a discreditable attribute, and alter deviant identities.

Selective Concealment

Selective concealment may be defined as the selective withholding or disclosure of information about self perceived as discreditable in cases where secrecy is the major stratagem for handling information about an attribute. Especially during the time period directly following their psychiatric treatment, the majority of non-chronics had a marked desire to conceal such information about their selves from all others. Decisions about disclosure and concealment were made on the basis of their perceptions of others, that is, whether they were "safe others" or "risky others." So too were decisions based on prior, negative experiences with "certain types" of others. Speaking of her classification of others into "trustworthy" and "untrustworthy" others, Davina, a 46 year old secretary, institutionalized on seven occasions, said:

> It's like this. There are two types of people out there, "trustworthy"
> ones—the people who will be understanding and supportive and "un-
> trustworthy" ones. Out of all of my friends and relations and even the
> people I work with at the company, I only decided to tell my friend Sue.

Moreover, there was a hierarchical pattern of selective disclosure based upon the individual's perceived degree of closeness and the ex-patient's revealing his/her discreditable attribute. In general, such information was most frequently revealed to family members, followed by close friends, and then, acquaintances—a pattern also reflected in the literature on epileptics (Schneider and Conrad 1980) and involuntary childless women (Miall 1986). As Sarah, a 36 year old mother of two, put it:

> When I was discharged, I didn't automatically hide it from everyone the fact that I was hospitalized for a nervous breakdown again. But I didn't go and tell everyone either. I phoned and told my relatives in "Logenport" and I confided in two of my close, good friends here in town.

Further, selective disclosures to normal others were frequently made to test reactions. Similar to Schneider and Conrad's (1980) epileptics, the continued disclosure of ex-patients' mental illness was contingent upon responses they received to previous disclosures. Rudy, a 39 year old male, hospitalized on ten occasions, stated:

> You learn through trial and error. When I was let out back in 1976, I was still naive, you know. I decided to tell a few people. Boy, was that a mistake. They acted as if I had AIDS. Nobody wanted anything further to do with me . . . Since then, I've pretty much dummied up and not told anyone!

In those cases where concealment was the dominant strategy of information management, ex-patients usually disclosed only to one or two individuals. As Simon, a 25 year old ex-patient, aptly expressed:

> I decided from the moment that my treatment ended, I would tell as few people as possible about my stay in the psychiatric hospital. I figured that it would be for the best to "keep it under a lid" for the most part. So, to this day, I've only confided in my friend, Paul and a neighbor who had a similar illness a while back.

The employment of concealment as a stratagem of information management took the following forms: avoidance of selected "normals;" redirection of conversations; withdrawal; the use of disidentifiers, and the avoidance of stigma symbols. Speaking on his efforts to redirect conversations, Mark, a 34 year old non-chronic, explained:

> Look, you've got to remain on your toes at all times. More often than not, somebody brings up the topic about my past and starts probing around. Sometimes these people won't let up ... I use the tactic where I change the subject, answer their question with a question . . . I try to manipulate the conversation so it works out in my favor.

For still others, concealment of their discreditable attribute was achieved through withdrawal. Over two-thirds of the ex-patients in this study engaged in withdrawal as a form of concealment, especially during the early months following discharge. Speaking of his use of this technique, Harry, a college junior, remarked:

Sometimes when I'm at a party or some type of gathering with a number of people, I just remain pretty reticent. I don't participate too much in the conversations . . . I'm really unsure how much to tell other people. For the most part, I just keep pretty quiet and remain a wallflower. People may think I'm shy or stuckup, but I'd rather deal with that than with the consequences of others finding out that I'm a mental patient.

A third technique employed by over one-third of the ex-patients to conceal their discreditable aspects of self from others involved the use of disidentifiers (Goffman 1963:44). That is, ex-patients utilized misleading verbal or physical symbols in an effort to prevent normal others from discovering their "failing." Similar to homosexuals (Carrier 1976; Delph 1978), unwed parents (Christensen 1953; Pfuhl 1978), and lesbians (Ponse 1978), who frequently made use of disidentifiers in their management work, non-chronic ex-patients also employed such techniques. Specifically, disidentifiers took the form of making jokes about psychiatric patients while in the presence of "normal" others, and participating in protests *against* the integration of ex-patients into the community. Mike, a 26 year old ex-patient, recently released after three hospitalizations, remarked (with some remorse) on his use of this tactic:

They wanted to use this house down the street for a group home for discharged patients. All the neighbors on the street were up in arms over it. It didn't upset me personally, but the neighbors made up this petition, and to protect myself, I not only signed it, but I also went door-to-door convincing other neighbors to sign it and "keep those mentals out"....I felt sort of bad afterwards, but what else could I do?

A final form of concealing information on the part of ex-patients was through the avoidance of stigma symbols (cf. Goffman 1963:43)—signs that would bring into the forefront or disclose individuals' discreditable attribute. It is interesting to note that the data presented here on non-chronics and their avoidance of stigma symbols supports observations made of other deviant groups, for example, transsexuals (Bogdan 1974; Kando 19773) and unwed fathers (Pfuhl 1978). Among the 146 ex-patients studied, over two-thirds avoided contact with such stigma symbols as other ex-mental patients with whom they had become friends while institutionalized, as well as self-help groups for ex-patients. So too, did they avoid frequenting drop-in centers, attending dances and bingos for ex-patients, and in general, placing themselves where other "patients and ex-patients hung out." For still others, avoidance of stigma symbols entailed not attending post-hospital therapy sessions. Margarette, a stocky middle-aged female of German descent, explained her avoidance of post-discharge therapy sessions in the following manner:

After I was released, my psychiatrist asked that I made appointments and see him every two weeks for follow-up maintenance treatments. But I never did go because I didn't want someone to see me going into the psychiatric department of "Meadowbrook Hospital" and sitting in the waiting room of the "Nut Wing." Two of my nosey neighbors are employed at that hospital and I just couldn't take the chance of them seeing me there one day.

In sum, as a strategy of information management, selective concealment of their attribute and past hospitalizations was done to protect themselves from the perceived negative consequences which might result from the revelation of their illness—an "offensive tactical maneuver" through which ex-patients attempted (although often unsuccessfully) to mitigate the stigma potential of mental illness on their daily lives.

Notably, employing concealment as a strategy of information management was a *temporal* process. The majority of ex-patients employed this strategy primarily during the first eight months following their discharge. During this time, in particular, they expressed feelings of anxiety, fear, and trepidation. However, as time passed, ex-patients began to test reactions, encountered both positive and negative responses from certain "normals," and their strong initial desires for secrecy were replaced by alternative strategies.

Therapeutic Disclosure

Therapeutic disclosure may be defined as the selective disclosure of a discreditable attribute to certain "trusted," "empathetic" supportive others in an effort to renegotiate personal perceptions of the stigma of "failing."

Similar to Miall's (1986) study on involuntary childless women and Schneider and Conrad's (1980) study on epileptics, 36 percent of the ex-patients felt that discussing their mental illnesses and past hospitalizations, getting it off their chests in a cathartic fashion, functioned to alleviate much of the burden of their loads. Attesting to the cathartic function disclosing served, Vincent, a 29 year old ex-patient remarked:

> Finally, letting it all out, after so many secrets, lies, it was so therapeutic for me. Keeping something like this all bottled up inside is self-destructive. When I came clean, this great burden was lifted from me!

Therapeutic disclosure was most often carried out with family members, close friends, and with other ex-psychiatric patients—individuals "sharing the same fate." Ida, a 52 year old, discussing the circumstances surrounding her disclosure to a neighbor who had also been hospitalized in a psychiatric facility at one time, said:

> At first, I was apprehensive to talk about it. But keeping it inside of you all bottled up is no good either. One day, I walked down the street to a neighbor of mine and she invited me in to have tea. I knew what had happened to her years ago (her deceased husband confided in my husband). I let out all my anxieties and fears to her that afternoon...I told her everything and she was so sympathetic...She knew exactly what I was going through. Once I let it all out, I felt so much better.

Even in cases where ex-patients disclosed to individuals who turned out to be unsympathetic and unsupportive, some considered this therapeutic:

> When I came out of hiding and told people about my sickness, not everyone embraced me. A lot of people are shocked and just tense up. Some just stare...A few never call you after that time or make up excuses not to meet with you...But I don't care, because overall, telling made me feel better.

Just as therapeutic disclosure functioned to relieve ex-patients' anxieties and frustrations, it also allowed for the renegotiation of personal perceptions of mental illness as a discreditable attribute. Speaking of the manner by which she came to redefine mental illness in her own mind as a less stigmatizing attribute, Edith explained:

> When I finally opened up and started talking about it, it really wasn't so bad after all. My Uncle John was very supportive and helped me to put my mind at rest, to realize that having mental illness isn't so bad; it's not like having cancer. He told me that thousands of people go into the hospital each year for psychiatric treatment and probably every third person I meet has had treatment...After much talking, I no longer think of myself as less human, but more normally...Having mental illness isn't the blight I thought it was.

In short, then, ex-patients employed therapeutic disclosure in order to relieve feelings of frustration and anxiety, to elevate their self-esteem, and to renegotiate (in their own minds) personal perceptions of mental illness as stigmatizing.

Preventive Disclosure

Preventive disclosure may be described as the selective disclosure to "normals" of a discreditable attribute in an effort to influence others' actions and/or perceptions about the ex-patient or about mental illness in general (cf. Miall 1986; Schneider and Conrad 1980). Preventive disclosure of their mental illness and past hospitalizations occurred in situations where ex-patients anticipated future rejection by "normal" others. In order to minimize the pain of subsequent rejection, 34 percent of the sample decided that the best strategy to employ with certain people was preventive disclosure *early* in their relationships. As Hector, a 40 year old janitor stated:

> I figured out that, for me, it is best to inform people right off the bat about my mental illness. Why? Because you don't waste a lot of time developing relationships and then are rejected later. That hurts too much. Tell them early and if they can't deal with it, and run away, you don't get hurt as much!

Preventive disclosure then, represented a way ex-patients attempted to prevent a drop in their status at a later date, or a way of testing acquaintances in an effort to establish friendship boundaries.

Just as non-chronics used preventive disclosure to avoid future stigma and rejection, so too did they employ this strategy to influence normals' attitudes about themselves and about mental illness in general. Specifically, ex-patients used the following devices: (a) medical disclaimers (cf. Hewitt and Stokes 1975; Miall 1986; and Schneider and Conrad 1980); (b) deception/ coaching (cf. Goffman 1963; Miall 1986; Schneider and Conrad 1980); (c) education (cf. Schneider and Conrad 1980); and (d) normalization (cf. Cogswell 1967; Davis 1961, 1963; Levitin 1975; McCaghy 1968; Scott 1969).

Medical Disclaimers—Similar to Schneider and Conrad's (1980) epileptics and Miall's (1986) involuntary childless women, 52 percent of the ex-patients frequently used medical disclaimers in their management work—"blameless, beyond-my-control medical interpretation(s)" developed in order to "... reduce the risk that more morally disreputable interpretations might be applied by naive others" discovering their failing (Schneider and Conrad 1980:41). Such interpretations were often used by ex-patients to evoke sympathy from others and to ensure that they would be treated in a charitable manner. As Dick, an unemployed laborer, put it:

> When I tell people about my hospitalization in a psychiatric hospital, I immediately emphasize that the problem isn't anything I did, it's a biological one. I didn't ask to get sick; it was just plain biology; or my genes that fucked me up. I try to tell people in a nice way so that they see mental illness just like other diseases—you know, cancer or the mumps. It's not my parents' fault or my own... I just tell them, "Don't blame me, blame my genes!"

Further, 11 ex-patients revealed their mental illness and past hospitalizations as a side effect of another medical problem or disease, such as childbirth, stroke, or heart disease, thereby legitimizing what otherwise might be considered a potentially-stigmatizing condition. As Rebecca, a 36 year old ex-patient confessed:

> I have had heart problems since birth. I was a very sick baby. I've had four operations since that time and I've been on all kinds of medications. The stress of dealing with such an illness led to my depression and subsequent breakdowns...When my friends hear about mental illness in this light, they are very empathetic.

While Sue spoke of her successes in influencing others' perceptions about her attribute and mental illness in general, Lenny lamented about his failure with the same strategy:

> Life's not easy for ex-nuts, you know. I tried telling two of my drinking buddies about my schizophrenia problem one night at the bar. I thought if I told 'em that it's a "disease" like having a heart problem that they

would understand and pat me on the butt and say it didn't matter to them and that I was o.k. Shit, it didn't work out like I planned; they flipped out on me. Sid couldn't handle it at all and just let out of there in a hurry; Jack stayed around me for about twenty minutes and then made some excuse and left.

In sum, through the use of medical disclaimers, ex-patients hoped to elevate their self-esteem and to renegotiate personal perceptions of mental illness as a non-stigmatizing attribute. *Deception/Coaching*—Deception differed from strategies of concealment in that with the former, ex-patients readily disclosed their illness and past hospital-izations but explicitly distorted the conditions or circumstances surrounding it. Similar to Miall's (1986) involuntary childless women and Schneider and Conrad's (1980) epileptics, about one-third of the ex-patients employed deceptive practices developed with the assistance of coaches. Coaches included parents, close friends, spouses, and other ex-patients sharing the same stigma. Coaches actively provided ex-patients with practical suggestions on how to disclose their attribute in the least stigmatizing manner and present themselves in a favorable light. Maureen, a 32 year old ex-patient, explained of her "coaching sessions" with relatives:

My parents and grandma really helped me out in terms of what I should say or tell others. They were so afraid I'd be hurt that they advised me what to tell my school mates, the manager at Woolco where I got hired. We had numerous practice exercises where we'd role-play and I'd rehearse what I would say to others...After a while I became quite convincing.

Moreover, it is interesting to note that about one quarter of the ex-patients employed deceptive practices together with medical disclaimers. As Benjamin, a 62-year-old ex-patient, aptly expressed:

To survive in this cruel, cold world, you've got to be sneaky. I mean, that you've got to try to win people over to your side. Whoever you decide to tell about your illness, you've got to make it clear that you had nothing to do with getting sick; nobody can place blame on anyone...And you've got to color the truth about how you ended up in the hospital by telling heart-sob stories to get people sympathetic to you. You never tell them the whole truth or they'll shun you like the plague!

Education— A third form of preventive disclosure used by ex-patients to influence others' perceptions of them and their ideas about mental illness was education. Similar to Schneider and Conrad's (1980) epileptics and Miall's (1986) involuntary childless women who revealed their attribute in an effort to educate others, 28 percent of the ex-patients revealed for the same educational purposes. Marge, a 39-year-old ex-patient, speaking on her efforts to educate friends and neighbors, stated:

I have this urge inside of me to teach people out there, to let them know that they've been misinformed about mental illness and mental patients. We're not the way the media has portrayed us. That's why people are afraid of us. I feel very strongly that someone has to tell people the truth . . . give them the facts . . . And when they hear it, they're amazed sometimes and begin to treat me without apprehension . . . Each time I make a breakthrough, I think more highly of myself too.

Ex-patients did not automatically attempt to educate everyone they encountered, but rather, based on subjective typification of normals, made value judgments about whom to "educate." Brenda, speaking on this matter, explained:

You just can't go ahead and tell everyone. You ponder who it is, what are the circumstances, and whether you think that they can be educated about it. There are some people that these efforts would be fatal and fruitless. Others however, you deem as a potential. And these are the people you work with.

While education proved successful for some ex-patients in their management activities with certain individuals, others found it less successful. Jim, recalling one disastrous experience with a former poker buddy, said:

I really thought he would learn something from my discussion of the facts. I really misjudged Fred. I thought him to be an open-minded kind of guy but perhaps just naive, so I sat him down one afternoon and made him my personal "mission." I laid out my past and then talked to him about all the kinds of mental illnesses that are out there. He reacted terrible; All his biases came out and he told me that all those people should be locked up and the key thrown away—that they were a danger to society. He was probably thinking the same thing about me too!

Following Goffman (1963:101), medical disclaimers, deception/coaching, and education are forms of "disclosure etiquette"—they are formulas for revealing a stigmatizing attribute ". . . in a matter of fact way, supporting the assumption that those present are above such concerns while preventing them from trapping themselves into showing that they are not." *Normalization*—A final form of preventive disclosure employed by ex-psychiatric patients to manage stigma was normalization. This concept is drawn from Davis' (1963) study on children with polio and is akin to deviance disavowal (cf. Davis 1961). Normalization is a strategy individuals use to deny that their behavior or attribute is deviant—it "seeks to render normal and morally acceptable that which has heretofore been regarded as abnormal and immoral" (Pfuhl 1986:163). Similar to observations made on pedophiles (McCahy 1968), the obese (Millman 1980), the visible handicapped (Levitin 1975) and paraplegics (Cogswell 1967), about one quarter of the ex-psychiatric patients I studied also employed this same strategy. Such persons were firmly committed to societal conceptions of normalcy and were aware that according to these standards, they were disqualified—they would never "measure up." Yet, ex-patients made active attempts at rationalizing and downplaying the stigma attached to their failing. So, for example, they participated in a full round of normal activities and aspired to normal attainments. They participated in amateur theater groups, played competitive sports such as hockey and tennis, they enrolled in college, etc. Ex-patients whose stigma could be considered "discreditable," that is, not readily or visibly apparent to others, would disclose such information for preventive reasons, thereby rendering them "discredited" in the eyes of others. They would then attempt to negotiate with normals for preferred images, attitudes, roles, and non-deviant conceptions of self, and definitions of mental illness as less-stigmatizing. Discussing his utilization of this technique, Weird Old Larry, a 59-year-old ex-patient, stated:

> The third time I got out [of the hospital], I tried to fit right in. I told some of my buddies and a couple of others about my sickness. It was easier to get it out in the open. But what I tried to show 'em was that I could do the same things they could, some of them, even better. I beat them at pool, at darts; I could out-drink them, I was holding down two jobs—one at the gas station and at K-Mart. I tried to show them I was normal. I was cured! The key to success is being up-front and making them believe you're just as normal as them . . . You can really change how they see and treat you.

If successfully carried out, this avowal normalized relations between ex-patients and others.

This is not to imply, however, that the strategy of normalization worked for all patients in all situations. Similar to Millman's (1980:78) overweight females who were accepted in certain roles but treated as deviant in others, many ex-patients expressed similar problems. Frederick, speaking on this problem with respect to co-workers, said:

> It's really tragic you know. When I told the other people at work that I was a manic depressive but was treated and released, I emphasize that I was completely normal in every way . . . but they only accepted me normally part of the time, like when we were in the office . . . But they never really accepted me as their friend, as one of 'the boys;" and they never invited me over to dinner with their wife and family—they still saw me as an ex-crazy, not as an equal to be worthy being invited to dinner, or playing with their kids.

It is interesting to note that just as ex-patients whose attribute was discreditable employed the strategy of normalization, so too, did other ex-patients with discrediting attributes (conditions *visibly apparent* or *known* to others) employ this same technique. Explaining how medication side-effects rendered him discredited and how he attempted to reduce the stigma of mental illness through normalization, Ross said:

> Taking all that dope the shirks dish out makes my hands tremble. Look at my shaking legs too. I never used to have these twitches in my face

either, but that's just the side-effects, a bonus you get. It really fucks things up though. If I wanted to hide my illness, I couldn't; everyone just looks at me and knows . . . So, what I do is to try to get people's attention and get them to see my positive side — that I can be quite normal, you know. I emphasize all the things that I can do!

In short, by presenting themselves as normals, ex-patients hoped to elicit positive responses from others whose reactions were deemed to be important. From a social psychological perspective, others accepted and reinforced a non-deviant image of self through this process of negotiation, allowing ex-patients to achieve more positive, non-deviant identities.

In many cases, ex-psychiatric patients progressed from one strategy to another as they managed information about themselves. Specifically, they moved from a strategy of initial selective concealment to disclosure for therapeutic and preventive reasons. According to the ex-patients, such a progression was linked to their increased adjustment to their attribute as well as the result of positive responses from others to the revelation of their mental illness.

Political Activism

Just as ex-psychiatric patients developed and employed a number of individualized forms of information management to deal with the stigma potential of mental illness, enhance self-images, and alter deviant identities, they also employed one collective management strategy[7] to achieve the same ends, namely, joining and participating in ex-mental patient activist groups (cf. Anspach, 1979). Such groups, with their goal of self-affirmation, represent what Kitsuse (1980:9) terms "tertiary deviation"— referring to "the deviant's conformation, assessment, and rejection of the negative identity embedded in secondary deviation, and the transformation of that identity into a positive and viable self-conception."

Political activism served a three-fold function for ex-patients: (1) it repudiated standards of normalcy (standards to which they couldn't measure up) and the deviant labels placed upon these individuals; (2) it provided them with a new, positive non-deviant identity, enhanced their self-respect, and afforded ex-patients a new sense of purpose; and (3) it served to propagate this new, positive image of ex-mental patient to individuals, groups, and organizations in society. The pay-off from political activism, was, then, both personal as well as social.

Similar to such activist groups as the Gay Liberation Front, the Disabled in Action, the Gray Panthers, or the Radical Feminist Movement, ex-mental patient activists rejected prevailing societal values of normalcy through participation in their groups. They repudiated the deviant identities, roles and statuses placed on them. Moreover, these individuals flatly rejected the stigma associated with their identities. Steve, a 51 year old, electrician aptly summed it up for most ex-patient activists when he stated:

The whole way society had conceived of right and wrong, normal and abnormal is all wrong. They somehow have made us believe that to be mentally ill is to be *ashamed* of something; that these people are to be feared, that they are to blame for their sickness. Well I don't accept this vein anymore.

Upon repudiating prevailing cultural values and deviant identities, ex-patient activists collectively redefined themselves in a more positive, non-deviant light according to their *own* newly-constructed set of standards. Speaking of her embracing a new non-deviant identity, Susan, a 39-year-old ex-patient who recently returned to teaching school, said:

I no longer agree to accept what society says is normal and what is not. It's been so unfair to psychiatric patients. Who are they to say, just because we don't conform, that we're rejects of humanity . . . The labels they've given us are degrading and make us feel sick . . . (the labels) have a negative connotation to them . . . So, we've gotten together and liberated ourselves. We've thrown away the old labels and negative images of self-worth and we give ourselves new labels and images of self-worth — as human beings who should be treated with decency and respect.

In contrast to other ex-patients who employed various individual management strategies to deal with what they perceived to be their *own personal* problems— personal failings—ex-patient activists saw their problems, not as personal failings or potentially-stigmatizing attributes but as *societal* problems. To the extent that ex-patients viewed their situations in this manner, it allowed them to develop more positive self-images. Speaking of this process as one of "stigma conversion," Humphreys (1972:142) stated:

In converting his stigma, the oppressed person does not merely exchange his social marginality for political marginality . . . Rather, he emerges from a stigmatized cocoon as a transformed creature, one characterized by the spreading of political wings. At some point in the process, the politicized "deviant" gains a new identity, an heroic self-image as crusader in a political cause.

Sally, a neophyte activist, placed the "blame" on society for her deviant self-image:

It's not any of our faults that we ended up the way we did. I felt guilty for a long time . . . I crouched away feeling that I had something that made me "different" from everyone else, a pock on my life . . . But I learned at the activist meetings that none of it was my fault. It was all society's fault—they're the one who can't deal with anything that is different. Now I realize that having mental illness is nothing to be ashamed of; it's nothing to hide. I'm now proud of who . . . and what I am!

Just as political activism, as contrasted with other adaptive responses to stigma, sought, in repudiating the dominant value system, to provide ex-patients with positive, non-deviant statuses, so too, did it attempt to propagate this new positive, normal image of ex-psychiatric patient to others in society. Thus, through such activities as rallies, demonstrations, protest marches, attendance at conferences on Human Rights for patients, lobbyist activities directed toward politicians and the medical profession, and the production of newsletters, ex-patient activists sought to promote social change. Specifically, they sought to counter or remove the stigma associated with their "differentness" and present society with an image of former psychiatric patients as "human beings" capable of self-determination and political action. Abe, the president of the activist group aptly summed up the aim of political activism during a speech to the selected political figures, media personnel, and "upstanding" citizens:

> Simply put, we're tired of being pushed around. We reject everything society says about us, because it's just not accurate. We reject the type of treatment we get . . . both in the hospital . . . and out. We don't like the meaning of the words (people) use to describe us — "mentals" and "nuts." We see ourselves differently, just as good and worthy as every-body out there. In our newsletter, we're trying to get across the idea that we're not the stereotypical mental patient you see in the movies. We're real people who want to be treated equally under the Charter of Rights. We're not sitting back now, we're fighting back!

In sum, then, through participation in political activist groups, many ex-patients internalized an ideology that repudiated societal values and conventional standards of normalcy, rejected their deviant identities and statuses, adopted more positive, non-deviant identities, and attempted to alter society's stereotypical perceptions about mental patients and mental illness in general.

Discussion: Becoming an "Ex-Crazy":—Role Exit and Reintegration

With the exception of a few studies (Adler 1992; Chambliss 1984; Shover 1985; Snodgrass 1982) little systematic attention has been given to individuals through their post-deviant careers. Centering on the lived experiences and accounts of 264 ex-psychiatric patients, this paper has dealt with the key elements and dimensions of their exit process and their (albeit, problematic) social reintegration. More generally, my research has attempted to make a contribution to the existing literature on deviant careers, the perception of stigmatizing attributes, stigma management strategies, and the reintegration of deviants.

When psychiatric patients are discharged from the institutions or psychiatric wards of general hospitals, their problems[8] are far from over. In fact, numerous problems lie ahead for such persons in their efforts to return to a conventional life. As Erikson (1966), Ebaugh (1988), and others have noted in their studies on role exit and the reintegration of deviants into society, there exist virtually no formal rights of passage to mark the ex-deviant's passage out of deviant identities and roles. While society has developed and employed various "degradation ceremonies" (Garfinkel 1956) marking the passage of individuals from "normal" to "deviant" identities and statuses, there are no such comparable ceremonies to re-instate the "transformed" or "ex-deviant." My findings suggest that ex-patients realized not only that no such ritualistic ceremonies existed to "transform them back," but also that they possessed a stigma that severely impeded such a transformation of self and endangered their future participation in society. In response to their undesirable post-hospital social situations, non-chronic ex-psychiatric patients employed five strategies, which if successfully carried out, lessened or mitigated the stigma of their failing, enhanced self-esteem, aided self-transformation and also allowed for renegotiation of societal conceptions of mental illness as a discreditable attribute. Strategies of stigma management have important consequences for social identities. Ebaugh (1984), in her study of nuns leaving the convent, spoke of the process of becoming an "ex-" in terms of the concepts of "role exit" and "self-transformation." Specifically, she asserted that ex-roles represent a unique sociological phenomenon in that definitions of self and societal expectations are shaped and often determined by a previous identity. That is, on the one hand, individuals are fighting to leave behind their *old* identities, statuses, and roles, while on the other hand, others are continually taking them into account when interacting with them. Ebaugh (1984:156) further pointed out that there are some ex-roles in our society that are fairly well-defined, such as "ex-president," but what we are seeing in society today are an increasing number of ex-roles for which there are few well-defined normative expectations. In these situations, the "ex's" themselves have to create role definitions as they play out their lives. Supporting others' (Glasser 1983; Ebaugh 1984; Irwin 1970; Meisenholder 1977; Shover 1983, 1985) documentations of role-exiting experiences that portrayed individuals' attempts to shake off their old roles and create new roles designed to reformulate societal expectations of their selves, I discovered a similar process operating with respect to discharged non-chronic patients. In their process of self-transformation, former patients struggled to cast off their deviant identities and roles—a decision prompted largely due to their perception of mental illness as a stigmatizing attribute. As Goffman (1963:78) stated: "The stigmatized individual tends to hold the same beliefs about identity that we do. His deepest feeling about what he is may be his sense of being a 'normal person,' a human being like anyone else, a person, therefore, who deserves a fair break. What is desired by the individual is what can be called acceptance." The creation of a new identity of "ex-crazy" or "ex-mental patient," a positive, non-deviant, non-stigmatizing identity arose then, through an ongoing process of negotiations with normals in a bid for "acceptance." In particular, ex-patients were successful in transforming their deviant aspects of self when (or if):[9] (a) they began to think of themselves in terms of current, non-deviant roles and when they began to project such an image to others, and (b) others began to relate to them in terms of their *new* roles.

My findings suggest, then, and are supported by other research on deviants (Hewitt and Stokes 1975; Levitin 1975; Miall 1986; Schneider and Conrad 1980, among others), that ex-psychiatric patients are not passive, powerless individuals; rather, they are strategists, expert managers and negotiators who play active (although not always successful) roles in the shaping of deviant outcomes. In other words, ex-patients have their hands in shaping their own social fates; they attempt to elicit desired reactions through their own behaviors, through the techniques of stigma management they employ, and through the expectations and images they project.

Moreover, my data demonstrate the relationship between self-labeling and the perception of mental illness as a stigmatizing attribute. Much of the empirical sociological work on the stigma of mental illness has assumed that (ex)-mental patients learn the meaning of their attribute primarily through societal reaction, specifically formal and/or informal disvaluing responses. With the exception of Thoits (1985), relatively little attention has been placed on the role of self-labeling. Self-labeling occurs when individuals recognize on the basis of internalizing of normative conceptions that other people may label their attributes as deviant if they learn of them (Lorber, 1967; Sagarin and Kelly 1980). The concept of self-labeling then, places importance not only on the normative order for self-definitions of stigma, but on the role of individuals' subjective perceptions in the definitional process.

My research also offers new insight into the various strategies that individuals use to manage potentially-stigmatizing information about themselves. Although the strategies employed by these ex-patients have been observed with respect to various other deviant groups, I documented an interesting difference. Specifically, I discovered that ex-patients perceived therapeutic disclosure to be helpful and desirable—even in those instances where audiences reacted in a negative, unsupportive manner.[10]

Future research on the stigma of mental illness should also focus on the families of ex-psychiatric patients, in terms of the dynamic of family interaction. While some studies (Freeman and Simons 1961; Lefton et al. 1962) have concentrated on such family interaction patterns as exclusion and rejection, it would be naive to conclude that these are the only two responses that develop. Future research needs to examine families' efforts at cooperation with ex-patients, and their efforts at attempting to reintegrate them into society, to manage stigma, etc. So too, should studies focus on the problems and frustrations experienced by family members in their efforts to cope with ex-patients. Specifically, studies should focus on the courtesy stigma potentially possessed by family and friends of ex-patients (Goffman 1963:30), and their attempts to deal with it.

Finally, future research would benefit from focusing on the relationship between social power, management strategies, and identity transformation. Following Becker (1963:17), those in positions of power—those having basic resources at their command—may deal with the stigma potential of mental illness in means different from those without such power. Those with powerful resources will likely be able to achieve more favorable outcomes than those without. Clearly, these factors merit future consideration with respect to ex-psychiatric patients.

REFERENCES

Adler, Patricia A. 1992, "The 'post' phase of deviant careers: Reintegrating drug traffickers." *Deviant Behavior* 13: 103–126.

Adler, Patricia A., and Peter Adler 1983. "Shifts and oscillations in deviant careers: The case of upper-level drug dealers and smugglers." *Social Problems* 31: 195–207.

Anspach, Renee. 1979. From Stigma to Identity Politics:Political Activism Among the Physically Disabled and Former Mental Patients. *Social Science and Medicine* 13A: 765–773.

Bar-Levav, Reuven. 1976. The Stigma of Seeing a Psychiatrist.*American Journal of Psychotherapy* 30 (3): 473–482.

Bartell, Gilbert D. 1971. *Group Sex: A Scientist's Eyewitness Report on the American Way of Swinging.* New York: Wyden.

Becker, H. S. 1963. *Outsiders: Studies in the Sociology of Deviance.* New York: Free Press.

Bell, Alan and Martin S. Weinberg. 1978. *Homosexualities: A study of Diversity Among Men and Women.* New York: Simon and Schuster.

Berger, P., and T. Luckmann. 1966. *The Social Construction of Reality.* New York: Doubleday.

Bogdan, Robert. 1974. *Being Different: The Autobiography of Jane Fry.* New York: Wiley and Sons.

Bord, Richard James. 1970. Rejection of the mentally ill: continuities and further developments. *Social Problems* 18: 490–512.

Braithwaite, John. 1989. *Crime, Shame and Reintegration.* Cambridge, England: Cambridge University Press.

Brown, J. David. 1991. The Professional Ex-: An Alternative for Exiting the Deviant Career. *The Sociological Quarterly* 32: 219–30.

Carrier, J. M. 1976. Family Attitudes and Mexican Male Homosexuality. *Urban Life* 50: 359–375.

Chambliss, William J. 1984. *Harry King: A Professional Thief's Journey.* New York: Wiley.

Cheadle, A. J., H. Freeman and J. Korer. 1978. Chronic Schizophrenic Patients in the Community. *British Journal of Psychiatry* 132: 221–227.

Christensen, Harold T. 1953. Studies in Child Spacing: Premarital Pregnancy as Measured by the Spacing of the First Birth from Marriage. *American Sociological Review* 18:53–59.

Clausen, John. 1981. Stigma and Mental Disorder: Phenomena and Terminology. *Psychiatry* 44(4): 287–296.

Cochrane, R., and K. Nieradzik. 1985. Public Attitudes Towards Mental Illness—The Effects of Behavior, Roles, and Psychiatric Labels. *The International Journal of Psychiatry* 31(1): 23–33.

Cogswell, B. 1967. Rehabilitation of the Paraplegic: Processes of Socialization. *Sociological Inquiry* 37: 11–26.

D'Arcy, Carl and Joan Brockman. 1977. Public Rejection of the Ex-Mental Patient: Are Attitudes Changing? *The Canadian Review of Sociology and Anthropology* 14(1): 68–80.

Davis, Fred. 1961. Deviance Disavowal: the Management of Strained Interaction by the Visibly Handicapped. *Social Problems* (9): 120–132.

———. 1963. *Passage Through Crisis: Polio Victims and Their Families.* Indianapolis: Bobbs-Merrill.

Davis, Nanette. 1975. *Sociological Constructions of Deviance: Perspectives and Issues in the Field.* Dubuque,Iowa: Wm. C. Brown and Company.

Delph, E. 1978. *The Silent Community: Public Homosexual Encounters.* Beverly Hills, California: Sage.

Doll, Wm., Edward Thompson Jr., and Mark Lefton. 1976. Beneath Acceptance: Dimensions of Family Affect Towards Former Mental Patients. *Social Science and Medicine* 10(6): 307–313.

Ebaugh, Helen Rose Fuchs. 1984. Leaving the Covent: Role Exit and Self-Transformation. Pp. 156–176 in J.A. Kotarba and A. Fontana (eds.) *The Existential Self in Society.* Chicago: University of Chicago Press.

———. 1988. *Becoming an Ex: The Process of Role Exit.* Chicago: University of Chicago Press.

Edgerton, Robert. 1967. *The Cloak of Competence: Stigma in the Lives of the Mentally Retarded.* Berkeley: University of California Press.

Erikson, Kai T. 1966. *Wayward Puritans.* New York: Wiley.

Estroff, Sue E. 1981. *Making It Crazy, An Ethnography of Psychiatric Clients in an American Community.* Berkeley: University of California Press.

Farina, Amerigo and Kenneth Ring. 1965. The Influence of Perceived Mental Illness on Interpersonal Relations. *Journal of Abnormal Psychology* 70: 47–51.

Faupel, Charles E. 1991. *Shooting Dope: Career Patterns of Hard-Core Heroin Users.* Gainesville: University of Florida Press.

Frazier, Charles. 1976. *Theoretical Approaches to Deviance*. Columbus: Charles Merrill.

Freeman, H.D., and O.G. Simmons. 1961. Feelings of Stigma Among Relatives of Former Mental Patients. *Social Problems* 8: 312–321.

Glassner, Barry and Margaret Ksander, Bruce Berg, Bruce D. Johnson. 1983. A note on the deterrent effect of juvenile vs. adult jurisdiction. *Social Problems* 31: 219–221.

Goffman, Erving. 1961. *Asylums*. New York:Doubleday.

———. 1963. *Stigma*. New Jersey: Prentice-Hall.

Goldmeir, J., M. Shore, and F. Mannino. 1977. Cooperative Apartments: New Programs in Community Mental Health. *Health and Social Work* 2 (1): 120–140.

Herman, Nancy J. 1981. *The Making of a Mental Patient: An Ethnographic Study of the Processes and Consequences of Institutionalization Upon Self-Images and Identities*. Unpublished Master's thesis, McMaster University, Hamilton, Ontario, Canada.

———. 1986 *Crazies in the Community: An Ethnographic Study of Ex-Psychiatric Clients in Canadian Society—Stigma, Management Strategies and Identity Transformation*. Unpublished Ph.D. dissertation, McMaster University, Hamilton, Ontario, Canada.

———. 1987. 'Mixed Nutters' and Looney Tuners:' The Emergence, Development, Nature, and Functions of Two Informal, Deviant Subcultures of Chronic, Ex-Psychiatric Patients. *Deviant Behavior* 8: 235–258.

Harris, Mervyn. 1973. *The Dilly Boys*. Rockville, MD: New Perspectives.

Hewitt, J. and R. Stokes. 1975. Disclaimers. Pp. 308–319 in J. L. Manis editors, *Symbolic Interactionism*. Boston: Allyn and Bacon.

Humphreys, Laud. 1972. *Out of the Closets, the Sociology of Homosexual Liberation*. New Jersey: Prentice-Hall.

Inciardi, James. 1975. *Careers in Crime*. Chicago: Rand McNally.

Irwin, John. 1970. *The Felon*. Englewood Cliffs: Prentice-Hall.

Kando, T. 1973. *Sex Change: the Achievement of Gender Identity Among Feminized Transsexuals*. Illinois: Charles C. Thomas.

Kitsuse, John. 1980. Presidential Address. *Society for the Study of Social Problems* 9: 1–13.

Kreisman, D.E. and V.D. Joy 1974. Family responses to the mental illness of a relative: A review of the literature. *Schizophrenia Bulletin* 1 (10): 34–57.

Lamb, J. and V. Goertzel. 1977. The Long-Term Patient in the Era of Community Treatment. *Archives of General Psychiatry* 34:679–682.

Lamy, Richard E. 1966. Social Consequences of Mental Illness. *Journal of Abnormal Psychology* 70:47–51.

Lefton, Mark, S. Angrist, S. Dinitz and B. Pasamanick. 1962. Social Class, Expectations and Performance of Mental Patients. *American Journal of Sociology* 68:79–87.

Levitin, T. 1975. Deviants as Active Participants in the Labelling Process: The Case of the Visibly Handicapped. *Social Problems* 22: 548–557.

Lorber, J. 1967. Deviance as Performance: The Case of Illness. *Social Problems* 14: 302–310.

Luckenbill, David F. and Joel Best. 1981. Careers in deviance and respectability: the analogy's limitations. *Social Problems* 29:197–206.

Lyman, Stanford M. 1970. *The Asian in the West*. Reno/Las Vegas, Nevada: Western Studies Center, Desert Research Institute.

McCaghy, Charles H. 1968. Drinking and Deviance Disavowal: The Case of Child Molesters. *Social Problems* 16:43–49.

Meisenhelder, Thomas. 1977. An exploratory study of exiting from criminal careers. *Criminology* 15:319–334.

Miall, Charlene E. 1984. *Women and Involuntary Childlessness: Perceptions of Stigma Associated with Infertility and Adoption*. Unpublished Ph.D. dissertation, York University, Toronto, Canada.

———. 1986. The Stigma of Involuntary Childlessness. *Social Problems* 33 (4):268–282.

Miller, Dorothy and Wm. Dawson. 1965. Effects of Stigma on Reemployment of Ex-mental patients. *Mental Hygiene* 49:281–287.

Millman, Marcia. 1980. *Such a Pretty Face*. New York:W.W. Norton.

Nunnally, J. 1961. *Popular Conceptions of Mental Health*. New York: Holt, Rinehart and Winston.

Pfuhl, Erdwin H., Jr. 1978. The Unwed Father: A 'Non-Deviant" Rule Breaker. *The Sociological Quarterly* 19 (Winter):113–128.

———. 1986. *The Deviance Process*, 2nd edition. Belmont: Wadsworth.

Ponse, Barbara. 1976. Secrecy in the Lesbian World. *Urban Life* 5:313–338.

Rabinowitz, Jonathon. 1982. Shared Ethnicity as a Correlation of Acceptance of the Formerly Hospitalized Mentally Ill. *Journal of Sociology and Social Welfare* 9 (3): 534–540.

Ray, Marsh. 1961. The cycle of abstinence and relapse among heroin addicts. *Social Problems* 9:132–140.

Reynolds, David K. and Norman Farberow. 1977. *Endangered Hope: Experiences in Psychiatric Aftercare Facilities*. Berkeley: University of California Press.

Robins, L. 1980. Alcoholism and Labeling Theory. Pp. 34–47 in W. Gove, editor, *The Labeling of Deviance*. 2nd edition. California: Sage.

Sagarin, E. and R. Kelly. 1980. Sexual Deviance and Labeling Perspectives. Pp. 347–379 in Walter Gove, editor, *The Labeling of Deviance*. California: Sage.

Scheff, Thomas. 1975. *Labelling Madness*. New Jersey: Prentice Hall.

———. 1984. *Being Mentally Ill: A Sociological Theory*. 2nd edition. Chicago: Aldine.

Schneider, J. and P. Conrad. 1980. In the Closet with Illness: Epilepsy, Stigma Potential and Information Control. *Social Problems* 28 (1): 32–44.

Schur, Edwin. 1979. *Interpreting Deviance: A Sociological Introduction*. New York: Harper and Row.

Scott, Robert. 1969. The Socialization of Blind Children. Pp. 23–37 in D. Goslin editor, *Handbook of Socialization Theory and Research*. Chicago: Rand McNally.

Segal, S.P., J. Baumohl and E.W. Moyles. 1980. Neighborhood types and community reaction to the Mentally Ill: A paradox of intensity. *Journal of Health and Social Behavior* 21: 345–359.

Shover, Neil. 1983. The later stages of ordinary property offenders careers. *Social Problems* 31: 208–218.

———. 1985. *Aging Criminals*. Newbury Park, CA: Sage.

Taylor, S. Martin, Michael Dear and G. Hall. 1979. Attitudes toward the Mentally Ill and Reactions to Mental Health Facilities. *Social Science and Medicine* 13D: 281–290.

Thoits, Peggy. 1985. Self-Labelling Processes in Mental Illness: The Role of Emotional Deviance. *American Journal of Sociology* 91: 221–249.

Thomas, W.I. 1931. *The Unadjusted Girl*. Boston: Little, Brown and Co.

Trute, B., and A. Loewen. 1978. Public attitudes toward the mentally ill as a function of prior personal experience. *Social Psychiatry* 13: 79–84.

Veevers, Jean. 1980. *Childless by Choice*. Toronto: Butterworths.

Webber, Avery and James D. Orcutt. 1982. Employers' Reaction to Racial and Psychiatric Stigmata: A Field Experiment. Paper presented at the 31st Annual Meetings of the Society for the Study of Social Problems, San Francisco, California.

Whatley, C.D. 1959. Social Attitudes Toward Discharged Mental Patients. *Social Problems* 6: 313–320.

NOTES

1. The stigmatized status of individuals and the information management strategies they employ have been well-documented on other groups such as: the retarded, (Edgerton 1967) epileptics (Schneider and Conrad 1980), secret homosexuals (Humphreys 1975), involuntary childless women (Miall 1986), swingers (Bartell 1971), and lesbians (Ponse 1976), among others.

2. Chronicity, for the purposes of this study, was defined *not* in diagnostic terms, i.e., "chronic schizophrenic;" rather, it was defined in terms of duration, continuity, and frequency of hospitalizations. Specifically, the term "non-chronic" refers to those individuals hospitalized for time-periods of less than two years, on a discontinuous basis, those hospitalized on less than five occasions, or those treated in psychiatric wards of general hospital facilities.

3. The term "chronic" ex-psychiatric patient refers to those institutionalized in psychiatric hospitals for time-periods of two years or more, institutionalized on a continual basis, or on five or more occasions.

4. The decision to stratify the sample by chronicity was based upon my interests and prior fieldwork activities. My earlier study (Herman 1981) indicated that when we speak of "deinstitutionalized" or "discharged" patients, we cannot merely assume that they are one homogeneous grouping of individuals

with like characteristics, similar post-hospital social situations, experiences and perceptions of reality. Rather, prior research led me to believe that there may be distinct subgroups of individuals with varying perceptions of reality and experiences (see Herman 1986).

5. In Estroff's (1981) ethnography on chronic ex-mental patients, she points out the catch-22 situation in which they find themselves. Ex-patients need to take their medications on a regular basis in order to remain on the outside. However, ironically, in an effort to become more like others, they take "meds" that make them "different." The various side effects reinforce their deviant identities.

6. See Herman (1986) for a detailed discussion of such other post-hospital problems.

7. Following Lyman's (1970) typology on deviant voluntary associations, ex-mental patient political activist groups represent an "instrumental-alienative" type of association. It is interesting to note that chronic ex-patients also employed one collective form of stigma management; specifically, they formed and participated in deviant subcultures (see Herman 1987).

8. For a detailed discussion of their problems as pre- and in- patients, see Herman (1986).

9. It is important to reiterate that transforming deviant identities is extremely difficult and complex. The implementation of the various strategies discussed in this paper in no way guaranteed success. Many times, ex-patients were unsure about when to use them, in which situations, with whom, etc. Even if they were used correctly, there was no guarantee that others would react in a positive manner, that is, they would accept proffered meanings and definitions.

10. One notable exception is Miall's (1986) study on involuntary childless women, but by and large, this finding has not been noted elsewhere with respect to therapeutic disclosure.

Chapter 46

DOUBLE STIGMA AND BOUNDARY MAINTENANCE: HOW GAY MEN DEAL WITH AIDS

Mark R. Kowalewski

This study is concerned with the responses of "normal" members of stigmatized groups to others who possess a second discredited characteristic—a double stigma. The presence of AIDS within the gay community provides a locus for examining the effects of double stigma. AIDS reinforces the stereotype of promiscuity that the broader society holds toward gays, and also adds a stigma of disease to the stigma of amoral character (Spenser, 1983).

A terminal illness, especially one medical authorities know little about, causes fears of contagion among those who are healthy (Sontag, 1979; Coleman, 1986). Barbarin (1986), in his study of childhood cancer, has noted that normals fear contagion even though they cannot develop the disease through contact with the sick. In conducting my research, I found that gay men not only attempt to avoid sexual contact with bearers of the AIDS virus, but fear even sociable interactions with persons with AIDS (PWAs), even though they cannot contract the virus through casual contact.

Through the influence of the media, the broader society has defined AIDS as a disease affecting a highly promiscuous segment of society (Albert, 1986a, 1986b). As a result, normals impute the "courtesy stigma" (Goffman, 1963) of disease and promiscuity to all gays. This study shows that a similar interpretation of AIDS has influenced gay men's perception of the illness and PWAs. In response, gay men differentiate between themselves and others who are at high risk for contracting a life-threatening disease, and are "stigma symbols" (Goffman, 1963) of a gay stereotype. In fact, PWAs are a subgroup such as pedophiles and transsexuals, who are stigmatized by "normal" gays (Warren, 1974).

While PWAs pose the threat of physical and social contamination to other gays, they also hold the status of the stigmatized's "own." Hughes (1945) stated that when faced with a dilemma of status, observers choose which characteristic of another person will be the basis of interaction, or the "master status" (Becker, 1963). Albert (1986a, 1986b) held that the larger society is ambivalent about the status of PWAs, conceiving of them simultaneously as "sinners" and "sick." In this study, I suggest that gay men also feel ambivalent about the contradiction of status PWAs present.

The medical community has produced a plethora of literature on the transmission and etiology of AIDS in its search for a vaccine and an effective treatment for the disease. The sociological and related literature on AIDS has focused on such diverse topics as transmission of AIDS among drug abusers (Des Jarlais et al. 1986; Marmor et al., 1984); the responses of physicians (Dosik, 1987), the media (Albert, 1986a,

1986b; Baker, 1986), and organized religion (Kayal, 1985); AIDS wards in hospitals (Lessor, 1987); and attitudes of college students toward the disease (Edwards and Hiday, 1987; Hamilton et al., 1987). Studies in the gay community have examined the effects of the AIDS antibody test on gay men (Spenser, 1983) and changes in sexual practice (Feldman, 1985; Kotarba and Lang, 1986). In this study, I will examine the effects AIDS has had on the structure of the gay community by discussing the strategies gay men employ to cope with their fears and ambivalence about AIDS and PWAs.

This study will show that the singly stigmatized maintain social fairness (Bogardus, 1959) from the doubly stigmatized by drawing both physical (Lyman and Scott, 1967) and symbolic (Scott, 1969) boundaries around interaction. By means of these boundary-maintaining strategies, the singly stigmatized seek either to separate themselves totally from the doubly stigmatized or to simply limit involvement with them.

In this article I first discuss the strategies gay men employ to cope with the threat of AIDS. These strategies include: restriction (of sexual interaction in general), avoidance (of the subject of AIDS), denial (of the disease's potential effect on them), and support (donating money to AIDS causes). Second, I discuss the interactional strategies gay men use when contact with PWAs occurs, such as avoiding them or limiting sexual and sociable involvement. I conclude by discussing structural factors affecting the ambivalent relations between singly and doubly stigmatized groups and their relation to the larger society....

Coping with the Threat of Aids

In an effort to avoid contact with the AIDS virus, all but 3 persons reported a reduction in the number of sexual partners and the variety of sexual techniques in which they engaged—a change also noted by Feldman (1985). Two persons stated that they had not changed their sexual behavior because they never did things to contract AIDS, while one felt he had not changed at all, or changed only slightly. As one 27-year-old man stated:

> I guess first of all, if I have sex, it's safe sex. And second of all, prior to the AIDS problem. I think everyone was freer about going home with people and doing what they wanted to. So certainly I have taken that stance, and most other people have as well. I guess...I guess there's just not as much free sex.

The phrase "safe sex" was used repeatedly by respondents, and has become part of the gay argot. It refers to a sexual encounter in which no body fluids are exchanged. Mutual masturbation and touching and kissing that do not involve the exchange of saliva are prescribed forms of "safe sex."

Members of the focus group said there were many sexual practices one could engage in without exchanging bodily fluids, such as using condoms during oral and anal sex. Some participants said that the sexual practices they found enjoyable had changed as a result of the restrictions "safe sex" placed on their behavior. One 26-year-old man noted that anal sex was no longer enjoyable for him:

> Anal sex is becoming desexualized for me. I learned over the years to be excited by it. Now I don't want it. It's a redefining of what is erotic for me. I want to do things that make me feel safe...I don't enjoy it anymore; I'm changing my behavior.

Anal sex became associated with contracting a terminal disease, and much like the redefinition process Becker (1963) noted among novice marijuana smokers, it became no longer pleasurable.

Members of the focus group stated that there was a hierarchy of practices they would be willing to give up. The one practice that group members reported they could not give up was deep kissing. A 26-year-old man maintained:

Kissing is so integral to the experience that I can't stop doing that. It wouldn't be romance.

Another 22-year-old man said: I can't stop kissing, especially if it's someone I care about, I'm willing to take that risk. I can't live my life in fear of what might happen.

Other members of the group agreed that even though deep kissing was dangerous, it would be difficult to give it up.

Two persons in the sample noted that they had started to "date," which for these men meant meeting someone for dinner or some other social activity not involving sex. Two other individuals who were involved in monogamous relationships noted that the threat of AIDS contributed to the maintenance of their relationships. One of these men noted:

> The possibility of my getting AIDS at this point is very slim, because the only sex I have is with my lover, and I think we're both healthy. That's one reason—this is a terrible thing to say—that's one good reason to stay in a relationship. Maybe I moved into a relationship a lot more quickly because of that fact. It was a good time to get into a relationship, because of the threat of AIDS.

Remaining in a monogamous relationship afforded a certain amount of security for these men.

Caution about short-term sexual relationships has become part of the gay culture. This is problematic, as sexual activity has had an identity-building function for gay men (Warren, 1974). However, one 26-year-old man maintained:

> My attitude is selfish. I suppose I'd be considered cavalier, but I have not altered my sex life...I don't know if it's the desperate disease it's made out to be. It's only affected a small amount of people; it's not the black plaque of the thirteen century.

In spite of the "cavalier" attitude he expressed when I first interviewed him, this person changed his views several months later when he found out that many of his friends in New York City had died of the disease.

While gay men sought to avoid contact with AIDS by taking prophylactic measures against the virus, they also avoided the subject of AIDS in an effort to ignore the possibility of contracting a terminal illness. As a 27-year-old man stated:

> You don't want to relate to it. That could happen to you, and I just don't want to think about it, and that just makes you think about it—having contact with a dying person.

In an effort to avoid confronting illness and their own mortality, this man avoided both the topic of AIDS and PWAs. Another man in his early thirties perceived that gays avoided the subject of AIDS because the disease challenged the cultural values of the gay community:

> Many gay men think of themselves as invulnerable. You know, beauty is very important—health, youth, everything that goes with that. I don't think they like to think about the future...Now is what matters—looking good...Getting old, God forbid getting old...AIDS is even worse; not only are you losing youth and vitality, you're dying. The physical aspects aren't that pleasant either, which is very difficult to deal with for a very vain community...It's not as easy to just fuck your way through life as it used to be. A lot of gay men...are having to look at their lives.

While youth, beauty, and sexuality were primary values for gays, this man noted that AIDS made gays reassess what was important to them. Many gays did not want to confront these questions. Such a reassessment of values would call into question the cultural boundaries of their community.

Another way gays coped with AIDS was to separate themselves from the types of people who had the potential for contracting it. AIDS would not strike them, since they were not like these stereotypical others. As one 35-year-old man stated:

> I don't worry about (AIDS). I don't go out of my way to get it, but I don't worry about it. I've always been a healthy person. I'm not afraid...I know, though, that my friend who had AIDS had a poor diet, didn't go out and go for a walk or get any air. He had very peculiar sleeping habits.

By retrospectively reinterpreting (Lofland, 1969) the biographies of PWAs to conform with a deviant gay identity, these men not only attempted to allay the fear that AIDS could affect them but, also avoided having to assume the double shame.

Gay men also used the stereotype of promiscuity to separate themselves from PWAs. A waiter in a restaurant frequented by gay men held that PWAs "got what they asked for," if they had led a promiscuous lifestyle. He continued:

> People getting AIDS...do drugs every weekend, then go to (an after-hours bar), then go to a bath house. My personal experience, what I see, is the element of our community who lead lifestyles of being gay in the fast lane...It's no surprise to me that they get sick.

This man joined the out-group of the larger society in what he perceived as its condemnation of the lifestyle that led to AIDS.

While gay men saw AIDS as a disease of gay "deviants," they also allayed the fear of double stigma by universalizing it as the problem of the whole society, and not simply as a gay disease:

> (Straight people) have an idea about why people got the disease, what kind of lifestyle led to it. Of course we know a person doesn't have to lead a promiscuous lifestyle, but I think the media has presented it as a disease which is picked up by a very promiscuous group...I think too you're seeing a few straight people—babies...Now that it's threatened their own, I think, I think people will be a little more concerned about it.

This person did not see AIDS as a reflection of the promiscuity of the gay community, but as a problem threatening gays and straights alike.

Another man, in his late thirties, spoke of a change in his perception:

> With time my perception has changed from, this is what one would expect when people abuse their body; to gee, this is a world-wide problem.

He went on to state that since that origin of AIDS can be traced to the third world, AIDS could be seen as:

> A result of a lack of concern that developed nations have had to underdeveloped nations in terms of trying to foster the standard of living to some minimum level that is at least hygienic.

Thus he perceived the responsibility for the AIDS crises to lie within the political economy of capitalist society.

A final coping strategy was to donate money to AIDS causes. Financial contributions were an adequate involvement of oneself in helping persons with AIDS. As one engineer admitted, however:

> I'm too involved in my own world to go out and march for AIDS; if there was a benefit I'd give money. Right now it's an abstraction, it's not a reality.

In these cases the individuals maintained their link to AIDS victims within their community through a financial relationship, but depersonalized the problem by maintaining social distance from PWAs.

Interacting with PWAs

All interviewed mentioned that they did not think people really faced the problem of AIDS until someone they knew contracted it or they contracted it themselves. If it did not "hit home," they could ignore the situation. A 26-year-old Latino admitted:

> I'm one of those people who deal with it indirectly, because it hasn't hit home. I know what AIDS is, and I know how you can get it, and my attitude is... I'm safe and I'm careful so it's not going to happen to me...It hasn't hit a chord, but if a friend had it...I guess it would break up my little world; I think my crystal ball would crack, because it means it's something I have to deal with. It's not reality; it's reality, but it's unreal for me.

In this case, the individual separated himself from gay people who had the stigma of disease because they were not close to him. Gay men predicted that if loved ones or close friends contracted the disease, they would confront it more directly. The PWAs gay men encountered were members of their "near group" (Yablonsky, 1959), yet they were strangers or casual acquaintances. In all but one case, gay men maintained high levels of social distance by insulating themselves physically and socially from PWAs.

While gay men attempted to avoid the subject of AIDS, they tried to avoid interaction with PWAs as well. A 21-year-old student stated that after he had met someone with AIDS, he did not want to deal with that person any longer:

> Actually I'm surprised at myself, I'm not a snob. I would have been his friend (a person he had met with AIDS). It's more, I don't have to deal with that, his life is really screwed up...cause he's gonna die. It means I don't need to get emotionally involved with someone who's gonna die.

Not wanting to confront death, this man dissociated himself from a dying person. "The dreaded, awful thing," as he put it, became the PWAs master status, overshadowing any other status he possessed. More commonly, respondents saw other gays and not themselves as avoiding and ignoring PWAs. A 21-year-old man observed:

> Well, I think they would prefer it if they (PWAs) didn't come out to the bars. I really think they don't want to see it, they just don't want to deal with it...They just didn't want to be reminded of it...A lot of people are very self-centered, and they wouldn't even want to bother giving anyone any support.

This man believed that gays did not want PWAs to go to gay bars, "home territories" (Lyman and Scott, 1967) for the gay community, since PWAs represent the stigma of AIDS.

Gay men may also interact with PWAs in restricted sociable, nonsexual ways. One 21-year-old man, John, recalled the first time he came in contact with someone who had AIDS:

> I met a guy this weekend, and I was attracted to him. He told me he had
> AIDS. My first impulse was to run, but before he told me this I had told
> him I would give him a ride home—so He told me he was a hustler. He
> wanted me to sleep with him, but no way though...He was so strong
> (emotionally) even though he was at a very weak point. He asked me into
> his house. I went in and tucked him into bed. I gave him a back rub, he
> went to sleep and I just looked at him for about 15 minutes cause it was
> just such a weird thing. Then I let myself out.

John was ambivalent when he found out his new acquaintance had AIDS. He was
attracted by some attributes of the individual, but at the same time, he feared
contracting AIDS or being emotionally involved with a dying person. Thus, he related
to this PWA in a physical, caring yet nonsexual way. While he spoke with his new
acquaintance once after this encounter, he decided the relationship was too uncomfortable. The ambiguity of the stigmatized status greatly inhibited the possibility of
interaction (Davis, 1961).

One 27-year-old man discussed the boundaries he placed around sociability:

> I was at a bar and someone pointed this person out to me as having AIDS.
> He seemed like a nice person; he was playing pool. I'd have played pool
> with him. I don't think I would have, this is terrible, asked him to my
> home.

In this case, relating to the person with AIDS was permitted as long as it remained at
a distance. This man believed that a gay bar was an acceptable place for social
encounters. However, he would not admit the stigmatized individual into the privacy
of his home—an extension of body space—out of fear of contamination (Scott, 1969).

One man in his early thirties chose an alternative strategy of embracing and
accepting persons with the disease, and went so far as to court physical danger in
doing so. He recalled:

> (AIDS) made me question what was important to me. Am I contributing
> to things? When AIDS came I jumped in helping...People thought I was
> crazy when I first started volunteering...had felt separated from the gay
> community. This was a way for me to be involved.

This man, Harry, felt linked to the gay community through his work with AIDS
organizations. Harry also related a story about becoming involved with a particular
PWA:

> I was at a party and one guy, when I met him I didn't know he had it. I
> had a physical attraction to find out who this guy was. He told me he had
> AIDS. When I found out, I had a sensation of finding someone and losing
> them all at the same time. I had volunteered with many people with

AIDS—didn't know them, never reacted to them. With this guy I felt incredibly sad. I'm attracted to people who are vulnerable and also strong. I had sex with him. We became good friends. I'm secondarily responsible for his care now.

About one month after this interview I found out Harry's friend had died.

Harry normally separated his emotional life from the PWAs he helped through a Los Angeles counseling center. When he became attracted to a PWA, however, the threat of physical contamination did not stand in the way of interaction. Harry's experience was rare; most men did not consider it necessary to endanger themselves physically in order to demonstrate acceptance for PWAs.

Personal involvement does not always mean accepting the problem of AIDS as something that can affect oneself. At the AIDS seminar mentioned above, an AIDS volunteer spoke about his involvement with PWAs. He mentioned that while he fought against AIDS through his involvement, he initially felt that PWAs were not like him. He kept a mental separation from them. Yet over time, he began to see himself as a member of a high-risk group. PWAs "look like me," he said.

Conclusion

AIDS threatens gay men with both physical danger and double stigma. In response, nearly all persons sought to put some kind of barrier between themselves and PWAs. In identifying with PWAs, gays not only confronted the possibility that they might get sick and die, but that they might by forced to assume the social stigma of AIDS. The thought that "I" might get AIDS, that AIDS "looks like me," was a reality perhaps too painful and too costly for gays to readily accept. At the same time, many gays felt ambivalent about PWAs within their community. While they could not fully embrace PWAs within their community, they could not forget them either.

Members of stigmatized groups who want to avoid the stereotypes attached to their stigma tend to separate themselves from others who are more stigmatized. They label themselves "normal" in relation to group members who exhibit the stigmatized characteristics of the group. For example, those who are hard of hearing set themselves apart from the deaf (Higgins, 1980) and the visually impaired from the blind (Criddle, 1953).

The AIDS crisis has caused outsiders to impute the double stigma of disease and promiscuity to all gays. As a result, "normal" gays have attempted to avoid this stigma by separating themselves from PWAs—their doubly stigmatized own.

One way gays have effected this separation is by joining the out-group in their condemnation of promiscuity. Thus, they blamed PWAs for their illness in much the same way as the larger society. Similarly, Reiss (1964) and Hencken (1985) have maintained that individuals who engage in homosexual acts but want to avoid the stigma of a homosexual label, employ elaborate explanations for their own behavior and espouse the conventional stereotypes about homosexuals. Other ways gays maintained separateness from the doubly stigmatized included physical distance, emotional distance, and distance through self-concept.

The problem of distancing oneself from others yet embracing one's own is not unique to gay men. Other stigmatized groups have experienced similar ambivalence. Frazier (1957) noted that blacks who entered the middle class in the first half of the twentieth century dissociated themselves from those blacks who were poor and did not accept white cultural values. While many more blacks entered the middle class during and after the 1960's, Glasgow (1980) and Lemann (1986) have both noted that these blacks dissociated themselves from the black "underclass." Lemann noted the ambivalence of middle-class blacks in that they felt solidarity with poor blacks, yet maintained distance from them.

Another stigmatized community, German Jews in the nineteenth century, constructed stereotypes of a "certain type of Jew" (Gay, 1978) from whom they dissociated themselves in order to assimilate into German society. German Jews also stigmatized the *ostijuden* or Eastern European Jews who immigrated to Germany. While these immigrants were both poor and culturally different, they were also their "own" and invoked a certain amount of solidarity.

In late nineteenth-century America, German Jewish immigrants who had already established themselves in the middle class once again dissociated themselves from the newly immigrated Eastern European Jews. German Jews perceived the newer immigrants as poor, crude, ignorant, and politically radical. German Jews believed their middle-class position would be jeopardized if the broader society attributed these traits to them. Most middle-class Jews sought to purify the immigrants by Americanizing them (Glazer, 1957; Howe, 1976; Waxman, 1983). Despite the stigma, however, the Germans felt a kinship with their fellows Jews.

The presence of doubly stigmatized group members threatened the limited status both the black and Jewish communities had achieved over time. In the same way, the stigma of AIDS has damaged the efforts of the gay community to gain status (Altman, 1986). All of these groups believed that creating distance would help maintain the social and economic gains they had achieved over time (Coleman, 1986; Schur, 1980). However, the common bonds they shared as a stigmatized community prevented them from severing all relationships with the doubly stigmatized.

While blacks and Jews could look forward to the future "normalization" of the doubly stigmatized members of their community through assimilation into the mainstream of middle-class society, PWAs cannot be relieved of the stigma of their disease. Even if AIDS becomes dissociated from the gay lifestyle, it is still a terminal disease. In light of our society's efforts to avoid confronting death and the terminally ill, the destigmatization of PWAs remains a remote possibility.

In the future, other minority communities will have to confront the added stigma presented by the AIDS crisis. The majority of heterosexual cases of AIDS have occurred in the black and Latino communities, and have been connected to intravenous drug-use—a complication involving yet another double stigma. In response, a new wave of racism in the broader society may accompany the spread of AIDS in minority communities, reinforcing the stereotypes of blacks and Hispanics as not only morally corrupt, but also diseased (Patton, 1985: 11–12). As a result, members of these groups may employ coping strategies like those mentioned above to insulate themselves from both a deadly disease and the social contamination attached to it.

REFERENCES

Albert, E.(1986a). "Acquired Immune Deficiency Syndrome: The Victim and The Press." *Studies in Communication* 3:135–58.

Albert, E. (1986b). "Illness and Deviance: The Responses of The Press to Aids". In D.A. Feldman and T.A. Johnson (eds.), *The Social Dimensions of Aids: Method and Theory*. New York: Praeger.

Altman, D. (1986). *AIDS In The Mind of America*. Garden City, New York: Anchor.

Barbarin, O.A. (1986). "Family Experience of Stigma in Childhood Cancer," Pp. 163–184 in S.C. Ainlay, G. Becker, and L.M. Coleman (eds.), *The Dilemma of Difference*. New York: Plenum.

Baker, A.J. (1986). "The Portrayal of AIDS in The Media: An Analysis of Articles in the New York Times," Pp. 179–194 in D.A. Feldman and T.M. Johnson (eds.), *The Social Dimensions of AIDS: Method and Theory*. New York: Praeger.

Biernacki, P. and D. Waldorf (1981). "Snowball Sampling: Problems and Techniques of Chain Referral Sampling." *Sociological Methods and Research* 10:141–63.

Birenbaum, A. (1970). "On Managing a Courtesy Stigma." *Journal of Health and Social Behavior* 11:196–206.

Bogardus, E.S. (1959). *Social Distance*. Yellow Springs, Ohio: Antioch.

Coleman, L.M. (1986). "Stigma: An Enigma Demystified," Pp. 211–232 in S.C. Ainlay, G. Becker, and L.M. Coleman (eds.), *Dilemma of Difference*. New York: Plenum.

Criddle, R. (1953). *Love is Not Blind*. New York: Norton.

Davis, F. (1961). "Deviance Disavowal: The Management of Strained Interaction by the Visibly Handicapped." *Social Problems* 9:120–32.

Des Jarlais, D.C., S.R. Friedman, and D. Strug (1986). "Aids and Needle Sharing Within The IV-Drug Use Subculture," Pp. 111–125 in D.A. Feldman and T. M. Johnson (eds.), *The Social Dimensions of AIDS: Method and Theory*. New York: Praeger.

Dosik, H. (1987). "The AIDS Doctors." Presented at the Annual Meeting of the American Sociological Association, Chicago.

Edwards, A. and V.A. Hiday (1987). "Attitudes Toward and Knowledge of AIDS," Presented at the annual meeting of the Society for the Study of Social Problems, Chicago.

Feldman, D.A. (1985). "AIDS and Social Change." *Human Organization* 44:343–348.

Frazier, E. F. (1957). *Black Bourgeoises*. New York: Free Press.

Gay, P. (1978). *Freud, Jews and Other Germans*. New York: Oxford University Press.

Glasgow, D.G. (1980). *The Black Underclass*. San Francisco: Jossey-Bass.

Glazer, N. (1957). *American Judaism*. Chicago: University of Chicago Press.

Goffman, E. (1963). *Stigma*. Englewood Cliffs, New Jersey: Prentice-Hall.

Hamilton, L.M., S. Perry, and V. Pratt (1987). "College Students and AIDS as a Social Issue." Presented at the annual meeting of Society for the Study of Social Problems, Chicago.

Hencken, J.D. (1985). "Conceptualizations of Homosexual Behavior Which Preclude Homosexual Self-labeling," Pp. 53–64 in J.P. DeCecco (ed.), *Gay Personality and Sexual Labeling*. New York: Harrington Park.

Higgins, P.C. (1980). *Outsiders in a Hearing World: A Sociology of Deafness*. Beverly Hills, California: Sage.

Howe, I. (1976). *World of Our Fathers*. New York: Harcourt Brace Jovanovich.

Hughes, E.C. (1945). "Dilemmas and Contradictions of Status." *American Journal of Sociology* 50:353–359.

Kayal, P.M. (1985)."Morals, Medicine and the AIDS Epidemic." *Journal of Religion and Health* 24:218–238.

Kitsuse, J.I. (1964). "Societal Reaction to Deviant Behavior: Problems of Theory and Method," Pp. 87–100 in H.S. Becker (ed.), *The Other Side: Perspectives on Deviance*. New York: Free Press of Glencoe.

Kotarba, J.A. and N.G. Lang (1986). "Gay Lifestyle Change and AIDS: Preventive Health Care," Pp. 127–143 in D.A. Feldman and T.N. Johnson (eds.), *The Social Dimension of AIDS: Method and Theory*. New York: Praeger.

Lemann, N. (1986). "The Origins of the Underclass." *Atlantic* 256 (6): 31–55.

Lessor, R. (1987). "AIDS and the Social Science: the case for verstehen research methodology," Presented at the annual meeting of the Society for the Study of Social Problems, Chicago.

Lofland, J. (1969). *Deviance and Identity*. Englewood Cliffs, New Jersey: Prentice-Hall.

Lyman, S. and M.B. Scott (1967). "Territory: a Neglected Sociological Dimension." *Social Problems* 15:236–252.

Marmor, M., D.C. Des Jarlais, S.R. Friedman, M. Lyden, and W. Elsadr (1984), "The Epidemic of Acquired Immunodeficiency Syndrome (AIDS) and Suggestions for its Control in Drug Abusers." *Journal of Substance Abuse Treatment* 1 (4) 237–247.

Morgan, D.L. and M.T. Spanish (1984). "Focus Groups: A New Tool for Qualitative Research." *Qualitative Sociology* 7:253–270.

Patton, C. (1985). *Sex and Germs: The Politics of AIDS*. Boston: South End.

Reiss, A. J., Jr. (1964). "The Social Integration of Peers and Queers," Pp. 181–210 in H.S. Becker (ed.), *The Other Side: Perspectives on Deviance*. New York: Free Press.

Schur, E.M. (1980). *The Politics of Deviance* Englewood Cliffs, New Jersey: Prentice-Hall.

Scott, R.A. (1969). *The Making of Blind Men*. New York: Russell Sage.

Sontag, S. (1979). *Illness as Metaphor*. New York: Random House.

Spenser, N. (1983). "Medical Anthropology and the AIDS Epidemic: A Case Study in San Francisco." *Urban Anthropology* 12:141–159.

Warren, C.A.B. (1974). *Identity and Community in the Gay World*. New York: Oxford University Press.

Waxman, C.I. (1983). *America's Jews in Transition*. Philadelphia: Temple University Press.

Yablonsky, L. (1959). "The Delinquent Gang as a Near Group." *Social Problems* 7:108–117.

Chapter 47

OSTOMATES:
NEGOTIATING AN INVOLUNTARY DEVIANT IDENTITY

Mark Nagler

This investigation examines, from a symbolic interactionist perspective, a case of spoiled identity. The research examines a segment of the physically disabled who are subject to ostomatic status.

Ostomies are becoming a common operation. Ostomy is a collective and generalized term used to refer to different types of bowel and urinary surgery. Common to all of these surgical procedures is the creation of an artificial body opening, located on the abdomen and called a "stoma." The term stoma is derived from two Greek words, *stomoun* meaning "to provide an opening" and *tome* which refers to a "cutting operation." This opening becomes the new body orifice from which body waste elimination occurs, replacing the anus and/or urethra. The waste is then disposed of into a collecting device known as an "appliance" or "bag," which is lightweight and often disposable. It is attached to the body in the frontal stomach region of the abdomen. A few drops of feces or urine flow from the stoma on a regular basis because there is no voluntary muscle in the stoma which can control excretion.

To a layman, explained in this manner, ostomy surgery appears to be relatively "simple." This surgery however, involves many complications, both physical and emotional. The patient in one way or another must come into direct contact with bodily wastes once the operation is performed, and it requires, to some degree, the alteration of one's life patterns. It necessitates major changes in order that a person might live a normal life without rectum or normal bladder function. The common concerns expressed by potential ostomates are: "Will I bulge?"; "Will my sexual functions be interfered with?"; and "Will I be able to resume various activities including sports?"

From a broad sociological perspective this investigation is one which focuses on identity. Identity has been an important sociological concern which had its beginnings with theorists such as Cooley, Mead, Thomas and Znaniecki, and Blumer. The tradition has continued in the present by the works of contemporary sociologists such as Becker, Goffman, Davis, Glazer and Strauss. Research on ostomates is part of the sociological tradition which analyzes the pattern by which actors victimized by involuntary spoiled identity cope with the physical consequences and the social meaning and reality of being subjected to instantaneous disability. This spoiled identity is often viewed and labelled by others in negative terms. The project investigated the ramifications of being accorded ostomatic status and examined the reactions of patients to their altered physical and social status.

From a conceptual perspective, spoiled identity evolves when an actor has had or believes he has had the attributes which normally define his presence in day to day interactions compromised, so that he is perceived by himself and/or others as possessing attributes which are often negatively defined or labelled deviant. Victims of stigma encounter difficulties in acceptance, maintaining and/or changing their personal identities.

The difficulties for many who are defined as disabled and/or involuntary deviants stem from the fact that they too accept the deviant label applied to them. For the victims, by accepting the self-fulfilling prophecy of ostomy status, the process becomes increasingly insidious. When this is the case, the ostomate is open to attack from within as well as from without.

This project is focused on a basic problem of sociology—the relationship between an individual's identity, the identity one presents to the world, and the reactions, real and imagined, of others towards the victim. As a consequence of socialization and one's achieved and ascribed status, one's identity is usually perceived as being continuous, consistent and in an established pattern fitting into an orderly career. The orderly career comprises sets of expectations as to how the actor will be treated in relationships with others. Deviations from established patterns cause spoiled identity.

By focusing on deviations produced by altered physical status as a result of surgery, we can observe how individuals often search for new identities. In viewing the process whereby disabled individuals attempt to regain normalcy or successful rehabilitation, one is able to analyze the patterns illustrated by actors attempting to come to terms with spoiled identity. One can thus ascertain the processes utilized by these actors (involuntary deviants) involved in an identity formation process or in an identity reformation process.

The Sample

Thirty-five patients were intensively investigated over the course of three and one half years. The participants were Caucasian and of Canadian citizenship of first to fourth generation, ranging in age from nine to eighty-six. Twenty of the subjects were male and all volunteers except two, one Jew and one agnostic, were from Protestant or Catholic backgrounds. These volunteers were representative of a wide range of socio-economic backgrounds. The sample included ten housewives, two executives, three students, three salesmen, thirteen blue collar workers and three retired subjects.

It was noted that there were no differences displayed in the types of problems and difficulties encountered or in the types of adjustments or adaptations that were subsequently illustrated after surgery. It appears that class backgrounds and education do not influence how actors react to being ostomates.

The patients experienced varying degrees of anxiety during the interview. Most patients seemed to be shy and reserved about matters of sexual intimacy.

This study was hampered by its relatively small sample size. The thirty-five patients consented to a series of in-depth interviews which in some instances commenced prior to surgery and extended over the course of the following three years. Their spouses, siblings and peers often contributed valuable data. In addition ninety-four other people were interviewed which included families of patients, doctors (General Practitioners, Internists and Surgeons), psychiatrists, medical social workers, psychiatric social workers, nurses and estomotherapists, who provided valuable insights into adaptive patterns illustrated by these involuntary deviants.

The limitations were offset by the breadth and intensity of the investigation into the ostomatic career of each individual. This investigation analyzed changes in the perception of self as the patient made the transition through seven basic stages; 1) minor symptoms phase; 2) major symptoms phase 3) diagnoses phase; 4) hospital preoperative phase; 5) hospital post operative phase; 6) adjustment phase— normalcy or disabled; and 7) an assessment of the patient in terms of normalcy, identity or renegotiated new identity.

Nine of the patients could not recall the signs that led to their eventual surgery. In four instances the patients were born with spina bifida and therefore had never known normal evacuative functions. Seven of the patients had been involved in severe injuries as the result of falls, traffic accidents and other events, during which their bladder and/or kidney had been severely ruptured, necessitating ostomy surgery. In six of these cases, the patients had never heard of ostomy status prior to surgery. They literally awoke from surgery with conditions which they never anticipated. Reactions were dramatic: "How could they do this to me?"; "They can't do this to a normal person"; "How can I live with this, my normal life will disappear?" "Marriage will be impossible." "Sex will be impossible."

These concerns afflict those who become ostomates as the result of instantaneous conditions. These are understandable concerns which are usually alleviated as one becomes familiar with the strategies of coping with ostomy status. The major concern for those between the ages of 15 and 30 center around the acceptability to the opposite sex and sexual activity. There are four normal and solvable problems after surgery, a) failure (of erection or orgasm) due to attempting intercourse before strength returns following surgery; b) serious anxiety about the ability to perform sexually, or about the attractiveness of one's altered body image, about the possibility of odor and the security of the appliance or stoma covering; c) depression which many people suffer following any surgery; d) excessive medication and/or alcohol. For most ostomates, where age is not a factor, these concerns and problems can usually be partially if not totally eliminated.

Eight individuals in the sample who had previously experienced normal sexual relations, encountered difficulties in reestablishing sexual activity. In seven of the eight cases, the difficulties were associated with the social and psychological implications of being an ostomate, of wearing a bag, of spillage, and of the escaping or possible escaping of urine, feces or gas. For the one patient the ability to have an erection after surgery was apparently a physiological impossibility. "They told me it beats dying, but that is very difficult for someone who is in love and has enjoyed a good sex life. I have never had any problems before, but last month my wife moved into another bedroom."

The new ostomate often perceives rejection by family, friends, medical and paramedical personnel during the immediate post- operative phase. It is at this stage that the patients are sometimes victimized by escaping gas, spillage, pain and pressure from nurses and/or estomotherapists to manage their own appliances. In other words, new patients are forced to take care of themselves. During this time, patients become acutely aware of their spoiled identities. The resulting anxieties often cause severe depression.

Some patients develop a myriad of physical, psychological and social problems. From a physiological perspective, in most cases when age is not a factor, a normal life may be resumed after ostomy surgery. From a medical perspective patients are considered cured. They encounter social stigma because they are "different" and their social adjustment to their spoiled identity is not easily accomplished.

The ostomate is constantly required to be involved in the management of the evacuation of bodily wastes. In many instances the new ostomate is repelled by spillage, escaping gas, skin irritation and accidents which plague most ostomates. The reality of being involved with the disposal of one's waste on a permanent basis forces many ostomates to radically redefine their images unless surgical resection occurs.

Many ostomates are negatively identified, as a consequence of the physiological effects of ostomy surgery, which hinders sociability and thus produces varying degrees of personal anxiety. Ostomates have become stereotyped and thus stereotyping leads to consequences which may be relatively severe. Some ostomates withdraw in varying degree from societal participation. Many new ostomates are inclined to accept the credibility of folklore, which defines their status as unacceptable. Hence some ostomates are often pressured to disguise their conditions.

The emotional reactions demonstrated by ostomy patients both at the time of the diagnosis and following surgery, are best examined by keeping in mind the importance of body image and North American values of cleanliness.

One of the human organism's earliest accomplishments is the control of waste elimination, a function which is surrounded by strong emotional components as a result of North American cultural values and body perceptions. An individual relinquishes these controls with varying degrees of anxiety. Objectively, having an ostomy appears to be a small price to pay for life itself. Nevertheless, all humans are creatures of their environment, and lack of control of body waste is often perceived as intolerable. Incontinence, through loss of this control, implies a return to infancy, a subsequent loss of self-esteem and resulting depression which may, in extreme cases, result in suicide.

The idea of having to manually expel body wastes is repugnant to most, even to many medical personnel. This patten of elimination evokes a sense of inadequacy, dirtiness and exposure. To the victims, there is a destruction of masculinity and femininity. Whether one loses a limb, an eye, or a breast, all mutilative surgeries frighten and outrage the patient as he or she faces a compromised physique. No longer are they capable of coming close to society's ideal which is that of the "body beautiful"; their physical appearance has been robbed of integrity. There is a high social premium placed on cleanliness. In mass media there is an emphasis on the ideal body image. Advertisements inform and indeed threaten that we will never find a job, a spouse or friends with the presence of odor or "sensual barriers." Ostomatic defects and other surgically produced conditions create insurmountable barriers to success. At all costs, we are told we must appear and smell attractive.

The symbolic identification of cleanliness and presumed acceptability of the clean individual is taken for granted. Being defined as dirty indicates low status and places the individual in the realm of the "unacceptable." Being seen as "dirty," therefore, has ramifications that are physical, psychological and social in nature.

Many patients solve the physical difficulties associated with being an ostomate, but encounter varying difficulties in establishing and/or maintaining social relationships. One 36-year old insurance salesman who had become an ostomate was subsequently separated and divorced from his wife. One day after having taken his five year old daughter for a birthday dinner he committed suicide. The daughter had accused him of being a "stinker." In this case the individual was able to cope with the physical difficulties but could not adapt to the social stigma produced by ostomy status.

Ostomy status can be conceptualized as stigmatized deviance. The physical impairment imposed by ostomy surgery involves some degree of spoiled identity with regard to the perceived, and usually, the physical performance of sexual and elimination functions. In most, if not all cases, this impairment penetrates the total interactional sphere of the victims. The existence of the physical stigma is a subjective and verbal aspect of one's self concept of identity and one's identity as perceived by many others. Personal cleanliness and sexual prowess are central themes of mass culture. These themes become significant parts of one's total identity.

Ostomates are involuntary deviants in a social milieu where the consequences of the deviance or perceived deviance becomes the central organizing factor in their patterns of social relationships. The ostomates are required to institute a series of strategies that establish, maintain or change many aspects of their relationships with their interacting counterparts.

The extent that these impairments are detectable affects the degree of perceived deviance. The nature of the impairment is different from other permanent impairments such as blindness, but the consequences for identity renegotiation are similar. Because of this similarity, findings about the renegotiated careers add to our knowledge about the careers of permanently stigmatized involuntary deviants.

With regard to structuring relationships, it is well known that *all* victims of disability—be it social or physical—*respond* to stigma producing situations *differently*. Contemporary symbolic interactionists such as Goffman (1963), Roth (1963) and Scott (1969) have illustrated that affected actors utilize a variety of responses to adapt or maladapt to the contingencies of new conditions. Whenever one examines the roles of ex-mental patients, polio victims, amputees or ostomates, victims of disability exhibit a consistent sequence or career of responses during renegotiation of identity. These responses range from denial, anger, resentment, bargaining, inevitability, to depression. For the stigmatized actors, renegotiation involves three stages: a fictional acceptance of one's new status and acceptance of the disability; the normalization of role taking which includes acceptance of self and awareness and understanding of one's limitations; and finally, institutionalization which is a stage where one not only accepts one's self for what he or she is, but where the actor is accepted by others.

The stigma engulfing potential of ostomy status is dramatic. Twenty of the adult ostomates interviewed had never heard of the procedures associated with ostomate surgery prior to diagnosis. In eleven of the instances cancer was a precipitating factor. The shock associated with diagnosis and the ramifications of ostomy status cannot be underestimated. Physicians have stated, "I'm sorry to tell you this but..." or "You will probably have to go through an extremely difficult surgical procedure"; or "Believe me if there were any other way..." or perhaps the most destructive of all, "It beats dying." Diagnosis conveyed in this way can hardly be expected to generate positive responses. Assessment of the medical literature indicates that as many as eight percent of various ostomy samples commit suicide as they are unable to contend with the physical and social consequences of their involuntary status.

The majority of patients initially chose to not disclose their anticipated status as they associated it with a deviant identity. Ostomates often encounter difficulty in their attempts to enter the so called ostomate subculture. Establishing an ostomate identity and/or public disclosure is plagued with many difficulties. The majority of patients in their relations with relatives, peers, the medical and paramedical fraternities encountered varying degrees of alienation because all parties are inclined to believe that the status of being an ostomate places one in a devalued group.

Being in a devalued group the motivation to closet one's deviant identity as an ostomate is often profitable. Because of the positive values of cleanliness and sexuality, and the negative attribution associated with body waste, one can understand why ostomates are inclined to believe that they should hide their spoiled identities.

One patient commented, "I feel like an ex-con with a great intellectual ability at mathematics but being unable to become a bank manager in spite of years of straight behavior. There is no possibility because of the reputation and it does not matter whether the reputation is legitimate." Another patient commented, "I felt like a criminal because for my job I lied and did not disclose that I was an ileostomate. If I had explained my condition, I would not have been hired. I was identified two and one half years after I had been working. Although I was not fired, the boss told me I should be ashamed because I was a liar and therefore my opportunities would be limited."

This incident illustrates the pressures for concealment. If ostomates desire normalcy many believe that it becomes mandatory to conceal their deviant identity. The possibility of coming out of the closet is plagued with many costs—economic, political, psychological and social. For the majority, after varying degrees of experimentation as an ostomate, it becomes operant to disclose the deviant status. Many patients have no choice as it is difficult if not impossible to camouflage their ostomy condition. For some of those who can camouflage ostomy status there are many positive gains to be achieved.

For the majority of patients the post-operative surgical experience, with experimentation in all realms—social, psychological, political, allows them to gain the skills needed to manage their new stigmatized identity. They become successful in conveying to others that they are not social and physical "cancers" and are "near normal human beings." A third group of ostomates, mainly those also afflicted with the difficulties of ageism are significantly disabled as the result of the new deviant status and are forced to relinquish many of their former roles. In some cases the relinquishment of these roles is not voluntary but a direct result of the problems associated with managing the limitations imposed by being an ostomate. A fourth group which is found amongst many other patients, who are plagued with stigmatizing conditions, are those who utilize their ostomy status to achieve secondary gains through illness. Two ostomates in the study opted for early retirement when apparently there was no physical need to do so. One subsequently committed suicide.

Ostomates often have similar anxieties to those encountered by homosexuals who contemplate coming out of the closet. The cost of coming out may be substantial even though the identity in and of itself may not be considered deviant in some quarters. The possibility of discrimination, isolation, alienation and honesty create an ambiguous social environment. Many ostomates view the costs and advantage of disclosure but are unwilling to make the choice.

The strategy of disclosure or concealment rests on a complex interaction of factors which the ostomate views as stigma-producing experiences or potentially stigmatizing experiences. This is enhanced by the ambiguity that there are always many who are prepared to accept a deviant identity and to normalize relationships while there are social contacts which are restructured if not destroyed as a consequence of disclosure. The victims find that they can never count on acceptance and thus the personal costs are seen as extreme.

Goffman, Glazer and Strauss, Becker and others have focused on the problems associated with the general sociological problems of how actors utilize strategies to manage what they see as discreditable in their self-concepts. Schneider and Conrad (1979) maintained: "We tried to see how people attempt to maintain favorable or at least neutral definitions of self, given a condition for which no new readily available supportive identity or subculture exists, and which most of the time, except for the occurrence of periodic seizures, is invisible." Ostomate status tends to be invisible, but the possibility of spillage, the odor of escaping gas, skin irritation and the negative reputation furnished by ostomate identity serve to pressure victims to closet their new, undesired, involuntary identities. This identity takes on extremely deviant perceptions because of contemporary values and the bizarre consequences of being an ostomate.

In addition to these difficulties, new ostomates often encounter difficulties in physically looking after themselves, in obtaining employment, in obtaining life insurance policies, and in establishing, maintaining and developing relationships. To the teenager or young adult the awareness of ostomy status and its consequences is often severe. As W.C. Fields maintained, "Some things are better then sex, and some things are worse but there is nothing exactly like it." The majority are able to have sex and to bear children.

The stigma associated with ostomy status is somewhat imprecise. In some instances patients encounter little difficulty and in other situations the efforts the patient must make to achieve normalcy may be described as monumental.

A stigmatized illness, be it mental illness, leprosy, cancer, tuberculosis, epilepsy and/or ostomy status tends to be an individualizing and privatizing experience. Persons with stigmatized illness are doubly insulated from one another, at least in one very important sense. Because there is no illness subculture they are separated, alone and unconnected with others sharing the same problems.

Although ostomy organizations which are self-help groups exist, the majority of new ostomates seldom have prolonged encounters with the organizations. They are prone to reject these organizations as making unwarranted intrusions into their private lives. Surgeons usually encourage patients to affiliate with ostomy organizations in order to learn the strategies of coping. Only two of the nine surgeons interviewed gave the name of new patients to ostomy associations. Most surgeons felt that it was not their obligation to become involved with the patients' subsequent social and psychological rehabilitative difficulties.

Conclusions

The study was undertaken to analyze the process by which the victims of spoiled identity (ostomates) form new identities. Because of the views of medical and paramedical personnel, patients, peers and society in general, it can be said that ostomy status can be perceived as stigmatized deviance.

Whether one examines the roles of ex-mental patients, polio victims, mastectomates or ostomates, victims of disability exhibit a consistent sequence or career of responses during renegotiation of new identity. These responses range from denial, anger, resentment, bargaining, inevitability, depression and usually renegotiation of a new identity and perhaps even to suicide. For the stigmatized actor renegotiation involves three strategies: a fictional acceptance of one's new status and acceptance of the disability; the normalization of role-taking which includes the acceptance of the disability, acceptance of self, awareness and understanding of one's limitations; and finally institutionalization which is the stage where one not only accepts oneself for what he or she is, but where the actor is accepted by others (Glazer and Strauss, 1967). In contrast for actors afflicted with an illness where recovery is possible, illness involves a non-stigmatizing deviance. There is an eventual return to the status quo as the actor encounters no social barriers as a consequence of illness. This pattern is revealed in Roth's (1963:14) study, *Timetables*. However, when an individual becomes disabled as the result of becoming blind or assuming the status of an ostomate, one discovers that one's disability is a stigmatized deviance.

For ostomates the career of renegotiating a new identity begins when an individual realizes that the physical transformation is about to be accomplished or is already accomplished. Before this point patients seldom realize the meaning of ostomatic status and its implications. The ability to build new identities is more or less modified by the severity of the disruption or change required in a new lifestyle and the result of ostomatic status. Older patients generally have more difficulty in addition to the difficulties imposed by becoming an ostomate. Ostomates acquire new identities more easily if they have the advantage of the following situations: 1) they are able to manage or conceal their physical conditions in interactions with significant others; 2) they were born into or acquire this deviant status at an early age so that they are not aware of the terms of their "abnormality"; 3) they are embedded in a familial situation characterized by the existence of strong positive primary relationships; 4) their status has already been established by virtue of achieved status in the community; 5) that they are married, past the child-bearing stage and physically able to cope with the consequences of their deviant status; 6) they are not required to relinquish any previously established roles; 7) they receive adequate counseling from medical and paramedical personnel, both prior to and following surgery (this seldom occurs).

The extent to which the above seven sociological preconditions are present usually determines the degree to which ostomates can successfully establish their identities.

Involuntary deviants, be they victims of physical, psychological or social stigma, seldom enjoy the consequences of their compromised identities except perhaps for those who utilize their acquired status to achieve secondary gains. For ostomates and other victims of spoiled identity their capacities for achieving acceptance are often limited by the stigma which the victims accept (self-fulfilling prophecy) or the stigma which is attributed by others to these involuntary deviants. They are the victims of a labelling process. As is known, deviance is viewed not as a property of an act itself, but rather as behavior which violates someone's conception of a rule and is identified as doing so (Becker, 1963). Here the distinction between voluntary and involuntary deviance is a useful and theoretically important distinction in the study of spoiled identity. In this context as Sagarin (1975:36) maintains, in speaking of the physically disabled,

> In the capacity of sociologist, therefore, one is no longer concerned with how people got that way but how and why they are defined in a devalued manner and with what consequences for all parties (1975:36).

Faced with the accusation that one is some kind of a different person (or not normal) the labelled person has two options: to attempt to fight the imposition of the label or to accept it. Acceptance of the label involves living up to or down to the expectations of the labellers. Ostomates, especially those who believe they have been seriously mutilated from a physical and social perspective become marginal actors. These marginal patients are seen as fulfilling a devalued position as they possess or are said to possess attributes which are different from the usual. Their life chances are often reduced because of spoiled identity. The problematic nature of their acceptance leads to renegotiation of new identities. The goal in renegotiating identity is to maintain and establish relationships which may otherwise be negatively affected.

The central sociological dimensions upon which the adjustment and the new identity formation of a disabled individual evolve is the fact that societal definitions of the disabled, be they correct, ambivalent or false, are often shared by the victims. Unlike the criminal deviant, the disabled involuntary deviant usually shares the values of the dominant society with regard to the stigma involved in the acquired status. The actor usually values and seeks legitimacy. Legitimacy is obtained most easily through minimizing the visibility and the relevance of the disability in the presence of one's self. The literature on deviant behavior and its utility for understanding the formation of identity, has limitations when applied to the case of the involuntary deviant. The involuntary deviant is like the Mertonion type who shares group norms but is blocked in the access to the means to conformity and either constantly attempts to conform, becomes the ritualist or retreatist, but in any instance it is not the rebel who, by choice, rejects the legitimacy to achieve goals (Merton 1959:131). The majority of ostomates opt for acceptance. When one examines the careers of the instantaneously blind (Scott), the severely burned (McGreggor) and ostomates, one generally finds that they pass through a series of stages which are theoretically critical in the subsequent identity formation process. Involuntary deviants illustrate that during the process undertaken in their renegotiation of identity they undergo a series of events where their awareness and patterns of acceptance of self and others are developed as a consequence of their patterns of interaction.

In the immediate post-operative phase, many involuntary deviants initially adapt to their altered conditions because the group that is paramount in determining their legitimacy, to a large extent in the immediate post-operative phase, is medical. However, interaction with others outside the medical realm subsequent to this phase often destroys the legitimate or normal interaction potential of ostomates. As a consequence of stigma their legitimate identity is damaged and perhaps even destroyed. It must be noted that interaction with others can also establish a positive base for establishment of identity.

By noting the stages which ostomates encounter, we discover the process through which they are assigned a social identity as involuntary deviants by others and subsequently enter upon ongoing careers as deviants. Lemert (1967:457–468) states:

> The empirical evidence now available makes it doubtful that the emer-
> gence of a new morality and procedure for defining deviance can be laid
> to the creation of any one group, class or elite. Rather they are products
> of the interaction of groups.

Once an individual has been a victim of involuntary deviance, problems arise in the managing of this new deviant identity. The involuntary deviant must decide how to integrate his social identity with his personal identity. With medical and paramedical personnel as well as with fellow ostomates, the ostomate is well advised to be open about his difficulties, but with non-ostomates the values of openness is problematic. How the ostomate, as an involuntary deviant manages his damaged identity affects how he fares in his deviant career. For involuntary deviance the effects of their careers, their successes and their failures depends on their social, psychological and physiological capacities to manage and adapt to their conditions.

Ostomates, like other involuntary deviants, are required to assume multiple roles with resulting strain on their personal images. For the involuntary deviants, knowledge of the legitimate as well as the illegitimate means of encountering the ramifications of this strain is important in their subsequent adaptations (Cloward 1959:164–176).

Renegotiating one's identity is often difficult because, like some other involuntary deviants, both patients and interacting audiences often possess different sets of expectations. The immediate consequences for all parties may not be as severe as first anticipated. The new ostomate, like the "new ex-mental patient" often discovers that he may not be able to exercise control over the image he wishes to portray to the same degree as was possible before the advent of spoiled identity. Initially, exchange between the new ostomate and others can be characterized as strained interaction. As illustrated by Glazer and Strauss the difficulty emanates from the patten of awareness existing between the ostomate and those who constitute his interacting spheres.

When actors find that they are unable to elicit desired patterns of treatment they encounter the consequences of stigma. Relationships between ostomates and normals often proceed under conditions of anxiety due to embarrassment, concern, pity, shock, revulsion and compassion. These conditions destroy the normal basis of interaction. This leads to the utilization of defense mechanisms amongst those who are subject to disabling conditions. Those subject to spoiled identity often are aware that the core of their being is totally regulated by expectations that subtly govern interaction between normals and those defined as disabled, inadequate or in some other ways discredited.

Ostomy status threatens personal esteem as one's body image has been significantly altered. A fairly serious maladjustment rate amongst ostomates and a significant suicide rate indicates a potentially productive area for research in endeavoring to eliminate the difficulties associated with serious cases of maladjustment and involuntary deviance. Ostomates illustrate the dramatic effects of involuntary deviance. Their stigma arises from two fundamental alterations of ability to perform bodily functions which in most societies tend to be strictly regulated—the sexual and the evacuational.

The renegotiation of new identities as experienced by people with this stigma under such intense social focus can contribute significantly to our understanding of the process of identity formation of those who belong to that segment of society defined as involuntary deviants.

REFERENCES

Becker, H. (1963). *The Outsiders: Studies in the Sociology Deviance.* New York: Free Press.
Blumer. (1962). "Symbolic Interaction." In A. Rose (ed.), *Human Behavior and Social Process.* Boston: Houghton-Mifflin.
Cloward, R.A. (April 1959). "Illegitimate Means, Anomie, and Deviant Behavior" *American Sociological Review XXIV.*
Cooley, C.H. (1902). "The looking Glass Self" as quoted in A.R. Lindesmith and A. Strauss, *Social Psychology.* New York, Holt, Rinehart and Winston.
Davis, Fred. (1963). *Passage Through Crisis: Polio Victims and their families.* New York, Bobbs-Merrill.
———. (1967). "Deviance Disavowal: The Management of Strained Interaction by the Visible Handicapped." In J. Manis and B.N. Meltzer (eds.), A Reader in Social Psychology. Boston: Allyn and Bacon.
Goffman, E. (1963). Stigma: *Notes on the Management of Spoiled Identity.* Englewood Cliffs, New Jersey: Prentice-Hall.
Glaser, B.G. and A.L. Strauss. (October 1967). "Awareness Contexts and Social Interaction". *American Sociological Review, XXIV:* 669–679.
Lemert, E.M. (1967). *Human Deviance, Social Problems and Social Control.* Englewood Cliffs, New Jersey: Prentice-Hall.
McGreggor, F.C. (1951). "Some Psychological Problems Associated with Facial Deformities." *American Sociological Review* 16:629–35.
Mead, G.H. (1913). "The Social Self" *Journal of Philosophy.*
Merton, R.K. (1959). "Social Structure and Anomie" Pp. 131–139 in R.K. Merton (ed.), *Social Theory and Social Structure.* Glencoe, Illinois: The Free Press.
W.C. Fields as quoted by B.D. Mullen and K.A. McGinn. (1980). *The Ostomy Book:* 139. Palo Alto: Bull Publishing Company.
Roth, J. (1963). *Timetables.* Indianapolis: Bobbs Merrill.
Sagarin, E. (1975). *Deviants and Deviance.* New York: Praeger Publishers.
Schneider, J.W. and P. Conrad. (1979). "In the Closet with Illness: Epilepsy, Stigma Potential and Information Control." In Delos Kelly (ed.), *Deviant Behavior.* New York: St. Martin's Press.
Scott, R.A. (1969). *The Making of Blind Men.* New York: Russell Sage Foundation.

Part X

TRANSFORMING DEVIANCE

In previous sections of this reader, we have demonstrated how an individual comes to acquire a deviant identity, develop a deviant career, become involved in deviant subcultures, and the various stratagems they employ to mitigate the stigma potential of their "failing" on their daily rounds. In this final section, we shall focus on transforming deviant identities or exiting deviant careers.

In general, although we have portrayed the social lives of the pre-deviant and deviant as stressful, undesirable and problematic in nature—especially those who entered deviant careers involuntarily, the existing literature suggests that the ex-deviant faces far greater problems when he/she desires to leave the deviant world behind. Upon release from "total" or "people-processing institutions," the deviant's problems are far from being over. So too, do problems prevail for individuals who have led voluntary careers as deviants, independent of official processing. In either case, numerous problems lie ahead for individuals attempting to return to lives of conventionality or normalcy.

This is not to imply, however, that all deviants are dissatisfied with their deviant careers and wish to renounce them. But some do come to the realization that their deviant activities are too stressful, too punishing, self-destructive, or that the rewards are too little and the negative consequences are too big a price to pay. One of the major social conditions leading to identity transformation or exiting deviance is an identity crisis. Feelings of remorse, guilt, stress, or desire to rid self of the "spoiled identity" pinned upon him/her, lead the person to attempt to resume normal identities and social statuses.

The first selection by Patricia Adler, *"The 'Post' Phase of Deviant Careers: Reintegrating Drug Traffickers,"* deals with the career paths of former occupational criminals. In particular, she analyzes the conditions affecting successful reintegration. Adler states that dealers return to mainstream society because they have evolved through the major phases of their dealing careers—they naturally move from an active to an inactive phase. Persons reintegrate due to various structural factors. Their involvement in the deviant world is no longer enjoyable, is too stressful and is anxiety-provoking. Adler demonstrates that the reintegration of former drug dealers is by no means an easy task. It is often difficult for them to find legitimate work. They may lack necessary experience, skills and social networks—essential prerequisites for entering legitimate occupations and professions. As a result, many resort to working in the entrepreneurial sector or in the employee sector.

As Erickson (1964), Ebaugh (1984), (1987), and others have noted in their studies on the reintegration of deviants into society, there exist virtually no formal rights of passage to mark the ex-deviants journey out of deviant identities and social roles. While society has developed various "degradation ceremonies" and "mortification" rituals marking the passage of individuals from "normal" to "deviant" identities and statuses, there are *no* such comparable ceremonies to reinstate the "reformed" or "*ex-deviant*."

In fact, even if a deviant expresses a sincere desire to exit deviant careers and identities, several factors may impede him/her from doing so. These include: (1) the deviant's distrust of "normal" others; (2) pressures from other deviants to return to the subculture and resume deviant activities; and (3) distrust, stigma, abandonment and social isolation on the part of normals.

Deviants desiring to return to conventional society realize that they possess a stigma—an attribute limiting future employment opportunities. Further, their stigmatizing attribute negatively affects their social relationships with normals. Some deviants not only find that their "spoiled identities" impede identity transformation (as we saw in the last section in Herman's article on ex-psychiatric clients). Other ex-mental patients, by virtue of their long-term institutionalization, are unable to cope in the larger community—they lack basic social living skills necessary to manage a conventional lifestyle. In the institution, everything is done for the person—all of their needs for clothing, shelter and food are met; the individual is no longer an autonomous being; the person does not have to think for him/herself. When released, the individual has tremendous difficulties resuming a life of normalcy as an autonomous being.

Deviants who desire to return to the "normal" or "straight" world, have the best chances of succeeding if they have social support from others who redefine the person in a non-deviant light, and allow him/her to resume normal social statuses and roles. Moreover, in some cases, it is important for officials to publically acclaim that the deviant is now an *ex*—that he or she is now "cured," is "rehabilitated," and is "no longer a threat to society." The paper by Thomas Meisenhelder, "*Becoming Normal: Certification as a Stage in Exiting from Crime*" discusses such issues. Specifically, the author discusses the importance of "*certification*" as the final stage in exiting a career in crime. Certification refers to the formal recognition on the part of a member from conventional society that the deviant has now changed, is reformed and is now to be considered a non-criminal. The major elements in this processes of certification are examined as are the implications for successful identity transformation.

Just as the process of certification may aid in the transformation of deviant identities, another important factor involves participating in a voluntary association with other ex-deviants with like intentions. Organizations such as Alcoholics Anonymous, Narcotics Anonymous, Recovery Inc., Gamblers Anonymous, and Overeaters Anonymous, reward members for making changes toward the conventional life and function to confirm their new identity as "ex-drinker," "ex-drug addict," "ex-mental patient" or "ex-gambler." The selection by Jack Haas deals with collective organizational attempts at identity transformation. In "*Recovery Through Self-Help*," the author discusses the social processes by which addicts become *ex's*. Individuals attempting to recover/transform their addict identities must first "hit bottom"—a necessary condition preparing the addict for change. Joining and participating in a twelve-step program contributes to successful identity transformation. Haas discusses the characteristics, recovery "rituals," and spiritual components of twelve-step programs which function to heal the "inner child"—a key component in achieving emotional sobriety. Moreover, the author addresses the social processes whereby an individual come to develop a positive, reintegrated self, and the implications for altering social statuses and identities.

In the article by Cliff English, *Gaining and Losing Weight: Identity Transformations*," the author begins by discussing some of the difficulties individuals experience when obese. Our society discriminates against overweight individuals; their stigma limits their occupational opportunities and social relationships. Moreover, other difficulties include *social isolation*. Cultural artifacts are designed for thin people—buses, public restrooms, restaurants, movie-theatre seats, and telephone booths deny the obese person full participation in society. Another difficulty involves interaction with *food pushers*—relatives and obese friends who explicitly or implicitly try to prevent the person from achieving or maintaining weight loss. A third difficulty involves interacting with *humiliators*—those who remind obese people of their weight in such a way that it causes them great embarrassment and lowers their self-esteem. A fourth problem involves interaction with *brutalizers*—those who directly attack the overweight person's identity.

Despite such difficulties however, persons do lose great amounts of weight. Once this occurs, doubts, confusion and negativity are perceived on the part of others. Significant others do not respond positively; they may feel threatened by the weight loss. Such fears and confusion are tied to the potential loss of a "master status." Moveover, the formerly heavy person also realizes that, even after the weight loss, he/she still possesses significant personal problems. Their anticipated expectations never materialize. Such factors may trigger a return to obesity. In short then, for the obese facing identity transformation, the major factors appear to be the reactions of others, interaction with others, and as a result, the degree to which the ex-obese views these changes as positive. If rewards are not forthcoming, then, an "identity erosion" occurs. The safety and comfort of the obese self is remembered, and it is likely that the person will relapse.

REFERENCES

Erickson, Kai T., (1964). "Notes on the Sociology of Deviance." Pp. 9–21 in H.S. Becker, ed., *The Other Side: Perspectives on Deviance*. New York: The Free Press.

Ebaugh, Helen Rose Fuchs (1984). "Leaving the Convent: Role Exit and Self Transformation. Pp. 156–76 in J.A. Kotarba and A. Fontana, eds., *The Existential Self in Society*. Chicago: University of Chicago Press.

———. (1988). *Becoming an Ex: The Process of Role Exit*. Chicago: University of Chicago Press.

Chapter 48

THE "POST" PHASE OF DEVIANT CAREERS: REINTEGRATING DRUG TRAFFICKERS

Patricia A. Adler

Scholars have noted that individuals' involvement in deviant or criminal activities displays many of the characteristics of legitimate careers, often compromising a beginning, an ascension, a peak, a decline, and an exit. The stages of these careers most often discussed in the literature are the entry and exit periods because they mark the boundaries of people's involvement in deviant worlds (Luckenbill and Best, 1981). Yet for many individuals, these careers encompass only a brief phase in their life span as they age and move out of deviance (Shover, 1985). What then happens to them? How do they make the transition into conventional society and its legitimate economy?

The issue of reintegrating deviants has received scant sociological attention. Braithwaite (1989) discussed the role of others in shaming individuals out of brief forays into deviance; Brown (1991) studied how people capitalize on their former deviant status and experiences to forge counseling careers; and Ebaugh (1988) analyzed the effects of previous roles on people's subsequent lives. Only a few studies (cf. Chambliss, 1984; Shover, 1985; Snodgrass, 1982) traced the lives of former deviants with the intent of discovering the paths they have taken and the effects of their former activities on their subsequent lives.

In this article, I offer a follow-up glimpse into the lives of 10 former upper level drug dealers and smugglers I studied in the 1970s. In my earlier writings, I described their active criminal careers and the attempts they made, often temporary and unsuccessful, to exit the drug world after years of trafficking and to find another way of making a living (Adler, 1985; Adler and Adler, 1983). Those members of my original sample whom I was able to locate in 1991 were all involved in other pursuits. Although they were, to varying degrees, reintegrated into more mainstream society, their lives had been indelibly affected by their years in trafficking. This, then, formed the postdealing phase of their deviant careers.

In this article, I contribute to the literature on deviant careers and the reintegration of deviants by describing the life paths of these former occupational criminals. I then analyze the factors affecting their degree of success in reintegration, the segments of society into which they move, and the influence of their years spent out of the mainstream in a criminal occupation and subculture.

I begin by describing my return to the field and the activities of my former subjects whom I was able to trace. I then discuss a range of factors that affected their reintegration into mainstream society and the legitimate economy once they finally

566

ended their careers in dealing. I conclude by considering those factors affecting the reintegrative stage of the deviant career.

Methods

Between 1974 and 1980, I had the fortunate opportunity to be allowed entry into a community of upper level drug dealers and smugglers in a southwestern region of the United States. For 6 years my husband, Peter Adler, and I lived among these drug traffickers as friends, neighbors, and confidants, gathering ethnographic data on their hopes and fears, motivations, life style, business operations, and careers. This research experience resulted in the 1985 publication of *Wheeling and Dealing*. In it I detailed the evolution of the marijuana- and cocaine-smuggling scene from the early mom-and-pop border-running days of vehicle and body concealment to the development of entrepreneurial crews working for smugglers, whose organization and business volume enabled them to remain active and profitable in the face of rising law-enforcement activities. Once across the border, these drugs were then brokered by high-level individual entrepreneurs who operated within a flexible and "disorganized" (Reuter, 1983) market, trading back and forth among a shifting group of dealers and varying quantities at free-market economy prices and relying on "fronted" credit and their reputation for reliability to stay in business. This was an enterprise supported by white, middle-class men and women aged 25 to 40 years, most of whom had quit other occupations to enter the drug business on this level and who relied more on threats and the withdrawal of business than on violence to enforce their deals. Their interest was in making money and living spontaneously and uninhibitedly, indulging themselves in their immediate passions for food, drugs, and sex without worrying about the future or deferring their gratifications. They snorted cocaine in large quantities, drank vast amounts of alcohol, and smoked only the highest quality marijuana. Near the end of our research, some began to indulge in smoking base, or what later came to be prepared and sold as crack cocaine.

More than 10 years have passed since I moved away and left behind these drug traffickers and their scene. Over those years, I have maintained contact with a couple of my closest respondents and through them have managed to stay somewhat current with a few more. Change has come rapidly to the drug scene since that time; many transformations have occurred in the popularity of various drugs, the strategies of law enforcement, and the structure and organization of the drug business. Ten years out seemed like a good time to return to the field to see what had become of my former friends and subjects and to consider the effects of their experiences in drug trafficking.

I therefore made a trip to "Southwest County" in the spring of 1991 to see whom I could find in person or by telephone. The scenes looked rather different; many of the stores and restaurants I had frequented were out of business. My informants had not worked in many legitimate concerns, so I could not begin my search for them in public establishments. Going from contact to contact, I picked up the trail as best I could, trying to track them down in their dispersed or hidden locations. Either directly or indirectly, I was able to get in touch with 10 of my former subjects in Southwest

County and around the country. Although my original group of subjects had never been a random or necessarily representative sample of all upper level drug traffickers, the sheer number of individuals I observed ensured that they covered a range of motivations, behavior, and social organization. This group had consisted of several different types of people: dealers and smugglers, pilots and drivers, money launderers, storage personnel, dope chicks and wives, hangers-on, and members of the general social circle. In addition, they were divided by their relation to Peter and myself; there was a core group with whom we were the most intimate (and saw at various points in time on a weekly or near-daily basis), and there were others who fell more in the range of acquaintances. Of the original 65 people in our sample, roughly 24 fell into this core group.

Despite its smaller size, the follow-up sample serves as a good representation of the original group for several reasons. First, the follow-up sample was drawn exclusively from among members of the core group. This core group had served as the center of the study, with others snowballing out from them. Their social and work styles were thus repeated, to a certain extent, within the more peripheral group. By not including these more peripheral members, I merely lost those who tended to replicate the core group's behavior. Second, the members encompassed the full range of dealing styles, from the successes to the failures, the lone operators to the organizers, the aggressive to the casual, the longer involved to the more briefly involved. They represented fairly well the entire spectrum of dealing activities that I had seen. Third, the new group was characterized by an appropriate gender diversity. Seven of the people who I recontacted were men and 3 were women (plus the wife of one of the men who had not, herself, been a dealer). This corresponded fairly accurately to the gender breakdown of the original sample. These factors thus gave me confidence that the group I found might be typical former Southwest County upper level dealers and smugglers.

Southwest County Revisited

Dave, my key informant, was the first person I contacted when I went back to Southwest County in 1991. From 1972 to 1976, he had worked as a money launderer for a major smuggler and then branched out into dealing in large quantities on his own. He had brokered a ton of marijuana at a time or up to 60 pounds of cocaine per shipment. Over time, however, he began consuming too much, his marriage fell apart, and he started dealing with more disreputable associates until he was eventually abandoned by most of his former connections. I found him in a dilapidated motel, scrounging money on a near-daily basis, and sharing a room with a 26-year-old transient he had met while operating a surf shop in Florida. He was down on his luck and was keeping a low profile, avoiding people to whom he owed money. Through him I was able to find other former respondents and to hear about a couple more I could not find. Given the covert, unsteady nature of the business, in which people commonly leave no forwarding address, I was not surprised to encounter such a small group out of my original sample.

I knew what Dave had been up to since I left Southwest County. He had bottomed out of the drug market after losing so much money and reneging on so many fronts that no one would do business with him. He tried to get back into the real estate business in which he had worked as an agent before he met the Southwest County dealers and smugglers. Unfortunately, his license had been revoked when he was sent to prison, and his numerous attempts over the years to petition the real estate board for reinstatement had been repeatedly turned down. He then transferred his entrepreneurial buying and selling skills first to the flea market and county fair business, where he sold a variety of temporarily hot but inexpensive items, and then to the import business, buying legitimate goods (mostly clothing) from Mexicans he had met while dealing. During these years, he lived on the road for several months at a time, buying beat-up old vans and crisscrossing the country with his merchandise. He lived out of cheap motels, ate greasy foods, and bartered with other road hustlers and salespeople.

He eventually opened up a series of his own surf stores under a variety of assumed names (for the credit rating), but these went bankrupt one after another. He never became as successful financially as he had been during the early drug years because he never found a product that consistently enjoyed the same high level of consumer demand, and his careless business practices failed to improve.

However, Dave was getting older. After years of consuming drugs in large quantities and failing to take care of himself, he was feeling tired and less resilient. His two boys, whom he had dragged around the country from shop to shop, were in their early 20s, living on their own, and trying to go to college part-time in between partying and chasing girls. They were torn between following their parents' lifestyle of one scam after another and trying to find something more stable.

In his mid-40s, Dave was no longer a party animal. He could not tolerate the effects of cocaine any more. After years of overuse, he found that it depressed and confused him, causing him difficulty in forming words and physical gestures. He explained:

> I just don't get the euphoria anymore. If I ever get some and I do it, then I become sorry right away that I did it. So because of that I have to really keep away from the people that do it.

Dave was definitely out of the drug business now, even as a sideline. This also signified a major change in his lifestyle. Nearly all of the people he had associated with had been "cokeheads" of one sort or another.

Dave was not only tired, he was bored. He confided:

> I miss being on the road. I haven't been out of town for 9 months, and I'm stuck here staring at the walls of this motel room. I have nowhere to go. I have all this [surfing] merchandise in storage, but when I try to open up a store, I can't break even. Even last Christmas season. The economy is just terrible.

Four other people whom I tracked down through Dave were also out of the drug business. Marty quit after being busted and then stayed away from his former dealing friends. He was a big dealer and had gotten "hot" while I knew him. He had been one of those people whose name showed up on a drug agent's list, so he knew they were watching him. He vowed to "be careful," but he was not careful enough. He had a new wife when he got busted, and her feelings, along with the weight of all these factors, made him decide to retire for good. He described his attitude following his arrest:

> It was like my life was smashed. It was all I could do to just hang in there. I was smoking three packs of cigarettes a day. So I just said to myself, "Marty, you just have to be Mr. Joe "Good Citizen." You just have to get your life together. When you stand up there in front of that judge, you really feel the full weight of the law.

Marty had been a schoolteacher before he began dealing, and he eventually settled down with his wife into a similar steady job.

Two others, Ted, a former pilot-dealer, and Ben, a major smuggler, ended up "hustling for a living." They had escaped without ever having been arrested, which put them among the fortunate ones. Now they were in business for themselves, pursuing whatever deals they could while never finding a permanent stake in any line of legitimate work. Ted worked on screenplays for a while, which he attempted to peddle in Hollywood, and then made some money traveling around the country taking slides of railroad train cars, which he sold to collectors. Ben opened a restaurant with some partners that closed after 6 months and then tried to broker Zodiac rafts to specialty groups with little better fortune. It especially surprised me that Ben ended up with so little investment to transfer into a legitimate world. He had been the most successful trafficker I knew, the one who introduced Dave to the business. Ben, who had owned car dealerships, restaurants, and other ventures during his heyday, had nothing to show for it. However, he had had a long decline. His best years were during the era of commercial marijuana importation. When the cocaine trade rose to prominence, he began to indulge in overuse and in reclusive behavior, and he became less careful about his business dealings. Ben stayed in the business for longer than anyone I knew. During his later years, people did business with him as a favor based on who he was and what he meant to them. Over time, these people, too, quit the business, and there was no one left who knew Ben from the old days. Eventually, his money evaporated, and his wife left him.

The fourth person, Barney, was in the airplane business. A "trust-funder" from an upper-middle class background, Barney had never held a steady, legitimate job. After college, he and his wife, Betty, moved to Southwest County, and they used the freedom afforded them by his family income to avoid the shackles of employment. After a short while, they were drawn into the fast life by former college friends as well as new friends. Barney had always been interested in flying, and he used his free time to get his pilot's license, transporting family and friends around the country for vacations. Within 2 years of his entry into the drug crowd, he was recruited by a smuggler to fly runs for him. He worked transporting cocaine and spent his time partying for several years but got caught in a near-bust in South America. Reacting quickly, he was able to escape, one step ahead of the drug agents. Terrified by this close call, he returned home and fled Southwest County with Betty, and, by this time, their two children. They moved to a new state and established themselves, and Betty got a job. Barney could not bring himself to resort to employment, however, or to quit hanging around airports. He eventually managed to create an entrepreneurial business for himself, buying and selling used airplanes. He supplemented this unsteady income with money from his continuing trust fund. He also changed his lifestyle, cutting down his drug use significantly.

With the help of Dave's boys, I then tracked down Dave's ex-wife, Jean. Along with her sister, Marsha, Jean had become a major cocaine dealer in her own right after she divorced Dave. Her situation had subsequently gone through more ups and downs. She had divorced Jim, her second husband and successful dealing partner, blaming the erosion of their relationship on drugs:

> Too much cocaine. We were always doing it. Seemed like we needed to do it to have a good time. But then we were doing it separately from each other. He would go into his study, where he kept his secret stash and toot it up. I would go into the bathroom, where I kept mine, and toot. Eventually we got so wired that we weren't connecting with each other at all.

After the divorce, they each tried to stay in the dealing business separately, but neither was successful. Together they had complemented each other, she providing the hard-driving business acumen and security-conscious rules, he serving as the nice guy to round out her hard edges and frame their operation with class and generosity. When they tried to operate alone, Jean drove people away by being too demanding and Jim lost money by being too lackadaisical. He eventually moved to Hollywood. Starting from scratch, he managed to establish a successful venture catering to "the stars." Catering had been his and Jean's former legal front during their heaviest dealing years, and they had always groomed it to serve as their line of work after retirement.

In the catering business, they had been partners with another couple, Bobby and Sandy, who had owned the local fish store. Jean and Jim, regular customers of the fish store, became friendly with Bobby and Sandy and then discovered that they were heavy cocaine dealers. Jean was struggling to establish herself as a dealer after breaking up with Dave, and she welcomed this connection. Jean and Jim first bought cocaine from Bobby and Sandy, but their rise to trafficking in larger quantities was so rapid that they were soon dealing on the same level, fluidly selling back and forth as availability and connections dictated. They also did business with Jean's sister, Marsha, who sold to her younger circle of friends. With Jean and Sandy's shared interest in food, they launched the catering business together and were soon joined by Jim. The catering business was fun and successful for several years. At this time, money was rolling in from the drug dealing so well that they did not need the extra income, and so the work was sporadic and seasonal. The catering venture came undone through drugs. Around 1980, both couples began to freebase rather heavily. Bobby used up all of his and Sandy's money on a 2-month run and then checked into a rehabilitation clinic. Sandy moved out and returned to live with her parents. They divorced. Jim and Jean had also gotten to the point at which they considered their drug use out of control. They were sneaking behind each other's backs to snort cocaine at all hours. They went on freebasing runs that made them forget their obligations. They could not keep up with the catering business.

Upon my return to Southwest County, I learned through Jean that Bobby had since moved to Hawaii and opened a fish store. Sandy was living in San Francisco, married a chef, and was cooking in his restaurant. Jean and Marsha had had a terrible fight over Marsha's boyfriend, Vince, and had not spoken for several years. On a lead, I was able to locate Marsha in another state, now married to her former boyfriend. He was still working as an artisan, selling blown glass to stores, in fairs, and in mall shows. She worked in an office but helped out with his business during the months preceding Christmas, when they did most of their yearly business.

After Jean split up with Jim, she hit the bar scene for a while, picking up men and drinking a lot. She moved into a remote area and got a job in bar where she had once worked right after her divorce from Dave. Over the years, she drifted from bar to bar, waitressing, bartending, and serving as a bar, restaurant, or country club manager. She was fired from most of these jobs once for having her hand in the till, other times for irregular attendance, and was arrested several times for drunk driving. When I spoke to her, she was employed at a country club as a bartender, working the club's catering events on the side. By her own admission, age had not dampened her ability to party; she could still get loose and have a good time far better than most of her contemporaries. After several years, she had settled into an on-again-off-again relationship with Cliff, a man who had a substance abuse problem. After drinking, he would get physically abusive in their relationship. She fled on several occasions, but she always returned because she had nowhere else to go. During their good times she spoke of getting married; during their bad times she hid from everyone.

Reflecting back on her dealing years in reference to her current life, she had mixed feelings:

> I wouldn't change a thing from the past, even if I could. Those years were great. Having as much money as we wanted, never having to worry about spending it. I really had a good time and I learned a lot from it. Not many people get to do all the things we did, and we did a lot of crazy things back then. But I'm not looking for the end of the rainbow anymore, all the scams and loose money. It was a wonderful thing to always have money, but we paid a price. I wouldn't want to live like that anymore. Now I like the comfort of my life. I like having a steady job. I like not having to worry about going to jail, having a driver's license that's legal.

My revisitation thus yielded results that were surprising in some ways and not in others. Direct or indirect follow-ups of 10 of my major subjects showed them all to be out of the drug business and involved in other ventures. As I originally described the scene, all of my subjects had been between the ages of 25 and 40 years. The people whom I returned to find were now well into their 40s and 50s and retired. Although their level of involvement in the drug business (carrying with it a greater potential for insulation and profit), coupled with the exit barriers they encountered (the treadmill of the dealing lifestyle and the removal of their credentials for legitimate professional work), might have hypothetically enabled or induced them to remain with the activity for even longer, they quit. Some quit with the help of Narcotics Anonymous or various detoxification programs. Some quit because they had near-arrest escapes. Some were killed while involved in dangerous work. Most of the people I knew, however, just quit on their own. They quit, first, because like Waldorf, Reinarman, and Murphy's (1991) cocaine users, their troubles, from the physical burnout, to the diminished excitement, to the outright paranoia associated with their activities mounted. They quit, second, because the rewards of dealing, from the thrills, to the power, to the money, to the unending drugs, became less gratifying. They finally decided, either at some major turning point or more commonly over a gradual period, that they were tired of or unable to traffick in large quantities any longer.

Their attempts at getting out were not all successful. Many factors continued to hold them to the drug world and undermined their success in the legitimate world (see Adler and Adler, 1983). Their exits, then, tended to be fragile and temporary followed by periods of relapse into dealing. Reintegration formed the mirror image to the shifts and oscillations they made out of dealing: a series of forays into the legitimate world, many of them unsuccessful and temporary, but that were often followed by subsequent re-endeavors. Each attempt at reintegration, however, brought them further back into society and away from the insulated world of the fast life. Yet even once made, their reattachment to conventional society was problematic because of their many years out of the mainstream economy.

Factors Affecting Reintegration

What factors affected these people's lives and employment in society subsequent to their exit from the drug trade? Some were able to reintegrate more readily than others, finding a steady line of work. Others floundered, moving from activity to activity, unsuccessful and unsatisfied. Their final exit from the drug trade also saw them move into a variety of different venues characterized by distinct patterns. Factors affecting dealers' reintegration were rooted in the periods before, during, and after their dealing careers.

Predealing

One element influencing dealers' ability to ultimately reintegrate themselves into legitimate society was the age of onset in illicit activities. Individuals who became active in drug trafficking or other aspects of the underground economy at a young age remove themselves from pathways to options of legitimate success. Like Williams's (1989) cocaine kids, they drop out of school and fail to accumulate years of experience toward work in a lawful occupation. Their attitudes are also shaped by their early drug world experiences, so that they lose patience for legitimate work and seek the immediate reward of the scam and quick fix. When they become disenchanted with drug trafficking or are scared enough to think about quitting, they have no reasonable alternatives to consider. In contrast, individuals who enter the drug world after they have completed more schooling or have established themselves in lawful occupations have more options to pursue.

Very few of the dealers I studied entered the drug world at an early age. In fact, of my original sample, only five people went directly from high school into supporting themselves through drug money. None of the members of my follow-up sample experienced the early-onset pattern. Those whom I recontacted had all been in their late 20s and early 30s before becoming drawn into the drug world. Nearly all of them had been to college, and over half had graduated. Nine had been married, and four had borne children. This introduced an element of stability and responsibility into their lives and gave them some years of investment in the legitimate world that they could draw on in their future.

Related to this were the prior interests and skills individuals developed in the legitimate economy before they began to earn most of their income from dealing drugs. Very often, maturation and growth involves an identity-forming process in which individuals gradually narrow the range of career or occupational options to those in which they are interested. During this time, they may begin to pursue one or more of these avenues and gain knowledge or experience in these areas. Such occupational experience is later helpful in aiding dealers' reintegration because it can offer them an area to which they can return, an educational foundation, or a base of legitimate working experience that provides some transferable knowledge of and confidence about the legitimate world.

In my follow-up sample, Dave had worked as a real estate agent for the 4 years immediately before entering the drug business. He had previously held jobs as an automobile mechanic, an appliance salesperson, and the editor and publisher of a surfing magazine. Jean had been a homemaker and mother for many years, with sales experience in retail stores. Jim had pursued a career as a photographer, holding a job on the staff of a major national news magazine for many years. Marty had been a teacher in the secondary school system, and Bobby and Sandy had owned a fish store. Later, a couple of them returned to these early roots. For instance, Bobby and Marty resumed their original jobs as a retail fish store owner and a teacher, respectively, and Dave spent several years operating surf shops on both coasts.

A third factor affecting dealers' reintegration was the social class in which they were born and raised. When people grow up and become accustomed to a certain standard of living, they are reluctant to engage in downward social mobility. One of the noteworthy aspects of the members of my sample is their middle-class background. They are likely representative of a more widespread, hidden, middle-class population that is involved in the illicit drug trade on either a full- or part-time basis (cf. Morley, 1989; Rice, 1989). Such people move into drug trafficking to enhance their middle-class, materialist lifestyle, and when they leave the fast-money world their ties to the middle-class lifestyle force them to reintegrate into legitimate society more quickly. All of my subjects had grown up in upper-middle-class, middle-class, or lower-middle-class backgrounds, with parents engaged in a variety of occupations from educators to career military to manufacturers and sales.

Concurrent Activities

The manner and style in which individuals comported their lives during the active phase of their trafficking careers also affected their later efforts at reintegrating. One of the most salient features toward this end was the dealers' degrees of outside involvement. A large number of drug dealers are engaged in other ventures in addition to trafficking. At both the upper and lower levels of the drug trade, individuals can participate in trafficking in either a part- or full-time manner. For example, Reuter et al. (1990) found that most of the arrested lower level crack dealers they surveyed in their Washington, DC sample were employed in full-time legitimate jobs but moonlighted as dealers to supplement their legitimate incomes. Similarly, at the upper levels, a whole coterie of accountants, bankers, lawyers, pilots, and other legitimate businesspeople are involved part-time in the drug economy, arranging smuggling runs or providing illicit services to full-time traffickers (Morley, 1989; Rice, 1989). These individuals who deal only part-time are likely to have more interpersonal, occupational, and economic factors tying them to society. When they renounce their dealing, they have fewer reintegration obstacles to face because they are already more fully integrated into the legitimate economy.

In contrast, those who deal full-time, like Williams's (1989) youthful Dominican-American dealers, Hamid's (1990) Caribbean-American dealers, and my white upper level dealers and smugglers, have more likely renounced their investment in socially sanctioned means of surviving financially. Of the 65 subjects in my original sample, nearly one third remained involved in their previous jobs for a significant period of time while they were dealing in large amounts. This was the case for all but one member of my follow-up sample as well. Eventually, they all renounced those jobs, however, and withdrew to dealing or smuggling as their primary activity and main source of economic support. Abandoning legitimate jobs or career tracks makes it significantly harder to re-enter these lines after several years away, and only Marty, the teacher, who remained in the classroom well into his dealing career, was able to subsequently find another job in his profession.

Yet, even while engaged in full-time trafficking, individuals can become involved with legitimate front businesses on the side. Because they were making so much money, nearly two thirds of my original sample had pretensions of being involved in a legitimate business (for the purpose of protecting themselves from the Internal Revenue Service). This figure roughly applies to the follow-up group as well. Jean, Jim, and Sandy worked in the catering business, Ben owned an automobile dealership, and Marsha ran an antique store. These occupations kept these people partially tied to the legitimate economy and made it subsequently easier for them to re-enter that economy on a serious basis. Maintaining some connection to the lawful world of work, as Meisenhelder (1977) noted, also implies a lifestyle commitment to keep some regular business hours. For these people, then, reintegration did not require as much of a lifestyle transformation as it did for those who had not worked at all. Thus, Jim eventually began his own successful catering business and Sandy worked in a restaurant, skills they had acquired in their legitimate front businesses.

Knowledge and experience about legitimate work that was potentially useful to individuals' later reintegration could come not only from outside involvements but from trafficking-related skills as well. For example, Barney took his piloting skills and turned them into an airplane-oriented business. At the very least, the dealers and smugglers I studied became educated and trained in handling money, working on credit, calculating profits and expenses, and living with the uncertainty of entrepreneurial business. Those with the discipline and business acumen to become successful in the drug world were often able to recreate some semblance of this outside arena. Others with less reputable and reliable approaches, who had survived in the drug business primarily on the selling strength of the product, did not usually fare as well.

Instrumental aspects of these dealers' lives were not the only significant factors affecting their later reintegration. The strength of these traffickers' outside associations were important as well. This included interpersonal relationships with their children, parents, siblings, close friends, and other family members. Such associations were important because they kept these dealers integrated, to some degree, into mainstream society. These upper level dealers and smugglers trod a delicate line, as they lived inside a conventional society and yet insulated themselves within it. That is, they ate at the same restaurants, sent their children to the same schools, and lived in the same housing developments as other people, yet they kept their social contacts with those outside the drug world to a minimum. For protection, they removed themselves from the inquisitive prying of people who would not accept their occupation and lifestyle. Some Southwest County smugglers and dealers went for long periods, then, without seeing former friends and relatives. Others, though, kept in touch with their most important associates, whether they lived locally or at a distance. Through these ties, they remained connected to individuals and social worlds outside of dealing. These associations would be crucial for them to draw on in their re-entry to the legitimate world.

Such outside associates are not likely to "steer individuals away" from their deviance, as Braithwaite (1989) suggested, nor are they likely to provide a ratio of definitions favorable to the law and thereby reorient dealers' and smugglers' normative attitudes, as Sutherland's differential association theory holds. Rather, they hold traffickers, to greater or lesser degree, from totally removing themselves from society and provide a bridge back into society when these individuals feel an internal push to re-enter it.

Both outside involvements and outside associations serve as the type of "bonds to society" described by Hirschi's control theory. Although people diminish these bonds during their careers in trafficking, they do not cut them entirely. They then reach out to strengthen them during their attempts to move out of dealing and reintegrate. Other deinsulating factors serve as bonds to society as well, maintaining these dealers' connections to the mainstream and easing them back. This included ties like sports and hobbies (cf. Irwin, 1970) and could have included potential others such as religion. The dealers and smugglers in my sample all held onto some vestiges of their sport and hobby interests, rooting for their favorite teams, pursuing sports such as tennis or skiing, and indulging themselves in collecting things such as antiques or travel mementos. Religion, however, was not a significant part of their lives. Some individuals had come from religious backgrounds, attending parochial schools and church regularly, but this ended even before the onset of their dealing careers.

Although most of my follow-up subjects continued their sport and hobby interests after they quit dealing, none returned to religion.

A final factor characterizing dealers' active career behavior that affected their success and type of reintegration was the degree of organizational sophistication associated with their trafficking activity. Drug traffickers' involvement in deviant associations may follow a continuum of organizational sophistication, beginning with lone operators ensconced in a collegial subculture at the lowest end and ascending to the loose associations of the crack house crews, with the more organized smuggling rings, the tighter and more serious delinquent gangs, and the deadly Colombian cartels or organized crime families at the highest end of the spectrum. We know from the broader study of deviance that individuals who are members of more organizationally sophisticated associations are more likely to be tied to those groups instead of integrated into society in a number of ways (see Best and Luckenbill, 1982).

The drug traffickers in my follow-up group, much like those from my original sample, represented a mixture of both dealers and smugglers. As such, their involvement in criminal organizations ranged from the lone operator to the member or leader of a smuggling ring. Although they were clearly drawn into this occupation and lifestyle, they made no lifetime commitment to the pursuit. Detaching and reintegrating into society required a major change of master status but had fewer unbreakable side bets.

Postdealing

Drug traffickers' success at reintegrating into society was also affected by several factors they could encounter subsequent to their involvement in dealing. As they oscillated back and forth between their phases of dealing and quitting, the availability of legitimate opportunities seriously affected their permanence of retiring. As Shover (1985) noted in his study of thieves, finding a satisfying job could tie an individual to a line of activity. A positive experience at a legitimate job can draw an individual back to more conventional peer associations, reinforce nondeviant identity, occupy significant amounts of time, and diminish the motivation to return to dealing. Although "straight" jobs were often looked upon with disdain by Southwest County dealers in their younger days, they were more likely to view them favorably at this later age. This was reflected in Jean's comments about her charged attitudes toward her current lifestyle and work.

The importance of opportunity structures illustrates the value of Cloward and Ohlin's differential opportunity theory for reintegrating drug traffickers. Those who had tried to oscillate out of dealing but could never find anything to support themselves in their hedonistic lifestyle returned to the drug world. Yet each time they attempted to quit reflected a greater dissatisfaction with the dealing life. After a while, a more somber job opportunity, even Jean's bartending and waitressing job, appeared attractive.

Some drug traffickers were aided in their societal reintegration by outside help. As Braithwaite (1989:100–01) noted, friends, associates, and acquaintances can aid former deviants' reintegration through "gestures of forgiveness" or "ceremonies to decertify offenders as deviant." Dealers may thus remove themselves from the scene, find a new life, make new friends, or meet a spouse (cf. Shover, 1985) who may help them start over. This begins the process of rebuilding the social bonds that tie individuals to legitimate society. For instance, Marty was strongly influenced in his move to reintegrate back into society by his new wife, who was opposed to his dealing activity, and Marsha was forcibly pulled from the dealing subculture by her boyfriend, Vince, who had never liked her hanging around with the dealing crowd.

The extent and type of dealers' reintegration into society were ultimately affected by their adaptability to the organizational world. In my revisitation to Southwest County, I observed a continuum, with those whose experiences in the days of the wheeling and dealing and the big money had left them permanently unsuited for work as an employee in the organizational or bureaucratic world at one end and those who sought and obtained jobs at the other. Some of my subjects could never stoop to getting a job. They had entered the dealing world to secure freedom for their "brute being," and they would not endure the shackles of becoming an employee. Others were willing to get back into the working world, even if it meant taking a job at the bottom. Interestingly, finding oneself in "dire straits," as Dave and several others had, proved an insufficient inducement to an entrepreneurial, freedom-seeking person to get a job. They all had their limits, below which they would not stoop.

None of the wheeler-dealers, then, entered the confines of the straight "work-a-day" employee world they had either fled or disdained in the first place. Like many legitimate entrepreneurs, they could not imagine themselves punching a clock or working for someone else. Having tasted the excitement of the drug world, the straight world seemed boring. For them, staying within the world of independent business was associated with the potential for freedom and adventure. They could still dream of making the big killing and retiring. This also enabled them to avoid the awkwardness of trying to explain on a resume how they had been earning a living during their dealing years. Like Dave and Barney, then, they became petty lawful entrepreneurs, leaving their glory days behind them.

In contrast, like Jean, some former dealers sought out a variety of jobs. Several of them had worked as employees before entering the drug world, whereas others tried to put together a legal business front that required them to work some regular hours during their dealing years. They did not feel uncomfortable, then, but rather enjoyed the assurance of a steady job and a predictable life. For them, quitting dealing and working became associated with security, domesticity, and freedom from paranoia. Their experiences with life as an employee, however, were never quite as predictable or as steady as the average worker.

Discussion

Although scholars have addressed the issue of exiting deviant careers (cf. Adler and Adler, 1983; Faupel, 1991; Frazier, 1976; Harris, 1973; Inciardi, 1975; Irwin, 1970; Meisenhelder, 1977; Petersilia, 1980; Ray, 1964; Shover, 1983, 1985), little has been written about the subsequent reintegration of former deviants into society. Brown (1991) suggested that one way they do this is to capitalize on their former deviant status and become "professional ex-'s," counseling and working to help others overcome their involvement in deviance. In his theory of crime, shame, and reintegration, Braithwaite (1989) argued that individuals are steered away from their former deviant activities by caring others who accept them as essentially good but who reject their bad behavior. Rather than labeling and isolating them as deviant, these friends, associates, and acquaintances aid former deviants' reintegration. Such reintegrative shaming, he argued, is effective only before individuals become ensconced in criminal subcultures, which support criminal behavior through their criminal opportunities, norms, values, and techniques of neutralization. At a more macro level, Braithwaite's theory suggested that "communitarian" cultures provide the most reintegrative form of shaming, by nurturing deviants within a network of attachments to conventional society.

Although Braithwaite's theory of reintegration sheds light on the process by which individuals can be steered out of minor forms of deviance before they have significantly invested their selves in these behaviors and subcultures, it does not deal with the problem of reintegrating individuals who have already entered into criminal subcultures and seriously committed themselves to deviant or criminal activities, groups, and lifestyles.

Yet much crime is committed by individuals who begin criminal activities in their relative youth, much like drug traffickers, without intending to remain criminals all their lives. They enter these activities thinking they will make a lot of money and retire into some less dangerous line of work. Studies of deviant careers, in fact, show that many criminals and deviants (especially those who have never been incarcerated) naturally burn out, bottom out, grow out, and quit (Harris, 1973; Irwin, 1970; Waldorf, 1983; Waldorf, Reinarman and Murphy, 1991). Once they have made the decision to exit deviance, their success depends largely on their ability to reintegrate into society. Braithwaite's theory, then, needs to be amended by a consideration of the reintegration of people who have passed the point on which he focused.

My research suggests that shaming plays no role in these individuals' decision to return to the more mainstream arena. Rather, they return because they have evolved through the typical phases of their dealing careers and, like their peers, progress past the active stage into the inactive stage. With variations on the theme unique to each individual, dealers experience a progression through their early entry and involvement in the drug world, a middle period in which they rise and experience shifts in their level and style of operation, an exit phase in which they suddenly or gradually withdraw from the drug world, and the last phase, in which they readapt themselves to the nondeviant world. Their eventual return to conventional society requires a process of reintegration, which is affected by the structural factors described here. They reintegrate, then, more because of "push" than "pull" factors, because the career of involvement in drug trafficking moves them beyond the point at which they find it enjoyable to the point at which it is wearing and anxiety provoking. Only once they have made the decision to leave the drug world, either temporarily or finally, do they reactivate their abandoned ties to the network of conventional society's attachments. This occurs, as Shover (1985) noted, after they change their orientational (self-conceptions, goals, sense of time, tiredness) and interpersonal (ties to people or activities) foci, finding it preferable to detach from their deviant and criminal commitment and to reblend with the conventional society.

Their reintegration into this society is difficult, however. The most difficult pursuit is finding legitimate work. Years "derailed" from the mainstream in the career-building stage of their lives have blocked their entry into the professions and caused a failure to accrue connections and experience in legitimate occupational realms. They work, then, primarily in the entrepreneurial sector and secondarily in the employee (sales, unskilled, or semiskilled labor) sector. Transferrable skills exist, but they are limited. Drug traffickers have gained experience working in the arena that functions more casually than most "straight" jobs. They could be irresponsible, be late, and be intoxicated for a drug deal, yet their connection would probably still wait for them because there was so much money to be made. Not many conventional jobs or deals are that profitable or forgiving. Former dealers then re-enter the legitimate economy at an older age, at which point they are no longer the freshest and most attractive employees or trainees, bearing the stigma of unexplainable employment years. This limits their range of work opportunities. Yet compared with others who abandon youthful "compressed careers" (Gallmeier, 1987) in such fields as sport, art, drama, or music, drug traffickers have at least had the benefit of working in a business arena.

The second hardest component of reintegrating is making the adjustment to the diminished lifestyle of the straight world. Although their new jobs do not pay as well, traffickers' ties to the drug world were never significantly to their work; relatively few individuals relished a deal well done or strove for intrinsic perfection in their operation. Rather, their satisfaction derived from the fast life and the easy money. They worked hard to play hard, not because they like work. Many appreciate the mundane security of the everyday world, yet they never attain their former level of disposable income, excitement, flexibility, and the pleasure, spontaneity and freedom they experienced during their halcyon days of drug trafficking. Some find a new identity and satisfaction in their postdealing lifestyle, value system, and relationships, but this occurs only after a painful period of readjustment, which includes feelings of relative deprivation and suffering.

Individuals' postdealing lives are thus profoundly affected by their years in the drug world. The attitudes, values, and lifestyle they adopted during the active phase of their dealing careers remain nascent within them. Most are straight for pragmatic rather then ideological or moral reasons. The "quick buck" and the "sweet" deal thus remain embedded within their vocabulary of motives. Although these individuals may be too old to keep up with their former drug-using pace or to return to the fast life, many still enjoy a touch of hedonism. In an era when most middle-aged people are former marijuana smokers, party drinkers, and general revelers, these ex-traffickers still like to have adventures. It remains a part of their lifestyle and new identity, carried over from earlier times. Thus, although they have shed the dealing occupation, may retain some proclivity for deviant attitudes and lifestyles. They are postdealers but not completely reformed deviants. They live near the fringes of conventional society, trying to draw from both within and outside of it.

REFERENCES

Adler, P.A. 1985. *Wheeling and Dealing*. New York: Columbia University Press.

Adler, P.A. and P. Adler. 1983. "Shifts and Oscillations in Deviant Careers: The Case of Upper-Level Drug Dealers and Smugglers." *Social Problems* 31:195–207.

Best, J. and D. Luckenbill. 1982. *Organizing Deviance*. Englewood Cliffs, New Jersey: Prentice-Hall.

Braithwaite, J. 1989. *Crime, Shame, and Reintegration*. Cambridge, England: Cambridge University Press.

Brown, J.D. 1991. "The Professional Ex-: An Alternative for Exiting the Deviant Career." *The Sociological Quarterly* 32:219–30.

Chambliss, W.J. 1984. *Harry King: A Professional Thief's Journey*. New York: Wiley.

Ebaugh, H.R. 1988. *Becoming an Ex*. Chicago: University of Chicago Press.

Faupel, C.E. 1991. *Shooting Dope: Career Patterns of Hard-Core Heroin Users*. Gainesville, Florida: University of Florida Press.

Frazier, C. 1976. *Theoretical Approaches to Deviance*. Columbus, Ohio: Charles Merrill.

Gallimeier, C.P. 1987. "Dinosaurs and Prospects: Toward a Sociology of the Compressed Career." Pp. 95–103 In K.M. Mahmoundi, B.W. Parlin, and M.E. Zusman (eds.), *Sociological Inquiry: A Humanistic Perspective*. Dubuque, Iowa: Kendall-Hunt.

Hamid, A. 1990. "The Political Economy of Crack-Related Violence." *Contemporary Drug Problems* 17:31–78.

Harris, M. 1973. *The Dilly Boys*. Rockville, Maryland: New Perspectives.

Inciardi, J. 1975. *Careers in Crime*. Chicago: Rand McNally.

Irwin, J. 1970. *The Felon*. Englewood Cliffs, New Jersey: Prentice-Hall.

Luckenbill, D. and J. Best. 1981. "Careers in Deviance and Respectability: The Analogy's Limitations." *Social Problems* 29:197–206.

Meisenhelder, T. 1977. "An Exploratory Study of Exiting from Criminal Careers." *Criminology* 15:319–34.

Morley, J. 1989. "Contradictions of Cocaine Capitalism." *The Nation*: 341–47.

Petersilia, J. 1980. "Criminal Career Research: A Review of Recent Evidence." Pp. 321–79 In N. Morris and M. Tonry (eds.), *Crime and Justice: An Annual Review of Research* (Vol. 2). Chicago: University of Chicago Press.

Ray, M. 1964. "The Cycle of Abstinence and Relapse Among Heroin Addicts." Pp. 163–77 in H.S. Becker (ed.), *The Other Side*. New York: Free Press.

Reuter, P. 1983. *Disorganized Crime*. Cambridge: MIT Press.

Reuter, P., R. McCoun, and P. Murphy. 1990. *Money from Crime*. Santa Monica: Rand.

Rice, B. 1989. *Trafficking*. New York: St. Martin's.

Shover, N. 1983. "The Latter Stages of Ordinary Property Offenders' Careers." *Social Problems* 31:208–18.

———. 1985. *Aging Criminals*. Newbury Park, California: Sage.

Snodgrass, J. 1982. *The Jack-Roller at Seventy: A Fifty-Year Follow-up*. Lexington, Massachusetts: Lexington Books.

Waldorf, D. 1983. "Natural Recovery from Opiate Addiction: Some Social Psychological Processes of Untreated Recovery." *Journal of Drug Issues* 13:237–80.

Waldorf, D., C. Reinarman and S. Murphy. 1991. *Cocaine Changes*. Philadelphia: Temple University Press.

Williams, T. 1989. *The Cocaine Kids*. Reading, Massachusetts: Addison-Wesley.

Chapter 49

BECOMING NORMAL:
CERTIFICATION AS A STAGE IN EXITING FROM CRIME

Thomas Meisenhelder

Introduction

The final aspect of the process of exiting from a career in crime can be termed "certification," which is briefly described as follows:

> The formal completion of a successful exiting project requires a symbolic component, certification. This final phase in exiting was required in order for the individual fully to achieve a social identity as a noncriminal. Certification is simply the social verification of the individual's "reform." Some recognized member(s) of the conventional community must publicly announce and certify that the offender has changed and that he is now to be considered essentially noncriminal (Meisenhelder, 1977:329).

This paper presents an expanded analysis of this final stage in the process of criminal change.[1]

The instigation of an exiting project by a criminal offender depends on the individual's decision to attempt to go "straight." This decision seems to be at least in part based on the individual's personal identity as a noncriminal. However, change within criminal careers also includes the social recognition (as perceived by ex-offenders themselves) of their abandonment of criminal activity. Thus change is not complete when individuals fully commit themselves to conventionality, rather, commitment must be supplemented by the social recognition of their reform. The process by which exiting from crime is conceived of as socially recognized is called certification. By certification, individuals convince themselves that they have convinced others to view them as conventional members of the community. They perceive by the reactions of others that they are defined as being largely conventional. They begin to feel trusted; that is, they feel that their contemporaries are likely to see them as normal and noncriminal. They no longer feel suspect (Matza, 1969:195). Certification, then, completes the exiting, or change, process by solidifying the self-concept of the ex-offender.

It is important to note that along with the impression of conventionality certification often produces an increased probability of noncriminal patterns of behavior. A social identity as noncriminal may regenerate and support the changed felon's commitment to conventionality. This may be so for several reasons. First, certification produces an integrated conception of the self as normal, and this congruence of self may facilitate the abandonment of crime (see Lofland, 1969:281). In addition, certification through the testimony of others often parallels the formation of strong interpersonal ties between the ex-offender and conventional others. These social bonds provide the changed criminal with meaningful reasons for staying "straight" (Meisenhelder, 1977).

In sum, certification is a process of social interaction through which the ex-offender's social identity is changed to one of noncriminality. Certification signals the end of exiting as a stage in the individual's biography. In the following pages this outline is filled out by a detailed description of how certification is experienced by the offenders themselves.

Methods

The research reported here has been conducted within a frame of reference that Matza (1969) has referred to as the "appreciative stance." Simply put, this point of view requires that the sociologist strive to grasp the experiential life-world of his or her subjects. In this case the stance of appreciation directs the researcher to attempt to understand the role of the process of certification within the larger exiting project and criminal career of the offender.

In line with this approach the data presented in this paper were collected during tape-recorded interview conversations with 25 male prison inmates (see Meisenhelder, 1977). These data originally formed part of a larger study of the stages in the development of criminal careers. Thus, as a whole, each interview was guided toward uncovering the phases of involvement in crime in the life history of the respondent. The interviews were ordered chronologically according to the respondent's cycle or cycles of criminal activity. They were conducted in two institutions (one in the eastern and one in the western United States), and they were largely unstructured or nonstandardized in form. At both research sites potential respondents were selected from the total inmate population through a review of inmate files. Inmates were chosen if they manifested offense histories composed entirely or largely of property crimes. Then each of the 48 selected inmates was briefly introduced to the general project, assured of its confidentiality, and asked to volunteer to be interviewed. It should be noted that participation in the study offered no advantage to the respondents, and they were clearly aware of the purely academic interests and position of the researcher.

All the interviewing was conducted by the author in a vacant office of the prison administrative building. The length of the interviews ranged from 1 to 3 hours, and the average interview was about 2 hours in length. Approximately 50 hours of tape recordings were produced by these sessions, which were completed during two 3-month periods approximately 1 year apart. Each recorded interview was fully transcribed prior to analysis of the data. The interviews were analyzed in order to reveal the patterned similarities (if any) shared across respondents as they reflected on their exiting experiences. During this analysis, the interviews were listened to and read several times in order to identify elements that respondents shared as they described the process of becoming certified as a noncriminal. The findings presented below are a result of that analysis and represent the most common and most significant aspects of the process of certification as the respondents described it.[2]

The Social and Personal Context of Certification

The social self is a central notion in modern sociology. In order to understand the process of certification, the self must be thought of as a dual identity. That is, each person is conscious of himself or herself in terms of both a social and a personal identity.[3] The self is both socially imputed and personally constructed.

Personal identity refers to the manner in which the individual defines his or her self. The concept concerns the judgmental, emotional, and cognitive categories into which the individual places himself or herself. Prior to certification, the typical respondent's personal identity was shakily noncriminal. He had constructed and committed himself to a personal identity as basically a conventional member of society. The men realized that they had been "in trouble"; yet they did not conclude from this concept that they were criminal types of persons. These feelings are revealed in the following statement taken from the interviews:

> Contrary to what you, they might think, I ain't no hard-down criminal.
> I just consider myself as an average person. But there is one difference,
> I got into some troubles, I've been to the joint.

Indeed the plan to exit from crime is in large part founded on this sense of the self as noncriminal.

> I try to be straight. If the people give me half a chance, I'll take it. I'm just
> like any other person, looking for stuff like settling down, having me an
> old lady, couple of kids.

Our sense of self entails more than a subjective definition of ourselves. Identity is also constructed on the basis of received evidence; that is, our self is socially imputed to us through our perception of the reactions of others. An awareness of social reactions results in a social identity, which may be defined as the self imputed to the individual by others (See Hawkins and Tiedeman, 1975:243). Laing and his co-workers (1966:6) refer to this as "my view of your view of me." Social identity is my perception of what type of person the other thinks I am.

Logically, then, one's sense of personal identity may conflict with one's perception of his or her social identity. As discussed earlier, the ex-felon felt that he was basically conventional, but he realized that many other people saw him as a criminal type. The respondents related that they sensed that many people "on the street" believed that they were simply, once and for all, criminals. Others are perceived by the ex-offender as seeing him as less than normal and not to be trusted. They believed that others expect him to behave and live in a fundamentally deviant fashion. These sentiments are evident in the following interview excerpt:

> You are no longer considered as being a man. Now that I've committed
> a crime, I got incarcerated, I don't get no respect. You just a plain criminal
> in their eyes. People in the streets are down on you all the time.

At best, the exiting ex-felon felt that others saw him as a deviant feigning conventionality (see also Matza, 1969:174).

Thus, the exiting ex-criminal experiences disagreement between his personal identity and other people's definition of his self. His social identity remains that of a criminal while his personal identity is noncriminal. Certification is essentially a process of constructing a conventional, or noncriminal, social identity for and by the ex-offender. Just as negative reactions may result in a criminal social identity, certification as an adjudication of conventionality labels the changing ex-offender as noncriminal.

Certification

Certification is the final social verification of the ex-offender's substantial reform. It can be described as a set of communicative actions through which the ex-offender impresses others with the conventionality of his motives, values, and personality (see Brim and Wheeler, 1966:42).[4] In certification, some recognized members of the conventional community publicly announce and verify that the ex-felon need no longer be considered a criminal but rather should now be treated as a normal member of the social group.

In order to impress others with their successful reform and to achieve certification, the respondents employed some adept forms of self-presentation and impression management. For instance, although they believed that change is an activity conceived and achieved by the individual, they were well aware that it must be finally verified through the testimony of others. In their own words, although all the men believed that "you rehabilitate yourself," they also knew that "you got to appear normal...It keeps them off your back," and "you have to, I had to, find someone to change me. To make me look good."

Further, the men related that the certification process involved manipulation of the image of oneself held by others rather than by any "real" personal or personality change (see Becker, 1964:42). Certification, then, can be seen as a specific instance of the general process that Goffman (1959) has described as the presentation of self. It too involves procedures, strategies, and tools that are used to present oneself as a particular sort of person. Here, the ex-offender must present his social audience with verbal and behavioral evidence of his normality. This evidence most typically includes others or a presentational team (Goffman, 1959:104) and social settings (Goffman, 1959:22). That is, by appearing with conventional others and in conventional places the exiting felon is able to demonstrate his change from crime. Likewise, by appearing with him others can testify to the individual's noncriminality and socially certify that he may be trusted to behave in a normal fashion. The phenomenological logic of certification seems to be that if one's associates seem reasonably normal and if they further seem to define one as trustworthy, others should and will do likewise. In short, as Schultz (1962) has noted, others assume that they would see things as one's close associates do if they were in their place. If he achieves certification and the construction of a noncriminal social identity, the individual no longer feels stigmatized. He has a chance to become anonymously conventional. He is now, for all practical purposes, typically conventional, and he has successfully (if temporarily) exited from crime.

In the following pages, a closer analysis of the certification process is presented. This analysis is ordered according to the most frequently mentioned tools of certification: other persons, physical settings or places, and formal agencies of correctional reform.

Certification Agencies

Certification may be achieved through participation in the rehabilitation programs of various social service and criminal justice agencies. Lofland (1969:288) has noted that these agencies provide the public with a reasonable accounting of their clients' criminality and subsequent reform. That is, they justify seeing the ex-offender as noncriminal.

However, it is easy to exaggerate the actual importance of these agencies to the ex-offender. The interviews reported here indicate that only a very few of the respondents used these agencies to demonstrate their reform. Further, most of these men used the programs in a manner far removed from their stated purposes.

> I tried the church thing, I'm not really religious, but I was gonna try it out. I'm gonna make people think that, like, I trying to change, which I was in my own way.
> Sure there are programs to help you, but it's, most people get into them account of it looks good. They see that you're in the program, they don't know that you ain't getting nothing out of it. They think you are changed.

As these comments suggest, formal agencies are often used purely as techniques of self-presentation.

From the point of view of the ex-offender, an important shortcoming of these agencies is that they are most often designed to effect some change in the personal identity of their clients. To the contrary, the exiting ex-offender already possesses a conventional personal identity and merely wants to use the program as ceremonial evidence for others in order to construct a similar social identity. Thus the ex-felon is forced to deceitfully manipulate his involvement in the program in order to demonstrate his commitment to change and in order to publicly announce and account for his presumed reform. The exiting experiences of "Ron," described below, illustrate the role of rehabilitation agencies in the certification process.

Ron is a middle-aged black male who has lived most of his years in the southwest and in California. As a youth he became involved in petty theft and some semiorganized shoplifting. As a result he has a fairly long juvenile arrest record that includes one substantial incarceration. As an adult Ron graduated into a career of property offenses, particularly in theft and burglary. He experienced one significant period of exiting that lasted about 14 months.

A prison-administered self-improvement program was a significant factor in Ron's exiting experiences. He clearly felt that this program both convinced him that he alone was responsible for his actions *and* changed his image for others: "You're trying to determine a new image so to speak, whether knowingly or unknowingly." Ron changed his image in the minds of others through his everyday behavior and through his participation and acceptance of the self-improvement course. While attending the program, which he did twice, Ron began to construct a new social identity. Besides altering his style of adjustment to prison toward that of a "square john" (Irwin, 1970) and beginning to associate with other model prisoners, Ron methodically catered to the image he presented to his environment. As he himself put it:

> I was very methodic about it. I didn't break no rules. And a lot of people
> I had known objected to how I began to react to situations. I knew what
> I was doing.

Ron's case provides us with an example of an individual consciously using an agency program to achieve certification. By his participation in the self-improvement course Ron loudly announced to his social environment at the time that he was a changed man. Admittedly a weak and partial case, Ron's is the exception rather than the rule among the respondents. More often certification was achieved through the informal testimony of conventional others and conventional places.

Certifying Settings

Certification of change may also occur via the physical places where the ex-offender can be observed to spend his time. As he continually appears in conventional surroundings, others may begin to define the person as non-criminal. As Lofland (1969:238) has suggested, "an Actor's places serve to communicate a part of what he 'is.'"

It seems that in the everyday world one's appearance in deviant places leads to the imputation of personal deviance, and one's appearance in conventional places indicates that one is normal or conventional. Thus, as revealed in the comments below, many of the respondents consciously attempted to avoid deviant surroundings and to put themselves in more normal social settings.

> Some places get you in trouble just by your being there...The wrong place
> at the wrong time.
> I always made it my business to try and get away from bad places.
> Places where I shouldn't be. I try to be more skeptical about where I
> would be.

A setting of primary import for certification is the person's place of employment. Appearance in a legitimate occupational setting for 8 hours a day, 5 days a week, is one of the most effective techniques of self-presentation available to the exiting ex-offender. The men interviewed were clearly cognizant of this fact. One respondent related that a conventional job made people accept him because

> They know what your job consists of, know what you is supposed to do.
> They think you is all cut and dry.

As Weber (1958) realized long ago, our culture seems to equate work with moral worth, and the changing offender's appearance in a conventional work setting strongly implies that he is worthy of trust. In short, he becomes as familiar as his job. Of course, work also gives the ex-offender practical economic aid and resources as he attempts to disengage from crime. But, beyond these practicalities, the work place also may lead others to impute conventionality to the ex-felon.

Places of leisure are also available as ways to achieve a certified non-criminal social identity. Being visible in churches, civic associations, and other socially recognized sites for the constructive use of leisure time can help the individual to become verified as having reformed. On the other hand, the exiting offender must not be seen frequenting pool halls, certain taverns, or other settings characterized by conventional others as the site of loitering, wasting time, and looking for trouble. Places such as these lead to the imputation of deviant and criminal social identity. As one respondent phrased it these kinds of places make "people look hard on you" or, even more to the point, "Pool halls and stuff, they's frustrating and full of trouble. And you looks bad there." Finally, as implied by the above, conventional places of leisure aid the exiting offender in a more practical way as a result of the fact that they are less likely to present the individual with the temptation to return to crime.

In sum, physical settings assist in the achievement of certification by providing evidence that leads others to label the ex-offender as noncriminal. That is, they can announce and verify the conventionality of those that work and play within them. The case of "Bob" highlights the role of places in the process of certification.

Bob is a middle-aged white male whose most frequent offense is passing and writing bad checks. He began his career in crime late in life (at the age of 30), and since then he has been incarcerated twice for passing bad checks. From 1965 to 1969, Bob "turned over a new leaf and went straight." In discussing these years of his life Bob continually pointed to the significance of his social and physical surroundings as a tool for achieving certification.

Bob stressed the negative impact of parole, for instance, as a symbolic place that is by definition reserved for criminals. Parole then involves the social imputation of criminality to the parolee. As Bob himself put it:

> Parole...is not beneficial to that man whatever. They (parole agents) come around, they'll sneak around, they peep on him. In some cases harass a man and cause him to do things he wouldn't normally do. If people, if they find out you're on parole they don't want to be around you. Parole doesn't help a man.

For these reasons Bob (and many other parolees) must actually skip parole in order to achieve certification as a noncriminal.[5]

After "running from parole," Bob achieved certification through his appearance in more conventional environments. He intentionally avoided known "bad" places where he might find the opportunity to "get into trouble" and where he surely would find the social imputation of deviance. Instead he began to associate with a more or less conventional group of people and to frequent conventional places. He "got involved with work." Beyond its mere economic effects, Bob's job was a place wherein he would be likely to be seen by others as normal and noncriminal.

> I was a cook in this restaurant in a small town. I enjoyed my work and the people I met were friendly. They saw me as a good cook, that's all.

Thus, through his appearance in the restaurant, Bob was able to achieve some degree of certification as a conventional person. His new associates and acquaintances did not know of his criminal past or present (he had skipped parole) and seeing him everyday "at work," they simply assumed that he was just like any other person in the community. That is, they imputed to Bob a normal social identity.

To further the process of certification Bob also acquired a car and a stable residence. Again these aspects of his daily life provided Bob with conventional surroundings. Driving his car to and from work, spending his nonwork time at his home, Bob became an accepted member of the community. It is extremely important to note the correctional paradox explicit in Bob's case. All these sources of certification might have been denied Bob if he had remained under parole supervision. However, by fleeing his parole (and thus violating the law) he was able to leave a deviant symbolic environment and adopt a new set of social places in the conventional world. As he acquired a new community, a conventional job, a car, and a home, Bob was defined as normal. He had achieved certification. But, ironically, in order to accomplish all this, Bob was forced to violate the law once more. Finally, the parole violation caught up with Bob, and he was returned to prison.

Bob's case is an example of the flow of the process of certification when it is primarily assisted by the individual's appearance in conventional settings. Equally important to certification are the people whom one finds in such environments.

Certifying Others

Places are, of course, peopled by others as well as by the ex-offender. Most social settings are normatively defined as the proper locations for particular types of persons and activities. For instance, the post office is a place thought to be inhabited primarily by post office employees and their customers. The respondents indicated in the interviews that they felt that the people with whom they associated were extremely important for their eventual certification.

The single most important group of others for the changing ex-offender is his family. A conventional family, newly formed or renewed, provided the individual with a significant group of close associates that could overtly testify to his noncriminality and trustworthiness. The importance of the family for exiting from crime was continually mentioned during the interviews. For example,

> They made me feel that I was doing right. I looked good while I was with them, living at home. And I stayed out of it for two years, with my family.

I got tired of the life, so I went back home. There I had a place to stay and people accepted me for myself. I was doing my best.

A family gives the changing ex-offender both a place that is recognized as conventional and others who announce to the public world that the family member has changed and is now to be considered noncriminal.

> It's very important, it keeps society from looking down on you. If you married and got kids, they think: "Well, he's rehabilitated. He's married and settled down, not wild anymore." Some people use it as a front, for others like me it ain't no cover up.

Of course, kin also present the ex-felon with much practical assistance, including job opportunities, financial loans, and simply "a place to start off from." Emotionally, families provide individuals with a sense of belonging, of being at home in the conventional world. Within his family the ex-felon is able to at least partially overcome his feelings of strangeness as he confronts the conventional world. By caring for him his kin create relational ties that are most important during the trials of exiting. These ties in turn represent an investment in conformity that works to keep the ex-offender "straight." The family, then, is defined as one of the primary rewards of settling down (Meisenhelder, 1977).

> The last nine months of my life, being with my wife and my son doing the things that normal people do is actually, seriously, have been the most important months of my life.

Besides these very important contributions to exiting, the family also provides the changing ex-offender with an effective means of self-presentation in order to achieve certification. Through his presence within a conventional family group, the individual announces that he is normal. At home and at ease in this most fundamental of social institutions, the ex-offender is seen by nonfamilial others as one to whom normality and respectability may be reasonably imputed (see Ball, 1970). The ex-felon's family members testify that he can be trusted and that he is not a dangerous person.

Nonfamilial associates also help to certify the individual's reform. Many of the respondents indicated the importance of carefully selecting one's friends and companions. Bad associates lead to the social imputation of personal deviance. On the other hand, conventional associates create an impression of conventionality. Recognizing this common practice, many of the respondents attempted to steer clear of "bad crowds."

I quit hanging around with bad crowds, that helped me. Police and folks didn't look at me the way they used to. If you hang around with a bad crowd, they would follow you more.

I always made it my business to try and get away from those kind of people. I wouldn't come in contact with those that look bad whatsoever.

By avoiding bad persons and by cultivating relationships with conventional people at work and at home, the changing offender presents himself as a noncriminal. By their acceptance of him, conventional acquaintances certify that the ex-felon can be considered a conforming member of the community.

Scott is a middle-aged white male whose varied career in crime includes theft, automobile theft, and check passing. Prior to his most successful change he was deeply involved in "checks." Scott experienced a 3-year disengagement from crime that ended with incarceration for auto theft and parole violation. His change experience provides a nice example of certification through others.

Scott decided to "get out of the life" because he was tired of "being on the run," a frequently noted hazard of check writing as an occupation. Passing checks forces the criminal into a very mobile existence, and Scott grew tired of this type of existence:

This was a time when I just got exhausted and said, "This ain't worth it." I just up and quit, tore up my check book.

He then went to a small town where he was "not known at all" and attempted to establish a normal life. In the process of doing so, Scott was able to get a job at a service station, and importantly, he established a meaningful relationship with a woman and her child. He related this experience:

I met a girl there that I became very interested in, her and her child. I decided to stay there, settle down with her. I was interested in her. She was something that I wanted to hold on to.

After he settled down in this family and became known in the area, Scott says that he began to feel accepted by the local community. People who knew him only as the new mate of "June" began to show that they trusted him with their friendship and with more material signs of acceptance. One such person loaned Scott a considerable sum of cash, and Scott's reaction to this event reveals that, to him, it was a meaningful sign of admission to the conventional world:

He entrusted me with that money. I could have just took that money and gone, I didn't. And by doing that it let me know *I was accepted for what I was.*

In short, by being seen around the community with his new girlfriend, a lifelong resident, Scott too received trust and acceptance from his new neighbors. Further, his own perception of these reactions from others led him to believe that he was no longer judged to be a criminal. The reactions of others, then, certified Scott's change. This is reflected in the comments below,

> I met some pretty nice people in that town. My wife's friends and all, and they went out of their way to make me feel at home. That was a place, a nice place to live, nice people. If I hadn't been violated, I'd still be working and living there.

Obviously, Scott felt that he succeeded in becoming an accepted member of a conventional community. His own recognition of the trusting reactions of others led him to believe in his own change and further pushed him along the path of exiting from crime. Here certification was clearly the result of relationships with conventional others.

Summary

In the preceding sections of the paper, the process of certification was reviewed by holding the tools or means of achieving certification analytically separate. In actuality, of course, some combination of places, others, and to a lesser extent agencies is evident in the total process. The ex-offender's continuing presence in conventional places and with conventional others forms an imputational process similar to that which Lofland (1969:227) has termed an "informal elevation ceremony." Such ceremonies made up of the behavioral evidence that testify to the conventionality of the ex-felon lead more and more people to categorize him as a conventional societal member. Having been seen with a "good job," a "fine family," and "respectable friends," the individual is presumed to be someone who can be trusted, someone,

> who is normal, who upholds social order and is deserving of order-maintaining and sustaining gestures of worth-acknowledgement from like-minded persons in society (Ball, 1970:339).

At this point, then, exiting is at least temporarily complete. The actor's self is consistently conventional, and he has developed a pattern of behavior and a style of life that, for the time being, are noncriminal.

Thus, certification is the final contingency in the abandonment of criminal behavior. Now the individual's social and personal identities join into a consistent sense of the self as noncriminal. The actor sees himself as normal and feels that others see him in the same fashion. However, it must be noted that certification is a process and as such is changeable and impermanent. Remission remains a possibility:

> It's a habit, like smoking. I thought I had it beat at one time. I was doing pretty good; got into a job that I loved doing, had a family, people began to accept me for myself, staying out of trouble. I thought I had it beat. I stayed out for one year and three months. Had a divorce, lost my job,

easiest thing for me to do was go back to my old habits. What I knew best, what I knew how to do.

Conclusions

Deviance is a social phenomenon involving both the deviant and his or her contemporaries. As Becker (1963:9) has declared, "deviant behavior is behavior that people so label." Likewise, conventionality is a social phenomenon that involves societal reactions. This paper has explored certification as the process by which people label ex-offenders as normal. It is an informal process of reality construction that results in the acceptance of the ex-felon as one who can be trusted. Certification revolves around the duel self of the actor and the use of others, places, agencies, and activities as means of self-presentation. These results in a sense confirm Davis' (1961) earlier conclusions concerning "deviance disavowal" among the visibly handicapped by revealing a similar process in the career of criminals. Certification is a way in which the stigmatized ex-offender attempts to resist a societal imputation of essential deviance and to deny that he is anything but a conventional person. The ex-felon, too, may be granted "fictional acceptance" at the onset of social encounters (Davis, 1961:126). He also uses settings, activities, and particularly others to encourage the other to identify with him through role-taking and thereby legitimate the ex-offender's non-criminal identity. Finally, like the visibly handicapped person (Davis, 1961:130–31), the ex-felon must sustain these normal relationships over some extended period. These parallels in the cases of two very different (ascribed versus achieved, for instance) kinds of deviant statuses and their normalization seems to lend support to the generalizability of the labeling position's emphasis on the interactional nature of social deviance. Any social reality is bounded by horizons of more or less open possibility. Through the process of certification, the individual has relegated criminality to the fringes of his life-world, but it does exist there as well as in his personal biography. Thus, criminal behavior remains, as it does for us all, a possibility.

REFERENCES

Ball, D.W. 1970. "The Problems of Respectability." Pp. 326–71 In Jack Douglas (ed.), *Deviance and Respectability*. New York: Basic Books.

Becker, H. 1963. *Outsiders*. New York: Free Press.

———. 1964. "Personal Change in Adult Life." *Sociometry* 27:40–53.

Berger, P. and T. Luckmann. 1968. *The Social Construction of Reality*. Garden City: Doubleday.

Brim, O. and S. Wheeler. 1966. *Socialization After Childhood*. New York: Wiley.

Davis, F. 1961. "Deviance Disavowal." *Social Problems* 9:120–32.

Goffman, E. 1959. *The Presentation of Self in Everyday Life*. Garden City, New York: Doubleday.

Hawkins, R. and G. Tiedeman. 1975. *The Creation of Deviance*. Columbus, Ohio: Charles Merrill.

Irwin, J. 1970. *The Felon*. Englewood Cliffs, New Jersey: Prentice-Hall.

Laing, R.D., H. Phillipson, and A.R. Lee. 1966. *Interpersonal Perception*. New York: Harper & Row.

Lofland, J. 1969. *Deviance and Identity*. Englewood Cliffs, New Jersey: Prentice-Hall.

Matza, D. 1969. *Becoming Deviant*. Englewood Cliffs, New Jersey: Prentice-Hall.

Meisenhelder, T. 1977. "An Exploratory Study of Exiting from Criminal Careers." *Criminology* 15:319–34.

Schutz, A. 1962. *Collected Papers I*. The Hague: Nijhoff.

Weber, M. 1958. *The Protestant Ethic and the Spirit of Capitalism*. New York: Scribner's.

NOTES

[1]As a process of social interaction, certification undoubtedly develops as a series of general steps or phases. Thus, as one *Deviant Behavior* reviewer has commented, it would be beneficial to be able to present a thorough "phrase analysis" of the process of certification. I assume this is possible and it should be done. However, the data collected in this study seemed more open to a somewhat static analytical framework. Therefore I have concentrated on uncovering the primary elements within the process rather than explicitly treating the stages of the process of certification. Still, in order to avoid a complete neglect of processual description, several case histories are presented in the text.

[2]The use of incarcerated respondents in a study such as this is of course controversial. However, all these men have, in their own minds, experienced a significant, though temporary, exit from crime. A more important question stems from the ethnomethodologist's notion of accounting. It must remain, at least for the time being, an open question whether certification is an event or the offender's way of accounting for a crime-free period in his biography.

[3]For a similar discussion of self, see Laing, Phillipson, and Lee (1966) and (1966) and Hawkins and Tiedeman (1975).

[4]In reference to Brim and Wheeler's work, and others on resocialization, it must be noted that these men do not think of themselves as having been resocialized. Neither do they think of themselves as in need of such a process. Although the general culture and much of the criminal justice system seems to attribute criminal behavior to the criminal's subjective deviance (motives and values), the men explain their pasts through more rational and practical contingencies. In other words, certification is more a process of self-presentation than of resocialization.

[5]Parole may be considered an agency, but the reference to it by the respondents continually reflected its status as a place for felons rather than an agency for reforming ex-convicts.

Chapter 50

RECOVERY THROUGH SELF-HELP

Jack Haas

Introduction

The process of recovery through participation in twelve-step programs includes a number of sociologically significant elements which facilitate healthy reintegration into wholesome living. This article describes those elements of the twelve-step fellowship found to be crucial for aiding recovery from compulsive behavior. Before discussing some of these key facilitating characteristics or processes provided by twelve-step programs it is necessary to outline the methodology of this research.

The methodology of participant observation best provides for a first-hand and intimate glimpse of addicts/alcoholics and this research involved extensive participant observation and informal interviewing of addicts in twelve-step groups over a ten year period. The main participants of the study have been alcoholics belonging to Alcoholics Anonymous, including members in Belgium, Canada, Germany, Great Britain, Scotland, and the United States. Other addicts in Narcotics Anonymous, Overeaters Anonymous, Sex and Love Addicts Anonymous, Sexaholics Anonymous, Emotions Anonymous, and co-dependents in Al Anon and Adult Children of Alcoholics have also been observed and informally interviewed. Additionally, published accounts and personal stories of these and other addictions, have been read and analyzed in the continuing search for a more general and theoretically enriched understanding of the processes of addiction and recovery.

Having observed thousands of meetings and talked with thousands of addict/alcoholics/co-dependents, I am confident that some of the integral elements of twelve-step recovery include: learning and adopting a set of integrative rituals to replace the alienating ritual of addiction; involvement in a group psychotherapeutic community of fellow sufferers; sharing one's perceptions and feelings through narrative as a form of identification, catharsis and healing of a shame and fear based personality; and learning and adopting a new set of core beliefs about oneself and using tools learned in the program for dealing with reality in a healthy and accepting way.

The Addictive Process

If we accept the stories of addicts at face value, as ones in which they perceive and experience much fear and pain, and thus have strong motivation for mood change, we can appreciate their move toward addictive behavior. When they find processes or substances that distort or alter reality, a reality that imprisons them and keeps them unhappy and suffering, they can be understood for seeking such relief and release. Their quest is for some freedom from their feelings, and obsessive-compulsive behavior and mind-altering substances or processes provide the release they desire. Once they experience the euphoria of freedom from the crippling feelings of their perceived reality and environment, they begin an insatiable quest to return to or heighten their release. The desire for an altered consciousness, and the experience of changed perceptions and feelings creates the lust for satiation and the next "fix," even in the face of harmful or disastrous consequences.

The development of a particular addiction or set of addictions is thus contingent upon the pattern of behavior meeting three attributes: 1)It blurs reality testing by diverting one's attention from a chronic aversive state; 2)It lowers self-criticism and self-consciousness, deflecting preoccupation from one's perceived inadequacies; and 3)it permits complimentary daydreams and wish-fulfilling fantasies about oneself (Jacobs, 1989: 46–47). The addicts seek and finds ways to create a self-induced dissociative condition which proves them temporary relief from their angst.

In order for recovery to commence the addict must, at first, "hit bottom." Twelve step programs emphasize this necessary phase of the addictive career because it is believed to prepare the addict for change. The addict is thought to be willful, selfish, and only preoccupied with the next fix, until, or when, the consequences of the addiction become so painful that the person reaches out for help. Without this willingness to change the addict can't be helped. This is not to say that "bottoms" can't be raised. Interventionists are sometimes able to arrange sessions with the addict which help cut through the addict's characteristic denial and bring home the present and future costs of using and abusing.

For those who do not hit bottom or who, for whatever reason, are unable to see the destructive results of their abusing, the prognosis for recovery is grim. The system of denial and loss of reality consciousness that pervades the practicing addict's life does not allow for ego weakness and admission that a serious problem exists. Instead the addict creates a denial system which includes blaming "people, places and things" for the difficulties and misfortunes that seemingly befall him/her. Unable to take responsibility and self-absorbed in maintaining the narcotic effect of the addiction, the practicing addict is stuck without any real choice. It is only when the denial system is overwhelmed with the crushing reality of the consequences of abusing that the addict may awaken to the desperation of the situation and the need to change.

The self-centeredness of the addict makes it difficult to accept the idea that there is a loss of control in using or abusing. Part of the defeat that hitting bottom implies includes some notion, vague or otherwise, that willpower has not worked for controlling the use or abuse. This incipient realization is fundamental for breaking down the system of denial and the prospective awareness that without help the destructive pattern will continue.

Ritual Ordeal and Radical Personal Change

Hitting bottom, the extreme of personal degradation and mortification, is initially important as the beginning point of dramatic personal change. The individual is now prepared for a ritual process of transcendence in which he/she is reconstituted into a new moral status of recovering or recovered addict. The conversion process takes place in twelve step recovery programs where individuals are related to with unconditional love and acceptance, provided new and healthy rituals of transcendence, and moved toward a new vision of themselves and their relationship to the world and matters spiritual.

Typically, in order for individuals or groups of individuals to undergo radical moral status and personality changes, societal institutions, e.g., schools, courts, mental institutions and prisons, armed forces training, etc., organize a process of ritual ordeal involving status degradation, and mortification before participants are elevated or demoted into their new and higher or lower moral status (Garfinkel, 1956; Glaser and Strauss, 1971; Goffman, 1959; Haas, 1989; Herman, 1981). Degradation and mortification are essential stripping processes whereby the "chosen," "damned" or "elect" are prepared for their new status through the stripping and loss of their old identities. The self is mortified as part of a necessary process of reconstituting the self with a new identity. The "old" self and identity is shorn and candidates are isolated and separated from lay culture as part of this process of resocialization and moral conversion.

Addiction continues until the addict "hits bottom," the beginning point of the process of recovery. Such "ego deflation at depth" is a necessary part of a ritual process of degradation and mortification that characterizes many forms of radical moral and personal change. Mortified and helpless the addict breaks through their elaborated system of denial and becomes more willing to admit powerlessness over their addiction and their need for help.

The dialectical extremes of "hitting bottom" and developing "emotional sobriety" describe the continuum range of the recovery career. For those who integrate the twelve-step program into their lives there is a process analogous to ritual rebirth, a "spiritual awakening" or radical personality change. The recovering or recovered addict develops a new and healthier set of "core beliefs" about self, others, and reality, and a more integrated self. The transition from addiction to recovery includes a "higher power" consciousness which is encouraged, developed and maintained in the transcendental and integrative practice of communal, and personal, spiritual rituals. What is unique in the reconstitution of self and transformations of identity which characterize the self-help programs of Alcoholics Anonymous and its derivatives is that the addiction itself promotes a career of degradation and mortification and the process of "hitting bottom" is usually self-promoted and does not necessarily require institutional support and reinforcement. As the individual sinks into a state of abject powerlessness over their addiction and the "fix" takes priority over other significant matters, helplessness, guilt and shame contribute to the mortification so necessary before recovery and radical personal change is possible. The ritual of addiction contributes in this sense to the ritual ordeal so necessary before recovery. As one proceeds to a bottoming out their prospects of breaking through the system of denial and the cycle of addiction are enhanced. The addictive cycle and the accompanying rituals of addiction produce feelings of despair and powerlessness so essential to a desire to change.

Addicts recounting of their experience of hitting bottom describe their ritual death and the beginning revelation of their sacred rebirth. The ordeal of "hitting bottom" is a necessary part of a ritual of recovery and the ideology of A.A. and its derivatives include the ritualistic telling and retelling at speaker meetings of "what it was like, what happened, and what it's like now." Speakers are advised to share "their experience, strength and hope" and part of the storytelling includes describing life before recovery and the process of "hitting bottom."

The ritualistic telling of personal accounts of degradation and mortification before elevation to a "recovering" or "recovered" status reinforces the cultural prerequisite of personal failure and surrender before change into a new way of life. The ritual death of the addict becomes interchangeable with transition toward a higher spiritual condition or regeneration. It is only through such a total crisis that the hope of beginning life over again through a genuine and total conversion takes place. Such conversions are rare in modern life because death is rarely given a positive value, but in the case of recovery from the desperation and despair of addiction, death or near death precedes the spiritual rebirth and transformation of the individual into a new being (Eliade, 1963).

Addicts recounting their experience of "what it was like" hitting their personal bottom essentially describe their ritual death and the revelation of the sacred, a process Eliade describes as time-honored and universal (transhistorical and metacultural) processes (1958: 102). The concrete death becomes interchangeable with transition toward a higher spiritual condition or regeneration. It is only through such a total crisis that the hope of beginning life over again through a genuine and total conversion takes place.

Ritual ordeal before elevation, as a process of radical personal change, underlies the recovery process and is supported by other transformative rituals that contribute to the individual's reintegration into society. These rituals require declarations of personal flaw, shame, guilt and/or failure. The transformative ritual begins in submission and after submission comes confession, purification and commitment to a new way of life based on the twelve steps of recovery and the learning and practice of integrative rituals.

Recovery Rituals

It is said that "man is a creature of habit." Such an idea is certainly confirmed, if one studies addicts, persons who essentially are victims or sufferers of such a principle of human life. Ritual, of course, provides us both the means to maintain ongoing structure and to effect transformations by integrating change into a basic form. Both types of ritual center the will in transcendental sources and anchor the immediate order in a realm that transcends it. No wonder then that pre-addict and addict, consumed with an insatiable appetite for mood change, would discover the transcendental qualities of ritual, and that the recovering addict would necessarily have to learn and practice substitute and integrative rituals to breakdown the perceptions and feelings of alienation which precipitate the desire to escape or alter feelings and perceptions of reality.

Perhaps we need emphasize our recognition of the prime place of ritual in providing people temporal relief and security in our early, at infancy, perception of complete dependence upon others. Ernest Becker writes of this early dependency and the concomitant anxiety it produces, and of the human fear of death and desire for immortality. These anxieties are quelled by the practice of ritual and basic to ritual is the idea that:

> ...man cannot impart life to himself but must get it from his fellow man. If ritual is a technique for generating life, then ritual organization is a necessary cooperation in order to make that technique work (1972:11).

It is, as Becker states, ritual organization, such as the twelve-step group, which provides integrative relationships with others and a more complete sense of wholeness. It is through communal and spiritual rituals that the addict gains freedom from emotional turmoil and feelings of aloneness.

Sigmund Freud took the position that the psychological mechanism responsible for the formation of obsessional-neurotic behavior was also responsible for the formation of apparently normal religious rituals. Freud states: "...one might describe neurosis as individual religiosity and religion as a universal neurosis" (Strachey, 1959:116). In comparing the salient features of obsessional neurosis with those of taboo behavior, Freud argued that religion and obsessional neurosis shared a genetic identity and that contemporary vestiges of religious ritual would under rational, scientific analysis disappear just as obsessional neurosis does with psychoanalytic treatment. Volney Gay correctly argues that Freud failed to prove that religious rituals are essentially obsessive-like behavior and, therefore, some religious rituals are of obvious benefit to some people (Gay, 1979: Chap. 1).

In the self-help example I would argue that the socially integrative rituals that are learned and practiced in self-help groups aid in the recentering of individuals, providing them a glimpse of non-alienated living and feeling. Participants are recentered in a world and reality they are learning that they cannot wholly control. Burdened with the self-centeredness of their dis-ease the recentering moves them to emphasize self-criticism, acceptance of personal limitations, and a general move from feelings of disequilibrium to harmony and emotional peace.

If the basis of transcendence is the practice of ritual, then the self-help meeting is obviously replete with opportunities for individuals and the collective to transcend or mood alter their feelings. Many participants report how they may come to a meeting burdened with the pain of everyday, or not so everyday living, and experience relief. For many the meetings are the 'medicine' for their dis-ease. There is a pervasive attitude of support in a "fellowship" of fellow sufferers who share a common fate and identity and who participate together in shared communal rituals in their search for acceptance, peace of mind, and serenity.

The very structure of the meeting is sociologically significant for producing a secure and comforting environment. By briefly describing some characteristics of a "typical" meeting the reader may relate to how well the meeting provides opportunity for ritual practice.

Most meetings take place in churches, usually church basement meeting rooms. Immediately, an ambience of sanctity, the idea of a special place and context is presented. Designated members arrive early to prepare the setting further by making coffee and tea, perhaps contributing food, a feature of "anniversary" or "birthday" meetings, arrange the chairs for the meeting (facing each other for discussion, usually around a table or tables, and in rows for a "speaker meeting"). Often one or more members serve as "greeters" at the door welcoming by handshake or hugs arriving participants.

A social occasion develops with a coffee social ritual prior to and after the meeting itself. Though this may be somewhat intimidating to the nervous newcomer, what is also obvious are the good feelings, conviviality, and friendliness of the members. Though the newcomer is a stranger to the group, there is a subtle attraction as one notes that these people, who are often thoroughly enjoying each others' company, are also people who share the same dis-ease which has brought the reluctant newcomer. These examples of healing are powerful symbols of identification and change and are, perhaps, at root for understanding the newcomer's motivation to change. The power of example of recovering addicts who have developed a new and healthy set of relationships with others and self, and positive attitudes towards life and living, contrasts dramatically, but provides hope, to the newcomer's suffering and despair.

What is also common to these meetings is the practice of communal rituals, particularly rituals which open and close the meeting. It is here that a certain solemnity is created and the seriousness of the matter at hand, recovery from co-dependence or the dis-ease of addiction, is impressed upon the participants. Solemn moments of silence, prayer and readings characterize this spiritual ambience. These shared rituals provide feelings of security and comfort as the mood is changed to one with which participants are familiar. The chanting of prayers, the steps and traditions of recovery, and other readings provide an assurance and reassurance that all is well, that there is predictability and safety, here and now.

The practice of such rituals has a tranquilizing quality because it has form which can be anticipated, thus assuring the participants of a predictable and secure process. The practice allows individuals to center themselves by lessening the distractions around them. As the ritual is engaged, it has somewhat of a mesmerizing effect and external stimuli become extraneous and filtered out of the prime perception of the ritual process. Individuals lose a sense of self-consciousness and find a peace in the concentration and rhythm of the ritual.

Recovery rituals are either communal or individual. The addict previously engaged in addictive rituals which, though they might be practiced in the presence of others, essentially separated self from others. Contrarily, communal recovery rituals require involvement and joining with others, and personal prayer and meditation rituals involve a concept of a relationship with a "higher power." Recovery rituals are therefore integrating and breakdown the perception and feeling of isolation and separateness.

Nowhere is the use of personal prayer ritual more significant as a substitute for addictive, ritualistic acting out than in twelve step members use of the "Serenity Prayer" (See Appendix C) in their daily life. Members frequently report how they use and repeat this prayer when they are experiencing turmoil. The saying of this prayer is virtually synonymous with twelve step membership and participants' reliance on it in times of crisis is a shared perspective of the fellowship.

The Serenity Prayer becomes for most members of twelve step groups both a connection or communication with their "Higher Power" and a ritual which provides them a temporary mood change. In the past a stressful context stimulated the addictive process but, in recovery, perceived stress is managed by reliance upon an integrative ritual. Schechner writes that the function of such ritual is "to keep people from thinking `too much'" (1987:1).

If one of ritual's main functions is to keep people from thinking too much then ritual, such as the reciting of the Serenity Prayer, short-circuits thought and promotes feelings of well-being and relief. The repetition of a few basic themes in very structured and predictable ways reinforces images, meanings or lessons and structure. Familiarity and a sense of integration with others and self replaces isolation, alienation and loneliness.

The recovering addict is then, like a religious person, able to both use ritual to gain contact with mysterious and "sacred" realities and/or to transform the lived reality. The repetitive nature of ritual focuses the individual by framing and shaping consciousness. George Coe in *The Psychology of Religion* describes prayer as:

> ...a way of getting one's self together, of mobilizing and concentrating one's dispersed capacities, of begetting the confidence that tends toward victory over difficulties. It produces in a distracted mind the repose that is power. It freshens a mind deadened by routine. It reveals new truth, because the mind is made more elastic and more capable of sustained attention (1917:312–13).

The third step of the twelve step program (Appendix D) suggests that individuals make "a decision to turn our will and our lives over to the care of God as we understood him." This step, like the Serenity Prayer, involves the individual's attempt to renounce personal autonomy and to experientially and cognitively place oneself in a divine order where the transcendentally centered meaning and purpose gains priority and emphasis.

As part of the personal rituals one is encouraged to engage, ritual prayer and meditation, to begin and close each day, are also given strong emphasis. These practices center the individual and temporarily reduce the perception of outside stimuli by quieting the mind. Many members begin and/or close their day with spiritual readings which again have the potential to move consciousness into another dimension of thought and feeling.

Spiritual rituals help promote the individual's sense of well-being and connection with a "Higher Power." Combined with communal and personal rituals, and a community of accepting others, the core beliefs of negativity and low self-esteem of the addictive personality are replaced by affirmative ways to perceive and experience life, the self, and others. Other ritual processes of Twelve Step programs add to and reinforce these changes. Processes of joining and participating in a group; celebrating "birthdays" based on one's date of sobriety where such anniversaries are ceremoniously celebrated with the awarding of pins and medallions, short congratulatory speeches by the "sponsor" and expressions of gratitude by the recipient, celebrations with food and birthday cake, and the singing of "Happy Birthday," etc. These and other rituals and the sharing about one's problems, interpretations of the program or the steps of recovery combine to reinforce and strengthen the move from emotional turmoil and dis-ease to "emotional sobriety." As Patrick Carnes in his book *Contrary to Love: Helping the Sex Addict* writes: "A sure sign of recovery is when the recovering person perceives the ongoing rituals as a symbol of a new life" (emphasis his) (1989:250).

Childhood Issues and Group Therapy

For many, the essence of recovery can be described as a reconstitution of self through the replacement of primary groups, where the "family of origin" and the lessons and scars of that relationship are replaced by a "family of choice," the self-help group or community which provides participants an opportunity to learn and adopt a valued conception of self. Though the "cracked mirror" and "diseased unions" of the past linger and lie dormant and can reemerge as enforcers of a negative conception of self, the recovering twelve-step member has an alternative source of affirmation and value from a loving and therapeutic "fellowship" or community of fellow sufferers. Alcoholism is often referred to as a "family disease" and although the medical concept of disease is inappropriate for describing the process or cause of addiction,[1] the idea that the alcoholic or addict affects other members of the family is useful and helps explain the cycle of addiction for children of addicts and the dysfunctional adaptations that make family members of the addict dis-eased as well. The dis-ease or "isms," the pattern of fear and denial that characterize the addictive family, are nicely summarized in terms of their attitudinal and behavioral outcomes in the fourteen characteristics of the Adult Children of Alcoholics [which are read at some adult children meetings], (See Appendix A). (See also Appendix B for the very similar characteristics of sex and love addicts.) The child of the alcoholic readily identifies with some or all of these characteristics, as would, I argue, adult children, pre-addicts and addicts, of all addictions.

How, then, does self-help provide healing through therapy?

The authors, Drs. Sophia Vinogradov and Irvin D. Yalom, of *The Concise Guide to Group Psychotherapy* (1989) provide practical criteria, specifically for psychiatrists and psychiatric residents, by outlining the demonstrable factors that makes group therapy work and participants change. In synthesizing empirically based information from a variety of social science researches they have outlined an eleven factor inventory of curative mechanisms operating in successful group psychotherapies which include: instillation of hope; universality; imparting of information; altruism; development of socializing techniques; imitative behavior; catharsis; corrective recapitulation of the primary family group; existential factors; and, group cohesiveness.

In reviewing these factors it is apparent that twelve step, self-help programs are really ideal-types for providing a context where such factors are abundantly available to willing participants. The important variable that remains is the openness of participants to the opportunities to learn and to change. For those who "work the program" the relevance and presence of these factors is significant for effecting life changes and a reconstitution of self.

Healing the Child Within

Though the concept of the "inner child" is a heuristic device, it symbolizes the powerful imprinting of early childhood socialization. The very direct relationship between perceived assaults on the child's self and adult addiction makes recovery critically linked, but oft ignored, to the healing of old wounds and scars of the self.

The "inner child" of the addict is the very hurt side of self that burdens the adult personality with pain and negativity. Having profoundly perceived the alienating experiences of abuse, neglect and/or abandonment, the "child within" lives in the pain and lessons of these memories, attempts to deny and hide these feelings from others and self through the creation of a "false self," and is motivated to escape the feelings and situations that are reminders or warnings of recurrence. The end result is a controlling and stifled self, crippled by fears and thus limited in response. Negative attitudes prejudge situations creating a self-fulfilling situation rooted in narrow and conditioned thinking. The spontaneous and free qualities of expression are stifled in the attempt to develop control over people, places and things. The frightened, insecure and damaged part of self denies the insanity of inappropriate choices and adaptations and is incapable of change until or unless the fiction is somehow challenged and a new awareness through the trough of desperation or "hitting bottom" produces the motivation and insight for change.

Recovery from the adaptations of addiction to the distorted perceptions of disease and alienation from self and others requires attending to that part of the self, the child, which maintains a co-starring role in defining and responding to life's situations. The adult may be successful by society's terms but the person suffers behind the mask and facade of the false self — a creation of the child to protect the wounded self. The lack of authenticity, the role playing and duplicity of a managed and manipulated self, further alienates the individual not only from others but, most importantly, from oneself. The crippling pressure to appease others by conforming, even against one's interests, needs and desires because of the desire to escape further hurts and rejections, makes for "soul-murder" and the further corrosion of self.

"Inner child" work or recovery therefore is a process of rediscovering the real self, identifying ongoing physical, mental-emotional and spiritual needs and practice getting these needs met with safe and supportive people. Most importantly, the healing depends on identifying, re-experiencing and grieving the pain of earlier losses and/or traumas and identifying and expressing "core issues" such as control, trust, feelings, being over-responsible, neglecting needs, all-or-nothing feeling and behavior, high tolerances for inappropriate behavior, low self-esteem, being authentic, grieving losses, fear of abandonment, difficulty risking conflict, and difficulty giving and receiving love, etc. (Whitfield, 1989:67).

Through processes of recovery the false self and the related core beliefs of inadequacy and self contempt are gradually replaced by an integrated wholeness and positively accepted sense of self. The addict moves from the struggle and pain of an alienated self to an integrated and authentic individual capable of the fuller acceptance and expression of feelings appropriate to a more clearly perceived reality.

The catharsis of rage and anger around perceptions of childhood maltreatment or neglect is a necessary prerequisite to a fuller honoring of these feelings and makes possible the forgiveness of self and others. Although it is not always possible, nor even desirable, to forgive behavior or people the individual finds beyond redemption, it is important that, at minimum, the addict move to self-forgiveness. The feelings of despair that accompany painful childhoods and the wasted years in addictive pursuits can produce extreme feelings of regret and remorse which no amount of self-flagellation can remove or correct. Instead, through individual and group therapy, the addict can properly understand negative adaptations as unwitting responses which are no longer relevant and are part of the past. What is imperative for a new life and well-being is acceptance of the past, forgiveness for past mistakes and ways, and an ongoing commitment to self-improvement.

Foremost in the process of recovery is the experiencing of the unconditional love of others. The self-help group is one place where such complete acceptance and reintegration is possible, it replaces the mirroring of the family of origin and is an alternative family of choice. The self-help group, particularly the twelve-step group, is an ideal-type psychotherapeutic group which meets a host of criteria for creating a healthy and nurturing environment for the reconstitution of self (Haas, 1991). Other sources of unconditional acceptance (counselor, friend, partner, etc.) can provide the nurturance that the child missed or didn't perceive while growing up. The negative perceptions about childhood may change as they are reinterpreted as the shortcomings of others who were handicapped by their own childhoods.

In a supportive and loving environment there is a real prospect for more genuine healing and dissolution of the false self and negative core beliefs, replaced by a healthy, integrated and authentic self. Recovery from addiction is reflected in a move from feelings of inadequacy and self-contempt to love of self, others and life itself. It is in a sense a rebirth as I have described elsewhere (Haas, 1990), but is contingent upon dealing with the scars of the past, the basis of the search for addictive release. Emotional sobriety and well-being fundamentally depend upon healing the child within.

Conclusion

For most sociologists the group is the focus for understanding human behavior and change. Joining, participating in, and leaving groups all have important consequences for the development of, and changes in, personal identity and conceptions of self. The significance of group effects on how individuals see themselves is very dramatic in the study of the twelve-step programs of Alcoholics Anonymous and its derivatives.

Though the process of recovery is not automatic and requires "honesty, openmindedness, and willingness" there are literally millions of recovering addicts whose lives and personalities have changed remarkably.

In examining the twelve-step program the focus is on those sociological features and processes which contribute to its success in aiding recovery. These include: the ritual character of this spiritual program and its psychotherapeutic nature, which implicitly aid the healing of the wounded "child within," a key to the development of "emotional sobriety"; opportunities for developing a valued and reintegrated self through processes that reduce feelings of alienation and; the learning of new attitudes and approaches to develop and maintain healthy ways of living. I also discuss the success of the twelve-step program for radically altering the status, identity and personality of participants.

APPENDIX A CHARACTERISTICS

1. We were isolated and afraid of people and authority figures.

2. We were approval seekers and lost our identity in the process.

3. We were frightened by angry people and any personal criticism.

4. We either became alcoholics, married them, or both, or found another compulsive personality such as a workaholic to fulfill our sick abandonment needs.

5. We lived life from the viewpoint of victims and were attracted by that weakness in our love and friendship relationships.

6. We had an overdeveloped sense of responsibility and it was easier for us to be concerned with others rather than ourselves; this enabled us not to look too closely at our faults.

7. We had guilt feelings when we stood up for ourselves instead of giving in to others.

8. We were addicted to excitement.

9. We confused love and pity and tended to "love" people we could pity and rescue.

10. We had stuffed our feelings from our traumatic childhoods and had lost the ability to feel or express our feelings because it hurt so much (DENIAL).

11. We judged ourselves harshly and had a very low sense of self-esteem.

12. We were dependent personalities who were terrified of abandonment and would do anything to hold on to a relationship in order not to experience painful abandonment feelings.

13. Alcoholism is a family disease and we Adult Children took on the characteristics of that disease even though we did not pick up the drink.

14. We were reactors rather than actors.

APPENDIX B ADAPTED COMMON CHARACTERISTICS OF SEX AND LOVE ADDICTION

1. We are addicted to emotional pain.

2. Terrified of abandonment, we will do anything to keep a relationship from dissolving.

3. Nothing is too much trouble, takes too much time, or is too expensive if it will "help" the person with whom we are involved.

4. We are willing to take more than 50 percent of the responsibility, guilt, and blame in any relationship.

5. We have a desperate need to control our relationships - and mask these efforts to control people and situations as "being helpful."

6. In a relationship we are much more in touch with our dream of how it could be than with the reality of the situation.

7. Accustomed to lack of love in personal relationships, we are willing to wait, hope, and try harder to please.

8. By being drawn to people with problems that need fixing, or being enmeshed in situations that are chaotic, uncertain, and emotionally painful, we avoid focusing on our responsibility to ourselves.

9. We tended to become immobilized by romantic obsessions.

10. We searched for some "magical" quality in others to make us feel complete. Other people were idealized and endowed with a powerful symbolism.

11. While constantly seeking intimacy with another person, the desperate quality of our need made true intimacy with anyone impossible. In trying to conceal our dependency demands from ourselves and others, we grew more isolated and alienated from ourselves, from God, and from the very people we longed to be close to.

12. We feared relationships, but continually searched for them. In a relationship, we feared abandonment and rejection, but out of one, we felt empty and incomplete.

13. We were drawn to people who were not available to us, or who would reject and abuse us.

14. We often developed unhealthy dependency relationships that eventually became unbearable.

APPENDIX C SERENITY PRAYER

God grant me the serenity to accept the things I cannot change, courage to change the things I can, and the wisdom to know the difference.

APPENDIX D THE TWELVE STEPS OF ALCOHOLICS ANONYMOUS

1. We admitted we were powerless over alcohol — that our lives had become unmanageable.

2. Came to believe that a Power greater than ourselves could restore us to sanity.

3. Made a decision to turn our will and our lives over to the care of God as we understood him.

4. Made a searching and fearless moral inventory of ourselves.

5. Admitted to God, to ourselves, and to another human being the exact nature of our wrongs.

6. Were entirely ready to have God remove all these defects of character.

7. Humbly asked Him to remove our shortcomings.

8. Made a list of all persons we had harmed, and became willing to make amends to them all.

9. Made direct amends to such people whenever possible, except when to do so would injure them or others.

10. Continued to take personal inventory and when we were wrong promptly admitted it.

11. Sought through prayer and meditation to improve our conscious contact with God as we understood Him, praying only for knowledge of His will for us and the power to carry that out.

12. Having had a spiritual awakening as a result of these steps, we tried to carry this message to alcoholics, and to practice these principles in all our affairs.

REFERENCES

Becker, Ernest, 1973. *The Denial of Death.* New York: Macmillan.
Carnes, Patrick, 1989. *Contrary to Love, Understanding Sexual Addiction: Helping the Sexual Addict.* Minneapolis, Minnesota: Comp Care Publications.
Coe, George, 1917. *The Psychology of Religion.* Chicago: Scribner's.
Eliade, Mircea, 1963. *Myth and Reality* New York: Harper and Row.
Eliade, Mircea, 1958. *The Sacred and the Profane: The Nature of Religion.* New York: Harcourt, Brace and World.
Freud, Sigmund, 1959 (1907b). "Obsessive Actions and Religious Practices," in James Strachey, *The Standard Edition of the Complete Psychological Works of Sigmund Freud,* 9: 116–127.
Garfinkel, Harold, 1967. "Conditions of Successful Degradation Ceremonies," *American Journal of Sociology* 61:420–24.
Gay, Volney P., 1979. *Freud on Ritual: Reconstruction and Critique.* Missoula, Montana: Scholars Press.
Glaser, Barney and Anselm Strauss, 1971. *Status Passage.* Chicago: Aldine, Atherton Press.
Goffman, Erving, 1959. "The Moral Career of the Mental Patient," *Psychiatry* 22:123–142.
Haas, Jack, 1990. "Addiction and Recovery as Ritual Processes of Transcendence," International Sociological Association, Madrid, Spain, July.
Haas, Jack, 1991. "How It Works: Self-Help Changing Self," Qualitative Research Conference, Carleton University, Ottawa, May.
Haas, Jack, 1989. "The Process of Apprenticeship: Ritual Ordeal and the Adoption of A Cloak of Competence" in M. Coy, *Apprenticeship: From Theory to Method and Back Again,* Albany: State University of New York Press.
Herman, Nancy J., 1981. "The Making of a Mental Patient: An Ethnographic Study of the Processes and Consequences of Institutionalization upon Self-Images and Identities." Unpublished Master's thesis, McMaster University, Hamilton, Ontario, Canada.
Jacobs, David F., 1989. "A General Theory of Addictions: Rationale for and Evidence Supporting a New Approach for Understanding and Treating Addictive Behaviors," Pp. 35–64 In Howard S. Shaffer, et. al., eds., *Compulsive Gambling.* Kentucky: Lexington Books.
Schechner, Richard, 1987. "The Future of Ritual," *Journal of Ritual Studies,* 1: pp. 5–33.
Vinogradov, Sophia and Irvin D. Yalom, 1989. *A Concise Guide to Group Psychotherapy.* Washington, D.C.: American Psychiatric Press, Inc.
Whitfield, Charles, 1987. *Healing the Child Within.* Deerfield Beach, Florida: Health Communications, Inc.

NOTES

[1] The concept of alcoholism as a disease is inappropriate for understanding the process or cause of alcoholism but helpful in terms of reducing stigma. Alcoholism and other addictions are examples of "accidental deviance" where individuals don't have a choice and willpower is not helpful. Addiction is better understood as symptoms reflecting dis-ease.

Chapter 51

GAINING AND LOSING WEIGHT: IDENTITY TRANSFORMATIONS

Cliff English

Introduction

An intriguing phenomenon associated with obesity is that heavy people do lose weight—often substantial amounts. Self reports from obese dieters indicate that losses of 35, 50, and even 100 pounds are not unusual. At the same time, heavy people frequently report subsequent weight gains that exceed their initial weight loss. Both heavy people and professionals who attempt to assist them in their efforts are aware of this phenomenon but are often puzzled by it. Nonobese people seem to be bewildered as to why anyone would return to an obese state after losing a large amount of weight, particularly given the difficulties obese people experience in dealing with our culture. There is, however, a growing recognition among professional clinicians and obese people that losing weight is only part of the battle; it is becoming increasingly clear that maintaining weight loss constitutes the ongoing battle.

Observations of weight-control therapy groups coupled with informal and formal interviews with fat people support the notion that weight loss maintenance is a real problem that plagues large numbers of heavy people. It is the contention here that both successful and unsuccessful efforts to maintain weight loss are related to a set of social variables.[1] The identification of these variables and an examination of the resulting interactions form the basis of this analysis.

Methodology

Data gathering for this study of obesity consisted of systematic observations of weight loss therapy groups in two phases, one during 1983 and one in 1989. The original research opportunity presented itself through the author's acquaintance with a psychotherapist who worked exclusively with overweight individuals. At the therapist's invitation, a year-long project that involved systematic observations of 24 therapy groups was conducted. Each group consisted of 15 members and met for 12 weeks each. The therapy program was a conservative approach to weight loss using behavioral self-control principles. Participants were advised that weight loss would be modest, but that they would learn techniques and strategies that would enable them to continue weight loss and control for the rest of their lives. The average weight of participants was 270 pounds, and 90% were female. Each participant selected a 1,000- to 1,200-calorie diet of her or his choice in consultation with a licensed nutritionist. The setting was similar to that of a college seminar with members seated around a table. The author sat off to one side and unobtrusively took field notes during each session.

In addition, both formal and informal interviews were conducted with heavy people in a variety of settings, including individual therapy sessions, bars, restaurants, parties, plane terminals, bus stations, and the researcher's office. Respondents were highly cooperative and openly shared their triumphs and failures in combating their weight problems. Respondents were so anxious to tell their story that it was not necessary to ask probing questions; rather the researcher was overwhelmed with biographical information that demanded a minimum amount of prompting and questioning. This allowed for use of the intensive interview approach, which has been described in the following manner:

> Its object is not to elicit choices between alternative answers to pre-formed questions but, rather to elicit from the interviews what she/he considers to be important questions of some situations being explored. Its object is to carry on a guided conversation and elicit rich, detailed materials that can be used in qualitative analysis. Its object is to find out what kind of things are happening, rather than determine the frequency of predetermined kinds of things that the researcher already believes can happen (Lofland, 1971:76).

The second phase involved the author's employment as a clinical sociologist in a medical clinic. Field notes were compiled on overweight patients.

Data analysis involved the construction of analytical categories that were developed around data clusters, which allowed for the identification of key variables that inhibit maintenance of weight loss. These variables are described below.

Findings

Social Isolation

In this culture fat people are socially isolated in subtle and not so subtle ways. One of the major difficulties they encounter is violation of territory (Lyman, 1978). Cultural artifacts are clearly constructed with the thin person in mind: narrow supermarket aisles and seats in buses, planes, taxicabs, trains, compact cars, and theaters are all designed to accommodate the thin person. Restaurant booths, tavern stools, hotel and motel beds, telephone booths, and conventional furniture all tend to pose difficulties for obese members of society, potentially denying them full participation in the culture. One of the respondents reported signing up for an adult education class only to discover that she could not fit into the conventional desk. The following episode demonstrates how an obese person can find him- or herself in situations that produce a high level of territory invasion:

> A few weeks ago I went on one of those bus tours with a group of girls from work. We went to Chicago, which was a 14-hour trip. The bus was

completely packed and I shared a seat with one of the girls who was really thin. Deciding who was going to sit down with whom was awkward, since I could tell no one really wanted to sit with me; however, my friend was really nice about it and volunteered to sit with me. There actually was not room for both of us, but we managed. In the afternoon we drank a couple of beers and then I had to go to the restroom—the problem was I was afraid the door was too narrow. My friend took off the sash she had on her dress and measured me sideways and then went to the restroom and measured the door; she came back and told me she was not sure if it was wide enough or not. I was very embarrassed and terribly uncomfortable for about a half hour. Finally we stopped for a snack, and while everybody was outside I went in to the restroom, and wouldn't you know it, I got stuck, and my friend had to pull me out. I will never go on a bus ride again!

This incident demonstrates one of the ways the physical organization of our culture excludes heavy people from full participation. The fear of territory violation forces the obese person to avoid certain social situations that "normal" people take for granted; this contributes significantly to the sense of social isolation.

Another factor that contributes to the sense of social isolation is the fear of public ridicule. As one respondent recounted:

I dread going to dinner at a home where small children are present. I know they do not mean anything by it, but they can say very embarrassing things. I remember going to dinner at the home of a woman from work, and she had a four-year-old child. The child took one look at me and said, "Mommy, this lady is so fat she's going to eat all our nice dinner and there won't be any for you and I."

This isolation and subsequent loneliness can interfere considerably with the heavy person's weight loss efforts. According to the respondents, excessive eating tends to take place when they are alone. Passive activities such as television viewing combined with constant snacking were typical leisure time pursuits. Respondents also reported devoting a considerable amount of their time to the elaborate preparation and consumption of food, which allowed food to take on heightened special meanings the general population does not share.

Social isolation is not the only factor that interferes with weight loss efforts. Close friends and relatives were frequently identified as an additional source of difficulty. In fact, these people were referred to by respondents as saboteurs, and dieters were often perplexed with how to deal with them. The situation is complicated even further by the saboteurs who, according to the respondents, are of three types, namely, food pushers, humiliators, and brutalizers.

Food Pushers

Relatives and other overweight friends wittingly or unwittingly create obstacles for the fat person trying to achieve and/or maintain weight loss. In some instances, food pushing is deliberate, as in the case of one husband who, for whatever reasons, does not want his wife to lose weight. Apparently this is not an uncommon phenomenon. For example:

> My ex-husband never wanted me to become thin, he really liked fat women. It was always Big Mama this and Big Mama that. Well, I finally threw that turkey out, but all my life I have been hurt by my weight.

Other food pushers are overweight friends and relatives who create temptations for the dieter. It appears that when the dieter loses a substantial amount of weight, questions are raised about the friend or relative's own ability to successfully diet. These temptations take the following forms:

> My best friend who is always heavy came by with these cookies. She knows I am in this program, but she goes, "Anne, you're lookin' so good I just had to bake you these cookies!" I told her to get out of here with those cookies.
>
> My mother who has been heavy all her life calls me every day and tells me what she is cooking for dinner. She knows how I enjoy eating. She never offers me any of it, but she does make it terribly hard on me. I just don't know what to say to her.
>
> My two cousins are always taking me out to dinner, particularly since I have been in the program. They are getting so jealous because they are afraid I will become more attractive than they are.

Humiliators

Humiliators remind fat people of their weight in a manner that creates embarrassment and lowers feelings of self-worth. The impact on the fat person frequently leads to excessive eating and/or intensifies social isolation. The humiliator is typically a thin person who is insensitive to the feelings of a fat person or an overzealous, well-intentioned friend or relative. An example of the former, and the resulting impact, is as follows:

> To go into a regular-size store and have the sales clerk act as if I did not belong there. I told her money did not know any size. Oh, if I could just buy in a regular-size store. I mean what business is it of hers? I might have been buying something for someone else, I could buy a size 3 if I wanted, it is none of her business. I really got even. I bought a large pizza, took it home, and ate the whole damn thing.

The overzealous friend or relative is frequently more difficult to deal with, since the person's comments appear well intended, taking the following forms:

> I am the only heavy person in my family and everyone knows I am in the program. I had decided I was going to let myself go on this day

[Thanksgiving]. My mother, though, was right on me the whole time. "Are you eating too much of this or that?" It really got to me.

I ate a very small portion of everything at dinner [Thanksgiving], but my husband kept pointing out that I was eating too much. It ruined the meal for me.

Brutalizers

Brutalizers are individuals who engage in a direct assault on the overweight person's identity. Previous research has documented that obese people are subjected to frequent stigmatization. It is this kind of interaction that contributes most to their social isolation:

I was mortified to death when I went to the movie *Elephant Man*, and on my way out a teenager said in an extremely loud voice, "Hey, there goes elephant woman."

My husband drinks too much, and when he gets drunk he calls me a "fat ass bitch." That's enough to set me off [excessive eating].

Last week I met what I thought was a real nice guy in a bar. We danced a couple of dances and talked a while. He told me he was recently divorced and talked about his kids and stuff like that. He had just bought a motorcycle and I told him I had never ridden on a motorcycle before. I have lost all this weight, and when he offered to take me for a ride I accepted. I would not have taken him up on it if I had not had a few drinks. Anyway, we went out and somehow I managed to get on the back. I was embarrassed about having so much trouble getting on, but I made a joke out of it. Once we got going I was really scared because he was wobbling all over the road. After a couple blocks a police car stopped us and the officer thought the guy was drunk. He probably was, but he said to the officer, "How do you expect me to drive this thing with a big old sweat hog on the back?" Both he and the officer laughed and the cop let him go, and [he] drove me back to the bar. I have felt just terrible. I do not know if I can bring myself to ever go back into a bar again. I am sure I will never accept a ride on a motorcycle again.

This latter incident, besides its brutalizing characteristics, brings up an additional obstacle associated with weight loss, namely, the extremely heavy person's inability to manage social situations once moderate weight loss has occurred. Even more difficult is the problem of managing the transformation of identity that occurs as weight loss becomes more dramatic.

Fat as a Master Status

Despite the difficulties obese people experience, as a consequence of their excessive weight, it is not unusual for them to experience severe reservations once significant weight loss takes place. Early weight loss efforts usually produce very minor results that may be noticeable only to the dieter; nevertheless, those changes are real and gratifying and intensify continued effort:

> I was delighted to get on the airplane two weeks ago, and for the first time in a long time I did not have to let the seat belt all the way out. Then when I put down the tray for the snacks, I was actually able to. There was room between the tray and my belly. I felt so good I had only one Tab on the whole trip. I just could not believe it!

However, once significant changes become apparent to others, doubts and confusion frequently emerge. What many respondents reported was a real change in the reaction of significant others. These changes were in some instances almost insignificant, whereas in others they were profound. The fears and confusion raised by these reactions are associated with the potential loss of a "master status" (Hughes, 1945).

The sheer size of the person can significantly shape the perception of others to the point of influencing their view of who the individual actually is. This master status of the obese person can form what Lofland (1969) has termed a pivotal category, which in extreme cases may even define that individual's core being as far as others are concerned. It would follow then that significant weight loss may produce intense ambiguity about the self that approaches a Durkheimian state of anomie. Although none of the respondents displayed this level of anxiety, they did articulate fears and concerns about this erosion of their master status.

In the case of obese people, there clearly are undesirable traits associated with their weight. Conversely, as indicated below, there are also certain desirable aspects to being heavy; these constitute secondary gains. The potential loss of certain identity documents associated with being heavy may produce a real identity crisis with which the individual is frequently ill prepared to deal. Respondents articulated these fears in a number of ways:

> I am good old lovable Aunt Mary to all my nieces and nephews. They really love me and always expect, and get, cookies and candy when they come over, to my house. Now that I have lost all of this weight, they do not seem to like me as much.
>
> We are experts, you know. We know more about calorie counts and diets than most doctors and nutritionists. People are always talking to me about their weight; what I think of this diet or that. If I get thin I am afraid I will not have anything to talk about.
>
> As long as I am heavy I do not have to worry about men. I have been married twice and neither one of them [former husbands] was worth a damn. Since I have gotten heavy, that is one problem I do not have to deal with.

The Coat Rack Effect

The coat rack phenomenon has one of the most devastating effects on the heavy person's efforts to continue and/or maintain weight loss. Given the person has been forced to focus so much attention on stigmatization, that individual perceives many of her or his life's difficulties as being a consequence of this status. Of course, everyone encounters "problems of living," but the stigmatized individual has the option of laying all his or her problems at the feet of his or her soiled identity. Goffman has been credited with observing how the deviant category can be a coat rack upon which are hung all manner of minor failings, disturbing feelings, and inappropriate acts (Lofland, 1969:184).

For the heavy person who is beginning to move from an extremely heavy state into a moderately heavy one, the realization that significant personal problems may still persist can prove to be a startling revelation. This may result in severe complications, as the following indicate:

> Once I lost 110 pounds, and expected that all those men who had been ignoring me would start paying attention to me. Well, they didn't, and I started eating again. Now I weigh twice what I weighed before.
>
> You know, since I've lost all this weight I am discovering that normal people are as mean and nasty to one another as they are to overweight folks. It makes me wonder why I am suffering so much if nothing is really going to change.

Clearly, this realization that life's problems may continue and even intensify, in spite of dramatic weight loss, can have far-reaching consequences. It is not surprising that only 10% of the respondents achieved goal weight. In fact, six months after leaving the program, 80% of the respondents had gained back all of the weight they had lost, and half were heavier than when they started the program. This escalation of weight gain after significant weight loss is a process that both heavy people and clinicians who treat obesity are well aware of, and puzzle over. Social factors contribute significantly to this phenomenon, particularly since dieters are engaged in a voluntary identity transformation rather than an involuntary one.

Discussion: Voluntary/Involuntary Identity Transformations

The decision to lose weight may be motivated by a dissatisfaction with one's physical appearance. Appearance has been documented as being a significant factor in shaping one's sense of self (Stone, 1981). Consistent with the symbolic interaction tradition, the self is continually constructed and reconstituted through social interaction (Mead, 1934; Cooley, 1964). For the extremely obese person, his or her physical size dominates the individual's presentation of self to the point that it becomes a powerful force in shaping the perceptions of others. The sheer size of the highly obese person can create what Goffman (1963) has termed a "virtual social identity." Correspondingly, the subsequent discreditation can reach such proportions that the individual becomes stigmatized. The actor who becomes a serious dieter clearly is attempting to shed this identity; hence the decision to join a therapeutic weight loss group.

A considerable amount of research has focused on involuntary identity transformations (Garfinkel, 1956; Goffman, 1961; Howsden, 1981), particularly as they occur within the total institution. The dieter's situation, however, is very different in that the dieter instigates the transformation process of his or her own volition. The dieter initially wants to become thin and achieve membership in the thin world. The dieter looks forward to the anticipated rewards of the stripping process, and yet all too frequently these expectations do not materialize. In fact, tremendous weight loss may lead to what Lemert (1972) has termed an "erosion of identity." This is frequently triggered by a significant shift in interactions with the dieter's "identity subculture." For example, the changes in appearance may have a disruptive effect on the relationship with a boyfriend or husband, the attractive thin friend may no longer look so striking in comparison, and as already pointed out, good old Aunt Mary may not have all those wonderful sweets around.

In some instances a return to obesity represents a return to normalcy. Old routines and relationships are reestablished; everything is as it once was. Secondary gains are most pronounced among the chronic obese person; individuals who have a life history of being overweight and have developed a master status from their obesity. Conversely, cases of reactive obesity involve individuals who have gained weight in response to a specific life situation, and once the situation is resolved these individuals rapidly lose the excess weight. For this group, the status of being heavy is so recent, and so generally short-lived, that the identity associated with being fat never has a chance to fully develop.

For the chronic obese person, however, substantial weight loss can become a frightening prospect. Significant others may not be supportive or comfortable with the changes that accompany the weight loss, which in turn triggers a retreat to the patterns deeply established prior to weight loss.

Stone (1981:188) adds further illumination into this process in his treatment of identity as socially situated:

> ...identity establishes what and where the person is in social terms....When one has identity he is situated—that is, cast in the shape of a social object by the acknowledgement of his participation or membership in social relations. One's identity is established when others place him as a social object...

Clearly Stone views the creation of identity as an outgrowth of social interactions. Research on other stigmatized populations has made similar observations and has called attention to the significance of the perceptions of others in influencing the course of identity transformation. For example, Ray (1961:434), in his classic study of heroin addicts, points out how relapse is related to social interactions:

> In the period following physical withdrawal from heroin, the addict attempts to enact a new social reality which coincides with his desired self-image as an abstainer, and he seeks ratification of his new identity from others....But the abstainer's social expectations during a period when he is off drugs are frequently not gratified....Socially disjunctive experiences bring about a questioning of the value of an abstainer's identity....

The recovering alcoholic also faces identity issues in terms of the response of others. Wiseman (1970:423), in her study of skid row alcoholics, points out the discrepancy between the identity issues that are faced once entry into respectable society is attempted:

...trying and failing to gain acceptance is much more ego debilitating than not trying at all....The skid row alcoholic, in his efforts to get back into society, may encounter a "reality shock" not intended by his rehabilitators—that of finding he is socially undesirable to the society he seeks, regardless of his efforts to the contrary.

Denzin (1987:161) in his study of recovering alcoholics, sees the destruction of the old self (alcoholic) and the creation of a new self (sobriety) as critical to recovery. Drawing upon the work of G.H. Mead, he points out that through involvement in Alcoholics Anonymous, "the sober 'I' learns how to be sober by taking the attitudes of sober 'selves' who are members of A.A. The A.A. group becomes a generalized 'other' for the other."

The loss of the established self clearly complicates the efforts of those individuals struggling with an identity transformation. The perceptions of others facilitate or inhibit how successful and/or traumatic this process is. One of the concerns that respondents raised was the loss of male companionship as their weight loss became increasingly more dramatic. Despite the cultural emphasis on thinness and female attractiveness, there exists a small subpopulation of males who are attracted to extremely heavy women. Female members of the therapy groups referred to these men as "fat admirers." A considerable amount of time was devoted to the discussion of "fat admirers" and expressing fears about losing their attention. After significant weight loss, respondents frequently complained of being caught in no-person land. One described this in the following manner:

My boyfriend just up and left me. He said I wasn't his type anymore, that I was getting too skinny. Now, what am I going to do? I am too thin for him and not thin enough for normal men.

Being thin was often viewed as entering an alien land. For the chronically obese person, there was considerable fear and trepidation about entry into this world. Comments such as the following were not uncommon:

I don't feel like myself anymore!

Conclusion

The problems faced by dieters regarding identity shifts are not unique to this group. It would appear that for many groups facing identity transformation, the critical variables appear to be the reactions of others, the interaction with others, and, as a consequence, the degree to which the individual views the changes as positive. If rewards and anticipated results are not forthcoming, then identity erosion can take place. The safety and comfort of the obese self is recalled with nostalgia, and relapse can become a reality.

The loss of weight involves only one distinct set of skills. Continuing and/or maintaining weight loss constitutes a different set. The failure of many commercial diet programs to recognize this limits long-term success of dieters. When the dieter begins to experience significant weight loss and the dieter's "master status" begins to erode, a focus on emerging issues in their social world might enhance that

Gaining and Losing Weight   617

individual's efforts. For example, to facilitate this, a number of therapies might be appropriate. Fundamental changes, such as learning how to make "normal" conversation and how to walk and present oneself as a thin person, may have to be developed. Learning how to accept responsibility for life's slings and arrows might be a threatening but necessary perspective. Social skills training, relationship training, and assertiveness training might prove to be instrumental in easing the transformation. Basic sex education, marriage counseling, and family therapy could possibly help the individual learn how to enter the world of thin people, and even to become a part of that world. Until dieters and therapists acknowledge and deal with the impact of the dieter's social world, programs will continue to have limited long-term success. Weight loss is only one issue the serious dieter encounters. The response of others is of equal, if not greater importance.

The loss of self can be a painful and frightening experience for anyone. Studies on divorce, retirement, death of a spouse, to name only a few instances, have documented this. What seems to be lacking in the field of deviance is a clear understanding of what the deviant individual experiences as he or she attempts to move from a deviant to a nondeviant identity. What the literature suggests is that this can be a traumatic experience. Further exploration into the dynamics of this phenomenon might yield important insights into why most treatment programs experience enormous frustration and limited success.

REFERENCES

Becker, H.S. 1973. *Outsiders*. New York: Free Press.
Cooley, C.H. 1964. *Human Nature and the Social Order*. New York: Schocken.
Denzin, N.K. 1987. *The Recovering Alcoholic*. Beverly Hills: Sage.
Garfinkel, H. 1956. "Conditions of Successful Degradation Ceremonies." *American Journal of Sociology* 61:420–24.
Goffman, E. 1961. *Asylums*. New York: Anchor.
———. 1963. *Stigma*. Englewood Cliffs, New Jersey: Prentice-Hall.
Howsden, J. 1981. *Work and the Helpless Self*. Washington, DC: University Press of America.
Hughes, E.C. 1945. "Dilemmas and Contradictions of Status." *American Journal of Sociology* 50:353–59.
Lemert, E.M. 1972. *Human Deviance, Social Problems, and Social Control*. Englewood Cliffs, New Jersey: Prentice-Hall.
Lofland, J. 1969. *Deviance and Identity*. Englewood Cliffs, New Jersey: Prentice-Hall.
———. 1971. *Analyzing Social Settings*. Belmont, California: Wadsworth.
Lyman, S.M. 1978. *The Seven Deadly Sins*. New York: St. Martin's.
Mead, G.H. 1934. *Mind, Self, and Society*. Chicago: University of Chicago Press.
Ray, M.B. 1961. "Abstinence Cycles and Heroin Addicts." *Social Problems* 9:132–40.
Stone, G.P. 1981. "Appearance and the Self: A Slightly Revised Version." Pp. 187–202 IN G.P. Stone and H.A. Farberman (eds.), *Social Psychology Through Symbolic Interaction*. New York: Wiley.
Wiseman, J.P. 1970. *Stations of the Lost: The Treatment of Skid Row Alcoholics*. Englewood Cliffs, New Jersey: Prentice-Hall.

NOTES

[1] Surprisingly none of the respondents cited "biological drives" as an explanation despite the growing body of literature linking the psychological and biochemical processes with weight control difficulties. It may be that since the research sample consisted of highly motivated adults in a behaviorally oriented program, such explanations would be self-defeating.

ABOUT THE EDITOR

Nancy J. Herman (Ph.D., McMaster University, Hamilton, Ontario Canada) is Associate Professor of Sociology at Central Michigan University. She has researched, written, and taught in the areas of deviance, social psychology, the sociology of mental illness and qualitative methods. In 1994, she co-edited with Larry T. Reynolds, *Symbolic Interaction: An Introduction to Social Psychology*. (New York: General Hall). Dr. Herman is currently the editor of the *Michigan Sociological Review*.

INDEX

LaVergne, TN USA
17 November 2010
205368LV00004B/91/P